12/05
12/07 (3/07)

SANTA ANA
PUBLIC LIBRARY

D0045076

# The Oxford Guide to PEOPLE & PLACES OF THE BIBLE

# The Oxford Guide to PEOPLE & PLACES OF THE BIBLE

*Edited by*

BRUCE M. METZGER
MICHAEL D. COOGAN

220.92 OXF
The Oxford guide to people &
places of the Bible
31994012651565

OXFORD
UNIVERSITY PRESS

## ADVISERS

**JO ANN HACKETT**
**BARBARA GELLER NATHANSON WILLIAM H. PROPP**
**PHILIP SELLEW**

Oxford University Press
Oxford New York
Athens Auckland Bangkok Bogotá Buenos Aires Calcutta
Cape Town Chennai Dar es Salaam Delhi Florence Hong Kong Istanbul
Karachi Kuala Lumpur Madrid Melbourne Mexico City Mumbai
Nairobi Paris São Paulo Shanghai Singapore Taipei Tokyo Toronto Warsaw

and associated companies in
Berlin Ibadan

Copyright © 2001 by Oxford University Press, Inc.

Published by Oxford University Press, Inc.
198 Madison Avenue, New York, NY 10016
http://www.oup.com

Oxford is a registered trademark of Oxford University Press.
All rights reserved. No part of this publication may be reproduced,
stored in a retrieval system, or transmitted, in any form or by any means,
electronic, mechanical, photocopying, recording, or otherwise, without the
prior written permission of Oxford University Press.

The editors and publisher gratefully acknowledge permission to quote from
the New Revised Standard Version Bible, copyright © 1989,
by the Division of Christian Education of the National Council of the
Churches of Christ in the U.S.A. Used by permission. All rights reserved.

Library of Congress Cataloging-in-Publication Data
The Oxford guide to people & places of the Bible /
edited by Bruce M. Metzger, Michael D. Coogan
p. cm.
Includes bibliographical references and index.
ISBN 0-19-514641-7 (alk. paper)
1. Bible—Biography—Encyclopedias. 2. Bible—Geography—Encyclopedias.
I. Metzger, Bruce Manning. II. Coogan, Michael David.
BS570.O94 2001
220.9'03—dc21 00-066900

3 5 7 9 8 6 4 2
Printed in the United States of America
on acid-free paper

# CONTENTS

# ACKNOWLEDGMENTS

In preparing this *Guide* we have had indispensable assistance from the staff of the trade reference department at Oxford University Press. We especially thank Katherine Adzima, who guided the *Guide* from idea through production. We are most grateful, of course, to the contributors, whose expert contributions are the essence of the volume; their names are listed after this introduction.

*Bruce M. Metzger*
*Michael D. Coogan*
September 2000

# INTRODUCTION

For nearly two millennia, the Bible has been the cardinal text for Judaism and Christianity. Its stories and characters are part of both the repertoire of Western literature and the vocabulary of educated women and men. It is, however, more than a collection of ancient tales. Even before a canonical list of books considered sacred scripture or holy writ was established, the writings we now call the Bible were considered normative: they laid down the essential principles of how human beings should deal with God and with each other. The practice of quoting from, and alluding to, earlier texts as authoritative is found within the Bible itself and has continued unabated in subsequent Jewish and Christian writings. At the same time, the Bible has also been formative; subsequent generations of believers have seen themselves as descended from, and in continuity with, those to whom God had spoken and for whom he had acted definitively in the past, and the recital of those words and events has been instrumental in shaping the religious communities of succeeding generations. The Bible has thus had an immeasurable influence on Judaism and Christianity, on the cultures of which they have formed a part, and on all those traditions in some ways derived from them, such as Islam.

Although the word Bible means "book," and the Bible has been treated as a single book for much of its history, it is in fact many books, an anthology of the literatures of ancient Israel, and, for Christians, also of earliest Christianity. The Bible thus speaks with many voices, and, from the time of its emergence as an authoritative sacred text, readers and interpreters have noted its many repetitions, inconsistencies, and contradictions. Since the Enlightenment especially, critical consideration of the Bible—that is, study of it insofar as possible without presuppositions—has irreversibly affected what may be called the "precritical" understanding of the Bible as simply a unified text, God's eternal, infallible, and complete word. Discoveries of ancient manuscripts (such as the Dead Sea Scrolls) and of literatures contemporaneous with, or earlier than, those preserved in the Bible (such as stories of creation and the Flood from ancient Babylonia and the gospels of Thomas and Philip from Nag Hammadi in Egypt), as well as innumerable archaeological finds, have deepened our understanding of the Bible and the historical and cultural contexts in which its constituent parts were written. This new understanding of the Bible has resulted in continuous scholarly attention and popular interest.

*The Oxford Guide to People & Places of the Bible* is derived from *The Oxford Companion to the Bible* (1993). We have selected entries from the original work to provide an authoritative reference to key persons and places of biblical times. The *Guide* provides up-to-date discussions of the interpretation of these topics by modern scholars, bringing to bear the most recent findings of archaeologists and current research methods from such disciplines as anthropology, sociology, and literary criticism. Like the *Companion,* the *Guide* is consciously pluralistic, and its contributors encompass a wide spectrum of intellectual and creedal perspectives. They represent the international community of scholars, coming from some dozen countries, on five continents. No attempt has been made by the editors to produce any dogmatic unanimity; readers should not be surprised to find differing interpretations in different entries. Contributors have been urged to present their own scholarly views while noting diverse perspectives. In general, the articles aim to present the consensus of interpretation, or the lack thereof, attained by the most recent scholarship, and to avoid partisanship and polemic.

In preparing the *Guide,* we have occasionally linked entries that were separate in the *Companion.* This can result in the inclusion under one major heading of contributors who have different views on related subjects. We have chosen to let this stand, just as we have not attempted to impose consistency between entries. Diversity of views will inform readers' understanding both of the issues involved and of the process of interpretation itself.

The *Guide* does not aim to be an encyclopedia or encyclopedic dictionary, and is not intended as a substitute either for the Bible itself or for a concordance to the Bible. Quotations from the Bible have deliberately been kept to a minimum, and biblical references are illustrative, not exhaustive. Nor have we included every name found in the Bible; rather, we have chosen only those judged important within the biblical traditions or by later readers. This is especially true of persons and places about which little if anything is known other than what appears in the Bible.

Within the scope of one volume, then, from **Aaron** to **Zion,** the *Guide* is a reliable resource for what the Bible says and how scholars have interpreted biblical traditions. The *Guide* is an authoritative and comprehensive reference for a wide audience, including general readers; students and teachers in high schools, colleges, seminaries, and divinity schools; rabbis, ministers, and religious educators; participants in religious education and Bible study programs; and scholars in the variety of disciplines for which the Bible is in some way pertinent.

## Use of the Guide

**Cross-references.** The *Guide* is arranged alphabetically. Extensive cross-references direct the reader to related entries; these cross-references are of three types:

1. Within an entry, the first occurrence of a name, word, or phrase that has its own entry is marked with an asterisk (*).
2. When a topic treated in an entry or a related topic is discussed elsewhere in the volume, the italicized words *see* or *see also* refer the reader to the appropriate entry term(s).
3. "Blind entries," that is, entry terms that have no accompanying text but are terms that readers might expect to find discussed, appear alphabetically in the volume and refer to the entries where the top-

ics are actually treated. Thus, the blind entry **Peter** refers readers to **Simon Peter.**

**Index.** Further investigation of particular topics is made possible by a detailed index, which provides page references for pertinent subjects and for ancient and modern proper names. There is also a set of maps at the end of the *Guide.* These maps have their own index, to enable readers to locate places named in the text more precisely.

**Bibliography.** At the end of the volume, there is an extensive annotated bibliography, which will enable readers to explore in more detail topics covered in the *Guide.* The bibliography is divided into categories for easier use, such as the history, geography, and archaeology of biblical times; anthologies of nonbiblical texts; critical and popular introductions to the Bible; reference works; surveys of the history of interpretation; and methodologies used in biblical scholarship.

**Translation.** The translation used in the *Guide* is *The New Revised Standard Version* (NRSV), the most recent authoritative translation of the Bible into English, produced by an interfaith committee of scholars and published in 1990. The renderings of the NRSV are the basis for entry titles. Within individual entries, contributors have on occasion used other published translations or their own; in these cases, differences from the NRSV are noted.

Following increasingly frequent practice, the term "Hebrew Bible" is used in preference to "Old Testament," and the abbreviations BCE (Before the Common Era) and CE (Common Era) are used in place of BC and AD.

# DIRECTORY OF CONTRIBUTORS

VALERIE ABRAHAMSEN, Waltham, Massachusetts

ELIZABETH ACHTEMEIER, Adjunct Professor of Bible and Homiletics, Union Theological Seminary, Richmond, Virginia

PAUL J. ACHTEMEIER, The Herbert Worth and Annie H. Jackson Professor of Biblical Interpretation, Union Theological Seminary, Richmond, Virginia

SUSAN ACKERMAN, Assistant Professor of Religion, Dartmouth College, Hanover, New Hampshire

PETER R. ACKROYD, Samuel Davidson Professor of Old Testament Studies, Emeritus, King's College, University of London, England

FRANCIS I. ANDERSEN, Professor of Old Testament, New College for Advanced Christian Studies, Berkeley, California

HECTOR IGNACIO AVALOS, Carolina Postdoctoral Fellow, Departments of Religious Studies and Anthropology, University of North Carolina at Chapel Hill

E. BADIAN, John Moors Cabot Professor of History, Harvard University, Cambridge, Massachusetts

WILLIAM H. BARNES, Associate Professor of Biblical Studies, Southeastern College of the Assemblies of God, Lakeland, Florida

MARKUS K. BARTH, Professor of New Testament, Emeritus, Universität Basel, Switzerland

JOHN R. BARTLETT, Principal, Church of Ireland Theological College, Dublin; Fellow, Emeritus, Trinity College, Dublin, Ireland

JOHN BARTON, Oriel and Laing Professor of the Interpretation of Holy Scripture, University of Oxford, England

JUDITH R. BASKIN, Chair, Department of Judaic Studies, State University of New York at Albany

RICHARD J. BAUCKHAM, Professor of New Testament Studies, University of St. Andrews, Scotland

CHRISTOPHER T. BEGG, Assistant Professor of Theology, Catholic University of America, Washington, D.C.

ROBERT A. BENNETT, JR., Professor of Old Testament, Episcopal Divinity School, Cambridge

ERNEST BEST, Professor of Divinity and Biblical Criticism, Emeritus, University of Glasgow, Scotland

OTTO BETZ, Professor and Lecturer of New Testament and Jewish Studies, Retired, Eberhard-Karls-Universität, Tübingen, Germany

PHYLLIS A. BIRD, Associate Professor of Old Testament Interpretation, Garrett Evangelical Theological Seminary, Evanston, Illinois

M. H. BLACK, Fellow, Clare Hall, University of Cambridge; former Publisher of Cambridge University Press, England

MATTHEW BLACK, Professor of Biblical Criticism, Emeritus, University of St. Andrews, Scotland

JOHN A. BRINKMAN, Charles H. Swift Distinguished Service Professor of Mesopotamian History, University of Chicago, Illinois

BERNADETTE J. BROOTEN, Kraft-Hiatt Chair of Christian Studies, New Eastern and Judaic Studies Department, Brandeis University, Waltham, Massachusetts

F. F. BRUCE, Rylands Professor of Biblical Criticism and Exegesis, University of Manchester, England, *deceased*

GEORGE WESLEY BUCHANAN, Professor of New Testament, Emeritus, Wesley Theological Seminary, Washington, D.C.

DAVID G. BURKE, Director, Translations Department, American Bible Society, New York, New York

EDWARD F. CAMPBELL, Francis A. McGaw Professor of Old Testament, McCormick Theological Seminary, Evanston, Illinois

RICHARD J. CLIFFORD, Professor of Old Testament, Weston School of Theology, Cambridge, Massachusetts

DAVID J. A. CLINES, Professor of Biblical Studies, University of Sheffield, England

AELRED CODY, O.S.B., Catholic Biblical Quarterly, St. Meinrad Archabbey, Indiana

RICHARD COGGINS, Senior Lecturer in Old Testament Studies, King's College, University of London, England

MICHAEL D. COOGAN, Professor of Religious Studies, Stonehill College, North Easton, Massachusetts

J. M. COOK, Professor of Ancient History and Classical Archaeology, Emeritus, University of Bristol, England

DERMOT COX, O.F.M., Professor of Old Testament Exegesis, Università Gregoriana, Rome, Italy

JAMES L. CRENSHAW, Professor of Old Testament, Duke University, Durham, North Carolina

PETER H. DAVIDS, Scholar in Residence, Langley Vineyard Christian Fellowship, British Columbia, Canada

ROBERT DAVIDSON, Professor of Old Testament Language and Literature, Emeritus, University of Glasgow, Scotland

ROBERT C. DENTAN, Professor of Old Testament, Emeritus, General Theological Seminary, New York, New York

ALEXANDER A. DILELLA, O.F.M., Professor of Biblical Studies, Catholic University of America, Washington, D.C.

JOHN W. DRANE, Director, Center for the Study of Christianity and Contemporary Society, University of Stirling, Scotland

CARL S. EHRLICH, Professor, Hochschule fäur jäudische Studien, Heidelberg, Germany

J. A. EMERTON, Regius Professor of Hebrew, and Fellow, St. John's College, University of Cambridge, England

F. CHARLES FENSHAM, Professor of Semitic Languages and Cultures, Emeritus, University of Stellenbosch, South Africa

JOSEPH A. FITZMYER, S.J., Professor of Biblical Studies, Emeritus, Catholic University of America, Washington, D.C.

DANIEL E. FLEMING, Assistant Professor, New York University, New York

EDWIN D. FREED, Professor of Biblical Literature and Religion, Emeritus, Gettysburg College, Pennsylvania

SEÁN FREYNE, Professor of Theology, Trinity College, Dublin, Ireland

STEVEN FRIESEN, Fellow, Program on Cultural Studies, East-West Center, Honolulu, Hawaii

REGINALD H. FULLER, Professor Emeritus, Virginia Theological Seminary, Richmond, Virginia

PROSPER GRECH, O.S.A., Professor of New Testament Exegesis, Augustinianum, Rome; Lecturer in Hermeneutics, Pontifical Biblical Institute, Rome, Italy

JOSEPH A. GREEN, Curator of Publications, Semitic Museum, Harvard University, Cambridge, Massachusetts

DAVID M. GUNN, Professor of Old Testament, Columbia Theological Seminary, Decatur, Georgia

JO ANN HACKETT, Professor, Department of Near Eastern Languages and Civilizations, Harvard University, Cambridge, Massachusetts

WILLIAM W. HALLO, The William M. Laffan Professor of Assyriology and Babylonian Literature, and Curator, Babylonian Collection, Yale University, New Haven, Connecticut

PHILIP C. HAMMOND, Professor of Anthropology, University of Utah, Salt Lake City

GERALD F. HAWTHORNE, Professor of Greek, Wheaton College, Illinois

DAVID M. HAY, Professor, Department of Religion and Philosophy, Coe College, Cedar Rapids, Iowa

JOHN H. HAYES, Professor of Old Testament, Candler School of Theology, Emory University, Atlanta, Georgia

RONALD S. HENDEL, Associate Professor, Department of Religious Studies, Southern Methodist University, Dallas, Texas

PAULA S. HIEBERT, Visting Professor of Theology, Boston College, Massachusetts

DAVID HILL, Reader in Biblical Studies, Retired, University of Sheffield, England

DELBERT R. HILLERS, W. W. Spence Professor of Semitic Languages, The Johns Hopkins University, Baltimore, Maryland

HAROLD W. HOEHNER, Chairman and Professor of New Testament Studies, and Director, Ph.D. Studies, Dallas Theological Seminary, Texas

CARL R. HOLLADAY, Professor, Candler School of Theology, Emory University, Atlanta, Georgia

MORNA D. HOOKER, Lady Margaret Professor of Divinity, University of Cambridge, England

LESLIE J. HOPPE, O.F.M., Professor of Old Testament, Catholic Theological Union, Chicago, Illinois

SHERMAN ELBRIDGE JOHNSON, Dean and Professor of New Testament, Emeritus, The Church Divinity School of the Pacific, Berkeley, California, *deceased*

EDWIN A. JUDGE, Macquarie University, North Ryde, New South Wales, Australia

ROBERT J. KARRIS, O.F.M., Rome, Italy

JACK DEAN KINGSBURY, Aubrey Lee Brooks Professor of Biblical Theology, Union Theological Seminary, Richmond, Virginia

DOUGLAS A. KNIGHT, Professor of Hebrew Bible, Vanderbilt University, Nashville, Tennessee

GARY N. KNOPPERS, Assistant Professor of Religious Studies, Pennsylvania State University, University Park

WILLIAM SANFORD LASOR, Professor, Fuller Theological Seminary, Pasadena, California, *deceased*

MARY JOAN WINN LEITH, Assistant Professor of Religious Studies, Stonehill College, North Easton, Massachusetts

AMY-JILL LEVINE, Professor, Department of Religion, Swarthmore College, Pennsylvania

LEE LEVINE, Professor of Jewish History and Archaeology, The Hebrew University of Jerusalem; Dean and Director, The Seminary of Judaic Studies, Jerusalem, Israel

ABRAHAM J. MALHERBE, Buckingham Professor of New Testament Criticism and Interpretation, Yale Divinity School, New Haven, Connecticut

I. HOWARD MARSHALL, Professor of New Testament Exegesis, University of Aberdeen, Scotland

REX MASON, University Lecturer in Old Testament and Hebrew, University of Oxford, England

GENE MCAFEE, Harvard Divinity School, Cambridge, Massachusetts

P. KYLE MCCARTER, JR., William Foxwell Albright Professor of Biblical and Ancient

Near Eastern Studies, The Johns Hopkins University, Baltimore, Maryland

STEVEN L. MCKENZIE, Associate Professor of Old Testament, Rhodes College, Memphis, Tennessee

PAULA M. MCNUTT, Assistant Professor of Religious Studies, Canisius College, Buffalo, New York

SAMUEL A. MEIER, Associate Professor of Hebrew and Comparative Semitics, Ohio State University, Columbus

BRUCE M. METZGER, George L. Collord Professor of New Testament Language and Literature, Emeritus, Princeton Theological Seminary, New Jersey

ISOBEL MACKAY METZGER, Princeton, New Jersey

CAROL L. MYERS, Professor of Biblical Studies and Archaeology, Duke University, Durham, North Carolina

ERIC M. MEYERS, Professor of Bible and Judaic Studies, Duke University, Durham, North Carolina

ALAN MILLARD, Rankin Professor of Hebrew and Ancient Semitic Languages, University of Liverpool, England

J. MAXWELL MILLER, Professor of Old Testament Studies, Emory University, Atlanta, Georgia

PAUL S. MINEAR, Winkley Professor of Biblical Theology, Emeritus, Yale University, New Haven, Connecticut

CAREY A. MOORE, Amanda Rupert Strong Professor of Religion, Gettysburg College, Pennsylvania

ROLAND E. MURPHY, O. Carm, George Washington Ivey Professor of Biblical Studies, Emeritus, Duke University, Durham, North Carolina

JEROME MURPHY-O'CONNOR, O.P., Professor of New Testament, École Biblique de Jérusalem, Israel

BARBARA GELLER NATHANSON, Professor, Department of Religion, Wellesley College, Massachusetts

WILLIAM B. NELSON, JR., Professor, Department of Religious Studies, Westmont College, Santa Barbara, California

ROBERT NORTH, S.J., *Elenchus* of *Biblica;* Professor of Archaeology, Emeritus, Pontificio Istituto Biblico, Rome, Italy

PETER T. O'BRIEN, Vice Principal and Head, New Testament Department, Moore Theological College, Newton, Australia

BEN C. OLLENBURGER, Professor of Religious Studies, Association of Mennonite Seminaries, Elkhart, Indiana

DENNIS T. OLSON, Assistant Professor of Old Testament, Princeton Theological Seminary, New Jersey

RICHARD E. OSTER, JR., Professor of New Testament, Harding University Graduate School of Religion, Memphis, Tennessee

J. ANDREW OVERMAN, Professor, Department of Religion and Classics, University of Rochester, New York

JOSEPH PATHRAPANKAL, C.M.I., Professor of New Testament and Theology, Dharmaran College, Bangalore, India

WAYNE T. PITARD, Associate Professor, Department of Religious Studies, University of Illinois at Urbana-Champaign

JAMES H. PLATT, Denver, Colorado

J. MARTIN PLUMLEY, Sir Herbert Thompson Professor of Egyptology, Emeritus, University of Cambridge, England

WILLIAM H. PROPP, Associate Professor of Near Eastern Languages and History, University of California at San Diego

JAMES M. REESE, O.S.F.S., Professor, Department of Theology, St. John's University, Jamaica, New York, *deceased*

BO REICKE, Universität Basel, Switzerland, *deceased*

JOHN RICHES, Professor of Divinity and Biblical Criticism, University of Glasgow, Scotland

GUY ROGERS, Associate Professor of Greek, Latin, and History, Wellesley College, Massachusetts

J. W. ROGERSON, Professor and Head, Department of Biblical Studies, University of Sheffield, England

DENIS BAIN SADDINGTON, Professor of Roman History and Archaeology, University of the Witwatersrand, South Africa

KATHARINE DOOB SAKENFELD, William Albright Eisenberger Professor of Old Testament Literature, Princeton Theological Seminary, New Jersey

RICHARD P. SALLER, Professor of History and Classics, University of Chicago, Illinois

JOHN, F. A. SAWYER, Professor, Department of Religious Studies, University of Newcastle upon Tyne, England

DANIEL N. SCHOWALTER, Associate Professor, Department of Religion, Carthage College, Kenosha, Wisconsin

PHILIP SELLEW, Associate Professor, Department of Classical and Near Eastern Studies, University of Minnesota, Minneapolis

DRORAH O'DONNELL SETEL, Seattle, Washington

GREGORY SHAW, Professor, Department of Religious Studies, Stonehill College, North Easton, Massachusetts

STEPHEN S. SMALLEY, Dean of Chester Cathedral, England

J. A. SOGGIN, Professor of Hebrew Language and Literature, Università di Roma, Italy

PHILIP STERN, White Plains, New York

ROBERT STOOPS, Associate Professor, Department of Liberal Studies, Western Washington University, Bellingham

G. M. STYLER, Fellow, Corpus Christi College, and University Lecturer in Divinity, 1950–1982, University of Cambridge, England

WILLARD M. SWARTLEY, Professor of New Testament, Associated Mennonite Biblical Seminaries, Elkhart, Indiana

JOHN SWEET, University Lecturer in Divinity, University of Cambridge, England

RON TAPPY, Assistant Professor of Archaeology and Literature of Ancient Israel, Westmont College, Santa Barbara, California

PATRICK A. TILLER, Visiting Lecturer on Greek, Harvard Divinity School, Cambridge, Massachusetts

W. SIBLEY TOWNER, The Reverend Archibald McFadyen Professor of Biblical Interpretation, Union Theological Seminary, Richmond, Virginia

GENE M. TUCKER, Professor of Old Testament, Candler School of Theology, Emory University, Atlanta, Georgia

DAVID H. VAN DAALEN, Minister, United Reformed Church, Huntingdon, England

BRUCE VAWTER, C.M., DePaul University, Illinois, *deceased*

JOHN D. W. WATTS, Donald L. Williams Professor of Old Testament, Southern Baptist Theological Seminary, Louisville, Kentucky

SIDNIE ANN WHITE, Assistant Professor of Religion, Albright College, Reading, Pennsylvania

R. N. WHYBRAY, Professor of Hebrew and Old Testament Studies, Emeritus, University of Hull, England

TIMOTHY M. WILLIS, Professor, Religion Division, Pepperdine University, Malibu, California

WALTER WINK, Professor of Biblical Interpretation, Auburn Theological Seminary, New York

DONALD J. WISEMAN, Professor of Assyriology, Emeritus, University of London, England

# ABBREVIATIONS

### ***Biblical Citations***

Chapter (chap.) and verse (v.) are separated by a period, and when a verse is subdivided, letters are used following the verse number; thus, Gen. 3.4a = the book of Genesis, chap. 3 v. 4, the first part. Biblical books are abbreviated in parenthetical references as follows:

| | | | |
|---|---|---|---|
| Acts | Acts of the Apostles | Josh. | Joshua |
| Amos | Amos | Jude | Jude |
| Bar. | Baruch | Judg. | Judges |
| Bel and the Dragon | Bel and the Dragon | Jth. | Judith |
| 1 Chron. | 1 Chronicles | 1 Kings | 1 Kings |
| 2 Chron. | 2 Chronicles | 2 Kings | 2 Kings |
| Col. | Colossians | Lam. | Lamentations |
| 1 Cor. | 1 Corinthians | Lev. | Leviticus |
| 2 Cor. | 2 Corinthians | Luke | Luke |
| Dan. | Daniel | 1 Macc. | 1 Maccabees |
| Deut. | Deuteronomy | 2 Macc. | 2 Maccabees |
| Eccles. | Ecclesiastes | 3 Macc. | 3 Maccabees |
| Eph. | Ephesians | 4 Macc. | 4 Maccabees |
| 1 Esd. | 1 Esdras | Mal. | Malachi |
| 2 Esd. | 2 Esdras | Mark | Mark |
| Esther | Esther | Matt. | Mathew |
| Exod. | Exodus | Mic. | Micah |
| Ezek. | Ezekiel | Nah. | Nahum |
| Ezra | Ezra | Neh. | Nehemiah |
| Gal. | Galatians | Num. | Numbers |
| Hab. | Habakkuk | Obad. | Obadiah |
| Hag. | Haggai | 1 Pet. | 1 Peter |
| Heb. | Hebrews | 2 Pet. | 2 Peter |
| Hos. | Hosea | Phil. | Philippians |
| Isa. | Isaiah | Philem. | Philemon |
| James | James | Pr. of Man. | Prayer of Manasseh |
| Jer. | Jeremiah | Prov. | Proverbs |
| Job | Job | Ps(s). | Psalm(s) |
| Joel | Joel | Rev. | Revelation |
| John | Gospel of John | Rom. | Romans |
| 1 John | 1 John | Ruth | Ruth |
| 2 John | 2 John | 1 Sam. | 1 Samuel |
| 3 John | 3 John | 2 Sam. | 2 Samuel |
| Jon. | Jonah | Sir. | Sirach |

| | | | |
|---|---|---|---|
| Song of Sol. | Song of Solomon | Titus | Titus |
| Sus. | Susanna | Tob. | Tobit |
| 1 Thess. | 1 Thessalonians | Wisd. of Solomon | Wisdom of Solomon |
| 2 Thess. | 2 Thessalonians | Zech. | Zechariah |
| 1 Tim. | 1 Timothy | Zeph. | Zephaniah |
| 2 Tim. | 2 Timothy | | |

### *Rabbinic Literature*

To distinguish tractates with the same name, the letters *m.* (Mishnah), *t.* (Tosepta), *b.* (Babylonian Talmud), and *y.* (Jerusalem Talmud) are used before the name of the tractate.

| | | | |
|---|---|---|---|
| *'Abod. Zar.* | *'Aboda Zara* | *Nez.* | *Neziqin* |
| *'Abot R. Nat.* | *'Abot de Rabbi Nathan* | *Nid.* | *Niddah* |
| *B. Bat.* | *Baba Batra* | *Pesaḥ.* | *Pesaḥim* |
| *Ber.* | *Berakot* | *Qoh. Rab.* | *Qohelet Rabbah* |
| *'Erub* | *'Erubin* | *Šabb.* | *Šabbat* |
| *Gen. Rab.* | *Genesis Rabbah* | *Sanh.* | *Sanhedrin* |
| *Ḥag.* | *Ḥagiga* | *Sukk.* | *Sukkot* |
| *Ketub.* | *Ketubot* | *Ta'an.* | *Ta'anit* |
| *Mek.* | *Mekilta* | *Yad.* | *Yadayim* |
| *Mid.* | *Middot* | *Zebaḥ.* | *Zebaḥim* |
| *Midr.* | *Midrash* | | |

### *Other Ancient Literature*

| | | | |
|---|---|---|---|
| *Adv. haer.* | Irenaeus, *Adversus haeresis* | 1QIsa[b] | Qumran Cave 1, Isaiah, second copy |
| *Ag. Ap.* | Josephus, *Against Apion* | 1QM | Qumran Cave 1, *Milḥāmāh (War Scroll)* |
| *Ant.* | Josephus, *Antiquities* | 1QpHab | Qumran Cave 1, *Pesher on Habakkuk* |
| *Apol.* | Justin, *Apology* | 1QS | Qumran Cave 1, *Serek hayyaḥad (Rule of the Community, Manual of Discipline* |
| *Bapt.* | Tertullian, *De baptismo* | 4Q246 | Qumran Cave 4, No. 246 |
| CD | Cairo Geniza, Damascus Document | 4Q503–509 | Qumran Cave 4, Nos. 503–509 |
| 1 Clem. | 1 Clement | 4QDeut[a] | Qumran Cave 4, Deuteronomy, first copy |
| *De Dec.* | Philo, *De Decalogo* | 4QMMT | Qumran Cave 4, *Miqsat Ma'aseh Torah* |
| *De spec. leg.* | Philo, *De specialibus legibus* | 4QpNah | Qumran Cave 4, *Pesher on Nahum* |
| Did. | Didache | 11QMelch | Qumran Cave 11, Melshizedek text |
| *Ep.* | Cyprian, *Epistles* | 11QTemple | Qumran Cave 11, *Temple Scroll* |
| *Exhort. Chast.* | Tertullian, *De exhortatione castitatis* | *Praescr.* | Tertullian, *De praescriptione haereticorum* |
| *Geog.* | Strabo, *Geographica* | Test. Abr. | Testament of Abraham |
| GT | Gospel of Thomas | T. Naph. | Testament of Naphtali |
| *Haer.* | Epiphanius, *Haereses* | *War* | Josephus, *Jewish War* |
| *Hist.* | Polybius, *Histories* | | |
| *Hist. eccl.* | Eusebius, *Historia ecclesiastica* | | |
| *Instit. Rhetor.* | Quintilian, *Institution of Rhetoric* | | |
| *Jov.* | Jerome, *Against Jovianum* | | |
| *Leg. ad Gaiiem* | Philo, *Legatio ad Gaium* | | |
| 1Q34 | Qumran Cave 1, No. 34 | | |
| 1QH | Qumran Cave 1, *Hôdāyôt (Thanksgiving Hymns)* | | |

### *Other Abbreviations*

| | |
|---|---|
| ABS | American Bible Society |
| AV | Authorized Version |
| BCE | Before the Common Era (the equivalent of BC) |
| BCP | Book of Common Prayer |
| BFPS | British and Foreign Bible Society |
| ca. | circa |
| CE | Common Era (the equivalent of AD) |
| chap(s). | chapter(s) |
| D | Deuteronomist source in the Pentateuch |
| E | Elohist source in the Pentateuch |
| EB | Early Bronze |
| GNB | Good News Bible |
| Grk. | Greek |
| H | Holiness Code |
| Hebr. | Hebrew |
| J | Yahwist source in the Pentateuch |
| KJV | King James Version |
| L | Special Lucan material |
| Lat. | Latin |
| LB | Late Bronze |
| LXX | Septuagint |
| M | Special Matthean material |
| MB | Middle Bronze |
| MSS | Manuscripts |
| MT | Masoretic Text |
| NBSS | National Bible Society of Scotland |
| NEB | New English Bible |
| NJV | New Jewish Version |
| NRSV | New Revised Standard Version |
| P | Priestly source in the Pentateuch |
| par. | parallel(s), used when two or more passages have essentially the same material, especially in the synoptic Gospels |
| Q | from German *Quelle,* "source," designating the hypothetical common source used by Matthew and Luke |
| REB | Revised English Bible |
| RSV | Revised Standard Version |
| RV | Revised Version |
| TDH | Two Document Hypothesis |
| UBS | United Bible Societies |
| v(v). | verse(s) |

# TRANSLITERATIONS

## HEBREW AND ARAMAIC

| *Transliteration* | *Pronunciation* | *Letter* |
|---|---|---|
| **Consonants** | | |
| ʾ | (now generally not pronounced; originally a glottal stop) | א |
| b | b (also sometimes v) | ב |
| g | g | ג |
| d | d | ד |
| h | h | ה |
| w | v (originally w) | ו |
| z | z | ז |
| ḥ | (not found in English; approximately like German -ch) | ח |
| ṭ | t (originally an emphatic t) | ט |
| y | y | י |
| k | k (also sometimes like German -ch) | כ, ך |
| l | l | ל |
| m | m | מ, ם |
| n | n | נ, ן |
| s | s | ס |
| ʿ | (now generally not pronounced; originally a voiced guttural) | ע |
| p | p (also sometimes f) | פ, ף |
| ṣ | ts | צ, ץ |
| q | k (originally an emphatic k) | ק |
| r | r | ר |
| ś | s | שׂ |
| š | sh | שׁ |
| t | t | ת |

| *Transliteration* | *Pronunciation* | *Hebrew Name* | *Symbol* |
|---|---|---|---|
| **Vowels** | | | |
| ă | father | *ḥāṭēp pataḥ* | ֲ |
| a | father | *pataḥ* | ַ |
| ā | father | *qāmeṣ* | ָ |

| *Transliteration* | *Pronunciation* | *Hebrew Name* | *Symbol* |
|---|---|---|---|
| â | father | *qāmeṣ* followed by *hē* | ָה |
| ĕ | petition | *šĕwā*, or *ḥāṭēp sĕgôl* | ְ , ֱ |
| e | bet | *sĕgôl* | ֶ |
| ē | they | *ṣērê* | ֵ |
| ê | they | *ṣērê* or *sĕgôl* followed by *yōd* | ֵי , ֶי |
| i, ī | machine | *ḥîreq* | ִ |
| î | machine | *ḥîreq* followed by *yōd* | ִי |
| ŏ | hope | *ḥāṭēp qāmeṣ* | ֳ |
| o | hope | *qāmeṣ ḥāṭûp* | ָ |
| o, ō | hope | *ḥôlem* | ֹ |
| ô | hope | *ḥôlem* with *wāw* | וֹ |
| u, ū | sure | *qibbûṣ* | ֻ |
| û | sure | *šûreq* | וּ |
| Other Semitic | | | |
| ḫ | (not found in English; approximately like German -ch) | | |

GREEK

| *Transliteration* | *Pronunciation* | *Letter* |
|---|---|---|
| a | a (father) | α |
| b | b | β |
| g | g | γ |
| d | d | δ |
| e | e (bet) | ϵ |
| z | z | ζ |
| ē | e (they) | η |
| th | th (thing) | θ |
| i | i (bit or machine) | ι |
| k | k | κ |
| l | l | λ |
| m | m | μ |
| n | n | ν |
| x | ks | ξ |
| o | o (off) | o |
| p | p | π |
| r | r | ρ |
| s | s | σ, ς |
| t | t | τ |
| y, u | u (like German ü), or part of a diphthong | υ |
| ph | ph (phase) | ϕ |
| ch | ch (like German -ch) | χ |
| ps | ps | ψ |
| ō | o (hope) | ω |
| h | h (hope): rough breathing | ῾ |

# The Oxford Guide to
# PEOPLE & PLACES OF THE BIBLE

# A

**AARON.** A major figure in Israel's origins and the first of its high priests. In very ancient narratives, he appears without specifically priestly features, as a leader with Hur, or as *Miriam's brother with no mention of their being related to *Moses, to whom they even appear opposed. Later, but still in fairly early stages of the Pentateuch's formation, Aaron is said to be Moses's brother and a *Levite, and he begins to appear with features that implicitly suggest a tie with priesthood. He is with Moses when Pharaoh asks for intercession with Israel's God; in Exodus 18.12, he may have been added to the account of the covenant between *Midian and Israel because a later editor may have felt that the covenant sacrifice required a priest; his presence with his sons Nadab and Abihu, reckoned elsewhere as priestly sons, seems also to have been added to the covenant-making scene at Sinai. The important question of Aaron's role in the episode of the golden calf is problematic. The incident is almost certainly told with the sanctuaries in mind established by Jeroboam I at Bethel and *Dan in the northern kingdom of Israel, but in the story Aaron is not presented as a priest or as a Levite; his guilt is brought out mainly in Exodus 32.25b, 35b, evident additions to a text in which the behavior of the people, looking to Aaron for leadership, was already contrasted negatively with the religiously correct zeal of Levites. In the Priestly components of the Pentateuch, Aaron's role as Moses's companion in Egypt and in the wilderness is heightened, but in P he is above all Israel's first high priest, and the other priests inaugurated with him are called his sons. The historical background of this development in the figure of Aaron is not clear. Although legitimate priests are called sons of *Zadok in Ezekiel, with Aaron's name quite unused in that exilic book, some suspect that the preexilic priesthood of *Jerusalem itself claimed an Aaronite origin; others believe that the first group to do so was the priesthood of Bethel, or a Levitical group in *Judah not originally identical with the priesthood of Jerusalem. In any case, the postexilic priests of Jerusalem settled peacefully into their own claim to be the sons of Aaron.

*Aelred Cody, O.S.B.*

**ABEL.** *See* Cain and Abel.

**ABRAHAM.** Abraham is the earliest biblical character who is delineated clearly enough to be correlated, to a limited extent, within world history. His homeland on the Fertile Crescent (possibly at Haran) and movements southeast toward Chaldean *Ur, then west to *Canaan and *Egypt, correspond to known *Amorite migratory and commercial routes. He may have been a caravan merchant, though the Bible presents him only as a pastoralist. This vague relation of Abraham to history does not exclude debate as to how much of his biography might have been worked up for vividness or as retrojection of a later tribal unity. More insistent claims of historicity presume contemporaneity with Hammurapi (despite the discredited equation of the latter with Amraphel). An even earlier date was put forward on the basis of some premature interpretations of *Sodom at Ebla. The name Abram (= Abiram, as Abner = Abiner), used in Genesis from 11.27 to 17.5, is there ritually changed to Abraham, a normal dialectal variant, though explained in relation to *ᵓab-hāmôn,* "father of many."

A certain unity in the whole Abraham saga involves a rich variety of peoples and individuals conditioning his activity; twenty-two separate episodes are discernible. Eleven are attributed to the Yahwist: base around Haran, Genesis 11.28–30; call westward, 12.1–3; Canaan pause, 12.4–9; separation from Lot, 13. 1–13; promise involving Mamre, 13.14–18; progeny like stars, covenant-incubation, 15.1–6, 7–24; *Hagar, 16; the three at Mamre, 18.1–15; vain plea for Sodom, 18.16–33; birth of *Isaac, 21.1–7; and old age, 24.1–25.11. Five other episodes suggest the Elohist: parts of the narrative of the covenant in chapter 15, especially verses 13–16; Gerar, 20; *Ishmael expelled, 21.6–21; Abimelech 21.22–34; and the call to sacrifice Isaac, 22. The Priestly additions include: journey to Canaan, parts of Genesis 11–12; birth of Ishmael, 16.1–16; covenant of El-Shaddai and circumcision, 17; birth of Isaac, 21.1–3; Machpelah, 23; death, 25.7–11; and, less clearly, the unique episode concerning *Melchizedek (chap. 14).

The three strands respectively see Abraham as "father of all nations"; "model of faith"; and "guarantor of Israel's survival." The covenant with Abraham is also a blessing for all the peoples of the earth and especially a bond of religious unity with his other descendants, the Ishmaelites. Abraham's progress from (Ur or) Haran through Canaan into Egypt involves numerous theophanies, justifying his eventual takeover of the whole area or, more sweepingly, the takeover by "his god" (El) of the cult of the local El, not clearly seen as either identical or different.

In Deuteronomy, Abraham is associated with Isaac and *Jacob; the three are often generalized as "your fathers," especially as those with whom God made a covenant, a covenant still in force. The Deuteronomic history recalls Abraham in Joshua 24.2–3; 1 Kings 18.36; 2 Kings 13.23; but it is surprising how seldom he is mentioned there, as well as in the Psalms and the preexilic prophets. The poorer classes of Judah who never were sent into exile justified their inheritance as the promise to Abraham, but the stronger group of returnees attributed their own liberation to God's faithfulness to Abraham "my friend" (Isa. 41.8, prominent in James 2.23 and in Muslim tradition, notably as the name of *Hebron, al-Halil). Abraham is often mentioned in the book of Jubilees and sometimes in other pseudepigrapha.

Abraham is second only to *Moses among New Testament mentions of biblical heroes. Sometimes this is in a slightly belittling sense, when he is claimed as father of the impious. More often the truly Abrahamic descent of the *Jews is acknowledged as a stimulus for them to live up to their heritage. This true but qualified descent from Abraham forms a key factor in *Paul's anguished efforts to determine how and in what sense Christianity can claim the promises made to Israel. Ultimately, as father of all believers, Abraham is to be looked to as a source of unity and harmony rather than dissent among Jews, *Christians, and Muslims.

*See also* Ancestors, The.

*Robert North*

**ABRAM.** *See* Abraham.

**ABSALOM.** Third son of King *David. The story of Absalom is presented as a subplot of the life of David, a consequence of David's adultery with *Bathsheba and murder of Uriah. He kills David's oldest son, Amnon (Absalom's half-brother), for raping his sister, Tamar. After a brief exile in Geshur, his mother's home, he is allowed to return to *Jerusalem. Apparently fearful that David's judicial inactivity is creating enough discontent to endanger his—or any son's—chances to succeed his father, Absalom conspires against David. He wins a sizable following in Israel, has himself declared king in *Hebron, and chases David out of Jerusalem. He soon attacks David in a wooded area of Ephraim, where he is defeated and, contrary to David's wishes, is killed by Joab, the commander of David's forces. David's grief at his son's death is characteristically intense. *Timothy M. Willis*

**ADAM.** Adam (possibly meaning "ruddy" or "earth") is the common noun in Hebrew for "human(-kind)"; only in Genesis 1–5 (when used without the article) and 1 Chronicles 1.1 is it the proper name for the first man. This usage highlights the unity of humankind, leaving no special apartness for Israel or Abraham. The stylized Priestly account of the creation of humans in Genesis 1.26 and more anthropomorphic narrative of the Yahwist in Genesis 2.7 neither disprove nor suggest (the) Adam's origin by evolution, a question that simply did not arise. God's image is in "the man" in Genesis 1.26, as "the man's" in turn is in Seth. Normal human toil and death as a punishment for (the) Adam's sin is the focus in Genesis 3 rather than either its propagation or the "protoevangelium." In the New Testament, Adam is chiefly a type of Christ in relation to release by resurrection from an original sin, perhaps taking up Adam as the ideal man.

*See also* Eve.

*Robert North*

**AFRICA.**

**Names and Words for Africa.** Africa appears throughout the Bible from Genesis 2.11–13, where the sources of the *Nile River are located in the garden of *Eden, to the apostle Philip's baptism of the African official in Acts 8.26–39. To recover these numerous references in the original Hebrew and Greek of the Bible, sometimes lost or obscured in English translation, one must first identify the key biblical names for Africa and its people.

"*Cush" in Hebrew and "Ethiopia" in Greek designate the land and people of the upper Nile River from modern southern Egypt into Sudan. The more indigenous term for this region is Nubia. "Ham" is another Hebrew term for the darker-hued people of antiquity. In Genesis 10, *Ham is son of *Noah who populates Africa, *Canaan, and *Arabia after the Flood. In poetry, the name Ham is a synonym for Egypt.

"Niger," the Latin word for "black," is used in Acts 13.1 to identify an African named Simeon. Simeon's companion Lucius was also African as is indicated by his place of origin, Cyrene, in Libya. Jesus's cross is carried by Simon, also from Cyrene.

In addition to Hebrew, Greek, and Latin terms for Africa, the Bible also uses Egyptian and Nubian names for the land and its people. The references to Africa encompass the length of the Nile Valley from the deep southern origins of the Nile down to the delta where it empties into the Mediterranean Sea. From the Lower Nile in the north to the Upper Nile in the south, the African skin color varied from brown to copper-brown to black. For the Egyptians used to these color variations, the term for their southern neighbors was *Neḥhesi,* "southerner," which eventually also came to mean "the black" or "the Nubian." This Egyptian root (*nḥhsj,* with the preformative *pꜣa* as a definite article) appears in Exodus 6.25 as the personal name of Aaron's grandson Phinehas (= *Pa-ne-ḥhas*). In Acts 8.27, the first non-Jewish convert to Christianity is an African official of the Nubian queen, whose title, Candace, meaning "queen mother," is mistaken for her personal name.

**Africa and Egypt.** *Egypt is in Africa, and both the Bible and the early Greek and Roman explorers and historians viewed this great civilization of the Nile as African. Before the modern idea of color prejudice, the distinctions noted in antiquity between the brown Egyptians and their darker-hued neighbors to the south did not contain the racial and cultural connotations that exist today. The Bible therefore classified Egypt, along with Canaan and Arabia, as African in the Genesis account of the restored family of peoples after the Flood.

This linkage between Egypt and its southern neighbor Nubia/Cush is reinforced by the presence of these darker southerners in Canaan during the ancestral period and afterward as major elements in the Egyptian army garrisoned there. The early-fourteenth-century BCE Amarna Letters, correspondence from Canaanite kings to Pharaoh Akhnaton, testify to the early African presence there. One letter, from Abdu-heba, king of pre-Israelite *Jerusalem, complains of the rebellious Nubian troops stationed there. One can speculate that an African presence remained in the area, and that maintaining their tradition of military prowess, later generations of Nubian/Cushites either became part of *David's forces which captured Jerusalem, or remained part of Jerusalem's militia which David incorporated as his own, as he did with the older *Jebusite priesthood.

Still later in Israelite history, during the reign of *Hezekiah of Judah (727–698 BCE), Nubia ruled Egypt as its Twenty-fifth Dynasty (751–656 BCE), and forged a close alliance with Judah in a common effort to ward off capture by the *Assyrians. Even as the prophet Isaiah protested that the king should trust in God rather than in the Egyptians for the defense of Jerusalem, his oracle on the Cushite emissaries fixed in biblical tradition the Egypt/African common identity. This same equation is expressed in Nahum's lament over the fall of the Egyptian capital Thebes, even as he exults over the destruction of Assyria's capital *Nineveh.

**Africa at the Royal Court and in the Wisdom Tradition.** The Africans who are named in the Hebrew Bible are closely aligned with the royal court and wisdom traditions of ancient Israel. One of David's Cushite soldiers brought news of the death of his son *Absalom, and *Solomon, already married to an Egyptian princess, entertained the Queen of *Sheba who had come to visit him on a trade mission. *Jeremiah was saved from death under King *Zedekiah by an African court official Ebed-melek ("servant of the king"), while in an earlier incident under King Jehoiakim a messenger of African heritage named Jehudi communicated with the prophet. The prophet *Zephaniah is called "son of Cushi" in his genealogy, which extends back to Hezekiah.

Solomon as patron of wisdom opened the door to Egyptian proverbs and poetry as evidenced in segments of the book of Proverbs modeled upon the Egyptian "Instructions of Amen-em-ope," and in Psalm 104, which echoes an Egyptian hymn to Aton. Hezekiah, who aligned himself with the Cushite Dynasty, is also listed as a royal patron of Israel's proverbial wisdom. The maiden in Song of Solomon 1.5 proclaims, "I am black and beautiful, O daughters of Jerusalem, like the tents of Kedar, like the curtains of Solomon." The dual imagery is clear: dark hue is paralleled by the black goat-skin tents, and beauty is matched by the sumptuous royal curtains. (The Hebrew connector *wĕ* is taken in its normal sense as a conjunctive "and" rather than the less usual disjunctive "but").

**Africa in Israelite Worship and Messianic Thought.** Among those known to God under the imagery of *Zion as mother of nations is Cush, who also brings tribute to the Temple. This concern for Cush and the other nations may extend from the formative experience of the Exodus and wilderness sojourn, where Hebrews were accompanied by a "mixed multitude," including Phinehas and *Moses's Cushite wife.

In prophetic literature, after God's wrath is vindicated on the nations of the earth, God will change their speech so all can worship God, and "from beyond the rivers of Ethiopia my suppliants, the daughter of my dispersed ones, shall bring my offering" (Zeph. 3.10). This refers to the African diaspora, to Israelite exiles in Africa returning with gifts of thanksgiving to God. Africa then with its people seen as converts shall come to worship God in Zion, along with dispersed Israelite exiles. It is in this context of God's universal reign that the prophet Amos proclaims, "Are you not like the Ethiopians to me, O people of Israel? says the Lord" (Amos 9.7). God is judge and ultimately redeemer of all nations.

The New Testament proclamation of Jesus as *Messiah continues in the early mission of the apostle Philip who baptizes the African official in Acts 8.26–39. It is significant that in this incident the term "messiah" is interpreted in light of Isaiah 53.7–8 as God's suffering servant. That the African was reading Isaiah suggests that the emissary was a recent convert or a *proselyte.

In the light of the Psalms and the prophets, then, Africans can be viewed both as diaspora and as proselytes among Israel's dispersed people, and also as forerunners of the conversion of all the nations of the earth. *Robert A. Bennett*

**AHAB.** The son and successor of Omri, Ahab ruled as one of Israel's most powerful kings from roughly 873 to 851 BCE. After expanding the summit of *Samaria, his capital city, he constructed a massive casemate fortification wall enclosing lavishly appointed royal buildings, including the "ivory house." Ahab brought Israel to the fore of international politics by marrying the Sidonian princess *Jezebel, fighting protracted wars against the Arameans of *Damascus, struggling for hegemony over Transjordan (Moabite Stone), and participating in the anti-Assyrian league at Qarqar in the Orontes Valley (Assyrian records). But deeply rooted north-south tensions and the Judahite perspective of the final Deuteronomic history resulted in a critical treatment of Ahab in the Bible; narratives describing the antagonism between Ahab and the prophet *Elijah constitute the sharpest polemic against him.

*See also* Israel.

*Ron Tappy*

**ALEXANDER III ("The Great").** Macedonian, born in 356 BCE. After the assassination of his father, Philip II, at Aegae in 336, Alexander ascended to the throne and took over his father's plan of a crusade to punish the *Persians for Xerxes' invasion of Greece almost a century and a half earlier. Alexander crossed the Hellespont with a total force of about fifty thousand in 334 and defeated the Persian army in three major battles, the last in 331.

These victories opened the heart of the Persian empire to Alexander. Persepolis was sacked and the palace of Xerxes burned. From Persepolis and Media, Alexander conquered Bactria and Sogdiana (330–329) and then extended his eastern frontier to the Hyphasis (Beas) and the lower Indus River (327–325). At the Hyphasis, the Macedonian army refused to march farther east. From the Indus Delta, Alexander marched west with part of his army across the Gedrosian desert, where his army suffered great losses during the fall of 325. He reached Susa in March of 324, where he and ninety-one members of his court married wives from the Persian nobility. During the final year of his life, Alexander discharged ten thousand Macedonian veterans at Opis, and then at *Babylon, in 323, made plans for future conquests (especially Arabia). He died, probably of a fever following a drinking party, on 10 June 323.

Alexander undoubtedly was the greatest general in Greek history; he made the army forged by his father into an irresistible force by a combination of uncanny strategic insight, versatility, and courage beyond reason. The cities he founded (reportedly over seventy) planted pockets of Hellenism throughout the Near East. He also made monarchy central to the politics of the Greek world; his kin and generals fought to establish themselves as his heir until about 275, when there emerged the three kingdoms that dominated the eastern Mediterranean until the advance of Rome: Macedon, ruled by the Antigonids until 168 BCE; *Egypt, ruled by the Ptolemies until 31 BCE; and *Syria, ruled by the Seleucids until 64 BCE. It is against the background of the origins of the Seleucid dynasty that the author of 1 *Maccabees presents a sketch of Alexander's conquests and the character of Antiochus Epiphanes.

*Guy MacLean Rogers*

**ALIEN.** Also translated "sojourner," "resident alien," and "stranger," an alien (Hebr. *gēr*) is technically a person in a community who is not part of its traditional lineages. In the Hebrew Bible, "aliens" usually are non-Israelites living ("sojourning") in Israel, but they can also be Israelites of one tribe sojourning in the territory of another tribe. Such persons were often financially distressed, forced to be dependents of "native" residents. Thus, aliens are often mentioned alongside *widows, *orphans, and the *poor as typically in need of assistance. Aliens could be subjected to manual labor; yet, special attention is given to accord them equal status with native Israelites, making them corecipients of God's blessings and curses. The Israelites are commanded to treat aliens well, because they were once aliens in Egypt. In fact, they are to view themselves as aliens sojourning on God's land, thereby furthering their sense of dependence on God.

New Testament writers describe their Israelite ancestors as aliens in Egypt and the exile in Babylon as the time of sojourning. In dealing with the problem of incorporating *gentiles into an all-Jewish community, Paul says that they are "no longer strangers and aliens, but . . . citizens . . . of the household of God" (Eph. 2.19). Any hint of separation is thereby eliminated. On the other hand, all who have become members of God's "people" must disavow allegiance to other groups, considering themselves aliens in the world around them. In this regard, *Abraham is held up as an ancient model.

*Timothy M. Willis*

**AMALEK.** One of Israel's most unrelenting enemies, at least in the early periods, Amalek is first referred to in Abraham's day, in Genesis 14.7, which speaks of the Amalekite field. But later in Genesis, Amalek is made the son of Eliphaz, son of *Esau, rendering the earlier reference anachronistic.

Shortly after the Exodus, the Amalekites attacked Israel, but Israel succeeded in repulsing the attack. The enmity created is reflected in the bloodthirsty declaration "I will blot out the name of Amalek. . . . The Lord's war against Amalek is from generation to generation" (Exod. 17.14, 16).

The Amalekites raided the Israelites in the days of the judges. Later, King *Saul made a concerted effort to destroy Amalek, following the prophet *Samuel's call for the ban, but enough Amalekites survived to destroy *David's city of Ziklag. Nevertheless, after Ziklag the Amalekites ceased to trouble Israel. 1 Chronicles 4.42–43 depicts the tribe of *Simeon as eradicating the remnant of Amalek, fulfilling God's earlier promise.

*Philip Stern*

**AMMON.** A tribal state located to the east of the *Jordan River that played a marginally significant role in the history of Palestine during the Iron Age. Relatively little is known about Ammon, its history, and its culture. Our main sources of information about it are the Bible and Assyrian inscriptions, both of which deal almost exclusively with Ammon's external affairs. Only a few substantive Ammonite inscriptions have been discovered so far, and excavations are just beginning to illuminate Ammonite culture.

The origins of the tribe of Ammon are obscure. Genesis 19:30–38 presents an artificial and satiric legend that portrays the eponymous ancestor of the Ammonites, Ben-ammi, as the offspring of the incestuous union of *Lot and his daughter. But this provides no insight into the initial development of Ammon. The region that became the land of Ammon was occupied fairly densely during the Middle and Late Bronze Ages, but there is no evidence whether the tribe of Ammon was already a distinct ethnic group during that time.

By the early part of the Iron Age (ca. 1200–1000 BCE), however, both archaeological and literary evidence indicates that a somewhat centralized state began to form around the capital city of Rabbat-bene-ammon ("Rabbah of the sons of Ammon"; modern Amman, Jordan). Conflict arose during this period between the Ammonites and the Israelites who lived to the east of the Jordan River. The earliest Ammonite king whose name is preserved is Nahash, who besieged the Israelite town of Jabesh-gilead and was defeated by Israelite troops rallied by the young *Saul. Nahash's son, Hanun, provoked a war with Israel during the reign of *David, which led to Ammon's defeat and incorporation into David's empire as a vassal.

After the death of *Solomon and the breakup of the united kingdom of Israel, Ammon presumably became independent again. Little is known of the kingdom during the ninth century, but it likely came under the domination of *Aram-Damascus, especially during the reign of Hazael (ca. 842–800 BCE), as did most of Palestine. During the eighth century, Damascus declined, and Israel and Judah experienced a resurgence of political power. Ammon appears to have come under the control of Judah during the reigns of Uzziah and Jotham, but with the arrival of the Assyrian king *Tiglath-pileser III, Ammon, like the other small kingdoms, became an Assyrian vassal.

The Assyrian period (late eighth to late seventh century) was a prosperous period for Ammon. The Assyrians guaranteed its position on the international trade routes and helped protect its flanks from the various nomadic groups that threatened the security of the routes. Excavations and Assyrian texts indicate that Ammon extended its boundaries during this period, westward to the Jordan River, northward into Gilead, and southward toward Heshbon. The most substantial ruins of the Iron Age date to this period, and seals, inscriptions, and statuary indicate the kingdom's wealth. A number of stone towers found in several regions of Ammon appear to date to this period. Once thought to be a system of Ammonite fortresses, recent studies now identify most of them as agricultural towers such as the one described in Isaiah 5.2.

There is uncertainty about the situation of Ammon during the Neo-Babylonian period. It is probable that Ammon was involved in the great rebellion against *Nebuchadrezzar in 589–586 BCE, and that, as a result, it was annexed into the Babylonian provincial system. By the succeeding Persian period only the name of the kingdom of Ammon survived, largely as a geographical rather than as a political term. Recent excavations and surveys indicate that a modest population continued to inhabit the region through this period.

Ammonite religion and culture remain little known. Even the characteristics of its patron deity, Milcom, are uncertain. *Wayne T. Pitard*

**AMORITES.** The Amorites were among the original inhabitants of *Canaan before the Israelite conquest, along with *Hittites, Canaanites, *Jebusites, and others. The entire aboriginal population of Canaan is also called "Amorite," and *Jerusalem was perhaps an Amorite town. There were Amorites east of the *Jordan River at Heshbon in *Ammon and at Bashan in Gilead. These were related to the Ammonites of central Transjordan, but not to the *Moabites or *Edomites in the south.

The Bible mentions Amorites as settled in Canaan and Transjordan. These were elements of an earlier, larger, more diverse Amorite group that originated apparently in the *Euphrates region of eastern Syria. Cuneiform texts of the third millennium BCE refer to a land west of the Euphrates known as MAR.TU in Sumerian or *Amurru* in Akkadian. Amurru included Syria and possibly parts of Palestine. Its inhabitants were considered foreign to Mesopotamia in language and culture. The Amorite language belongs to the linguistic family of Northwest Semitic, like Ugaritic, Aramaic, and Hebrew, and Amorite material culture in Syria shows affinities with that of Palestine in the Middle Bronze Age (first half of the second millennium BCE). Mari, a second-millennium Syrian city on the Euphrates, can be considered an Amorite town, though the Akkadian-language Mari texts do not refer to the city's inhabitants specifically as "Amorites." Some Amorites were not town-dwellers but *nomads, and the Mari texts frequently mention one such group, the "Banu-yamina," who resembled, in name and nomadic habits, the later biblical Benjaminites. *Joseph A. Greene*

**AMOS.** The early *prophets of Israel—*Samuel, *Elijah, *Elisha, and many others—are known from stories included in the historical books of Samuel and Kings. Amos was the first of the prophets whose name goes with a book entirely concerned with his life and message; nothing is known about him from any other source. The composition of his prophecy represented the creation of a new kind of literature. It was followed by other books that carry the names of a succession of prophets: three large books ("major" prophets) and twelve small ones ("minor").

The authors behind these shorter books were by no means "minor" in stature. Amos himself is one of the giants of the ancient world, one of the most powerful of the biblical prophets. He brought the prophetic word against social injustice and international terrorism and he preached repentance—and, when that failed, he denounced the impenitents. As a visionary ("seer") he located the domestic wrongs within Israel, and the crimes within the community of nations in a global, indeed cosmic setting. He held the rulers responsible for the evils in the world and addressed his messages primarily to them. He placed Israel, the chosen people of Yahweh, on the same footing as other nations. God expects the same morality from them all; but the words of reproach, condemnation, and judgment are addressed most directly to Israel because of its domestic wrongs.

Amos was not only a prophet of doom; he also called the people to reform, and when they failed and disaster became inescapable, he pointed to the hope of future restoration.

Amos's career is set in the time of two kings, Uzziah of Judah and Jeroboam II of Israel. Both monarchs had exceptionally long reigns, covering most of the first half of the eighth century BCE. Many scholars date Amos toward the end of that period (about 750 BCE), or even later; but recent research into the political situation disclosed by the book suggests that it could be earlier than that. *Assyria is nowhere recognized as a factor (except in the Septuagint text of 3.9), and the six nations surrounding Israel are addressed in 1.3–2.3 as if they are all still independent: this more accurately describes the early decades of the eighth century. The historical perspective is likewise vast. God's dealings with Israel are reviewed in the light of events that have taken place over centuries, with the Exodus as a major point of reference.

The book of Amos falls into three distinct sections, each with its own message and mood. The last, the Book of Visions, contains the only narrative material. This autobiographical report of five visions provides a framework that carries the dramatic report of Amos's confrontation with Amaziah, priest of Bethel, as well as prophetic oracles.

In the first pair of visions, Amos is able to secure a reprieve for Israel by his intercession. There is still time for repentance. The plagues reported in chap. 4 were intended as chastisements that would lead to contrition and reparation; but they failed to achieve this, and turned into destructive judgments.

In the second pair of visions the situation has completely changed. There is no intercession; rather, the Lord says twice that he will never pass by them again. This new attitude corresponds to the message of certain doom that pervades the first four chapters, and especially the opening speech, with its note of finality. The situation has become hopeless. Amos's early messages, corresponding to the intercessions of the first two visions, are presented in the middle of the final book (chaps. 5–6); his final message comes first (chaps. 1–2), with the following material analyzing the causes and justifying the decision.

The major cause of the change in attitude between the first and second pairs of visions, the final proof that repentance will never be forthcoming, is the refusal to listen to the prophets, and worse, the attempt to silence them altogether. Amaziah's ban is the turning point: when the highest religious leader rejects the word of God and his messenger, judgment is inevitable. The fifth vision and the oracles that go with it predict the total destruction of "all the sinners of my people" (9.10).

That is not the end of everything, however. As elsewhere in the Bible, death can be overcome by the miracle of resurrection; and Amos promises the recovery of Israel's life and institutions in a new age of prosperity and bliss.

*Francis I. Andersen*

**ANANIAS.** Three different characters in the book of Acts are named Ananias:

(1) A member of the Jerusalem church who violates its communal principles and is struck down after denying the transgression.

(2) The disciple who reluctantly restores Saul's vision after the road to Damascus experience (*see* Paul).

(3) The high priest who presides when Paul is brought before the Council in Jerusalem. Later this Ananias leads a delegation from the Council to the governor in Caesarea to plead for Paul's condemnation. *Daniel N. Schowalter*

**ANCESTORS, THE.** Genesis 12–50 relates in the fullest form the traditions about the ancestors of Israel, frequently called the patriarchs (*Abraham, *Isaac, and *Jacob) and the matriarchs (*Sarah, *Rebekah, *Leah, *Rachel, Bilhah, and Zilpah). These chapters are part of a larger narrative that covers the period from the creation of the world to the fall of Jerusalem in 587/586 BCE, and they have the specific purpose of presenting the story of the *Hebrews from their beginnings, with the call of Abraham, to their presence in Egypt following *Joseph's rise to power.

Within Genesis 12–50 can be discerned the Abraham cycle, the Isaac cycle, the Jacob cycle, and the Joseph story. Each section differs markedly from the others. The Joseph story is a highly artistic and skilled narrative, leading to a climax in which Joseph, the ruler of Egypt, discloses his identity to his brothers, who had sold him into slavery. The Isaac cycle is by far the shortest, and the only one of its narratives that deals exclusively with Isaac closely resembles two stories about Abraham. While the Abraham and Jacob cycles show every sign of having been compiled from traditions that were originally separate, the Jacob cycle has the more integrated narrative structure.

The predominant theological theme that runs through these disparate sections is that of the fulfillment of God's purpose and promise in spite of all hindrances. After God has promised to Abraham that he will become a great nation, Abraham goes to Egypt, where God must intervene to rescue Sarah from the Pharaoh's harem. Sarah is next presented as being sterile, and in order to get offspring, Abraham considers adoption, only to produce a son by Sarah's Egyptian maid *Hagar. When Sarah finally produces a son it is in her old age; almost immediately, though, Abraham is ordered to offer the son, Isaac, as a sacrifice. Abraham's obedience is rewarded by the sparing of Isaac's life, and the first cycle ends with Rebekah being brought from Abraham's home of northeast *Mesopotamia as a wife for Isaac.

Rebekah is also sterile, so that her children, like Sarah's child, are a special divine gift. The Isaac cycle is quickly swallowed up into the conflict between his sons Jacob and *Esau, with the latter threatening the life of Jacob, who is designated as the successor of Abraham and Isaac. In Haran, Abraham's original home to which Jacob flees, Jacob comes into conflict with his uncle Laban, and is tricked into marrying Leah before he can obtain his true love, Rachel. Like Sarah and Rebekah, Rachel turns out to be barren; the son she eventually does have, Joseph, will later be sold into slavery by his brothers, some of whom would have preferred to kill him. In the meantime Jacob, who has fled from Laban and is returning home, must survive the danger of being reunited with Esau. Prior to this meeting, his name is changed by God to *Israel.

Joseph's words to his brothers, "It was not you who sent me here, but God" (Gen. 45.8), sums up the main theological theme of the ancestral narratives: God's fulfillment of his purpose and promise. But there are subsidiary themes, prominent among which is God's rejection of parts of Abraham's family. His nephew, *Lot, has two sons who are the ancestors of the nations *Moab and *Ammon; but their rejection is indicated by their incestuous origin. Similarly, Esau, the ancestor of the nation of *Edom, is rejected for marrying non-Hebrew wives. Jacob's triumphs over Laban indicate the rejection of the northeastern branch of the family.

This subsidiary theme no doubt reflects the political realities of the time in which the narratives were being combined, the period of *David or *Solomon. In the tenth century BCE, Ammon, Moab, Edom, and kingdoms to the northeast were subject to Israelite rule. This raises the question of the relation between the ancestors as historical figures and the traditions about them. Although some scholars argue that the ancestral narratives were not written until after the exile (which is certainly when they reached their final form), a majority would accept that Abraham and Jacob were ancestors around whom traditions gathered in Israel's premonarchic period. It should be noted that Abraham is associated with *Hebron while Jacob is connected with Bethel and his sons with *Shechem. This suggests that Abraham was an ancestor of the tribe of *Judah, and had migrated from northeast Mesopotamia together with groups that later became Moab and Ammon. Jacob was the ancestor of Israel, which was originally an association of tribes, not including Judah, in the central highlands of Canaan. The odd fact that, whereas Jacob is the ancestor of Israel, the real father of the nation is the Judahite figure Abraham, is best explained by Judah's dominant position over Israel when the Abraham and Jacob traditions were united in the tenth century BCE. For a people experiencing relief from oppression for the first time in many decades, the figures of the ancestors provided the focus for stories that articulated the identity of the people, marked them off from their neighbors, and interpreted their peace and their possession of the land as the fulfillment of a divinely executed promise. *J. W. Rogerson*

**ANDREW.** A disciple of *Jesus and brother of *Simon Peter. The two are pictured as fishermen working beside the sea when Jesus summons them to follow him and become "fishers of people." In John's gospel Andrew first appears as a disciple of *John the Baptist.

Although less prominent than his brother, Andrew is present for Jesus's bread miracle and the apocalyptic speech on the Mount of Olives. Lists of the *Twelve name Andrew second or fourth. According to late medieval tradition, Andrew was martyred by being crucified on an X-shaped cross, which later appears on the flag of Great Britain representing Scotland, whose patron is Andrew. *Philip Sellew*

**ANGELS.** In Israel's early traditions, God was perceived as administering the cosmos with a retinue of divine assistants. The members of this divine council were identified generally as "*sons of God" and "morning stars," "gods" or the "host of heaven," and they functioned as God's vicegerents and administrators in a hierarchical bureaucracy over the world. Where Israel's polytheistic neighbors perceived these beings as simply a part of the pantheon, the Bible depicts them as subordinate and in no way comparable to the God of Israel.

The most ancient Israelites would probably have felt uncomfortable in describing all these beings as "angels," for the English word "angel" comes from the Greek *aggelos,* which at first simply meant "messenger" (as does the Hebrew term for angel, *malʾāk*). God's divine assistants were often more than mere messengers. *Cherubim and *seraphim, for example, never function as God's messengers, for their bizarre appearance would unnecessarily frighten humans. On the contrary, God is frequently depicted in early narratives as dispensing with divine messengers, for he deals directly with humans without intermediaries.

As time passed, however, an increasing emphasis on God's transcendence correlated with an increasing need for divine mediators. These beings who brought God's messages to humans are typically portrayed as anthropomorphic in form, and such a being may often be called a "man." The members of God's council are the envoys who relay God's messages and perform tasks appropriate to their status as messengers. In some narratives of encounters with supernatural beings, there is reluctance to identify them by name. But as these messengers become more and more frequent, they eventually are provided with individual names and assigned increasingly specific tasks that go beyond that of a messenger. The only two angels named in the Hebrew Bible are in the book of *Daniel: *Gabriel reveals the future while *Michael has a more combative role, opposing the forces of evil. The angelic hierarchy becomes more and more explicit and elaborate (*see* Archangels), and each human being has his or her own protecting angel. The term "messenger" (Grk. *aggelos;* Hebr. *malʾāk*) is used so frequently to depict these beings in their encounters with humans that it becomes a generic term to describe all supernatural beings apart from God, whether or not they actually functioned as messengers.

Angels are depicted as having the freedom to make moral choices, for they require judicial supervision and God himself is reluctant to trust them. The Bible records a number of angelic rebellions or perversions, as a result of which some rebel angels are already incarcerated.

"The Angel [or Messenger] of the Lord" is a problematic figure. The ambiguous Hebrew phrase is best translated without the definite article, that is, "an angel [messenger] of Yahweh" (as do the Septuagint and NJV). Later Christian theology tended to see the preincarnate Christ in this figure (hence the definite article), but the phrase probably referred vaguely to any mediator sent by God. He may be human. When the figure is clearly referred to as superhuman, he does not always function as a messenger but instead talks and behaves as if he were God, even failing to introduce his words as the message of another who sent him. Since early stories are internally inconsistent, identifying the figure as both God and God's messenger, it is probable that some of these stories originally described God at work but were modified through time to accommodate God's increasing transcendence as one who no longer casually confronted humankind.

The increasing role played by angels in the later stages of the Hebrew Bible is found everywhere in the New Testament. The voice of God (the Father) is only exceptionally heard in the New Testament, unlike earlier biblical traditions. Instead, angels bring God's message to humans and assist Jesus and his followers. Angels have limited knowledge, and when they appear to human beings, they may be described as descending from heaven. Although Jesus alludes to the absence of the institution of marriage among angels, angels are sexual beings. Some *Jews, particularly the most conservative, denied their existence. But among Jews and *Christians in general, angelology continued to develop so that not only was *Satan provided with his own retinue of angels as a counterpart to God, but hundreds of names and functions are also applied to angels in extrabiblical texts such as the books of *Enoch. *Samuel A. Meier*

**ANTICHRIST.** The word "antichrist" occurs in the Bible only in 1 and 2 John. The prefix *anti-* in Greek means "over against," "instead of," and so may imply usurpation as well as substitution. In 1 John, the coming of Antichrist is referred to as a standard sign of the "last hour," which has already happened in people who deny that Jesus is the Christ who has come in the flesh, and have seceded from the community; they are "false prophets" who embody the "spirit of antichrist." (*See also* John.)

On the other hand, 2 *Thessalonians warns, again as standard teaching, that the day of the Lord cannot come until the "lawless one," "the one destined for destruction," has appeared. He will usurp God's place in his Temple, and deceive people with Satan-inspired signs and wonders, until the Lord Jesus appears and destroys him. There are links with the prophecies of a desolating sacrilege in the holy place, and of false messiahs and false prophets, which must precede the coming of the Son of Man. Luke has historicized the picture in terms of the fall of Jerusalem in 70 CE; and John sees the "one destined for destruction" not as a future figure but as *Judas Iscariot (17.12).

The marks of the figure of Thessalonians recur in the two beasts of Revelation 13: the beast from the sea, which in its death and resurrection is a parody of Christ and claims divine honors; and the beast from the earth, which deceives people into worshiping the first beast, and with its lamblike voice and signs and wonders is a parody of the Holy Spirit. But there is also here an element of political coercion, and the sea beast's healed wound and his number identify him as Nero, returned from the dead, the persecuting emperor who was worshiped as a god.

The antecedents of this figure lie in Daniel 7, which was immensely important for New Testament writers. This vision relates that before the coming of God's kingdom there would be a time of disasters, persecution, and apostasy, and that opposition to God and his people would be summed up in a nation or person, human or superhuman, whom God or his agent would destroy. The vision is related to the Near Eastern myth of God's conflict with the dragon of the chaos waters, out of which this world was created. The myth celebrated the victory of order over chaos in nature; in some biblical passages the powers of chaos were historicized as nations opposed to God and his people—*Egypt and *Babylon—and in Daniel 7 the four beasts arising out of the sea (on which the sea beast of Rev. 13 is modeled) represent persecuting empires. They culminate in the "little horn" on the fourth beast, which represents the Greek king Antiochus Epiphanes, who tried to hellenize Judaism, and set up his statue in the Temple (the desolating sacrilege referred to at Mark 13.14 and Matt. 24.15). The book of Revelation updates this picture in terms of the Roman empire, the emperor cult, and collaborating *Christians.

On the other hand, those who accepted the state as God's ordinance saw the expected Antichrist as the embodiment of a specious spirit of lawlessness, which the state was keeping in check (according to one interpretation). After the Christianization of the Roman empire, this understanding became popular and even Revelation was read in this light, but corruptions in church and state led people back to Revelation's original sense.

The Antichrist expectation, with its attendant disasters, apostasy, and martyrdom of the faithful, dominated the Middle Ages and the sixteenth and seventeenth centuries. The myth expresses both the speciousness of evil and its apparent omnipotence, while asserting the imminence of God's final victory and the value of faithful witness in its achievement. From another point of view, it has provided a forceful way of characterizing opponents in church or state, and dignifying resistance to them.

*John Sweet*

**ANTIOCH OF SYRIA.** Present-day Antakya in Turkey, to be distinguished from the less important Antioch in Pisidia. In the first century CE, Antioch was the third-largest city of the Roman empire and capital of the proconsular province of Syria. Seleucus I Nicator founded it shortly after 300 BCE and named it for his father, Antiochus the Great. Antioch was settled by Macedonians, Greeks, native Syrians, and Jewish veterans of the army of Seleucus I. Located in the fertile Amuk plain on the Orontes River, which could be navigated to this point, it was at the junction of trade routes to *Damascus, Palestine, *Egypt, and the Aegean. By the second century BCE, it had a great public library, and under Antiochus IV Epiphanes (175–164/163 BCE) and the emperors Augustus and Tiberius fine public buildings were constructed. Excavations have disclosed splendid mosaic floors and a colonnaded main street.

The large Jewish population was generally loyal to the Seleucid monarchs and the *Roman empire. According to Acts, a *Christian mission among Antiochene *Jews began when refugees from persecution arrived after the martyrdom of *Stephen. Soon gentiles were also evangelized, and here the term "Christians" was first used. The new church subsequently sent *Barnabas and *Paul to Jerusalem with famine relief, as well as to discuss the issue of observance of the Law by gentile converts.

For many centuries, Antioch was a great center of Christian learning. Ignatius, who was martyred early in the second century CE, was its third *bishop according to tradition.

*Sherman Elbridge Johnson*

**APOLLOS.** The book of Acts records that an Alexandrian *Jew named Apollos was active as a missionary in *Ephesus and Achaia. Although skillful in communicating and knowledgeable concerning scripture, his teaching on baptism was incomplete. Priscilla and Aquila needed to provide him with a "more accurate" understanding, and when *Paul visited Ephesus after Apollos's departure, he had to rebaptize some people who had known John's baptism for repentance but not baptism in the name of Jesus.

In 1 Corinthians, Paul's references to Apollos and his teachings betray some tension between the two leaders.

*Daniel N. Schowalter*

**APOSTLE.** The Greek word *apostolos* ("someone who has been sent") is seldom used in classical Greek, but it occurs eighty times in the New Testament, where it means "delegate" of Jesus Christ and "messenger" of the gospel. Paul lists apostles first among the members of the body of Christ.

The corresponding word in Hebrew (*šālîaḥ*) was especially used to denote someone given full authority, for some particular purpose and for a limited time, to represent the person or persons from whom the delegate comes; the rabbis said that "a man's *šālîaḥ* is as himself." The legal status of such a delegate has its roots in Semitic customs pertaining to a messenger. The mission of *Paul to *Damascus and the delegation of *Barnabas and Paul by the church of *Antioch are to be understood in terms of a *rabbinic *šālîaḥ*. The same holds true for the sending of the disciples by Jesus, who included the apostles." They went two by two; their task of proclaiming the gospel and casting out *demons was limited as to sphere and time, and they had to return to the sender and report about their task.

Although Jesus is called "apostle" only once in the New Testament, in his "Son of man" sayings he presents himself as the agent of God for salvation. The divine commission of the Son is elaborated in the gospel of John, where the evangelist more than once uses the law concerning the authority of the *šālîaḥ*.

The status of a post-Easter apostle of Christ transcends that of a Jewish *šālîaḥ*. In his letters, Paul often defends and defines his apostolic authority. He mentions the apostles before him, specifying *Peter, the *twelve, James, and all the apostles. Though Paul was called last of all and considered himself to be the least of them, he was convinced that God had set him apart before he was born; thus, Paul repeated the claim of the prophet Jeremiah and of the servant of the Lord (Isa. 49.1–5). This means that the apostles of Christ had to serve during their whole lives as did the biblical *prophets, who were called by God and spoke as his messengers. Paul may have used the narrative of Isaiah's call as a key for interpreting his vision near Damascus. The motifs of Isaiah 6 can be discovered in scattered statements in which Paul speaks about the call and about the nature of his apostleship. The rhetorical questions "Am I not an apostle? Have I not seen Jesus our Lord?" (1 Cor. 9.1) get their force from Isa. 6.1, 8: "I saw the

Lord . . . send me!" Moreover, Paul understood his call to apostleship as an act of the grace of God. As a persecutor of the *Christians he was not worthy of it; in a similar way, Isaiah had confessed his unworthiness. Isaiah had been told to bring a message of doom to the Israelites that would harden them; Paul experienced disobedience to the gospel by his fellow *Jews, which is why he brought it to the gentiles. He felt the necessity to preach his message as Jeremiah had.

Besides the limited group of apostles (the twelve) in Jerusalem, Paul knew another circle of apostolic preachers. Therefore, one may distinguish between two types of New Testament apostles in Paul's view: those called through an appearance of the risen Lord; and charismatic preachers, who were delegated by a church such as that at Antioch, including both men and women (*see* Junia). But both types were united in a figure such as Paul. On the other hand, Luke reserves the designation "apostle" for the twelve disciples of Jesus who became the leaders of the Jerusalem church. For him, the apostle has to be a companion of Jesus and a witness to the resurrection. This seems to be the view of Mark as well as that of Matthew. *Otto Betz*

**ARABIA.** Arabia is a large, predominately arid peninsula bounded on the east by Mesopotamia and the Persian Gulf, on the north by the Mediterranean coastal highlands of Syria and Palestine, and on the west and south by the *Red Sea and Indian Ocean. Northwest Arabia is mountainous, stony desert. Like the neighboring *Negeb, it is desolate but habitable for sheep/goat nomads. The sandy deserts of interior Arabia remained impenetrable until domestication of the camel allowed its scattered oases to be linked by means of caravan routes in the first millennium BCE. Southern Arabia (Yemen) is, by contrast, a well-watered highland where terraced agriculture has supported permanent settlement from at least the second millennium BCE.

The Bible reflects close familiarity with the desert places and nomadic peoples of northwestern Arabia, and southern Arabia (*Sheba) was also known as a source of camels, gold, frankincense, and myrrh. Some places, like Dumah and Tema, can be identified with sites in northern Arabia; however, recent attempts to relocate the ancestral narratives wholesale from Palestine to northern Arabia must be rejected. The Hebrew word *ᶜărābâ* means "desert," but in one form it also means "*nomad." The phrase "all the kings of Arabia" can mean "all the kings of the Arabs" or "all the kings of the nomads." Few of the numerous nomadic peoples mentioned in the Bible are called "Arabs," and only rarely is their territory called "Arabia." Rather, they are identified by their geographic or ethnic origin: Amalekites, Ishmaelites, Midianites.

In the New Testament, "Arabians" (denoting probably Arabic speakers) were among the polyglot crowd gathered in Jerusalem at Pentecost. For a time after his call, *Paul "went away into Arabia," perhaps to eastern Syria or Transjordan. *Joseph A. Greene*

**ARAM.** Aram is a name of both places and persons. As a place name it refers usually to Aram-Damascus, a powerful Aramean state in southern Syria during the early first millennium BCE (*see* Damascus). Aram also designates other contemporary Aramean states along the northern border of Israel, including Aram-zobah northeast of the Antilebanon mountains and Aram-maachah in the upper Jordan valley. Some English translations follow the Septuagint and put "Syria" or "Syrian" where the Hebrew text has "Aram" (place) or "Arami" (person of Aram, an Aramean). The Greek words, however, are not precise equivalents of the Hebrew (*see* Syria).

As a personal name, Aram is one of the five sons of Shem and the eponymous ancestor of the Arameans. Genesis 22.20–21 identifies another Aram as son of Kemuel and grandson of Nahor, brother of the patriarch *Abraham. Abraham's son *Isaac married a granddaughter of Nahor who was sister to Laban "the Aramean." Abraham's grandson *Jacob wed *Rachel and *Leah, both daughters of this same Laban. These and other accounts in Genesis that associate the *ancestors of Israel with people and places in the upper *Euphrates region (Aram-naharaim, translated "*Mesopotamia," or Paddan-aram) suggest a close relationship between the Israelite ancestors and the Arameans.

Outside the Bible, Aram is mentioned in a cuneiform inscription of Naram-Sin of Akkad (ca. 2300 BCE) as a place along the upper Euphrates. Cuneiform texts from Drehem in southern Mesopotamia also name Aram as a city in the upper Euphrates region ca. 2000 BCE. Annals of the Assyrian king Tiglath-pileser I speak of punitive campaigns in his fourth year of reign (1112 BCE) against nomadic Ahlamu-Arameans who reached as far west as Tadmor (Palmyra in Syria) and the Lebanon mountains.

In the reign of *David (tenth century BCE), Aram-zobah ruled southern Syria but was eventually defeated by the Israelite king. Aram-Damascus assumed control of southern Syria during the reign of *Solomon and was a recurrent opponent of Israel throughout ninth-eighth centuries BCE, although it was also sometimes Israel's ally against the *Assyrians. Aram-Damascus and the other Aramean cities of Syria were ultimately destroyed by the Assyrians in the late eighth century BCE.

In both biblical and extrabiblical sources, Aram denotes lands occupied by speakers of Aramaic, a Northwest Semitic language related to Hebrew and Phoenician that was widely spoken in Syria in the first millennium BCE. Aramaic language and script survived the destruction of the Aramean states in Syria. Aramaic became the lingua franca of The Persian empire, and dialects of Aramaic continued to be widely spoken in Palestine and Syria into the Roman period.

*Joseph A. Greene*

**ARARAT.** A mountainous country surrounding Lake Van in Armenia. It is commonly referred to as Urartu in *Assyrian texts, in which it first appears as a conglomeration of kingdoms in the thirteenth century BCE. A unified kingdom reached its zenith in the late ninth century under the dynasty founded by Sarduri I; its decline began when Sarduri II was defeated by *Tiglath-pileser III in 743 BCE. The end came in the early sixth century, when Urartu was conquered by the *Medes. In the Bible Ararat can be an enemy of Assyria or Babylon. It is best known, however, as the region ("the mountains of Ararat," not "Mount Ararat") in which *Noah's ark came to rest after the Flood. In spite of later Jewish, *Christian, and Muslim traditions that sought to identify the mountain on which Noah landed, all attempts to do so have ended in failure.

*Carl S. Ehrlich*

**ARCHANGELS.** From Greek *archaggeloi,* "chief angels" or "angels of high rank." The plural form is not found in the Bible, but in Tobit 12.15, *Raphael describes himself as "one of the seven angels who stand ready and enter before the glory of the Lord" (cf. Rev. 8.2). Further information concerning these seven angels is found in 1 *Enoch 20, whose Greek version describes them as "archangels" and lists their names as follows: Uriel, Raphael, Raguel, *Michael, Sariel, *Gabriel, and Remiel, the last name probably corresponding to the "archangel Jeremiel" of 2 Esdras 4.36. In the New Testament there are two references to individual archangels: in 1 Thessalonians 4.16 the call of the (unnamed) archangel is to herald the Lord's return, and in Jude 9 reference is made to the archangel Michael's contending with the devil over the body of Moses. But the paucity of these scriptural references is in sharp contrast to the elaborately developed angelology of the later church fathers.

*See also* Angels.

*William H. Barnes*

**AREOPAGUS.** This term refers both to the "Hill of Ares" located northwest of the Acropolis in *Athens and to the Council that met on the hill until the fourth century CE. During the seventh century BCE, the Council probably watched over the laws of the city; in 462/461 BCE, the Areopagus lost its guardianship of the laws. According to the author of the Athenian Constitution, it retained the power to hear cases of deliberate wounding, homicide, poisoning that resulted in death, arson, and digging up or cutting down of the sacred olive trees of Athena. During the late fourth century BCE, the Council investigated allegations of treasonable offenses.

The judicial functions of the Council were extended during the Roman imperial period. In Acts 17.16–21, *Paul is reported to have been brought to the Hill of Ares by some *Epicurean and *Stoic philosophers because he was preaching about *Jesus and the resurrection; there he delivered his speech about the altar of the unknown god. The scene of Paul on the Areopagus constructed by the author of Acts does not reflect an official judicial procedure or inquiry. Rather, the author of Acts has created an idealized scene of Athenian life, based upon stock motifs of Athenian topography, culture, and history, intended especially to recall the trial of Socrates. In this scene, Paul has been cast as a latter-day Socrates who discloses the true identity and plans of the unknown god to the listening gentiles.

*Guy MacLean Rogers*

**ARMAGEDDON.** A place name found only in Revelation 16.16, where it is identified as the "Hebrew" name for the location where the kings of the earth will assemble to fight against God. Scholars generally explain Armageddon (NRSV: "Harmagedon") as a Greek transliteration of the Hebrew phrase *har mĕgiddô* ("the mountain of Megiddo"). The city of Megiddo, strategically located in the western part of the Esdraelon valley at the crossroads of two trade routes, was the site of several important battles in ancient times. The reference to the "mountain" of Megiddo is, however, more problematic, corresponding to no evident geographical feature in the area. Although Armageddon appears only once in the Bible, it has become a familiar designation for the future final battle between the forces of good and evil. *William H. Barnes*

**ARTEMIS OF THE EPHESIANS.** Artemis was the Greek goddess of the woods and hunting, as well as the patron of women in childbirth, identified with the Roman goddess Diana. The early background of Artemis of the Ephesians is hidden in legends and sources related to the Greek colonization of Ionia. It seems reasonable, however, to conclude that the original goddess was an amalgam of the imported Greek Artemis and an indigenous goddess, perhaps an Anatolian mother goddess.

The Ephesian Artemis functioned primarily as the tutelary deity of *Ephesus. Although she was the deity "whom all Asia and the whole world worship (Acts 19.27)," her central shrine was located in and protected by the city. Religious artifacts from this cult have been found as far west as Spain and as far east as Palestine, but only "the city of the Ephesians [was] the temple keeper of the great Artemis, and of the statue that fell from heaven (Acts 19.35)."

There has been much confusion and misunderstanding of the goddess, arising largely from a polemical Christian misnomer that labeled the egg-shaped objects attached to certain depictions of the goddess as female breasts. From the epithet "multi-breasted" it was a short, but incorrect, leap to the conclusion that the goddess was primarily a fertility goddess. In fact, there is no scholarly consensus that the egg-shaped objects attached to the goddess represented breasts. Even if they did and this mammary/fertility symbol lay at the heart of the religion, it is difficult to explain why this depiction appeared so late in the development of the cult. In addition, the Ephesians, particularly in the Greco-Roman era, associated their goddess with the chaste Greek Artemis rather than a mother goddess of Anatolia or one of the fertility goddesses of the East. The primary internal sources of the religion itself, such as texts, coins, statuary, and inscriptions, offer no cogent evidence for depicting this goddess or her cult as principally a symbol of sexuality and fecundity.

The goddess was well known for her wealth, which stemmed from two circumstances. Her temple served as a bank both for the safe deposit of others' wealth and for loans at a profitable rate of interest. The goddess also owned extensive lands and fisheries that contributed to her great wealth. Others, such as manufacturers of devotional items involving the goddess, received income as long as the goddess's reputation flourished.

Because of its size and wealth, the temple of Artemis was acclaimed as one of the seven wonders of the ancient world. It was constructed of marble (127 columns, each 60 ft [18 m] tall), possessed an external horseshoe-shaped altar (96 by 66 ft [29 by 20 m]) and was the largest Greek temple in antiquity (20 by 425 ft [67 by 130 m]). It was damaged by invading Gothic raiders during the mid-third century CE and finally fell into disuse because of Christian ascendancy in the fourth and fifth centuries. The temple no longer stands, and its exact location was unknown for centuries until its foundations were unearthed in the late nineteenth century.

*Richard E. Oster, Jr.*

**ASHER.** The second son of *Jacob and Zilpah, *Leah's maid, and one of the twelve *tribes of Israel. In Genesis 30.13, the name Asher is associated with the Hebrew word for blessing, but many scholars associate the name's origin with the goddess *Asherah.

According to Joshua 19.24–31, the tribe of Asher settled in northwest *Canaan. Biblical sources praise Asher's fertile land. The authors of Judges claim that Asher failed to occupy all of its territory. *Solomon reorganized Asher's territory into an administrative district and later ceded twenty Galilean cities to the king of Tyre. After the Assyrian exile Asher's territory remained in foreign hands, but the tribe, as witnessed by its genealogies, endured.

*Gary N. Knoppers*

**ASHERAH.** The Canaanite mother goddess, associated with lions, serpents, and sacred trees. The word "asherah" in the Bible most often refers to a stylized wooden tree.

The biblical writers generally condemn worship of the goddess, but there is evidence that many in Israel devoted themselves to Asherah, perhaps even worshiping her as consort of Yahweh. At several times an asherah stood in Yahweh's *Temple in Jerusalem; there were in the Temple, moreover, vessels dedicated to Asherah and a compound in which women wove garments for her. An asherah also stood in *Samaria, the capital of the northern kingdom of Israel and in Yahweh's temple in Bethel. Recent archaeological discoveries have confirmed that the cult of Asherah was a part of Yahwistic tradition for at least some Israelites. *Susan Ackerman*

**ASHTAROTH; ASHTORETH.** *See* Astarte.

**ASIA.** In the Hellenistic period, Asia is a term for the Seleucid Empire. In the Roman period, Asia means the province of that name, in the western part of what is now Turkey. It was an important province, containing within its boundaries a number of wealthy cities, including *Ephesus, its capital. The *seven churches of the opening chapters of the book of Revelation are all in the province of Asia, as is Colossae, to whose church the letter to the *Colossians was sent. *Michael D. Coogan*

**ASSYRIA.** The ancient land of Assyria, located in what is now northeastern Iraq, drew its name from the small settlement of Assur (or Ashur) built on a sandstone cliff on the west bank of the Tigris about 24 mi (35 km) north of its confluence with the lower Zab River. Situated at a major river crossing but outside the zone for reliable annual rainfall, Assur early attracted settlements by pastoralists, since it was easily defensible and had ready access to water. Early levels of a small shrine there dating to ca. 2800–2200 BCE show affinities with *Sumerian culture to the south in furnishings and statuary.

The earliest independent ruler of the city-state of Assur attested in a contemporary inscription is Shalim-ahum, who reigned about 1900 BCE. At this time, firms of merchants in Assur established branches in several Anatolian cities and traded textiles and tin from Assur for silver.

About 1813 BCE, Shamshi-Adad I, an Amorite prince from the middle Euphrates, took possession of Assur and subsequently founded an empire with its capital at Shubat-Enlil (modern Tell Leilan in northeast Syria), with two sons reigning as subkings in *Mari and in Ekallate (just north of Assur). Under Shamshi-Adad's son Ishme-Dagan I, the empire was quickly lost; and the dynasty of Shamshi-Adad was replaced within a few decades by native Assyrians, who ruled—in relative obscurity—during the next four centuries, at times as vassals of Mitanni.

Under the dynamic Ashur-uballit I (1364–1328 BCE), Assyria reemerged as a major power, and in the next century conquered and gradually annexed much of the old heartland of Mitanni to the west, setting up an extensive provincial system and then briefly taking over much of Babylonia to the south. Its imperialist ethic was embodied in the Middle Assyrian coronation ritual, in which the officiating priest solemnly charged the king: "Expand your land!" After 1200 BCE, amid widespread upheavals and population movements in Western Asia, the Middle Assyrian empire declined both politically and territorially. An extensive if short-lived revival in the time of Tiglath-pileser I (1115–1076 BCE) dissipated under the pressure of invading Arameans, who confined Assyrian political power to a narrow strip along the Tigris until the late tenth century.

After 935 BCE, Assyrian kings reclaimed lost sections of the Assyrian heartland from the Arameans and began to expand militarily, especially to the west. Over the next three centuries, these monarchs created an extensive Neo-Assyrian empire, which at its height (ca. 660 BCE) embraced a substantial part of the ancient Near East from southern Egypt, Cyprus, and western Anatolia through Palestine-Syria and Mesopotamia to Elam and the Iranian plateau. The foundations of Assyrian imperial power were effectively laid by Ashurnasirpal II (884–859 BCE), who built a splendid new capital at Calah (Nimrud), restructured the Assyrian army into a fighting force without peer in southwestern Asia, reorganized the Assyrian provincial system, and earned a reputation for ruthless treatment of rebels and prisoners. His massive deportations from conquered lands, continued by his successors, brought large numbers of western Arameans into the heartland of Assyria, swelling the ranks of the court and army, influencing artistic and architectural styles, and, by the early seventh century, replacing the Assyrian language with *Aramaic as the vernacular. Ashurnasirpal's campaigns consolidated Assyrian territorial gains as far west as the Upper Euphrates and extracted tribute from these areas; his trading ventures, with military escort, succeeded in reaching the Mediterranean. His son, Shalmaneser II (859–824 BCE), began to extend Assyrian control into northern Syria; but his advance was checked temporarily at the battle of Qarqar (853 BCE) by a broad coalition of states led by *Damascus and Hamath and including Arab tribes and Israel (under *Ahab). Shalmaneser's subsequent campaigns, which reached into Cilicia, secured north Syria and brought the *Phoenician cities Tyre and Sidon into the Assyrian orbit. Despite a revolt of the major cities in Assyria (827–821 BCE) and an ensuing weakness in monarchic power, Assyria continued to be active in the west until about 785 BCE.

Meanwhile, in the late ninth and early eighth centuries in the mountains to the north of Assyria, the rival power of Urartu had risen to prominence. As the fortunes of Assyria declined after 783 BCE under weak kings and strong provincial governors, the Urartians pushed south into Iran and west across the Euphrates into northern Syria. By 745 BCE, Urartu had conquered or concluded alliances with most of the important states in south-central Anatolia and northern Syria and had assumed hegemony over the region. A revolt in Calah brought to the Assyrian throne *Tiglath-pileser III (745–727 BCE), a vigorous monarch who checked encroaching Aramean and Chaldean tribesmen in *Babylonia, restricted Urartu to its homeland, and marched across Syria and Palestine (once in response to a request from Ahaz of Judah for intervention) as far as Gaza. His son, *Shalmaneser V (727–722 BCE), besieged Tyre and captured *Samaria, bringing the kingdom of *Israel to an end. Sargon II (722–705 BCE), a usurper, deported the population of Israel to various parts of the empire, campaigned as far as the border of Egypt, brought Babylonia under his control, and built a magnificent capital at Dur-Sharrukin (Khorsabad) in the north of the country. His son, *Sennacherib (705–681 BCE), expanded further into Anatolia. Faced with perennial unrest in Babylonia (fomented for the most part by Merodach-baladan and his fellow Chaldeans) and smarting from the murder of his crown prince, Ashur-nadin-shumi, who had been king there from 700 to 694 BCE, Sennacherib eventually sacked and depopulated Babylon. In Palestine, he received the submission of *Hezekiah, who had rebelled in collusion with Merodach-baladan, and, after a siege, extracted tribute from *Jerusalem. Assassinated by one of his sons, Sennacherib was succeeded by another son, Esarhaddon (681–669 BCE), who invaded the Iranian plateau and Egypt, but died prematurely of illness while on campaign. His empire was inherited principally by his son Ashurbanipal (669–627 BCE), who reigned in Assyria; but another son, Shamash-shum-ukin (668–648 BCE), was installed as king in Babylon. Ashurbanipal campaigned extensively in Egypt, reaching as far as Thebes, and brought the empire to its territorial apogee in about 660 BCE. In 652 BCE, Shamash-shum-ukin launched a massive revolt, which won support from Elamites, Arabs, and other disaffected Assyrian subjects. Ashurbanipal spent more than ten years defeating and wreaking reprisals on the dissidents, exhausting the empire in the process.

After Ashurbanipal's death in 627 BCE, civil war broke out in Assyria between three contenders for the throne; it took several years before Sin-shar-ishkun (623?–612 BCE) emerged as the victor. Within a decade he was faced with a coalition of *Medes and Babylonians, who invaded and destroyed the central provinces of Assyria. A final king, Ashur-uballit II (612–609 BCE), ruled briefly in the western provincial capital of Haran with the support of Egyptian armies; but he was driven out by the Babylonians. The fledgling empires of Babylon and Media divided the territories of the Assyrian empire, which disappeared with barely a trace even in its former heartland.

Assyria in the first millennium BCE, though renowned primarily as a massive military power that overwhelmed and intimidated much of southwestern Asia, had a vigorous cultural and economic life. In the decorative arts, its craftsmen displayed creative sensitivity in such diverse media as ivories, seals, and palace wall reliefs; the latter depict an astonishing variety of subjects, including formal protective deities, scenes of battlefield and siege, daily life at court, and the botanical zoological parks created in and around the Assyrian capitals. Literature also flourished, its most notable monument being the large library amassed by Ashurbanipal (669–627 BCE) at *Nineveh, whose excavation in the mid-nineteenth century led to the rediscovery of Mesopotamian literature. On the economic side, trade prospered throughout the empire as new markets were opened to entrepreneurs even from the conquered territories. Booty, tribute, and trade goods poured into the Assyrian heartland, financing the erection and renovation of resplendent urban capitals as well as the maintenance of the military machine that made the empire possible.

*John A. Brinkman*

**ASTARTE** (AV: Ashtoreth, Ashtaroth). The Greek form of Ashtart, one of the three great Canaanite goddesses. Astarte was primarily a goddess of fertility and love, the counterpart of Greek Aphrodite. She was also associated with war, and, like her Mesopotamian equivalent Ishtar, had astral features.

In the Bible, worship of the goddess is repeatedly condemned: twice in the book of Judges the Israelites are punished for straying after the *Baals and Astartes; *Solomon is criticized for worshiping Astarte; and Jeremiah castigates the people for making offerings to the *Queen of Heaven, a syncretism of Astarte and Ishtar. *Susan Ackerman*

**ATHENS.** Excavations of ancient Athens (named after its patron goddess Athena) reveal its settlement since the Neolithic period. The easy defense of the Acropolis and the proximity of the Saronic Gulf to the south explain the importance of the site in the history of Attica. In the fifth century BCE, despite defeats in the Peloponnesian War, Athens emerged as the cultural and intellectual center of the Greek world. Innovative techniques in art and sculpture, powerful developments in Greek drama, and significant progress in political reform characterized the glory of fifth-century Athens. The wellspring for later Greek philosophical inquiry flowed from the life and thought of Socrates (ca. 470–399). Ironically, the virtual destruction of the Acropolis in the early fifth century by the Persians made way for an era of architectural creativity in the last half of the century, when the Parthenon, Erechtheion, and numerous other temples were constructed on the Acropolis.

Acts 17.16–34 contains the only extended reference in the New Testament to Athens. The plot of this narrative is structured around some of the best-known aspects of Athenian culture and local color. The city's religiousness, expressed in temples, shrines, and altars, was proverbial in both Greek and Roman thought. The travelogue composed by the Greek geographer Pausanias (second century CE) depicts a city replete with sacred edifices and statues. This facet of Athenian culture is reflected in Luke's statement that "the city was full of idols" and *Paul's reference to the Athenians' piety and an altar "to an unknown god."

From the time of Socrates until the emperor Justinian closed the schools of philosophy in 529 CE, the name of Athens was synonymous with philosophical pursuit of truth. The city had, in fact, been the home not only for Socrates but also for Plato's Academy, Aristotle's Lyceum, the Painted Porch of Stoicism, and the Gardens of Epicurus. As a university town in Paul's time, Athens continued to attract philosophical and philhellenic intellectuals. The account of Paul's efforts there is interwoven with allusions to the city's philosophical traditions. Paul encounters "Epicurean and Stoic philosophers" (17.18), argues for the true nature of God on the basis of natural revelation, and quotes the Stoic poet Aratus. (*See also* Epicureans; Stoics.) The scrutiny of Paul's doctrine of God by the council of the *Areopagus deliberately echoes the trial of Socrates for proclaiming new deities and leading the populace to question its beliefs in the traditional gods.

Beyond Acts 17, 1 Thessalonians 3.1, in which Paul mentions his stay in Athens, is the only other New Testament reference to the city. Athens was the home of several second-century Christian apologists, but otherwise did not exert much direct influence in early Christian history. *Richard E. Oster, Jr.*

**AZARIAH (THE THREE YOUNG MEN).** The Greek translation (Septuagint) of the book of *Daniel inserts between vv. 23 and 24 of chap. 3 a section embracing sixty-eight verses, which is not found in the Semitic original; this section is seen by Protestants as one of the Apocrypha, but is considered deuterocanonical by Roman Catholics and some Orthodox churches. It consists of a brief connecting narrative and two (or perhaps more correctly three) poems of liturgical character. The poems purport to be the words recited or sung by the three young men whom King *Nebuchadrezzar caused to be thrown into a fiery furnace when they refused to worship the golden image that he had set up.

The first of the poems is in the form of a prayer and is placed upon the lips of Azariah, the Hebrew name of the youth also called by his Babylonian name, Abednego. The prayer is not specifically appropriate to the situation of the fiery furnace, being simply a national lament like Psalms 74 and 79, which are petitions for the deliverance of Israel after the destruction of the Jerusalem *Temple. The prayer differs from these psalms by stating that the disaster was a justified punishment for the sins of the nation, an emphasis quite incongruous with the situation of the young men, who were being punished precisely for their religious integrity. The concluding verses of the prayer would be suitable for anyone suffering oppression and are doubtless the reason the prayer was felt to be suitable.

The much longer poem that begins in verse 29 also is a prayer in the form of a hymn of praise, recited by Azariah and his companions Hananiah (Shadrach) and Mishael (Meshach). It too is irrelevant to the particular situation of the youths, except for v. 66, which may well have been added when the hymn was interpolated into the book of Daniel.

With regard to the date of composition of the poems, there is no clear evidence, except for v. 15, which speaks of the absence of civil government and the cessation of Temple worship. In their present context, of course, the words are intended to apply to the putative situation of the youths in the Babylonian exile, but they would be even more appropriate in the early second century BCE when Antiochus Epiphanes desecrated the Temple (164 BCE) and when, indeed, there was no prophet or native government. *Robert C. Dentan*

**AZAZEL.** Appears only in the Day of Atonement ritual in Leviticus 16. Two goats were designated by lot, one for the Lord and one for Azazel, perhaps the name of a *demon. The Lord's goat became a sacrificial sin-offering, while the scapegoat was sent into the *wilderness after *Aaron placed his hands on it and confessed the people's sins. Verse 21 uses three words for sin, but does not mention impurity. Thus, the scapegoat ritual is for sins alone, and reveals the sacrificial cult's inability to achieve complete atonement by itself.

Some scholars suspect that the scapegoat was added to the chapter; if so, it has been well integrated into the text. In 16.17, Aaron makes atonement "for the assembly of Israel," making the scapegoat seem unnecessary. Yet it was necessary: this involves the riddance of something profoundly unwanted. The sin offering could not carry the sins away like the scapegoat. The magical Azazel ritual assured that the sins were sent away.

The Septuagint rendered Azazel as "sending away." In the Ethiopic book of *Enoch, Azazel is a fallen *angel. The Midrash and many modern commentators see Azazel as the demon to whom the scapegoat was sent. In the Mishnah, the practice was to throw the scapegoat over a cliff; the *rabbis derived from this an etymology, accepted by some (NEB: Azazel = "precipice"). Scholars have proposed other etymologies, but the origin and meaning of Azazel remain uncertain. *Philip Stern*

# B

**BAAL.** A common Semitic word meaning "owner, lord, husband." As "lord" it is applied to various *Canaanite gods, such as the Baal of Peor and the Baals, which were largely local manifestations of the storm god Baal. Although the head of the Canaanite pantheon was El, Baal was the most important god because of his association with the storms that annually brought revival of vegetation and fertility. Baal is prominent in the great complex of fifteenth century BCE Ugaritic epics, where he is called son of *Dagon and is named some 250 times, sometimes interchangeably with Hadad, the widely known Semitic storm god whose symbol, like Baal's, was the bull.

In art, Baal is depicted as the storm god Aliyan ("triumphant") Baal, who holds a thunderbolt in one hand and swings a mace with the other. Baal is the champion of divine order over earthly chaos—over deadly drought, represented by the deity Mot ("death"), and the unruly forces of the sea (the god Yamm). The Ugaritic epics tell how Baal defeats these powers and wins the title "rider on the clouds" (the same title ascribed to the God of Israel in Ps. 68.4).

The theme of opposition to Baal worship runs throughout the Deuteronomic literature and the *prophets. By the ninth century BCE, Baalism had deeply pervaded Israelite life. Personal names formed with Baal appear already in the time of the Judges. Even *Saul and *David had sons with Baal names. Intense conflict appeared with the introduction of the Baal of Tyre into Israel by *Ahab's queen, *Jezebel, daughter of Ethbaal of Sidon. Even as late as the time of *Manasseh, altars to Baal were still among the appointments in the Jerusalem *Temple.

Opposition to Baalism was led by Israel's prophets. The fertility rites associated with Baal worship corrupted the faith in Yahweh, and the myths undergirding them wrongly deified aspects of nature. The prophets endeavored to show Yahweh as a transcendent, universal God who provides rains and fertility yet who is no "nature god" trapped in unvarying seasonal cycles. Because agriculture was so vital and so precariously dependent on the weather, it became important to show that Yahweh, not Baal, was the one who rode the clouds, controlled the storms, and brought freshening rains. That the struggle against Baalism was finally successful is signalled by the replacement of the Baal element in some proper names by the word *bōšet* ("shame").

*David G. Burke*

**BAAL-ZEBUB.** The *Phoenician god at Ekron consulted by King Ahaziah. The name in Hebrew means "Lord of Flies," but no evidence exists for a

*Philistine god who either drove off flies or gave oracles through their buzzing. The Hebrew form is probably a derogatory transformation of Baal-zebul, which appears in Ugaritic texts meaning "Lord *Baal," but could also be understood as "Master of the Heavenly House" (cf. Matt. 10.25). In *Aramaic, Beel-zebul may have been construed as "Lord of Dung," Beel-zebub possibly as "Enemy." During the Greco-Roman period, Beel-zebul came to be used for a leader among the *demons opposed to God. Jesus denies that he casts out demons by authority of Beelzebul, the ruler of demons. Some translations employ Beelzebub in the New Testament passages, following the text of 2 Kings. Christian interpreters identified Beelzebul with *Satan on the basis of the Gospel passages. *Robert Stoops*

**BABEL, TOWER OF.** Babel is the Hebrew word for *Babylon, which the Babylonians themselves explained as meaning "gate of God." This etymology is probably not original, but the meaning is significant for a famous city whose central temple tower was said to reach the heavens. In Genesis 11.9 the meaning of Babel is explained by the Hebrew verb *bālal,* "to confuse, mix," and the confusion of speech.

The brief narrative in Genesis 11.1–9 also explains how there could exist such a variety of languages among the earth's people. The understanding that the earliest humans shared a common language is found in the *Sumerian *Enmerkar Epic.* Genesis 11.1–9 tells how *Noah's descendants wandered to the plain of Shinar (Babylonia), where they perfected the techniques for monumental brick architecture and built the renowned tower of Babel. Building the tower is interpreted as an act of arrogance, and human history is here understood to take a decisive turn from a common thread to many strands as God descends to confuse human speech and scatter the people all over the earth.

The enormous ziggurats of Mesopotamia could easily have symbolized the presumptuousness of the urban elite, and their ruin the judgment of God. Even as ruins their massive dimensions would have been striking. The Sumerian temple tower of the moon god Nanna at *Ur could have been the model for the tower of Babel. This huge terraced mountain of brick, with the god's temple on top, at least 70 ft (21 m) above ground level, was built ca. 2100 BCE. Of similar construction, the great temple of Marduk in Babylon, the E-sagila, is possibly the referent of the Genesis narrative; according to the Babylonian epic *Enuma Elish,* it took a year just to make the bricks for this colossally high structure.

*David G. Burke*

**BABYLON.** Babylon is the rendering of Akkadian Babilum (Babilim), the city that for centuries served as capital of the "land of Babylon." Cuneiform sources interpret its name as *bāb-ilim,* "gate of the deity." The Bible rejected this popular etymology in favor of a more scurrilous one that linked the name to the confusion of tongues (Hebr. *bālal,* "[God] confused"), and so the city is called Babel.

Not until around 1900 BCE did an independent dynasty establish itself at Babylon. Like most of their contemporaries, its rulers bore Amorite (Northwest Semitic) names, but unlike some of them, they enjoyed lengthy reigns, passing the succession from father to son without a break; this may have helped Babylon survive its rivals in the period of warring states (ca. 1860–1760 BCE).

Under the adroit Hammurapi (ca. 1792–1750 BCE), Babylon succeeded in restoring the unity of Mesopotamia under its own hegemony.

Babylon's triumph was short-lived, though: under its next king, Samsu-iluna (ca. 1749–1712 BCE), the extreme south was lost to the new Sealand Dynasty and the north to the Kassites at Hana. About 1600 BCE, the city itself was sacked by an invading army of Hittites from distant Anatolia (modern Turkey), and these rivals took it over, the Sealanders only briefly, but the Kassites for almost half a millennium (ca. 1590–1160 BCE).

It remained for the Second Dynasty of Isin (ca. 1156–1025 BCE) to restore Babylon to its earlier prominence. The recapture of the cult statue of Marduk from Elamite captivity by Nebuchadrezzar I (ca. 1124–1103 BCE) probably capped this development. Babylon was henceforth regarded as the heir to the millennial traditions of the ancient Sumerian centers of cult and culture. Marduk, the local patron deity of Babylon, was endowed with the attributes of the ancient Sumerian deities of those centers—notably Enki of Eridu and Enlil of Nippur—and exalted to the head of the pantheon. This exaltation was celebrated in new compositions such as *enuma elish* ("when above"; conventionally known as the "Babylonian Epic of Creation") and can be compared in certain respects with the exaltation of the God of Israel as celebrated in the roughly contemporary Song of the Sea.

In the early first millennium, Babylon could not sustain a military and political posture to match these cultural and religious pretensions, and it gradually declined into the status of a vassal state to *Assyria, the powerful neighbor to the north. Occasional alliances with Elam in the east or, notably under Marduk-apal-iddina II (the biblical Merodach-baladan), with Judah in the west, provided brief periods of precarious independence. The city was devastated by the Assyrian king *Sennacherib (704–681 BCE) not long after his abortive siege of *Jerusalem in 701 BCE. It was restored by that king's son and successor Esarhaddon (680–669 BCE), only to be caught up again in the violent civil war (652–648 BCE) between the two sons of Esarhaddon that pitted Shamash-shum-ukin of Babylonia against Assurbanipal of Assyria. The resultant weakening of the Assyrian empire no doubt helped clear the path for the accession of the last and in some ways greatest Babylonian dynasty, that of the Chaldeans, sometimes referred to as the Tenth Babylonian Dynasty (625–539 BCE).

With this restoration, Babylon ranked as one of the major cities, indeed, in Greek eyes, as one or even two of the seven wonders of the ancient world, by virtue of its walls in some accounts and invariably for its famous "hanging gardens." The gardens were more likely the work of Marduk-apal-iddina II than of *Nebuchadrezzar II (as claimed by Berossos in one Hellenistic tradition), but the latter certainly rebuilt the city most grandly during his forty-four-year reign (605–562 BCE). He is remembered in biblical historiography as the conqueror of Jerusalem in 597 and 587/586 BCE. The biblical record is supported and supplemented by the Babylonian Chronicle and other cuneiform documents. But the stories told in the book of Daniel about Nebuchadrezzar, as well as about *Belshazzar, should rather be referred to Nabonidus, who proved to be not only the last king of the dynasty (555–539 BCE) but the last ruler of any independent polity in Babylon. The city surrendered to *Cyrus the Persian in a bloodless takeover and thereafter, while continuing as a metropolis of the successive Achaemenid, Seleucid, and Parthian empires, ceased to play an independent role in ancient politics.

In the Bible, Babylon plays a dual role, positively as the setting for a potentially creative *diaspora, negatively as a metaphor for certain forms of degeneracy. The "Babylonian exile" imposed by Nebuchadrezzar on the Judeans removed the center of Jewish life to Babylon for fifty or sixty years, if not the seventy predicted by the prophet Jeremiah. The exiled king Jehoiachin was released from prison by Nebuchadrezzar's son and successor Amel-Marduk, the Evil-merodach of 2 Kings 25.27, and provided for from the royal stores, as indicated also by cuneiform sources. Jeremiah wrote to the exiles in God's name, advising them to enjoy the positive aspects of life in Babylon and to pray for its welfare. Ezekiel lived among the exiles and prepared them for the restoration, while Second Isaiah welcomed the arrival of Cyrus, which paved the way for the return of those exiles who chose to accept his proclamation.

Under Persian rule, Babylon continued to flourish as the seat of one of the most important satrapies of the Persian empire, and the Achaemenid Artaxerxes I could still be called "king of Babylon." The *Jews who chose to remain there enjoyed considerable prosperity, as indicated by business documents from nearby Nippur in which individuals identified as Judeans or bearing Jewish names (in Hebrew or Aramaic) engage in various agricultural and commercial activities. The foundations were thus laid for the creative role that Babylonia was to play in the Jewish life of the postbiblical period.

The Bible also reflects a negative view of Babylon. Already in the primeval history, the *tower of Babel uses the traditional ziggurat present in each city of *Sumer as a metaphor for the excesses of human ambition that led to, and accounted for, the confusion of tongues and dispersion of peoples. The Psalmists emphasized the negative aspects of exile, and the fall of the "arrogant" city and "its sinners" was predicted confidently, even gleefully, by the prophets. In the New Testament, Babylon became the epitome of wickedness and a symbolic name for Rome.

*William W. Hallo*

**BALAAM.** A non-Israelite *prophet who figures most prominently in the narratives of Numbers 22–24; there is also a lengthy prophecy of the same Balaam in the text from Deir ᶜAllā in the Jordan Valley dating to around 700 BCE.

The Bible evaluates Balaam's character in two quite different ways. On the one hand, Balaam is often portrayed as an example of an evil diviner who would sell his prophetic powers to the highest bidder, often in conflict with God's will. In a particularly humorous scene, Numbers 22.21–35 makes fun of Balaam's powers as a seer; he is repeatedly unable to see the divine messenger that even his donkey can see.

On the other hand, Numbers 22–24 as a whole portrays Balaam in a favorable light. When the *Moabite king Balak hires Balaam to curse his enemy Israel as they cross his territory on the way to the *Promised Land, Balaam replies piously that as a prophet he can speak only the words that God gives to him.

On four occasions when Balak asks Balaam to curse the Israelites, Balaam instead obeys God and speaks only words of great blessing upon Israel. The most famous of these oracles of blessing includes a prophecy about a great future king or *messiah of Israel. The oracle may originally have applied to *David, but later it was interpreted as the promise of a ruler who would come as a deliverer in the end time. Using royal images, Balaam proclaims, "A star shall come out of Jacob, and a scepter shall rise out of Israel"; this text probably underlies the account of the star followed by the *Magi.

A passage from Balaam's final oracle was quoted in the first telegraph message: "What hath God wrought!"

*Dennis T. Olson*

**BARABBAS.** Outside the Gospels nothing is known of Barabbas. His name is Aramaic and means "son of the father" (Abba), ironically denoting the status given exclusively to Jesus. Barabbas was imprisoned for robbery or for insurrection and murder, crimes not uncommon in the turbulent Palestine of the first century CE. In the account of the trial of Jesus, the Roman prefect Pontius *Pilate is portrayed sympathetically, finding no fault in Jesus and recognizing that Jewish priests plotted his arrest. Following a Passover custom unknown outside the Gospels, Pilate offered to free a Jewish prisoner and suggested Jesus, but the crowd (in John, "the Jews") demanded that Pilate release Barabbas and crucify Jesus. This helped establish a negative attitude toward Jews in *Christian tradition. *Gregory Shaw*

**BARNABAS.** Acts describes Joseph "Barnabas" as a Hellenized *Jew from Cyprus who played a leading role in the gentile mission. The apostles call this Joseph "son of encouragement" when he makes a large donation to the Jerusalem church. Barnabas introduces Saul (*Paul) to Jesus's original apostles in Acts 9.27 and journeys to *Antioch in Acts 11.22–24 as their representative.

In the letter to the *Galatians, Paul describes how he and Barnabas were given "the right hand of fellowship" by the Jerusalem leadership and had their mission to the gentiles approved. Acts portrays Barnabas as Paul's senior partner in evangelizing Cyprus and Iconium until their split over the role of John Mark (15.36–41: probably the Mark called Barnabas's cousin in Col. 4.10). Although Barnabas plays no further role in the New Testament, the second-century *Epistle of Barnabas* is written in his name. *Philip Sellew*

**BARTHOLOMEW.** A follower of Jesus and one of the *Twelve. Other than his Aramaic name, which means "son of Tolmai," nothing is recorded about him in the New Testament. Because Nathanael is not mentioned in the synoptic Gospels, and Bartholomew does not occur in the gospel of John, but both are linked with Philip, it has been suggested that they are the same person, in which case Bartholomew would be Nathanael's patronymic. Later tradition ascribes an apocryphal gospel to Bartholomew and describes his missionary activities in Egypt, Persia, India, and Armenia, where he was reportedly martyred by being flayed alive. Hence he is the patron of tanners.

*Michael D. Coogan*

**BARUCH.** Son of Neriah, the scribe of *Jeremiah, and the purported author of the book of Baruch. The name is a shortened form of names like Berechiah and Barachel; all three forms are well attested in biblical and extrabiblical sources. In its full form Baruch's name also occurs on a clay seal impression (bulla) from the late seventh century BCE. The full inscription reads "[belonging] to Berechiah, son of Neriah, the scribe" and is a relatively rare example of the occurrence of the name of a biblical person in a nonbiblical source from the individual's own time. Other bullae from the same period name Seriah, Baruch's brother, and Gemariah, son of Shaphan.

According to the Roman Catholic and Eastern Orthodox churches, the book of Baruch is a work of canonical scripture, but Protestants include it among the Apocrypha. As even the casual reader will note, it is divided into at least three distinct parts, each with its characteristic style and point of view. This observation leads naturally to the view that Baruch is not a unified composition, but a compendium of works from several authors. The only unifying factor is the supposed common background of the Babylonian exile.

The first part (1.1–3.8) is in prose and tells how Baruch, in Babylon, composed a prayer of confession and petition, which he read to the deposed king, Jeconiah (or Jehoiachin), and the other exiles. The prayer was then sent to Jerusalem, with an explanatory letter giving directions as to when it should be used. The second part (3.9–4.4) is a poem in the style of the wisdom literature, in which Israel is reproached for having forsaken the wisdom that God had given her, which is then identified with the Mosaic Law, the Torah. This act of apostasy is said to explain Israel's unhappy lot in exile. The third part (4.5–5.9) is a poem, partly in the style of Isaiah 40–66, encouraging the exiles to believe that God will not only deliver them but provide for them a glorious future.

The fact that the book was never accepted into the Jewish canon is strong evidence against any part of it being the work of Baruch, Jeremiah's companion. Modern commentators are almost unanimous in regarding this attribution as fictitious and the work as a typical pseudepigraphon. While the dates of the various sections of the book cannot be determined with any precision, most scholars would date them within the second or early first century BCE.

Despite the ostensible setting of Baruch in the Babylonian exile, its purpose seems to have been to bring a message of reconciliation and hope to the worldwide Jewish community of the Hellenistic period, in which exile, in a sense, had become permanent. In addition to this book of Baruch, several other books of that name were at one time in circulation, of which by far the most important is an apocalypse in Syriac, often designated as 2 Baruch and generally dated late in the first century CE.

*Michael D. Coogan, Robert C. Dentan*

**BATHSHEBA.** Wife of King *David, mother of *Solomon. Bathsheba was the wife of Uriah the Hittite, one of David's "mighty men," but she became David's wife after David killed Uriah to cover up his affair with her. God's displeasure over the affair is seen when the child conceived in the affair dies as an infant. However, Solomon, David and Bathsheba's fourth child, succeeds David to the throne. Solomon's successful bid for the throne is attributed in part to the efforts of Bathsheba, who apparently had risen to the status of *queen mother. *Timothy M. Willis*

**BEELZEBUB.** *See* Baal-zebub.

**BEELZEBUL.** *See* Baal-zebub.

**BEHEMOTH.** A mythical beast described in Job 40.15–24 as the first of God's creations, an animal of enormous strength that inhabits the river valleys. Although frequently identified with the hippopotamus (as *Leviathan is with the crocodile), not all the details of the creature's physiology fit that well-known mammal. In view of the references to Behemoth in the apocrypha and pseudepigrapha, it is more likely that it is a form of the primeval monster of chaos, defeated by Yahweh at the beginning of the process of creation; in fact, according to Job 40.24, the monster is represented as tamed by him and with a ring through his lip, so that like Leviathan he has become a divine pet. According to later Jewish tradition, at the end time Behemoth and Leviathan will become food for the righteous.

*Michael D. Coogan*

**BEL AND THE DRAGON.** This small "book" of the Apocrypha is one of the three additions to the book of *Daniel found only in its Greek translation (the Septuagint), but not in the original Hebrew-Aramaic text; the other two are the Prayer of *Azariah and the Song of the Three Young Men, and *Susanna. Unlike Susanna, which is a well-told, plausible story, these two tales of Daniel's detective work in exposing the fraudulent claims of the priests of Bel and his destruction of the dragon (or, better, "snake") are obvious polemical fabrications intended to demonstrate the foolishness of Babylonian religion and the superiority of the faith of Israel. The story of Bel is at least a good story, but the story of the dragon is so preposterous as to verge on the grotesque.

Bel, equivalent to Hebrew *Baal, was another name for Marduk, the chief god of Babylon. When challenged by the king (*Cyrus!) for his failure to worship Bel, who each day proves himself to be truly a god by the enormous quantity of food he consumes, Daniel undertakes to demonstrate that Bel does nothing of the kind. After the priests have set out the regular offering of food in the temple for the god's enjoyment, Daniel sprinkles the floor with ashes in the presence of the king alone. When they return the next morning, they see in the ashes the footprints of the priests and their families who had entered by a secret trap door during the night and consumed the food. The king then, acknowledging that Daniel was right, has the priests and their families executed and gives Daniel permission to demolish the statue and the temple.

The other story tells how Daniel destroyed the living snake (the "dragon"), though there is no evidence from antiquity that the worship of live snakes was ever a feature of Babylonian religion. Daniel feeds the snake a mixture of pitch, fat, and hair (an unpleasant but hardly lethal concoction), which, it is said, causes the snake to explode. Under compulsion from the snake's worshipers, the king has Daniel thrown into a lions' den for six days (a device borrowed from chap. 6 of the book of Daniel). While there he is fed by the prophet *Habakkuk, who is miraculously transported from Judea for the purpose. On the seventh day, an unharmed Daniel is released by the king, who immediately confesses that there is no god but the God of Daniel.

Like the other stories in Daniel 1–6, these two are examples of a partly satirical polemic against other religions, which must have been popular in the later Hellenistic period, when the attraction of Greek culture for Jews was strong. The strength of the appeal is illustrated by a passage such as 1 Maccabees 1.11–15, which describes the apostasy of a segment of the Jewish population of Jerusalem.

There is no external evidence as to the original language of the stories, but it was presumably Hebrew, less likely Aramaic. Palestine was probably the place of their composition, although one can point to no unambiguous clues. The time of writing is probably the second century BCE; the writer is, of course, unknown. Some critics profess to find in the stories faint echoes of the story of Marduk and his slaying of the monster Tiamat in Babylonian mythology, or of some early version of the story of Saint George and the dragon, but the points of contact are few and remote. The manner of Habakkuk's miraculous journey to Babylon is an outright borrowing from Ezekiel 8.3.

*Robert C. Dentan*

**BELIAL.** A word that occurs two dozen times in the Hebrew Bible, frequently in the pseudepigrapha and other Jewish literature of the Greco-Roman period, and once in the New Testament. In the Hebrew Bible it is used to characterize the wicked or worthless, such as idolaters, the men of Gibeah, the sons of Eli, Nabal, and Shimei; in later literature it is a title of *Satan. The etymology of the term is unclear. The most widely held view is that it is a compound meaning "without worth." Another possibility is to understand it as a term for the underworld, literally, "[the place of] no return." More recent translations generally paraphrase the word, while older translations more often transliterated it. In the KJV, for example, "Belial" occurs fifteen times, whereas in the NRSV it is found only in 2 Corinthians 6.15, in the variant form Beliar. *Michael D. Coogan*

**BELSHAZZAR.** The name of the eldest son of the last Neo-Babylonian king, Nabonidus (556–539 BCE), who for ten years acted as co-regent during his father's absence in Arabia. Belshazzar (Babylonian Bēl-sharra-uṣur, "Bel has protected the kingship") follows the Aramaic form of the name; elsewhere he is referred to as Balthasar or Baltasar (Josephus), but he should not be confused with the name Belteshazzar applied to Daniel in Babylon.

In his third regnal year, Nabonidus entrusted his army to his eldest son and put under his command troops levied from all lands. The king relinquished all control and entrusted the kingship to Belshazzar while he himself went on a long journey to Tema in the West (Persian Verse Account). Belshazzar, as crown prince and co-regent, exercised genuine royal powers; he is named in texts dated early in Nabonidus's reign (first, fifth, and seventh years) as controlling his own household and business, and he is associated with Nabonidus in oaths taken by their names in legal transactions in his twelfth–thirteenth regnal years. He issued an edict outlining a scheme in which land would be managed by specified chief revenue officials. Belshazzar's death at the time of the fall of Babylon to *Cyrus in October 539 BCE is likely, though not mentioned in the Babylonian (Nabonidus) Chronicle, which does refer specifically to the capture but not the death of Nabonidus (he was exiled to Carmania). Attempts to read a broken passage of the Chronicle as telling of Belshazzar's death a month after the Persian entry into Babylon in 539 BCE remain conjectural. There is no extrabiblical confirmation of Belshazzar's feast.

*See* Daniel.

*Donald J. Wiseman*

**BENJAMIN.** The youngest son of *Jacob, by *Rachel; *Joseph's full brother;

and the ancestor of the tribe of Benjamin. The name means literally "son of the right hand," and should be understood geographically, in the sense of "southern"; the same name is used of a different group in the *Mari texts. Though the smallest of the tribes, it had an importance disproportionate to its size. The narratives in Joshua 3–9 are all set in Benjaminite territory, and members of the tribe were reputed to be fierce warriors. Notable Benjaminites include Ehud the judge; *Saul, the first king of Israel; *Jeremiah the prophet; and *Paul.

*See also* Tribes of Israel.

*Michael D. Coogan*

**BETHLEHEM.** Village in Judah, ca. 6 mi (10 km) south of *Jerusalem. The site was settled in the Paleolithic era, but is first mentioned in the Amarna letters (fourteenth century BCE); the meaning of its name is probably "house of (the deity) Lahmu" rather than the traditional "house of bread." It appears first in the Bible as home of a Levite who became a household priest in the hill country of Ephraim and was carried off by the Danites to their new city *Dan. *Ruth came to Bethlehem with her mother Naomi, married Boaz, and became the ancestor of *David.

One account of how David's career began says that he was brought to play the lyre for *Saul, the other that he was a shepherd whom *Samuel anointed as king. Hope for a king like David persisted in the postexilic period, and Micah 5.2–4 prophesies a shepherd king from Bethlehem. According to Matthew 2 and Luke 2, *Jesus was born in Bethlehem, and Matthew interpreted this as the fulfillment of Micah's prophecy.

*Christian tradition, perhaps as early as the second century CE, identified a cave as the site of Jesus's birth. About 338 CE, Constantine had a church built over the grotto (and Justinian reconstructed it in the early sixth century). Jerome settled in Bethlehem in 386; here he made the Latin Vulgate translation of the Bible.

Among other traditional sites in or near Bethlehem are the shepherds' field, the tomb of *Rachel, and the well from which David's warriors brought him water.

*Sherman Elbridge Johnson*

**BISHOP.** In pre-Christian and extra-Christian usage the Greek word rendered "bishop," *episkopos,* and its cognates, refers primarily to caring for something or someone. This can involve a person's oversight of a task or a group of people, such as priests in a temple, or God's own oversight of a person or an event.

The word occurs rarely in the New Testament and only in later documents with the exception of Philippians 1.1; the other passages are Acts 1.20; 20.28; 1 Peter 2.25; 1 Timothy 3.1–2; Titus 1.7. Acts 1.20 is a citation from Psalm 109.8 used to legitimate the selection of a replacement for Judas among the disciples. Acts 20.28 is from a speech by Paul encouraging his audience to "keep watch . . . over all the flock, of which the Holy Spirit has made you overseers to shepherd the church of God." The three citations from the Pastoral Letters have to do with requirements for the position or role of *episkopos* within the church.

Much of the debate about the usage of the term in the New Testament and early Christianity has been concerned with the evolution of an office called "bishop." Is it an authoritative role within the church that existed from apostolic times? Or should it be understood as a general term giving some measure of honor and perhaps authority to any believer? Naturally, different *Christian traditions have various stakes in how these questions are answered.

With the exception of Philippians 1.1, all of the texts cited above probably come from the very end of the first or the beginning of the second century CE. Acts 20.28 and the citations from the Pastoral Letters seem to have in mind a specific group of leaders who look out for the well-being of the larger church. Philippians 1.1 seems to have a similar sense; the overseers are mentioned together with *deacons, but there is no further indication of how they might have functioned. The Pastorals associate certain responsibilities with the office. The *episkopos* is a teacher, a good host, possesses only one wife, is above reproach, and perhaps is good in a debate; there is no evidence that this overseer had responsibility outside the local church.

The letters of Clement of Rome (ca. 95 CE) and Ignatius of Antioch (ca. 115 CE) demonstrate the development of a hierarchical office that eventually became dominant. The office of bishop is thus an indicator of the evolution of Christianity from a popular Palestinian movement to a sophisticated institution with offices, authorities, and hierarchy. *J. Andrew Overman*

**BROTHERS AND SISTERS OF JESUS.** Siblings of *Jesus are referred to collectively twice in the Gospels. In the account of the "true kindred," Jesus's mother and brothers come to speak to him while he is teaching. Jesus refuses to see them, however, saying that his true sister, brother, and mother are those who do the will of God.

When Jesus teaches at the *synagogue in his hometown of *Nazareth, the listeners react angrily to his wisdom and mighty works. The crowd doubts that a local person could be endowed with such power, and they cite the presence of his parents, brothers, and sisters as proof. The brothers are listed by name (*James, Joseph; Mark reads Joses; Simon, and Judas) but the sisters only as a group. In Luke 4.22, the crowd asks simply, "Is not this Joseph's son?"

References to brothers and sisters of Jesus conflict with some understandings of the virgin birth. For those who feel that Jesus's mother *Mary remained a virgin for life, brothers and sisters must be read as cousins or as stepbrothers and stepsisters fathered by *Joseph in another, unmentioned, marriage.

*Daniel N. Schowalter*

# C

**CAIAPHAS.** Also named Joseph, Caiaphas was high priest at the time of Jesus's death. According to Josephus, he was appointed in 18 CE by Valerius Gratus, the Roman procurator before *Pilate; his father-in-law, Annas, had preceded him, as had, for very short terms, several of Annas's sons. He was removed from office in 37 CE and replaced by another of Annas's sons. There is some confusion in the New Testament about whether Annas or Caiaphas was high priest at the end of Jesus's life and about their role in his death, but the Gospels are consistent in their depiction of hostility toward Jesus by the high priest.

In 1990 the family tomb of Caiaphas was found in Jerusalem. It contained twelve ossuaries, one of which had inscriptions with the full name of Caiaphas in Aramaic (*yhwsp br qypʾ* and *yhwsp br qpʾ*: Joseph, son of Caiaphas), and another with simply the family name (*qpʾ*). *Michael D. Coogan*

**CAIN AND ABEL.** Genesis 4.1–16 relates the curious story of Cain and Abel. Cain (meaning perhaps "smith," possibly related to the *Kenites), is the firstborn of *Adam and *Eve, and Abel (meaning "emptiness") is his younger brother or twin. As is generally the case among biblical siblings, they come into conflict. Cain, a farmer, offers a sacrifice of grain to Yahweh, while Abel, a shepherd, offers a sacrifice from the firstborn of his flocks. For no obvious reason, Yahweh rejects Cain's sacrifice; this appears to be a literary gap or blank. After some moral advice from Yahweh, Cain murders Abel in the field, which Yahweh discovers from Abel's blood "crying out" from the ground. Yahweh confronts Cain with Abel's absence, to which Cain feigns ignorance. As punishment, Yahweh condemns Cain to wander the earth, decreeing that the earth will no longer bear crops for him. In fear for his life, Cain pleads for mercy, which Yahweh grants by placing an unspecified sign on Cain so that no one will murder him. Cain finally departs to wander in a land called Nod ("wandering"), east of *Eden.

Many themes appear in this story, including sibling rivalry, the attraction of sin, crime met with punishment, the futility of pretense before God, and the moral distinction between civilization and barbarism. Cain begins as a farmer, plying the fruitful earth, and because of his unchecked passion he commits a heinous crime, only to separate himself and be separated—morally, economically, and geographically—from the proper realm of civilized life. Only a plea for God's mercy (perhaps implying a degree of repentance) saves his life, signaling the small worth of life outside of civilization, where one is "hidden" from God's face.

In later interpretation, the cause of Cain's evil nature is frequently explored, with a tendency to identify Cain as the son of either *Satan, the wicked angel Sammael (Targum Pseudo-Jonathan), or the serpent in Eden. Other gaps in the story also receive much attention, such as the origin of Cain's wife (in Jubilees 4.9 she is his sister, Awan, meaning "Wickedness") and the fate of Cain and his offspring (identified as demons in the *Zohar* and medieval legend). An early gnostic sect, the Cainites, may have regarded Cain as a savior figure.

In the New Testament, Abel is the prototypical martyr, who died for his faith. *Ronald S. Hendel*

**CAIN'S WIFE.** *See* Names for the Nameless.

**CALVARY.** *See* Golgotha.

**CANAAN.** An ancient name for the region occupied today by Lebanon and Israel. The origin of the term "Canaan" is obscure. It was used at Nuzi in Upper *Mesopotamia as a term for red or purple dye, a product for which the coastal Canaanites were famous. Although it has been suggested that the geographical name Canaan was derived from the name of the dye, it is more likely that the Nuzi dyes were named for their Canaanite manufacturers. Similarly, the rare meaning "merchants" for "Canaanites" in biblical Hebrew is probably a secondary development, based on the mercantile reputation of the coastal Canaanites, rather than a clue to the origin of the word.

"Canaan" was in use as a geographical designation as early as the third millennium BCE. In the latter half of the second millennium it referred to a province of the *Egyptian empire in western Asia. The province of Canaan was bordered on the north by the land of Amurru, which lay in southern *Syria west of the middle Orontes, and on the east by the province of Upe, which included the region of *Damascus and northern Transjordan. The Israelites seem to have adopted this older usage of the name when they took control of the land. The frontiers of Canaan described in Numbers 34.1–12 correspond closely to those of the Egyptian province; the eastern and western boundaries are formed by the Mediterranean coast and the Jordan rift respectively, the southern boundary extends from the southern end of the Dead Sea west to the Wadi of Egypt near Gaza, and the northern boundary traverses the Pass of Hamath on the upper Orontes north of the Lebanon.

The biblical writers sometimes use "Canaanites" as a general designation for all indigenous inhabitants of ancient Palestine without ethnic or political distinction. Elsewhere the same peoples are collectively called "*Amorites." This general usage of "Canaanites" was most important as a term marking ethnic boundaries, distinguishing the Israelites from the indigenous peoples with whom intermarriage was to be avoided. The ethnic position in which the Israelites placed the Canaanites is expressed genealogically in Genesis 10.6, 15–18, in which Canaan is said to have been a son of *Noah's second son *Ham, a brother of *Cush (Ethiopia), Egypt, and Put (Libya?), and the father of the Sidonians (the *Phoenicians), the *Hittites, the *Jebusites, the Amorites, and the other pre-Israelite inhabitants of Canaan.

Elsewhere in the Bible, the *Promised Land is thought of as having been ethnically diverse, and the Canaanites are presented as one of several peoples who lived there before the arrival of Israel. According to Deuteronomy 7.1, the Canaanites were one of seven nations driven out before the Israelites. In still other passages the pre-Israelite population is said to have had regional ethnic divisions, of which the Canaanites were the coastal component. In this last usage the term "Canaanites" corresponds exactly to "Phoenicians."

The biblical story of the conquest of Canaan is found in Joshua 1–11 and Judges 1. The Joshua account continues the story of the conquest of the Transjordan given in Numbers 21; it depicts the conquest as quick and complete. The Israelites cross into Canaan and capture *Jericho and Ai. Although tricked into an alliance with the Gibeonites, they defeat a coalition of cities led by *Jerusalem and sweep through the southern part of the country, destroying everything in their path. This southern campaign is followed by a victory over an alliance of northern cities led by *Hazor. The subjugation of Canaan takes only five years, and most of the indigenous population is destroyed. Judges 1, however, gives the impression that the conquest was a matter of individual tribal actions occurring over an extended period and often with inconclusive results.

Modern historians have attempted to describe the process by which Israel came into control of Canaan. It seems to have had two phases, one of peaceful settlement in the hills and one of conflict with the cities of the lowlands. Surveys of Israel and Jordan show that the central highlands were sparsely populated before 1200 BCE, when a marked expansion began. Most of the newcomers were agriculturalists, not nomads. They seem to have been of mixed origin, arriving from several directions and settling in villages. Certain continuities in material culture, including pottery and architecture, suggest that a substantial number came from the Canaanite cities of the lowlands. These peoples made up the bulk of the population of later Israel. They aligned themselves with an existing group called Israel, who were already living in the region, as shown by a reference made to them in about 1207 BCE by the Egyptian king Merneptah. The resulting larger community developed a strong sense of ethnic identity, sharply separating themselves from the peoples of the neighboring lowland cities, whom they eventually grew strong enough to conquer or assimilate in a process that was not complete until *David's capture of Jerusalem in the tenth century BCE. It was probably the memory of this process that gave rise to the tradition of *Joshua's conquest.

Archaeology has cast doubt on the historicity of many of the specific victories described in Joshua, including especially the battle of Jericho, which was not fortified at the time of the Israelites' arrival. The story of the crossing of the *Jordan and the first victory serves the theological purpose of presenting the conquest as a part of Yahweh's plan for Israel, the means by which the land promised to the ancestors was acquired. The crossing into the sacred realm and siege of the first Canaanite city are presented in ritual terms, while the divine participation in the war is made clear.

*P. Kyle McCarter, Jr.*

**CAPERNAUM.** A village on the northwest shore of the Sea of Galilee. The Greek name *Kapharnaoum* evidently represents a Semitic original, "village of Nahum." It is identified as Tell Hum, a mound that has now been extensively excavated.

Jesus is reported to have settled in Capernaum and made his home there at the beginning of his ministry. From here he carried on his early preaching and healed many, beginning with an exorcism in the synagogue. Here he healed the slave of the centurion who had built the synagogue. The synagogue is also the scene of the discourse on the bread of life.

The first archaeological discovery was a magnificent synagogue, now dated to the fourth century CE. It is constructed of limestone, enclosed by columns, and adorned with fine carvings, and the facade faces Jerusalem.

More recently a large area has been excavated, in which single-story basalt dwellings were grouped in squares, with streets in between. In this complex there is an octagonal church from about 450 CE. Beneath it is a house church (about 350 CE), which was remodeled from a dwelling that the Franciscan archaeologists identify as Peter's house. Near the great synagogue there is a smaller one, built of basalt, probably from the first century CE.

Capernaum was evidently a fishing village when its houses were built in the first century BCE and had a population of not more than one thousand.

*Sherman Elbridge*

**CENTURION.** A century in the *Roman army was nominally a hundred, in practice usually eighty strong. There were sixty centurions in a Roman legion. They were of officer rank, corresponding to company commanders. They were men of status in the community and had a wide range of expertise and experience. Their duties often ranged beyond the strictly regimental, even to judicial functions and the administration of small military districts.

Centurions were also found in the auxiliary regiments supplementing the legions. These were either promoted from the ranks or transferred from a legion, and they might be Roman citizens (often recently enfranchised) or noncitizens.

The centurion at *Capernaum was probably a member of the armed forces of the *tetrarch Herod, organized on the Roman pattern. The centurion at the death of Jesus was serving in a Roman auxiliary unit, as were the centurions at the arrest of Paul. So too were Cornelius and Julius, both probably Roman citizens.

*Denis Bain Saddington*

**CHALDEANS, UR OF THE.** *See* Ur of the Chaldeans.

**CHERETHITES AND PELETHITES.** A group of mercenaries loyal to *David. As a military unit separate from the regular army, the Cherethites and the Pelethites were under the command of Benaiah. They followed David on his flight from *Absalom, fought for him during the revolt of Sheba, and supported Benaiah's efforts to crown *Solomon as his father's successor. Although this personal mercenary unit seems to disappear after David's death and the elevation of Benaiah to commander-in-chief of Solomon's army, some scholars connect the Cherethites with the Carites mentioned in 2 Kings 11.4, 19.

Research on the Cherethites and the Pelethites has focused on their origins and ethnic affiliations. Most commonly, but by no means universally, the terms are understood as Cretans and *Philistines, respectively. In two later prophetic passages the Cherethites appear in poetic parallelism with the Philistines. Oracles of doom against the Philistines also make use of word play on the Hebrew root *krt,* "to (be) cut off," with which the word for Cherethites was associated. From 1 Samuel 30.14 it can be surmised that the Cherethites were settled in southern Philistia and were engaged by David while he was in Ziklag as a vassal to Achish, the Philistine king of Gath. Although the exact relationship between the Cherethites and the Pelethites and the Philistines is unresolved, it is likely that they were all descended from the various sea peoples of Aegean origin who first settled on the southwestern coastal strip of Palestine at the beginning of the Iron Age (twelfth century BCE). *Carl S. Ehrlich*

**CHERUB, CHERUBIM.** Hebrew singular and plural for hybrid supernatural creatures associated with the presence of God, and in postbiblical tradition identified as one of the choirs of *angels. Among the nearly one hundred occurrences of the word in the Bible, the usual image is that of a huge eagle-winged, human-faced bull-lion, iconographic features familiar in Assyrian and Canaanite sources. Four interrelated roles for the cherubim can be identified.

**Guardians of Paradise.** As guardians of the entrance to *Eden they are the functional counterparts of the colossal, human-faced winged bulls used in Mesopotamian architecture to guard the entrance to temples and palaces.

**Protective Bearers of God's Throne.** In descriptions of the ark, a three-dimensional cherub stands at either side with wings protectively outstretched over its cover. Before the *Temple was built, when the ark was still a portable shrine and housed in the tent of meeting, the Lord spoke to Moses "from between the two cherubim," where he was understood to sit invisibly. Portable shrines similar to Israel's ark are known from Egypt, Mesopotamia, Canaan, and Arabia, and some also feature cherubim as a decorative motif. In Solomon's Temple the ark became a permanent fixture, and the size of the cherubim increased dramatically. Notable Canaanite parallels are the Megiddo ivory reliefs (ca. 1200 BCE) and the Ahiram sarcophagus from Phoenicia (ca. 1000), both of which depict winged cherubim supporting the throne of the local king.

**Decorative Elements.** The walls and doors of the Temple were carved with cherubim and palm trees. In many ways the art and symbolism of the Temple replicated the garden of Eden, where the cherubim guarded the tree of life, widely depicted as the date palm.

**Means of Yahweh's Mobility.** In the theophanic visions of Ezekiel 1 and 10, the cherubim become the power by which God's chariot-throne is able to fly. In 2 Samuel 22.11 the Lord is said to ride on a cherub, equated in poetic parallelism with flying on the wings of the wind.

The etymology of the Hebrew word *kĕrûb* is uncertain, but some connection with Akkadian *kāribu,* the intercessor guardian creature, seems probable. The cherubim of the Bible have no relationship with the winged infants or *putti* often featured in Renaissance art.

*David G. Burke*

**CHRISTIAN.** According to Acts 11.26, *Jesus's disciples were first called Christians in *Antioch. Elsewhere in the New Testament the word "Christian" occurs in Acts 26.28 and 1 Peter 4.14–16.

The origin of the term "Christian" is uncertain. It comprises the word "Christ," the Greek word meaning "anointed one" (*see* Messiah) with an ending meaning "followers of" or "partisans of." *Jews who did not accept Jesus as the Messiah would hardly refer to Jesus's disciples as Christians—the Messiah's followers. According to Acts 24.5, such Jews referred to Jesus's followers as "the sect of the Nazarenes," apparently regarding Christians as a Jewish group.

Because followers of Jesus used "*saints," "brothers," "the Way," "*disciples," and other designations when referring to themselves, it is unlikely that the term "Christian" originated among Christians.

In Acts 26.28 Agrippa uses "Christian" sarcastically; in 1 Peter 4.14–16 it is a term of reproach used during persecution. Thus, the term seems to have been derogatory. The contemporary Roman historians Tacitus and Suetonius use the term that way. Tacitus refers to Christians as people hated for their evil deeds, and Suetonius calls them "a new and evil superstition."

If first applied to Jesus's followers in Antioch, Roman officials may have coined the word to distinguish the Christian group from Judaism. Perhaps "Christian" was used to designate the Christian movement as hostile toward Agrippa. No matter where the term originated, it was first a word of scorn or ridicule. But by the end of the first century CE Christians accepted the name as a comforting sign of God's glory.

*Edwin D. Freed*

**CITIES OF REFUGE.** Six cities set aside to provide safe haven for someone guilty of an accidental killing. There is some uncertainty about who decided the fate of the manslayer, whether the *elders of his hometown or the elders of the city to which he had fled or "the congregation." In any case, if the killing was judged to be premeditated, the manslayer was returned to his hometown for execution; if it was judged accidental, he was allowed to reside in the city of refuge until the death of the high priest (which constituted, in a sense, exile).

Most scholars agree that in the Bible the basic principle of asylum evolved into the specification of six cities of refuge and into the linking of these with the forty-eight levitical cities. Opinions as to the historicity of the actual use of these cities of refuge vary. Some hold that these cities never actually served as cities of refuge but were part of a utopian restoration program developed by priestly circles after the destruction of Judah (ca. 550–400 BCE). Others think that they served as part of the reform of King *Josiah (ca. 640–609 BCE). A third group believes that this institution was a reality, but fully so only during the United Monarchy (ca. 1025–925 BCE), because some of the cities were lost to invaders after the kingdom split. One nagging question for proponents of each view is the exclusion of *Jerusalem from the lists of cities of refuge, particularly after *David had moved the central altar there.

*Timothy M. Willis*

**COLOSSAE.** Colossae was located in western Asia Minor, south of the Maeander (modern Menderes) River, 4 mi (6.4 km) east of Denizli in present-day Turkey. It was a trading town until subsumed by nearby Laodicea, and was the home of the *Christian community to which the letter to the Colossians is addressed.

Colossians is one of three or four letters written by *Paul at about the same time and sent to various churches in the Roman province of *Asia. The Christian community at Colossae came into existence during a period of vigorous missionary activity associated with Paul's

Ephesian ministry (ca. 52–55 CE), recorded in Acts 19. Paul was assisted by several coworkers through whom a number of churches were planted in the province of Asia. Among these were the congregations of the Lycus Valley, Colossae, Laodicea, and Hierapolis, which were the fruit of Epaphras's endeavor. A native of Colossae who probably became a Christian during a visit to *Ephesus, Epaphras was "a faithful minister of Christ;" as Paul's representative he had taught the Colossians the gospel.

Paul was in prison (probably in Rome) when he wrote the letters, and so they are called the captivity epistles. Colossians seems to have been written fairly early in Paul's imprisonment, about 60–61 CE. Epaphras had paid Paul a visit in Rome and informed him of the state of the churches in the Lycus Valley. While much of the report was encouraging, one disquieting feature was the attractive but false teaching recently introduced into the congregation; if unchecked, it would subvert the gospel and bring the Colossians into spiritual bondage. Paul's letter, then, is written as a response to this urgent need.

The letter's many allusions to the former lives of the readers suggest that most were gentile converts. They had once been utterly out of harmony with God, enmeshed in idolatry and slavery to sin, but God had reconciled them to himself. The picture is thus drawn of a Christian congregation obedient to the apostolic gospel, and for which the apostle can give heartfelt thanks to God. He knows of their "love in the Spirit" and is delighted to learn of their orderly Christian lives and the stability of their faith in Christ. *Peter T. O'Brien*

**CORINTH.** A major city in Greece and the home of the *Christian community to which the two letters of *Paul to the Corinthians are addressed. Corinth is mentioned in the *Iliad* and was occupied throughout most of the first millennium BCE and until 521 CE. Located on the isthmus separating the harbor towns of Lechaeum on the Corinthian Gulf from Cenchreae on the Saronic Gulf, Corinth owed much to its geography. Even though efforts to connect the two gulfs by a canal failed in antiquity, Corinth was still located at a crossroads of travel and commerce. Another important geographical factor was the citadel of the Acrocorinth (elevation ca. 1,800 ft [550 m]), situated directly south of Corinth.

Among important events in the city's history were its destruction by the Roman consul Mummius in 146 BCE and its reestablishment as a Roman colony in 44 BCE by Julius Caesar. Archaeological excavations have demonstrated that the traditional picture of Corinth as a city totally deserted during the period 146–44 BCE is inaccurate. Not only was the site populated, although sparsely, but several structures (e.g., stoas, archaic temple, Asclepieum, and the sanctuary of Demeter and Kore) were still in use after the defeat of the city in 146.

Certain aspects of Corinthian culture complement our understanding of nascent Christianity there. The city was apparently the provincial capital of the Roman province of Achaia and therefore the residence of the proconsul Gallio. This explains the importance of the city in Paul's ministry and why a circular letter to "all the *saints throughout Achaia" would be addressed to Corinth.

Though edited as two separate letters, the canonical letters of 1 and 2 Corinthians most likely consist of several shorter letters or notes written by Paul to the church at Corinth in the early 50s CE. Because of their length, content, and influence they rank among the major Pauline letters. Except for certain subsections, Pauline authorship is undisputed.

Not only do the letters contain reminiscences of his founding visit, but the narrative account in Acts 18 also provides independent confirmation of certain details about the church's beginning. Especially valuable for dating the letters is the mention in Acts of Paul's appearance before Gallio, whose proconsulship is reliably dated ca. 51–53 CE on the basis of an inscription discovered in 1905 at Delphi. Accordingly, Paul's founding visit, which lasted eighteen months, could have occurred as early as 50–51 CE during his ministry in the Aegean. After Paul's departure from Corinth, he remained in continual contact with the church, even though he was engaged in a mission in *Ephesus, from which he wrote 1 Corinthians and at least part of 2 Corinthians. The letters reflect at least two different stages in Paul's relationship to the church after his founding visit.

The problem of sexual immorality (incest and fornication) among Paul's converts in Corinth is noteworthy, as illustrated by the fact that one of the Greek verbs meaning "to practice fornication" was *korinthiazomai,* a derivative of the city's name. The city's reputation in this matter probably owed more to being adjacent to two bustling seaports than to its temple of Aphrodite.

The practice of certain Christian men at Corinth of wearing head coverings while praying and prophesying probably mirrors the widespread Roman custom of wearing devotional head coverings during worship. Another practice mentioned by Paul as having disruptive consequences was that "strong" Christians at Corinth would be participants at meals in an idol's temple, thereby creating a scandal in the eyes of "weak" Christians. Numerous banquet halls attached to temples have been excavated at Corinth. The specific location, the physical size, and the social function of these banquet rooms associated with a "temple of an idol" shed light on Paul's discussion of the strong and weak consciences of his converts.

Against the backdrop of a plethora of cults, where claims of miracles, healings, ecstatic prophecies, interpretations of prophecies, and visions abounded, one understands how gentile Christians in Corinth could easily be ignorant and misinformed about their own spiritual gifts.

Although Acts 18 refers to a synagogue in Corinth, the famous synagogue lintel inscription found there ("Synagogue of the Hebrews") cannot be dated precisely.

*Carl R. Holladay, Richard E. Oster, Jr.*

**CUSH.** Often translated "Ethiopia," Cush refers principally to the land of Nubia, south of Egypt. Cush's political apex came when the Nubians conquered and ruled *Egypt as its Dynasty XXV (716–656 BCE). According to 2 Kings 19.9, the Cushites saved King *Hezekiah of Judah from the *Assyrians in 701 BCE. In Genesis 2.13, Cush probably refers to *Babylon, which was occupied by Kassites in the second half of the first millennium BCE, and in Genesis 10.6–14 Cush (Babylon) has been confused with Cush (Nubia).

If *Moses's Cushite wife was Zipporah, there may have been another Cush in *Midian (whose poetic parallel is Cushan). But *Miriam's becoming "as white as snow" with leprosy (Num. 12.10) seems appropriately ironic punishment for her criticism of Moses's marriage to a black woman. Jeremiah 13.23 contends that Judah can no more change its penchant to sin than a Cushite can change skin color. Amos 9.7 mentions the Cushites as an example of God's universal concern. The name of Phinehas, *Aaron's grandson, is Egyptian for "the Nubian."

*See also* Africa.

*Steven L. McKenzie*

**CYRUS.** Cyrus (II) "the Great" founded the Persian (Achemenid) empire in 559 BCE and controlled the ancient Near East by the time of his death in 530. "Cyrus" may have been a dynastic rather than a personal name, for his grandfather Cyrus (I) was king of Anshan and a contemporary of Ashurbanipal, king of *Assyria (669–627 BCE). Cyrus took over the territories of the *Medes around 550 BCE and united them into a strong alliance, which clashed with Croesus of Lydia and captured Sardis, thus inaugurating a prolonged war with the Greek states. Cyrus's empire, which extended far to the east as well, was administered by local district governors (satraps).

In October 539, Cyrus defeated the *Babylonians at Opis, and his troops took control of the capital into which the gods from surrounding cult centers had been withdrawn for safety. When Cyrus entered the city he was warmly welcomed as a man of peace, and he demonstrated his religious tolerance with decrees returning the exiled deities to their shrines. In an edict he allowed the exiled Judeans to return home and later supported the restoration of the *Temple in Jerusalem. The references to Cyrus in *Isaiah are significant, both for the usual dating of Isaiah 40–55 ("Second Isaiah") to the mid-sixth century BCE and for their description of him as the divinely designated shepherd and as the Lord's anointed ("*messiah"), the agent of the divine plan for Israel. Parts of the narrative of the book of *Daniel are also set in the reign of Cyrus, but this has been interpreted as the use of Cyrus as a dynastic name, as is the case with Darius in the same context.

Cyrus is depicted on sculptures in his palace at Susa. He was buried in Pasargadae in 530 BCE and succeeded by his son and co-regent, Cambyses II.

*See also* Persia.

*Donald J. Wiseman*

# D

**DAGON.** The national god of the *Philistines, according to the Bible. Judges 16.23 identifies a temple of Dagon at Gaza, which *Samson pulls down; the captured ark of Yahweh is placed in another temple of Dagon at Ashdod. The divine name also appears in the town name Beth-dagon. Dagon is not mentioned in inscriptions from southern Syria or Palestine, but occurs frequently in texts from north Syria and Mesopotamia as Dagan, the chief god of the middle Euphrates region; in the Ugaritic tablets, *Baal is often referred to by the patronymic "son of Dagan." The Philistines thus probably borrowed the Semitic deity through direct contact with the coast of Syria rather than from southern Canaan. *Daniel E. Fleming*

**DAMASCUS.** A city of *Syria (*Aram. It lies in an oasis formed by the Nahr el-Barada, which flows through the city from the anti-Lebanon range, and the Nahr el-A$^{c}$waj south of Damascus, fed by springs on Mount *Hermon. These are the Abana and Pharpar of 2 Kings 5.12. The region has been inhabited since prehistoric times, and the city is mentioned in nonbiblical sources by the mid-second millennium BCE. A comprehensive history is difficult to establish because no major excavations have taken place within the city, in part because it has been continuously inhabited.

*David subjected Damascus to tribute, but only briefly. Several wars were fought between the Aramean kingdom and Israel and Judah, and at one time Jeroboam II conquered Damascus. *Tiglath-pileser III brought it into the *Assyrian empire (732 BCE), and subsequently it was under Neo-Babylonian and *Persian rule. After *Alexander the Great's conquests it fell to his successors, the Seleucids, until in 85 BCE it became briefly the capital of a *Nabatean kingdom. Rome conquered Syria in 65 BCE. Under the *Roman empire, Damascus was considered one of the city-states of the *Decapolis.

By the mid-first century CE there was a Jewish community in Damascus, among whom were *Christians. Damascus was evidently under the control of the Nabatean King Aretas IV when *Paul escaped from his local governor.

A temple of Jupiter Damascenus was built on the site of the old temple of Hadad-Rimmon. This was superseded by the Church of Saint John the Baptist, built by Theodosius the Great (late fourth century CE), which was remodeled to become the Great Mosque.

*Sherman Elbridge*

**DAN.** The fifth son of *Jacob and one of the twelve *tribes of Israel. Dan's mother is *Rachel's maid Bilhah. The name Dan seems to be derived from the

Hebrew verb meaning "to judge or vindicate." The tribe of Dan's first settlement is depicted as lying between the territories of Ephraim to the north, Benjamin to the east, and Judah to the south. Dan was renowned for its verve.

Already at an early time, a majority of the tribe migrated northward to a site near the source of the *Jordan river. Hence, Dan often marks the northern border of Israel. If the stories of the Danite hero *Samson and the song of *Deborah have a historical core, however, some members of the tribe must have remained in the south. With the rise of the monarchy, these southern clans were apparently assimilated into the kingdoms of Israel and Judah.

Dan can also refer to a city, originally called Laish or Leshem, which was captured and renamed by the Danite tribe. Dan's northern clans were probably located around this city. The ancient sanctuary at Dan was designated by King Jeroboam I of Israel as one of his two national shrines. Archaeological work at Dan has revealed a substantial cult center dating to the tenth century BCE, the era of Jeroboam I. During the reign of Pekah, king of Israel, the territories of Dan and *Naphtali were conquered by *Tiglath-pileser III of Assyria, who exiled many of their residents.

*Gary N. Knoppers*

**DANIEL.** According to the book that bears his name, Daniel was a pious and wise Jewish youth who was deported to *Babylon by King *Nebuchadrezzar (Nebuchadnezzar in the book), together with his three young friends, Shadrach, Meshach, and Abednego, the royal household, and other prominent citizens. Presumably, this was the first deportation ordered by Nebuchadrezzar in 597 BCE. In Ezekiel 14.14, 20, a Daniel is mentioned alongside *Noah and *Job as one of the outstandingly righteous men of history; in Ezekiel 28.3, the wisdom of the king of Tyre is said to exceed even that of this Daniel. Many commentators believe that the Daniel of the Ezekiel text is to be identified with the Canaanite Danʾil of "The Tale of Aqhat" preserved among the fourteenth-century BCE texts found at Ras Shamra (Ugarit) in Syria. There, Dan'il is described as one who "judges the cause of the *widow / tries the case of the *orphan." It would therefore appear that Daniel was a legendary figure, represented in this book as a youth of outstanding wisdom and piety who matures into a seer capable of receiving visions of the future.

In the six tales that comprise the first half of the book, Daniel and his companions are shown to be observant *Jews. God protects them and endows them with wisdom that surpasses that of the Babylonian courtiers and magicians. Having requested a vegetarian diet in order to avoid eating non-kosher food, they become healthier than their non-Jewish counterparts. Daniel is a divinely gifted interpreter of dreams and even knows the king's dream of a composite statue without being told what it is. He likewise interprets the king's dream of a felled tree as prophetic of the king's temporary insanity, sent by God to teach him of the divine preeminence. And when Nebuchadrezzar's successor, *Belshazzar, is terrified during a banquet by writing on a wall, Daniel can interpret the mysterious words. Finally, during the reign of the Persian king *Darius I (522–486 BCE), Daniel survives a plot concocted by his rivals at court to have him killed in a den of lions for failure to worship the king. These episodes are relatively independent and are part of a larger cycle of tales about Daniel as a model Jew in exile.

In the second half of the book (chaps. 7–12), Daniel is an apocalyptic seer, granted detailed visions of the future. In highly symbolic imagery, clarified by angelic interpreters, the ultimate defeat of the successive kingdoms of the Babylonians, *Medes, *Persians, and Greeks is announced, to be followed by a rule of "the holy ones of the Most High."

The internal dates throughout the book show that the narratives of chaps. 1–6 partially overlap the visions of chaps. 7–12. The latter culminate in the final vision dated in "the third year of King Cyrus of Persia" (10.1), 535 BCE. In effect, the book records both the external and the internal history of Daniel, the former consisting of the stories of his virtuous deeds and wonders, and the latter his visionary experiences and revelations regarding the future of the world.

The artful arrangement of the diverse subject matter of the book might suggest a single redaction, if not a single author. But the problem is further complicated by the circumstance that the book of Daniel is written in two languages. The Hebrew text of Daniel 2.4a begins: "The Chaldeans said to the king (in Aramaic)." From that point until the end of chap. 7, Daniel is written entirely in Aramaic, in the same dialect as that found in the other Aramaic texts of the Hebrew Bible. Why the text of Daniel switches so suddenly from Hebrew to Aramaic and back again, no one has ever been able to determine. One obvious solution would be that another writer composed those chapters. Or perhaps a single writer of Daniel freely moved from Hebrew to Aramaic to tell the stories of the Babylonian *Diaspora in the language used there at the time.

The strongest arguments for multiple authorship are these. First, the literary style of chaps. 1–6 differs radically from that of chaps. 7–12. The former have all the flavor of heroic tales of the kind that would emanate from courtly or wisdom circles (compare Daniel 2 with the *Joseph story and with *Esther); the latter chapters belong to that late descendant of prophetic eschatology, apocalyptic literature. Second, the stories about Daniel in chapters 1–6 reflect a Diaspora outlook. By their language and their knowledge of cultural details, they show considerable exposure to both Persian and Hellenistic influences. In their essentials, these stories are assumed to come from the third century BCE or even somewhat earlier. The apocalypses of Daniel 7–12, on the other hand, focus on *Judah, *Jerusalem, and the sanctuary. The writers of these chapters knew of the earlier cycle of Daniel stories and used that collection as a basis from which to extend its ministry into their own realm of apocalyptic dreams and visions.

The lengthy apocalypse of Daniel 10–12 provides the best evidence for date and authorship. This great review of the political maelstrom of ancient Near Eastern politics swirling around the tiny Judean community accurately portrays history from the rise of the Persian empire down to a time somewhat after the desecration of the Jerusalem *Temple and the erection there of the "abomination that makes desolate" (Dan. 11.31) in the late autumn of 167 BCE by the Greco-Syrian king *Antiochus IV Epiphanes. The portrayal is expressed as prophecy about the future course of events, given by a seer in Babylonian captivity; however, the prevailing scholarly opinion is that this is mostly prophecy after the fact. Only from 11.39 onward does the historical survey cease accurately to reproduce the events known to have taken place in the latter years of the reign of Antiochus IV. Had the writer known about the success of the Jewish freedom fighters led by Judas *Maccabeus in driving the garrison of the hated Antiochus from the Temple precincts (an event that occurred on 25 Kislev, 164 BCE, according to 1 Macc. 4.34–31), the fact would surely have been mentioned. But evidently it had not yet happened. The book of Daniel is thus the latest of all the books of the Hebrew Bible.

The heroes of the stories of chaps. 1–6 were observant Jews, heroes of the faith who refused to compromise with idolatry. Modern commentators have frequently identified the authors of Daniel and the audience to which they spoke with the observant party of the "Hasideans" or hasidim, a title variously translated "the righteous ones," "the godly ones," or even "the *saints," who joined in the war of liberation raised by the Maccabean rebels. According to some scholars, their descendants among the observant wing of Judaism of the first century BCE branched into the covenanters at Qumran, on the one hand, and into the *Pharisees, and perhaps even the *Zealots, on the other.

*Michael D. Coogan, W. Sibley Towner*

**DARIUS.** The son of Hystaspes, an Achaemenid, Darius was ruler of the *Persian empire from 522 BCE (when he usurped the kingship in Parsa) until his death in 486 BCE. After a year spent quelling revolts in Mesopotamia, Elam, Iran, and Armenia, he conquered the Indus Valley (about 516 BCE), invaded Scythia north of the Danube without success, and conquered the southeastern corner of Europe (about 514–512 BCE). Part of Libya was subdued; but campaigns against Greece in 492 and 490 failed, and with Egypt in revolt (486) Darius died before his final expedition could be launched. Under his rule, the Persian empire reached its greatest extent.

He had a talent for administration. The empire was divided by him into twenty provinces (satrapies) whose governors (satraps) were responsible for law and order, the delivery of fixed tribute, and local military operations. A leading part was played by an elite increasingly composed of Persian nobles; but in *Egypt and *Babylonia natives could hold important offices, and in Syria and *Phoenicia city kings and local rulers were responsible to the satrap. For provincial affairs, Darius seems also to have used expert advisers whom he could keep beside him or send out as agents. To *Jerusalem *Zerubbabel seems to have been dispatched as local governor; and the *Temple, whose reconstruction had been ordered by *Cyrus and allowed to lapse, was completed under his rule in 515 BCE. The prophets *Haggai and *Zechariah prophesied during his reign.

In his court style, Darius seems to have set himself on a pinnacle high above his subjects. He had a script invented for his royal inscriptions (in Old Persian), in which he showed himself remarkably introspective. Presumably a Zoroastrian by upbringing, he claimed an intimate relationship with the god Ahuramazda, whose universal omnipotence was matched by his own on earth. He could be called a monotheist, but he supported the established religions of the conquered peoples (including that of Yahweh). As a ruler he was dynamic (his own words at Behistun were "What was said to them by me, night and day it was done"), and though implacable he was generally just. He molded an imperial system that his successors, who prided themselves on their descent from him, were too inclined to preserve unchanged.

He was born either about 550 BCE or some eight years earlier. His principal palace was at Susa, but his rock-cut tomb is near Persepolis.

Two later Persian kings of the same name were Darius II (423–404 BCE) and Darius III (336–330 BCE). The reference in Nehemiah 12.22 to Darius the Persian could be to either Darius II or Darius III. "Darius the Mede," mentioned only in Daniel 5.31 and 9.1, is understood by most scholars to be a composite created by the author of the book of *Daniel because, they argue, texts like Isaiah 13.17 and 21.2, as well as Jeremiah 51.11, had looked forward to a Median capture of *Babylon.

*J. M. Cook*

**DAVID.** One of the best-known biblical characters, David is a curiously elusive figure. The Bible tells of his carving out an empire unmatched in ancient Israel's history. Elsewhere, however, in historical records from near that period (tenth century BCE), he is not so much as mentioned. He is known to generations of scripture readers as "the sweet psalmist of Israel (2 Sam 23.1 KJV)" and the man whom God had chosen. Yet his story in the books of *Samuel pivots on the episode of his adultery with *Bathsheba and murder of her husband, Uriah.

**The Books of Samuel and Kings.** David's story emerges primarily in the books of Samuel, concluding in 1 Kings 1–2. Scholarly attempts to reconstruct the history of the composition of these books remain highly speculative. On the one hand, there is general agreement that the final form of the work belongs to the period of exile in the sixth century BCE. On the other hand, dates for individual component units of the work vary from near the time of the events depicted to the time of final compilation, a span of some five hundred years.

Few critics, however, would deny David a significant place in the history of the ancient Israelite state. Recent scholarship views him as a paramount chief with a genius for mediation, a man supremely able to command diverse tribal, economic, and cultic allegiances and to consolidate them into the centralized power needed for the formation of a nation-state.

According to Samuel and Kings, this youngest son of a Bethlehem farmer is sought out and anointed by the prophet *Samuel on behalf of the Lord. He gains access to the court of *Saul, first king of Israel, initially by virtue of his musical prowess and then by defeating the Philistine champion *Goliath; there is some inconsistency in the plot here. Jonathan, Saul's son, loves him. A period of deadly rivalry with Saul, however, ensues. During this time, he marries Saul's daughter, Michal, and establishes his own independent military power as an outlaw in the Judean wilderness and as an ally of the *Philistines.

After Saul's death, David becomes king over *Judah in the south and then over *Israel in the north, hence king over "all Israel." In 2 Samuel 5–10, he is depicted as coming to the peak of his power: he wins victories over external enemies, including the Philistines, establishes *Jerusalem as a capital and a cult center, and is assured by the prophet *Nathan of an enduring dynasty. His dealings with *Bathsheba and Uriah, however, elicit divine denunciation, conveyed by Nathan. Rape and murder now erupt within David's own house, his son *Absalom rebels, and civil war ensues.

A coda of short stories, anecdotes, and poetry, connected to what has preceded by theme and allusion rather than by plot, caps the books of Samuel. The main plot itself is brought to a close with the story of David's death and *Solomon's succession at the beginning of the next book.

This story of David belongs to the larger story, told in Genesis through 2 Kings, of Israel's origins, nationhood, and eventual removal from the *Promised Land. David's story belongs with the account of the emerging nation-state's attempt to adapt religious and political institutions, especially leadership, to changing circumstances. His story is also part of the story of Yahweh's attempt to maintain or re-create a relationship of loyalty between deity and people. The people's desire for a human king is taken as a rejection of divine sovereignty. Thus Saul, designated by God at the people's insistence, must be rejected in favor of David, the one whom God has chosen freely.

In a sense, the reader's first glimpse of David comes even earlier in 1 Samuel. The childless Hannah gives thanks for the gift of a baby (Samuel) and speaks, prophetically, of the king, the "anointed one" (*see* Messiah) to whom Yahweh will give power. As the child is a special gift to the woman, so the kingdom is a special gift to David. Both gifts are freely given by God.

Giving and grasping lie at the story's heart. At critical moments David seems to allow choice to rest with others, especially Yahweh. At those moments he moves with a favorable tide; he may provoke a reader to contemplate forbearance, to consider providence as reality. At other times he falters, unwilling to take the risk or to accept injured esteem issuing from rejection. In these instances, a reader may be confronted with a more familiar reality, the reality of deceit, greed, and violence that makes many judge the David story in Samuel realistic and plausible.

God gives David the kingdom, the house of Israel and Judah. David's life, however, has a private as well as public dimension. What happens, privately, in his own house (palace and family) impinges on the nation. While his mighty men are besieging Rabbah, the *Ammonite capital, David seizes Bathsheba. Thus, as the one house (the house of Israel) is secured, another (the house of David) begins to crumble. In the brutal story of Amnon, Tamar, and *Absalom that follows, first Tamar, David's daughter, then both family and nation will be rent.

The kingship arose out of the people's search for security, but security readily generates corruption. David's son, the builder of Yahweh's house, falters in turn: the great Solomon falls prey to the expanding glory of his own house. Kingship—even Davidic kingship, Yahweh's gift—turns out to be no talisman. In Yahweh alone, the story suggests, is true power and security to be found. The larger story ends with the house of Yahweh ruined, the people dispersed. A brief note about the house (dynasty) of David concludes the work: the exiled Davidic king sits powerless in the house of his *Babylonian conqueror, like Mephibosheth, grandson of Saul, in the house of David. The wheel has turned full circle. The promise of an enduring house for David seems, in 2 Samuel 7, to be unconditional. It turns out to have limits; Yahweh, after all, is unwilling to be taken for granted.

The New Testament designation of *Jesus as "son of David" has predisposed many Christian readers to idealize the king. Yet David in Samuel and Kings is a complex character. Often, to be sure, the narrator elicits for David the admiration of readers—as the heroic slayer of Goliath, for example, or the man who twice spares Saul, his persecutor, or the king who denounces Joab for killing Abner, the enemy general, or who grants life to the cursing Shimei. Yet, equally, the narrator opens other possible perspectives even in these same narratives; David is a man with an eye for the main chance, adept at clothing his power-seeking and self-interest in the rhetoric of piety and morality, but exposed for all to see in the story of Bathsheba and Uriah.

The undercutting of the hero is ubiquitous. The account of his incarceration ("until the day of their death") of the ten concubines whom he abandoned to be raped on the roof of the house he fled hardly conjures a character of courage or responsibility. The story of Solomon's accession in 1 Kings 1 pictures the king in gray tones as the dupe of a Solomonic faction's power play. His dying charge to Solomon to kill Joab, his long-serving general, and Shimei, to whom he had granted pardon, evokes admiration only for its tidy ruthlessness. Or the coda to 2 Samuel may prompt a reader to ponder, for example, the difference between Rizpah's courage and David's compliance, or the incongruity between David's treatment of Bathsheba and Uriah and the psalmist king's proclamation of his innocent righteousness ("I was blameless before [Yahweh] and I kept myself from guilt"). Is this perhaps not righteousness but self-righteousness, not piety but hypocrisy? Even the tale of the slaying of Goliath, the foundation story of the heroic David, is placed in question by the coda. Without warning, tucked in amongst miscellaneous anecdotes, is the narrator's devastating remark that it was Elhanan who slew the mighty Gittite.

In the subsequent narrative David is viewed as a standard by which most other kings are judged unfavorably, yet even these passages harbor a sardonic quality. David, the narrator informs us, "did what was right in the sight of Yahweh and did not turn aside from anything that he commanded him all the days of his life, except in the matter of Uriah the Hittite." That little word "except" is powerfully subversive.

In Samuel and Kings the tensions in the depiction of David are never resolved. They are, perhaps, what give him life.

**The Books of Chronicles.** 1 and 2 Chronicles offer quite a different version of David's life. This work is later than Samuel-Kings, composed perhaps in the fifth century BCE, and draws upon a version of those books which it revises and supplements.

After a genealogical prologue, the main story line starts with the death of Saul and David's crowning as king of all Israel; gone are the divisions between north and south. Jerusalem is taken. A great muster of mighty men is transformed into a cultic congregation conducting David and the ark to the new capital with singing and celebration. Battles and plague are mentioned but bracketed by this greater purpose of establishing the place where Yahweh will be worshiped. From 1 Chronicles 22 to the end of the book and David's death, the focus is upon worship. David gathers the congregation once more and issues plans for the building of Yahweh's house and the organization of those who will sustain it. Priests and *Levites, musicians and gatekeepers, commanders of this, chief officers of that, all are ordered to such an end. It is in ordering and implementing the great praise due to God that David finds life in the Chronicler's narrative.

**The Psalms.** Elsewhere in the Bible, the theme of a promise to continue David's line (the Davidic covenant) surfaces, for example, in the prophecy of Isaiah 9.7 and in Isaiah 55.3–4, a message of hope addressed to the Judean community in exile. Otherwise, David's presence is most marked in the Psalms where many of the psalm titles use the term *lĕdāwīd*—of, to, or about David.

Modern scholars (and a few in ancient times) have generally considered these psalm ascriptions to be later additions to material that is itself mostly post-Davidic. Most interpreters over the centuries, however, have read the psalms in the light of these Davidic titles. In western iconography, for example, David is instantly recognizable as the man with crown and harp or psaltery, David the psalmist king; in popular culture he is often found with these attributes as the king of spades in playing cards. The image connects with the story of David's coming to Saul's court in 1 Samuel 16, but much more with 1 Chronicles, where the king's concern with the promulgation of music in the temple worship is such a dominant theme. Moreover, one psalm is shared by both the Psalter and 2 Samuel.

Davidic authorship of the psalms has a special attraction for those who would flesh out the inner life of David, especially the David of Samuel-Kings whose piety is so tenuously pictured. Thus Psalm 51, linked by its title to the crucial Bathsheba episode, may be read as a window into the soul of the great king. His repentance, indicated in the narrative with but a few words, is here paraded impressively. Problems of interpretation remain, however. The last verses of Psalm 51, for example, conjure a postexilic context (sixth century BCE or later) and strain any reading that takes the poem too literally as the outpourings of the tenth-century king.

**The New Testament.** The New Testament shows little interest in the personality of David, though the account of Jesus's plucking of the ears of grain on the Sabbath explicitly recalls David's taking the holy bread from the priest at Nob and is in character with the David of the books of Samuel. In the Gospels, Jesus is linked to the royal dynasty of Judah and to the Davidic covenant by both genealogy and address—he is called son of David, mostly in the context of healing/exorcism stories. Above all, in the New Testament, David is author—and prophet—of the psalms, which are interpreted where possible as messianic prophecies fulfilled by Jesus.

*See also* Israel; Judah, The Kingdom of.

*David M. Gunn*

**DEACONS.** The Greek noun *diakonos* underlying the English word "deacon" has in general usage the meaning of "servant," especially in the sense of one who waits on tables. Perhaps the word was originally applied to early *Christian leaders who assisted at celebrations of the Lord's supper. It has often been suggested that the establishment of the diaconate is sketched in Acts 6.1–6, and this may be Luke's intention, although neither here nor elsewhere does he use the noun *diakonos* (*see* Seven, The).

The understanding of *Jesus as servant (e.g., Mark 10.45, using the verb *diakonein*) informs later Christian concepts of ministry, though the New Testament applies *diakonos* to Jesus in a positive sense only once. The term occurs twenty-eight other times in the New Testament but only rarely in relation to a special church office.

In Philippians 1.1 Paul addresses a letter to all the Philippian *saints "with the *bishops and *deacons." Generally the Pauline letters do not imply the existence of fixed church offices with distinctive functions, but in this passage "deacons" clearly refers to a particular group of church leaders. No function is specified, but perhaps Paul mentions them here (along with bishops) because they helped provide the material assistance that partly occasions his letter.

In Romans 16.1–3 Paul mentions a certain Phoebe as a *diakonos* of the church at Cenchreae (a port city of *Corinth) and "benefactor" of many Christians, himself included. Nothing specific is said about her work, but there is no indication that she is a deacon in a lesser or different sense from that of the persons addressed in Philippians 1.1.

One passage in the Pastoral letters follows a list of qualifications for bishops with those for deacons. Deacons must be of good character, not avaricious, and good managers of their private households. Such requirements suggest that deacons are administrators with special responsibility for money. Nothing is said about teaching ability. A sentence about *women may allude to women deacons or to the wives of male deacons.

Although the Pastoral letters seem to reflect an advanced stage in the development of church organization and differentiation of clerical roles, it is noteworthy that here and elsewhere *diakonos* can also be used as a general term for Christian "minister." Paul several times applies the term in this broad sense to himself and to other church leaders.

*David M. Hay*

**DEBORAH.** A name which means "bee" in Hebrew, Deborah is the name of two women mentioned in the Hebrew Bible. Two passages call Rebekah's nurse Deborah. Much more prominent is the Deborah mentioned in Judges 4 and 5, whose fame in the biblical record emerges from her role as a military leader. With her general, Barak, she successfully led a coalition of Israelite tribal militias to victory over a superior Canaanite army commanded by Sisera. The battle was fought in the plain of Esdraelon, and the mortal blow to the Canaanite general was delivered by another female figure, Jael.

The account of this war, ending with an important victory for the Israelites in their struggle to control central and northern Palestine, is recounted in two versions, a prose narrative in Judges 4 and a poetic form in Judges 5. The literary and chronological relationship of these two versions is a matter of debate; but most scholars see in the archaic language of the poem evidence that it comes from a very early stage of biblical literature and may be the oldest extant Israelite poem, perhaps dating from the late twelfth century BCE, not long after the battle it recounts.

Deborah occupies a unique role in Israelite history. Not only is she a judge in the sense of a military leader, but also she is the only judge in the law-court sense of that title in the book of *Judges. Of all the military leaders of the book, only Deborah is called a "prophet." She is also the only judge to "sing" of the victory, illustrating the creative role played by women as shapers of tradition. While some would see Deborah, a female, as an anomaly in all these roles, her contributions should be set alongside those of other women who are pivotal figures in the premonarchic period (*Miriam, Jael, Jephthah's daughter, *Samson's mother). All emerge as strong women with no negative valuation, perhaps because during the period of the judges, a time of social and political crisis, able people of any status could contribute to group efforts. In the rural, agrarian setting of the period of the judges, with the family as the dominant social institution, the important role of women in family life was more readily transferred to matters of public concern than during the monarchy, with its more formal and hierarchical power structures. Deborah as a strong woman reflects her own gifts as well as a relatively open phase of Israelite society.

*Carol L. Meyers*

**DECAPOLIS.** The Decapolis was a league of ten cities founded by *Alexander the Great and his successors around 323 BCE. By the first century CE, according to both the Gospels and Pliny, the term refers both to the cities and to the region in which they were situated. The earliest list of the cities appears in Pliny; most scholars agree on these ten: Scythopolis/Beth-shan, Hippo, Philadelphia (modern Amman), Gerasa (Jerash), Gadara, Pella, Dion, Canatha, Raphana, and *Damascus. According to both Josephus and Polybius, by the dawn of Seleucid rule in the region of Palestine and the Transjordan at least four of the cities were of real importance (Gadara, Scythopolis, Pella, and Abila).

This region is perhaps the paramount example of the role of urbanization in the development and dominance of the Greek East by colonial empires. In both the Ptolemaic (ca. 300–200 BCE) and the Seleucid periods (200–130 BCE) these cities were built or expanded. With the conquest of the region by Pompey on behalf of Rome (ca. 63 BCE), their importance increased. They were a vital means of Roman control, both economic and military. Pompey made the capital of the league, Scythopolis/Beth-shan, the seat of the regional court (the *Sanhedrin) and utilized other cities in the region in a similar fashion. These urban centers almost invariably sided with the colonial power in revolts by the indigenous population (whether Maccabean, resistance to Pompey, or the First Jewish Revolt against Rome in 66–70 CE) and frequently put down native resistance brutally.

A number of the cities have been excavated (Pella, Gerasa, Abila), with the most recent significant project being at Scythopolis/Beth-shan. Excavations at these sites reflect a diverse, cosmopolitan milieu. Several languages were used (Greek, *Hebrew, and *Aramaic), temples and monuments stood almost side by side with *synagogues and early churches, and local culture and trade took place within the larger setting of Roman military and economic hegemony. *J. Andrew Overman*

**DEMONS.** In all cultures, fabulous notions may be found about the work of evil spirits, more or less capricious, more or less baleful. Such concepts are also found in the Bible, at times echoing extrabiblical thinking, at times reverberating with overtones characteristic of the Bible.

Ideas about demons in the Hebrew Bible are too diverse to be systematized. Animistic notions may be discerned in the recognition of spirits inhabiting trees, animals, mountains, rivers, and storms. Allusions are found to belief in fertility deities, or in divine beings, who, through sinning, lost their heavenly home (*see* Sons of God). More often the narratives focus upon the role of evil spirits in producing erratic and unexpected behavior; they arouse explosive jealousies, powerful desires for vengeance, or shocking mental confusions. The words of a prophet could be attributed to lying spirits sent by God. The worship of idols could be explained by the influence of such spirits on the gullible.

In the New Testament, though, the picture is different. References are much more numerous, reflecting developments in the Hellenistic and Roman periods. Attitudes are more unified, reflecting the influence of stories about *Jesus. Now demons are viewed as evil by nature, since they are obedient servants of *Satan who is the ultimate adversary of God. Their power to deceive and torment is viewed as coterminous with "this evil age," so that any restriction on their movements is viewed as an intrusion of a new age.

It was the authority of Jesus over demons that posed this possibility. According to the Gospels, that authority was first demonstrated when Jesus overcame Satan's most persuasive offers. This victory qualified him to begin evicting demons from their human homes. Those spirits manifested their evil power by causing spiritual and physical blindness, deafness, paralysis, epilepsy, and madness. Debates over Jesus's healings centered not on whether they were real but on the authority by which they were accomplished: were they a sign of Satan's fall from heaven, of God's own intervention into human affairs, of faith in Jesus's word, or were they rather a sign of Jesus's affilation with *Beelzebul, the ruler of demons?

The first option was the conviction of the Gospel narrators. And for them, the healings were not limited to Jesus. Even before his death he had shared with disciples the power over demons; after his death they continued his work. Evil spirits continued to resist the power of the Holy Spirit, but faith continued to bring liberation. As a result, a more or less standard attitude toward demons emerged: (1) Their primary activity lies in blinding and paralyzing human beings, who become captives of Satan. (2) Demons are forces external to human beings, yet their power also depends on internal forces operating at subconscious levels. (3) This conjunction of demonic and human wills creates a captivity that has been granted by God and can therefore be terminated by God. (4) That is why God's word, by evoking the faith of captives, can liberate them from their demonic captors. (5) The exorcisms attributed to Jesus point to him as authorized to speak that word. (6) After his death and resurrection, the Holy Spirit enabled his representatives to continue that work of liberation; this gift did not, however, make them immune to demonic counterattack. (7) There was a widespread expectation that this counterattack would reach its deceptive maximum in the endtime, immediately before the return of the *Messiah.

*Paul S. Minear*

**DEVIL.** *See* Satan.

**DIANA OF THE EPHESIANS.** *See* Artemis of the Ephesians.

**DIASPORA.** *See* Dispersion, Diaspora.

**DINAH.** *Jacob and *Leah's daughter, Leah's seventh child, born after her six sons; her name, like that of her half-brother *Dan, is derived from a root meaning "to judge." In Genesis 34, Dinah is raped by Shechem, who then falls in love and wants to marry her. Enraged at their sister's treatment, Dinah's brothers agree to intermarriage, but only if the men of *Shechem (the city) will be circumcised. While they recuperate, *Simeon and *Levi (full brothers to Dinah) kill them, and Jacob's other sons plunder the city, taking women and children as well as wealth and livestock and risking retaliation from neighboring groups.

The narrative in Genesis 34 gives a remarkable glimpse into Israelite history and customs, including the complicated relationships between the "sons of Israel" and the inhabitants of the land of *Canaan and the association of circumcision with marriage. *Jo Ann Hackett*

**DISCIPLE.** The term *disciple* (Grk. *mathētēs*) occurs many times in the New Testament, but only in the Gospels and Acts. It is used both of the *twelve who according to the Gospels originally followed *Jesus, and also of a wide range of Jesus's followers. The Gospels speak not only of disciples of Jesus but also of *Moses, *John the Baptist, and the *Pharisees. But above all the term refers to followers of Jesus, who are literally "learners," students of Jesus of Nazareth.

The somewhat amorphous group called disciples constitutes a vital feature of all the Gospel narratives, but the authors used the term to communicate different aspects of being a follower of Jesus. In *Mark the disciples are agents of instruction for the author, but as negative examples. They teach the audience or readers, but mostly through the things they do wrong or fail to understand. The constant questions and concerns of the disciples, particularly in the central section of Mark's gospel, provide an opportunity for the author to explain the purpose of Jesus's mission and the hidden meanings of his teaching. Discipleship in Mark involves fear, doubt, and suffering, as 8.31, 9.31, and 10.33 make explicit; nowhere is this more poignantly captured than in the character of *Simon Peter. The disciples in Mark, whomever this broad term may include, never fully understand and never quite overcome their fear and apprehensions. There is actually the hint in Mark that the disciples' fear is in some sense the beginning of wisdom.

The gospel of *Matthew on the other hand offers a rather different portrayal of the band of disciples, a term he uses with much greater frequency than the other Gospels (forty-five times without parallel in Mark or Luke). A disciple in Matthew is one who understands, teaches, and does what Jesus taught and did. Discipleship in Matthew is not a distinctive office or role but rather describes the life of an ordinary follower of Jesus in the Matthean community. Disciples have authority to teach, and so naturally, unlike the Marcan disciples, they understand the teachings of Jesus, himself portrayed as the authoritative teacher, as the Sermon on the Mount illustrates. Matthew alone among the Gospel writers ascribes the authority to forgive sins to the disciples. As in Mark, the figure of Peter embodies all aspects of discipleship, but in contrast to the Marcan Peter, in Matthew he understands, can teach, and is granted unusual authority.

The meaning and content of the term "disciple" varies in the four Gospels. Each writer uses this broad term, which tends simply to designate a follower of Jesus, in ways that support the writer's understanding of the community of the followers of Jesus and impress on the reader the contours and complexities of the life of a contemporary disciple. *J. Andrew Overman*

**DISPERSION, DIASPORA.** Diaspora is a Greek word meaning "dispersion." The first dispersion of Israel followed the *Assyrian conquest of the northern kingdom in 722 BCE; the deportees did not, however, form a living diaspora community. It was the deportation of a part of the population of *Judah by the *Babylonians in 597 and 587/586 BCE that resulted in the creation of a permanent community, which later produced the Babylonian Talmud. The prophet *Jeremiah advised the new exiles to pray for Babylon, "for in its welfare will be your welfare (Jer 29.7)." The prophet *Ezekiel preached to Israel from the newly formed Babylonian Diaspora.

After the Babylonian empire fell, the Persian king *Cyrus allowed the Judeans to return home. A commonwealth of exiles was created. The books of *Ezra and *Nehemiah treat only the returned exiles as legitimate Israelites. Those who had remained in the land or who lived elsewhere were disenfranchised. It was at this time that Judaism in effect began. Despite the return, a Jewish community continued in Babylon. Diaspora had become a way of life, one that would continue into the Greco-Roman period, when Jews were scattered over much of the ancient world. The first book of *Maccabees records a letter of the Roman Senate that reflects Jewish habitation in Egypt, Syria, Pergamum, Parthia, Cappadocia, and many individual Greek cities and islands. Jews had begun to take pride in diaspora, although Judith 5.19 still reflects the pain, speaking of a repentance followed by a return from all the places of the dispersion to retake Jerusalem and other places left deserted. Here the dispersion is portrayed as something to be overcome.

In the New Testament, James 1.1 identifies its recipients as "the twelve tribes in the Dispersion." This may mean Jewish *Christians of the Diaspora, but may also be symbolic; 1 *Peter, a letter clearly written to gentiles, is similarly addressed. *Philip Stern*

**DIVES.** In the parable of the rich man and Lazarus, one character is named (probably to facilitate dialogue between the rich man and Abraham), but the other is not. This has led to various attempts to supply the perceived deficiency. In relatively modern times, the rich man has traditionally been called "Dives," the Latin word for "rich" used in the Vulgate. Names assigned in antiquity include Nineves (or Neves), Finaeus, Tantalus, and Amonofis.

*See also* Names for the Nameless.

*Patrick A. Tiller*

# E

**ECCLESIASTES.** The pseudonym used for the author of the book of Ecclesiastes. The title of the book in Hebrew is *qōhelet* (also transliterated *qōheleth* and *koheleth*), a particular form of the verb "to assemble," which led to the Septuagint translation *Ekklēsiastēs,* one who addresses an assembly, frequently rendered "The Preacher." The content of this short treatise, however, is less ecclesial than sapiential, displaying a skepticism and dry wit that would be incongruous in a formal religious gathering. Even the ethical theory of moderation smacks of the academic, and the editorial epilogue, by another hand, shows the author in the guise of a scribe-teacher, adding the definite article: *haqqôhelet,* or "The Assembler," suggesting that it may well be a student's nickname for a well-known character.

Written probably in the third century BCE, the book is philosophical more than religious and consists of a sequence of reactions to the question presented in Ecclesiastes 1.2–3: "What does one gain by all one's toil?" Beginning and ending with this theme, the book falls into two parts: a philosophical treatise on life and the absurd (chaps. 1–6), and an ethical discussion on how one should live one's life as a result (chaps. 7–12). Adopting the mantle of *Solomon and thus vested with perfect wisdom, the author looks for meaning where traditionally it is to be found: in pleasure, in riches, in work. All end in death. Even wisdom itself avails nothing. Absurdity remains, and not simply in personal experience but rooted in human nature: "God has given to human beings" the innate urge to reason why, but even this is "vanity." Paradoxically, the inevitability of death focuses the mind on the "now," and so human life, with its limitations and pleasures, takes center stage. The author presents an enjoyment ethic, but he is quite careful to impose restrictions on the enjoyment of life's good things, which must never exceed human limits. Abuse is never acceptable. Pleasure is a practical ideal, not an absolute. This appears to be the best solution to the vanity of things.

Ecclesiastes represents an individual's experiential view of the world and human existence and a resultant ethic based on reason applied to that experience. Without rejecting his tradition, the author's rational, universalistic tendencies made blind allegiance to that tradition impossible. God remains the God of Judaism, but the author sees him rather as Elohim, the universal creator and sovereign who remains beyond human understanding. It is this that makes the ethic so important; in an unpredictable world one maintains human values of integrity and decency. One maintains one's humanity, and perhaps this is the only certain value.

How this book found a place in the Hebrew canon remains a puzzle. Perhaps it is a tribute to the fact that a religious scholar, heir to a tradition, could face a world of cultural ferment and make a personal contribution by offering an intellectually valid answer to the problem of existence.

*Dermot Cox, O.F.M.*

**ECCLESIASTICUS.** *See* Sirach (Ecclesiasticus).

**EDEN, THE GARDEN OF.** A garden of trees and lush vegetation planted by God and occupied by *Adam and *Eve. The meaning of the word "Eden" in Hebrew is uncertain. Some scholars connect it with a Sumerian word meaning "wilderness" or "plain," while others have proposed a derivation from the Hebrew word for "delight" or "pleasure." Thus, Eden came to be identified as an ideal garden of delight, or paradise.

The location of the garden of Eden that the author of Genesis had in mind is difficult to determine. Genesis 2.8 places the garden "in the east," which in general indicates *Mesopotamia. Genesis 2.10–14 appears to draw from a Near Eastern tradition of an idyllic garden from which rivers flowed. Two of the four rivers named in Genesis are known, the Tigris and the Euphrates. The other two are not known (although Gihon, meaning "gusher," is also the name of *Jerusalem's primary spring), making any precise geographical location hypothetical.

In Genesis 2–3, the garden of Eden has at its center the tree of life and the tree of the knowledge of good and evil. The garden is not simply a luxurious paradise but a place created by God in which human beings live and eat and work. Eden functioned as a paradigm of the unbroken relationships between God and humans, and between humans and nature, which no longer obtained after the first couple's disobedience.

The image of the garden of Eden reappears in somewhat altered form in the later prophets. The expulsion from Eden functions as a metaphor for the coming judgment against the nations (Tyre and Egypt), and for the coming judgment of the day of the Lord. The garden of Eden is also an image of promise: in parallel with "the garden of the Lord," Eden appears in Isaiah 51.3 as a metaphor for the renewal of the land of Israel after the Babylonian exile.

*Dennis T. Olson*

**EDOM.** A kingdom that neighbored Judah on its southeastern border during the Iron Age. It encompassed the area southward from the Wadi Hesa in Jordan to the Gulf of Aqaba, and, during part of this period, included the area called Seir, southwest of the Dead Sea and south of Kadesh-barnea.

Very little is known about Edom. Virtually no Edomite inscriptions have been found, apart from some seals and a few ostraca. The primary literary source for the history of Edom is the Bible, but only the barest outline can be constructed from that source. Some information comes from Assyrian records, and archaeological excavations and surveys have enabled a general picture of the development of the region to be sketched.

The early development of Edom remains largely unknown. The stories in Genesis that describe family relationships between Israel's *ancestors and those of all the surrounding kingdoms are generally understood to be artificial. For Edom this is particularly clear, since the connection between *Isaac's brother

*Esau and Edom is tenuous and awkward in the narratives of Genesis 25:19–34 and is almost certainly a later imposition on the stories.

Archaeological surveys indicate that the land of Edom was occupied fairly sparsely during the Late Bronze Age (ca. 1550–1200 BCE), with only a few small fortified towns and some tiny villages. The geographic name Edom appears for the first time in an Egyptian document of the thirteenth century BCE.

Numbers 20.14–21 suggests that Edom was already a monarchy at the time of the Exodus in the thirteenth century. Recent studies, however, have cast considerable doubt about the historicity of this and related stories. Even the so-called Edomite king list in Genesis 36.31–39 has been shown to be garbled and unreliable.

*Saul is said to have fought Edom successfully, but it was *David who conquered it and incorporated it into his empire, setting up garrisons throughout the land. Although a certain Hadad tried to rebel against *Solomon, he does not appear to have been successful. Edom remained under Israelite control, ruled by an Israelite governor until the reign of Jehoram of Judah in the mid-ninth century. At that time the Edomites successfully rebelled and set up their own king.

During the reigns of Amaziah of Judah (797–769) and Uzziah (769–734) Edom again came under Judean domination. Uzziah recaptured and rebuilt Elath on the Gulf of Aqaba early in his reign. But in the reign of Ahaz Edom decisively threw off Judean control and remained independent of Judah from that time on.

In Judah's place, however, came *Assyrian domination, but as was the case also for *Ammon and *Moab, the Assyrian presence appears to have been economically and politically beneficial to Edom. Excavations at Buseira (probably the Edomite capital Bozrah), Tawilan, and Tell el-Kheleifeh (Elath), show that the late eighth through the mid-sixth centuries BCE saw the peak of Edomite prosperity and expansion. It is from these centuries that monumental architecture is known, and there are indications that Edom expanded its influence into the southern hinterlands of Judah.

Edom seems to have survived the violence of the *Babylonian campaigns under *Nebuchadrezzar, and, although Buseira, Tawilan, and other sites suffered destruction later in the sixth century, the region recovered and continued to play a role in international trade during the Persian period. With the rise of the *Nabateans, a significant proportion of the Edomites seem to have moved westward, so that, by the Hellenistic period, Idumea (the Greek form of Edom) was the name of the region directly to the south of Judah. The most famous Idumean was *Herod the Great.

Attested Edomite names suggest that the Edomites worshiped the well-known West Semitic gods, Hadad/*Baal and El. But it appears that the primary deity of Edom was a god named Qaus/Qos. Little is known of this god, and even his basic characteristics (is he a war god or a storm god?) are debated. Some scholars have speculated that in the late second/early first millennium BCE, Yahweh may have been an important deity in Edomite religion, since a few biblical passages link Yahweh closely with Edom and Seir.

Although Deuteronomy 23.8 expresses a tolerant attitude toward the Edomites, most biblical passages dealing with the kingdom display a severe hostility toward it, reflecting the almost constant conflict between Judah and Edom. Considerable bitterness is evident in the biblical texts concerning Edom's attitudes and actions after the destruction of Jerusalem in 587/586 BCE. Edom, in fact, became a symbol of Israel's enemies in postexilic literature. *Wayne T. Pitard*

**EGYPT.** The name is derived from the Greek *Aiguptos,* itself a rendering of the Egyptian *Ḥwt-Ptaḥ,* "Temple of Ptah." The Egyptian name for the country was *Keme,* "the Black Land"; in Hebrew it appears as *Miṣrayim.*

Apart from the delta region, formed by silt deposited for millennia by the *Nile, the rest of Egypt consists of a narrow river valley, bounded on its eastern and western sides by vast arid and inhospitable deserts. The delta is similarly bounded on the east by the Sinai desert and on the west by the Libyan desert. In the south, the turbulent waters of the First Cataract at Aswan form a natural boundary, as does the Mediterranean Sea in the north. In ancient times these natural geographical borders effectively isolated Egypt from the rest of the Near East, thereby favoring the uninterrupted development of the civilization distinctive to the Egyptians, generally undisturbed by foreign invasions. Blessed with a stable climate and extremely fertile lands, regularly watered by the river Nile, the Egyptians developed a rich agricultural economy, producing wheat, barley, vegetables of many kinds, various fruits, and grapes. Very early on, Egypt became the granary of the ancient Near East, especially in times of famine. Although rich in fine types of stone suitable for building and carving—among them, limestone, alabaster, sandstone, and granite—Egypt was poor in metal ores workable at the time. The one exception was gold from the eastern desert, Nubia, and the northern Sudan. Egypt also was and still is poor in trees suitable for woodworking. External trade in this commodity dates back to early times.

The exact origin of the Egyptians is uncertain. They themselves claimed that their ancestors migrated northward from a region bordering on the Red Sea. Their language, essentially Hamitic, nevertheless reveals certain affinities with the Semitic family of languages. The latest form of Egyptian is Coptic, developed during the early period of Christianity in Egypt. It is still used in the liturgy of the Coptic church, though since the Arab conquest in the seventh century CE the ordinary language of the people has been Arabic.

Egypt's geography, largely a river valley some six hundred miles in length, led to the development of many local dialects of the native language. During the early pharaonic era, in order to overcome the difficulties caused by this diversity of speech, a special form of writing was developed. Based on many hieroglyphic figures, it was a kind of Mandarin written language, strictly consonantal but capable of coping with the vocalic differences of the various dialects. The work of interpreting and more particularly writing the hieroglyphs was performed by a large body of trained scribes, who might be described as forming an early civil service that maintained the successful administration of Egypt.

Both from original sources and from a history written in Greek ca. 300 BCE by an Egyptian priest, Manetho, it appears that the unification of the two ancient kingdoms of the north and the south was effected by Menes, the founder of the first historical dynasty and the builder of the city of Memphis. In his history, Manetho lists the rulers of Egypt under thirty dynasties, but many of the kings he names have left no tangible records of their reigns. A simpler scheme of the long history is provided by these divisions: the Archaic Period, ca. 3100–2700 BCE; the Old Kingdom, ca. 2700–2500 BCE; the Middle Kingdom, ca. 2134–1786 BCE; the New Kingdom, ca. 1575–1087 BCE; the Late Period, until the beginning of the Greek or Ptolemaic Period, ca. 1087–332 BCE. The Old Kingdom was a period of remarkable building and artistic excellence. In particular, the rulers of Dynasty IV erected the immense pyramids at Giza, reckoned by classical antiquity as one of the seven wonders of the world. The drain on the kingdom's economy in building the pyramids, intended as the secure burial places of the rulers, eventually so weakened the succeeding dynasties that at the end of Dynasty VI a period of anarchy and decline occurred.

Able monarchs, originating from Thebes, during Dynasty XI established effective control over the whole of Egypt and founded the Middle Kingdom. The most powerful rulers were those of Dynasty XII, who conquered and held Nubia. During the Middle Kingdom there was a revival of artistic excellence, especially in portraiture.

As had been the case with the Old Kingdom, toward the end of the Middle Kingdom a period of weakness in the central government allowed the entry into the delta region of a group of foreigners, known as the Hyksos or "Chieftains of Foreign Lands," probably of pastoral origin. They were powerful enough to hold northern Egypt for a considerable time; some ancient and modern scholars regard this period as the setting of the *Joseph narratives in Genesis. During the same period, people from Nubia (the northern Sudan) overran most of the region south of Aswan.

Despite these reverses, the rulers of Thebes eventually succeeded in defeating the forces in Nubia and expelling the Hyksos from the delta. With the founding of the powerful Dynasty XVIII, a period of military advance into Palestine and Syria began. Under warlike kings such as Tuthmose I and his later successor Tuthmose III, greatest of all the pharaohs, Egyptian armies advanced as far as the headwaters of the Euphrates. Conquest brought vast quantities of booty into Egypt to swell the treasury of the state god, Amun-Re. This period also witnessed the entry of many foreign artisans into the country, and with them new ideas. Toward the end of the dynasty, internal religious strife and external administrative weakness followed the accession of Amenhotep IV, better known as Akhnaton (also spelled Akhenaton and Ikhnaton). He attempted to change the long-established religion, bitterly opposing the priesthood and eventually removing his capital city from Thebes to Tell el-Amarna. Opinions about Akhnaton have varied from seeing him as the first monotheist to a pleasure-loving materialist. It is not easy to form a just assessment, for after his death his capital city was abandoned, the ancient religion restored, and every possible record of him destroyed. Some correspondence with Asiatic rulers in such cities as Byblos, *Jerusalem, and *Shechem has survived and is known as the *Amarna letters; it is an important source for our understanding of Syria-Palestine in this period. Among his successors was the youthful Tutankhamun, who reigned briefly, and whose tomb, filled with splendid treasures, was found in the Valley of the Kings by Howard Carter in 1922.

A significant restoration of Egypt's former glory was achieved during Dynasty XIX under the Kings Seti I and his son Ramesses II, both of whom advanced once more into Palestine and Syria; the Exodus of the Hebrews from Egypt is dated to this period by many scholars. Ramesses warred inconclusively with the *Hittites in northern Syria, but his greatest achievements during a long reign were his building projects, especially at Thebes, and his massive rock-cut temples at Abu Simbel in Nubia. His successor, Merneptah, had to deal with foreign invasion in the north. On a triumphal stele from his reign occurs the first mention of the name of Israel, as a defeated people (*see* Israel). In Dynasty XX, a far more serious invasion of northern Egypt by land and sea occurred. This was crushed by Ramesses III, not generally recognized as militarily the greatest of the kings bearing that name. Among the various people who attempted the invasion by sea were the group known in the Bible as the *Philistines.

A succession of kings bearing the name Ramesses followed, but each proved weaker than his predecessor, and Egypt declined in power. The geographical barriers that in times past ensured so many centuries of isolation no longer sufficed to prevent foreign invasion. Thus, Dynasty XXII was founded by a Libyan general, Sheshonq I. Called Shishak in the Bible, he invaded Palestine during the reign of Rehoboam, ca. 920 BCE, removing some of the vessels of the Temple. A record of some of the places he claimed to have captured appears on one of the walls of the temple at Karnak. Dynasty XXV originated from Nubia. In the time of Taharqa (the Tirhakah of 2 Kings 19.9), the fourth ruler of the Dynasty, Egypt faced invasions by the *Assyrians. During the last of the Assyrian invasions in the time of Taharqa's successor, in 663 BCE, the great city of Thebes, No-Amon, was captured and sacked.

For a period after the withdrawal of the Assyrians, Egypt revived under a number of able rulers only to fall eventually to the *Persians under Cambyses. In 332 BCE *Alexander the Great was welcomed by the Egyptians as their deliverer from the rule of the hated Persians. Following Alexander's death and the division of his empire among his generals, Ptolemy gained Egypt in 322 BCE, becoming the first ruler of the Ptolemaic or Greek Dynasty. The last of the Dynasty was Cleopatra, who like her lover Antony committed suicide after their defeat at the Battle of Actium (31 CE). Egypt then became part of the *Roman empire.

Under the Pharaohs, the government of Egypt was essentially theocratic, the king as a child of the gods being semidivine, and as such high priest of the land. His general title, pharaoh, meaning "the Great House," can be compared with "the Palace" or "the Sublime Porte." It is not until the time of the Pharaoh Sheshonq that the throne name of the ruler of Egypt is recorded in the Bible. Two other names of rulers recorded are So and Neco. The order of precedence in Egyptian society can be illustrated by the figure of a pyramid: the pharaoh at the apex, and, in descending layers, the royal family and the local princes, the priests, the scribes, the artisans, and at the base the workers of the land.

To modern minds, the religion of ancient Egypt appears to be a strange, chaotic mixture of pantheism and animal worship, frequently full of contradictory beliefs. Long isolation from the rest of the ancient Near East had tended to breed in the Egyptians a strongly conservative outlook with a deep reverence for the past, so that what might seem to be contradictory was accepted as complementary. Over the centuries, purely local deities merged into larger groupings so that the god of one locality might be regarded as the husband of the goddess of another locality. In some instances, the deity of a third locality, merged into a larger grouping, might be regarded as the child of a divine marriage, thus creating a triad. In many instances, the only clues to the former existence of local gods are their names alone. It should be noted that the many gods of Egypt were essentially deities of the Nile Valley, and that of their vast number only one, the goddess Isis, was successfully translated abroad.

The many temples, supported by great estates, were established to serve the various gods, who in their turn served humankind by preserving the physical fabric of the world. The temples were in fact state institutions and not places of individual devotion and prayer. The temples played a very practical role by training able boys, regardless of their social standing, to become scribes in the service of the state. There was a widespread belief in a resurrection and a future realm of rewards and punishments, presided over by the god Osiris, who had been slain by his evil brother Set, but who was afterward restored to life. From various writings it appears that at all times there existed a sense of personal religious morality as distinct from the state religion. *J. Martin Plumley*

**ELDER.** The designation and role of the elder (Hebr. *zāqēn;* Grk. *presbyteros*) dates to premonarchic times in Israel. In the legislation concerning the Passover in Exodus 12.21 Moses addresses "all the elders of Israel." Similarly, in Numbers 11.16 Moses is commanded to gather together "seventy of the elders of Israel whom you know to be the elders of the people and officers over them" and bring them to the tent of meeting. As this passage and others suggest, the elder, as head of the extended family, had authority over it and also represented it in larger assemblies. These elders functioned primarily on the local level as judges, leaders in battle, and intermediaries between the people and their leaders or God. These functions continued during the monarchy, as the story of Naboth's vineyard (1 Kings 21.8–14) and other passages make clear, and in the Second Temple period as well, both in Judea and in the *Diaspora.

In the New Testament, the "elders of the people" figure throughout the Gospels and Acts as leaders of the Judean community who frequently counsel with other leadership groups and have some role in judging capital crimes. Perhaps related to such a group is the phrase "the tradition of the elders" against which Jesus argues and which is associated with the *Pharisees in both the Gospels and Josephus.

When Christianity began to institutionalize in a formal sense, it understandably drew on Jewish tradition to accomplish this task; thus the title and office of elder make their way into New Testament history and texts. Though not found in the authentic Pauline letters, there are elders mentioned in Acts in the churches at *Antioch, *Jerusalem, and *Ephesus. The author of 2 and 3 John identifies himself as a *presbyteros,* as does the writer of 1 Peter. The office of elder occurs frequently in the Pastoral Letters. 1 Timothy 5.1 uses the term in the context of one who is deserving of respect, but not necessarily as a technical term; in 5.17, however, an office is clearly meant, and an elder is defined as one who both teaches and preaches. Functions such as laying on of hands, anointing the sick, and general governance are also mentioned. There are also repeated references to the office of elder in the apostolic fathers, but as time went on hierarchical episcopacy became the normative form of church administration (*see* Bishop); the English word "*priest," however, is ultimately derived from the Greek word *presbyteros.*

The title, and to some extent the functions, of elder were revived by the sixteenth-century reformer John Calvin, and the Greek word was adopted for the name of the Presbyterian church. *J. Andrew Overman*

**ELIJAH.** Elijah ("Yah[weh] is my God") was a prophet in the northern kingdom of the divided monarchy during the reigns of Ahab, Ahaziah, and Jehoram (873–843 BCE). The circumstances of his birth and early life are not recorded, nor, somewhat unusually, is the name of his father. He was a native of Tishbe in Gilead, an unknown Transjordanian site.

The stories about Elijah, which once circulated separately, have been incorporated into the Deuteronomic history as part of its extensive account of the reign of Ahab of Israel and of its briefer account of the reign of his short-lived son Ahaziah. Elijah's translation to heaven and his succession by *Elisha in 2 Kings 2.1–18 are outside the regnal frame and are part of the Elisha cycle; they take place sometime in Jehoram's reign.

The Elijah cycle records the battle in the north for the survival of authentic Yahwism. Both Ahab and his successor Ahaziah looked not only to Yahweh but also to *Baal and to his consort *Asherah for the winter rains and summer dew that fertilized the land, and for healing. Elijah had to contend not only with the many prophets of Baal and Asherah but with other prophets of Yahweh; 1 Kings 20 and 22 (though not mentioning Elijah) show disagreements among prophets speaking in Yahweh's name. To Elijah, Yahwism involved more than proper worship; the king was accountable to Yahweh's word delivered through prophets such as Elijah and was bound by Mosaic laws protecting the *poor. The royal house, influenced by the Phoenician Queen *Jezebel, looked to non-Israelite models of kingship, in which the patron gods supported the dynasty.

The section 1 Kings 17–19 is artfully arranged from short stories into a coherent demonstration of Yahweh's control of fertility and protection of his prophet. Elijah announces a drought in 17.1, then in 17.2–24 is protected from its effects and from the king. In 18.1–40 Elijah challenged Ahab and his prophets to a contest to determine which deity could end the drought. Yahweh's consumption of the bull offered to him proves that he alone is God; the rain of vv. 40–46 is therefore from Yahweh and not from Baal.

The prophetic word ending the drought, like the word that began it (17.1), puts Elijah in danger from the king. Chap. 19 tells how Yahweh protected Elijah at *Horeb, the source of authentic Yahwism. Like Moses, he encounters God. The theophany, however, is not in the traditional storm but in "a still small voice" (19.12; NRSV: "a sound of sheer silence"), commissioning him to anoint new kings in Syria and Israel (Hazael in place of Ben-Hadad and *Jehu in place of Ahab), and a prophetic successor, Elisha. The sole divinity of Yahweh, proved in the drought-ending storm at Carmel, is asserted in a different way at Horeb; the God of Israel has authority to reject and appoint kings and to provide for a continuing prophetic word.

Chap. 21 is another confrontation of king and prophet, this time about the judicial murder of Naboth, who, in accord with the Israelite conception of land tenure, had refused to sell his family plot to Ahab. Elijah's curse upon Ahab takes effect only in the next generation, occasioning Elijah's last recorded confrontation, with Ahaziah in 2 Kings 1. The king in his illness had sent to Baal of Ekron for healing, and so he must die.

Outside the books of Kings, the Chronicler reports a letter from Elijah condemning Jeroboam. Malachi identifies the messenger of the last days with Elijah; taken up to heaven, the prophet shall return to prepare the nation for the day of the Lord in judgment. Elijah's role as precursor continues in Jewish tradition, with the development of messianic expectations; at the Passover table a place is set for Elijah in case he returns to inaugurate the messianic age. This belief is also present in the New Testament; Mark and John speak of Elijah as the precursor of the last days. The Elijah of the book of Kings appears in Luke 4.25–27; Rom. 11.2; James 5.17; and is dramatically presented in Felix Mendelssohn's oratorio *Elijah.*

*Richard J. Clifford*

**ELISHA.** Elisha ("God has granted salvation"), son of Shaphat, a native of Abel-Meholah in the northern kingdom of Israel, was a prophet during the reigns of Jehoram, Jehu, Jehoahaz, and Joash (849–785 BCE). The stories about him in 2 Kings 2–9 and 13.14–21 directly continue those about his prophetic predecessor *Elijah in 1 Kings 17—2 Kings 1. The Deuteronomic history, a vast work narrating the story of Israel from Moses to Josiah and into the sixth century BCE, incorporated these stories with little editing. Most scholars assume there was once a cycle of stories about Elisha, perhaps more extensive than those preserved in 2 Kings, which was then joined to the slightly older Elijah cycle before being incorporated into the Deuteronomic history. Elisha is portrayed as a disciple of Elijah. Elisha, however, is quite different from the solitary Elijah with his unswerving hostility toward the house of Omri. He leads prophetic guilds, "the sons of the prophets" (NRSV: "company of prophets"), and is sometimes, though by no means always, in friendly contact with the Israelite kings.

Elisha is first mentioned in 1 Kings 19. Elijah, renewed by his visit to the source of Yahwism at Mount *Horeb, is commissioned to three momentous tasks: to anoint Hazael to be king of Syria in place of Ben-Hadad, to anoint Jehu to be king in Israel in place of Jehoram, and to anoint Elisha "as prophet in your place . . . and whoever who escapes from the sword of Jehu, Elisha shall kill." Elijah thereupon seeks out Elisha, who is plowing, and casts his mantle, the symbol of his prophetic office, upon him; Elisha becomes his servant and eventually his successor, when Elijah's mantle definitively is given into his hands. The first two tasks given to Elijah—the anointing of Hazael in 2 Kings 8.7–15 and of Jehu in 2 Kings 9—were in fact performed by Elisha.

There are two types of Elisha stories. One type is the lengthy narratives in which the prophet, sometimes with his servant Gehazi, is involved with the great figures of the day. He advises the kings of Israel, Judah, and Edom in their war with Moab; he assists the king of Israel in the matter of Naaman the Syrian; he plays a role in wars between Syria and Israel; and he foments the rebellion of *Jehu. The other type is brief stories in which Elisha alleviates the distress of individuals: he makes a spring's water nontoxic; he punishes irreverent boys; he feeds the Shunammite *widow and raises her son from the dead; he detoxifies a cooking pot and multiplies loaves of bread; and he makes an ax head float. Both types of stories, especially the latter, emphasize the miraculous. Their emphasis upon the extraordinary resembles that of the Elijah stories and the plague narratives in Exodus; biblical signs and wonders, generally, are more soberly portrayed.

Elisha is mentioned only once in the New Testament, in Luke 4.27, which cites the cure of Naaman the Syrian as an instance of God's caring for non-Israelites. The miracles of Elisha, like those of Elijah, have, however, influenced the narratives of Jesus's miracles, especially in Luke, such as the raising of the widow's son and the multiplication of loaves.

*Richard J. Clifford*

**EMPEROR.** The English word "emperor" is derived from Latin *imperator,* first given by soldiers in the field to a successful general, later a permanent title of Julius Caesar (100–44 BCE) and his successors, the equivalent of "commander-in-chief." It has no exact correspondent in Greek and is not used in the New Testament. In the NRSV, "emperor" is used to translate two different terms. The most frequent is the Greek word *kaisar,* itself a transliteration of the Latin *Caesar.* This was the family name of Julius Caesar, assumed by his great-nephew Octavius (Augustus) (63 BCE–14 CE) and used as a title by subsequent Roman rulers. "Emperor" is also used for Greek *basileus,* "king," in 1 Peter 2.13, 17. In neither case is the NRSV's use of emperor entirely accurate.

*See also* Roman Empire.

*Michael D. Coogan*

**ENOCH.** Of this Old Testament patriarch it is recorded only that he is son of Jared and father of *Methuselah (not to be confused with Enoch, son of Cain) and it is written that, after walking "with God" for 365 years, "he was no more, because God took him." From these words has grown the Enoch legend and its literature, the books of Enoch. Traces of the legend are found in Hebrews 11.5, where Enoch has become a hero of faith. The brief reference in Genesis is further elaborated in Jewish Midrashic tradition; his wife's name was Edni, and he spent hidden years with the *angels before he was taken up to heaven. There are parallels to the latter in Greek and Near Eastern sources, and the later picture of Enoch as omniscient sage and seer probably owes more to Babylonian than to Israelite ideas.

The Ethiopic book of Enoch, or 1 Enoch, is a collection of mainly apocalyptic traditions, arranged as a pentateuch. The collection is now generally dated to about the first century BCE or the first century CE.

The Slavonic Enoch, or 2 Enoch, is found only in Old Slavonic manuscripts, none earlier than the fourteenth century CE. The date of the work is uncertain, with proposals ranging from the first century CE (the prevailing view), or even earlier, down to the Middle Ages.

The Hebrew Enoch, or 3 Enoch, is a heterogeneous collection of qabbalistic materials attributed to Rabbi Ishmael (second century CE). The author is familiar with 1 and 2 Enoch, but the date of composition is uncertain. Recent research suggests the fifth to sixth century CE.

*Matthew Black*

**EPHESUS.** A city on the western coast of Asia Minor and the home of the *Christian community to which the letter to the Ephesians is addressed. Commonly acknowledged to be the first and greatest metropolis of the Roman province of *Asia, Ephesus played a historic part in the movement of Christianity from *Palestine to Rome. Acts depicts Ephesus as the zenith of *Paul's missionary activity, and it was from Ephesus that Paul wrote the Corinthian letters. The Pastoral letters and the book of Revelation associate the city with *Timothy and *John, respectively. Later traditions held that *Mary, the mother of Jesus, lived and died there.

From the classical into the Byzantine period, Ephesus exercised hegemony in the Ionian region. It was well known for its philosophers, artists, poets, historians, and rhetoricians. Ephesus made distinctive contributions to intellectual and religious history from the pre-Socratic period down to the philosophical revivals of the later Roman empire. Small wonder that Paul is seen teaching "daily in the lecture hall of Tyrannus" at Ephesus for two years (Acts 19.9), that *John reportedly wrote the Fourth Gospel at Ephesus, and that this was the site of the conversion of Justin Martyr, the first Christian philosopher.

The importance of Ephesus stemmed from its location on the western coast of Asia Minor at the nexus of river, land, and sea routes. The city's size at the time of early Christianity has been estimated at 250,000, and during the early empire it was one of the fastest-growing urban and commercial centers in the Roman east. Although the harbors at Ephesus were plagued by alluvium, they were still serviceable in the later empire and early Byzantine period.

According to Josephus there was a significant Jewish community there, although few Jewish material remains have been discovered. The city was famous as a site for magic and thaumaturgy. The Greek phrase *Ephesia grammata* (Ephesian letters) became a generic label for all types of magical words and apotropaic incantations. The city attracted Jewish exorcists as well as their gentile counterparts, such as Apollonius of Tyana.

Although the Greek and Egyptian pantheons were well represented in imperial Ephesus, the religious focal point of the city was the goddess *Artemis of Ephesus. From Ephesus her worship had spread throughout the Mediterranean basin, and her Ephesian sanctuary was widely recognized as one of the seven wonders of antiquity. The site of Ephesus is exceptionally well excavated and reconstructed. Most of the excavated areas shed light on the Roman and Byzantine city rather than the Hellenistic one. Noteworthy monuments include the foundations of the Artemis temple and its altar, the 25,000-seat theater, temples for the imperial cult, the library of Celsus, numerous baths and gymnasia, the "slope houses" dating from the early empire to the Byzantine era, and the temple of the Egyptian deities. The thousands of coins and inscriptions that have been found have illuminated many facets of the history and culture of Ephesus that was contemporary with early Christianity. Prominent Christian monuments date from the Byzantine era and include the Church of Saint John, purportedly constructed over the site of the apostle's grave, the Church of Saint Mary, traditionally claimed as the site of the Council of Ephesus in 431 CE, and the legendary Cave of the Seven Sleepers.

According to Ephesians 1.1; 3.1–13; 4.1; and 6.19–22, the letter to the Ephesians was written while Paul was in prison. A very few postscripts to ancient Greek manuscripts state that Ephesians was written in Rome; if this is true, the date of the letter would be about 61–63 CE. However, the Caesarean imprisonment of the apostle (between 58 and 60?) and an Ephesian captivity (in the mid 50s) have also been suggested.

In 1792 the English divine Edward Evanson first questioned Pauline authorship. During the nineteenth century, German scholars gathered arguments in favor of pseudonymous origin, and today most researchers treat the letter as non-Pauline, dating it between 70 and 100 CE, mainly in the 90s. Some think that the author was Onesimus, the runaway slave mentioned in Paul's letter to *Philemon, who is then further identified with the *bishop of Ephesus bearing the name Onesimus (mentioned in Ignatius's letter to the Ephesians).

*Markus K. Barth, Richard E. Oster, Jr.*

**EPHRAIM.** Ephraim first appears in the Bible as the name of the younger son of *Joseph, born to him in Egypt of his wife Asenath. In Genesis 48 the dying patriarch *Jacob blesses Joseph's two sons, *Manasseh and Ephraim, crossing his hands and giving the birthright to Ephraim. This continues the well-known biblical pattern of the lesser inheriting before the elder (Abel, Isaac, Jacob, Joseph, etc.). In the case of Ephraim this probably reflects the eventual domination of the tribe of Manasseh by the tribe of Ephraim, both of which claimed descent from the respective sons of Joseph (*see* Tribes of Israel). The tribe of Ephraim came to inhabit the central hill country of Canaan north of Jerusalem, the so-called hill country of Ephraim (from which the tribe probably received its name. The ancient cities of Bethel, *Shechem, and Shiloh are all to be found in its territory. Its importance is highlighted by the use of the name of Ephraim as an alternate literary designation for the whole northern kingdom of *Israel by the mid-eighth century BCE. This pivotal position is underlined by the names of some of the tribe's leading personages: *Joshua, *Deborah, *Samuel, and Jeroboam I, the founder of the secessionist northern kingdom. A town by the name of Ephraim is mentioned in 2 Samuel 13.23; it may be the same as the Ephraim to which Jesus went after raising Lazarus.

*Carl S. Ehrlich*

**EPICUREANS.** Epicurus (341–270 BCE) formed a community of friends in *Athens, who held that philosophy had the practical aim of securing happiness. Believing that pleasure is the sum total of happiness, they conceived of pleasure not as sensual indulgence, as their opponents charged, but as a tranquility like that of the gods. Contrary to the popular view, they claimed that the gods exercised no providential oversight in human affairs. People therefore need not fear the gods, nor need they fear death, for it simply marks the end of human existence and should have no bearing on one's manner of life. The Epicureans sought security in organized communities where, in the company of friends, including women and slaves, they sought to "live unnoticed" by withdrawing from society, which they held in contempt. Opposition to the Epicureans was sharp and slanderous. Because they did not believe in the popular gods they were called atheists or, at best, believers in gods who were idle or asleep; their social attitude was regarded as misanthropic and irresponsible; and the motto "eat, drink" (because there is no life after death), became a shorthand reference to supposed Epicurean hedonism.

Epicureans were associated with Gadara, Gaza, and Caesarea, and it is not surprising that traces of Epicureanism have been detected in biblical and other Jewish writings dating from the third century BCE onward. Epicureanism was not, as some have maintained, a bridge between Greek philosophy, on the one hand, and Christianity and rabbinic Judaism, on the other; some Jews and Christians, however, were aware of the alternative options presented by Epicureans and of the polemic against them. The pessimistic view of death in *Ecclesiastes and the advice to eat, drink, and find enjoyment in this life have been thought to reflect Epicurean influence, despite the expressed conviction that it is God who makes enjoyment possible. On the other hand, *Sirach's opposition to libertinism and to the view that God does not intervene in human affairs suggests that the author rejects behavior and views like those attributed to Epicureans.

The only explicit reference to Epicureans in the Bible is Acts 17.18, where *Paul is described as encountering Epicureans and *Stoics in Athens. These were the two major philosophical sects of the time, and they presented radically opposed views. Paul is portrayed as more congenial to the Stoic view of divine providence, which is reflected in both his argument and the sources he quotes in the sermon that follows. Paul also uses language derived from anti-Epicurean polemic in 1 Corinthians 15.32–34, where he clarifies the hope of resurrection and opposes libertinism. The attack in 2 *Peter on teachers who reject divine providence similarly reflects such polemic, particularly in the denial that the Lord is slow and that their destruction by God is asleep. Despite these views, Christians' emphasis on love between members of their communities, their opposition to popular religion, and their reputation for antisocial behavior caused them on occasion to be lumped together with the Epicureans.

*Abraham J. Malherbe*

**ESAU.** The older son of *Isaac and *Rebekah, and the twin brother of *Jacob. His ruddy and hairy appearance, as well as his preference for hunting and the outdoor life, distinguished him from his brother. Despite the apparent connection between his name and his hairiness in Genesis 25.25, the etymology of Esau remains uncertain. Esau also is considered the ancestor of the *Edomites.

Genesis 25.29–34 relates how Esau foolishly sold his birthright to Jacob for the price of a meal whose name in Hebrew *(ʾādōm)* resembles Edom, another name for Esau. Jacob, acting on the advice of Rebekah, then tricked Isaac into making him the principal heir by disguising himself as his older brother and obtaining his father's blessing. Esau eventually shunned revenge, was reconciled with Jacob, and settled in Seir.

Most scholars view the stories of Jacob and Esau not only as folktales about fraternal relationships and reversals of fortune but also as Israelite depictions of the ambivalent and sometimes treacherous relationship between Edomites (sons of Esau) and Israelites (sons of Jacob) over territorial claims and other ethnopolitical issues. Ethnopolitical relationships are ostensibly reflected in notices about Esau's marriages to women of various ethnic origins and about his progeny.

Within Christianity Esau became a central example in debates concerning the right of *Christians to the blessings promised by God to the descendants of Isaac and in debates about predestination.

*Hector Ignacio Avalos*

**ESDRAS.** The Greek form of the name *Ezra, used in the traditional titles of the books of 1 Esdras and 2 Esdras in the Apocrypha. There is no connection between the two books beyond the fact that Esdras is a central figure in each.

**1 Esdras.** 1 Esdras is a book of history, though it has sometimes been doubted that it should be called a book at all, since it may quite plausibly be regarded as a mere torso. The nature, history, and purpose of the book are among the perennial, and perhaps insoluble, problems of apocryphal literature.

In simplest terms, the book is an alternative version of the canonical book of Ezra, to which are prefixed and subjoined brief sections of, respectively, the books of Chronicles and *Nehemiah; it also contains one major section (3.1–5.6) not found in the Hebrew Bible at all. In manuscripts of the Greek Septuagint this composite book (called Esdras A) stands just before the book called Esdras B, which is in fact a literal, unexpanded translation of the canonical Hebrew Ezra-Nehemiah. In effect, then, the Septuagint contains two versions of the book of Ezra, one of which (1 Esdras) diverges considerably in matters of detail from the canonical book. Eventually, 1 Esdras was dropped from the canon of the western church and is included in the standard Apocrypha only because it appears, for purely historical reasons (under the title of 3 Esdras) in an appendix to the Latin Vulgate. It is not counted as one of the deuterocanonical books by the Roman Catholic church, but it is recognized as such by some Orthodox churches.

**2 Esdras**. 2 Esdras is commonly referred to as "4 Ezra" after the enumeration in many manuscripts and the Latin Vulgate, where it has stood since 1560 in an appendix after the New Testament. The book was never a part of the Hebrew or Greek canon. Our principal authority is the Latin text, of which there are several old manuscripts and many late ones. It was translated from a Greek text, of which a few scattered verses remain, preserved on papyrus or in patristic citations.

The core of the book (chaps. 3–14) is a Jewish apocalypse, originally written around 100 CE in Hebrew or Aramaic. The date is indicated roughly by the historical allusions in chap. 12, and more precisely by the phrase "the thirtieth year after the destruction" of *Jerusalem (3.1); this is doubtless a veiled reference to the calamity of 70 CE, though ostensibly it refers to that of 587/586 BCE.

The first two chapters are generally held to be a *Christian addition, preserved in two Old Latin recensions. The replacement of Israel by a new people is foretold in language reminiscent both of the prophets and of the New Testament. The last two chapters (15–16) are a further addition, with dire warnings and invective against enemies of God's people; they appear to reflect a knowledge of events in the third century CE. In the manuscripts, these pairs of chapters are often designated 2 Esdras and 5 Esdras respectively, and modern scholars have sometimes advocated these or similar labels.

**The Ezra-Apocalypse** (chaps. 3–14) relates revelations given to Ezra in seven visions by the angel Uriel. The general theme is the suffering and restoration of Israel in light of God's justice and mercy, but it is widened to include the sin and destiny of all humanity and the fate of individual souls. In the first three visions, these problems are examined at length. Ezra begins each time by pouring out his troubled thoughts and prayers; one of these has been particularly admired (8.20–36), and many manuscripts of the Vulgate include it among other canticles as a separate item entitled "Confession of Ezra." The angel replies with arguments and discourses, often illustrated with parables or riddles. With Ezra pressing his questions, this is the most valuable part of the book.

In the fourth vision (9.26–10.59), Ezra encounters a woman mourning for her husband and son; she represents

*Zion in her desolation, and is transformed into a glorious new city. The fifth vision (chaps. 11–12) is closely modeled on Daniel 7, where the fourth beast with many horns symbolizes Hellenistic kings; the image here is of an eagle with many wings and three heads, evidently representing Roman emperors and usurpers, from Julius Caesar to Domitian. The eagle's doom is pronounced by a lion, symbol of the *Messiah, who comes to destroy the godless and to deliver the righteous remnant. In the sixth vision (chap. 13), the Messiah is depicted as a man rising from the sea (some of the language reflects Dan. 7.13), and his victory is described in some detail; standing on a huge mountain, he confronts a great concourse of enemies and destroys them, not with any weapon but with a stream of fire from his mouth.

In the final vision (chap. 14), the tone changes; Ezra becomes the inspired writer who dictates ninety-four books to five scribes. Twenty-four of them are the canonical scriptures, which (it is said) had been burned when the *Temple was destroyed; these are now restored and published in a new script (i.e., the Aramaic square characters now used for writing Hebrew); the other seventy books are esoteric writings for "the wise" alone to read, for they contain the secrets that had been revealed to Ezra.

Ezra is portrayed as a man of great piety, who prepares for his visions by seven-day fasts; he is called "the prophet" and is the shepherd, as it were, on whom the people depend for leadership and support. But the picture is a conventional one and has little in common with the historical Ezra of the Hebrew Bible; there is perhaps one deliberate point of contact in the story of the restoration of the scriptures, since the historical Ezra was scribe of the law of Moses. "Ezra" is in fact a pen name, in accordance with the custom of apocalyptic writers, who present their insights in the form of discourses to holy men of old. Like *Enoch and *Elijah (and *Moses according to postbiblical tradition), Ezra is destined not to die but to be "taken up" (8.19; 14.9).

2 Esdras is an important book for students of Jewish apocalyptic; it throws light on developments parallel to Christianity, and therefore, at least indirectly, on *Christian origins.

*Robert C. Dentan, G. M. Styler*

**ESTHER.** The heroine of the book of Esther, whose author is unknown. The book presents the story of an unsuccessful attempt to kill the *Jews living in the *Persian empire during the reign of a certain Ahasuerus, probably meant to be Xerxes (486–465 BCE). The threat was averted by the courage and shrewdness of Esther and her cousin Mordecai, with the aid of a series of fortuitous circumstances. Since it purports to explain the origin of the festival of Purim, the book has been read aloud in the *synagogue at that feast since antiquity.

Neither the date nor the location of the book's composition can be determined with any precision. While it is clearly one of the latest books in the Hebrew Bible, the absence of clear historical allusions or perspectives renders the questions uncertain; nor is there sufficient linguistic evidence to resolve them. It may be as late as the second century BCE, just before the Maccabean period, or as early as the late fifth century, from the Persian period. Doubtless, it contains traditions and information that go back to the Persian period. In part because of its lack of interest in Palestinian religious institutions and its concern with the problems of Jews in foreign lands, it is likely that the book was composed in the eastern *diaspora.

Although the details of its setting are entirely plausible and the story may even have some basis in actual events, in terms of literary genre the book is not history. Nor is it legend, though the sequence of events is as unlikely as those in legends, and folkloristic traditions probably underlie the story. Missing are the conventional legendary features of the miraculous, as are characters who reveal the power of God in human affairs and thereby serve as models for future generations. Rather, because of the extended and well-developed plot and its point of view, the book is best understood as a novella, a type that arose not as oral tradition but as a written composition. The closest biblical parallels are the story of *Joseph and the books of *Ruth, *Jonah, and *Tobit.

By means of a relatively straightforward plot, the book of Esther tells the story of how the Jews were saved from persecution and death. It is a simple story of the triumph of good over evil, but the narrator takes some care to pace the tale, keeping the outcome in doubt as long as possible. Ironic twists appear—first, when Haman hears the king ask, "What shall be done for the man whom the king wishes to honor?" and, assuming the monarch has him in mind, he answers, only to discover that the king intends to honor Mordecai. The final irony for Haman is that he is hanged on the gallows he had built for Mordecai. Moreover, the story is not without humor, and possibly satire as well, particularly in the portrayal of Ahasuerus.

The first two chapters set the scene and mood for the events of the story itself. In chap. 1, though the main characters have not yet appeared, we learn how the king, Ahasuerus, behaves capriciously, how much plotting and conflict there is in the court, and that when the king banishes Vashti he will need a new queen. Two events equally important for the outcome of the story are reported in chap. 2: after an empirewide search, the Jewish girl Esther becomes the queen (as in the book of Ruth, intermarriage between Jews and *gentiles is not only condoned but even approved); and her cousin Mordecai discovers a plot against Ahasuerus and reports it.

Two distinct but related threads run through the body of the story: the threat against Mordecai and the threat against the Jewish people as a whole. The first is set in motion when Mordecai refuses to bow down before Haman, thus disobeying one of the king's laws. The story does not state directly why Mordecai puts his life in danger, but it implies that he does so because he is a Jew. When Haman learns this, he vows to kill all the Jews. Then Haman schemes to accomplish his goal, bribing the king to proclaim the destruction of the Jews on a date set by the casting of a lot (Hebr. *pûr;* hence the festival is called Purim [the plural form]). The first thread of the plot is brought to a climax when Ahasuerus, finding Haman in what he takes to be a compromising position with Esther, decrees Haman's death. It was not just Esther's appeal but a chance encounter that brought the enemy's downfall.

Still, the terrifying danger hangs over the Jews, for the king's edict has gone out and cannot be recalled. As the book stresses more than once, royal proclamations cannot be changed. Ahasuerus can and does, however, promulgate another edict, this one authorizing the Jews to defend themselves. When this document is circulated, the main plot has reached its resolution. What follows, including the extermination of the Jews' enemies, is the denouement of the conclusion's results.

**Additions to the Book of Esther.** Jerome, in preparing his Latin Vulgate, recognized some 107 verses as additions to the book of Esther. Since the passages in question appeared in his Greek text but not in the Hebrew, he removed them from the body of the book and placed them at its end. A further step was taken during the Protestant Reformation, when the Apocrypha was created by placing in a separate part of the Bible those books found in the Greek Old Testament but not in the Hebrew. It was then that the Additions to the Book of Esther became a separate book.

The additions make the book of Esther a dramatically different work and indicate that some of those who transmitted it were uneasy with the original. What had been a tale of the triumph of good over evil through the skills and courage of the hero and heroine, assisted by fortuitous circumstances, becomes a religious story stressing piety and the will of God. Whereas the book of Esther does not mention God, the additions constantly refer to the deity, to prayer, and to the sacred traditions and practices of Judaism. The important human qualities are not shrewdness or power or royal position, but piety and humility.

*Gene M. Tucker*

**ETHNARCH.** *See* Tetrarch.

**EUNUCH.** A castrated male. The Hebrew word *sārîs* is derived from an Akkadian phrase, *ša rēši,* literally, "(the one) of the head," meaning a royal attendant or official. Context largely determines whether the Hebrew should be translated "eunuch" or simply "official."

In early biblical writings, eunuchs appear as members of the royal court with no mention of their physical condition. The first references occur in texts coincident with the Davidic monarchy of the tenth century BCE. References increase in the seventh-century Deuteronomic history and are most frequent in literature of the sixth century BCE and later, especially in narratives depicting the Babylonian and Persian courts. This distribution does not support the view that the use of eunuchs was a custom imported into Israel from neighboring cultures. The inclusion of eunuchs among the royal entourage suggests that eunuchs were native to ancient Israel.

Later writings are preoccupied with the physical condition of the eunuch. In Isaiah 56.5, the eunuch who fears oblivion because of his childlessness is reassured that the eschatological commonwealth holds for him a "monument and a name *(yād wāšēm)* better than sons and daughters." In Sirach 30.20, the eunuch's inability to consummate his desire is a metaphor for an invalid's frustration in enjoying life.

In the New Testament, the eunuch is a potent ascetic symbol. Matthew 19.12 recognizes that eunuchs come from differing circumstances, including those "who have made themselves eunuchs for the sake of the kingdom of heaven." In Acts 8.27, Philip converts an Ethiopian court eunuch who is reading from the book of Isaiah; the passage may be an allusion to the eunuch of Isaiah 56.

*Gene McAfee*

**EUPHRATES.** The southernmost of the two rivers that, along with the Tigris, define *Mesopotamia. The Euphrates begins from two tributaries in mountainous eastern Turkey, crosses into Syria at Carchemish, and flows south roughly 100 mi (160 km) from the Mediterranean before turning east at Emar. It then proceeds southeast past *Mari to *Babylonia and into the Persian Gulf. This portion of the river served as an important trade route between Egypt, Syria-Palestine, and southern Mesopotamia.

In the Bible, the Euphrates is treated as the farthest northern horizon of Israelite territory in the promise to *Abraham (*see* Promised Land), in the conquest instructions to *Moses and *Joshua, and in the description of *David's success in *Syria. Though Israelite territory never properly extended across Syria, the ambitious ideal suggests a sense of vocation to be the major inland power between Egypt and the Euphrates, as David and *Solomon may briefly have been. The river boundary did not assume control of the northern coast, which belonged to the *Phoenicians. The Euphrates boundary is also evident in the Persian province in Syria-Palestine called "Beyond the River," which included the district of Yehud, in earlier Judah.

*Daniel E. Fleming*

**EVANGELIST.** Evangelist (Grk. *euaggelistēs*) derived from the verb *euaggelizomai,* meaning "to announce good news" *(euaggelion),* is a primary New Testament concept. In the Hebrew Bible we find a similar figure in the messenger who brings good news *(mĕbaśśēr)* and proclaims peace. The "prophet of consolation" in Second Isaiah is also a messenger of good news, announcing the deliverance of the people. Consequently, Jerusalem is exhorted to convey the good news to the neighboring cities that their God is coming to take care of his flock and to bring with him peace, happiness, and salvation.

In the Greco-Roman world the words *euaggelion* and *euaggelizomai* had acquired technical connotations associated with important events in the *Roman empire. In the New Testament the word *euaggelistēs* occurs only three times, whereas the substantive *euaggelion* and the verb *euaggelizomai* occur seventy-six and fifty-four times respectively. In the Gospels, *Jesus is presented as a preacher of the good news of the kingdom of God. He tells the disciples of *John the Baptist that the *poor are being evangelized, recalling Isaiah 61.1; the same text is referred to in Luke 4.17–19.

Outside the Gospels, the word "evangelist" has three different meanings. First, it was a title for early preachers of the gospel. In a certain sense, all *apostles were evangelists, since their duty was to preach the gospel. Gradually, the term came to be confined to the disciples of the apostles. In Ephesians 4.11, "evangelist" is third in a list of offices in the church, after *apostles and *prophets but before pastors and teachers. *Timothy is referred to as someone performing the work of an evangelist, probably because of the role he played in establishing the believers in their faith. Philip, one of the *seven, is also called an evangelist because he preached the gospel to the *Samaritans and those outside Judea. In a more restricted sense, the word denotes the author of one of the four canonical Gospels; this usage first appears in the third century CE. Traditionally, the four evangelists are symbolized by a man, a lion, an ox, and an eagle, on the basis of Revelation 4.6–10. Finally, in modern times, the word has developed a more specialized meaning, referring to a traveling preacher or revivalist.

*Joseph Pathrapankal, C.M.I.*

**EVE.** The name given to the first woman by the first man. The Bible interprets this name to mean "the mother of all living," both because Eve is, through her sons, the female ancestor of the entire human race and because the name sounds similar to the Hebrew word for "living being." The wordplay is probably etymologically incorrect, and later rabbinic tradition proposed a connection with the *Aramaic word for "serpent." The actual linguistic derivation of the name remains uncertain. According to the account in Genesis 2–3, the woman is created to be a companion corresponding to (not originally subordinate to) the man. Because the two of them eat the forbidden fruit, the man is destined to toil as a farmer in fields of thorns and thistles, and the woman is destined to suffer pain in childbearing. It is in the aftermath of these divine pronouncements that the man names the woman as he had earlier named the animals, thus indicating dominion over her.

Both Jewish tradition and the New Testament offer a very negative view of Eve, presenting her as representative of the alleged weaknesses of women. Paul feared that the Corinthian Christians would be led astray from Christ as Eve was deceived by the serpent. In 1 Timothy 2.13–15, Eve's deception by the serpent and also her creation subsequent to the man are cited as reasons that women must keep silent in church and hold no authority over men. Early Christian theologians contrasted Eve's sinfulness with the perfection of the "new Eve," *Mary, the mother of Jesus.

This traditional emphasis on the gullibility of Eve and her tendency toward sin is one possible interpretation of the Genesis narrative; it is not, however, inherent in the text of the narrative itself. Genesis 3 gives no indication why the serpent addressed the woman and even indicates that the man and the woman were together when the serpent spoke. It has been suggested that the serpent might have addressed the woman as provider of food or as theological thinker, not as the more gullible of the couple, and that the woman's addition to the divine prohibition about the fruit ("we may not touch it") represents not a lie, but a desirable exaggeration meant to make sure that the basic command would not be broken. The man and the woman together discover their nakedness, together make fig leaf garments, and together hide from the deity. Both are destined to a life of pain (neither is cursed) because of their actions, and together they are expelled from the garden. Thus, once the reader sets aside the portrait of Eve based on later traditions, the great skill of the Genesis narrator in presenting a character open to diverse interpretation becomes apparent.

*See also* Adam; Eden, The Garden of; Lilith; Women.

*Katharine Doob Sakenfeld*

**EZEKIEL.** A priest and prophet of the early sixth-century BCE, to whom is attributed the book of Ezekiel.

The book of Ezekiel tells relatively little that is explicit concerning the figure for whom it is named, and apart from brief references in Sirach and 4 Maccabees he is not mentioned elsewhere in the Bible. Ezekiel, whose name means "God strengthens," was of priestly lineage, son of Buzi. Along with other Judeans, he suffered deportation to *Babylon following the surrender of Jehoiachin in 598/597 BCE. Ezekiel received his prophetic calling in Babylon in 593; his age at the time is not recorded. It is disputed whether some or even all of Ezekiel's ministry actually took place in *Jerusalem rather than in Babylonia, as various of his words could suggest. According to the book's dates, he continued to receive divine communications until at least 571. Nothing is mentioned in the Bible concerning the circumstances of his death; much later tradition states that he was murdered by one of the leaders of the exiles whose idolatry he had denounced, and that he was buried near Babylon.

Unlike his near contemporary *Jeremiah, Ezekiel appears as an outwardly stoical, highly self-controlled and somewhat passive personality, who, for example, follows without demur Yahweh's directive not to mourn the death of his beloved wife. On occasion, however, he does venture a protest or appeal in the face of what is communicated to him. It is likewise clear that Ezekiel's call to herald *Judah's doom caused him profound distress. The response to Ezekiel's message seems to have been much less overtly hostile than was true in the case of Jeremiah. In fact, there are several references to his being respectfully consulted by the leaders of the exiles. Finally, the content of Ezekiel's book reveals him as a man of wide learning.

Ezekiel's God is above all a "holy" being, that is, one who utterly transcends human comprehension, manipulation, and calculation. This quality of Yahweh finds manifold expression throughout the book. Ezekiel refrains from any direct claims to have seen the deity. Yahweh remains free to rebuff human inquiries; he can void the schemes of practitioners of magic. The movements and fates of the great world powers, such as Babylon and *Gog, are just as much under his control as is the destiny of Israel itself. Yahweh has the capacity to manifest himself outside the land of Israel; he is able to withdraw his presence from the *Temple, and later to return there as he wills. He acts, unconstrained by any human claim, for his own purposes.

At the same time, however, the holy Yahweh is also a God who has freely but passionately and irrevocably committed himself to the people of Israel. Like *Hosea and Jeremiah, Ezekiel develops this dimension of Yahweh's being and activity by using conjugal imagery. Yahweh carefully and tenderly nourished the cast-off child Israel as his future bride. At present, he is punishing her for her persistent infidelities, but ultimately he will not abandon his spouse to her misery and sinfulness. Rather, he will restore her prosperity and give her the inner capacity to live in faithfulness to him. In all of this, the transcendent God is intimately and continuously involved in human history, to the end that, finally, both Israel and the nations will know him as the sole, truly efficacious deity.

Ezekiel's anthropology is characterized by an underlying unresolved tension. On the one hand, he is the Hebrew Bible's great advocate of individual responsibility. Ezekiel is likewise commissioned precisely in order to summon his hearers to conscious decision about their behavior options. On the other hand, however, Ezekiel's words disclose an overwhelming pessimism concerning the people's capacity ever to choose rightly. For him, unlike Hosea and Jeremiah, there never was a honeymoon period in Israel's relation to Yahweh. Already during her time in Egypt, as well as ever since, Israel has consistently chosen other gods in preference to Yahweh. Judah learned nothing from Yahweh's punishment of the northern kingdom, only redoubling her own idolatry in the face of that experience. Although Ezekiel's hearers may not actively persecute him, neither do they give much attention to his warnings. Such circumstances suggest that the exhortations

Ezekiel is sent to deliver are futile; what is needed, rather, is a direct intervention by Yahweh that will produce a transformed, obedient heart in his people. Ultimately, like so many theologians after him, Ezekiel is left affirming both realities, human freedom and divine grace, without being fully able to account for their interplay.

*Christopher T. Begg*

**EZRA.** Son of Seriah, Ezra was a *priest and a *scribe who played a significant role in the reform of Judaism in the fifth century BCE. The book of Ezra is named for him, and he is a principal character in the book of *Nehemiah.

Ezra 7–10 tells of the return of Ezra and a certain group of *Jews to Judah in the time of the Persian king Artaxerxes (presumably Artaxerxes I, 465–424 BCE). It is clear from these chapters that Ezra was dispatched by the Persian king Artaxerxes to Jerusalem to establish the Israelite law (Torah) among the Jews. A number of exiles returned with Ezra, a kind of ideal group consisting of, among others, priests and *Levites. To his dismay, Ezra discovered that there had been intermarriage with the neighboring nations, and he ordered all foreign wives to be repudiated, so as to keep the religion of Jews pure of contamination by the worship of different gods.

An important source in Ezra 7–10 is the Ezra memoir, written in the first person with some parts in the third person. It is probable that we have here an actual memoir of Ezra himself used by the Chronicler. In the sections using the first person, the Chronicler has quoted from the memoir, and in those parts using the third person he has rendered it in his own words.

*See also* Esdras.

*F. Charles Fensham*

# G

**GABRIEL.** Gabriel is one of the most prominent *angels in postexilic Jewish literature and in *Christian texts, especially extracanonical literature. He is portrayed as one of the seven *archangels in 1 Enoch 20.7; elsewhere he is one of the four angels close to God's throne. This proximity to God results in his distinctive functions. Gabriel intercedes with God for those oppressed by evil, he brings *Enoch into God's very presence, he explains mysteries about future political events, and he delivers special revelations from God to individuals. Jewish and Christian interpreters have sometimes concluded that biblical texts with unnamed divine messengers refer to the archangels Gabriel and Michael. In general, *Michael is described as a warrior, while Gabriel more often functions as an intermediary or an interpreter of dreams. *Steven Friesen*

**GAD.** Son of Zilpah, *Leah's maid, and *Jacob, and one of the twelve *tribes of Israel. The name Gad is associated with the Hebrew word for fortune. In early Israel Gad is both populous and adept in battle. The Gadites, together with *Reuben and half of *Manasseh, settle in the Transjordan, an area suited for their abundant cattle. The Gadites support *Saul and his family, aid *David, and participate in his administration.

Gad fares poorly during the divided monarchy. King Mesha of Moab (ca. 835 BCE) claims that he dealt harshly with the Gadites of Ataroth. Hazael of Damascus (Syria) devastates Gad. Subsequently, *Tiglath-pileser III of Assyria exiles the Transjordanian tribes.

Gad can also refer to a foreign deity, a seer during the time of David, or an organizer of levitical service and chronicler of David's life. *Gary N. Knoppers*

**GALATIA.** A region in central Asia Minor (around modern Ankara, in Turkey). Galatia was the location of several churches to which *Paul addressed his letter to the Galatians. The "churches of Galatia" addressed in this letter were situated in the Roman province of Galatia, but which part of the province is a matter of dispute. Until 25 BCE the area had been the kingdom of Galatia. The original Galatians were Celts from central Europe who invaded Asia Minor and established themselves there in the third century BCE. But the rulers of Galatia extended their authority over neighboring territories populated by other ethnic groups; these groups were included in the province of Galatia and were Galatians in the political but not in the ethnic sense. To some of these groups belonged the cities of Pisidian Antioch, Iconium, Lystra, and Derbe, which were evangelized by Paul and Barnabas around 47 CE.

One view is that the churches of those cities were recipients of the letter. Another view is that the recipients were churches established later in the northern part of the Roman province, among the ethnic Galatians. It is true that Acts makes no mention of Paul's visiting north Galatia, but Acts does not give a complete account of his missionary activity. The precise identity of the recipients does not greatly affect the argument of the letter.

The letter is a sustained and passionate expostulation with a group of churches whose members were in danger of abandoning the gospel that they had received from Paul. They were inclined to pay heed to certain teachers who urged them to add to their faith in Christ some distinctive features of Judaism, particularly circumcision. These teachers also endeavored to diminish Paul's authority by insisting that he was indebted to the Jerusalem church leaders for his apostolic commission and had no right to deviate from Jerusalem practice.

The traditional view, accepted here, is that those against whom Paul polemicizes in Galatians were judaizing intruders, eager to make the churches in Galatia, which were mainly gentile in composition, conform to the Jewish way of life and probably also to bring them under the control of the church of Jerusalem.

The letter can be read against the background of revived militant nationalism in Judea in the years after 44 CE. These militants (who came to be called Zealots) treated Jews who fraternized with gentiles as traitors. Jerusalem *Christians were sensitive to the charge that some of their leaders, if not they themselves, practiced such fraternization. Hence, perhaps, the representations to Peter at Antioch, which made him break off his table fellowship with gentile Christians in that city; hence too, perhaps, the judaizing mission to Galatia. For if gentile converts could be persuaded to accept circumcision and conform to Jewish customs in other ways, for example, by observing the sacred calendar, the militants (it was hoped) would be pacified.

The response of the churches of Galatia to the letter is unrecorded.

The date of the letter has been fixed at various points between 48 and 55 CE. If it was sent to the churches of Pisidian Antioch, Iconium, Lystra, and Derbe, a date around 48 CE is possible, even probable; if it was sent to churches in ethnic Galatia, its date would be later.

*F. F. Bruce*

**GALILEE.** The name for the northern region of Palestine, meaning literally either the circle or the district. According to Joshua 19, this area was allotted to the tribes of Naphtali, Zebulun, and Dan, although the accounts of the tribal settlements suggest that the older population continued in the more prosperous regions such as the valley and the coast. Archaeological data, especially from surveys, add evidence of many new settlements throughout the region in the early Iron Age, as farther south in the central hill country (*see* Canaan). Galilee, together with some of its major cities, especially *Hazor, is only sporadically mentioned in biblical and nonbiblical sources in the first half of the first millennium BCE. After the fall of the northern kingdom in 722 BCE Galilee was included in the Assyrian province of *Samaria, but it is unlikely that the whole Israelite population was ever completely uprooted in this largely rural area. While drawing a distinction between Upper and Lower Galilee, later writers, such as Josephus and Pliny, extol the fertility and the variety of its agricultural produce.

The region receives more attention beginning in the Hellenistic period, when Simon, one of the Maccabean brothers, went there to rescue some fellow Jews during the persecution that followed Antiochus IV's Hellenistic reform in the mid-second century BCE. This episode has suggested to many scholars that Galilee was then a thoroughly gentile region, but this may not be an accurate assessment. Scattered references from the Persian period indicate a continued Jewish presence there in Persian times. Archaeological surveys suggest that the region was not densely populated in the early Hellenistic period, and the episode involving Simon seems to have been confined to the region of Ptolemais. Josephus informs us that the Hasmonean Aristobulus I forcibly circumcised the Iturean people as part of the campaign to reestablish control of the old Israelite territory. This episode may have involved some of those dwelling in Upper Galilee but can scarcely be considered to have involved all Galilean Jews of the first century BCE.

The population of Galilee seems to have increased under the Hasmoneans by a process of "internal colonization," giving rise to a densely populated province by the first century CE. This "Jewish Galilee" emerged as a separate administrative unity when Pompey, the Roman general, carved up the Hasmonean kingdom, and its identity was further enhanced by the setting up of an administrative council for the region at Sepphoris by his successor Gavinius in 57 BCE. This center, and its rival Tiberias, founded by Herod Antipas in 19 CE, continued to dominate the whole of Lower Galilee administratively, whereas Upper Galilee retained a largely village culture into late Roman and Byzantine times.

Galilee's separate identity also emerged when the Romans once again intervened to carve up *Herod the Great's kingdom on his death in 4 BCE. The region, together with Perea, was entrusted to his son Herod Antipas, whose long reign (4 BCE to 39 CE) covered the career of Jesus of Nazareth. By contrast with Judea in the south, which came under direct Roman rule in 6 CE, with the consequent deterioration of social relations there, Antipas's reign appears to have brought stability to Jewish Galilee. Galilee also came under direct Roman rule, probably on the death of Herod Agrippa in 44 CE, although part of the region—Tiberias and Tarichaeae and their territories—had been given by Nero to Agrippa's son, Agrippa II, whose territory had previously been confined to Trachonitis in Transjordan. In the First Jewish Revolt (66–70 CE), the Jewish revolutionary council appointed Josephus as governor of Galilee at the outbreak of hostilities with Rome, but apart from a few centers such as Gischala, Gamala (situated in the Golan, although closely associated with Galilee), and Tiberias, the campaign was quickly brought to an end by the advancing Roman legions, and Josephus was captured after his last stand at the fortress of Jotapata, an account of which is highly embellished to extol his own military prowess. Galilee does not seem to have been involved in the Second Jewish Revolt (132–35 CE), and as part of the Roman settlement Jews from the south were forced northward. Thus, from the second century CE on, Galilee became a home of Jewish learning and piety in the land of Israel. It was there that the great scribal schools flourished at Usha, Sepphoris, and Tiberias, producing the Mishnah and later the Palestinian Talmud *(Yerushalmi)*. Jews from all over the Mediterranean world were buried at Beth Shearim in Galilee. The excavated remains of the *synagogue there suggest a thriving local community with an independent religious life down to the Arab conquests of the seventh century CE, despite the increased Christian presence after Constantine's conversion.

This sketch of Galilean political and religious history should help to correct some false impressions of Galilee and Galileans that are often found in accounts of the career of *Jesus of Nazareth. Galilean life was relatively stable politically, especially in contrast to Judea, and so it is incorrect to see Galilee as the home of the *Zealots or as a hotbed of revolutionaries, at once more radical and more charismatic in the expressions of their Jewish religious loyalties. Nor were Galileans generally socially deprived or marginalized. The natural fertility of the region, its strategic location on the caravan routes to the East, as well as its role as a hinterland for the Phoenician trading centers, meant that its inhabitants were in a position to enjoy at least some of the benefits that the Hellenistic age brought to the East.

Galilee and Galileans are associated particularly with Jesus of Nazareth and his movement. While each of the four Gospels treats the region differently within the overall purposes of its narrative and does not give us the kind of detailed information about the region that one can glean from Josephus's *Life,* for example, many of their underlying social and religious assumptions are realistic on the basis of what can be reconstructed historically from other sources. For the evangelists also Galilee is thoroughly Jewish in its religious affiliation. Tensions between the religious claims on the region from Jerusalem and the distinctive regional ethos are recognized. The rural setting predominates, and the lake region with its busy commercial life is highlighted. This picture, highly selective in its coloring, corresponds remarkably well with a more detailed profile that can be established with the aid of other sources. Galilee did indeed function as a symbol of the newness of Jesus's vision in contrast to the more established circles of Jewish belief for the early Christians, but all the indications are that the symbolic reference was grounded in an actual ministry that was conducted in the real Galilee of the first century CE. *Seán Freyne*

**GALILEE, SEA OF.** A large, heart-shaped expanse of water, 12.5 mi (20 km) long by 7 mi (11 km) wide at its maximum points. It forms a deep basin surrounded by mountains on both sides and a narrow, shoreline plain where several important cities and towns are located. This pattern is broken only at the northwestern corner, where this strip opens out into the plain of Gennesar, the fertility of which was extolled by Josephus. The lake surface itself is ca. 700 ft (210 m) below sea level, thus forming a large basin for the waters of the *Jordan River. According to Josephus and Pliny its original name was the Lake of Gennesaret, although both authors are aware that it was also called the Lake of Tiberias (Josephus) or the Lake of Tarichaeae (Pliny), after two of the more important settlements on its shores in Roman times.

The gospels of Matthew (eleven times) and Mark (seven times) call it the Sea of Galilee, a designation also found in John 6 and 21. This may reflect the Hebrew *(yam),* which can mean either a freshwater lake or the sea properly understood. It has been suggested, however, that Mark's usage (followed by Matthew) has a more symbolic significance in terms of Jesus's control of the forces of evil that are associated with the deep. Luke reserves the word "sea" for the Mediterranean and always speaks of the "lake of Gennesaret" or "the lake" when referring to the Sea of Galilee. The significance of this usage is that it suggests that Luke, although presumably not a native of Palestine, was able to project himself into that context and accurately reflect local usage in differentiating between sea and lake.

The lake provided a natural boundary between Jewish Galilee and the largely gentile territories of Gaulanitis and the *Decapolis directly across. Despite differences of religious affiliation among the population on either side of the lake, archaeological evidence suggests a real continuity in terms of lifestyles, trading, and other relations. The Gospels also testify to this frequent movement, even when it is not always possible to detect accurately the points of embarkation and arrival. Josephus too mentions fleets of boats on the lake, thus suggesting a busy and thriving subregion within Galilee and linking it with the larger region.

In addition, the lake was a natural resource for Galilee because of the fish industry. Strabo, Josephus, and Pliny, as well as the Gospels, all mention the plentiful supply of fish in the lake. Both Bethsaida and Tarichaeae are generally believed to have derived their names from the fish industry; the latter is most probably the Greek name for Magdala and is derived from the Greek term for preservation. Salting of fish, which made their export possible on a much wider scale, was, we know, a technical skill that was developed during the Hellenistic age. It is likely, therefore, that there was a genuine expansion of this industry in Palestine also. Josephus mentions one type of fish, the *coracin* belonging to the eel family, which was also found in the Nile, suggesting perhaps that the early Ptolemaic rulers had expanded the fish industry to Galilee as a commercial enterprise. In this regard it is worth noting that James and John, the sons of Zebedee, would appear to have abandoned a thriving business when they left their father and his hired servants to follow the call of Jesus. *Seán Freyne*

**GAMALIEL.** Gamaliel the *elder was a first-century CE teacher. Although he is not often quoted in the *Mishnah, it is said that "when he died the glory of the Torah ended."

Gamaliel is best known outside the Mishnah for his brief speech in Acts 5.35–39. Identified as a *Pharisee respected by the people, Gamaliel counsels the *Sanhedrin to leave the early Christian leaders alone: "If this plan or this undertaking is of human origin, it will fail; but if it is of God, you will not be able to overthrow them." He is also identified as *Paul's teacher in Acts 22.3.

*J. Andrew Overman*

**GARDEN OF EDEN.** *See* Eden, Garden of.

**GEHENNA.** The place where, according to Jesus in the synoptic Gospels, sinners are punished after death. A few times Hades is also treated as such a place of punishment, but it is cited more often as the realm of death in general. (The NRSV translates Grk. *geenna* as "hell.")

Gehenna was originally the Hebrew name of a valley just south of *Jerusalem's southwestern hill called "the valley of Hinnom" (*gēʾ hinnōm*) or "the valley of Hinnom's son(s)" (*gēʾ ben(ê) hinnōm*). Under the influence of the Aramaic form *gēhinnā(m)*, the Greek transliteration of the word became *geenna*. "Hinnom" may be understood as the representative of a *Jebusite group that once dominated the place in question, but the Bible mentions only the valley. In boundary lists it forms the border between Judah and Benjamin south of the Jebusite city, implying that Jerusalem belonged to Benjamin.

The later view of Gehenna as a place of punishment, especially by fire, is anticipated in an Isaianic reference to a large *topheth, or burning place, near Jerusalem, said to be lit by the Lord to punish the *Assyrians and their king. A further stage in the development of the relevant concepts is reached in the report concerning King *Josiah's cultic reform of 622 BCE, which implied a desecration of similar topheths in Judah, especially one found in the valley of Hinnom and dedicated to Molech for children. The elimination ordered by Josiah was not entirely successful, for somewhat later Jeremiah made repeated attacks on the topheth and said the valley of Hinnom would become a general burial place.

On the basis of such passages and influenced by parallelism with Persian ideas of a judgment in fire, Jewish apocalypticism made the valley of Hinnom a place of punishment within an eschatological milieu. In a vision ascribed to *Enoch a cavity was depicted, into which the faithful Jews, gathered on the holy mountain, would look down to see the righteous judgment and eternal punishment of all godless and cursed people. No name appears here, but since the details of the picture indicate the topography of Jerusalem, the cavity in question must have been meant as the valley of Hinnom. The joining of the eschatological perspective to Jerusalem then led to an explicit use of the name Gehenna for that place of punishment, a usage that emerges in texts of the first century CE in the New Testament and in Jewish apocalypse (e.g., in the Latin translation "Gehenna"). In the Mishnah and later rabbinic texts, the name Gehenna *(gēˀ hinnōm)* has superseded the older term for the underworld (Sheol). Gehenna is also the ordinary term in the Qur'ān for the place of ultimate punishment. *Bo Reicke*

**GENTILES.** From the Latin *gens* (literally, "nation;" Hebr. *gôy;* Grk. *ethnos*), "gentile" refers to a non-Jew or, more broadly, anyone outside the covenant community of Israel. Postexilic times witness references to individual gentiles as opposed to nations; concurrently, the possibility of conversion to Judaism appears. Gentiles depicted in the Bible are as diverse as are Jews: From *Rahab to *Ruth, Haman to Holofernes, they come from various locations and play various roles—helpers, oppressors, witnesses, tempters.

Joshua 24.11 mentions the seven nations from whom the covenant community is to maintain separation. Yet a "mixed multitude" accompanies the community escaping Egypt, and rules for the resident *alien permit the circumcised sojourner to participate in Israel's religious life. The so-called promise motif insists that by *Abraham "all the families of the earth will bless themselves/be blessed"; Isaiah 42.6 calls Israel "a light to the nations"; and *Jonah is commissioned to preach to *Nineveh. Yet *Ezra and *Nehemiah require divorce of gentile wives, and the condemnation of gentile nations is a common prophetic motif. The Hebrew book of *Esther does not decry intermarriage, and the book of Ruth celebrates the union of a Judean man to a *Moabite woman, but the Greek additions to Esther and the book of *Tobit value endogamy.

Connections between Jewish and gentile communities existed in politics, trade, and even religious practices. Some gentiles became *proselytes; others were attracted to Jewish practices and *synagogues (the "God-fearers"). The pseudepigraphical book of Joseph and Asenath presents the Egyptian priest's daughter whom Joseph marries as the archetypal proselyte. Gentiles also participated in worship in the Herodian *Temple.

Jewish reactions to gentiles are also diverse. Most Jewish groups in the Hellenistic and early Roman periods believed that the righteous among the gentiles would achieve salvation, but they would do so as gentiles and by divine decree at the end of time. Such dual soteriology may also underlie Romans 9–11. *Genesis Rabbah* 34.8 lists the Noachide commandments incumbent on gentiles. *Tosepta Sanhedrin* 13.2 mentions gentiles who receive a place in the world to come. Jews were to deal honestly with gentiles and relieve their *poor even as they were warned against associating with idolaters. Neither scriptural warrant nor unambiguous historical evidence exists for an organized Jewish program to convert gentiles. Distinctions were to be kept between Jew and gentile, but the manner in which separation was maintained varied economically, socially, geographically, ritually, and philosophically.

Early Christian views of gentiles are generally positive; this is not surprising, given that the church found gentile territory fertile soil for its messages and that most of its canonical documents are addressed to gentile or partially gentile communities. Matthew's genealogy includes gentiles, and the gospel concludes with the command to make disciples of all the nations (or gentiles, *panta ta ethnē*); Luke has *Simeon predict that Jesus will be "a light for revelation to the Gentiles (2.32)." *Paul is the apostle to the gentiles both in Acts and in his own letters. How Jesus himself regarded gentiles is not clear. In Matthew 10.5b–6; 15.24, he forbids his disciples to engage in a gentile mission (see also Rom. 15.8), but Luke 4 depicts his early willingness to extend the good news to non-Jews. And both comments may be redactional inserts.

Anticipated by the conversion of Cornelius in Acts 10, behavior incumbent on gentile Christians is confirmed by the Apostolic Council in Jerusalem: gentiles were to follow what was likely a combination of Noachide commandments and the laws incumbent on the resident alien. Scholars debate whether Paul himself insisted that all ritual law was abrogated in light of the Christ event, or whether ethic Jews could retain ritual practices. Within a century, this debate ended: Christianity became predominantly gentile, and Jewish practices were labeled heresies. Today, especially in the United States, "gentile" is often viewed as synonymous with "Christian." This is not, however, the case among members of the Church of Jesus Christ of Latter-day Saints (Mormons), who refer to those outside their community (including Jews) as "gentiles."

*Amy-Jill Levine*

**GETHSEMANE.** The name of the place in *Jerusalem where, according to Matthew 26.36 and Mark 14.32, Jesus was arrested. John does not name it but calls it a garden. This fits the name's meaning, "oil-press," as does its location on the lower slopes of the Mount of Olives, in the general vicinity of the several churches there today.

*Michael D. Coogan*

**GEZER.** A major city in antiquity and the object of important archaeological excavations in this century, Gezer lies on the border between the Judean foothills and the Shephelah, in the tribal territory of Ephraim. Mentioned in inscriptions of Pharaohs Tuthmose III (first half of fifteenth century BCE) and Merneptah (end of thirteenth century), as well as in the Amarna letters (mid-fourteenth century), Gezer came under Israelite control at a relatively late date. Although the Israelites had failed to conquer the Canaanite city, it passed to their control when it was ceded to *Solomon by Egypt, ostensibly as a dowry for his wife, the pharaoh's daughter. The siege of Gezer by the *Assyrians is depicted on a relief from the palace of *Tiglath-pileser III in Nimrud (ancient Calah). During the Maccabean period Gezer (called Gazara) was an important Seleucid stronghold until its capture by Simon in 143 BCE.

*Carl S. Ehrlich*

**GIDEON.** Also called "Jerubbaal," Gideon is a judge-deliverer from *Manasseh who leads the central highland tribes to victory over *Midianite raiders. His story illustrates the theme of total dependence on God: at divine command, he reduced his army from thirty-two thousand to three hundred before attacking the enemy. Gideon's story also reveals tensions in premonarchic Israel. Intertribal rivalry is evident, as the tribe of *Ephraim shows its jealousy toward Gideon's tribe of Manasseh as a result of Gideon's success. Also, there is tension over Israel's form of government. After his victory, the people move to make Gideon king; but he refuses, saying they should look on God as their king. By contrast, when Gideon's son Abimelech tries to adopt kingship for himself (after his father's death), he is rejected by the people and killed.

*See also* Judges.

*Timothy M. Willis*

**GOG.** Described in Ezekiel 38–39 as ruler of the land of Magog, Gog is also "chief prince" of the lands of two tribes in Asia Minor, Meshech and Tubal; the specific location of Magog is unknown. Gog, leading a coalition of nations from virtually all points of the compass, is summoned by Yahweh, the God of Israel, to attack Israel itself. Yahweh nonetheless promises to intervene on Israel's behalf, destroying the enemy coalition by means of stupendous natural disasters. The book of Revelation refers to a Satanic invasion of "Gog and Magog," curiously placing it after the promised millennium (the thousand-year period of the reign of the *Messiah).

*William H. Barnes*

**GOLGOTHA.** The site of the crucifixion of Jesus in *Jerusalem; the tomb in which Jesus was buried was apparently nearby. The name is Aramaic, and means "the skull," a translation given after the Aramaic in Matthew 27.33, Mark 15.22, and John 19.17. Luke 23.33 gives only the Greek translation. In the Vulgate a Latin word for "skull," *calvaria,* is used; this is the source of the English word "Calvary," used in the KJV of Luke 23.33. The origin of the name Golgotha is obscure; suggestions include its location in a cemetery and its being a site for executions. The great biblical scholar Origen (third century CE) thought it was the burial place of *Adam; following this view, artists have frequently placed a skull at the base of the cross in representations of the crucifixion.

The precise location of Golgotha and of the tomb of Jesus is not certain, but the most likely candidate is the present site of the Church of the Holy Sepulcher, though traditions identifying it as the place of Jesus's death and burial are apparently no earlier than the fourth century CE. *Michael D. Coogan*

**GOLIATH.** The heavily armed *Philistine warrior from Gath who, according to 1 Samuel 17, was slain by *David while the latter was still a young shepherd who was armed only with a slingstone and faith in Yahweh. Goliath's height is given in the MT of 1 Samuel 17.4 as six cubits and a span (ca. 9 ft 9 in [3 m]), although textual traditions represented in the *Dead Sea Scrolls and the Septuagint give four cubits and a span (ca. 6 ft 9 in [2 m]). 1 Samuel 21.8–10 implies, perhaps ironically, that David returned to Gath with Goliath's sword.

In 2 Samuel 21.19 a warrior named Elhanan killed Goliath, a descendant of the giants of Gath, in a battle at Gob. The AV attempts to harmonize the discrepancy by reading: "Elhanan . . . slew the brother of Goliath," following an ancient tendency already found in 1 Chronicles 20.5. However, these discrepancies suggest that the attribution of Goliath's slaying to David may not be original. *Hector Ignacio Avalos*

**GOMORRAH.** *See* Sodom and Gomorrah.

# H

**HABAKKUK.** A prophet to whom is attributed the book that bears his name. Little is known about Habakkuk himself, though he figures as a minor character in *Bel and the Dragon. The central theme of the book of Habakkuk has to do with God's purpose. It was composed between 609 and 598 BCE, when the Babylonian armies under *Nebuchadrezzar marched into and captured the Palestinian landbridge. Habakkuk resides in the southern Israelite kingdom of *Judah, and unlike the prophets who preceded him, Habakkuk addresses his words not to his compatriots but to God. His principal question is: When will God fulfill his purpose and bring in his reign of justice, righteousness, and peace on the earth? When is the kingdom of God going to come?

In the first oracle, Habakkuk raises his initial lament. He sees in Judean society around him nothing but violence and evil—the oppression of the weak, endless strife and litigations, moral wrongs of every kind. And despite Habakkuk's continual pleading with God to end the wrong, God seems to ignore him and to leave the righteous helpless to correct it.

But then God does answer his prophet. He tells Habakkuk that he is rousing the Babylonians to march through the Fertile Crescent and to subdue Judah, as punishment for her sin. The nation that has rejected God's order and rule will find itself subjected to the order and rule of Babylonia and her gods.

In the third section, the prophet acknowledges the justice of God's punishment of Judah. And because God's judgment is always finally an act on the way to salvation, Habakkuk knows that Judah will not die. But his problem remains, because the Babylonians, in their cruel conquests, are even more unrighteous than Judah has been. When will God bring that unrighteousness to an end?

To seek an answer, Habakkuk stations himself on his watchtower, a symbol of his complete openness to God. And God answers him, assuring him that the "vision"—that is, God's righteous rule, God's kingdom—will come, in faithfulness to the divine promise. Indeed, the fulfillment of God's purpose hastens to its goal. It may seem delayed to human beings, but it will surely come, in God's appointed time. In the meantime, the righteous are to live in faithfulness to God, trusting his promise, obeying his commands, and acting in a manner commensurate with the coming kingdom. Only those who live such trusting and obedient lives will have fullness of life. Those who rely on themselves and their own prowess, who are proud and self-sufficient, and who have no regard for the ways and will of God, will not prosper but will sow the seeds of their own destruction.

The hymn of 3.3–15, with its introduction, confirms the message of 2.2–3. The prophet is granted a vision of God's final, future judgment of all, and of the establishment of God's rule over all the earth. From such a vision of God's future triumph, Habakkuk has found his certainty. He therefore sings the magnificent song of faith with which the book closes. The prophet's external circumstances have not changed. Violence and injustice still mar his community, strife still abounds, nations still rage and devour the weak, and the proud still strut through the earth. But Habakkuk has been given to see the final outcome of human history. God is at work, behind all events, fulfilling his purpose. His kingdom will come, in its appointed time, when every enemy will be vanquished, and God's order of righteousness and good will be established over all the earth.

*Elizabeth Achtemeier*

**HAGAR.** An Egyptian servant of Sarah, featured in the Genesis narratives about *Sarah and *Abraham. According to custom, Sarah, who was sterile, presented Hagar to Abraham so that Hagar might conceive and provide Abraham with an heir.

Two Hagar stories appear in the Bible. The first describes the expulsion of the pregnant Hagar from Sarah's household, her conversation in the wilderness with a messenger of God who urges her to return to the household, and the subsequent birth of her son *Ishmael. In the second Hagar story, set more than fourteen years later, when Sarah herself had at last borne a son (*Isaac) and was celebrating the day of his being weaned, Hagar and Ishmael are cast out from Sarah's household into the wilderness. A divine messenger rescues them when their water supply runs out, and he proclaims that Ishmael will become a great nation.

The literary and chronological relationship of these two narratives is problematic, but certain themes common to both can be recognized. One is that Sarah is the dominant figure in the household with respect to management of domestic affairs, including determining the fate of household staff. In both narratives, Sarah makes a decision about Hagar's fate and Abraham acquiesces. Another theme is the tension between the main wife and a concubine or servant wife with respect to inheritance. Parallels with Babylonian laws suggest that Isaac, though born later, could still be considered firstborn. Sarah's desire to exclude Ishmael from any inheritance at all is partly to satisfy the narrative of Genesis 17, in which Sarah will be the mother of the covenantal heir; it may also reflect the difficult personal relations that arise when one son receives all.

A fourth theme involves the way in which disadvantaged individuals are portrayed as surviving and being blessed with the promise of great prominence. A final theme concerns the special role of Ishmael in biblical history. The Hagar stories establish the close relationship of the Ishmaelites ("the descendants of Hagar," according to Bar. 3:23) to the Israelites, relegating them to a separate territory but recognizing that God has protected and sustained their eponymous ancestor, the son of Hagar and Abraham. Finally, the narratives, while making Hagar a heroic figure, are also sensitive to her vulnerability as a woman, a foreigner, and a servant.

Paul interprets the Hagar stories with a tendentious allegory in Galatians 4:21–31.

*Carol L. Meyers*

**HAGGAI.** A late-fifth-century BCE prophet. We know nothing about Haggai himself. The book that is named after him tells us that Haggai prophesied in the second year of *Darius the Persian (i.e., 520 BCE), his recorded ministry spanning a period of only three months, from the sixth to the ninth month of that year. The book shows that Haggai was seen as a prophet who assured the immediate postexilic community that earlier prophecies would be fulfilled and the hopes of the Zion/David theology of preexilic Jerusalem would be renewed. The *Temple was completed in 515 BCE, but we learn no more about or from Haggai after his three months of preaching spanning the dates given in the book (Ezra 5.1–2 adds nothing new). The addition of a gloss in 2.5 alluding to the presence of God in terms of the pillar of fire and cloud that accompanied the Israelites at the time of the Exodus, and the description of the response of Haggai's hearers in terms reminiscent of that of the Exodus community to *Moses, suggests that his oracles were handed down among those who saw the return from exile as a second Exodus (as Second *Isaiah had done) and Haggai as having exercised the ministry of a second Moses.

A series of brief oracles in chap. 1 reveals the hardship of the situation of the pioneers, who were struggling to rebuild Judah after the Babylonian exile. The promises of *Ezekiel and Second Isaiah, which must have spurred on many of the returning exiles, seemed not to have been fulfilled. The community had known repeated droughts and failed harvests, with consequent famine, poverty, and inflation.

Haggai challenged the community about their priorities. He replies to their protests that they are too poor to rebuild the Temple by saying that it is because they have not rebuilt it that they are so poor. He thus draws on the old covenant traditions that had threatened the people, if they broke the Law, with drought, pestilence, famine, and the frustration of all their activity. Similarly, the *Zion tradition had linked God's presence in his Temple at Jerusalem with peace and prosperity for the land and community. He therefore calls on them to rebuild the Temple.

A short narrative section (1.12–15) tells how the whole community under the leadership of *Zerubbabel, the governor, and Joshua, the high priest (the Jeshua of Ezra and Nehemiah), was energized by Haggai's preaching to begin work, encouraged by a further assurance of Yahweh's presence by the prophet.

Evidently some grew discouraged in the work; they were not helped by the cynicism of those who had seen the grandeur of Solomon's Temple. The following verses show Haggai again encouraging them, not only by assuring them of Yahweh's presence in the task but also with the promise that this Temple, once completed, would be the scene of Yahweh's reign as universal king. Earlier prophetic promises are taken up again, together with themes from the psalms that celebrate Yahweh's rule as king (the so-called enthronement psalms). So God appears, as on Mount *Sinai, accompanied by earthquake and cosmic upheavals; the nations come in pilgrimage to Zion, bringing tribute to God as king. God will fill the Temple with his "glory" as he dwells there again. That is why the new Temple will excel even the first and that is why it is worth building.

The oracle based on a priestly directive in 2.10–14 shows that the postexilic prophets were seen as serving in a sanctuary setting and yet also were deeply concerned with ethical and moral purity.

In 2.15–19 the prophet describes the marked contrast in fortunes that he believed would be experienced after the Temple was rebuilt. The promises of 2.6–9 are renewed in 2.20–22, while 2.23 shows that Haggai saw Zerubbabel as continuing the line of the preexilic Davidic dynasty, which, it was believed, God had promised would last forever. The picture of the Davidic king as God's "signet ring" echoes what was said of Jehoiachin earlier. Haggai thus seems to have centered some kind of messianic hope on Zerubbabel. *Rex Mason*

**HAM.** One of the sons of *Noah. According to Genesis 9.20–27, Ham saw his father, Noah, lying drunk and naked in his tent, and Noah later cursed Ham's son *Canaan, pronouncing him a slave to his brothers. Ham's precise offense has been interpreted as castration, sexual assault, and incest. But the simplest explanation seems best: in failing to cover his naked father, Ham was disrespectful. Still, it is not Ham but his son, Canaan, whom Noah cursed, almost certainly because the story served to legitimate Israel's conquest of Canaan and the destruction of its inhabitants.

This passage has more recently been used to support another kind of racism. Because some of Ham's descendants, notably *Cush, are black, the "curse on Ham" has been interpreted as black (Negroid) skin color and features in order to legitimate slavery and oppression of people of African origin. This interpretation is reflected in the postbiblical Christian tradition of three *Magi, one of whom is black, in parallel to Noah's three sons. Yet it was neither Ham nor Cush who was cursed, but Canaan, the "brother" of Cush and the "son" of Ham. *Steven L. McKenzie*

**HAZOR.** Located north of the Sea of *Galilee, Hazor was occupied from the early third millennium to the second century BCE. The city's 30-acre (12-hectare) acropolis and 175-acre (70-hectare) "Lower City," which was enclosed by earthen ramparts, gained international prominence during the second millennium. Texts mention Hazor as an enemy of Middle Kingdom *Egypt (Execration Texts), a destination for tin shipments from the east (*Mari archives), and a military objective of New Kingdom Pharaohs (Dynasties XVIII–XIX). Destruction of those levels dating from the Late Bronze Age (1550–1200), with their successive Canaanite temples, may relate to Israelite conquest traditions. Hazor's Iron Age acropolis continued as headquarters for Canaanite alliances until *Solomon and *Ahab made it a garrison city. Despite damage by the Arameans in the ninth century and an earthquake in the eighth, Hazor prospered under Jeroboam II before the *Assyrians razed it in 732 BCE, leaving destruction debris one meter thick. *Ron Tappy*

**HEBREWS.** A name applied occasionally to the early Israelites, primarily to distinguish them from other cultures and peoples of the ancient Near East. An ethnic term, it antedated the common sociopolitical names *Israel or *Judah in the monarchic period, as well as the more ethnoreligious appellative *Jew in later times. The word Hebrews, used thirty-three times in the Hebrew Bible, appears in only four texts describing the period after the time of the Davidic kingdom. Contemporary sources outside the Hebrew Bible refer to the people not as Hebrews but as Israel.

The derivation of the word Hebrew (Hebr. *ᶜibrî*) is uncertain. It may be related to the verb *ᶜābar,* "to cross over or beyond." Thus, the Hebrews would be understood as "those who crossed over" or "the ones from beyond," meaning probably from the other side of the *Euphrates River or perhaps the *Jordan River. Along this line, the Septuagint translates "Abram the Hebrew" in Genesis 14.13 as "Abram, the one who crossed over."

A second possible etymology is based on the genealogies that identify Eber, the grandson of Shem, as one of the ancestors of *Abraham and all his descendants, thus the "Eberites." No such explicit tie, however, is made in the Bible, and this connection would suggest that other peoples who are thought to derive from Abraham, including *Edomites, *Moabites, and Arabic tribes, should also be called Hebrews. The connections with Eber on the one hand and the motif of "crossing over" on the other, as well as a third possibility mentioned below, remain suggestive but inconclusive. Virtually every reference to the Hebrews in the Hebrew Bible occurs in a context in which the purpose is to differentiate these people from those of neighboring countries, usually the Egyptians and the Philistines. *Joseph, stemming from "the land of the Hebrews," is identified by this name in the story recounting his rise to prominence under the Pharaoh. A later Egyptian ruler charges the Hebrew midwives to kill all sons born to the Hebrews, but they refuse to do so, reporting deceitfully to the Pharaoh that "the Hebrew women are not like the Egyptian women; for they are vigorous and give birth before the midwife comes to them." Moses is recognized by the Pharaoh's daughter as a Hebrew child, and she calls for a Hebrew woman to nurse him. Subsequently, Moses defends a Hebrew, "one of his people," from a beating at the hands of an Egyptian and then flees the land when he learns that other Hebrews have heard of it. In confronting the Pharaoh to demand release of his people, Moses makes reference to "the Lord, the God of the Hebrews." At all these points, the ethnic name serves to distinguish this people from the Egyptians, who are shown as using this designation as well. Genesis 43.32 reports that the Egyptians even considered it an "abomination" to eat with Hebrews, a custom for which there is no record in Egyptian sources.

In their dealings with the *Philistines, the people are also often called Hebrews, especially by the Philistines themselves. At times it seems to be used as a term of contempt, parallel to the tradition in Genesis 43.32. In 1 Samuel 4.6, 9, the Philistines speak derisively of their opponents in battle and urge each other to fight courageously "in order not to become slaves to the Hebrews as they have been to you." In a later episode the Philistines, considering the Hebrews to be unworthy fighters who cower in caves, are easily routed by the bravery of Jonathan and his armor bearer. This story also raises the question of whether the Hebrews and the Israelites are identical groups. When *Saul issues the battle cry "Let the Hebrews hear," the text states that "all Israel heard"—which may not be the same as saying that all the Hebrews responded. It is in fact later reported that a number of Hebrews had previously attached themselves to the Philistines, and that after Jonathan's rout they disaffected and joined the Israelites. This text may retain an ancient distinction that in later periods no longer applied: Hebrews as a larger socioeconomic group extending beyond Israel, and Israelites as the particular ones who banded together in the Canaanite highlands to form a new nation. In that case, the Philistines may have simply considered the Israelites to be part of the larger class of Hebrews whom they were attempting to control, for example by restricting their access to metal-working. A similar confusion occurs in 1 Samuel 29.3 when the Philistines prohibit *David, who has been living with them, from joining them in battle against the Israelites—not because he is an Israelite but because he is considered a Hebrew.

There are only two other similar references to Hebrews in the Hebrew Bible. In Genesis 14.13, a context in which numerous peoples are mentioned, "Abram [Abraham] the Hebrew" appears parallel to "Mamre the Amorite." In a much later period, the prophet *Jonah, when pressed by sailors of the boat on which he sought escape, calls himself a Hebrew and a believer in the Lord who created the sea and land.

The ethnic and sociopolitical origin of the Hebrews remains a contested point. In many respects the $^{c}$*apiru* (or $^{c}$*Habiru;* in Sumerian *SA.GAZ*) seem to be a close counterpart, and it is often suggested that the word Hebrew is derived from $^{c}$*apiru* (rather than from Eber or from the verb "to cross over," as indicated above). The $^{c}$*apiru* were a diverse group of people with an inferior social status, living mostly on the fringes of settled civilizations from Mesopotamia to Egypt, and there is evidence of them in numerous sources throughout the second millennium BCE. They frequently were hired as mercenaries or sold themselves into servitude in order to survive. The *Amarna letters (fourteenth century BCE) place them in the area of Syria-Palestine and describe them as basically outlaws and raiders, but such antagonism with resident populations may not have been common.

While there is no basis for equating the Hebrews with the $^{c}$*apiru,* the proto-Israelites were probably a conglomeration of various Semitic groups, of which the $^{c}$*apiru* was certainly one. Another was the *shasu,* pastoral nomads and plunderers also known to have been dwelling in Syria-Palestine as well as elsewhere in the region. The tradition of a "mixed multitude" or "rabble" led by Moses through the wilderness is consistent with this picture of the early Israelites as an amalgamation of diverse peoples. Calling them "Hebrews" is an early means of distinguishing this new entity from other existing ethnic groups.

Hebrews are mentioned in one other notable context in the Hebrew Bible. Two laws dealing with slavery distinguish those who are Hebrews from others who are not. Exodus 21.2–11 provides for the release of every male Hebrew slave after a seven-year period of service unless he should choose to remain for life with his master. Special rights are also reserved for a daughter who has to be sold into slavery. Deuteronomy 15.12–18 extends the law of manumission to include both male and female Hebrew slaves, stipulating that they are to be given ample provisions for starting their new life of freedom. Immediately before the fall of Jerusalem in 587/586 BCE, according to Jeremiah 34.8–22, King Zedekiah proclaimed the release of all male and female Hebrew (here also called Judean) slaves, but after this was accomplished the Israelite masters took them back, eliciting from Jeremiah an ominous pronouncement of doom. It may be that these Hebrew slaves, especially in the earlier laws, are reminiscent of the often-enslaved $^{c}$*apiru,* but the Bible perceives them as compatriot Israelites deserving of treatment better than that normally afforded foreigners.

The name Hebrew, used rarely in the Hebrew Bible, thus occurs primarily to distinguish Israelites ethnically from non-Israelites. At times it is applied by foreigners (mainly Egyptians and Philistines); in other instances, by the Hebrews themselves when addressing foreigners. Except for the slave laws, Israelites normally identify themselves to each other—and often to others as well—as the people of Israel and Judah. Similar usage continues in later literature.

In the New Testament, the term designates *Jews, hence Jewish Christians who maintained their ties with the Jewish heritage and the Aramaic or Hebrew language. Acts 6.1 contrasts them with Hellenists, perhaps Jewish Christians who accommodated more to the Hellenistic culture by speaking Greek and following certain Greek customs. *Paul, born in Tarsus, proudly identifies himself as "a Hebrew born of Hebrews."

In modern usage, the term Hebrew is generally applied only to the language of ancient and modern Israel and of Jewish scriptures and tradition.

*Douglas A. Knight*

**HEBRON.** A major city of Judah, located ca. 19 mi (31 km) south of Jerusalem. In biblical traditions it is especially associated with the *ancestors of Israel. *Abraham is said to have built an altar there, and Abraham and *Sarah, *Isaac and *Rebekah, and *Jacob and *Leah were buried there in the cave of Machpelah. An enclosure wall built by *Herod the Great surrounds the traditional burial site, now incorporated into a mosque that was originally a church. Hebron's modern Arabic name reflects this association; it is called Halil, for Abraham, the "friend" of God.

Also associated with Caleb and *Samson, Hebron served as *David's first capital and continued to have symbolic importance in the early monarchy. But once *Jerusalem became established as the capital of the kingdom, Hebron's importance diminished.

*Michael D. Coogan*

**HERMON, MOUNT.** The mountain that formed Israel's northern boundary. With an elevation of over 9,200 ft (2,800 m), it dominates the landscape of northern *Galilee and is snow-covered virtually year-round. In antiquity it was apparently the home of lions and leopards. Its name means "set apart" and indicates its sacred character, suitable for a peak from whose base flow the sources of the *Jordan River. Hermon was associated with the Canaanite god *Baal; just below it there is a later shrine to the Greek deity Pan (modern Banias), identified with Caesarea Philippi. Some have proposed Mount Hermon as the setting for the transfiguration of Jesus, although Tabor is the traditional location.

*Michael D. Coogan*

**HERODIAN DYNASTY.** Several members of the family of Herod governed Jewish Palestine during the period of Roman domination.

**Sources.** The primary source for the Herods is Josephus; for the later Herods, especially Herod Antipas, Agrippa I, and Agrippa II, the New Testament makes a small contribution to our knowledge. Josephus's two main works, *The Jewish War* and *The Jewish Antiquities,* overlap in their coverage of the Herods. Regarding Antipater and Herod the Great, Josephus depended primarily on Nicolaus of Damascus, who was Herod's court historiographer. For the period from Herod's death (4 BCE) to the First Jewish Revolt (66–70 CE), Josephus relied for the most part on oral tradition and hence has far fewer historical particulars. There has been debate about Josephus's historical credibility, but most would grant him to be reliable, taking note, however, of his biases. Archaeological discoveries in *Jerusalem, at Qumran, and elsewhere have supported many details of his works.

**Origin of the Herodian Dynasty.** After the Maccabean Revolt (167–164 BCE), in 142 BCE the Jews became politically independent under the rule of the Hasmonean family. It was the Hasmonean Alexander Janneus (103–76 BCE) who appointed the Herodian Antipater, Herod the Great's grandfather, as governor of Idumea. After Alexander's death in the struggle for power among his family members, Hyrcanus II, his eldest son, after ruling only three months as king and high priest, was forced out by his younger brother, Aristobulus II (67 BCE). In 63 BCE Antipater II, son of Antipater and father of Herod the Great, was instrumental in having Hyrcanus II reinstated and in deposing his younger brother. With Rome's intervention in Palestine (63 BCE), both brothers appealed for Roman support, and Pompey sided with Hyrcanus II, reinstating him as high priest. Later Julius Caesar, who had defeated Pompey (48 BCE), reconfirmed Hyrcanus II as high priest and granted Antipater II Roman citizenship with tax exemption, making him procurator of Judea. Antipater II appointed his sons Phasael as governor of *Jerusalem and Herod as governor of *Galilee (47 BCE).

**Herod the Great (47–4 BCE).** ***Governor of Galilee*** **(47–37 BCE).** Although Herod was only twenty-five years old when he became governor of Galilee, he displayed efficient leadership. After the murder of Caesar in 44 BCE, Cassius, the Roman leader of Syria, appointed him as governor of Coele-Syria. After Antony defeated Cassius (42 BCE), he appointed both Herod and Phasael as *tetrarchs of Judea.

In 40 BCE troubles arose for the two new tetrarchs. When the Parthians arrived in Syria, they joined with Antigonus (the son of Hyrcanus II's deposed brother Aristobulus II) to depose Hyrcanus II. The Parthians besieged Jerusalem and sued for peace. Herod was suspicious of the offer, but Hyrcanus II and Phasael went to meet the Parthian king, who put them in chains. On hearing of this treachery, Herod, his family, and his troops moved to Masada and then to Petra. Antigonus mutilated his uncle Hyrcanus II's ears to prevent his being reinstated as high priest and sent him to Parthia. Phasael died of either poisoning or suicide.

Herod departed for Rome, where Antony, Octavius, and the senate declared him king of Judea. On returning to Palestine, Herod was able to regain Galilee and eventually to lay siege to Jerusalem in the spring of 37 BCE. Meanwhile, before the fall of Jerusalem he married Mariamne, niece of Antigonus, to whom he had been betrothed for five years. He did this not only to spite Antigonus but also to strengthen his claim to the throne, since she was a Hasmonean. In the summer of 37, Herod defeated Antigonus and became de facto the king of the Jews.

***King of the Jews*** **(37–4 BCE).** Herod's reign can be divided into three periods: consolidation (37–25 BCE), prosperity (25–14 BCE), and domestic troubles (14–4 BCE).

To consolidate his rule, Herod had to contend with four adversaries: the Pharisees, the aristocracy, the Hasmonean family, and Cleopatra of Egypt. The *Pharisees, who disliked Herod because he was an Idumean, a half-Jew, and a friend of the Romans, had great influence over the majority of the people. Herod punished both the Pharisees and their followers who opposed him and rewarded those who were loyal to him. The Sadducean aristocracy, most of whom were members of the *Sanhedrin, were pro-Antigonus. Herod executed forty-five of them and confiscated their property in order to pay the demands that Antony placed on him. The Hasmonean family was upset because Herod had replaced the mutilated high priest Hyrcanus II with Ananel of the Aaronic line. Herod's mother-in-law Alexandra successfully connived to have Ananel replaced with her seventeen-year old son Aristobulus (late 36 or early 35 BCE). Later Herod managed to have him drowned "accidentally," and soon after he put Alexandra in chains. His last adversary was Cleopatra, who wanted to eliminate Herod and Malchus of Arabia and confiscate their lands. When civil war broke out between Octavius and Antony (32 BCE), Herod was prevented from helping Antony because Cleopatra wanted Herod to make war against Malchus, hoping to weaken both and acquire their territories.

After the defeat of Antony at the battle of Actium (31 BCE) Herod proceeded to cultivate Octavius's friendship. Convinced of his loyalty, Octavius returned Jericho to him and also gave him Gadara, Hippos, *Samaria, Gaza, Anthedon, Joppa, and Strato's Tower (later Caesarea).

The last years of consolidation saw much tension in Herod's domestic affairs. Owing to a bizarre series of events, Herod executed his wife Mariamne (29 BCE), his mother-in-law Alexandra (28 BCE) after she attempted to overthrow him, and his brother-in-law Costobarus (25 BCE). Hence, all male relatives of Hyrcanus II were now removed, leaving no rival for Herod's throne.

The period from 25 to 14 BCE was marked largely by success, although there were still occasions of stress. Herod constructed theaters, amphitheaters, and hippodromes and introduced quinquennial games in honor of Caesar, thus violating Jewish law. On the site of Strato's Tower a large urban port was built and named Caesarea. In 24 BCE he built a royal palace in Jerusalem. His crowning achievement in construction was his plan to rebuild the Jewish *Temple; work on this began ca. 20 BCE and was completed in 63 CE. Herod's territory was also greatly expanded in this period with the addition of Trachonitis, Batanea, Auranitis, the area between Trachonitis and Galilee containing Ulatha and Paneas, the area north and northeast of the *Sea of Galilee, and Perea. To gain the good will of the people, in 20 BCE he lowered taxes by a third and in 14 BCE by a fourth.

As Herod grew older a considerable amount of intrigue engulfed his life, much of which arose from his ten wives, each of whom wanted her son(s) to become his successor. This is evident in his changing his will six times. His first wife was Doris, by whom he had Antipater; he repudiated them when he married his second wife, Mariamne (37 BCE), by whom he had five children, of whom only Alexander and Aristobulus were notable. In 24/23 BCE he married his third wife, Mariamne II, by whom he had Herod (Philip). His fourth wife was a *Samaritan, Malthace (23/22 BCE), by whom he had Archelaus and Antipas. In 22 he took as his fifth wife Cleopatra of Jerusalem, who became the mother of Philip the tetrarch. Of the other five wives, none were significant and the names of only three are known.

The main rivalry was between Mariamne's two sons Alexander and Aristobulus and Doris's son Antipater. In 22 BCE Herod made his first will naming Alexander and Aristobulus as his successors. Because of the alleged plots of these two sons, Herod made a second will in 13 BCE, naming Antipater as sole heir. Later there was reconciliation between Herod and Alexander and Aristobulus, and in 12 BCE he made out his third will naming Antipater as the first successor and next after him Alexander and Aristobulus. Because Alexander and Aristobulus became hostile in their attitude toward Herod, he finally ordered them to be executed by strangulation in 7 BCE. Immediately after their execution Herod drew up his fourth will, naming Antipater as sole heir, and, in the event of his death, Herod (Philip) as his successor. With the discovery of Antipater's plan to kill Herod, he was tried and imprisoned. A fifth will was made in which Herod passed over the next two oldest sons, Archelaus and Philip, because Antipater had influenced him against them, and he selected Antipas as sole heir. Five days before Herod's death, he executed Antipater and made his sixth will, in which he designated Archelaus as king, his brother Antipas as tetrarch of Galilee and Perea, and their half-brother Philip as tetrarch of Gaulanitis, Trachonitis, Batanea, and Paneas. It is during this last period of Herod's life, complicated by illness and plots to obtain his throne, that the narrative of the *Magi is set (Matt. 2.1–16).

In conclusion, although Herod was a successful king who was highly regarded by the Romans, his personal life was plagued by domestic troubles. After the death of Herod the Great in the spring of 4 BCE, Antipas and Archelaus contested his last two wills before the emperor in Rome. Antipas favored the fifth will because in it he was sole heir; Archelaus, of course, preferred the sixth. After some delay the emperor made Archelaus ruler over Idumea, Judea, and Samaria with the title of ethnarch, promising that he could become king if he showed good leadership. He appointed Antipas tetrarch over Galilee and Perea and Philip tetrarch over Gaulanitis, Auranitis, Trachonitis, Batanea, Paneas, and Iturea.

**Archelaus (4 BCE–6 CE).** Archelaus, the son of Herod and Malthace, was made ethnarch over Idumea, Judea, and Samaria in 4 BCE. Before he left for Rome to contest his father's will he was given control of the realm and proceeded to kill about three thousand people; after this there was a prolonged revolt at the feast of Pentecost. On his return he treated both Jews and Samaritans with brutality and tyranny; this is the background of Matthew 2.20–23. Archelaus continued the building policy of his father, but his rule became intolerable. Finally, in 6 CE, the emperor deposed him and exiled him to Gaul. His domain became an imperial province governed by prefects appointed by the emperor.

**Antipas (4 BCE–39 CE).** Antipas, the son of Herod and Malthace and a full brother of Archelaus, was appointed tetrarch over Galilee and Perea in 4 BCE. After Archelaus had been deposed, Antipas was given the dynastic title *Herod,* which had great political significance at home and in Rome. He rebuilt what had been destroyed in the widespread revolt after his father's death, including the largest city, Sepphoris, and moved his capital to a new city, Tiberias (named in honor of the emperor Tiberius).

Herod Antipas's greatest notoriety is the imprisonment and beheading of *John the Baptist. This incident occurred after he had married Herodias, who was his niece and the wife of his brother Herod (Philip). John the Baptist boldly criticized the marriage, for according to the Mosaic law it was unlawful to marry a brother's wife, except for levirate marriage (Deut. 25.5). As a result, John was imprisoned, and eventually, at the instigation of Herodias with *Salome's help, Herod beheaded John at Machaerus in 31 or 32 CE.

According to the Gospels, Antipas thought that Jesus was John the Baptist resurrected and desired to see him, but Jesus withdrew from his territories. Later, during Jesus's final journey to Jerusalem, the Pharisees warned him to leave Galilee because Herod wanted to kill him. According to Luke, during Jesus's trial *Pilate sent Jesus to Herod when he heard that Jesus was from Galilee.

In 36 CE the *Nabatean king Aretas IV defeated Antipas in retaliation for Antipas's deserting his daughter to marry Herodias. Although Antipas had hoped to get help from Rome, it was not forthcoming because of the change of emperors. On his accession, Caligula (37 CE) gave his friend Agrippa I, brother of Herodias as well as nephew of Antipas, the territories of Philip the tetrarch, who had died in 34 CE, and granted Lysanius the coveted title of king. His sister Herodias became intensely jealous and urged her husband to seek the title of king for his long, faithful service. When Antipas and Herodias went to Rome in 39 CE to request the title, Agrippa brought charges against Antipas, and consequently Caligula banished him to Gaul. Agrippa I obtained his territories.

**Philip the Tetrarch (4 BCE–34 CE).** Philip was the son of Herod the Great and Cleopatra of Jerusalem. In the settlement of Herod's will, he was appointed tetrarch over northern Transjordan, including Gaulinitis, Auranitis, Trachonitis, Bananea, Paneas, and Iturea. He rebuilt two cities: Paneas, which he renamed Caesarea Philippi, the site of Peter's confession of Christ, and Bethsaida, where Jesus healed a blind man. Philip married Herodias's daughter Salome, but they had no offspring. When he died in 34 CE, Tiberias annexed his territories to Syria and, when Caligula became emperor (37 CE), they were given to Agrippa I, Herodias's brother.

**Agrippa I (37–44 CE).** Agrippa I, the son of Aristobulus (son of Herod the Great and Mariamne) and Bernice (daughter of Herod's sister, Salome, and Costobarus) and the brother of Herodias, was born in 10 BCE. He lived extravagantly and with creditors pursuing him. Sometime ca. 27–30 CE Antipas provided him with a home and a position as inspector of markets in Antipas's new capital, Tiberias. Not long afterward he went to Rome and befriended Gaius Caligula. Owing to an unwise remark favoring Caligula as emperor, Tiberius put him in prison, where he remained until Tiberius's death six months later. In 37 CE when Caligula became emperor, he released Agrippa I and gave him a gold chain equal in weight to his prison chain. He also gave him the territories of Philip the tetrarch and of Lysanius, with the coveted title king. On Caligula's death in 41 CE, Claudius confirmed the rule of Agrippa I and added Judea and Samaria to his kingdom.

Of all the Herods, Agrippa I was the most liked by the Jews and, according to Acts 2, was a persecutor of early *Christians. In 44 CE he died suddenly in Caesarea. Because Agrippa's son was only seventeen years old, his territories were reduced to a Roman province. His daughter Drusilla eventually married the Roman procurator Felix.

**Agrippa II (50–100 CE).** Agrippa II, son of Agrippa I and Cypros, daughter of Phasael (Herod the Great's nephew), was born in 27 CE. Because of his young age he was not allowed to rule immediately, but in 50 CE Claudius appointed him king of Chalcis. In 53

Claudius gave him Abilene, Trachonitis, and Arca in exchange for Chalcis. Shortly after the accession of Nero in 54 CE, he acquired the Galilean cities of Tiberias and Tarichea, with their surrounding areas, and the Perean cities of Julias (or Betharamphtha) and Abila, with their surrounding land.

The private life of Agrippa II was not exemplary, for he had an incestuous relationship with his sister Bernice. In his public life he was in charge of the vestments of the high priest and could appoint him. The Romans would seek his counsel on religious issues, and this may be why Festus asked him to hear Paul at Caesarea.

Agrippa II failed to quell the Jewish revolt against Rome in 66 CE and sided with the Romans throughout the war of 66–70. He died childless ca. 100 CE; with his death, the Herodian dynasty ended.

**Conclusion.** Herodian rule brought stability to the region. With its domination of the eastern parts of the Mediterranean Sea, it was important for Rome to have a peaceful Palestine, because it acted as a buffer state between Rome and the Parthians and was crucial for the trade routes north and south of Palestine. To be a ruler of the Jews was difficult primarily because of their religion. Although the Herods were enamored of Hellenism and adopted some of its elements, they were aware of Jewish religious sensitivities. After the deposition of Archelaus, direct Roman rule of Judea by prefects like Pilate brought instability, much of it due to lack of understanding of Judaism.

Although each of the Herods (except possibly Archelaus) contributed to this stability, it was the pioneering rule of Herod the Great that laid its foundation. As a vassal king, he made it possible for Judea to be somewhat independent. Rome allowed this because he brought stability to the area and because he had proved his loyalty to Rome both militarily and financially.

*See also* Roman Empire.

*Harold W. Hoehner*

**HEZEKIAH** ("Yah[weh] strengthens"). King of Judah ("the finest") 715–698 (or 727–686) BCE. Like his later successor *Josiah, while young he worked closely with the priesthood and sought unification with the northern kingdom of Israel (left kingless), inviting the northern tribes to an ecumenical Passover (perhaps a midrashic embroidering of his reforms). At first he paid tribute to *Assyria, remaining submissive until 705; but apparently as part of his revolt he set about fortifying *Jerusalem. The year of *Sennacherib's punitive invasion (*see* Lachish), Hezekiah's fourteenth year in 2 Kings 18.14, was 701, whence the beginning of his reign in 715, a date incompatible with 2 Kings 18.10, in which his sixth year was that of the fall of Samaria in 722 (whence the inauguration date of 727). Assyria's general appealed to Jerusalem's populace in their own language over the king's head; but trouble in the army (perhaps a plague) forced Sennacherib's sudden withdrawal. A second Assyrian campaign has been proposed on the basis of 2 Kings 18.17–19.36, to collect the immense sum Sennacherib claimed from Judah; but *Isaiah may have induced Hezekiah just to send off the money and end his years in peace. *Robert North*

**HITTITES.** Among the people Israel found in *Canaan were the "sons of Heth," members of a Canaanite family. *Esau had married two of their women, and later Ezekiel decried Israel's religious faithlessness by calling her a descendant from a Canaanite and a Hittite.

Ephron the Hittite sold his field and cave near *Hebron to *Abraham. The names given for these Hittites are all Semitic, and it is likely that all were members of a local Canaanite tribe.

The Hittites of Anatolia (modern Turkey) were another people, forgotten until excavations at Boghazköy were begun in 1906. This was the site of their capital, Hattusha, containing a palace and temples. Clay tablets inscribed with Babylonian cuneiform writing preserve their language, the oldest recorded member of the Indo-European family. Inscriptions show that the Hittites set up their kingdom about 1750 BCE, and that from about 1380 to 1200 BCE they rivaled the Egyptians and the Babylonians in international affairs. Their armies marched into Syria, where they faced Egyptian forces. After decades of war, the battle of Qadesh (ca. 1259 BCE) led to a treaty that established a line across northern Lebanon, the frontier between their zones of influence. This line provided the limit for Israel's territory.

Hittite archives include many rituals for temple services with precise instructions for kings and priests, displaying concern for ritual purity and complexity of detail similar to the ritual laws of the Pentateuch. Treaties made by Hittite kings with vassal kings present a formula also found in biblical covenants, especially those made before the monarchy. Beside records in cuneiform, Hittite scribes used their own hieroglyphic script for royal monuments and perhaps on wooden tablets that have perished.

After the Hittite empire had collapsed under attacks from migrant tribes (possibly including *Philistines among the Sea Peoples), several princes held on to certain cities and created local kingdoms (e.g., Carchemish, Hamath), identified today by carved monuments with Hittite hieroglyphic inscriptions. These "neo-Hittite" states were finally overwhelmed by *Assyria in the ninth and eighth centuries BCE. Before that time they supplied wives for *Solomon, perhaps soldiers for *David (Uriah the Hittite, *see* Bathsheba), and presented a threat to Israel's Aramean enemies.

*Alan Millard*

**HOREB.** The alternate name of the mountain of revelation more frequently referred to as *Sinai. The name is derived from a root meaning to be dry, an appropriate characterization of the Sinai desert. The designation "Horeb" is characteristic of the Elohist tradition in the Pentateuch and of the book of Deuteronomy and the Deuteronomic history. The identity of Sinai and Horeb is recognized in Sirach 48.7, suggesting that an attempt to locate two different peaks is misguided. *Michael D. Coogan*

**HOSEA.** Hosea is the second of the eighth-century BCE *prophets whose messages became a separate book (*see also* Amos). Nothing is known about Hosea outside the book of Hosea.

The first three chapters of the book tell the story of the prophet and his family. Hosea, the son of Beeri, was instructed by God to marry a woman, Gomer, who is described as adulterous, either because she was already immoral or in anticipation of her unfaithfulness. The three children carry the same stigma, and they are given bizarre names to symbolize their degraded status, "Not pitied," and "Not my people."

The similarity between Hosea's experience with his wife and Yahweh's experience with Israel is worked out in the book in all its dimensions—heartbreak, enraged rejection, efforts at reconciliation. All these are interwoven in an allegory in chap. 2. The stories are really the same, because the sin of Gomer against Hosea is identical with Israel's sin against Yahweh: unfaithfulness to the covenanted relationship by resorting to the cult of *Baal, the god of the Canaanites. This rival religion provided sexual activity as part of its ritual, at once literal and spiritual adultery. In spite of the hopeless situation, which called for the most drastic discipline and even for the death penalty for both the mother and the children, the Lord was quite unwilling to give up the covenant relationship. Strenuous efforts were made to renew the marriage, to begin all over again.

We do not know the outcome of Hosea's private tragedy and his heroic measures to recover his wife. He buys Gomer back, but we are not told how she responded. In God's parallel dealings with Israel, the book everywhere threatens and announces death as the inevitable punishment for sin. But that will not be the end; once God's anger has been vented, the way of return is open. They may repent; then there will be healing and renewed love. Nothing less than resurrection from the dead can achieve this, and this is what is promised.

The story and the prophecy operate on several different levels at once, and it is impossible to separate the strands. The oracles have multiple meanings, personal and individual, national and historical. The figures of estrangement/reconciliation, sickness/recovery, death/resurrection are both literal and symbolic, realistic and fantastic. Beginning with one man's private tragedy and agony, the presentation expands to an analysis of Israel's past history and future destiny, reaching from the *ancestors to the eschaton.

None of the oracles is dated, so we cannot attach them to the political developments of the period. The military activity described briefly in 5.8–12 has been identified as one of the *Assyrian invasions, but it could be one of the many wars between the two kingdoms of *Israel and *Judah. Many of the criticisms of the religious life of Israel could have been made at most times in its history; but the deterioration of the situation fits well with the third quarter of the eighth century, when the northern kingdom went into a rapid decline after the death of Jeroboam II (745 BCE), whom Hosea evidently regarded as the last real king of the north. The discourses reflect the chaos and lawlessness that marked the last two decades of the Samarian regime, the anarchy that set in after the death of Jeroboam II in which many of his successors lost their lives through assassination or revolution.

*Francis I. Andersen*

# I

**IMMANUEL (EMMANUEL).** Israelite *prophets could give names to individuals in accord with a specific message that they were trying to communicate. In the same way that *Hosea named his three children to correspond with his message, so *Isaiah noted, "I and the children whom Yahweh has given me are for signs": Shear-jashub, meaning "a remnant will return"; Maher-shalal-hash-baz, meaning "swift is the booty, speedy is the prey"; and Immanuel, meaning "God is with us."

The time between the birth and the maturation of Immanuel is the specific focus of Isaiah's prophecy. Isaiah claims that before the boy reaches a certain age, Judah's enemies in *Damascus and *Samaria will be driven back by *Assyria. Assyrian sources affirm that in 732 BCE the two kings reigning in those cities were killed and their kingdoms subdued by Assyria.

This larger context makes it probable that Immanuel was a son of Isaiah. However, because Isaiah laconically says that Immanuel will be born to "the young woman," some suggest that the mother is someone other than Isaiah's wife, whom he refers to elsewhere as "the prophetess." Some propose that the mother is a queen (a wife of King Ahaz, to whom Isaiah is speaking), an unidentified bystander to whom Isaiah points, or a cult figure. The traditional Christian interpretation that "the young woman" is an intentional reference to *Mary, the mother of *Jesus, does not do justice to the immediate prophecy, which required fulfillment in the eighth century BCE.

The gospel of *Matthew applies Isaiah 7.14 to Jesus in the same way that Matthew applies other events that had already happened in Israel's history to Jesus's life. Because Immanuel is one of the few names for which Matthew supplied a translation ("God with us"), it is clear that Matthew wished to stress that in the miraculous birth of Jesus there was a dimension of Isaiah's words appropriate only to Jesus. The echo of the name Immanuel in Jesus's last words in the gospel, "I am with you," is a literary recapitulation of the promise of the birth. *Samuel A. Meier*

**ISAAC.** Son of *Abraham and father of *Esau and *Jacob. The principal stories about Isaac are found in Genesis 21–28. Isaac is a more shadowy figure than the other patriarchs, and little if anything can be said of him as a historical figure. He is said to have been born when his parents were both advanced in years as a fulfillment of God's promise to Abraham to grant him posterity against all human expectation. In Genesis 22 God himself seems to challenge his own promise by demanding that Isaac be offered as a human sacrifice, but rewards Abraham's unquestioning obedience by providing a ram as a substitute at the last possible moment. This story (the Aqedah) has been important in Judaism as a reminder of the precariousness of Israel's election and yet the sure promises of God, as well as in Christianity as a "type" of the sacrifice of Christ.

Of Isaac's maturity we learn little. Genesis 24 tells how he acquired a wife (*Rebekah), but the principal characters in this tale are Isaac's servant and Rebekah's family. In Genesis 26 Isaac and Rebekah are involved in an incident with "Abimelech king of the Philistines" (an anachronistic reference), who takes Rebekah into his harem—essentially the same incident twice reported of Abraham and *Sarah. Isaac next appears as an old man, deceived by Jacob into giving him the blessing of the firstborn that should by right have been Esau's. The stories about Isaac locate him at Beer-sheba in the far south of Judah and associate him with the worship of the God El-roi, while Jacob later swears by "the Fear of his father Isaac," perhaps an old divine name (*see* Names of God in the Hebrew Bible).

*See also* Ancestors, The.

*John Barton*

**ISAIAH.** The eighth-century prophet from *Jerusalem to whom is attributed the book of Isaiah.

**Author.** All that is known of Isaiah son of Amoz, the prophet to whom the book is attributed, is found in the book itself. He is not referred to elsewhere in the Bible apart from parallel passages in Kings and Chronicles (2 Kings 19–20; 2 Chron. 29–32). The book contains a few biographical details, which present the picture of a prophet in the traditional pattern: a glimpse into the heavenly court; the giving of symbolic names to his children; dramatic appearances at the courts of kings; prophesying through symbolic actions; the performing of miracles; and the condemnation of injustice and oppression. According to an extrabiblical legend, he was martyred ("sawn in two") in the reign of *Manasseh.

The title informs us that he lived during the reigns of four kings of *Judah (Uzziah, Jotham, Ahaz, and Hezekiah), that is to say, during the second half of the eighth century BCE. This was a period during which Judah's fortunes changed from affluence under Uzziah to defeat and humiliation at the hands of the *Assyrians in 701 BCE. Many passages clearly reflect those traumatic years—the approaching Assyrian army, the devastation of the land of Judah, the folly of Judah's leaders—and were probably composed at that time. Perhaps the hopes accompanying the coronation of *Hezekiah in 715 BCE are expressed in the dynastic hymn 9.1–7.

A few sections of narrative, however, clearly reflect later ideas and attitudes. The story of Jerusalem's miraculous deliverance from the Assyrian army under *Sennacherib in 701 (chaps. 36–37), for example, though based on the fact that Jerusalem was not destroyed on that occasion, probably owes much to an upsurge of national confidence during the reign of *Josiah (626–609) when the Assyrian empire collapsed. The annals of Sennacherib, and 2 Kings 18.14–16 (omitted from the Isaianic version), suggest that the reality was very different.

Some passages, mainly in chaps. 40–66, contain no references at all to the Assyrians, but frequently allude to events and conditions in the Babylonian period (605–538 BCE): Jerusalem and the *Temple in ruins; *Babylonian idols; a Jewish colony at Syene (Elephantine) in Egypt; *Cyrus. The bulk of the book was thus probably composed more than a century after the lifetime of Isaiah. The popular division into three sections, First Isaiah (chaps. 1–39) dated to the eighth century BCE, Second (Deutero-) Isaiah (chaps. 40–55) to the sixth, and Third Isaiah (chaps. 56–66) to the fifth, is a crude oversimplification. The literary and theological unity of the whole book is unmistakable; and some parts of First Isaiah, notably the two Babylonian chapters (13–14) and the Isaiah apocalypse (24–27), manifestly belong to the sixth century or later. Chaps. 24–27 should probably be dated to the fourth century BCE, contemporary with *Joel. Each passage must be handled on its own, though both as a product of its age and in the context of the Isaianic corpus as a whole.

**The Book.** Isaiah is the first of the Major Prophets in both Jewish and Christian tradition. The book consists of sixty-six chapters that can be divided into five sections of roughly the same length (1–12; 13–27; 28–39; 40–55; 56–66). All except one begin with an attack on arrogance and an appeal for justice and culminate in a hymn or prophecy of salvation, and all except one are addressed to the people of Jerusalem. The one exception is chapters 40–55, which begins "Comfort, O comfort my people," and is addressed to an exiled community in Babylon during the sixth century BCE.

**Contents.** Chaps. 1–12 consist of prolonged and bitter attacks on the arrogance and hypocrisy of Jerusalem's leaders ("rulers of Sodom," 1.10), interspersed with prophecies of a better age to come when swords will be beaten into plowshares and "the wolf shall live with the lamb" (11.6). As the title suggests, the prophet's visions place special emphasis on the role of Jerusalem and a royal savior from the line of *David. In such a context, it was inevitable that 7.14 would be interpreted as referring to the birth of either a royal savior, Hezekiah, or a future *messiah.

These chapters also contain a memorable account, like those of other prophets, of Isaiah's glimpse into the heavenly court where he was confronted by the awesome holiness of God and commissioned to convey God's judgment to his unhearing and unseeing people (chap. 6). This judgment theme continues into the narrative of his confrontation with King Ahaz during the Syro-Ephraimite crisis. Like other eighth-century prophets, Isaiah prophesies that the Assyrians are the real danger and that they will sweep like a mighty river over the northern kingdoms and into Judah. He calls for faith and sees beyond present gloom and anguish to future victory. Assyria is a tool in God's hand. Both the terror of a confrontation between human power and God's power, and the hope of the eventual victory of God's people, are expressed in the richly emotive term *Immanuel, "God is with us" (7.14; 8.8; 8.10). The section ends with a short hymn of thanksgiving.

Chaps. 13–27 further proclaim God's sovereignty over history. Isaiah's oracles concerning the nations begin with Babylon and end with the entire earth. In addition to the customary taunts and mock laments (e.g., "How you are fallen from heaven, O Day Star, son of Dawn!" 14.12), this series contains some unusual material: expressions of sympathy for the survivors of *Moab, an unexpected blessing for *Egypt and Assyria, and another glimpse into the trauma of a prophet's visionary experience.

The oracle concerning Tyre (chap. 23), an international seaport in contact with every part of the world (*see* Phoenicia), leads logically into the last part of this section in which the subject is the entire earth (24–27). These four chapters are often known as the "Isaiah apocalypse": although they do not have the literary characteristics of the book of Revelation and other true apocalypses, they do contain apocalyptic language and imagery. The whole earth is depicted as desolate, twisted, despoiled, and polluted; sun and moon are eclipsed; and the passage pictures an eschatological banquet, the resurrection of the dead, and God's ultimate victory over the host of heaven, *Leviathan, the "fleeing . . . twisting serpent," and the "dragon that is in the sea" (27.1). The passage belongs firmly to Isaianic tradition, however, as is indicated by such recurring motifs as the city, the mountain of the Lord, and the vineyard.

In chaps. 28–39, the prophet first directs the full force of his rhetoric against Israel and Judah again, just as *Amos does after his oracles concerning the foreign nations. The whole preceding section (13–27) functions merely as a foil for this final condemnation of his own people. He takes up where he left off in 1–12: "Ah, the proud garland of the drunkards of Ephraim" (28.1; cf. 5.11–12). "The mighty flood" of an Assyrian invasion reappears from chap. 8, and the call for faith and courage in a city under siege is repeated. This time the crisis is that of 701 BCE, when Sennacherib invaded Judah and Hezekiah was tempted to join forces with Egypt. Chaps. 36–37 tell the story of a miraculous victory over the Assyrians in that year, highlighting Isaiah's role. There were two other crises in the same year, Hezekiah's illness, when the prophet performs a solar miracle reminiscent of Joshua's at Gibeon, and the visit of Babylonian ambassadors to Jerusalem, during which he foretells the Babylonian exile (chap. 39). Like chap. 39, the central chapters of this section, especially 34 and 35, point forward to the next section.

Chaps. 40–55 are often known as the "Babylonian chapters." They constitute the most distinctive and homogeneous part of the book, both stylistically and theologically, and are for that reason commonly referred to as "Second Isaiah" or "Deutero-Isaiah." Repetition is frequent. The exiled community in Babylon is described and addressed collectively as "Zion" and "my servant." The rise of Cyrus, king of the *Medes and *Persians, is described, as are the fall of Babylon and the return of the exiles to Jerusalem in a new Exodus. The sheer scale of God's power in history and in creation is another recurring theme in these chapters, as are explicit monotheism, the ridicule of idolatry, and feminine images for God. Finally, the concept of healing and victory through the vicarious suffering of "the servant of the Lord" (52.13–53.12) marks out this section as unique in biblical prophecy. The final section of the book is mainly concerned with the return of the exiles to Jerusalem and the building of a new society there. "Justice" and "righteousness" are again key motifs here as they were at the beginning. Foreigners and *eunuchs will be admitted into the Temple. The *poor and the oppressed will be set free, and Temple sacrifice is finally rejected in favor of humility and repentance. The feminine imagery, introduced in chaps. 40–55, is further elaborated. God is addressed as father, and a striking variation on the God-as-warrior theme is the famous "grapes of wrath" passage (63.1–6) in which he is portrayed as a somewhat reluctant victor, limping home from war, bloodstained and stooping (v. 1; NRSV: "marching"). The last verse of the book, one of the few biblical texts on which a doctrine of hellfire can be based (66.24), is so gruesome that in Jewish custom the preceding verses about "the new heavens and the new earth" are repeated after it, to end the reading on a more hopeful and at the same time more characteristically Isaianic note. *John F. A. Sawyer*

**ISHMAEL.** Son of *Abraham and *Hagar. A generally positive attitude toward Ishmael and thus toward his descendants is found in the Genesis traditions. He is the recipient of a special divine blessing and is present at the burial of Abraham. Like Jacob, Ishmael is the father of twelve sons, the ancestors of twelve tribes. Another indication of the generally favorable view of this patriarch is the fact that several other later Israelites have the same name. There are, however, hints of ethnic tension in the narratives as well. Like *Cain, Ishmael is depicted as an outcast and prone to violence and as a wanderer (note the opening words of Melville's *Moby Dick*). The Ishmaelites are elsewhere described as leading a typically nomadic life. The story of Ishmael and Hagar's separation from Abraham's household contains the kind of scurrilous sexual innuendo found elsewhere in J's etiological narratives concerning Israel's neighbors.

In Muslim tradition, the Arabs trace their ancestry back to Abraham through Ishmael. Because Ishmael was circumcised, so are most Muslims. And, analogous to Paul's reversal of the figures of *Isaac and Ishmael, Muslim tradition makes Ishmael rather than Isaac the son Abraham was commanded to sacrifice.

*Michael D. Coogan*

**ISRAEL.**

**The Biblical Story of Israel.** Genesis 32.28 reports God's words to *Jacob: "You shall no longer be called Jacob, but Israel, for you have striven with God and with humans, and have prevailed." As the biblical narrative continues, one reads that Jacob/Israel immigrated with his family to *Egypt where, during a long sojourn, his twelve sons fathered twelve *tribes. Eventually, these twelve "Israelite" tribes were led out of Egypt by *Moses, wandered for forty years in the wilderness, and finally reached the plains of *Moab east of the *Jordan River. At that point in the biblical narrative, *Joshua succeeded Moses and led the tribes across the Jordan into *Canaan, where they took possession of the land and divided it among themselves. The book of *Judges finds the tribes settled in Canaan following Joshua's death, without stable leadership and often oppressed by surrounding peoples. "In those days there was no king in Israel; all the people did what was right in their own eyes" (Judg. 17.6).

In the time of the prophet *Samuel, when the *Philistines were oppressing Israel, the people cried out to Samuel to give them a king. Against his better judgment, Samuel accommodated their desire by anointing *Saul to be the first king of Israel. Thus Saul, followed by *David and then *Solomon, ruled over a kingdom that consisted primarily of the twelve Israelite tribes with their respective territories. When Solomon died, this Israelite monarchy split into two rival kingdoms—a northern kingdom, composed of ten tribes, which kept the name Israel, and a southern kingdom, composed of the two remaining tribes, *Judah and *Benjamin, which took the name Judah. These two kingdoms existed side-by-side for two centuries, sometimes at war with each other, sometimes at peace, until the northern kingdom was conquered by *Assyria and its territory annexed by that great empire (722 BCE). Judah also fell under

Assyrian domination, but it maintained its political identity for almost a century and a half, until it fell to the *Babylonians (587/586 BCE).

Hopes of national recovery remained alive during the long years of Assyrian and Babylonian domination, however, and continued in the Jewish community (the remnant of the kingdom of Judah) that struggled for survival under *Persian rule. These hopes are expressed in the prophetical books of the Hebrew Bible. Moreover, the hope was not just for recovery of Judah but for a united Israel as it had existed in the "golden age" of David and Solomon.

Thus, the biblical writers use the name Israel in different ways. It can refer to the patriarch Jacob; to the twelve tribes (constantly referred to as "the children of Israel" in the books Exodus through Judges); to the early united monarchy ruled over by Saul, David, and Solomon; to the northern kingdom after the split of the united monarchy; or to the restored nation hoped for in the future.

**Historical Uncertainties and Extrabiblical Sources.** The biblical story of Israel, when examined in detail, presents numerous internal inconsistencies—for example, the several enumerations of the Israelite tribes do not always identify the same twelve, nor do they take into account other important tribal groups such as the Calebites and Kenizzites. Moreover, the story presupposes concepts that were generally accepted in ancient times but not today, such as the idea that each of the world's nations descended from a single individual (see Gen. 10).

An Egyptian inscription from the reign of Pharaoh Merneptah (ca. 1200 BCE) provides the earliest known nonbiblical reference to Israel, and the only such reference earlier than the ninth century BCE. The Merneptah inscription is a royal monumental text inscribed on a stele discovered at the site of ancient Thebes. Unfortunately, we learn no more from it regarding Israel than that a people known by that name was on the scene in Palestine by the end of the thirteenth century. Later texts from the ninth century are also royal inscriptions, one commissioned by King Mesha of Moab (see 2 Kings 3 and Moabite Stone), and several others from the reign of an Assyrian king, Shalmaneser III (858–824 BCE). Israel and Judah were separate kingdoms by the ninth century, and it is Israel that figures in these texts. Mesha reports that King Omri of Israel had "humbled" Moab and claims recovery of Moabite independence among the accomplishments of his own reign. Shalmaneser reports a series of military campaigns into Syria-Palestine and mentions in that context two Israelite kings, *Ahab and *Jehu. Occasional references to Israelite and Judean kings appear in later Assyrian and Babylonian documents, usually in the context of military campaign reports. These references in extrabiblical documents are especially useful for establishing a chronological framework for the Israelite and Judean kings and for correlating biblical history with international affairs.

Archaeological excavations at Palestinian sites provide information about the material culture of biblical times and also allow for some correlations. For example, the time of the "judges" in Israel would seem to correspond roughly to the opening centuries of the Iron Age (ca. 1200–1000 BCE), which was a period of transition and change in Palestine. Many of the old cities that had flourished during the Bronze Age, especially in the lowlands, were destroyed. Most of them were rebuilt but on a much smaller scale. At the same time, there was a marked increase in the number of small village settlements in areas such as the central hill country, which seem to have been only sparsely populated during the Bronze Age. Note that most of the stories of the book of Judges have their setting among the villages in the north-central (Ephraimite) hill country. (*See* Canaan.)

The writer of 2 Kings 9.10–14 credits Solomon with building (or fortifying) several cities including *Hazor, *Megiddo, and *Gezer. Excavations at all three of these places have unearthed remains of buildings and fortifications that date from approximately 1000 BCE; their relatively impressive scale is suggestive of royal architecture, and for this reason archaeologists generally associate them with Solomon. A somewhat more impressive royal building program from approximately the ninth century seems to be indicated by the ruins at Hazor, Megiddo, and *Samaria. This second building program generally is associated with the Omride rulers of Israel, particularly Omri and Ahab. Remains from later phases of the cities and villages of Israel and Judah show a marked decline in material wealth, many of them ending finally with destruction in approximately the seventh and early sixth centuries BCE. No doubt these later phases correspond to the years of foreign domination by the Syrians, Assyrians, and Babylonians.

**Contemporary Views Regarding the History of Israel.** Given the uncertainties that arise from the biblical story, the paucity of references to Israel or Israelites in extrabiblical documents, and the very generalized nature of evidence from artifacts, it is not surprising that present-day scholars hold widely divergent views concerning Israel's history. At one extreme are those who hold that the biblical story is an essentially accurate portrayal of Israel's past; at the other are those who see the Bible as a virtually useless source for historical information and regard it as futile even to speculate on the details of Israelite history. Most biblical scholars and ancient historians hold a moderate position between these two extremes. There seems to be a growing consensus, for example, on the following points.

Nothing can be said with certainty about the origin of the various tribes and clans that composed early Israel and Judah. For the most part, these tribal groupings probably emerged gradually from the diffuse population of Late Bronze and early Iron Age Palestine rather than having entered the land from elsewhere. The name Israel probably referred in premonarchic times primarily to the tribe of *Ephraim, settled in the north-central hill country, but would have been understood to include certain surrounding tribes (such as Benjamin, *Manasseh, and Gilead) that Ephraim dominated. This Ephraim/Israel tribal group would have been the Israel to which the Merneptah inscription refers; most of the stories in the book of Judges have to do with this tribal group; and it was the core of Saul's kingdom, which he appropriately called Israel.

One should not think of Saul's Israel as a highly organized kingdom with precisely defined boundaries. Moreover, loyalty to him probably varied from region to region, with Saul's strongest base of support being the Ephraim-Benjamin-Gilead-Manasseh zone. There is nothing to suggest that the Galilean tribes were part of his kingdom. His campaign against the *Amalekites implies thoroughfare through Judahite territory. Saul also received some Judean support in his attempts to arrest David. This, however, does not necessarily mean that he exercised any sort of permanent control over Judah. In Judah, as in other peripheral areas, Saul's authority probably lasted only as long as he was present with his troops or the local people needed his protection against some other threat.

The battle of Gilboa, in which Saul and Jonathan were killed, left the kingdom on the verge of collapse. A surviving son (Ishbaal; Ishbosheth) claimed the throne but transferred his residency to Mahanaim in Transjordan and soon was assassinated. Thereupon the *elders of Israel went to David, who in the meantime had established a kingdom in the south-central "Judean" hill country, and recognized him as their ruler also. Later David would make *Jerusalem his capital and expand his realm to include much of Palestine.

Thus, the Davidic-Solomonic monarchy was not exactly continuous with Saul's Israel. Moreover, the Israelites appear to have maintained their separate identity under David and Solomon—for example, there was some rivalry between the Israelites and the Judahites, as well as ongoing opposition to Davidic rule. The Israelites played a central role in both *Absalom's and Sheba's rebellions against David; Solomon subjected them to forced labor in connection with his royal building projects; and when Solomon died they rebelled again, this time successfully. Thus was established the northern Israelite kingdom, which the biblical writers depict as a rebel and apostate state, but which the rebels themselves no doubt regarded as a restoration of pre-Davidic Israel. At the core of the rebel (or restored) kingdom was the old Ephraim/Israel tribal area, but it included additional territories (e.g., Jezreel and *Galilee) and cities (e.g., *Shechem) that had been annexed by David. The small tribal area of Benjamin became a disputed frontier between the rival kingdoms of Israel and Judah.

The northern kingdom of Israel lasted approximately two centuries (ca. 924–722 BCE), which may be divided into four phases.

***Unstable beginnings (ca. 924–885).*** Separation left both Israel and Judah weak, while mutual warfare drained their strength even further. Moreover, Israel suffered dynastic instability that resulted finally in civil war.

***The Omride dynasty (ca. 885–843).*** Omri, who emerged victorious from the civil war, founded a dynasty that continued through four kings. Under Omri and his son Ahab, Israel enjoyed a period of international prestige and internal prosperity that may have surpassed that of Solomon's day. Israel clearly overshadowed and probably dominated Judah during this period. Omri built a new capital for the kingdom, which he named Samaria. The Omride period was remembered, however, as a time of economic and social injustice, and of conflict between Baalism and Yahwism. *Elijah and *Jezebel were colorful characters of the Omride era.

***The Jehu dynasty (ca. 843–745).*** Simultaneous and related palace coups brought a new ruler to the thrones of both Israel and Judah in approximately 843 BCE. *Jehu, who seized power in Israel under the banner of Yahwism, founded a dynasty that lasted approximately a century. *Damascus, however, was already on the rise when Jehu seized the throne, and it totally dominated Israel during the reigns of Jehu and his son, Jehoahaz. Damascus, faced with problems from the direction of Assyria, eventually lost its hold on Israel, and Israel in turn enjoyed a brief period of recovery and prosperity. The moment of prosperity is to be associated especially with the reign of Jeroboam II. The *Elisha stories reflect the difficult times experienced by the people of Israel during the early years of the Jehu dynasty, the years of Syrian domination. The book of *Amos reflects the situation during the later years, when Israel is enjoying a recovery of prosperity, and implies that the problems of economic and social injustice remained. Zechariah, son of Jeroboam II, was assassinated soon after coming to the throne in approximately 745 BCE, and *Tiglath-pileser III ascended the Assyrian throne the following year. Israel's end was near.

***Assyrian conquest and annexation (745–722).*** Already during the Omride era, Assyrian kings had threatened the little kingdoms of Syria-Palestine in general and Israel in particular. Now Assyria turned its attention to the west and, under Tiglath-pileser III (744–727), secured a firm grip on the whole region. Israel, which offered some resistance at first in coordination with Damascus, was reduced to vassal status and Hoshea confirmed as king. After Tiglath-pileser's death, however, Hoshea attempted to throw off the Assyrian yoke. This was a disastrous move: Assyria conquered Samaria, annexed the kingdom's territory, exiled thousands of its leading citizens, and replaced them with foreigners from other conquered lands.

The remnants of the kingdom of Israel usually are referred to in later literature as *Samaritans, after the name of the kingdom's chief city founded by Omri. A small group of Samaritans still survives in the vicinity of Nablus.

(*For a chronological table of the Kings of Israel and Judah, see* Judah, The Kingdom of.)

*J. Maxwell Miller*

**ISSACHAR.** A son of *Leah and *Jacob and one of the twelve *tribes of Israel. The name combines Hebrew words for "man" and "wages"; hence Leah's exclamation "God has given me my hire." The territory allotted to Issachar lies in the plain of Jezreel. References to Issachar suggest close associations between it and *Zebulun. Issachar, the probable home of *Deborah, played an essential role in her campaign against Sisera. The territory of Issachar was conquered by the *Assyrians in 732 BCE

*Gary N. Knoppers*

# J

**JACOB.** Son of *Isaac and *Rebekah and younger brother of *Esau. The Bible presents Jacob in a double light. On the one hand, he is the revered ancestor of the people of Israel, and indeed the name "*Israel" is said to have been given him by God after he had wrestled with God himself at Penuel; on the other, he is a trickster, who deceives his brother into parting with his birthright and his father into giving him the blessing of the firstborn that should have belonged to Esau. Hosea 12.2–6 and Isaiah 43.27 may well indicate that Jacob's acts were later regarded as sinful, although the accounts in Genesis seem to record them without censure. Jacob is presented as a pastoralist, whereas Esau is a hunter, and the stories about them may reflect rivalries between these two groups in later times, as with the story of *Cain and *Abel; equally, they are contrasted as the ancestors respectively of Israelites and *Edomites.

Jacob, like his father Isaac, seeks a wife in Mesopotamia. On the way Jacob encamps at Bethel and there in a dream sees divine messengers ascending and descending on a staircase between earth and heaven (*see* Angels) and erects a pillar to commemorate the incident—perhaps a story to explain why Israelites worshiped at what had been a Canaanite sanctuary. Jacob the trickster is himself tricked by his uncle Laban into working fourteen years to obtain the wife he desires, *Rachel; Jacob contracts to work for seven years but at the end of that time is given *Leah, her elder sister, instead. Jacob has his revenge on Laban by swindling him out of large flocks and herds and flees from Laban's house to return to the land of *Canaan but is finally reconciled with his uncle. After the mysterious incident at Penuel there follows a reconciliation also with Esau.

The remaining stories of Jacob focus on the deeds of his children, the ancestors of the twelve *tribes of Israel. Jacob appears as an old man in the story of *Joseph, where the theme of trickery recurs in the deceit by which he is robbed of his favorite son by Joseph's jealous brothers. Eventually Jacob goes down to Egypt with his sons and dies there (Gen. 49.33), but his embalmed body is taken for burial to the land of Canaan by Joseph and his brothers. The blessing of Jacob is widely held to contain some of the oldest poetry in the Bible. *John Barton*

**JAMBRES.** *See* Jannes and Jambres.

**JAMES.** Four persons in the New Testament have the name "James" (Greek *Iakōbos*), which is one of two Greek forms of the Hebrew name Jacob (the other being the simple transliteration *Iakōb*). Since *Jacob was a revered ancestor of Israel, James was a common name among Jews in the Roman period.

**James, Son of Zebedee,** was a Galilean fisherman in the area of *Capernaum on the Sea of *Galilee, a partner (along with his brother *John) of *Simon Peter. He was working in the family business headed by his father when called by Jesus to be his disciple. James and John along with Peter formed the inner core of three among the *twelve apostles; they witnessed the raising of Jairus's daughter, were present at the transfiguration, and observed (and partially slept through) Jesus's agony in *Gethsemane.

Apparently James and John either expressed themselves explosively or expected God to bring sudden judgment on the enemies of Jesus, for they were nicknamed "Boanerges" ("sons of thunder"). Their request to sit at Jesus's right and left hand in his kingdom earned them the anger of the other apostles and a mild rebuke from Jesus.

Outside the synoptic Gospels James, son of Zebedee, appears only in Acts. He was present in the upper room with the group waiting for Pentecost. The only other reference to him in the New Testament is the cryptic note that Herod (Agrippa I) had him killed. He was thus the second recorded martyr of the church (after *Stephen) and the first of the apostolic band to die (except for *Judas Iscariot, who had been replaced as an apostle).

**James, Son of Alphaeus,** was a Galilean Jew and one of the twelve; many believe he is the same person as James the younger. The Greek term translated "the younger" can also be translated "the little," which probably gives the correct meaning (i.e., he was shorter than James, son of Zebedee). If this identification is correct, this otherwise unknown apostle had a mother named Mary who was present at the crucifixion and was a witness of the Resurrection and a brother Joseph (or Joses) who was probably a well-known early Christian.

**James, Father (KJV "brother") of the Apostle Judas (not Iscariot),** is mentioned only by Luke. Nothing further is known about him.

**James, Brother of Jesus,** is named in Matthew 13.55 and Mark 6.3 along with three other brothers of Jesus (*see* Brothers and Sisters of Jesus). The Gospels indicate that neither James nor his brothers were followers of Jesus before the crucifixion. After the Resurrection, however, these same brothers are mentioned among the group of believers at prayer before Pentecost. *Paul explains the reason for this change of heart (at least in James) in the statement that the risen Jesus had appeared personally to James. James apparently rose quickly in the ranks of the church. In Acts 15.13 it is James, not Peter, who is named as the preeminent leader who summed up the deliberations of the council at Jerusalem (49 or 50 CE). Thus, he is viewed as the person who presided over the compromise that allowed Jewish and gentile Christians to remain unified without either forcing gentiles to become Jews or violating Jewish cultural sensibilities.

In his letter to the *Galatians, Paul mentions James along with Peter and John, son of Zebedee, as "acknowledged pillars" of the church at Jerusalem. James's authority appears clearly in Galatians 2.12, for emissaries from Jerusalem are said to come "from James" and apparently therefore had authority as his official representatives. Scholars are divided over whether the effort of the emissaries to split Jewish from gentile congregations was James's position (in which case Paul and Acts give differing pictures of James) or whether he had sent them for some other purpose.

In 61 CE James suffered martyrdom at the instigation of the high priest Ananus after the sudden death in office of the procurator Festus. In the following centuries legends about James developed. For example, Hegesippus reports that James was known as "James the Just" because of his exemplary piety, and Jerome connects him with the lost apocryphal *Gospel according to the Hebrews.* But other than the fact of his martyrdom and its approximate date, there is little evidence that any of these legends are accurate, and most are certainly apocryphal.

James's leadership was well enough known so that the letter of James is attributed to him with a simple "James, a servant of God and of the Lord Jesus Christ" (James 1.1), and the author of the letter of *Jude identifies himself as "Jude, a servant of Jesus Christ and brother of James." While the attribution of both these letters is debated, there is reason to believe that at least the material in the letter of James, if not the writing itself, stems from the brother of Jesus, and this material reveals an authoritative leader in a Palestinian context.

The letter may be a collection of sermons and sayings from James (and possibly from Jesus as well, from whom James 5.12 unquestionably comes) edited into letter form. If the material comes from James and reflects his setting, then the most likely place of editing is Jerusalem or at least Judea. Some of the material probably dates from before Paul's activity became well known in Jerusalem (49 CE or earlier), for it shows no awareness of Pauline formulations or at best knows only distorted oral reports of his teaching. But the final editing was probably triggered by the martyrdom of James and the desire to preserve and spread his teaching, that is, after 61 CE but probably before the fall of Jerusalem in 70 CE.

James is writing in the context of a church under pressure, not facing impending martyrdom but discrimination and economic persecution. He is concerned about two tendencies, adopting the mores of the oppressors (e.g., valuing money over community) and attacking other members of the community (e.g., gossip, criticism). Thus his chief concern is the unity of the community and turning the community back from practices that threaten to disrupt it.

James writes on several major themes. The first is testing. Only true commitment to God will resist the overtures of the devil made through the impulses of internal cravings. The second is wisdom. God offers people the gift of wisdom to help them stand firm in the test. The third theme is wealth. In the culture in which James lives, the wealthy are by and large the oppressors of the Christians, many of whom are poor. Christians, however, must not accept the world's values or view their material poverty with concern; if they are truly committed to God, they will show it in generous charity and in seeking God's will in all their business plans.

Because of the famous section in James 2.14–26, James has often been seen as opposing Paul's stress on justification by faith without the deeds of the Law. This appears true until one realizes that James uses his critical terms in ways that differ from Paul; in fact, James is using terminology in its older, original sense. Works for Paul are works of the Law, that is, ritual acts such as circumcision; works for James are deeds of charity such as, according to Jewish tradition, those that *Abraham performed. Faith for Paul is a commitment to God, which produces good works; for James faith (i.e., in James 2.14–26, for he uses the term in two or three different ways elsewhere in the letter) is mere intellectual belief, lacking commitment. Finally, "justified" for Paul means the pronouncing of a sinner righteous; "justified" for James means the declaration that a person did in fact act justly. Paul, of course, would have agreed with James that "faith" that does not produce appropriate deeds is a false faith.

Given such differences in usage of common terminology, how are these two authors related? Two possibilities may be mentioned: either James is reacting to a misunderstood and badly distorted Paulinism, perhaps not even knowing who had originated it; or James is speaking to the fault of making intellectual religious commitments without the corresponding amendment of life. In neither case is James opposing Paul; he is simply arguing in his own context what Paul taught in his.

*Peter H. Davids*

**JANNES AND JAMBRES** (the latter sometimes Mamre). They are mentioned in late antique Jewish, Christian, and Greco-Roman (Pliny, Apuleius, Numenius) sources as Egyptian magicians; the earliest citation is the first-century BCE "Damascus Document" of the Dead Sea Scrolls. They are identified in Jewish midrash and the New Testament (2 Tim. 3.8) as among Pharaoh's unnamed wise men who duplicated *Moses's and *Aaron's miracles. In both traditions, they symbolize false prophecy and heretical obstruction; several Jewish sources describe them as *Balaam's sons. The sixth-century CE Christian work "Decree of Gelasius" mentions an apocryphal book, now lost, about their exploits and ultimate conversion.

*Judith R. Baskin*

**JEBUSITES.** The Jebusites were one of several groups of people living on the land that Israel eventually conquered. According to Genesis 10.15–16 and 1 Chronicles 1.14, the Jebusites were related to the *Canaanites. But these passages may indicate a geopolitical relationship rather than an ethnic one; since the Jebusites shared the same territory as the Canaanites, they were perceived to be from the same stock, though they probably were not. In fact, the biblical writers normally distinguish the Jebusites from the Canaanites and from other peoples as well.

*Jerusalem is sometimes identified as Jebus. From this one might infer that Jebus was the pre-Israelite name of the city. The name Jerusalem, however, predates the Israelite conquest by several centuries, and the city was not appropriated by Israel until the tenth century BCE. Therefore it seems best to take Jebus as an alternate Israelite designation for Jerusalem. The people, then, were not called Jebusites because they lived in Jebus; rather, the city of Jerusalem was sometimes called Jebus because the Jebusites controlled it.

Although there is a brief account of a victory over Jerusalem in the early tribal league period, the Israelites did not take possession of the city at that time, for it is later mentioned as still being a foreign city of the Jebusites. *David captured Jerusalem from them and made it his capital. Apparently he did not kill or drive out all the local inhabitants, because subsequently, when he needed land on which to build an altar, he purchased it from Araunah the Jebusite (2 Sam. 24.18–24; 1 Chron. 21.18–27 has the name Ornan for Araunah). *Solomon built the *Temple on that plot of ground; he also enslaved the remainder of the Jebusites and other non-Israelites. Ultimately, they must have assimilated into Israel; Zechariah 9.7 likens them to a Judean clan.

Some have seen Jebusite origins for the changes in Israel's political structure and religious ideology that occurred with the establishment of kingship, but there is little evidence to support such a hypothesis. *William B. Nelson, Jr.*

**JEHOSHAPHAT.** The fourth king of *Judah (ca. 874–850 BCE). His reign is given only brief attention in Kings, but he is one of the Chronicler's favorite monarchs. Jehoshaphat reverses the policy of his predecessors by entering into military, maritime, and marital alliances with kings of Israel. Jehoshaphat's achievements as a reformer are accentuated in Chronicles. He reorganizes the judiciary, sending ministers, *Levites, and priests to the towns of Judah "to teach the law of the Lord," appoints judges for the towns of Judah, and establishes a court in Jerusalem. Jehoshaphat also reorganizes the army and fortifies cities within his domain.

The reference to the "valley of Jehoshaphat" in Joel 3.2, 12 plays on Jehoshaphat's name ("the Lord has judged"). It is unclear whether Joel is designating geography (e.g., the Wadi Kidron) or dramatizing a future judgment.

*Gary N. Knoppers*

**JEHOVAH.** An artificially constructed name for Israel's God first attested in sixteenth-century CE Christian texts. The new construction was the result of changing attitudes toward the use of God's name. The Hebrew name "Yahweh" was not normally pronounced after about the third century BCE out of respect for its holiness. In its place, readers of the Hebrew used *ʾădōnāy*, "Lord." When vowels were added to the consonantal text of the Hebrew Bible (ca. 1000 CE), the consonants of Yahweh were preserved but the vowels of *ʾădōnāy* were used as a reminder to readers. Renaissance Christian tradition erroneously combined the consonants of Yahweh and the vowels of *ʾădōnāy* to produce "Jehovah," which is used occasionally in the King James Version and regularly in some revisions of it. More recent English translations tend to use LORD rather than "Jehovah."

*See also* Names of God in the Hebrew Bible.

*Steven Friesen*

**JEHU.** The son of Nimshi, Jehu was king of Israel ca. 843–816 BCE. 2 Kings 9–10 describes how, under prophetic mandate, Jehu led a bloody military revolt to seize the throne of Israel. He killed the kings of both Israel (Jehoram) and Judah (Ahaziah), had *Jezebel executed, annihilated the dynasty of Omri, and obliterated the worship of *Baal in Israel. Yahweh rewarded Jehu's faithfulness by allowing his dynasty to last five generations.

However historical its base, the account in 2 Kings 9–10 is strongly influenced by the ideology of the Deuteronomic historian. Quite a different perspective on Jehu's revolt is found in Hosea 1.4–5, where the house of Jehu is threatened with punishment for the bloodshed of Jezreel.

The annals of the Assyrian king Shalmaneser III mention and his "Black Obelisk" depicts a "Ia-ú-a/Ia-a-ú son of Omri" paying tribute to him. This individual is probably Jehu, though his predecessor Jehoram has also been proposed; in any case, it is the only contemporary picture we have of a king of Israel.

*See also* Israel.

*Steven L. McKenzie*

**JEREMIAH.** Son of Hilkiah, a priest and a prophet of the late seventh century BCE. Little is known about Jeremiah except from the book that bears his name. He was from the village of Anathoth, north of Jerusalem, and prophesied during the tumultuous last days of the kingdom of *Judah in the late seventh and early sixth centuries BCE. Although occasionally consulted by King *Zedekiah, he was also imprisoned by him. After the fall of Jerusalem in 587/586 BCE, he was forced to move to Egypt, where, according to a later tradition, he was killed.

**The Book of Jeremiah.** The editorial introduction to the book of Jeremiah, 1.1–3, informs us that the book contains "the words of Jeremiah," that is, what Jeremiah said and did—the Hebrew term translated "words" can cover both—from the beginning of his prophetic ministry in the thirteenth year of the reign of *Josiah, 627 BCE, until the fall of Jerusalem to the *Babylonians in 587/586 BCE. This is not strictly an accurate account of the contents of the present book since chaps. 40–44 describe the activity of the prophet both in *Judah and in Egypt after the fall of Jerusalem. Nevertheless the last forty years of the independent Judean state are the stage on which Jeremiah played out his major prophetic role. The book of Jeremiah depicts a man who consistently protested against political and religious policies that sealed the fate of his country, a prophet who in the eyes of the establishment of his day was both traitor and heretic.

**Content and Sources.** It is generally agreed that the material in the book of Jeremiah falls into three categories, each stemming from different sources or circles.

***Poetic material,*** to be found in the main interspersed with prose passages in chaps. 1–25. These poetic sections consist largely of oracles in which the prophet functions as God's messenger, speaking in the name of God. They cover a variety of themes, including the nation's infidelity to the Lord and the call to repentance, with attacks on the religious and political establishment of the day. These poetic passages are on the whole undated and are given no clearly defined context, but it is widely held that in such passages we are in touch with the teaching of the prophet Jeremiah, and that much of the material in chaps. 1–25 represents the earliest stage of the book of Jeremiah. Such passages may well have been part of the scroll that King Jehoiakim, according to chap. 36, insolently consigned to the flames in the winter of 604 BCE, whereupon Jeremiah redictated the scroll to the scribe *Baruch and for good measure added similar words. Certainly there is little in such poetic oracles that could not have come from the early years of the prophet's ministry between the time of his call (627 BCE according to 1.2) and 604 BCE.

In addition to these oracles in which the prophet speaks the word of God to his people, there are other poetic passages in 1–25 that are in the form of intensely personal poems that have been called Jeremiah's confessions or his spiritual diary (see 11.18–12.6; 15.10–21; 17.5–10, 14–18; 18.18–23; 20.7–18). Here we listen not to the word of God on the lips of the prophet but to a man baring his own soul and exposing some of the tensions involved in being a prophet. These passages are without parallel in prophetic literature. There seems little reason to doubt that they reflect Jeremiah's experience. As such they are of the highest significance and interest. They show us that behind the apparently untroubled certainty of "Thus says the Lord" there may lie a host of unresolved questions and deep inner turmoil. This is a very human prophet committed to a vocation that tears him apart, agonizing over the apparent failure of his ministry, on the verge of giving up, consumed by a savage bitterness against those who opposed or ignored what he had to say, accusing God of betraying him. There are two other blocks of material in the book outside chaps. 1–25 that similarly contain poetic prophetic oracles, often interspersed with and expanded by prose sections.

*a)* Chaps. 30, 31 and 33, the so-called book of consolation, consisting of oracles whose basic theme is that of hope beyond national disaster. This material is probably of very varied origin. The influence of an earlier prophet, Hosea, is very marked in some sections (e.g., 31.1–6), while the language and thought of other passages have close links with a later prophet, the author of Isaiah 40–55 (e.g., 31.10–14). That some of the material in this section goes back to Jeremiah, however, we need not doubt.

*b)* Chaps. 46–51, the oracles against the nations. The tradition of oracles against other nations, particularly those that threaten the existence of Israel, is one that can be traced back to Amos 1.3–2.3; such oracles occur also in other prophetic books. Inasmuch as Jeremiah was called, according to 1.5, to be "a prophet to the nations," it is hardly surprising that a substantial collection of such oracles appears in the book. Such oracles affirm that the God of Israel is lord over all nations and pronounce judgment on them not only for their treatment of Israel, but for the arrogant self-confidence that assumes that might is right and for actions that sacrifice justice and human rights to imperial ambitions. How much of this material can be traced back to Jeremiah himself is a highly contentious issue.

***Biographical narratives*** that claim to recount key incidents in the life of the prophet. There are two notable features of these narratives. First, there are more such narratives in the book of Jeremiah than in any other prophetic book, and thus, if authentic, they provide us with more information about Jeremiah than is available for any other prophet. Such narratives are to be found in chaps. 26–29, 32, 34–44. Second, these narratives are usually provided with precise dating, the earliest dated to 609 BCE (26:1). If therefore we assume, following 1.2, that Jeremiah's prophetic ministry began in 627 BCE, we have no such narrative for almost the first twenty years of his ministry. This, allied to the lack of any clear evidence in the book for Jeremiah's attitude to the key religious event of this period, the reformation under King Josiah in 621 BCE, has led a variety of scholars to believe that his ministry did not begin until 612 BCE or 609 BCE, with 627 BCE being the possible date of his birth. This is not, however, a necessary inference. The biographical narratives are often linked with the scribe Baruch, who appears in Jeremiah's company in chaps. 32, 36, 43, and 45. We could argue from the lack of biographical material prior to 609 BCE that Baruch first came into contact with Jeremiah in 609; perhaps he was drawn to Jeremiah as the result of the Temple sermon that chap. 26 dates to that year. We have spoken of biographical narratives, but we must not assume from this that it is possible to write a satisfactory biography of Jeremiah, even from 609 BCE onward. The narratives do not appear in chronological sequence, nor do they do any more than highlight what are taken to be certain key incidents that reveal the prophet often locked in conflict with the religious and political establishment of the day. It is no more possible to write a satisfactory biography of Jeremiah on the basis of these narratives than it is to write a life of Jesus on the basis of the gospel narratives. If we push this analogy further we would have to say that it is the events leading up to and surrounding the destruction of Jerusalem in 587 BCE that occupy in the book of Jeremiah the central place that the passion narratives occupy in the Gospels. It is perhaps not surprising that the book of Jeremiah ends in chap. 52 with an account of the fall of Jerusalem, derived in the main from 2 Kings 24–25.

***Prose passages*** occur throughout the book, sometimes in the form of sermons or speeches attributed to Jeremiah, which are usually called Deuteronomic (or Deuteronomistic), since they reflect the style, language, and thought of the book of Deuteronomy and the Deuteronomic editors who shaped the history of Israel that we find in the books of Judges to 2 Kings. Typical examples of this material are the Temple sermon in chap. 7 and the covenant passage in 11.1–17. It is these Deuteronomic passages that have provoked the greatest controversy in the study of the book of Jeremiah. Some would trace them to Jeremiah himself; others argue that they reflect the characteristic rhetorical prose style of Jeremiah's day and present a tradition of Jeremiah's teaching as handed down in circles familiar with this style and sympathetic to the theology of the book of Deuteronomy. A variation of this view is to regard such passages as conventional scribal compositions and attribute them to Baruch. All such views trace the material in its present form back to the time of Jeremiah. Others, however, believe that such passages are later, either emanating from Deuteronomic preachers during the period of the exile in Babylon in the sixth century BCE or reflecting theological issues of a still later date during the Persian period. It is doubtful whether in their present form such passages can be attributed to Jeremiah, but it is unduly skeptical to deny that they may well have their roots in a tradition that builds on what Jeremiah said and did.

How or when such varied material came together to form the book of Jeremiah, either in its shorter or its longer form, we do not know, but it must have taken many decades, or even centuries, after Jeremiah's life. The very nature of the book—its varied components, the clear evidence of editing within it, the amalgamation of different traditions—raises the question as to what extent the book provides us with reliable historical data concerning the life, words, and deeds of the prophet. Some deny that the book provides us with any access to the historical Jeremiah. Behind the editing, however, and in and through the varied material, there does seem to emerge a prophetic figure of striking individuality, God's spokesman to Judah at a major crisis point in the life of the nation.

**The Letter of Jeremiah.** One of the Apocrypha, considered deuterocanonical by Roman Catholics and by some Orthodox churches. According to Jeremiah 29, Jeremiah wrote from Jerusalem a letter addressed to the Judeans who had been carried off to exile in Babylon in the first deportation in 597 BCE. In that letter Jeremiah gives the people instruction as to their conduct in Babylon and warns them against false prophets in their midst. It was no doubt this passage that inspired an unknown author, living probably rather late in the Hellenistic age, to write a similar letter in the prophet's name, to be delivered, supposedly, to those condemned to exile either in 597 BCE or the final disaster of 587/586 BCE before they departed from

Jerusalem. The purpose of the letter is to warn the deportees against the temptation that would confront them in Babylon to worship other gods. The danger of apostasy was, of course, also acute in the Hellenistic period, when, presumably, the letter was actually written.

The manner in which the theme is treated was very likely suggested by Jeremiah 10.1–16, and particularly by v. 11, the only verse in Jeremiah written in Aramaic, which says, "The gods who did not make heaven and earth shall perish from the earth and from under the heavens." The author may have been further inspired by Isaiah 44.9–20.

**The Lamentations of Jeremiah.** The book of Lamentations, also commonly known as the Lamentations of Jeremiah, consists of five poems occasioned by the siege and fall of Jerusalem in 587/586 BCE. Beginning with very early times, perhaps not long after the events, these laments have been used in Jewish, and later in Christian worship, as an expression of grief at the destruction of the city and also for more generalized sorrow, as in Christian liturgies of Good Friday, as well as an appeal for divine mercy. The book has attracted special interest among biblical scholars because of its relatively strict poetic form, all the chapters being alphabetic acrostics or related in some way to the alphabet.

One ancient tradition ascribes the book of Lamentations to the prophet Jeremiah, and this has even affected the traditional depiction of Jeremiah in western art as the "weeping prophet." Another ancient tradition, however, is silent as to the authorship of the book, thus implying that the author was unknown, and this is also the commonly held modern critical opinion.

The Septuagint, the ancient Greek translation of the Hebrew Bible, groups Lamentations with the book of Jeremiah, and prefaces the book with these words: " . . . Jeremiah sat weeping and composed this lament over Jerusalem and said . . ." Other ancient versions, as well as rabbinic sources, make the same ascription to the prophet. Although there is no explicit warrant for this in the Bible, there is a kind of basis for it in the comment in 2 Chronicles 35.25 that Jeremiah produced a "lament" or "laments" for King Josiah.

In the Hebrew scriptures themselves, Lamentations is not placed with Jeremiah. It is always placed not among the Prophets but with the Writings, the third division of the Jewish canon. This position is significant testimony to the original anonymity of Lamentations, for it is difficult to see why the book was separated from that of Jeremiah if from the beginning it was understood to have been composed by the prophet. In modern times, scholars have pointed out elements in Lamentations that seem so much at odds with the views and personality of the prophet Jeremiah that it becomes very difficult to think of him as their author. Lamentations 1.10 refers to the enemies' entry into the Temple as a thing forbidden by God, whereas Jeremiah (7.14) had predicted it. Jeremiah foresaw the failure of foreign alliances (2.18; 37.5–10), but the author of Lamentations 4.17 shared with his people a frustrated longing for help from "a nation that could not save." Still further evidence of this sort may be pointed out, leading to the common opinion that the book's author—or authors, since the work is not strongly unified—is best regarded as unknown.

It is clear that Lamentations was written after the fall of Jerusalem in 587/586 BCE, but otherwise the date is uncertain. Since it expresses no clear hope for relief from conditions of bondage and humiliation, it probably dates to a time well before 538, when *Cyrus permitted the Jews to return from exile. The book may have been written in Judah (rather than Babylon or Egypt), since it displays no interest in any other locale.

*Robert Davidson, Robert C. Dentan, Delbert R. Hillers*

**JERICHO.** Jericho, whose name probably means "Moon (City)" (Hebr. *yārēaḥ*), is located 8 mi (12 km) north of the Dead Sea at the foot of the western escarpment of the *Jordan valley. At 840 ft (258 m) below sea level it is the lowest city on earth. Today a thriving market town, its ten-thousand-year history has been documented principally by the excavations of Kathleen Kenyon at Tell es-Sultan.

Mesolithic hunters were attracted to the area in the ninth millennium BCE by the abundant perennial spring of Ein es-Sultan. By about 8000 BCE a permanent settlement of some two thousand people had been established just beside it. Its irrigation system and the large tower and defense wall imply a social organization that justifies Jericho's title as the oldest city in the world. Sometime around 6800 BCE the original settlers were displaced by another Neolithic people, whose most distinctive cultural achievement was a series of skulls with individualized features restored in plaster. This group, however, had not yet discovered pottery, which first appeared around 4500 BCE when another group took possession of the site. The site was then occupied more or less continuously until the middle of the Late Bronze Age, when the city was devastated. This destruction is too early to be attributed to *Joshua (*see* Canaan), but in harmony with his words the site was abandoned until the seventh century BCE, a date that is too late to coincide with the reoccupation mentioned in 1 Kings 16.34 as having occurred in the ninth century BCE. The Iron Age city visited by *Elijah and *Elisha was known as the city of palm trees.

After the Babylonian exile Tell es-Sultan was abandoned, but there must have been a settlement elsewhere in the oasis, because in the late sixth century BCE Jericho was a Persian administrative center, a role it retained in later periods. In the Hellenistic period the area was considered a private royal domain, and this inhibited any real urbanization; its fortifications guarded the eastern frontier.

The Hasmoneans extended the cultivated area by building an aqueduct from Ein Qilt. The agricultural wealth of the enlarged oasis is extolled by Josephus and Strabo. The delightful winter climate inspired Alexander Janneus to build a palace on the north bank of the Wadi Qilt. *Herod the Great had Aristobulus III, his last serious rival for the crown of Judea, drowned in its great swimming pool in 35 BCE. During the years 34–30 BCE, when he was forced to rent the plantations from Cleopatra to whom they had been given by Mark Antony, Herod built a winter residence south of the Wadi Qilt. Once Octavian (Augustus) had transferred Jericho to Herod's control in 30 BCE, the latter remodeled the Hasmonean palace, constructed the theater-hippodrome complex at Tell es-Samrat, and later erected more buildings on both sides of the Wadi Qilt. The vast quantities of water required by the palace were supplied by three new aqueducts, two on the south wall of the Wadi Qilt and the third coming from Ein Duk at Naaran. Security was guaranteed by Kypros, a fortress on a cliff to the west.

Herod lived in the palace during his last terrible illness, but the medicinal springs of Callirhoe on the east side of the Dead Sea gave him no relief, and he died in Jericho shortly before Passover in 4 BCE. Josephus's reports that the palace was burnt by Simeon and rebuilt by Archelaus have not been confirmed by recent excavations.

After the dismissal of Archelaus in 6 CE, a garrison occupied Kypros. Burials in the cliffs north of the palace continued to 68 CE. Wealthy families from Jerusalem presumably returned each winter to their villas, some of whose foundations have been traced in the plantations south of the palace. This provides the background for the preaching of *John the Baptist in this area, for the plantation slaves who were the only permanent population are unlikely to have been his primary audience. The presence of Jesus in Jericho is explained by the fact that, to avoid passing through *Samaritan territory, Galilean pilgrims to Jerusalem followed a route down the Jordan valley to Jericho.

*Jerome Murphy-O'Connor*

**JERUBBAAL.** *See* Gideon.

**JERUSALEM.** *This entry consists of two articles, the first on the* History *of Jerusalem and the second on the city's* Symbolism. *For additional discussion of these topics, see* Zion.

### *History*

**Name and Description.** The earliest attestation of Jerusalem's name is in the Egyptian Execration Texts of the nineteenth and eighteenth centuries BCE in a form that must be a transcription of the Semitic *Urusalim,* which appears in the *Amarna letters of the fourteenth century BCE. It is a combination of two elements meaning "the foundation of [the god] Shalem." The second element, rendered Salem, is used alone in Genesis 14.18 and Psalm 76.2. The pronunciation of the Hebrew name is reflected in the Greek *Ierousalem,* which predominates in the Septuagint. In 1 *Esdras, *Tobit, and 1–4 *Maccabees, however, the Septuagint has the strongly Hellenized *Hierosolyma.* Both forms appear in the New Testament.

The biblical city spreads across two hills (average altitude 2,500 ft [750 m]) in the central mountain range. It is limited on the west and south by the Hinnom valley, and on the east by the Kidron valley, which separates it from the *Mount of Olives. Josephus alone records that the central valley was called the Tyropoeon ("Cheesemakers"). The western hill is slightly higher than the eastern hill, and both slope to the south. There are two springs, Gihon ("gusher") and Ein Rogel ("the fuller's spring"), in the Kidron valley. The climate is temperate, and all the rain (annual average 22 in [560 mm]) falls during the four-month winter (December to March). It occasionally snows.

**Before the Exile.** The original city was on the southern extension of the eastern hill known as Ophel, excavated principally by Kathleen Kenyon and Yigal Shiloh. Scattered pottery attests occupation from the third millennium BCE and the site was defended by a heavy wall from about 1800 BCE. Houses built on artificial terraces climbed the slope to the acropolis. After the Israelite conquest the territory of Jerusalem was absorbed by the tribe of *Benjamin, but the city of the *Jebusites, with its mixed population of *Amorites and *Hittites, was left alone. It thus served *David's need for a capital independent of the twelve tribes. He took it ca. 1000 BCE and made it an effective center by bringing into it the ark of the covenant, to which all the tribes gave allegiance. In order to house the ark appropriately David bought a threshing floor to the north of the City of David from one Araunah, which is both a title ("lord") in Hittite and a personal name in Ugaritic. Here *Solomon built the First *Temple ca. 960 BCE, which he linked to the city by a palace, effectively doubling the size of the original Jebusite city. The Jebusite water-shaft was retained for use in military emergencies, but Solomon dug a tunnel from Gihon along the edge of the hill. Sluice gates at intervals facilitated irrigation of the King's Garden in the Kidron valley. The population of Davidic and Solomonic Jerusalem was a few thousand at most.

The excavations of Nahman Avigad in the Jewish Quarter have unearthed evidence, notably a massive wall 23 ft (7 m) wide, that the city had expanded to cover the western hill in the late eighth century BCE. When *Sennacherib menaced Jerusalem, King *Hezekiah built the wall to protect refugees from the northern kingdom of Israel, who had settled outside the crowded city. He thus created two new quarters, the *mišneh* ("second") on the western hill, and the *maktēš* ("mortar") in the Tyropoeon valley. The City of David was given a new wall just inside the Jebusite wall that had served for a thousand years. In order to guarantee the water supply, Hezekiah dug a 1,750 ft (533 m) tunnel from Gihon through the Ophel ridge to the pool of Siloam in the Tyropoeon valley. An inscription found inside the exit details the construction technique. A new wall was built to protect the vulnerable north side of the city in the seventh century BCE. Both it and houses in the City of David bear traces of the savage attack that brought Jerusalem under *Babylonian control in 587/586 BCE.

**After the Exile.** The Israelites who returned from the exile in 538 BCE rebuilt the Temple under the direction of *Zerubbabel, but were authorized to reconstruct the walls only when the *Persians appointed the first Jewish governor, *Nehemiah, about 445 BCE. A complete description of these walls is given in Nehemiah 3, but the passage abounds in textual problems, and it has proved impossible to translate the data into a precise line on the ground. The complete absence of Hellenistic remains on the western hill, however, indicates that they encompassed an area barely equal to that of the city of David and Solomon.

Jerusalem suffered three sieges in the wars between the Ptolemies of Egypt and the Seleucids of Syria (201, 199, and 198 BCE). Sirach 50.1–4 praises the high priest Simon (220–195 BCE) for his rebuilding program, but the differences between the Hebrew and Greek versions create a certain obscurity as to what he actually achieved. After Jerusalem passed into the hands of the Seleucids in 198 BCE, the Hellenizing faction among the Jews built a gymnasium in the city. In 167 BCE Antiochus IV Epiphanes forbade all Jewish religious practices. In order to forestall any resistance he threw down the walls of Jerusalem, and built a great fortress, the Akra, to hold a Syrian garrison. Nine different sites have been proposed for the Akra, but it seems likely that it was south of the Temple. It is not to be confused with the Baris sited northwest of the Temple.

The refortification of the city was begun by Jonathan Maccabeus and completed by his brother Simon, i.e., between 160 and 134 BCE. Josephus's description of this line, which he calls the First Wall, has been given precision by excavations. It ran due west from the Temple along the southern edge of a tributary of the Tyropoeon valley, followed the rim of the Hinnom valley, and mounted the eastern edge of the Ophel ridge to join the Temple. Descriptions of the Hasmonean city appear in the *Letter of Aristeas* and in Josephus, but both must be used with great caution. The date of the information in the former is uncertain, and the latter is at times guilty of anachronism.

**The Herodian City.** The Romans, who asserted their authority over Palestine in 63 BCE, appointed *Herod the Great king of Judea in 40 BCE. A three-year campaign to establish his sovereignty culminated with the capture of Jerusalem in the summer of 37 BCE. The fact that he had to break two walls in order to reach the Lower City suggests that what Josephus calls the Second Wall, which ran from the Gennath Gate in the First Wall to the northwest corner of the Temple, was already in existence at this time. No certain elements of this wall have been discovered, but the section running north from the First Wall cannot be farther west than the present Suq Khan ez-Zeit. Excavations beneath the Holy Sepulcher and in the Muristan reveal that this area was not within the city of the late first century BCE or early first century CE. There is unambiguous evidence that it was an abandoned quarry. A Jewish catacomb was cut in the west wall. The six kokhim graves still visible in the Holy Sepulcher are typical of the first centuries BCE and CE. A projecting corner in the south wall, which sloped to the southeast, was called *Golgotha ("[the place of] the skull"). The relationship of these two elements corresponds perfectly with the descriptions of Jesus's crucifixion and burial in John 19.17–42.

While he presumably repaired, and in some cases certainly strengthened, the walls of the city, Herod did not alter the lines he had inherited. The prime contemporary written source for data on the area they enclosed is Josephus's *Jewish War.* The principal passages are 5.4.136–83 and 6.4.220–10.442, but other topographical references are scattered throughout the work. He consistently refers to the western hill as the Upper City and alludes to the old City of David on Ophel as the Lower City. Cemeteries bordered the city on the north and east; the tombs of the families of Herod the Great and of the high priest *Caiaphas have been located west of the city.

**Herod's Buildings.** Herod's first concern was for his own security. On the site of the Hasmonean Baris at the northwest corner of the Temple he built the Antonia fortress. Since it was named for Mark Antony, it must have been completed prior to the latter's defeat in 31 BCE. Paul was imprisoned there. The Roman garrison based there after 6 CE may have influenced the growth of the healing shrine outside the walls to the east, which figures in John 5.1–9. For the entertainment of his supporters Herod built a theater and an amphitheater. The latter has not been located, but the former was in a little valley south of the Hinnom. The hippodrome must have been in the Kidron valley. The quadrennial contests for which these were built gave great offense to pious Jews. In order to further elevate his splendid palace, excavations show that Herod erected a podium at the highest point of the Upper City. It was protected by three great towers, Hippicus, Mariamne, and Phasaelis. The latter surpassed the Pharos of Alexandria, one of the seven wonders of the ancient world. Its great base (today part of the Citadel) is the only element of the palace to have survived.

After the Romans assumed direct control of Palestine in 6 CE, Herod's palace became the residence of the procurators when they came to Jerusalem; Philo calls it "the house of the procurators" (*Leg. ad Gaium* 306). It is here then that we must locate the praetorium in which Pontius *Pilate judged Jesus. This is confirmed by the geographic term used in John 19.13, because Gabbatha ("high point") can only apply to this part of the Herodian city. At this stage the descendants of Herod used the Hasmonean palace on the western edge of the Tyropoeon valley.

Starting in 20 BCE it took Herod nine and a half years to complete rebuilding the *Temple on a much grander scale than its predecessor on the same site. Nothing remains except the huge retaining walls supporting the platform, the western side of which became a site for Jewish prayer (the "Wailing Wall") after the destruction of the Temple. Such building activity inspired others, and the quality of life of the wealthy in first century CE Jerusalem is nowhere more evident than in the magnificent mansions excavated in the Jewish Quarter.

The sources make no mention of any concern on the part of Herod for the water supply of the city, but Josephus's mention of the Serpent's Pool (today Birkat es-Sultan), which served a large catchment area west of the city, probably implies the existence of the serpentine 42 mi (67 km) low-level aqueduct that brought water from Arrub via Solomon's Pools to the Temple. Herod certainly constructed the great reservoir, Birkat Israel, against the north wall of the Temple, and it is likely that he refurbished the Pool of Siloam. Other known reservoirs are Struthion, adjacent to the Antonia, and Amygdalon, just north of the palace; the latter was fed by aqueducts from Mamilla and from the north. When the water stored in house cisterns is added, it has been calculated that the population ceiling must have been about seventy thousand.

**After Herod the Great.** Pilate is credited with having constructed a new aqueduct soon after 26 CE, but it cannot be identified with the 9 mi (15 km) high-level aqueduct from Bir el-Daraj that supplied the Upper City, and which inscriptions date to 195 CE. The prosperity of Jerusalem increased the demand on space, and the climate of peace meant that there was no risk in building outside the Second Wall. Herod Agrippa I (41–44 CE) tried to wall in this New City or suburb of Bezetha, but the attempt was blocked by the Emperor Claudius. This wall, completed by the rebels during the First Revolt (66–70 CE), is the famous Third Wall of Josephus, which has given rise to intense debate, because the data given by Josephus are both vague and incoherent. Only two elements have been identified archaeologically, the north gate beneath the present Damascus Gate, and the east gate, which is the Ecce Homo arch near the Antonia. When eighteen thousand men were made redundant on the completion of work on the Temple in 62–64 CE, Herod Agrippa II employed them to pave the city with white stone.

The Roman siege began at Passover 70 CE, while internecine warfare raged in the city. All Jerusalem was in the hand of the legions by late August. By order of Titus it was levelled to the ground, the only exceptions being the great towers, Phasaelis, Hippicus, and Mariamne, which were left as a memorial to Jerusalem's former strength and glory.

*Jerome Murphy-O'Connor*

### *Symbolism*

Although the sixteenth century was a period of great scientific advances among

European mapmakers, one of the best known maps of that period is more imaginative than accurate: a woodcut in the form of a cloverleaf, with Jerusalem depicted as the center of the world from which emanate the continents of Europe, Asia, and Africa. The idea of the centrality of Jerusalem has been a mainstay in Christianity, in various ways, since its inception. It has also been integral to Judaism since the time of King *David in the tenth century BCE and, together with the sacred cities of Mecca and Medina, to Islam since its beginnings in the seventh century CE. In the modern era of nation-states, Jerusalem is both the capital of Israel and, for Palestinians, the capital of the state of Palestine. Thus, Jerusalem has long been a focus of powerful and intertwined passions of religion and politics. Although its name probably originally meant "foundation of [the god] Shalem," it has often been interpreted to mean "city of peace" (*ᶜîr šālōm*). But peace has remained an elusive goal for most of Jerusalem's nearly four-thousand year history.

In his meditation on this most holy and painful city (*Jerusalem: City of Mirrors,* [Boston, 1989]), the "capital of memory," the Israeli writer Amos Elon observed that it is as if the very name Jerusalem (Hebr. *yĕrûšālaim*) is a reflection of the city's contradictory, even dualistic nature (*aim* is the Hebrew suffix indicating a dual or pair), manifesting itself even in its location on the boundary between Israel's cultivated grasslands and arid desert regions. There has always been a tension between the present and the future, the earthly and the heavenly, the real and the ideal Jerusalem, a city of diverse peoples struggling to accomplish their daily activities and the city of religious visionaries.

The name Jerusalem occurs 660 times in the Hebrew Bible; *Zion, often used as synonymous with Jerusalem, especially in biblical poetry, occurs another 154 times. The former appears most frequently in the historical narratives of 2 Samuel, Kings, Chronicles, Ezra, and Nehemiah, and in the prophetic books of Isaiah, Jeremiah, Ezekiel, and Zechariah. Except for Salem in Genesis 14.18, it is absent from the Pentateuch, achieving importance in ancient Israel's self-understanding only after David brought the ark of the covenant, symbol of God's presence, to the newly conquered city. The ark would find its permanent home in the Jerusalem *Temple, the house of God, completed by David's son *Solomon, and strategically situated very near to the house of God's loyal servant, the king. The belief in the inviolability of Jerusalem, the chosen dwelling place of God, was challenged by such prophets as Micah and Jeremiah, who warned that the city would be destroyed as a result of its transgressions. But after the *Babylonian destruction of Jerusalem and its Temple in 587/586 BCE, the exilic prophets envisioned a new Jerusalem, which was simultaneously a rebuilding and restoration of the old and also an idealized city, both grander and more enduring than its predecessor, offering its inhabitants a relationship with God and concomitant peace and prosperity. For Jeremiah, the rebuilt Jerusalem was well grounded in the old, even in its physical contours. Ezekiel, who understood Jerusalem as "in the center of the nations, with countries all around her (5.5)" celebrates a new city and a new Temple, areas of radiating holiness, fruitfulness, and well-being, where God's glory will again reside: "And the name of the city from that time on shall be, The Lord is There (48.35)." Second Isaiah is consoling in its assertion that Jerusalem "has served her term, that her penalty is paid (Isa. 40.2)." The gates of the new city will always be open, and the Lord will be its everlasting light. "No more shall there be in it an infant that lives but a few days, or an old person who does not live out a lifetime (65.20)."

The hopes and expectations of the exilic prophets were realized in part with the rebuilding of the city and Temple during the latter half of the sixth century BCE, the first generation of Persian rule. Both, however, would be destroyed by the Roman army in 70 CE. The Temple was never rebuilt. In the generation before its destruction, the Alexandrian Jewish philosopher and statesman Philo wrote that the Jews "hold the Holy City where stands the sacred Temple of the most high God to be their mother city" (*Flaccum* 46). The destruction of the Temple and "mother city" was both a great blow and a great challenge to Jews, inside and outside of Israel. Some Jewish apocalyptic texts from this period envisioned that at the end time, the heavenly Jerusalem, fashioned by God, would descend to earth; others envisioned a heavenly Jerusalem that awaited the righteous above. In either case, the renewal of Jerusalem was integral to the vision of the end time, a role already suggested in the eschatological visions of the exilic and postexilic prophets.

The formative texts of rabbinic Judaism, which date from roughly the third to the seventh centuries CE, share with the earlier apocalyptic texts both the centrality of the renewal of Jerusalem in the messianic age, and a lack of uniformity in the description of that future, ideal city; in some texts, an earthly Jerusalem, and in others a heavenly city; in some an earthly city that ascends to heaven, and in others a heavenly city that descends to earth. What is striking, however, are the linkages and interdependencies between the earthly and the heavenly Jerusalem. In the anti-Roman messianic Palestinian Jewish revolt of Bar Kochba (132–135 CE), the rebels struck coins with the image of the Temple facade and the inscription "of the freedom of Jerusalem," indicating their hopes for the rebuilding of Jerusalem and its Temple. Similarly, the Jewish rebels of the First Revolt (66–70 CE), with their constellation of religious, nationalist, and messianic apocalyptic motivations, issued coins with the inscription, "Jerusalem the holy." As noted above, however, the consequence of the first revolt was not the reinvigoration of Jerusalem, but rather its destruction.

Early rabbinic literature did not focus only on the Jerusalem of the messianic age. The Mishnah, Talmuds, and midrashic collections celebrated the memory of the historic Jerusalem as well. Some texts describe Jerusalem as the center or "navel" of the world; others depict in glowing language the grandeur and uniqueness of the city. Jerusalem's uniqueness was reflected also in the halakhic requirements associated with the city, most of which were not practiced, given the destruction of the Temple and city, and the banning of Jews from Jerusalem by the Roman emperor Hadrian, in the aftermath of the war of Bar Kochba.

As if in response to the words of the psalmist of a long-gone era, "If I forget you, O Jerusalem, let my right hand wither," the memory of Jerusalem and its Temple and the hope for their restoration were reflected in evolving Jewish liturgy, to be evoked on occasions of joy and mourning and perhaps, most importantly, to be recited as part of the Grace after Meals and the daily Amidah prayer, which together with the Shema, constitute, in a sense, the foundation of Jewish liturgy. The ninth of the month of Av developed as a day of fasting and mourning for the destruction of the First and Second Temples, becoming associated also with other calamitous events in Jewish history.

It is not clear to what degree and for how long Hadrian's decree banning Jews from Jerusalem was enforced. Jews were permitted to reside in Jerusalem, however, during its many centuries of Muslim rule, beginning with its conquest by Caliph Umar in 638, interrupted only by the brief and, in many ways, violent rule of the twelfth-century Crusader Kingdom of Jerusalem. During the years of Ottoman rule (1517–1917), notwithstanding the rebuilding of Jerusalem's walls (1537–1541) by Suleiman I, Jerusalem remained a small and impoverished city. Only in the mid-to-late nineteenth century did the Jews, Latin Christians, Armenian Christians, and Muslims leave their traditional quarters in the walled city to establish new ongoing neighborhoods, the Jews settling generally to the west of the Old City.

The expansion of Jerusalem outside of the walled city developed at roughly the same time as European Zionism. Many factors contributed to the evolution of the latter, including the anti-Jewish policies of the Russian czarist governments, the overall political, social, and economic conditions of Eastern European Jewry, the evolution of anti-Semitic movements and agitation in Western Europe, and the presence and vitality of other European nationalist movements. Notwithstanding the generally nontraditional religious orientation of most of the early Zionist leaders, one cannot underestimate the significance for them of Jewish historical connections with the land of Israel and the city of Jerusalem, suggested even in the term "Zionism." Nonetheless, many of the early Zionist leaders expressed a kind of ambivalence about Jerusalem, reacting seemingly both to the physical squalor of the city and, from their perspectives, to Jerusalem's tired and outdated Jewish religious practices and passions. The ultra-Orthodox Jewish communities of Jerusalem were a counterpoint to the Zionists' visions of a transformed Jewish society. As late as 1947, the Zionist leadership was willing to accept the United Nations resolution to partition Palestine into a Jewish state and an Arab state, and to make Jerusalem a separate political entity under international administration. Following the war of 1948 and the bloody battle for Jerusalem, however, neither the internationalization of Jerusalem nor the Arab state in Palestine was established. Instead, the land fell under Israeli or Jordanian rule with western Jerusalem under Israeli control and eastern Jerusalem, including the Old City and its holy places, under Jordanian control. Jerusalem was declared the official capital of Israel in December 1949. As a result of the 1967 Six Day War, Israel began to govern formerly Jordanian-held East Jerusalem, which was later officially annexed and incorporated by the Israeli government into the state of Israel. Within the Old City stood the Western or Wailing Wall, a retaining wall from the Second Temple as renovated by *Herod in the first century BCE. It continues to function as a complex religious-national symbol, a focus of prayer, and an object of pilgrimage for Jews inside and outside of Israel. Today, even most of the significant number of Israeli Jews who support territorial compromise with the Palestinians in exchange for peace, including the establishment of a Palestinian state in the West Bank and Gaza, are reluctant to give up any portion of Jerusalem, or to see the city come under international rule or be divided again. Analogously, the significant number of Palestinians who also support a "two state solution" insist that eastern Jerusalem serve as the capital of Palestine. Thus the "city of peace" remains a stumbling block in Arab-Israeli and Palestinian-Israeli negotiations.

Although the Christian population of Jerusalem, two to three percent of the total, has been in decline for the last fifty years, the number of Christian visitors and pilgrims to Jerusalem remains very large. The roots of this fascination with Jerusalem date both to the origins of Christianity as a first-century Palestinian Jewish apocalyptic movement and to the depictions of the ministry, death, and resurrection of Jesus in the four New Testament Gospels. The Gospels mention Jerusalem sixty-seven times. Matthew refers to it as the "holy city." Although the texts vary, each of the Gospels depicts Jesus as moving seemingly inevitably to Jerusalem, the site of the pivotal events of the life of Jesus and of Christianity's self-understanding, that is Jesus's death and resurrection; and, for first-century Palestinian Jewry, their national and religious center.

As was the case with other kinds of Judaism of this period, early Christianity knew of both an earthly and a heavenly Jerusalem. The book of Revelation, drawing heavily on Ezekiel's vision of the new Jerusalem and very reminiscent of contemporary Jewish apocalyptic texts, describes "the holy city, the new Jerusalem, coming down out of heaven from God (21.2)." Unlike Ezekiel's city, however, this Jerusalem has no Temple, "for its temple is the Lord God the Almighty and the Lamb (21.22)." As Robert Wilken has noted, speculation concerning God's future kingdom on earth with Jerusalem as its center dominated Christian eschatology of the first and second centuries, as, for example, in the writings of Justin Martyr and Irenaeus. Later church fathers, however, such as Origen, who spent more than twenty years in third-century Caesarea, disputed both the teachings of Justin Martyr and Irenaeus, as well as Jewish beliefs in the future restoration of some kind of Jerusalem on earth, to speak only of the heavenly Jerusalem, which remained above and entirely separate from the earthly city.

The fourth century was a period of tremendous change for Christianity. It entered the century as the religion of a persecuted minority, and exited as the official state religion of the Roman empire. Emperor Constantine made Christianity a legal religion in 313, and became its patron and protector. Palestine and in particular Jerusalem became a Christian showplace of sorts. From the time of Constantine, massive church building projects were undertaken to create a visible and glorious manifestation of the legitimacy and permanence of Christian rule—an outward sign of the truth and victory of Christianity. Money poured in from both the government and private persons, bringing with it increased material prosperity and cosmopolitanism for all of fourth- and fifth-century Palestine. Hadrian's Jerusalem, Roman Aelia Capitolina, named after the emperor and the gods of the Capitoline in Rome, would be transformed into a Christian Jerusalem. Constantine himself sponsored the building of three major Palestinian churches, all connected with the life of Jesus, and two of which were in Jerusalem: the Church of the Holy Sepulcher; a church on the Mount of Olives; and the Church of the Nativity in nearby *Bethlehem. Already, in the writings of Eusebius, the early fourth-century Caesarean church historian, one can see intimations of the Palestinian church's understanding of itself as guardian of a very earthly Christian Palestine with its center at Jerusalem—a land in which Christians lived and visited, and in which one could see and touch the very places in which the saving events of biblical history had taken place.

Christian pilgrimage to Palestine and especially Jerusalem became widespread in the fourth century. Early pilgrims included Helena, the mother of Constantine. Fourth-century Christian pilgrims, as part of their quest for perfection, would undertake the dangers of travel to Palestine to visit the holy places, and therein both confirm and strengthen their faith. As pilgrimage flourished, some church leaders questioned its value, drawing attention to the contrast between "Jerusalem the Holy" and the city that awaited the pilgrim. For example, Gregory of Nyssa in his "Letter on Pilgrimage" pointed to the "shameful practices" of the people of Jerusalem as evidence that God's grace was no more abundant in Jerusalem than elsewhere.

Echoes of early Christian speculations on the role and nature of Jerusalem in the end time, as well as an interest in the earthly city itself, can be found both in the constellation of factors that shaped the Crusades of medieval Europe, and in the voyages of Columbus who, influenced by late fifteenth-century apocalyptic thought, sought to acquire the gold to finance the final crusade, which would capture Jerusalem and place it again in Christian hands—all part of God's plan for the end time.

Columbus failed in his plans, but Christian interest in and pilgrimage to Jerusalem has endured. For many pilgrims, the Church of the Holy Sepulcher, consecrated in 335, was the highlight of their trip. Today it remains the major Christian holy place in Jerusalem, although most of what can be seen dates from the period of the Crusades, the Church having been destroyed and rebuilt several times since the time of Constantine. Several Christian denominations have rights to various sections of the Church. In their stories of conflict and cooperation, they are illustrative of the diversity within Christianity and the long, complex, and vital history of the Christian community in Jerusalem.

Although an overview of the symbolism and significance of Jerusalem for Islam is beyond the scope of this article, one must note both the importance of Jerusalem for Islam, and the importance of the city's Muslim communities since their inception in the seventh century CE for the history of Jerusalem, in Arabic "al-Quds," "the Holy." Today, Jerusalem's major Muslim holy place, the magnificent Dome of the Rock, a rotunda on an octagonal base, built by the Umayyad Caliph Abd al-Malik and completed in 691/692, dominates the Haram al-Sharif, or Noble Sanctuary, also the site of the Temple Mount of the Jews. The Dome, reminiscent on a grander scale of the nearby Church of the Holy Sepulcher, was constructed in the architectural style of the Byzantine martyrium to serve as a shrine for the holy rock beneath it—a rock which by the time of the Muslim conquest of Jerusalem in 638 was already associated with the Temple and with *Abraham, the common traditional ancestor of Judaism, Christianity, and Islam. The Dome affirmed the triumph of Islam in the midst of the Christian show place, Jerusalem, "The Holy City," and in a place, atop the Temple Mount, which the Byzantine Christians had kept in ruins to concretize Christian beliefs that the destruction of the Jerusalem Temple was both a fulfillment of prophecy and a proof of the victory and truth claims of the "New Israel."

The sanctity for Islam of the Rock, the Haram, and Jerusalem, in general, was strengthened by the identification by early Muslim authorities of Jerusalem as the destiny of the Prophet Muhammad's night journey, and the Rock as the place from which he ascended to heaven. As in Judaism and Christianity, Jerusalem assumed an important role in Muslim beliefs concerning the end time and the day of judgment. So too, Muslim sources reflect the tensions between the holy city, setting of the last judgment, and Jerusalem in its daily activities. Thus Muqaddasi, a tenth-century geographer and historian, and a native of Jerusalem, would celebrate Jerusalem as "the most illustrious of cities" where the advantages of the present and the next world meet, and also describe the city as a place oppressive to the *poor, lacking in learned men, "a golden basin filled with scorpions."

Jerusalem is today a city of more than 650,000 people, a city which both celebrates and is haunted by its history, a city in which the tensions between the ideal and the real Jerusalem are lived and witnessed daily, and in which the rages and passions of religion and politics bring to mind the words of the psalmist, "Pray for the peace of Jerusalem."

*Barbara Geller Nathanson*

## JESUS CHRIST.

**Life and Teaching.** ***Introduction: critical method.*** By accepting the modern critical method of studying the New Testament, we need not attempt to write a life of Jesus in the modern sense of a psychological study. We can hope only to reconstruct the barest outline of his career and to give some account of his message and teaching.

We shall assume that *Mark is the earliest of the four Gospels and that, apart from the passion narrative (14.1–16.8), the individual units of material are arranged in an order determined more by subject matter than by historical or chronological concerns. Moreover, these units of material (stories about Jesus, pronouncement stories, miracle stories, parables, and aphorisms) were adapted to the needs of the post-Easter community and circulated in oral tradition for some forty years before Mark was written down. The authors of the two later synoptic Gospels, *Matthew, and *Luke, used Mark as their primary source, plus a common source consisting mostly of sayings, unknown to Mark. This source is hypothetical and only recoverable by reconstructing the non-Marcan material common to Matthew and Luke. It is generally known as Q, from the German word *Quelle,* "source." In addition, Matthew and Luke have their own special traditions. Like Mark, the three sources—Q, Special Matthew, and Special Luke—contain material previously passed on orally for some fifty years. The evangelists, in their use of sources and oral traditions, shaped them according to their theological interests; this editorial work is known as redaction. Thus, the synoptic Gospels contain material that developed in three stages: authentic words and memories of Jesus himself (stage I), materials shaped and transmitted in oral tradition (stage II), and the evangelists' redaction (stage III). The gospel of *John, however, is very different. It contains some stage I and stage II materials independent of the synoptics that can be used sometimes to confirm or supplement the synoptic evidence in reconstructing the career and teaching of Jesus. But the Fourth Gospel contains much more material belonging to stage III. In reconstructing our account of Jesus, we shall attempt to recover stage I materials from all four Gospels. We shall be assisted by certain tests of authenticity. We may be reasonably certain that materials go back to stage I if they meet some or all of the following criteria: (1) have multiple attestation (i.e., are attested in more than one source or in more than one type of material); (2) are distinctive to Jesus (i.e., they are without parallel in Judaism or in the post-Easter community; this test should be used with caution and generally applied to confirm rather than exclude; principle of dissimilarity); (3) cohere with other accepted Jesus traditions (test of coherence); and/or (4) exhibit indications of originating in Aramaic (in the case of sayings), since this was Jesus's normal language (though he probably knew some Greek), or in a Palestinian milieu or social setting.

***The birth and upbringing of Jesus.*** The birth stories in Matthew and Luke are relatively late, and belong to stages II and III. But they contain certain items that go back to earlier tradition. Some of these are clearly theological: Davidic descent, conception through the Holy Spirit while his mother remained a virgin, homage at birth. Factual data in these common items include: the date of Jesus's birth in the last years of the reign of *Herod the Great (died 4 BCE); the names of Jesus's parents, *Mary and *Joseph; the fact that the child was conceived between betrothal and wedding; the birth at *Bethlehem (though this may be a theological assertion, associated with the Davidic descent). In any case, Jesus was brought up in *Nazareth. His father is said to have been a carpenter, and Jesus is said to have been one himself. Since sons habitually followed their father's trade, this is not improbable. Presumably, Jesus received the education of the devout poor in Israel, with thorough instruction in the Hebrew scriptures.

***The beginning of Jesus's public ministry: his message.*** Jesus's public career began when he left home for the *Jordan River to be baptized by *John the Baptist. Jesus looked back to the Baptist as the source of his mission and authority. For a time, he appears to have conducted a ministry of baptizing parallel to that of the Baptist, presumably continuing the Baptist's message by demanding repentance from Israel in view of the impending advent of God's kingdom. After the Baptist's arrest, Jesus embarked upon a new kind of ministry. The message of the kingdom acquired a new urgency, perhaps as a result of the temptation, which included a vision of God's victory over *Satan. Abandoning the practice of baptism, Jesus went to the *synagogues for a time and then spoke in the open air, reaching out to the people instead of waiting for them to come to him; but still like the Baptist, he continued preaching the coming kingdom. Jesus never defined what he meant by the kingdom, but it means God's coming in saving power and strength, defeating the powers of evil and inaugurating salvation for Israel. It is basically future ("your kingdom come" in the Lord's Prayer) but also presently operative in Jesus's words and works. In the parables of the kingdom, Jesus seeks to engage his hearers, persuading them to see the present operation of the kingdom in his own words and works, and to secure from them the response of faith and confidence in its future consummation—parables of the sower, the seed growing secretly, the mustard seed; also the leaven.

An inescapable conclusion is that Jesus was influenced by the prophecies of Isaiah 40–66, where the coming of the reign of God is a central theme. Indeed, much of Jesus's teaching is shot through with allusions to Isaiah 40–66. Jesus is represented as quoting Isaiah 61.1–2 and 58.6 in the inaugural sermon in the synagogue at Nazareth

(Luke 4.18–19), but the content of the sermon was probably shaped in stage II or III. There are, however, clear echoes of these passages in the Beatitudes and in the answer to John. Jesus thus appeared first and foremost as eschatological prophet, one who announced the definitive coming of God's kingly rule, the salvation of the end time.

***Jesus's teaching: ethics.*** Jesus was also recognized as a *rabbi and teacher. Like the rabbis, he taught in synagogues, collected a band of disciples, and discussed Torah with them as well as with inquirers and critics. The forms of his teachings were similar to those employed by Pharisaic teachers: parables and aphorisms, that is, sayings, often of a wisdom type, enunciating general truths about human life and manners. Like the *Pharisees, Jesus took the authority of the Hebrew Bible for granted. It enunciates the demands of God: prohibition of divorce; the second tablet of the Ten Commandments; the Shema and the summary of the Law.

Yet there are differences between Jesus's teaching and those of the Pharisees. He emphasizes more strongly than they that God demands not just outward conformity to the Law but the whole person, and not just love of neighbor but love of enemy (see the antitheses of the Sermon on the Mount). The rich young man must not only keep the commandments but sell all he has and follow Jesus.

For Jesus, God's demand is summed up in the double commandment of love. This raises the question of the relationship between Jesus's preaching of the kingdom and his enunciation of God's demand, between his prophetic preaching and his wisdom teaching. Jesus never relates the two; in fact, he relates his wisdom teaching to creation rather than to the coming of God's kingly rule. Thus, the command to love one's enemy is based on the fact that God causes the rain to fall and the sun to shine upon the just and the unjust alike. Similarly, the absolute prohibition of divorce shows that the reversion to the situation at creation is now possible because of the shift in the ages: the age of *Moses is coming to an end, and God's kingly rule is coming. Therefore, Jesus's prophetic preaching presupposes his wisdom teaching. The coming of that rule makes possible the realization of God's original intent in creation. The same unspoken presupposition operates in the double commandment of love: only the coming of God's kingly rule makes it possible for people to love God in radical obedience and to love one's neighbor, including one's enemy. For God's coming in his kingly rule is an act of mercy and forgiveness (an important aspect of Jesus's message); and forgiveness as a human response to God's forgiveness is the supreme expression of love. Jesus's prophetic message is the indicative and his enunciation of the will of God is the imperative that the indicative implies.

***Jesus's teaching about God.*** Jesus brought no new teaching about God. God is the creator, though this is understood in an immediate way. God did not merely create the world in the beginning, rather, it comes from him as his creation in every moment. For Jesus, God is also the God who acts in history, the climax of which is the coming of the kingdom. Also, Jesus frequently adduced biblical characters whose situation in their day was analogous to the situation of his contemporaries in the face of the coming kingdom (e.g., Lot and his wife, the Queen of *Sheba, *Jonah).

Although the address of God as Father is not unknown in the Hebrew

Bible and Judaism, and even the familiar "abba" is not completely without precedent, that usage was characteristic of Jesus. He did not enunciate the fatherhood of God as an abstract doctrine or a general truth but himself experienced God as his own Father (i.e., in his call to his unique mission mediated through his baptism and temptations), and he offered to those who responded to his prophetic message a similar experience and the privilege of addressing God as abba (note the opening address of the Lord's Prayer in its original Lucan form, Luke 11.2).

***Jesus's conduct.*** Jesus appeared as a charismatic healer as well as a preacher and teacher. This was a further implementation of the prophetic mission set forth in Isaiah 35 and 61. Jesus performed exorcisms, which he claimed were the action in him of the Spirit (Matthew) or finger (Luke) of God. To deny this spirit at work in his exorcisms was blasphemy, a sin for which there would be no forgiveness. Thus, both healings and exorcisms are related to his message. The actual miracle stories may not be direct reports, but they reflect a general memory that Jesus did do such things. More problematic are the so-called nature miracles. There are three raising stories—Jairus's daughter, the widow's son at Nain, and Lazarus—but all these belong to stage II. The answer to John (Matt. 11.5–6 || Luke 7.22–23), however, may enable us to take back the fact of resuscitations to stage I, in which case the three stories of the raising may rest upon a general memory that Jesus did perform such deeds. Another special instance of a nature miracle is the feeding of the multitude. This miracle has multiple attestation. The shaping of the stories originated early in stage II, where they were modeled partly on the eucharistic tradition and partly on the *Elisha story (2 Kings 4.42–44, whence the miraculous multiplication of the loaves derives). But such a meal itself may well be historical: Jesus met with his followers in a remote place and ate with them. This meal may have been one of a series of events constituting a crisis at the climax of the Galilean ministry (see below).

Jesus also celebrated meals with the outcast, and for this too there is multiple attestation. In the parables of the lost (Luke 15), Jesus interprets this action as a celebration in advance of the joy of the great banquet of the kingdom of God.

Like John the Baptist, Jesus addressed his message of repentance in view of the coming kingdom to Israel as a whole. But he called some to follow him, accompany him, and share in the work of proclaiming the message. From these he selected *twelve to symbolize the restoration of Israel. It would seem that much of Jesus's radical demand was intended for these followers, who constituted a band of wandering charismatic preachers and therefore had to dispense, as he did, with the normal securities of human life, including family ties.

***The central crisis.*** It is clear that at one point Jesus broke off his Galilean ministry and transferred his activities to *Jerusalem. There are indications of a series of events starting with the feeding of the multitude, followed by a withdrawal from the crowds, a crossing of the lake, and a period of solitary communication with his disciples (represented by the confession of *Peter and the Transfiguration), after which Jesus set out for Jerusalem. We may suppose that during this period of solitude Jesus resolved that it was now God's plan for him to go to Jerusalem and carry his message to Israel at the very center of its life. Two circumstances may have contributed to this decision. First, Jesus's ministry evoked a dangerous messianic enthusiasm among the crowds. Second, the execution of John the Baptist made Jesus fear that Herod Antipas might arrest him before he could challenge the authorities in Jerusalem.

***The chronology of the Galilean ministry.*** Since Mark mentions only one Passover during Jesus's public career, it is often supposed that his entire ministry lasted but a few months, less than one year. True, John mentions two Passovers before the final one, but these references belong to stage III. There are, however, indications of two springs during the Galilean ministry. In Mark 2.23, Jesus's disciples plucked ears of grain, while in the first feeding the crowds sit on the "green grass" (6.39). If we can trust these items and if they do not refer to the same spring, it would permit us to conclude that the Galilean ministry lasted over a year, for the grainfields episode requires that Jesus should have had time to collect a band of followers, and the feeding presumes a longer ministry. According to Luke 3.1, the Baptist's ministry began in the fifteenth year of Tiberius's reign (27 CE). Jesus's baptism could have occurred in that year, his Judean ministry would have covered the intervening period, and the Galilean ministry would have begun in late 27 or early 28 and ended after the spring of 29. But this is highly speculative.

***The journey to Jerusalem.*** John's gospel has obscured the decisiveness of Jesus's final journey to Jerusalem by bringing him to the holy city on two earlier occasions, but these episodes probably belonged to the final Jerusalem period. John may be right, though, in making the Jerusalem ministry last for several months rather than for a single week, as it does in Mark. Indeed, Luke 13.34 offers some support for a longer Jerusalem ministry. This would mean that the journey would have occurred some months earlier than the final Passover, perhaps bringing Jesus to Jerusalem in time for the feast of tabernacles. This would be in the fall of 29 CE.

The purpose of the trip is stated in Mark's three passion predictions (8.31; 9.31; 10.33–34). It is generally agreed that these predictions in their present form are prophecies after the event and therefore reflect a knowledge of the passion story (stage II). But they may well contain an authentic nucleus (stage I), such as "the Son of man will be delivered into the hands of men" (Mark 9.31), where we have an Aramaic play on words (Son of man/men). Jesus hardly went up to Jerusalem in order to die; that, it has been suggested, would be tantamount to suicide. But he may well have realized that death would be the inevitable outcome of his mission.

***The ministry in Jerusalem.*** Jesus continued to preach and teach in Jerusalem as he had done in Galilee. He also engaged in conflicts with his adversaries. These conflicts, Mark indicates, were of a different kind from the earlier ones in Galilee. Jesus is now a marked man and his enemies engage him on specific issues, seeking to entrap him into self-incrimination. John likewise presents Jesus as engaged in theological conflict with the religious authorities in Jerusalem.

Jesus's challenge reached its climax in his entry to Jerusalem and the "cleansing" of the *Temple (so the Synoptics; John shifts the "cleansing" for theological reasons to the beginning of the ministry). It is not at all clear what the precise issues were that led the *Sanhedrin to plot Jesus's execution. The Synoptics attribute the plot against Jesus to the Sanhedrin's reaction to the cleansing of the Temple, while John, less convincingly, attributes it to the raising of Lazarus. Yet John's report of the Sanhedrin meeting seems to be based on reliable tradition: the Sanhedrin decided to get rid of Jesus out of fear that any disturbance of the peace would lead to Roman intervention and destroy the delicate balance between Jewish and Roman power.

On the eve of Passover (following the more plausible chronology of John), Jesus celebrated a farewell meal with his disciples. In the course of it, he interpreted his impending death as the climax of his life of self-giving service. The exact words Jesus spoke over the bread and cup are impossible to recover, since the various accounts of the institution have been colored by liturgical developments in the post-Easter community. But they all agree that Jesus associated the bread with his body (i.e., his person) and the wine with his blood (i.e., the giving of his life in death) and with the inauguration of a (new) covenant. He also assured his disciples that beyond his death lay the coming of the kingdom of God.

After the supper, Jesus and the disciples went out to the garden of *Gethsemane where he was arrested by Temple police, and also, if John 18.3 is correct, by Roman soldiers. This would indicate that the priestly party and the Roman prefect *Pilate were in close collusion over the matter. A preliminary investigation was held before the Jewish authorities. This was not a formal trial, but more like a grand jury proceeding. By this investigation they established to their satisfaction that there was sufficient ground to warrant an accusation of high treason before Pilate's court. There Jesus was condemned to death as a messianic pretender. He was then taken out to *Golgotha and crucified with two criminals who were guilty of sedition. Jesus died later that same day and was buried, according to the gospel tradition, by sympathizers. This marks the end of his earthly career.

***Jesus's self-understanding.*** While Jesus's career evoked messianic hopes among his followers and fears among his enemies, stage I material shows him reluctant to assert any overt messianic claim. The self-designation he uses is "son of man." This is so widely attested in the gospel tradition and occurs (with one or two negligible exceptions) only on the lips of Jesus himself, that it satisfies the major tests of authenticity. It occurs in all primary strata of the gospel tradition (Mark, Q, Special Matthew, Special Luke, and the pre-Gospel tradition in John). It is not attested as a messianic title in earlier Judaism and occurs only once outside the gospels, in Acts 7.56. So there should be no reasonable doubt that it was a characteristic self-designation of the historical Jesus. It is not a title but means "human one," and it is best understood as a self-effacing self-reference. It is used in contexts where Jesus spoke of his mission, fate, and final vindication.

Jesus certainly thought of himself as a prophet, but there was a final quality about his message and work that entitles us to conclude that he thought of himself as God's final, definitive emissary to Israel. He was more interested in what God was doing through him than in what he was in himself. He did not obtrude his own ego, yet his own ego was included as part of his message: "Whoever welcomes you welcomes me, and whoever welcomes me welcomes the one who sent me" (Matt. 10.40 || Luke 10.16 Q); "Follow me" (Mark 1.17; etc.); "Those who are ashamed of me . . ." (Mark 8.38); "Blessed is anyone who takes no offense at me" (Matt. 11.6 || Luke 7.23 Q); "If it is by the Spirit [Luke: "finger"] of God that I cast out demons . . ." (Matt. 12.28 || Luke 11.20

Q). Jesus dared to speak and act for God. This is clear in the antitheses of the Sermon on the Mount (Matt. 5.21–48: "It was said to those of ancient times . . . but I say to you"), in his pronouncement of the forgiveness of sins (which only God could do), his acceptance of the outcast and healing of lepers who were shunned under the Law. Coupled with such features is the tremendous authority with which Jesus spoke and acted, an authority for which he offers no credentials save that it is intimately bound up with the authority of the Baptist and rests upon God's final vindication. Jesus does not claim overtly to be Son of God in any unique sense. Passages in which he appears to do so belong to stage II or III of the tradition. But he does call God "abba" in an unusual way, which points to God's call to which he has responded in full obedience, and therefore we may speak of his unique sense of sonship. But we must bear in mind that in this Palestinian milieu sonship denoted not a metaphysical quality but rather a historical call and obedience. Jesus did challenge his disciples to say who they thought he was, which elicited from Peter the response that he was the Christ or *Messiah. According to Mark, he neither accepted nor rejected Peter's assertion. What did Peter mean, and in what sense did Jesus take it? It is commonly thought that it was meant in a political-nationalist sense and that Jesus rejected this. It seems more likely, however, that Peter meant it in the sense of the anointed prophet of Isaiah 61.1. Such a response to Jesus would have been wholly appropriate as far as it went. What Peter and the other disciples did not realize, of course, was that this mission extended beyond the terms of Isaiah 61 and that it also involved rejection, suffering, and death. It is possible, though much disputed, that Jesus modeled this further insight upon the figure of the suffering servant in Isaiah 53. We could be sure of this if Mark 10.45b belongs to stage I.

A very early tradition (Rom. 1.3) asserted that the earthly Jesus was of a family descended from the royal line of David. We cannot be sure that this played any role in his self-understanding. For the post-Easter community this title was important as qualifying him for the messianic role he assumed after his exaltation.

The use of "Rabbi" and "my Lord" in addressing Jesus during his earthly ministry did not denote majesty: these were titles of respect accorded a charismatic person. However, as the conviction grew among his followers that he was the final emissary of God, these terms would acquire a heightened meaning.

In sum, we find in the Synoptics only limited evidence for an explicit Christology in Jesus's self-understanding, and such evidence as there is is critically suspect. He was more concerned with what God was doing in him than who he was, especially in any metaphysical sense. But what God was doing through him in his earthly ministry provided the raw materials for the christological evaluation of Jesus after the Easter event.

**Person and Work.** ***Introduction: critical presuppositions.*** In reconstructing the New Testament interpretation of the person (Christology) and work (soteriology) of Jesus, we are concerned with the Christian community's response to the Christ event in its totality. This event embraces both his earthly career, culminating in his crucifixion, and also the Easter event, that is, the community's subsequent experiences, the empty tomb, and the appearances, together with their ongoing sense of his presence and the hope of his coming again.

The earliest Christian writings we have are those letters of *Paul that are beyond question authentic, namely, 1 *Thessalonians, *Galatians, 1 and 2 *Corinthians, Romans, *Philemon, and *Philippians. These letters contain formulae that give us evidence of the theology of the pre-Pauline communities. Some of these formulae go back to the earliest Palestinian community, others to the Hellenistic communities (Greek-speaking communities before Paul). In addition, we have the kerygmatic speeches, proclamations of the Christ event, in Acts; though composed by the author of Luke-Acts, they probably enshrine samples of early Christian preaching. Putting the evidence afforded by these materials together, we can form a general idea of the Christologies and soteriologies of the early communities. The letters of Paul provide ample evidence for the apostle's understanding of these matters. We have no other writings that can be said with any certainty to derive from the apostolic age, but there are a number of New Testament writings that, though ascribed to apostolic authors, were probably written in the subapostolic age (i.e., the period from ca. 70 to 110 CE). This would include the "deutero-Pauline" letters, that is, those letters which though ascribed to Paul were with varying degrees of probability written by later writers. Their purpose was to perpetuate Paul's teaching after his death. They consist of 2 *Thessalonians, *Colossians, *Ephesians, and 1 and 2 *Timothy and *Titus. Other writings for this period are Hebrews, together with the catholic letters (James, 1 and 2 Peter, 1, 2, and 3 John, Jude, Revelation), and stage III of the four Gospels.

***The person of Christ.*** The Easter event established in the first disciples the conviction that, despite Jesus's crucifixion, God had vindicated him and his message. The Christ event was indeed God's saving act. The earliest Christians expressed this conviction by ascribing to Jesus titles of majesty, such as Messiah (Grk. *christos,* Eng. "Christ," which was originally a title and is not a proper name), Lord *(kyrios),* and Son of God. Some of the early christological patterns suggest that Jesus was "appointed" Christ, Lord, or Son of God at his exaltation. These patterns are often called "adoptionist," but this is misleading. The meaning is not that Jesus became something he was not before, for example, a divine person; rather, he was appointed to a new office and function, that of being the one in whom God would finally judge and save the world, and through whom he was already offering salvation after Easter in the church's proclamation. Moreover, this type of Christology does not mean that the earthly life of Jesus had no christological or salvific significance. It was not nonmessianic, for God was present and acting in the earthly Jesus. But its messianic significance was initially expressed by a different set of terms, such as the end-time prophet promised in Deuteronomy 18.15. It is notable that the emphasis of these Christologies is on the end of Jesus's career; in short, they are paschal Christologies.

Over time, the titles that were first applied to the post-Easter phase of Jesus's saving activity were pushed back into his earthly life. This was notably the case with the title Son of God. As the story of Jesus's baptism developed in stage II, this title was featured in a heavenly voice ("You are my Son," Mark 1.11), perhaps replacing an earlier use of "servant" in this context. Later in the birth stories, the title Son of God is pushed back to the moment of Jesus's conception or birth. This does not mean that some sort of metaphysical divinity is being ascribed to Jesus. In a Jewish context, it meant that like the kings of Israel Jesus was chosen for a unique role in history. Jesus's conception through the Holy Spirit is not meant to imply any metaphysical quality; it means, rather, that Jesus was a historical person elected from the womb for his unique role through the direct intervention of God.

A similar type of Christology is expressed in the so-called sending formulae. These follow a regular pattern: a verb of sending with God as the subject and the son as the object, followed by a purpose clause stating the saving intention behind the sending. The earliest occurrence of such a formula is: "God sent his Son . . . to redeem those . . ." (Gal. 4.4–5). From such formulae it will be clear that the title "son" denotes a historical person with a saving mission. Notice that, unlike the paschal type, this type of Christology focuses upon the beginning rather than the end of Jesus's career.

In Hellenistic Christianity, a new pattern began to develop in which Christ existed in heaven before his birth. Here is a Christology of preexistence and incarnation. It is generally agreed that this pattern developed from the identification of Jesus with the *wisdom of God. In Judaism, especially in the Greek-speaking world, the notion of the wisdom of God had undergone a remarkable development. Originally it had been no more than the personification of a divine attribute, like God's righteousness or salvation. In the later wisdom literature, however, and in the writings of Philo, the concept of the wisdom or Word (logos) of God developed in the direction of hypostatization—it became the distinct personal entity within the being of God, something like a person in the sense in which that term was later used in the Christian dogma of the Trinity. Wisdom or "Word" was that aspect of the being of God which was God turned toward the world in creative, revelatory, and saving activity.

The ground for this identification of Jesus with the hypostatized wisdom of God was the fact that Jesus himself had appeared as a sage or wise man and had used the speech forms of wisdom literature (see above). He thus came to be regarded not merely as a spokesperson of wisdom but as wisdom's final envoy who acted as the mouthpiece of wisdom. From there, it was but a short step to identify him in person with wisdom itself. This happened first in certain christological hymns (Phil. 2.6–11; 1 Cor. 8.6; Col. 1.15–18a; Heb. 1.3–4; John 1.1–18). In these hymns, the same grammatical subject, usually the relative pronoun "who," governs all the verbs that speak of wisdom's activity before the incarnation, of the activity of the incarnate one in history, and of the exalted one after Easter. Thus, we now have a three-step Christology: (1) wisdom's activity in creation, revelation, providence, and salvation history before Christ; (2) the career of the historical Jesus; (3) the exalted life of Jesus after Easter. Like the sending formulae, this Christology focuses upon the origin rather than the fate of Jesus.

Outside the Fourth Gospel and the Letters of John, this preexistence-incarnation Christology is for the most part confined to hymns. It does not widely affect the christological thinking of Paul, the deutero-Pauline writings, or Hebrews outside the hymns. There are, however, a few exceptional passages where we do see the influence of this type of Christology. When Paul says that the rock that followed the Israelites in the *wilderness was Christ, this implies the identification of Christ with a preexistent wisdom who was active in Israel's salvation history, especially in the exodus. Again, when Paul says that God sent his Son in the "likeness of sinful flesh" (Rom 8.3), the sending formula has apparently been widened to include the idea not just of historical sending but of preexistence and incarnation.

Hebrews also shows the influence of this incarnation Christology when the author applies Ps. 8.5–7 to Jesus's career in 2.6–9, and goes on to say "since, therefore, the children share flesh and blood, he himself [Christ] likewise shared the same things" (Heb. 2.14). There are signs in Hebrews that the three-step Christology is beginning to be integrated into the author's thinking.

It is in the gospel of John, however, that the preexistence-incarnation Christology was fully integrated into the thought of the evangelist. True, the Fourth Gospel does contain earlier materials reflecting the more primitive sending formula (e.g., John 12.44, a pre-Johannine saying with synoptic parallels). There are also passages in John where, like Matthew 11.28–30, Jesus is presented as the spokesperson of wisdom (e.g., John 6.35, 37). This may also have been the original sense of the great "I am" sayings, including John 8.58, which originally was intended not to be a personal utterance of Jesus but of God's wisdom speaking through Jesus. Other parts of the evangelist's stage III materials, however, present Christ as one who was personally preexistent. He came down from heaven. God sent him into the world. He came into the world. At the Last Supper, Jesus prays that he may resume the glory that he had before the world was made. Thus, in the later phases of stage III, John moves beyond the idea of Christ as wisdom's spokesperson to the idea that he is the personal incarnation of the eternal wisdom of God. This doubtless affected the understanding of the earlier sending formulae and the sayings in which Jesus is the spokesperson of wisdom. He is now perceived to be the incarnation of wisdom in person. But never does John call Jesus the wisdom of God; rather, the titles that describe him as such are "son" and, in the prologue, Word (Grk. *logos*). The consequence is that the title Son of God, or son, which had earlier been used functionally to denote historic mission, now acquired a metaphysical sense. We may now properly speak of the divinity, or better, the deity, of Christ. In three instances the Johannine writings actually call Jesus "God" (John 1.18; 20.28; 1 John 5.20). Other instances of this in the New Testament are doubtful on textual or interpretative grounds. When we call Jesus God, it must be carefully nuanced: Jesus is not all that God is. He is the incarnation of that aspect of the divine being which is God going forth from himself in creative, revelatory, and saving activity. In terms of later dogma, he is the incarnation of the Second, not of the First, person of the Trinity.

We may ask what motives propelled Christian writers to such a high Christology within such a relatively short period. The God whose presence had been discerned in the Christ event was the same God they had known all along, the God who created the world, the God who was known in general human experience, and, above all, the God who was known in Israel's salvation history. The Christ event was an experience of recognition. Also creation and salvation were closely related. Salvation was not salvation out of the world but salvation of the world.

***The work of Christ.*** By the work of Christ is meant the saving significance of the Christ event (soteriology). The earliest Christian preaching as recorded in Acts (chaps 2, 3, 10) does not highlight the death of Christ, but speaks of the Christ event in its totality as God's act of salvation. These speeches do feature the death of Christ, but always in the so-called contrast scheme: the death of Christ was Israel's rejection of God's offer, and the Resurrection was God's act of vindicating his offer. Mark's passion predictions, which in their present form belong to stage II, have the same contrast scheme. Yet these passages also state that Israel's rejection of the Messiah was in accordance with God's purpose (Acts 2.23 and the "must" of the passion predictions). It was also explicitly predicted in scripture. Thus, the way was prepared for conceiving the death of Christ not only as Israel's active refusal but also as God's act of salvation.

It was the celebration of the Lord's Supper which appears to have provided the context for reflection on the saving significance of Christ's death. The earliest traditions that do so consist of liturgical materials. First, we have the expansion of the cup word in the Supper tradition itself (Mark 14.24; cf. Mark 10.45b). Here we get for the first time the so-called *hyper*-formula (Grk. *hyper*), which asserts that the death of Christ was for us. Next, the *hyper*-formula appears in creedal or catechetical traditions (1 Cor. 15.4).

Over the course of time, more precise imagery was introduced to interpret the meaning of Christ's death. One pre-Pauline hymn compares the death of Christ and its effects with the ritual of the Day of Atonement. We are "justified . . . through the redemption that is in Christ Jesus, whom God put forward as a sacrifice of atonement by his blood . . . He did this to show his righteousness, because in his divine forbearance he had passed over sins previously committed" (Rom. 3.24–25). "Justify" is a metaphor from the law courts referring to the judge's pronouncement of the verdict "not guilty." This is another way of saying that Christ's death conveyed the forgiveness of sins, an idea that occurs later in the hymn when it speaks of God's "passing over sins." Christ's death is then described as an act of "redemption" (Grk. *apolytrōsis*). Although this word is often thought to derive from the manumission of slaves, it has a more likely background in salvation history. God redeemed Israel by bringing it out of the land of Egypt and by restoring it after the exile, and Israel continued to hope for redemption at the end. The Song of Zechariah announces the fulfillment of this hope. Redemption thus came to denote deliverance from all the ills of history in the messianic age.

Next we have the word translated "sacrifice of atonement" (Grk. *hilastērion*). Its precise meaning is disputed. Some translate it "propitiation," which suggests appeasing or placating an angry deity—a notion hardly compatible with biblical thought and rarely occurring in that sense in the Hebrew Bible. It requires God as its object, whereas in this hymn God is the subject: "whom God put forward." Luther translated it as "mercy seat," an item of the Temple furniture which was sprinkled with blood on the Day of Atonement. But applied to Jesus the metaphor would be confused: Jesus did not cleanse himself through his own blood as the priest did with the mercy seat on the Day of Atonement. Accordingly, the rendering "expiation" is the most probable. In Israelite sacrifices, especially those of the Day of Atonement, sins were expiated, that is, they were covered over or cleansed and thus removed. This seems to give the best meaning in Romans 3.24–25. There is, however, an element of truth in the idea of propitiation, for it calls attention to the fact that sin is not only a defilement but a breach of the human relationship with God. As a result of Christ's saving work, this broken relationship has been restored. The last soteriological term in this hymn is the word "blood." This comes from the cup word in the supper tradition and denotes not a substance but the death of Christ as a sacrificial and saving event. Another early formula is found in Romans 4.25: Christ "was handed over to death for our trespasses and was raised for our justification."

Paul took over these earlier traditions about the saving work of Christ and developed them significantly in two directions. He speaks both of the work of Christ in itself (the objective side) and of the work of Christ in believers (the subjective side). Here we will be concerned with the former, the objective side.

The central term in Paul's soteriology is justification. Together with its cognates, including "righteousness" as applied to God, it occurs some forty-eight times in the undisputed letters. It is the major focus of Paul's arguments in Galatians 3–4 and in Romans 3.21–5.11. It is almost synonymous with reconciliation. This gives it a more personal twist, for reconciliation is a metaphor derived not from the law court but from relationships between persons and between social groups. Thus, justification comes to mean not merely to pronounce not guilty but also to bring into a right relationship with God. Paul tries to explain how this happened. On the cross Christ took upon himself the curse of the Law and endured its consequences. God made his son to be "sin" for us. Christ put himself in the place of sinners, and as the sinless one he exhausted God's wrath against sin, thus making it possible for humanity to enter into a right relationship with God. The metaphor reconciliation also gives a social and cosmic dimension to justification. These dimensions received further emphasis in the deutero-Pauline letters.

Paul occasionally speaks of Christ's death as a sacrifice but only in traditional formulae. He once uses the term "blood" as shorthand for Christ's death as a saving event, in the phrase "justified by his blood" (Rom. 5.9). Otherwise, in the genuine Pauline letters "blood" occurs only in connection with the Lord's Supper.

Christ's death is also regarded by Paul as a victory over the powers of evil, another item that comes from earlier tradition. In speaking about victory, however, Paul is careful to emphasize that the powers, though decisively defeated, await final subjugation at the end. The apostle includes among the powers of evil not only cosmic forces but existential realities like law, sin, and death. This victory-soteriology becomes more important in the deutero-Pauline letters, which abandon Paul's reservation about its present incompleteness. All that remains is for everything to be united (NRSV: "gathered up") in Christ at the end (Eph. 1.10).

In itself, the term "salvation," with its cognates "save" and "savior," is a rather colorless word in the Pauline writings. As with the other words we have studied, its background is found in the Hebrew Bible, where it is applied to the Exodus and to the restoration from exile. Like similar words, it also became part of Israel's hope for the end. Paul uses this word group in an all-embracing way. Believers have been saved, though only in hope; they are being saved; and they will be saved at the end. Once again, the deutero-Pauline letters abandon this reserve and insist that believers have already been saved.

The only New Testament work to develop the doctrine of Christ's saving work is the letter to the Hebrews. This letter makes an elaborate comparison between the levitical high priests and their sacrifices, on the one hand, and Christ and his sacrifice, on the other. The author took up certain items from earlier Christian tradition. One was the comparison of Good Friday with the Day of Atonement, which we have already seen in Romans 3.24–25 (note the expression "sacrifice of atonement"). Another was the supper tradition with its language about blood and covenant. Yet a third theme, that of Christ as high priest after the order of *Melchizedek, was suggested by Psalm 110, which led the author on to verse 4.

In developing his argument, the author of Hebrews had first to prove that Jesus was qualified to be a high priest despite his lack of levitical descent. Then, in the central part of his work, he compares Jesus and his sacrifice point by point with the levitical high priests and their sacrifices, demonstrating at every point the superiority of Jesus and his self-offering. As the comparison with the Day of Atonement shows, Christ's sacrifice is not confined to his death but includes also his ascension into heaven. For the action of the priest in taking the blood of the victim into the Holy of Holies was an essential part of the ritual, in which the slaying of the victim was only a preliminary. Thus, Christ's sacrifice was completed only when he entered into the presence of God and sat down at his right hand. Henceforth, Christ lives to make intercession for us.

How does the author of Hebrews understand Christ's sacrifice to be effective in taking away sin? He follows the biblical belief that sin is a ritual defilement that can be cleansed only with the blood of a victim. Yet he points beyond a merely cultic interpretation of this imagery when he observes that Christ's death was the offering of a perfect obedience of his human will. On the strength of his perfect obedience, believers too can draw near to God's presence and offer the sacrifice of praise that leads to the obedience of a holy life.

The author of 1 Peter takes over the earlier tradition that compared Christ's sacrifice to that of the Passover lamb. In a remarkable hymnlike passage (1 Pet. 2.21–25), the author describes Christ's passion in terms of the suffering servant of Isaiah 53. Christ's sufferings are to serve as the example for Christian slaves to follow. This treatment of the death of Christ as an example is characteristic of the moralism of the subapostolic age.

We turn now to the treatment of the death of Christ in stage III of the four Gospels. Each evangelist presents the death of Christ from his own perspective. For Mark, the death of Jesus was the occasion for the unveiling of the messianic secret. Only at the crucifixion could he be publicly acknowledged as the Son of God. Mark was probably countering the view that overemphasized the miracles as revelations of Christ's deity. The miracles are important to Mark but only as prefigurations of the supreme act of salvation on the cross.

For Matthew, the cross was Israel's rejection of the Messiah. Because of it, God's judgment came upon the nation at the fall of Jerusalem in 70 CE. A new nation, the Christian church, would arise in Israel's place. Meanwhile, Matthew emphasizes the saving significance of the cross by adding to the cup word at the supper the phrase "for the forgiveness of sins" (Matt. 26.28).

For Luke, the death of Jesus at Jerusalem and his consequent assumption into heaven constituted a major turning point in salvation history, inaugurating the new period of the church and its universal mission. This period would be covered by the book of Acts. Luke is wrestling with the problem created by the delay in Christ's second coming. The time of the church will be marked by persecution and martyrdom, and Christ's passion is presented as an example for Christian martyrs to follow, such as Stephen in Acts 6–7.

John seems to shift his interest away from the cross to the revelation that Jesus brings in his earthly life. The death of Jesus seems to be no more than the occasion when he returned to the Father from whom he came. But this is to underestimate the importance of Christ's death in the Fourth Gospel. The words and works of Christ are all overshadowed by the hour of the passion. The signs or miracles point to what Christ would finally accomplish on the cross. It is there that he brings in the new order symbolized by the changing of the water into wine. It is there that he makes his flesh available for the life of the world, that he cures the blindness of human life, and that he confers eternal life. It is also in the cross that all the claims made in the great "I am" sayings are substantiated. It is because of the cross that he is the true bread that comes down from heaven, that he is the light of the world, the door of the sheep, the good shepherd, the resurrection and the life, the way, the truth, and the life, and the true vine. Moreover, it is through the cross that the Spirit-Paraclete is released which leads the Johannine community into all truth. Thus it was the death of Christ and his glorification that made it possible for the Fourth Gospel to ascribe the "I am" sayings to Jesus.

Despite the apparent preoccupation of the author of Revelation with the events leading up to the end and with the new heaven and the new earth that lie beyond, the cross for him plays a crucial role in salvation history. The central christological image in Revelation is the Lamb that was slain. In the cross, the Lamb has conquered and taken his seat beside the Father on the throne of heaven. Because of that victory, the Lamb alone is qualified to open the scroll and its seven seals. In other words, his victorious death determines the future course of history. It becomes clear that the cross is the central and controlling event of the whole book. Meanwhile, Christ has "ransomed" believers "from every tribe and language and people and nation, and . . . made them to be a kingdom and priests serving our God" (Rev. 5.9–10). *Reginald H. Fuller*

**JEW.** The English word "Jew" is derived from Hebrew *yĕhûdî* (fem. *yĕhûdît*, "Judith"), meaning "Judean," by way of Greek *ioudaios* and Latin *judaeus.* The term is first used of citizens of the southern kingdom of *Judah in 2 Kings 16.6; previously, male inhabitants of the kingdom, or of the tribe of Judah from which the kingdom took its name, were referred to as *ʾîš yĕhûdâ,* literally "man [men] of Judah." As a consequence of the exile of many members of the upper classes of Judah by the Babylonians in 597 and 587/586 BCE, many Jews were forcibly settled in Mesopotamia. Others, including the prophet Jeremiah, fled to Egypt. This was the beginning of the Jewish *dispersion, or Diaspora, across the globe, which continues to this day. After the exile the term Jew came to be used for all descended from or identified with this ethnic or religious group, whatever their race or nationality. Thus, in Esther 2.5, Mordecai is identified both as a Jew and as a member of the tribe of *Benjamin. The term "Jew" thus began to parallel the much more ancient designation "Israelite."

The Jews who returned from exile after 538 BCE settled in the Persian province of Yehud, which eventually became the Roman province of Judea and preserved its name until it was suppressed by the Romans in reaction to Jewish revolts of 66–73 and 132–135 CE.

In the New Testament "Jew" can designate both Jesus and many of his followers, as well as some of his adversaries. However, the rivalry between Christianity and Judaism, coupled with the often uncomplimentary portrait of Jews in the New Testament and the similarity in sound to the name of Judas, often made the word *Jew* pejorative in the Christian world.

The question of how to define a Jew, put more simply as "who is a Jew," has engendered much discussion through the ages. Are the Jews to be understood as a social, religious, national, or ethnic community? Basically, the answer of the Jewish tradition, the *halakhah,* has been that one born of a Jewish mother or one converted to Judaism is a Jew. But this definition has been challenged in recent years. The murder of many of Jewish descent who, however, were not halakhically Jewish during the Holocaust has raised questions regarding inclusion and exclusion in the Jewish community. The high court of Israel, in the Brother Daniel Rufeisen case, has ruled that an apostate from Judaism cannot apply for automatic citizenship as a Jew under the Law of Return. And in recent years the American Jewish Reform movement has attempted to redefine the term *Jew* to include, in addition to converts, anyone of Jewish descent, whether that descent be matrilineal (the halakhic position) or patrilineal (excluded by *halakhah*), who practices Judaism and identifies himself or herself as a Jew. A strict definition is therefore impossible to reach. *Carl S. Ehrlich*

**JEZEBEL.** Princess of Tyre who married *Ahab, king of Israel (mid ninth century BCE). Jezebel was the daughter of Ethbaal, king of Tyre ("Sidonians" in 1 Kings 16.31 is a biblical term for *Phoenicians in general); according to genealogies given in Josephus and other classical sources, this would make her the great-aunt of Dido, the founder of Carthage. Jezebel was an ardent worshiper of *Baal and *Asherah who supported their worship from the throne in Israel; her name is best understood as meaning "Where is the Prince?," the cry of Baal's divine and human subjects when he is in the underworld. Jezebel exercised royal prerogatives to acquire Naboth's vineyard for her husband by plotting to have Naboth executed. This incident prompted *Elijah to predict that dogs would eat Jezebel's corpse in Jezreel. *Jehu, the commander of King Joram's army in Israel, was anointed king in Ramoth-gilead in order to destroy Ahab's house because of what Jezebel had done to the prophets and the faithful of Yahweh. When Jehu met King Joram, son of Ahab and Jezebel, to kill him, he remarked that there could be no peace in Israel while the "whoredoms [=apostasy] and sorceries" of Jezebel continued. After killing Joram of Israel and King Ahaziah of Judah (Ahab and Jezebel's grandson), he went to Jezreel to kill Jezebel. Adorned like a queen, she appeared to him in a window, regally defiant in the face of his violence. She was thrown out of the window by her own attendants, who sided with Jehu, and was trampled to death.

Jezebel's sons and daughter also ruled. Ahaziah was king of Israel for two years after Ahab died and Joram succeeded him. Jezebel and Ahab's daughter Athaliah married Jehoram of Judah, and was the mother of Ahaziah, king of Judah. When her son was killed by Jehu, Athaliah set out to kill all his heirs, and she herself ruled for six years.

Jezebel later becomes an insulting epithet for a woman, and is used in Revelation 2.20 of a prophet in Thyatira of whose teaching and practice the author disapproves.

*See also* Queen and Queen Mother.

*Jo Ann Hackett*

**JOB.** The hero of the book that bears his name. Originally a charracter in folklore, in the biblical book Job is from Uz, probably in northern Arabia. He is thus apparently a non-Jew, indicative of the universal issues that the book addresses. Neither his wife nor his original ten children are named in the book (see Names for the Nameless).

The book of Job is an extended discussion of one theological issue, the question of suffering. Its chief literary feature is that it does not expound or defend a dogma from one point of view, but portrays a debate in which conflicting points of view are put forward, none of them unambiguously presented as preferable. In design the book has both the form of an unsophisticated prose narrative, which nonetheless contains intriguing surprises, and that of a series of subtle speeches in poetry of great delicacy and power. The interplay between prose and poetry, between näiveté and rhetorical finesse, mirrors the interplay among the six participants in the book: Job, the four friends, God—and the narrator.

In the first part of the narrative framework, or prologue of the book (1.1–2.13), Job is introduced as a perfect and perfectly pious person, and a wealthy one as well. His family is large, and while his three daughters apparently still live at home, his seven sons each have their own homes, where they host gala celebrations for their siblings. The scene abruptly shifts to the divine council, the meeting of the "*sons of God," one of whom is the "*satan." In his role as presider, Yahweh initiates the proceedings by questioning the satan about his servant Job. The satan shrewdly observes that Job's piety is linked to his prosperity, and challenges Yahweh to strike Job down. Yahweh delivers Job into the satan's power.

The third scene returns to Job. All the children are in their oldest brother's house, but the narration is localized with Job; in the manner of a Greek tragedy, four messengers in succession describe the loss of Job's livestock and the annihilation of his children. Marauding bands of Sabeans and Chaldeans cause the first and third disasters, but the second and fourth are of divine origin: fire from heaven and a great wind from the eastern desert. This pattern mirrors the shifts in locale of the prologue as a whole. Job's reaction to the disasters is pious resignation and praise of Yahweh; his uprightness endures.

Without transition the scene returns to the court of Yahweh. Once again, Yahweh calls Job's piety to the satan's attention, and once again, the satan questions its depth. If Yahweh will strike Job's person, then Job will curse him. So this time Job himself is stricken, with a terrible skin disease. Nevertheless, despite his wife's bitter suggestion, he refuses to speak impiously.

Finally, three friends of Job, Eliphaz the Temanite, Bildad the Shuhite, and Zophar the Naamathite, arrive to console him. Even from a distance, the sight of the stricken patriarch is horrible. The friends mourn and in silent sympathy sit with Job for a week.

The poetic core of the book (3.1–42.6) is a series of dialogues, first between Job and his friends, and then between Yahweh and Job. In the first set, Job complains bitterly about his suffering, and ultimately challenges God to explain why this has happened to him. His friends rehearse the clichés of tradition: God rewards goodness and punishes wickedness, and if Job is suffering, it must be deserved. All that Job has to do is confess his sins and ask for divine mercy, and his troubles will be over. Job passionately reiterates his case: despite his innocence, God has unjustly turned against him, and he demands a hearing.

Toward the end of the dialogues, the alternating pattern of speeches breaks down, and there are what appear to be later additions to the original book, including a set of speeches by a previously unmentioned fourth friend, Elihu, in chaps. 32–37.

Finally, in chaps. 38–41, Yahweh does speak to Job. In magnificent poetry, he catalogues the wonders of creation, over which no human can exercise control, and in derisive rhetorical questions reminds Job of human fragility and ignorance. In his final speech (42.1–6) Job apparently capitulates. The prose framework resumes with an epilogue in which Yahweh rebukes the three original friends for not having spoken correctly and restores Job's fortunes, including his children.

The earliest reference to Job outside the book is found in Ezekiel 14.14, 20, where Job is mentioned along with *Noah and Danel (probably not Daniel; *see* Daniel) as an ancient hero. But this sixth-century reference may well be not to the book of Job but to the more ancient folktale that underlies the prose framework. In later traditions it is the Job of this framework who is generally remembered, as in the admonition of the letter of James to imitate the "patience of Job" (James 5.11 [KJV]).

*David J. A. Clines, Michael D. Coogan*

**JOEL.** A prophet to whom is attributed the book that bears his name. We know nothing about the person of Joel (whose name means "Yahweh is God") other than that he is identified as the son of an equally unknown Pethuel. All the knowledge that we can derive about him and his times comes from the examination of his prophecy.

In both the Hebrew and the Greek canons of the Bible, the book of Joel appears in proximity to that of the eighth-century BCE prophet *Amos, a circumstance that is easily explained by the close correspondence between Joel 3.16–18 and Amos 1.2; 9.13. There can hardly be any doubt that this correspondence is the result of the dependence of the text of Joel on that of Amos; from internal evidence it seems clear that the book of Joel is the work of a late postexilic prophet who was indebted for his images and metaphors to the much older prophetic traditions to which he laid claim and in which he presumed to participate.

Joel is much concerned with the proprieties of the Temple worship, a trait that connects him very closely with the anonymous prophet *Malachi, who was possibly one of the very last to appear in the Judahite prophetic tradition. This trait, however, was by no means characteristic of preexilic prophecy of either Israel or Judah. Joel presupposes, therefore, the existence of a Temple—presumably the Second Temple of *Zerubbabel, which came to be in the aftermath of the initial return from exile following the liberating decree of *Cyrus the Persian after his defeat of the Babylonian empire in 539 BCE. Furthermore, contrary to the picture drawn in the preexilic Deuteronomic history of Israel and Judah, so much concerned with kings and politics, and even contrary to that of the Chronicler's depiction of the period of *Ezra and *Nehemiah (ca. 458–443 BCE), when Judah and Jerusalem, still under the domination of the Persian empire, were regaining a relative political autonomy with a secular (although concomitantly religious) leadership of native governors (like Nehemiah), Joel's text seems to presuppose a polity not unlike that presupposed by *Sirach or the book of *Judith, where it is taken for granted that the political leadership of the *Jews has, by default, devolved upon the high priesthood. Since there is no hint of a disruption in Joel of this peaceful coexistence between religion and alien domination, we are probably not far off the mark when we assign this work to the latter stage of the Persian period of Palestine, which was disrupted only by the conquests of *Alexander the Great beginning in 333 BCE. These considerations would date Joel about 400 BCE.

The book of Joel consists of two sharply distinguished parts. There is, first of all, the graphic and highly descriptive depiction of a locust plague and a drought (the Hebrew vocabulary for "locusts" is virtually exhausted in 1.4) that descends on Judah and Jerusalem, demanding of everyone, class by class, profession by profession, repentance and prayer as the price of the Lord's continual toleration of a recalcitrant people. In the second part (2.28–3.21 [3.1–4.21 in the Hebrew Bible]), the Day of the Lord is announced in apocalyptic language. There is a series of salvation prophecies: Judah and Jerusalem will be restored, Israel will triumph over her enemies, and the gentiles will be requited for their misdeeds.

Is Joel a prophet of judgment (against Israel) or of salvation (of Israel in the face of its gentile enemies)? It is really difficult to say. Was the locust plague of the first verses an attempt to describe a real happening, as in Amos 7.1–3, or is it merely a literary device borrowed from the text of a prophetic predecessor? Is this plague a cloak for physical invasion of Israel or simply a symbol of national disintegration? Is the lifting of the plague potential or real? How much and to what extent is the repeated "Day of the Lord" intended to apply to Israel's future destiny and its relation to the gentile world? Whether Joel is to be considered a "cult" or "nationalist" prophet, a prophet of "judgment" or of "salvation," are questions that truly indicate that we have not yet fully comprehended the phenomenon of Israelite prophecy. *Bruce Vawter, C.M.*

**JOHN THE APOSTLE.** The apostle John, the son of Zebedee and brother of *James, one of the *twelve. John and his brother were in the fishing business with their father. After their call by *Jesus, they became, together with *Peter, Jesus's closest followers. John was present along with Peter and James at the Transfiguration and in the garden of *Gethsemane. This special position seems to have caused some envy among Jesus's other followers. Jesus gave John and his brother the nickname "sons of thunder" (Mark 3.18).

After Jesus's death, John was one of the leaders of the church in Jerusalem, along with Peter and James the brother of Jesus. Later Christian traditions report that John subsequently lived at *Ephesus in Asia Minor, where he died of natural causes at an advanced age, and identify John as the author of the Gospel According to John, the Letters of John, and the book of Revelation.

**The Gospel According to John.** ***Structure and Content.*** The story of Jesus in John's gospel is presented as a drama, consisting of a prologue, two main acts, and an epilogue. By considering the gospel in this light, its distinctive character may be understood and its teaching illuminated.

The prologue (chap. 1 as a whole) introduces the main theological themes developed in the body of the gospel, such as "life," "light," and "glory." It also includes the leading characters who are to be involved in the main action. *John the Baptist is there, and so are the disciples who will form the nucleus of the early Christian community: *Andrew and *Peter, Philip and Nathanael. But the stage is dominated by the central character of Jesus himself, whose identity begins already to be disclosed, for in this single chapter he is described as Word, Son, Christ (*Messiah), Son of God, King of Israel, and Son of man. The climax of the prologue is reached in 1.51 ("you will see heaven opened, and the angels of God ascending and descending upon the Son of man"). Jesus, as the incarnate and exalted Son of man and Son of God, joins earth and heaven decisively together and makes it possible, even in this world, for every believer to share the life of eternity.

Act I (chaps. 2–12) describes the revelation of the Word of God to the world. For those with eyes to see, Jesus during his ministry reveals through his words and actions the glory of God the Father. To demonstrate this truth, John makes his own selection from the miracles, or "signs," that Jesus performed and narrates six of them dramatically. To these six signs are attached explanatory discourses, all of which deal with the leading theme of "life" through Christ, and several memorable "I am" sayings, which act as a text for each sermon.

Act 2 of John's drama (chaps. 13–20) deals with the glorification of God's Word for the world. At its heart is the story of the passion and resurrection of Jesus, prepared for by the farewell address to the disciples, a discourse that deals with the life of the believer.

The drama ends with an epilogue, chap. 21, which may have been written later but is now firmly related to the body of the gospel. This final section narrates the seventh sign, the catch of 153 fish, and the recalling of Peter. Together these incidents point to the unlimited scope of the Christian good news, an idea retained throughout John's gospel, and provide an agenda for the church of the future. The mission of the disciples to the world can now begin on the basis of the revelation and glorification of the messianic Word of God.

Throughout his dramatic portrayal of the ministry, death, and exaltation of Jesus, John is anxious that readers should "see" the identity of the central character as Christ and Son of God (20.29–31) and "hear" his words. Verbs of seeing and hearing are important in John and are close in meaning to the activity of believing. As in a courtroom, witnesses are called throughout the drama to bear testimony to the life-giving Christ; and the sources of this evidence are divine (the Father, 5.37; the Spirit, 15.26; the scriptures, 5.39) as well as human (John the Baptist, 1.29–36; the Samaritan woman, 4.29, 39–42; the blind man, 9.35–38; Martha, 11.27; and, supremely, *Thomas, 20.28).

John thus moves beyond the witness of the other gospel writers in exploring the nature of Jesus in relation to God and humanity, and the grounds for Christian belief and for the spiritual life that is its consequence. Jesus, in John's portrait, is both one with the Father and one with his church on earth.

***Origin.*** We have already noted that John's gospel is a literary unit, which may be analyzed in terms of its dramatic structure. But, despite the unity of the gospel as we now have it, there are some features that suggest it was composed in edited stages. What follows is a suggested description of those stages.

First, John the apostle, who was traditionally identified as the "beloved disciple," transmitted orally to his followers an account of the deeds (especially the miracles, or "signs") and sayings of Jesus and of his death and resurrection. As we have already seen, these reminiscences preserved historical information about the ministry of Jesus in both Judea and Galilee.

Second, the beloved disciple and his circle of followers moved to *Ephesus (a city associated, by strong tradition, with John), where the nucleus of the Johannine church was established. While there, John's disciples committed to writing the traditions preserved in their community for the purposes of worship and instruction. In this first draft of the final gospel what may now be recognized as distinctively Johannine thought emerged, as the ideas handed on by the apostle were dramatically treated and theologically developed by the fourth evangelist and his colleagues.

Third, after the death of John his church at Ephesus published a final edited version of the gospel. This included a summary introduction (1.1–18), based on a community hymn and now tied securely to the remainder of the chapter, some editing of the discourses, possibly the addition of the prayer of consecration in chap. 17, and an epilogue (chap. 21). The whole gospel thus assembled then carried an authenticating postscript (21.24–25).

***Date.*** Even if the Johannine tradition may be dated to the early first century CE, this still leaves open the question of the date of the gospel's publication in its final form. An upper limit may set at 150 CE or a little earlier. Two manuscripts, written on papyrus and discovered in Egypt, are relevant to dating the gospel. One, known as the Rylands Papyrus, contains a few verses of John 18 and may be dated to 135–150 CE. A second papyrus (Egerton 2) includes part of an unknown gospel that probably used John as well as Mark, Matthew, and Luke; this manuscript dates from ca. 150 CE. The existence of these witnesses suggests that John's gospel must have been written at the very latest by the beginning of the second century CE, and probably earlier.

**The Letters of John.** ***Situation.*** The three letters in the New Testament that bear the name of John form a composite unit. Although each possesses individual features, all have common characteristics of style, language, and thought and appear to belong to the same situation.

1 John, in contrast to 2 and 3 John, does not at first look like a personal letter. But it was evidently addressed to a particular church situation, in which problems of belief and behavior were being encountered. Indeed, a crisis had arisen, precipitated by some members of the Johannine circle who were spreading false teaching and encouraging secession from the community. As a result, dissident groups had already been established. In the face of division, John (as we may for convenience call the writer[s] of these three epistles) composed a "letter" that was designed to correct the inadequate and erroneous views of his readers and to recall them to the fundamental elements in the apostolic gospel.

The plea for love and unity, however, evident in both the Fourth Gospel and

1 John, seems not to have been widely heeded. The divisions in the community, already apparent when 1 John was written, deepened; and from 2 John we learn that "many deceivers" had gone back into the world. Perhaps these were predominantly docetic in outlook, although, again, there is nothing in the Johannine letters to suggest that docetism is the only tendency in view.

By the time 3 John appeared, the unity of the Johannine circle seems to have been threatened from an organizational, as well as doctrinal, point of view. Diotrephes was "putting himself first" and excluding orthodox members from the church, and the writer's concern that the influence of such leaders should not increase suggests that he feared the final dissolution of the Johannine community. What actually happened we can only guess. Some of the group presumably went further into gnosticism; the Jewish secessionists may have returned to Judaism, while the orthodox adherents no doubt became absorbed into the life of the great church. At that time John's gospel, with the discussion of its doctrine provided by 1 John (supplemented by 2 and 3 John), came into its own, and the teaching of John's circle was finally secured for the cause of orthodoxy.

***Authorship.*** The identity of the author of the Johannine letters is a matter of considerable debate and raises the issue of the relationship between these documents and both the gospel and Revelation of John. The following scheme, which attempts to take account of all the relevant data, is only one solution to the problem.

The inspiration behind the tradition and distinctive theology of the Fourth Gospel came from John the apostle, the beloved disciple, himself. In 70 CE he wrote Revelation in order to encourage the members of his community to remain steadfast in the faith. Some of his followers later undertook the final publication of the gospel. A leading Johannine Christian (who may possibly have been involved in the composition of John's gospel) in due course wrote 1 John. An *elder, close to the author of 1 John (or possibly the same person), was then responsible for 2 and 3 John.

All the Johannine documents in the New Testament are associated in some way, even if at times the links between them seem tenuous. That association is probably best accounted for by tracing their origin to a specific community, gathered in some way around John the apostle. Whatever answers are given to the question of authorship, therefore, the origin of the letters (as of the other parts of the Johannine literature) can well be assigned ultimately to an authoritative, apostolic tradition.

***Date and Place of Origin.*** There are conflicting opinions among scholars about when and where the Johannine letters appeared. Assuming that 1, 2, and 3 John followed the gospel of John, the letters of John may be dated to the last decade of the first century CE. This allows time for a sharpening of the heterodox opinions within John's circle and for the first moves on the part of the secessionists.

Although some scholars have suggested Syria as the place of publication, the view that 1, 2, and 3 John were addressed to Johannine communities in Asia Minor, with their center in *Ephesus, is more probable. This is the traditional setting for the birth of John's gospel; it could easily have produced the controversy with Judaism and Hellenism that may be detected in both the Johannine gospel and the letters; and its religious syncretism would readily have nurtured the tendencies in the situation behind the letters.

**The Book of Revelation.** ***Content.*** The book calls itself an apocalypse or revelation, which Jesus gave, for his servants, through his angel to John, but it begins in letter form, "John to the seven churches that are in Asia, grace to you and peace" (1.4), and ends like a Pauline letter with the "grace" (22.21). The risen Christ appears to John on the island of Patmos, off the coast of the Roman province of *Asia, and orders him to write to the *seven churches (chaps. 2–3); the messages warn the complacent and the worldly, and encourage the faithful. Summoned up into heaven, John sees God enthroned, holding a sealed scroll no one can open. He hears that the lion of the tribe of *Judah has won the right to open it, and he sees standing by the throne a lamb bearing the marks of sacrificial slaughter.

The Lamb's opening of the seals unleashes the first of three series of disasters, which represent God's wrath against an idolatrous and impenitent world: seven seals opened, seven trumpets blown, and seven bowls poured out. Symbolic visions in between depict the opposing forces in cosmic war, which comes to a climax in chap. 19: the Lamb and the 144,000 who bear his name and God's seal, over against the seven-headed beast, Satan's emissary (the *Antichrist), and those who bear his mark. The beast's city, *Babylon, the "great whore," is destroyed, the beast is defeated, *Satan is bound and the saints reign for a thousand years (the millennium), until Satan is released for his final assault. Then follows God's judgment of the world, and a new heaven and earth replace the old. The holy city, *Jerusalem, the bride, comes down from God, and all earth's splendor is gathered into it.

***Recipients.*** At first sight, John is writing to seven particular congregations; many other cities in the Roman province of Asia are known to have had Christians. But seven is the number symbolic of wholeness, and these churches probably represent the whole church. The seven cities were all centers of communication, set on a circular route beginning at Ephesus, the nearest to Patmos. The writer knows the geography and traditions of each city, and clearly is acquainted with the circumstances of each church. But the particular warnings and encouragements add up to a message for all the churches, and he claims divine authority for his book.

***Author and Sources.*** Irenaeus and most later writers assumed that the author was the John who wrote the Gospel and letters, and that he was the son of Zebedee. But some, like Dionysius of Alexandria (third century), anticipated the majority of modern scholars by questioning this identification because of differences of thought, style, and language. Dionysius relied on hints that there had been two writers named John in Ephesus; and Papias (ca. 140 CE) mentions a John who was an *elder, as well as the apostle.

Another possibility is that Revelation is pseudonymous, claiming a great figure of the past as author, like much other apocalyptic literature. There is a later tradition that the apostle John was martyred as his brother James had been; as one of the inner circle, associated as he was with Jesus at the Transfiguration and on the Mount of Olives, he would have been a good figurehead for an apocalypse calling Christians to face martyrdom. If it was published ca. 95 CE, its later acceptance as genuine could have given rise to the widely held belief that John lived to a great age in Ephesus.

But the evidence for John's martyrdom is flimsy, and if "John" is a fiction, it is odd that no capital is made out of it;

the author is simply "your brother," and mentions the twelve apostles of the Lamb without hint that he is one of them. The only status he claims is, by implication, that of *prophet. This tells also against genuinely apostolic authorship, but not decisively; and Dionysius's comment concerning differences in thought and style may be due to differences in situation and genre; there are also many marks of Johannine theology and expression.

The whole book purports to be what John has seen and heard, but it is clear that his visionary experience has been shaped both by canonical and apocalyptic writings. There are allusions to or echoes of practically every book in the Hebrew Bible. Probably it is a mixture of genuine experience and literary elaboration. Revelation is a rereading of biblical tradition in the light of the death of Jesus, and though no doubt Jewish, the author is also a citizen of the Greco-Roman world and knows its myths and astrology.

*Stephen S. Smalley, John Sweet*

**JOHN THE BAPTIST.** If John was born of priestly parentage, he must have abandoned the priesthood and taken up an ascetic mode of life in the Judean wilderness, where he subsisted on locusts and wild honey. Those who came out to him encountered a man dressed in camel-hair homespun with a leather belt around his waist, the explicit garb of a prophet. With prophetic zeal he preached a new message and offered a new rite. The message was that lineal descent from *Abraham would not guarantee salvation. Abraham's merits would not suffice, but only an act of repentance that included the renunciation of all presumptions based on election or ethnicity. The God that had called Israel out of Egypt and led it across the *Jordan River was now creating a new people by passing them through the waters of baptism in that same river. The twelve stones that had been set up to mark Israel's crossing of the parted Jordan would themselves be raised up into twelve new tribes if the people of Israel would not repent. John was not founding a new religion but attacking the use of all religiousness as a defense against the demand of God for authenticity and justice.

This message of radical repentance was enacted in a rite of immersion in which the sin of presumption and the whole of one's old life were washed away. Those who rose out of the waters were as newborn infants, or as those who had passed from death to life, having been buried and raised from the dead. These later Christian interpretations seem to have carried forward at least Jesus's own understanding of what John was about, for he spoke of his own baptism not as an event in the past but as a metaphor for his own approaching death.

John himself may have shared the idea, common in that period, that the last judgment would be enacted by a river of fire through which everyone would have to walk. In anticipation of that imminent judgment, John was inviting one and all to submit to God's judgment now, and by undergoing baptism to cleanse themselves of sin now, in advance of that terrible day. Those who had surrendered themselves to this washing would be preserved through the coming tribulation. They would be wheat gathered into God's granary, while the rest would be chaff burned in unquenchable fire.

John's message fell on Israel like fire on stubble. The Gospels report that "all" went out to hear him, and Josephus comments that he was highly regarded by the whole Jewish people. The crowds that attended him included tax collectors and *prostitutes. This simple act of immersion, unlike circumcision, made salvation accessible even to women. It was John, not Jesus, who opened a way to God for those who before had felt themselves excluded. And by his dress and diet, even by the metaphors he chose (a tree cutter, a thresher), John identified himself, and the one whom he awaited, with the lowly.

Judaism had never encountered anything quite like this, yet virtually everything recorded of John had parallels in *Isaiah. These parallels include the following: an eschatological outpouring of the Holy Spirit associated with the wilderness; a spirit-endowed one to come who will act as judge; Israelites as children of Abraham; unfaithful Israel portrayed as a brood of vipers or as trees that God will hew down with an axe; wind/breath/spirit (Hebr. *rûaḥ*), and fire compared to a river in which one is immersed; Israel as the threshed and winnowed one; Israel washed clean; and works of righteousness mandated subsequent to washing.

Despite such extensive parallels, John burst on the scene as a virtual mutant, for his rite of baptism, though outwardly similar to Temple lustrations, was wholly without precedent in its meaning. Nowhere in any Jewish source is rebirth made a metaphor for redemption. One is born a Jew. *Proselytes might be "reborn" as Jews, but proselyte baptism was not practiced in the first century CE, applied only to non-Jews, lacked an eschatological setting, and did not require running water. John's rite was so unique that he was named by it ("the Baptizer"), and Jesus clearly regards it as given to John by revelation from God. It circumvented the Temple and its rites; perhaps John's rejection of the priesthood is related to widespread revulsion against the corruption of the Temple and its priesthood in the first century CE.

John's presence in the wilderness has suggested to some that he might have at one time belonged to the community at *Qumran, possibly even being raised by them as an *orphan (his parents were elderly at his birth). Both John and the settlers at Qumran glowed with eschatological fervor, expecting an imminent judgment and preparing for it in the wilderness. Both called on all Israel to repent, denying that mere Jewishness could save. Both used washings, broke with the Temple cultus, taught prayer and fasting, and focused on Isaiah as their guide to the future. But these qualities seem to have been shared by other sectarians who had located in the wilderness. The Jerusalem Talmud indicates that twenty-four such distinct sects had come into existence by 70 CE (*Sanh.* 29c). And much of what John and Qumran held in common derives from Isaiah.

In key respects, moreover, John was quite different from the community at Qumran. They wore white linen; he dressed like the *poor, in homespun. His disciples did not settle a community but wandered about with him. John required no three-year period of probation but accepted whoever came, and they returned home rather than remaining with him in the wilderness. He was prophetic, public, missionary, inclusive; Qumran was exclusive, secretive, and withdrawn. His opening of salvation to prostitutes, tax collectors, and sinners must have scandalized that sacerdotal sect. Qumran's ethic applied only to its own community; John's was addressed to the entire nation, even the king. He called not for the communal sharing of goods but for sharing with the wretched who had nothing. Instead of demanding that his hearers abandon lives of moral ambiguity and move to the desert, John offered an ideal attainable in society by people unable to abandon everything. John's baptism, unlike Qumran's washings, was not daily, but once for all, and was not intended to achieve levitical purity, but to secure the forgiveness of sins in anticipation of the coming day of wrath. Even their common use of Isaiah 40.3 was different. Qumran interpreted it to mean that the preparation for the Lord's way was to be done in the wilderness by moving there and studying scripture. John seems to have understood the wilderness only as the place where the voice cries out. And Qumran expected a prophet, a messiah of Aaron, and a messiah of Israel; John expected only a coming judge different from all three.

The evangelists each employ the traditions about John in the service of the proclamation of Jesus. Each handles him differently, but all see him as the one who stands at the beginning of the gospel story, demanding of the hearer a beginner's mind and the jettisoning of all previous securities, so that a new word can be heard. *Walter Wink*

**JONAH.** The antihero of the book of Jonah is mentioned in 2 Kings 14.25 as a prophet of salvation during the expansionistic era of Jeroboam II. The choice of this prophet as the target of didactic satire is doubly appropriate, first because he proclaimed nationalistic oracles on behalf of Israel and second because his name means "dove [of faithfulness or truthfulness]." The author wrote a short parable characterized by fantastic events to poke fun indirectly at a little man whose inner thoughts remain virtually hidden. Although certain similarities exist between this story and the prophetic legends of *Elijah and *Elisha, a greater kinship is with 1 Kings 13, which involves an unnamed prophet. Neither Jonah nor this unnamed man of God is intended for emulation; hence the term "legend" is not entirely appropriate.

The book of Jonah resembles later midrash, for it interprets biblical texts explicitly and implicitly. In each instance the issue is the nature of Jonah's God: Is divine mercy a more powerful attribute than justice? Can the deity actually repent? Does God's preference to grant life rather than death extend beyond Israel's borders?

Jonah's resistance to the divine call exceeds the usual reluctance, exemplified by *Moses, *Amos, and *Jeremiah. When Yahweh calls Jonah to go to *Nineveh to preach, Jonah disobeys and actually flees by sea. There he is thrown overboard and swallowed by a fish, from which he escapes after three days and nights. After the deity has shown him the futility of his ways, he carries out the task with a vengeance. Then he resents the sparing of repentant Ninevites and argues that justice ought to prevail, although he has experienced undeserved compassion. This picture of Israelite prophecy is not flattering, for Jonah is unrepentant to the end. Furthermore, his manipulation of the facts in answering the sailors renders the prophet suspect and extols their superior ethics. When he does resort to prayer, Jonah exalts the ego and uses the occasion to accuse God. He is also spiteful, hoping that the sailors' repentance will be short-lived, and he eagerly awaits the destruction of Nineveh.

The strange behavior on Jonah's part is given a rationale from sacred tradition. Jonah quotes Exodus 34.6, the cultic confession that the Lord is both compassionate and just, as the reason for his flight from the divine presence. This conscious reflection on the nature of God offers a decisive clue to the purpose of the book. The conflict between Jonah and God concerns theodicy. Is it fair for the wicked inhabitants of Nineveh to escape the deity's wrath by repenting of their sins? Linguistic features link Nineveh and the cities *Sodom and Gomorrah, a comparison in which the Israelites could concur because of the suffering inflicted on them by Assyrian hordes. Nevertheless, the object lesson involving a fast-growing plant that perished just as quickly offers a justification for God's repentance. The closing question addressed to the sulking prophet throws into relief divine compassion for all creatures in Nineveh.

The author may have had more than one purpose. The great prophets had predicted the destruction of foreign nations, but these oracles had failed to come true. Were the prophets false? No, this book suggests, for the Assyrians gained time by repenting. Again, from the perspective of several prophets, Israelites were entirely unrepentant. How could the nation escape God's wrath? By turning from their evil ways and evoking the Lord's pity. Is it too late for that? No, for God is so eager to save them that repentance even by the wicked Ninevites would result in forgiveness. Although the portrait of Israelite prophecy is troubling, the radical self-criticism goes a long way toward redeeming the profession.

*James L. Crenshaw*

**JORDAN RIVER.** The major river in ancient Palestine, linking the two major inland lakes of Kinneret (the Sea of *Galilee) and the Dead Sea (also known as the Salt Sea). The principal source of the Jordan is the precipitation on Mount *Hermon and the three springs near Tel Dan, Banias, and Hasbaya. In antiquity some of the headwaters of the Jordan River flowed through the Huleh Valley, a lake until modern times, which is some 985 ft (300 m) higher than the Sea of Galilee; this rapid drop in elevation, which continues farther south, probably explains the river's name (from Hebr. *yāarad,* "to go down"). These sources combine near the northern edge of the Huleh Valley, and from that point the river is called the Jordan.

The river flows out of Kinneret at its southern tip, possibly an artificial outflow; 6 mi (10 km) south the Jordan is joined by its main tributary, the Yarmuk. Another tributary from the east is the Jabbok, in the Wadi Zarqa, 35 mi (56 km) farther south. The Jordan valley receives virtually no direct rainfall south of the Yarmuk. The total annual flow of the river into the Dead Sea, another 600 ft (194 m) lower than the Sea of Galilee, is 3 billion gal (1.2 billion $m^3$) of water. Despite this volume, the Jordan River has rarely served as a source of irrigation. The river bluffs of the flood plain of the Rift Valley (Arabic *Ghor*), which line both sides of the Jordan, are 1,500–3,000 ft (500–1,000 m) wide and constantly crumbling and rise at least 60–150 ft (20–50 m) above the river bottom. These factors constitute a serious impediment to irrigation, since the technology of pumping is fairly recent. The flood plain (Arabic *Zor*) is called "pride of the Jordan" (NRSV: "thicket").

Because of the intense heat of the Rift Valley and the availability of moisture from the Jordan along its river banks, much of the vegetation there has the characteristic of a tropical jungle, which is typical of regions as far south as the Sudan. One plant that grows freely there is the papyrus. In addition there is much tamarisk and *spina Christi* on the river banks. In antiquity it was a haven for many wild animals, including lions. The river is fairly narrow and easy to cross, though the current is often swift.

Much of the importance of the Jordan River in the Bible derives from the fact that it assumes so central a place in the geographical nomenclature. It forms a natural boundary, so that *Moab is "beyond the Jordan" and hence the Israelites must cross the Jordan in order to enter the *Promised Land. Although Israel often controlled territory east of the Jordan, the Jordan forms a natural eastern border, and Ezekiel's idealized nation is entirely to its west. Jesus is reported to be baptized at "Bethany across the Jordan." It is thus both as a primary water source, especially in the northern Ghor, and as a central feature of the Palestinian landscape that the Jordan River derives its importance.

*Eric M. Meyers*

**JOSEPH (HUSBAND OF MARY).** According to the opening chapters of the gospels of *Matthew and *Luke, *Mary, the mother of *Jesus, was engaged before his birth to Joseph, son of Jacob or of Heli. Matthew's infancy story is written largely from Joseph's point of view, even narrating his receiving messages from *angels in his dreams. These dreams portray his struggle to determine how to deal justly with his fiancée's unexpected pregnancy and how to respond to threats against the infant Jesus.

Matthew and Luke agree in their genealogies of Jesus that Joseph was a descendent of King *David. These genealogies imply that Joseph was in some way Jesus's father. Joseph is gone from the scene when the Gospels describe Jesus's adult life, though he was apparently remembered by those around Jesus as his father and as a carpenter. The gospel of Mark makes no mention of Jesus's father, and calls him instead "Mary's son." The second-century *Protevangelium of James* provides additional information of a legendary character. Later Christian tradition comes to view Joseph as an elderly widower, so that the "*brothers and sisters of Jesus" in such passages as Mark 6.3 could be understood as Joseph's children from a previous marriage, not his children with Mary; later, he came to be seen as a saintly ascetic with no interest in sex, and Jesus's siblings as "cousins."

*Philip Sellew*

**JOSEPH (SON OF JACOB).** Joseph, whose name means "May God give increase," was the son of *Jacob and *Rachel, and the eponymous ancestor of the house of Joseph, one of the twelve *tribes of Israel. Genesis 37–50 portrays Joseph as a patriarch through whom the promises to *Abraham, *Isaac, and Jacob are transmitted to later Israel. The God of the ancestors is not, however, called the God of Joseph, and Joseph the patriarch is seldom mentioned in the Bible outside Genesis.

The Joseph story begins in Genesis 37.1, "Jacob settled in the land where his father had lived as an *alien, the land of Canaan," and comes to its preliminary end in 47.27, where the opening formula is transformed, "Thus Israel settled in the land of Egypt, in the region of Goshen." Its unity comes not from a single theme, but from sophisticated art, narrating the interaction of the human characters; God's direct action is hardly mentioned.

The story begins with the young, self-centered Joseph announcing to his father and brothers his double dreams of their obeisance to him. The doubling of his dreams here and later proves their divine origin. Joseph later goes out to visit his brothers who are caring for their father's flock, apparently a rare event since he does not even know where they are camped. As he comes upon his brothers, they decide to kill him, but at the intercession of Reuben and Judah, he is spared; he ultimately falls into the hands of traders who sell him to the Egyptian Potiphar, captain of the guard. His brothers, however, tell Jacob that his son is dead, and offer as evidence his blood-stained garment, a preferential gift from his father (traditionally, although probably erroneously, translated as "a coat of many colors"). As if to indicate the passing of time and to build suspense about Joseph's fate, chap. 38 tells the story of Judah, the ancestor of the southern kingdom, a counterbalance to Joseph, the ancestor of the northern kingdom. Chap. 39 opens with Joseph as overseer of Potiphar's house. Even in prison, to which he is unjustly condemned, God protects him. His ability to interpret dreams brings him to Pharaoh's notice. He interprets Pharaoh's dream correctly as seven years of plenty and seven years of famine, and he is put in charge of preparing for the seven years of famine. That famine causes Jacob to send all his sons but *Benjamin (the other son of his beloved Rachel) to Egypt to buy grain. In the first visit of his brothers, Joseph tests them by treating them roughly, holding Simeon as hostage, putting their money back in their grain sacks, and demanding that they return with Benjamin on their next visit. Joseph, the cool courtier, wants to learn his brothers' attitude toward him, his full brother Benjamin, and their father. The second visit of the now uneasy brothers is even more eventful: Joseph surprises them by seating them at a banquet according to the order of their birth, Benjamin is arrested on a ruse, and, finally, Judah as spokesman for the group expresses the pain the family disunity has caused. Joseph, by now emotionally drawn into the family's crisis, reveals himself to his brothers, acknowledging that God, despite the selfish behavior of the family members, "sent me before you to preserve life" (45.5). The last chapters narrate Jacob's blessing of his grandsons *Ephraim and *Manasseh, his testament, his death, and Joseph's final days.

At one level, chaps. 37–50 explain how the sons of Jacob got to Egypt through the agency of Joseph. On a deeper level, the chapters tell movingly how God kept a disintegrating family united by the repentance and restraint of its members. The lesson is an important one for Israel because its unity is often threatened by the claims of one tribe against another.

The tribe of Joseph is divided into the tribes of Ephraim and Manasseh. "House of Joseph" may designate the northern kingdom as distinguished from the southern kingdom of Judah, or it may designate all Israel.

In the New Testament, Hebrews 11.22 lists Joseph as a hero of faith; Stephen in his speech summarizes his career in Acts 7.13–17. Some have seen in Mark's episode of the youth who left his cloak behind an echo of Genesis 39.11–12. Among noteworthy modern retellings of the Joseph story is Thomas Mann's *Joseph and His Brothers.*

*Richard J. Clifford*

**JOSEPH OF ARIMATHEA.** Unanticipated, Joseph enters all four passion narratives to request Jesus's body from Pilate to entomb it. Mark 15.43–46 depicts a respected council member awaiting the reign of God. His Joseph buys a linen cloth, removes the body from the cross, wraps and buries it, and rolls the stone against the tomb. Possibly a disciple, he adheres to commandments concerning burial. Matthew's "rich disciple" displays higher righteousness by placing Jesus's body in his own new tomb. Luke's "good and righteous" Joseph (23.50–53) explicitly dissents from the council's action against Jesus, and John's Joseph, paired with the Pharisee Nicodemus, hides his discipleship for fear of the Jews. Apocryphal writings variously present Joseph as caring for *Mary after the Ascension, as the patron of Glastonbury, England, and as involved in the Grail saga. *Amy-Jill Levine*

**JOSHUA.** The son of Nun and the protagonist of the book of Joshua. Joshua is first mentioned in the narratives of the events following the Exodus, where he appears as *Moses's assistant. As such, he leads the battle against *Amalek, accompanies Moses up Mount *Sinai, and is the custodian of the tent of meeting. In the narrative of the spies (Num. 13–14), Joshua and Caleb are the only spies who bring back a favorable report, and they are exempted from the punishment that none of the generation of the Exodus will be permitted to enter the *Promised Land. As Moses's life nears its end, Yahweh instructs him to appoint Joshua as his successor, and at Moses's death the divine commission is affirmed.

The book of Joshua is a narrative that reports how Joshua, following the death of Moses, led the people of Israel in occupying the Promised Land, apportioned it to the twelve *tribes, and led them in the renewal of their covenant with Yahweh. In terms of the present arrangement of the biblical books, it continues the story begun in Genesis and brings to full circle the traditions of the Pentateuch, recording the fulfillment of the promises to the *ancestors reported in Genesis 12–50. At the same time, the book of Joshua is the second major section of a Deuteronomic history, the account of Israel's past that includes the books of Deuteronomy through 2 Kings.

This pivotal literary position has affected the portrait of Joshua. He is presented as the ideal leader of Israel, in the pattern established by Moses, leading an Israel united both in war and in exclusive worship of Yahweh. In various ways, the life of Joshua is shown to parallel that of Moses: as Moses led the people through the sea, Joshua led them across the *Jordan River, and both men led the people in the establishment and renewal of the covenant with their God. Moreover, like Moses, Joshua sends spies into the land, intercedes with Yahweh for Israelites who have offended God, and delivers a lengthy address just before his death. Joshua is also the prototype of the ideal king, who, like *David, *Hezekiah, and especially *Josiah, keeps the law of Moses, and a foil to Israel's first king, *Saul, who unlike Joshua violated both the rules of holy warfare and the oath made with the Gibeonites.

The result of these and other parallels is that it is difficult to determine to what extent the figure of Joshua is historical. Most of the individual stories in Joshua 1–12 relate to events in a single region, that of the tribe of *Benjamin and the area near Gilgal, an old sanctuary. What at first glance is an account of the conquest of the entire land turns out to concern the occupation of a small region, with a focus on the cities of *Jericho, Ai, and Gibeon. It seems very likely, then, that the traditions of the tribe of Benjamin and of the sanctuary at Gilgal formed an old collection that became the core of other stories. Joshua himself may have been a local hero, like many of the *judges, and was probably from *Ephraim, as Joshua 24.30 suggests. Like the era in which he lived, he has been magnified and idealized by the Deuteronomic historians in their presentation of the history of Israel in the land.

*Michael D. Coogan, Gene M. Tucker*

**JOSIAH.** King of *Judah (640–609 BCE). His reign is described in 2 Kings 22.1–23.30. He became king at the age of eight after the assassination of his father, Amon, and is hailed as the most faithful of Judah's kings.

Because of the decline of the *Assyrian empire, Josiah was able to promote the interests of Judah during his reign. He is praised by the biblical writers primarily for his religious reform, in which he sought to eliminate all non-Yahwistic practices and sanctuaries in Judah. Although the reform may have begun several years earlier, its major impetus was the discovery of "the book of the law" (thought to be the law code of Deuteronomy) in 621. Some scholars also believe that an early edition of the books of Joshua–Kings (the Deuteronomic history) was compiled in conjunction with this reform to reinforce Josiah's measures.

In 609, Pharaoh Neco of Egypt marched through Judah on his way to Carchemish to fight alongside the *Assyrians against *Babylon. Josiah intercepted the Egyptians at *Megiddo, where he was killed. His religious reform was abandoned after his death.

*Timothy M. Willis*

**JUDAH, THE KINGDOM OF.**

**The Tribe of Judah.** The tribe of Judah, which occupied the hill country between the vicinity of *Jerusalem and *Hebron, plays a minor role in the biblical narratives that pertain to premonarchic times. In the book of Judges, for example, there are only occasional mentions of Judah, and this tribe seems to have been very much on the fringe of *Saul's kingdom. Judah comes into prominence, however, with David's rise to power, *David himself being a Judean from the village of *Bethlehem. Before conquering Jerusalem and transferring his residency there, David ruled over a kingdom centered at Hebron and consisting primarily of the tribe of Judah. Later, the tribal territory of Judah was to be the core of the southern kingdom, which remained loyal to the Davidic dynasty following *Solomon's death.

Thus the name "Judah," like the name "*Israel," is used in different ways in the Bible. It can refer to the eponymous ancestor of the tribe of Judah (Judah is the name of the son of *Jacob and *Leah), to the tribe itself, and to the kingdom of Judah, which covered more extensive territory and included peoples of other tribal origins. These distinctions are not always clear in the biblical story. For example, the tribal boundaries and cities recorded for the tribe of Judah in the book of *Joshua actually represent the ideal territorial extent of the kingdom of Judah. Likewise, the biblical genealogies tend to subsume under Judah various other southern tribal groups, such as the Calebites, which became constituents of the kingdom of Judah (*see* Tribes of Israel).

**David's Judean Kingdom.** David gained popularity as a *Philistine fighter under Saul's command. Later he broke with Saul and led a rebel army that operated along the frontier of Judean territory. First we hear of David and his men camped at Adullam (1 Sam. 22.1–4). When Saul learned of their presence there, David and his followers moved to the barren slopes of the hill country southeast of Hebron. Apparently, they received little support from the local population in either area; on the contrary, the villagers reported their whereabouts to Saul on more than one occasion.

Eventually, David found it necessary to move to Philistine territory, where he placed himself and his army under the command of Achish, the Philistine king of Gath. Thus it happened that David was allied with the Philistines when they defeated Saul's army at the battle of Gilboa, the battle at which Saul and Jonathan lost their lives. Saul's Israelite kingdom was left on the verge of collapse and without leadership. The crown fell to Ishbaal (Ishbosheth) who, realizing that the whole central hill country was now vulnerable to Philistine encroachment, moved his residency (and accordingly the administrative center of the kingdom) to Mahanaim, east of the Jordan. Thereupon David, presumably with Philistine approval, occupied the city of Hebron and its surrounding villages. His kingship over the region was formalized when "the people of Judah came [to Hebron] and there they anointed David king over the house of Judah" (2 Sam. 2.4).

Thus, for the next seven years, according to 2 Samuel 5.4–5 and 1 Kings 2.11, David ruled over a kingdom centered in the hill country south of Jerusalem, composed largely of the tribe of Judah, with Hebron as its capital. David's realm of influence expanded rapidly during these years of rule from Hebron, so that by the time he conquered Jerusalem and moved his residency there, the tribe of Judah was only one constituent part of the kingdom. This was to remain true throughout the reign of Solomon. Among other constituent elements of the Davidic-Solomonic kingdom, for example, were the Israelites.

**The Post-Solomonic Kingdom of Judah.** Following Solomon's death, the Israelites rebelled and established an independent kingdom of "Israel." No doubt, many of them understood this as a restoration of the old Saulide kingdom. The people of Jerusalem and of the southern hill country, however, remained loyal to the Davidic dynasty, specifically to Solomon's son, Rehoboam, who was next in line for the throne. While Rehoboam continued to rule from Jerusalem, his realm of authority consisted essentially of the area that David had ruled from Hebron, that is, the old tribal territory of Judah and immediately adjacent regions—the southern hill country, the "wilderness" region between the hill country and the Dead Sea, some of the *Negeb, and some of the Shephelah. Not surprisingly, this post-Solomonic kingdom came to be called Judah, even though its territory and population extended well beyond those of the tribe of Judah.

This post-Solomonic kingdom of Judah remained in existence for almost three and a half centuries, from Solomon's death in approximately 925 BCE to the destruction of Jerusalem in 587/586 BCE. During the first two hundred years of this period, the kingdoms of Israel and Judah existed side by side, sometimes at peace, sometimes at war; and for much of this time, during the Omride period for example, Judah was overshadowed by, and possibly subject to, Israel.

The article in this volume on "Israel" summarizes key political developments during the two centuries that the two kingdoms existed alongside each other. The following summary covers some of the same material, but focuses on Judah and extends to the destruction of Jerusalem in 587/586.

***Unstable beginnings (ca. 924–855).*** Rehoboam was left with a small and weak kingdom. Hostilities with Israel, whose frontier was only about 10 mi (17 km) from Jerusalem, would have drained his resources even more. As if that were not enough, the Egyptian pharaoh Shishak raided Palestine during the fifth year of Rehoboam's reign. Rather than challenge Shishak, Rehoboam paid a heavy ransom from the Temple treasury.

Apparently, Shishak's raid was a temporary episode with no lasting effect. The hostilities with Israel continued for four decades, however, through the reign of Rehoboam's grandson, Asa (ca. 905–874). 1 Kings 15.16–24 reports that Asa negotiated an agreement with Ben-hadad, the Aramean king of *Damascus, which called for an Aramean attack on Israel's northern border. With Israel's king (Baasha, ca. 902–886) thus distracted, Asa secured his own northern frontier with fortifications at Mizpah and Geba.

***In the shadow of the Omrides (ca. 885–843).*** Under the Omride rulers during the second quarter of the ninth century, Israel emerged as a powerful kingdom. *Jehoshaphat of Judah (ca. 874–850) was roughly contemporary with the two most outstanding of the Omride kings, Omri and *Ahab; and the biblical records suggest that he was an unwavering supporter of their military undertakings; probably he had little choice. Moreover, the two royal families were joined by the marriage of Jehoshaphat's son Jehoram (ruled ca. 850–843) to Omri's daughter (or granddaughter; compare 2 Kings 8.18 with 8.26). When the Omride dynasty fell, therefore, in approximately 843 BCE, there were significant political repercussions in Judah as well.

The circumstances are described in horrible detail in 2 Kings 8.28–10.27. On an occasion when Israel's troops were defending northern Transjordan against Aramean encroachment, *Jehu, commander of the troops, assassinated the king of Israel (also named Jehoram, a son of Ahab), seized the government, and massacred the whole Omride family. Ahaziah, who by that time had succeeded Jehoram son of Jehoshaphat to the throne in Judah, also was assassinated, while visiting his Omride relatives in Israel.

***A century of instability and decline (ca. 843–745).*** Jehu's coup initiated a period of hard times in both Israel and Judah. In fact, all of Syria-Palestine seems to have been dominated for the next four decades by the Aramean kings of Damascus. Judah was troubled as well with dynastic instability. After Ahaziah, who had been assassinated in connection with the Omride massacre, the next three Judean rulers (Athaliah, Joash, and Amaziah) were each executed or assassinated.

Athaliah, the Omride *queen mother, seized the throne for herself at Ahaziah's death and ordered the execution of all others in Judah who could possibly have any claim to it. Her own downfall and execution, after seven years of rule, resulted from a palace coup orchestrated by a priest named Jehoiada. Joash, whom Jehoiada placed on the throne in her stead, was a seven-year-old child, supposedly a son of Ahaziah who had escaped the bloodletting at the time of his father's death. Not surprisingly, Joash was much influenced during the early years of his reign (ca. 837–?) by Jehoiada and the Jerusalem priests. Later, however, as Joash reached adulthood and especially after Jehoiada died, he began to exert more independence over the priests. Eventually he too was assassinated, apparently by persons in the royal court.

By the time that Amaziah, the son of Joash, ascended the throne (sometime near the end of the ninth century BCE), the Aramean domination of Syria-Palestine had begun to relax. Once again, conflict erupted between Israel and Judah, with Israel overwhelmingly victorious. Not only was Amaziah unable to defend his frontier against Jehoahaz of Israel, but Jehoahaz captured Jerusalem, destroyed a large section of the city wall, and took royal Judean hostages to *Samaria. Soon thereafter, Amaziah was assassinated by his own countrymen, and Judah probably remained essentially a vassal to Israel through the reigns of Uzziah and Jotham.

Dates for the Judean kings of this period are impossible to establish with any degree of precision. Uzziah and Jotham would have lived during the latter part of the eighth and first part of the seventh centuries BCE respectively. The prophets *Amos and *Hosea also belong to this period, as does the early career of *Isaiah.

***Assyrian domination (ca. 745–627).*** Judah, along with all the other little city-states and kingdoms of Syria-Palestine, succumbed to Assyrian domination during the latter half of the eighth century BCE. Unlike Israel, however, whose national existence came to an end at that time and whose territory was annexed by the *Assyrian empire, Judah survived for another quarter of a century after the Assyrian empire itself collapsed. This does not mean, however, that Judah continued to enjoy any significant degree of independence. On the contrary, *Tiglath-pileser's Palestinian campaigns in 734–732 left Judah a subject nation, and this situation remained essentially unchanged until the fall of Jerusalem in 587/586. When *Hezekiah and certain other allied kings dared to challenge Assyrian domination during the reign of *Sennacherib (705–681), the attempt failed miserably, and numerous Judean cities and villages were destroyed. Jerusalem itself narrowly escaped destruction, which was regarded as a miracle. The prophets Isaiah and *Micah were active during these years of Assyrian domination.

***Egyptian domination (627–605).*** Although the specific circumstances are not well known, it seems that the Assyrians and Egyptians established an alliance during the latter years of the Assyrian empire. As the Assyrians began to relax their grip on Syria-Palestine, the Egyptians tightened theirs. Specifically, Judah seems to have been subject to Egypt from approximately the end of the reign of Ashurbanipal (668–627 BCE) until the battle of Carchemish in 605. This was the political context of *Josiah's cultic reform, his execution by Pharaoh Neco, and *Jeremiah's early career.

***Babylonian domination and the end of the kingdom of Judah (605–587/586).*** The *Babylonians, by defeating the Assyrians and their Egyptian allies at the battle of Carchemish in 605 BCE, became masters of Syria-Palestine as well as of Mesopotamia. Unfortunately, the Judeans persisted in challenging the new master, which resulted in the end of their kingdom. Jehoiakim (605–598) died while Jerusalem was under Babylonian siege. Jehoiakim's son Jehoiachin was on the throne when the city fell in 597 and was exiled to Babylon with many other prominent Judeans. The Babylonians placed *Zedekiah on the throne; when he too proved disloyal, they conquered Jerusalem again, sacked the city, sent many more Judeans into exile, and placed one Gedaliah in charge of the region.

The exact status of Gedaliah, who resided at Mizpah, is unclear—whether he was regarded as a vassal king or as a military governor over annexed territory. Apparently he was not, however, of the Davidic family; soon he was assassinated by a nationalistic group who presumably wished to restore the Davidic line. Very little is known about the situation in Palestine in the aftermath of Gedaliah's assassination, but certainly by this time Judah had ceased to exist as a kingdom.

**The Hasmonean Kingdom of Judah.** Mention should be made finally of the revolt of the *Maccabees against the Seleucid rulers during the second century BCE. Not only was the revolt successful in throwing off the Seleucid yoke, but it resulted in a Judean kingdom with Jerusalem as its capital, lasting for a century—from the Maccabean recovery of Jerusalem in 164 BCE to Pompey's eastern campaigns in 64–63 BCE. Ruled by the Hasmonean dynasty, the family of Judas Maccabeus, this kingdom included virtually all of Palestine when it reached its greatest territorial expansion under John Hyrcanus I (134–104 BCE) and Alexander Janneus (103–76 BCE).

*J. Maxwell Miller*

**APPROXIMATE CHRONOLOGY OF THE KINGS OF ISRAEL AND JUDAH**

Saul, David, and Solomon lived ca. 1000 BCE. The following dates may be regarded as accurate within ten years for the earlier kings and within two years for the later ones.

| JUDAH | ISRAEL | JUDAH | ISRAEL |
|---|---|---|---|
| Rehoboam (924–907) | Jeroboam I (924–903) | Jotham (?–742) | |
| Abijam (Abijah) (907–906) | | | Shallum (745) |
| Asa (905–874) | Nadab (903–902) | | Menahem (745–736) |
| | Baasha (902–886) | Jehoahaz I (Ahaz) (742–727) | Pekahiah (736–735) |
| | Elah (886–885) | | Pekah (735–732) |
| | Omri (885–873) | Hezekiah (727–698) | Hoshea (732–723) |
| Jehoshaphat (874–850) | Ahab (873–851) | | *Fall of Samaria* (722) |
| Jehoram (850–843) | Ahaziah (851–849) | Manasseh (697–642) | |
| Ahaziah (843) | Jehoram (849–843) | Amon (642–640) | |
| Athaliah (843–837) | | Josiah (639–609) | |
| Joash (Jehoash) (837–?) | Jehu (843–816) | Jehoahaz II (609) | |
| Amaziah (?–?) | Jehoahaz (816–800) | Jehoiachin (608–598) | |
| | Joash (800–785) | Jehoiachim (598–597) | |
| Uzziah (Azariah) | Jeroboam II (785–745) | Zedekiah (597–587/586) | |
| | Zechariah (745) | *Destruction of Jerusalem* (587/586) | |

**JUDAS ISCARIOT.** Judas Iscariot is mentioned only in the Gospels and Acts. The name Iscariot probably means "man from Kerioth" (a village in southern Judea) because "from" is used with the name in John and because similar names occur in Josephus.

Only in John is Judas called Simon's son, and Simon is also Iscariot. So was the name Iscariot given to Judas or to his father or to both? Only John says that Judas was "a thief" and "kept the common purse" (12.6; 13.29). Unlike the *synoptic Gospels, John does not mention the kiss to indicate the one whom the authorities sought.

Judas was remembered for his betrayal of Jesus, an incident on which the sources agree. The motives for Judas's behavior cannot be precisely determined. Mark and Luke report that Jewish authorities promised Judas money for his action, but Matthew says that they paid him thirty pieces of silver immediately, a particular derived from the Hebrew Bible. Judas repented, returned the money, and hanged himself. The authorities used the money to buy the "Field of Blood," but Acts 1.18–19 reports that Judas himself bought the field with his blood money and that he died as the result of a fall when "all his bowels gushed out." According to Acts 1.16, 20, his end was predicted in Psalms 69.25 and 109.8.

According to John 13.18, Jesus chose Judas deliberately so that the scripture might be fulfilled by his betrayal. John agrees with the Synoptics that at the Last Supper Jesus predicted his betrayal by Judas; but John, unlike the Synoptics, does not leave the identity of the traitor in doubt, since "the devil had already put it into the heart of Judas . . . to betray him." Luke also attributes Judas's action to Satan's influence.

Accounts of Judas are varied, inconsistent, and influenced by theological opinions of the writers, the belief in the fulfillment of scripture, and the idea that God brings death to ungodly persons. It is therefore difficult to assess the historicity of Judas and his action. Why, for example, does Mark not mention the name of Judas in the story of the traitor? Yet all sources list him among Jesus's disciples and know him as Jesus's betrayer. Perhaps as tradition grew the name of Judas became more infamous and the details of his demise more appalling.

*Edwin D. Freed*

**JUDE.** An apostle, one of the *twelve and brother of Jesus. Jude is identified by ancient tradition as the author of the letter of Jude, which was written to an unknown church or group of churches to combat the danger posed by certain charismatic teachers who were preaching and practicing moral libertinism. The author seeks to expose these teachers as ungodly people whose condemnation has been prophesied, and he urges his readers to maintain the apostolic gospel by living according to its moral demands. Despite its brevity, the letter is rich in content, owing to its masterly composition and its economy of expression, which at times achieves an almost poetic effect.

Most scholars are agreed that the Jude (a shortened form of Judas, the author's actual name, which few English translations use because of the association with *Judas Iscariot) to whom this letter is attributed is Judas the brother of Jesus. This identification is strongly implied by the phrase "brother of James" (v. 1), which distinguishes this Judas from others of the same name by mentioning his relation to *James the brother of the Lord (*see* Brothers and Sisters of Jesus). A majority of modern scholars think the letter is pseudepigraphical, written by a later

Christian who attributed his work to Jesus's brother, but a strong case for authenticity is made by others, who point to features that may place the letter in the context of Palestinian Jewish Christianity.

The author evidently had great respect for the book of *Enoch, quoted in vv. 14–15 and echoed elsewhere. V. 9 refers to an apocryphal text no longer extant, perhaps the lost ending of the Testament of Moses. The use of such literature may locate the letter in a Palestinian Jewish context, in which these works were highly valued. Other indications that point in the direction of Palestinian Jewish Christianity as the milieu in which Jude wrote are his exegetical methods, his dependence on the Hebrew text of the Bible rather than its Greek translation (the Septuagint), his emphasis on the importance of ethical obligation rather than doctrinal orthodoxy, and his apocalyptic outlook, which expects the parousia in the near future. Some scholars therefore regard Jude as a relatively early work that affords a rare glimpse of early Jewish Christianity. But many other scholars date Jude relatively late (up to ca. 120 CE) and consider it an example of the post-Pauline development of early Christianity represented by such works as the Pastoral letters and Luke-Acts. *Richard J. Bauckham*

**JUDGES.** The judges are the tribal heroes who led Israel during the late second millennium BCE, between the death of *Joshua and the establishment of the monarchy. According to the book of Judges, under Joshua's strong and effective leadership, the *tribes of Israel enjoyed unity and success. No leader comparable to Joshua took his place, with the result that the unity of the tribes was broken: apostasy soon followed, then military defeat. Israel was faithful to Yahweh during Joshua's lifetime; after his death it fell away. Because Israel turned to other gods, it placed itself in mortal danger. The stories of the judges show how a number of tribal heroes were able to ward off this danger—but only for a time. The book of Judges is a collection of stories about these heroes; the chronological sequence of the stories is certainly artificial, and the fact that the total number of heroes is twelve also suggests editorial design.

The stories about the savior-judges portray them as heroes who led single tribes or groups of tribes in military campaigns in order to liberate Israel from periodic oppression by its enemies. Their rule was temporary. They led certain tribes in a specific military campaign and then, after the military threat was removed, they returned home. None of the judges succeeded in gaining the allegiance of all the tribes. They held power briefly and the area under their effective control was limited. In the present framework, however, these stories receive greater significance. They are not simply tribal sagas about famous heroes of the past; they have become testimonies to the power of Yahweh, who frees Israel when it repents and calls out for deliverance.

The predominant motif in these stories is Yahweh's deliverance of Israel through the judges. The judges are charismatic leaders upon whom has come the "spirit of Yahweh" (Judg. 6.34; 11.29; 14.6,19; 15.14). This spirit enables them to accomplish what is apparently beyond their natural abilities. In Gideon's story, this receives special emphasis through the narrative about his call (Judg. 6.11–23).

The first of the judges was Othniel, whose portrait (Judg. 3.7–11) is rather ill-defined, though it follows the Deuteronomic pattern that is the interpretive framework of the book as a whole: Israel sinned by worshiping the gods of Canaan; God gave Israel into the hands of its enemies for a time; the people repented and God raised up a warrior to deliver them; then Israel had rest for forty years. The story about Ehud (Judg. 3.12–30) is a coarse Benjaminite saga about one of that tribe's ancient heroes who outwitted and then killed Eglon, king of *Moab. There is no narrative connected with Shamgar but only the statement that he "delivered Israel" (3.31).

The story of the prophet *Deborah and the commander Barak is told in both prose and poetry. The poem of Judges 5 is known as the Song of Deborah and is the most authentic literary source from the period of the judges, probably composed a short time after the victory it celebrates. The story of Deborah and Barak exposes the conflicts that took place when the Israelite tribes that originally settled in the largely unoccupied highlands attempted to make their way into the more fertile and therefore more populated valleys. The tribal forces led by Deborah and Barak defeated a Canaanite army and secured the Esdraelon Valley for Israel. Archaeology has shown that Taanach was violently destroyed about 1125 BCE, when *Megiddo was occupied.

The story of *Gideon (Judg. 6.1–8.35), also known as Jerubbaal, describes the fear with which Israelite farmers lived. There was the constant danger of having their harvest stolen by raiders. Gideon defeated the *Midianites, whose raids threatened the Israelite population in central Canaan, but he refused the offer of kingship that the grateful tribes made. Gideon's son Abimelech, however, was quite different; he became king of *Shechem. Abimelech was not really a judge but served as commander of the tribal militia. His story (9.1–57) describes the folly of the monarchy. When the people of Shechem withdrew their support from him, Abimelech did not hesitate to turn his army against them. The remains of ancient Shechem (Tell Balatah) give evidence of a violent destruction in the twelfth century BCE. Abimelech's story was recounted by those who considered the monarchy an infringement upon the rights of Yahweh.

Following Abimelech's story, there is a short note about Tola and Jair (Judg. 10.1–4). They are credited with no military exploits. The lack of any information about their activities stands in marked contrast with the stories about the exploits of the savior-judges. The two mentioned here, along with three others cited in Judg. 12.8–15, had some type of judicial and administrative authority during the period before the monarchy and therefore were known as judges; because details of their activity are so scant, they are sometimes called "minor judges." Later their title was given to military heroes whose exploits are recounted in the major portion of the book; these are the "major judges."

The story of Jephthah (Judg. 10.6–12.7) shows that social class posed no barriers to exercising leadership within the Israelite community at this period; Jephthah was a son of a *prostitute. He led a mercenary army in the north and was called by the *elders of Gilead to deal with the *Ammonites. Jephthah is remembered for the sacrifice of his daughter to fulfill a vow and for his use of the password *shibboleth* during a civil war with the tribe of Ephraim.

Before the stories about Samson begin, there is another note about three judges who engaged in no military exploits but who, like Tola and Jair, were famous tribal leaders: Ibzan, Elon, and Abdon (Judg. 12.8–15).

*Samson hardly fits the figure of a judge. His stories (Judg. 13.1–16.31) do not describe leadership he provided for the Israelite tribes against their enemies; rather, they recount a series of personal battles he fought with the *Philistines. None of Samson's adventures have anything to do with the fate of Israel as a whole; he led no organized military campaigns. Samson is a tragic figure who was consumed in a Pyrrhic victory over his enemies. He is included among the judges because his final victory over the Philistines was remembered as a reaffirmation of God's presence with Israel.

*Leslie J. Hoppe, O.F.M.*

**JUDITH.** The heroine of the book of Judith, which is regarded by Jews and Protestants as apocryphal and by Roman Catholics and some Orthodox churches as deuterocanonical. Judith is a beautiful and wealthy *widow who, in defense of God and country, first captivates and then decapitates Holofernes, the Assyrian general besieging her hometown, Bethulia of Samaria. Often characterized as a type of novel, the book is best understood as a folktale about a pious widow who, strengthened by her faith in the God of Israel, courageously (and literally) took matters into her own hands and so saved Israel and Jerusalem.

The moral and ethical views of the storyteller have frequently been censured, especially the treatment and obvious approval of the character and conduct of the heroine who, at least in her dealings with Holofernes, showed herself to be a shameless flatterer, a bold-faced liar, and a ruthless assassin who seemingly follows two highly popular but debatable axioms: "all's fair in love and war" and "the end justifies the means."

Yet both before and after her murderous (and salvific) act, Judith is regarded by her people as a *saint, that is, one who is totally devoted to the Lord: diligent both in prayer and in fasting, observant of the dietary laws, honoring her husband's memory by remaining forever celibate after his death and honored by all, and fearing the Lord. In the eyes of the storyteller, at least, Judith was the saint who murdered for her people and her God; she is the ideal Jewish woman, as her name, which is simply the feminine form of the word for "Jewish," suggests.

No other biblical book, in either its parts or its totality, is as quintessentially ironic as Judith. Given the sexist and patriarchal character of the day, its central theme is most ironic: "The Lord Almighty has foiled them by the hand of a woman" (16.5); this echoes, probably deliberately, the story of Jael (Judg. 4.17–22; 5.24–27). The storyteller probably intended even the opening verse to be understood as ironic, and certainly all the major scenes and characters are.

A beautiful, desirable, but childless widow, Judith lived a celibate life after her husband's death; yet she gave political and spiritual rebirth to her people. Very feminine in appearance, she herself murdered the general, praying even as she decapitated him! Neither King *Nebuchadrezzar, lord of the whole world, nor Holofernes, the master of the west, could master Bethulia. The Ammonite Achior, a seasoned warrior who early in the story displayed more faith in Israel's God than did Uzziah, the chief elder of Bethulia, fainted on seeing the head that Judith had cut off with her own two hands. The Assyrian patrol that captured Judith and her maid were so captivated by their captive that they escorted her into the well-protected tent of her intended victim.

The scenes featuring conversations between Holofernes and Achior and between Holofernes and Judith abound in punctual ironies (i.e., irony at more or less isolated points) and, when taken together, are what literary critics call "episodic irony." These episodes result in a thematic irony in the book as a whole: Achior spoke the complete truth to Holofernes but was not believed, while Judith dissimulated, equivocated, and lied—and was totally believed! Holofernes had intended to have his way with Judith, but as Judith's song so eloquently expresses it, the exact opposite happened: "Her sandal ravished his eyes; her beauty captivated his mind; and the sword severed his neck" (16.9). Not surprisingly, this dramatic climax is a favorite theme of Renaissance artists.

Whatever the original language of the Judith story, the basis of the Greek version, as its many Hebraisms attest, was Hebrew. In view of this fact, as well as the storyteller's Pharisaic theology and greater knowledge of Palestinian geography, one may infer that the author was a Palestinian *Pharisee.

As for the book's date of composition, though the story has a postexilic setting and a significant number of Persian nouns and personal names, it also has unmistakable Hellenistic features, as well as distinctively Maccabean/Hasmonean elements. All this, plus the fact that the book has none of the anti-Sadducean spirit so characteristic of Pharisees in the days of Alexander Jannaeus (104–78 BCE), suggests that the book was composed in the days of John Hyrcanus I (135–105 BCE).

*Carey A. Moore*

**JUNIA.** The only woman called an *apostle in the New Testament. *Paul's relative or compatriot, Junia had been in prison, perhaps for the gospel. Her name suggests that she may have been a freedwoman or a descendant of a slave freed by a member of the Junian clan. As an apostle, Junia must have claimed to have seen the risen Jesus and have engaged in missionary work.

Although previous scholars interpreted the name Junia as masculine, church fathers, including Origen, John Chrysostom, and Jerome, identified her as a woman. Further, while the hypothetical male name Junias is unattested in ancient inscriptions, the female Latin name Junia occurs over 250 times in Greek and Latin inscriptions found in Rome alone. Therefore scholars today generally interpret the name as feminine.

*Bernadette J. Brooten*

# K

**KENITES.** The Kenites are portrayed in biblical tradition as staunch supporters of Israel and Yahwism who were never fully incorporated into Israelite society. Their status as a marginal group is implied in Judges 4.17–22 and 5.24–27, where the house of Heber the Kenite is portrayed as having peaceful relations with the tribes of Israel as well as Jabin the king of *Hazor, Israel's enemy. Some relation to Israel is also suggested in Judges 1.16, where the Kenites are said to have settled with the people of Judah in the Negeb near Arad. The positive relationship between the Israelites and the Kenites is further affirmed in 1 Samuel 15.6; 30.29.

The Kenites may have had some connection with nomadic or seminomadic metalsmiths, although they are never explicitly identified as such. A nomadic or seminomadic mode of life is suggested by references to their presence in various locations throughout Palestine, possibly including northern Sinai, a region of copper mining and smelting in ancient times. The association with metalworking has been postulated on the basis of the linguistic similarity between their name and *Cain's, the ancestor of Tubal-cain, the first "forger of all instruments of bronze and iron." The marginal status of the Kenites also supports this hypothesis, as marginality is characteristic of metalworking groups in many traditional societies throughout the Middle East and Africa.

Some interpreters have hypothesized that the Kenites were responsible for introducing Yahwism to the Israelites (the "Kenite hypothesis"). This proposal is based on the traditions that *Moses first encountered Yahweh while in the service of the priest Jethro, who praises and offers sacrifice to Yahweh and instructs Moses regarding delegation of authority.

The Kenites are not mentioned in traditions about the later history of Israel. They may, however, have been related to the *Rechabites, another socially marginal group that was fiercely supportive of Yahwism, and to the *Midianites. Moses's father-in-law is identified as a Midianite in the Exodus traditions but as a Kenite in Judges 1.16 and 4.11. And in 1 Samuel 15.6, the Kenites are remembered as loyal supporters of Israel during the Exodus, a role attributed to the *Midianites in the Pentateuchal narratives.

In Numbers 24.21–22, it is foretold that the Kenites will perish. This is the one instance in which they are viewed unfavorably. *Paula M. McNutt*

**KOHELETH.** *See* Ecclesiastes.

# L

**LACHISH.** Modern Tell ed-Duweir, one of the major fortified cities in Israel in the second and first millennia BCE. It has been the focus of several excavations, which have both illuminated and been illuminated by its frequent mention in written and pictorial sources. In biblical traditions, Lachish features prominently in accounts of the conquest, and as *Sennacherib's headquarters for his campaign against Judah in 701 BCE; its capture by the Assyrian king is depicted in detail in reliefs from *Nineveh.

Among the most significant discoveries at the site are the Lachish ostraca. In the excavations of J. L. Starcky in the mid-1930s, eighteen inscribed potsherds, apparently military dispatches, were discovered in the ashy debris of a room in the city's gate. They are dated to the final months of the kingdom of *Judah. Their servile tone—for example, "who is your servant but a dog"—shows that they were sent from an inferior to a superior, presumably the garrison commander. Letter 3 briefly reports on a mission to Egypt and alludes to an unnamed prophet who delivered a letter of warning from a royal official. The most famous, Letter 4, ends in pathos: "We are looking for the signals of Lachish, according to all the indications my lord has given, because we do not see Azekah." This letter must have been written just after Jeremiah 34.1–5, an oracle of doom and comfort delivered by the prophet to King Zedekiah "when the army of the king of Babylon was fighting against Jerusalem and against all the cities of Judah that were left, Lachish and Azekah; for these were the only fortified cities of Judah that remained." Soon, in 587/586, *Nebuchadrezzar would take *Jerusalem and raze the *Temple. The Lachish ostraca are valuable to paleographers, since they can be precisely dated, but their chief importance is as mementos of a tragic era in Israelite history.

*William H. Propp*

**LAWYER.** Lawyer is a term used in the gospels of Matthew and Luke for a certain portion of the Jewish leadership portrayed as hostile to Jesus. There is not enough information to determine the role of these lawyers in first-century CE Roman Palestine. Doubtless they were literate officials in or around the corridors of power in the colonial setting of the Greek East. The Greek term for lawyer *(nomikos)* is found only once in Matthew, and even there it is textually uncertain. Luke seems to have replaced other stereotyped members of the opposition to Jesus, such as the *Sadducees, with the lawyers. Alongside the *Pharisees in Luke, the reader can depend on a *nomikos* to ask a question that provokes Jesus's instruction or condemnation or a parable illustrating the nature of the kingdom of God.

*J. Andrew Overman*

**LEAH.** Leah, whose name means "cow," was one of the matriarchs of Israel. She is said to have been buried in the cave at Machpelah. Leah, with "weak" or "delicate" eyes, is contrasted with her younger sister *Rachel, who is "graceful and beautiful." Because of their father Laban's wedding night deception, *Jacob marries both sisters, but loves Rachel more than Leah. Yahweh takes pity on Leah because she is unloved and gives her many children: *Reuben, *Simeon, *Levi, *Judah; *Issachar, *Zebulun, and *Dinah, as well as *Gad and *Asher, the children her maid Zilpah bears to Jacob. Although Leah was the first wife and had several sons, she apparently did not have automatic marital rights, since in one case she is said to bargain with Rachel for Jacob's time by giving Rachel mandrakes to promote conception. *Jo Ann Hackett*

**LEBANON.** A range of coastal mountains with elevations up to 10,000 ft (3,000 m) stretching northward from Sidon to near Homs, Syria. The name means "white," referring probably to its snowcapped peaks in winter. Lebanon already appears as a place name in the mid-third-millennium BCE *Ebla texts. In the Bible, Lebanon denotes both the mountains and the country around them, although it is distinct from the *Phoenician cities in the neighboring coastal plain. The Lebanon and Anti-lebanon mountains (a parallel range on the east) enclose the Biqa$^{c}$ valley (the "Valley of Lebanon"). Mount *Hermon, the highest peak in the southern Anti-lebanon chain, stands at the headwaters of the Jordan River. The Bible mentions Lebanon chiefly as a source of timber for large buildings. *Solomon's palace and *Temple were built with Lebanon cedar. The Egyptians and Assyrians also knew Lebanon for its cedar and cypress. *Joseph A. Greene*

**LEVI.** Son of *Jacob and *Leah, and one of the twelve *tribes of Israel. Leah associates Levi with the verb "to join." Aside from his involvement with *Simeon in the attack against *Shechem, Levi is best known for the sacerdotal functions of his descendants. The *Levites play a prominent role in assisting Moses quell the golden calf rebellion. Whatever Aaron's ancestry, his sons, and not Levi's, dominate the Jerusalem cult from the time of *Solomon until the overthrow of Onias III by the Seleucids in 174 BCE.

Biblical sources depict the Levites as porters, carrying the ark and the tabernacle. Given no inheritance of their own, the Levites were to reside in forty-eight designated cities. Israelites were to support the Levites through tithes and offerings.

Scholars disagree whether Levi was originally a secular tribe or whether the Levites were supposed to have secondary status. P prescribes a rigid division of duties for the descendants of Levi's sons, Gershon, Kohath, and Merari. Barred as priests, the Levites function under Aaronid supervision. Similarly, Ezekiel denounces the Levites and confirms their lesser status.

In contrast, Deuteronomy defines a priest as a levitical priest and accords Levites an equal share at the central shrine. In Deuteronomy Levites are judges, guardians of the torah scroll, and they assist in covenant renewal. In a postexilic context, *Malachi predicts Levite renaissance, because of priestly corruption at the Jerusalem *Temple. Chronicles strikes a mediating position, depicting cooperation between the dominant Aaronids and the Levites and stressing levitical responsibilities as Temple singers, gatekeepers, and teachers of torah.

Many commentators see competition between the Levites and the Aaronids as the most plausible explanation for the different duties and kinds of status ascribed to these groups by biblical writers. *Gary N. Knoppers*

**LEVIATHAN.** A mythological sea monster who is one of the primeval adversaries of the storm god. In the Ugaritic texts, *Baal defeats Lothan (*ltn,* a linguistic variant of Leviathan), described as a seven-headed serpent, apparently identified with Baal's adversary Prince Sea. In the Bible Leviathan is also identified with the Sea and has many heads, and his defeat by God is a prelude to creation. According to apocalyptic literature, that battle will be rejoined in the end time when the evil Leviathan will be finally defeated, and, according to later tradition, given along with *Behemoth as food to the elect, another recalling of creation. In Job 41, Leviathan is described as fully under God's control, a divine pet. Many commentators have equated the Leviathan of Job 41 with the crocodile, and some elements of the description seem to fit this identification. But others, like his breathing fire, do not; in light of the other biblical references as well as the Canaanite antecedents it is better to understand Leviathan as a mythological creature.

In Thomas Hobbes's work by this title (1651), Leviathan is the symbolic name for the absolute power of the political commonwealth, to whose sovereign people must be subordinate but which is ultimately subject to divine control.

*Michael D. Coogan*

**LEVITES.** Priests in ancient Israel were considered descendants of the tribe of *Levi, or, in a broad sense, Levites. Whether such a tribe ever existed is debated. To the tribe they are connected only by genealogies: some perhaps ancient, one at least the product of postexilic times, drawn up in order to legitimize the existing conditions and the privileges of the *Zadokites. For the word Levite no clear etymology has been found; the most suitable meaning is "devoted to the Lord." Levites, then, are those who are given or have given themselves for the service of the Lord; this is their role in traditions of early Israel.

Although Levitical priests are the descendants of Aaron, the Zadokites claimed and eventually obtained the Levitical priesthood. Thus, in general biblical usage, the Levites are subordinate Temple officials who never obtained full priesthood. They are prominent in later phases of biblical tradition, especially in Deuteronomy, P, and Chronicles. They were charged with the more menial tasks in the Temple cult. This secondary position seems to have started with King *Josiah's reform; after the suppression of the country shrines, where it is often assumed (but is unproven) that they officiated and from which they drew their income, they were deprived of their powers and that income, thus reducing them to poverty. In Deuteronomy they are therefore often mentioned together with *aliens, *widows, and *orphans. The Jerusalem priesthood, on the contrary, increased through the reform in power, dignity, and wealth, which they refused to share. Although Deuteronomy 18.1–8 had granted equal dignity and rights to all members of the tribe of Levi, the Jerusalem priesthood succeeded in nullifying this principle, limiting the Levites as priests of the high places. Such a division into an upper and a lower clergy was first codified in the reconstruction program of *Ezekiel, where the Zadokites were granted the privileges of the Temple and the sacrifices. This hierarchy is confirmed by P and may explain why relatively few Levites returned from the exile.

As to the length of their service, we have contrasting information. According to an older stratum of P, they started at thirty years of age and finished at fifty; according to a later stratum they started at twenty-five, while Ezra 3.8 and 1 Chronicles 23.24, 27 mention the twentieth year.

In Chronicles we find traces of a struggle by the Levites to obtain equal dignity with the Zadokites, which would have meant sharing in the sacrifices. This was not obtained, however, and the Levites had to content themselves with sharing in the liturgy only. The struggle between the two groups continued until the destruction of the Second Temple (70 CE), with the Levites trying to improve their position and the Zadokites trying to deprive them of the little they had, such as the revenues of the tithes.

*J.A. Soggin*

**LILITH.** A female demon who appears in Isaiah 34.14 as part of a description of the Lord's day of vengeance. The figure of Lilith may have evolved out of Babylonian demonology. In some postbiblical Jewish midrashic texts, she is depicted as a slayer of infants and women in pregnancy and childbirth, for which reason amulets were used against her destructive powers. The early medieval *Alphabet of Ben Sira* draws on traditions that *Adam had a first wife who preceded *Eve and identifies her with Lilith. Noting that both she and Adam were created from the earth, Lilith flies away from Adam after unsuccessfully demanding that she be regarded as his equal. Feminist readings of this and other texts about Lilith have observed that the male authors of the Lilith material created an antithesis to Eve, who is depicted here as more docile and dependent and, unlike Lilith, as a begetter and nurturer of children. These readings also draw positive attention to Lilith's self-reliance and demand for equality in societies in which women were legally and socially subordinated to men.

*Barbara Geller Nathanson*

**LOT.** The nephew of *Abraham and ancestor of *Moab and *Ammon. Because Abraham was the oldest son of Terah, and Lot's father, Abraham's brother Haran, had died, Abraham was the head of the extended family and Lot was his dependent. As such, he traveled with Abraham to the land of *Canaan; when a dispute arose between the two branches of the family over grazing land, Abraham arbitrated it, giving Lot first choice, and enabling him to settle in the *Jordan Valley, in the vicinity of *Sodom. When Lot was captured by raiding kings, Abraham led a campaign to rescue him, and when Sodom was about to be destroyed, Lot was spared, presumably because of his association with Abraham. Throughout these stories, Lot is portrayed as a less than heroic figure, who has no respect in his own family, is hesitant, and is tricked by his daughters.

This familial history is intertwined with etiological narratives that explain topographic features (the pillar of salt and the desolation of the Dead Sea region) and several names, especially Moab and Ammon. The account of the incestuous origin of these neighbors of Israel is both a genealogical recognition of shared ethnicity and a scurrilous rationalization of Israelite superiority.

In later literature, Lot is recalled as a righteous man, whose goodness saved him from Sodom's punishment.

*Michael D. Coogan*

**LUKE.** A companion and coworker of *Paul, called "the beloved physician" in Colossians 4.11. Ancient Christian tradition locates Luke at *Antioch and identifies him as the author of the Gospel According to Luke and of Acts of the Apostles. If this tradition is accepted, then the first-person sections of Acts may be an account of some of his travels with Paul; see further below.

**The Gospel According to Luke.** The third gospel is "the first volume" (Acts 1.1) of a two-part work, Luke-Acts, composed by the same author and dedicated to Theophilus. In content, this gospel is related to the Marcan and Matthean gospels; collectively, these three Gospels form the group usually called synoptic, i.e., the tradition that developed independently of the gospel according to *John.

***Content.*** The content of the Lucan gospel may be summarized under eight headings. (1) A brief *prologue* (1.1–4), written in a stylized periodic sentence, states the author's purpose in writing. (2) Two chapters are devoted to an *infancy narrative* (1.5–2.52), recounting in studied parallelism the birth and childhood of *John the Baptist and those of *Jesus. (3) One and a half chapters (3.1–4.13) set forth the appearance of John in the desert, his preaching and baptist career, and his imprisonment by Herod Antipas as a *prelude to the events inaugurating Jesus's public career,* namely, the latter's baptism, sojourn in the desert, and temptation by the devil. (4) The story of *Jesus's Galilean ministry* (4.14–9.50) begins programmatically in a *synagogue in his hometown, *Nazareth, and moves on to *Capernaum and other towns and villages, as Jesus preaches the kingdom of God, heals those who are afflicted, and associates himself with disciples whom he gradually trains. This Galilean activity serves also as the starting point for his "exodus," or transit to the Father through death, burial, and resurrection. (5) There follows the *travel account* (9.51–19.27), which has both a specifically Lucan form and another form in 18.15–19.27 that parallels Mark 10.13–52. In this account, Jesus is depicted not only as moving without distraction toward *Jerusalem, the city of destiny, but also as instructing crowds of people and especially the disciples, who would become the foreordained witnesses of his ministry, career, and destiny in Jerusalem. (6) At the end of the travel account, Jesus is accorded a regal welcome as he enters Jerusalem itself, purges its *Temple, and initiates there a period of *ministry and teaching in the Temple* (19.28–21.38), which serves as a prelude to the events of his last days. (7) The *passion narrative* (22.1–23.56a) forms the climax of his exodus, as the Jerusalem leaders conspire with Judas against him, and as he eats his last meal with the *twelve and foretells Peter's denial of him. After praying on the Mount of *Olives, Jesus is arrested, brought before a morning session of the *Sanhedrin, delivered to *Pilate, sent to *Herod, and finally handed over for crucifixion. This narrative ends with the notice of Jesus's death and burial. (8) The Lucan *resurrection narrative* (23.56b–24.53) tells of the women who discover the empty tomb and of Jesus's appearance as risen to followers on the road to Emmaus and in Jerusalem itself. The Lucan gospel ends with Jesus giving a final commission to the eleven and others and with his ascension (apparently on the night of the day of the discovery of the empty tomb).

***Authorship.*** Unlike the Pauline letters, which bear the Apostle's name, the third gospel is anonymous, as are the other gospels. Ancient church tradition attributed the third gospel to Luke.

Most modern commentators on the Lucan gospel, however, are skeptical about the validity of this traditional attribution. They regard the tradition as based largely on inferences from the text of the New Testament made when people were first beginning to wonder who had written the Gospels. A minority of commentators, however, retain the traditional attribution as substantially correct. They recognize that in this tradition one must distinguish between what could have been inferred from the text of the New Testament and what could not have been so inferred. Many of the latter details are legendary and of no value; but the substance of the tradition—that the author of the third gospel and Acts was Luke, an inhabitant of *Antioch in Syria and a companion of Paul—is far from being untenable. If the gospel and Acts were not originally written by him, there is no obvious reason why they should have been associated with him.

***Sources.*** The prologue of the gospel reveals that Luke depends on other gospel narratives and on information gathered from "eyewitnesses" and "servants of the word" (who may or may not represent two distinct sources for him). From an internal analysis of the gospel, one recognizes that Luke used mainly three sources: the Marcan gospel (in a form more or less as we know it today), a postulated Greek written source, often called Q (some 230 verses common to his and the Matthean gospel but not found in Mark), and a unique source, often designated L, either written or oral (episodes exclusive to the third gospel).

Attempts are sometimes made to associate L with specific persons from whom Luke would have derived information: *Mary, the mother of Jesus; the disciples of *John the Baptist; Joanna, "wife of Chuza, Herod's steward"; Cleopas. Luke could have obtained information from such sources, but such a list of candidates is based on speculation, more pious than critical, about possible informants.

***Date and Place of Composition.*** If the Marcan gospel is rightly included among the sources used by Luke in composing his gospel, then the latter is to be dated after Mark. The Marcan gospel is commonly dated ca. 65–70 CE. How much later is the Lucan gospel? One cannot say for certain. Luke 1.1 refers to "many" others who had previously tried to write the Jesus story; even if Mark is included among the "many," more time must be allowed for the others to whom Luke alludes. Again, since the Lucan Jesus refers to Jerusalem as an "abandoned" house, this and other references to Jerusalem ("surrounded by camps" with earthworks erected against it) would suggest a date for Luke after the fall of Jerusalem in 70 CE. Some have sought to interpret these references as merely literary imitations of biblical descriptions of the fall of Jerusalem under Nebuchadrezzar, hence lacking in historical references to the Roman destruction. But this interpretation is not without its problems. In any case, it is widely held that the Lucan gospel was composed ca. 80–85 CE, even though one cannot maintain this dating with certainty.

Nothing in the Lucan gospel hints at the place where it was composed. The author's knowledge of Palestine is at times defective, which would suggest that it was not composed there. Ancient tradition mentions Achaia, Boeotia, and Rome; modern conjectures include Caesarea, the *Decapolis, or Asia Minor. No one really knows where it was written.

**Acts of the Apostles.** The fifth book of the New Testament in the common arrangement, Acts records certain phases of the progress of Christianity for a period of some thirty years after Jesus's death and resurrection. Acts was originally written as a sequel to the gospel of Luke; both are clearly from the same author, who apparently planned the complete work from the outset.

***Content.*** Seven main divisions may be discerned in Acts: the formation and development of the church of Jerusalem (Acts 1.1–5.42); the rise and activity of the Hellenists in the church, which led to their persecution and expulsion from Jerusalem (Acts 6.1–8.3); the dissemination of the gospel by these Hellenists, culminating in the evangelizing of gentiles in the Syrian city of Antioch (Acts 8.4–12.25); the extension of gentile Christianity from Antioch into Cyprus and Asia Minor (Acts 13.1–14.28); the decision reached by the Jerusalem church on problems raised by the influx of gentile converts (Acts 15.1–16.5); the carrying of the gospel by Paul and his colleagues to the provinces bordering on the Aegean Sea (Acts 16.6–19.20); Paul's last journey to Jerusalem, his arrest there, and his journey to Rome under armed guard to have his case heard before the emperor (Acts 19.21–28.31).

Acts, in short, is concerned with the advance of the gospel from Jerusalem to Rome; its simultaneous advance in other directions is ignored. The narrative reaches its goal when Paul arrives in Rome and, while under house arrest, preaches the gospel there without interference to all who came to visit him (Acts 28.30–31).

***Authorship.*** For Acts, as for the gospel of Luke, the author was dependent on the information handed down by others. But he probably made further inquiry on his own account, and he may have been present at some of the events recorded in the later part of the book of Acts. This is the prima facie inference to be drawn from the "we" sections—those sections in which the third-person pronouns "they" and "them" give way to the first-person "we" and "us." There are three such sections: Acts 16.10–17; Acts 20.5–21.18; Acts 27.1–28.16. All three are largely devoted to journeys by sea—from Troas to Neapolis, and then by road to Philippi; from Philippi (Neapolis) to Caesarea, and then by road to Jerusalem; from Caesarea to Puteoli, and then by road to Rome—and may have been extracted from a travel diary. The traditional view, which still has much to commend it, is that the "we" of those sections includes the "I" of Acts 1.1—that the transition from "they" to "we" is the author's unobtrusive way of indicating that he himself was a participant in the events he narrates.

Ever since the second century CE the author has been traditionally identified with the Luke mentioned in Colossians 4.14 as "Luke the beloved physician." The attribution of the twofold work to such an obscure New Testament character has been thought to speak for the genuineness of the tradition. The only question of consequence to be considered is the degree of likelihood that the author of Acts was personally acquainted with Paul, whose missionary activity forms the main subject of the second half of the book. The critical judgment of several scholars is that such personal acquaintance is highly unlikely—that the "Paulinism" of

Acts is too dissimilar to the teaching of Paul's letters for the idea to be entertained that the author of Acts knew Paul or spent any time in his company. On the other hand, many authorities maintain that, when account is taken of the difference between the picture of him as seen through the eyes of an admirer and, indeed, hero-worshiper, the Paul of Acts is identical with the real Paul.

***Date.*** The latest event to be recorded in Acts is Paul's spending two years under house arrest in Rome (Acts 28.30). This period begins with his arrival in the city, probably in the early spring of 60 CE. Most of the book deals with the twenty years preceding that date, and the book as a whole is true to its "dramatic" date, that is, it reflects the situation of the middle of the first century CE, especially with regard to the administration of the Roman empire. But the date of writing is not the same as the "dramatic" date. Some scholars have argued that it was written very shortly after that event, possibly even before Paul's appeal came up for hearing in the imperial court. Paul's death is not recorded: would it not have been mentioned (it is asked) if in fact it had taken place?

But the goal of Luke's narrative is not the outcome of Paul's appeal, whether favorable or otherwise, or the end of Paul's life: it is Paul's unmolested preaching of the gospel at the heart of the empire. In fact Paul's death is alluded to, by implication, in his speech to the *elders of the Ephesian church, in a manner that suggests that Luke knew of it. And in general Luke appears to record the apostolic history from a perspective of one or two decades after the events. By the time he wrote, Paul, Peter, and James had all died; and the controversies in which they were involved, while important enough at the time (as Paul's letters bear witness), had lost much of their relevance for Luke's purpose, so he ignored them.

The date of Acts cannot be considered in isolation from that of the gospel of Luke. A date later rather than earlier than 70 CE is probable for the gospel. If we date the composition of the twofold work toward the end of Vespasian's rule (69–79 CE), most of the evidence will be satisfied.

***Intended Readers.*** The one recipient of Acts named explicitly is Theophilus, to whom Luke's gospel also was dedicated (Luke 1.3). We know virtually nothing about him. His designation "most excellent" may mark him as a member of the equestrian order (the second-highest order in Roman society), or it may simply be a courtesy title.

One could regard him as a representative of the intelligent middle-class public of Rome, to whom Luke wished to present a reliable account of the rise and progress of Christianity. As late as the time when Tacitus, Suetonius, and Pliny were writing (ca. 110 CE), Christians enjoyed no good repute in Roman society; writing some decades earlier, Luke hoped to bring his readers to a less prejudiced judgment. There is much to be said for the view of Martin Dibelius that, unlike the other New Testament books, Luke and Acts were written for the book market. Perhaps there was already a positive interest in Christianity in the class of readers Luke had in mind; this could account for the substantial theological content of the work, especially its emphasis on the Holy Spirit.

Rome is the most likely place for the first publication of the work. Not only is Rome the goal toward which it moves, but with Paul's arrival there, Rome implicitly replaces Jerusalem as the center from which the faith is to spread.

*F. F. Bruce, Joseph A. Fitzmyer, S.J.*

# M

**MACCABEES, THE.** The family of Mattathias and his sons, who led the Jewish revolt against the Seleucid rulers of *Judah, beginning in about 166 BCE.

In 200 BCE, Antiochus III of *Syria defeated Ptolemy V of *Egypt at Paneion, thus finally winning the Levant, including Judah, for the Seleucid empire. He won Jewish support by granting tax concessions and the right to live in accordance with traditional Jewish law (Antiochus IV's later removal of this concession precipitated rebellion). Antiochus III then tried to extend his empire into Greece, but came into conflict with Rome, which had similar interests. He was defeated and forced in the Peace of Apamea (188 BCE) to pay ruinous indemnities. Syria's financial desperation was another factor contributing to the Jewish rebellion: it caused Seleucus IV (187–175 BCE) to send his minister Heliodorus to raid the Jerusalem *Temple for money, and it caused his successor Antiochus IV (175–164 BCE) to accept bribes from successive candidates for the Jerusalem high priesthood. Rivalry for this office was itself a major factor in the ensuing struggle. When the high priest Onias III, slandered by his rivals, went to Syria to defend his position before Antiochus IV, his brother Jason usurped him by offering to pay more tribute and to turn *Jerusalem into a more typical Hellenistic city-state, of the kind Antiochus favored as conducive to the unity and stability of his empire. In 171 BCE Jason himself was similarly ousted by Menelaus, who, though not of the high priestly family, offered a yet higher tribute to Antiochus and raided the Temple plate to pay it, much to the anger of the people. However, the systemic change brought about by Jason and exacerbated by Menelaus subtly affected the agreement by which the Jews were allowed to regulate their lives by their own laws; a Hellenistic Jerusalem might be expected to organize itself like other cities of the Greek world, with an assembly, a voting citizen body, a gymnasium, and an ephebeion for training young men who would take part in athletic contests at home and abroad. In short, the Jews were under pressure to conform to the life-style of the surrounding world; and this too was a factor in the Maccabean struggle.

The attempt to regularize Jerusalem's position in the Seleucid empire was important to Antiochus because Judah lay between Syria and Egypt, which Antiochus wished to annex. In 172 BCE, the guardians of the newly enthroned minor Ptolemy VI declared war on Antiochus, who sent a diplomat to Rome to meet Roman objections and invaded Egypt in 169 BCE; when he did so again in 168 BCE, the Romans ejected him. Jason meanwhile had attacked Menelaus and tried to reinstate himself in Jerusalem. Antiochus, seeing this as rebellion, attacked Jerusalem and looted the Temple, leaving a commissioner in charge. In 167 BCE, the Syrians made an unexpected and vicious attack and established a military garrison in Jerusalem. Clearly, Antiochus was determined to control Judah, although Egypt, for the time being, was closed to him.

Antiochus's determination led him to one further disastrous political error. In 167 BCE he tried "to compel the Jews to forsake the laws of their ancestors and no longer to live by the laws of God, also to pollute the temple in Jerusalem and to call it the temple of Olympian Zeus" (2 Macc. 6.1–2). According to 1 Maccabees 1.41–50, the king decreed the Jews "to follow customs strange to the land, to forbid burnt offerings and sacrifices and drink offerings in the sanctuary, to profane sabbaths and festivals, to defile the sanctuary and the priests, to build altars and sacred precincts and shrines for idols, to sacrifice swine and other unclean animals, and to leave their sons uncircumcised." This was followed in December 167 BCE by the erection of "a desolating sacrilege upon the altar of burnt offering" (1 Macc. 1.54), the erection of altars throughout Judah, and the proscription of the Jewish Law. These descriptions show that in Jewish eyes the king was persecuting Jewish religion by attacking the Law and the Temple. By his "decree," however, Antiochus presumably (his original wording is not extant) was withdrawing the Jewish right of self-rule by Jewish law and opening the Jerusalem Temple to all worshipers (as any other Hellenistic city temple would be); but, worse, he was making the positive practice of Jewish law punishable. It has been argued that Antiochus saw the Jews much as the Romans saw the followers of the god Bacchus—as dangerous religious fanatics—and wished to suppress them, but Antiochus was not giving way to mere prejudice; he was punishing the Jews for political rebellion by prohibiting precisely those things that constituted Jewish independence—the concession of self-rule by ancestral laws, and the exclusivity of the Jerusalem Temple.

The result was rebellion, led by Judas called "Maccabeus" ("hammerlike"), son of Mattathias, from Modin, 17 mi (20 km) northwest of Jerusalem. The rebellion is described in detail in 1 Maccabees (see below). In outline, however, affairs developed as follows: After several local victories in Judah, Judas occupied the Temple area, purged it of non-Jewish cultic activities, and rededicated it (December 164 BCE); this was the institution of the festival of Hanukkah (called the feast of the Dedication). The following year he widened his military activities to Idumea, Galilee, Transjordan, and Philistia; the Seleucid army responded, but, after an initially successful campaign preempted by an attempted coup d'état in Syria, the Syrians offered Judas terms, withdrawing the edict of 167 BCE, but leaving the Syrian garrison in Jerusalem and destroying Judas's Temple defenses. They also executed the high priest Menelaus. Thus, in theory the Jews had regained religious independence (with no clear leadership to exercise it), and the Syrians retained political control (with inadequate popular support to maintain it). In 162–161 BCE a new Syrian king, Demetrius, and a new high priest, Alcimus, collaborated to eliminate Judas and his supporters. Judas defeated the new general sent against him, Nicanor, but fell before the more experienced Bacchides in 160 BCE. Bacchides fortified Judah, but failed to make progress against Judas's successor Jonathan and finally withdrew. Alcimus died, and power remained de facto with Jonathan, who began to "judge" the people from his home in Michmash; the historian deliberately compares Jonathan with the rulers who preceded the monarchy in Israel. Constitutionally, however, Judah was still under Seleucid rule, symbolized by the garrison in Jerusalem.

Jonathan now proceeded to steer Judah toward independence by diplomacy, bargaining with successive Seleucid rulers for political concessions. In return for Jonathan's support, the Seleucid pretender Alexander Balas gave him the high priesthood (to which Jonathan had no hereditary right) in 152 BCE. Jonathan refused to support Demetrius I and defeated Demetrius II in 147 BCE (thus earning new honors and more territory from Balas); but when Balas was killed in 145 BCE, Jonathan shifted his allegiance to Demetrius II, for which Demetrius transferred to Jonathan three districts from *Samaria. When Antiochus VI and Trypho ousted Demetrius in 145 BCE, they confirmed Jonathan in his position and made his brother Simon governor of the coastal region. Jonathan and Simon now began rapidly to develop Judah's position. The Seleucid garrison at Beth-zur was replaced by a Jewish one, Joppa was garrisoned, Adida fortified, Gaza captured, the Seleucid garrison in Jerusalem blockaded, and the walls of Jerusalem and the fortresses of Judah repaired. Jonathan renewed both the diplomatic links with Rome initiated by Judas in 161 BCE and the links of brotherhood and friendship with Sparta which supposedly were established several generations earlier by Onias the high priest and Arius, king of Sparta. Jonathan campaigned, ostensibly against Demetrius II, in Syrian territory near Hamath. Trypho, naturally anxious at this Jewish resurgence, captured Jonathan by treachery, and Simon took over the Jewish leadership. He completed Jonathan's military and diplomatic program, crowning his achievements by expelling the Seleucid garrison from Jerusalem and negotiating the formal abolition of tribute payable to Syria with Demetrius II. In effect, this meant the end of Seleucid rule of Judah, and 1 Maccabees 13.41 notes that in 142 BCE "the yoke of the gentiles was removed from Israel, and the people began to write in their documents and contracts, 'In the first year of Simon the great high priest and commander and leader of the Jews.'" This was the beginning of a new era, which was to last until 63 BCE, when Pompey the Great claimed Judah for Rome.

**The Books of the Maccabees.** The four books of the Maccabees are independent works. 1 and 2 Maccabees separately record the Maccabean rebellion and the events leading up to it; 3 Maccabees is a historical novel, which became associated with 1 and 2 Maccabees for thematic reasons; and 4 Maccabees is a discourse on reason which took its cue from the story of the Maccabean martyrs. Because they were either not written or not preserved in Hebrew, they are not part of the Jewish and Protestant canons, but are accorded varying degrees of canonicity by Roman Catholic and Orthodox churches. They differ greatly in aims and presentation, scope and detail. They also differ in matters of chronology, so reconstructing the precise course of events and their political background has been a major scholarly pursuit. *John R. Bartlett*

**MAGI.** The term "magi" customarily refers to the anonymous wise men who followed a star until it led them to *Bethlehem. While in Luke's gospel shepherds come to worship the child, Matthew introduces mysterious figures from the east who offer gifts from their treasure boxes.

Many details about the Magi are supplied by later tradition. In western Christianity they are assumed to have been three in number since three gifts are mentioned; eastern tradition gives their number as twelve. They traveled by camel, as is normal practice in the desert regions even today. Their names (Balthasar, Melchior, and Caspar, in the west) are supplied later. The fact that they are wealthy and converse with King *Herod leads to their identification as three kings. (*See also* Names for the Nameless.)

In fact, the Greek word from which "magi" is derived does not refer to royalty but to practitioners of eastern magical arts. The connection between magic and astrology is reflected in the visitors' fascination with the star that had led them to Bethlehem. Elsewhere in the Bible the portrayal of magi is not so positive. Greek versions of the book of *Daniel refer to magi who were ineffective advisers to King *Nebuchadrezzar. In Acts, apostles interact with Simon, a magician in *Samaria, and Bar-Jesus who was a magician and false prophet on Cyprus. *Daniel N. Schowalter*

**MALACHI.** Since Malachi in Hebrew means "my messenger," it is unclear whether this is the name of the prophet or a description of his office. Usually the book is dated after the time of *Haggai and *Zechariah but before the coming of *Ezra and *Nehemiah in the mid-fifth century BCE. A postexilic date is indicated by the reference to a "governor" and the fact that the *Temple is standing. The abuses Malachi attacks are thought to show the need for the reforms that Ezra and Nehemiah were soon to carry out.

Malachi's question-and-answer style usually begins with a statement from the prophet of some theological truth followed by a question from his hearers. His answer then expounds the original theme. This is a literary device but may contain echoes of the teaching and preaching practices current in the Second Temple.

A theme prominent in the book is covenant. The stark expression in 1.1–5 of the teaching that God chose Jacob (i.e., Israel) while rejecting *Edom, a nation that became a symbol of oppression during and after the exile, is elaborated in the manner of earlier *prophets, that divine choice is not a ground for complacency but for obedience. The *priests, for all their status under the covenant, have been less zealous in their duties toward God than to the governor. Malachi thinks it would be better for such Temple worship to stop altogether and even contrasts it unfavorably with the offerings of other nations. The whole nation has violated the covenant in their cruel treatment of each other, denying their family status as children of the one God, especially in their practice of casual divorce (a warning against intermarriage with foreigners has been inserted into this section).

Later, Malachi charges them with neglect of payment of tithes for the upkeep of the Temple and its personnel. Obedience here will result in material prosperity (cf. the words of Haggai about the rebuilding of the Temple). It is important to see that, for Malachi, proper observance of cultic worship was an expression of a true relationship to God ("Return to me," 3.7).

The book ends with a call to keep the Law of Moses and a promise that God will send *Elijah the prophet to prepare the people for the final "day of the Lord" (4.5–6) so that it may prove to be a day of salvation and not a repetition of the old judgment of the "curse" (Hebr. *ḥērem*). Perhaps Elijah was thought of in this role because he had not died but had been taken up to heaven. This idea was repeated in Sirach 48.10 and in Mark 9.11.

Malachi shows how the postexilic prophets were deeply concerned for the Temple and its worship and yet held such concern in creative tension with a call for right ethical living. They recognized the dangers the preexilic prophets had warned against, whereby external worship could easily become a substitute for genuine relationship with God, yet challenged their hearers with the call to hold both aspects of the religious life together. Their call was not for mercy rather than sacrifice but for mercy and sacrifice. They also held together concern for obedience to the Law and a strong eschatological hope of God's future saving action. *Rex Mason*

**MANASSEH.**

**1.** Eldest son of *Joseph, brother of *Ephraim, and ancestor of the tribe of Manasseh. According to various territorial lists, the tribe of Manasseh was settled on both sides of the Jordan River, on the east, north of the Jabbok, and on the west, in the central hill country. It was in its later history weaker than Ephraim; this political fact is reflected in the story of Jacob's blessing, in which he reverses the birth order. Manasseh is also described as the father of Machir, a genealogical explanation of a more complicated history between two apparently separate tribal entities; note that in Judges 5.14, Machir is mentioned along with Ephraim, but Manasseh is not named. (*See also* Tribes of Israel.)

**2.** King of *Judah. His reign was the longest of any Israelite or Judean king, and in the difficult times of Assyrian domination he achieved a measure of autonomy for Judah. This apparently involved some compromises with older ideals, for Manasseh is condemned by the Deuteronomic history as the worst of the Davidic kings, whose "sin" was responsible for God's punishment of Judah. His portrayal in Chronicles is less harsh. (*See* Judah, The Kingdom of.)

The account of Manasseh's reign over Judah in 2 Chronicles 33 contains the account of an episode, almost certainly legendary, in which Manasseh was taken captive by the *Assyrians and carried off to *Babylon where, in his trouble, he became a loyal worshiper of the God of his people. This story, which has no parallel in the older account in 2 Kings 21.1–18, was no doubt told to give a theological explanation for the length and prosperity of the career of one whose policy was to promote idolatry: for in theory, he should have been punished by God with political failure and come to a disastrous end. The author of Chronicles, having explained the king's paradoxical and puzzling success by a story of his eventual return to the worship of Yahweh, also mentions that his prayer was preserved in "the Annals of the Kings of Israel." A devout writer from a much later period, probably the late Hellenistic age, composed a prayer such as the king might have used. The result was the small "book" called the Prayer of Manasseh.

*Michael D. Coogan, Robert C. Dentan*

**MARK.** The traditional author of the Gospel According to Mark. The ascription of the gospel of Mark goes back at least to Papias, *bishop of Hierapolis, who in about 130 CE reported that he had been told that it was written by Mark "the interpreter of Peter"; this is presumably the Mark referred to in 1 Peter 5.13 as "my son Mark." Traditionally, he has been identified with the John Mark mentioned in Acts 12.12, but the latter was associated with *Paul and *Barnabas, not Peter, and the name "Mark" was one of the most common in the ancient world.

Mark is the shortest of the four canonical Gospels and was almost certainly the first to be written. Although the use of narrative to record God's salvation of *Israel is common in the Hebrew Bible and although there is an obvious correspondence between the story told by Mark and the very brief summaries of the gospel found elsewhere in the New Testament, there are no parallels to this precise literary form before early Christianity. In all probability, therefore, the author of this book was responsible for creating the literary genre we know as "gospel."

This gospel is usually dated between 65 and 75 CE. The first of these dates is set by Irenaeus (late second century CE), who said that Mark wrote after Peter's death. If we accept Marcan priority, then we must allow time between the composition of Mark and that of *Matthew and *Luke, which suggests a date before about 75 CE. The only clue in the gospel itself is chap. 13, which predicts the destruction of the *Temple; many commentators contrast the vague references to the fate of *Jerusalem in Mark 13 with the clear reference to the siege of the city in Luke 21.20 and suggest that this indicates that Mark was written before 70 CE. But Mark 13 is concerned to separate the disasters that are going to overwhelm Judea from the supernatural chaos at the end, and it is arguable that it was written in the period following the former to explain why the end was "still to come." The gospel of Mark was probably written, therefore, either immediately before or immediately after the destruction of Jerusalem in 70 CE.

Tradition at least as early as Irenaeus held that it was composed in Rome, but this may have been a deduction from the association with Peter. Support for a Roman origin is sometimes found in Mark's use of Latinisms, but these were probably familiar throughout the *Roman empire. Explanations of Jewish words and customs, together with a poor knowledge of Palestinian geography, suggest that Mark was writing for gentiles living outside Palestine, but they do not point to any particular place. The emphasis on the inevitability of suffering for Jesus's followers could well be explained if this gospel were written for a community that was suffering for its faith: although the Roman church was persecuted in the time of Nero, it was by no means alone, since persecution of Christians was common at the time.

*Morna D. Hooker*

**MARY MAGDALENE.** Mary Magdalene is one of the inner circle of the followers of *Jesus in the Gospel narratives. Her name suggests that she came from Magdala, a large city on the western shore of the Sea of Galilee, also called Taricheae. Magdala was known for its salt trade, for its administrative role as a toparchy, and as a large urban center that was part of the contiguous cities and large villages along the western shore of the lake from Tiberias to Bethsaida/Chorazin.

Mary Magdalene is mentioned sparingly but at crucial points in all four Gospels. During the events surrounding the crucifixion of Jesus, she is depicted as watching the proceedings and waiting near the tomb to attend to the body. She is also one of the first witnesses to the resurrection. These passages probably gave rise to the romantic portrayals of Mary as the devoted follower whom Jesus had saved from her errant ways.

Contrary to subsequent Christian interpretation, reflected in popular belief and recent films, there is no evidence from the Gospels that Mary Magdalene was a *prostitute or for the later identification of Mary Magdalene with the women who anoint Jesus's feet or with Mary of Bethany. In Luke 8.2 it is said that Mary Magdalene was healed of seven evil spirits by Jesus. But this is in the context of a list of women who were followers of Jesus, who had also been healed, and who supplied the material support for his mission. Since Mary Magdalene, Chuza (the wife of a steward of Herod) and Susanna are the only women mentioned, it is likely that these three were the benefactors of the Jesus movement according to Luke.

*J. Andrew Overman*

**MARY, MOTHER OF JESUS.** According to ancient Christian sources, Mary was the child of Jewish parents Joachim and Anne and was born in Jerusalem or Sepphoris in Galilee. If, as the sources suggest, Mary's first child *Jesus was born around 4 BCE and she was espoused around the age of fourteen, as was common, then Mary was probably born in 18 or 20 BCE.

During her childhood she lived in *Nazareth, where she became engaged to the carpenter *Joseph, who was descended from King *David. The gospel of *Luke relates that an *angel of God appeared to Mary and told her that she would become pregnant with God's son by the Holy Spirit, even though she was not yet married. Mary and Joseph traveled to *Bethlehem where Jesus was born in a stable or, according to later traditions, a cave. As was Jewish custom, Jesus was circumcised and then presented at the Temple in Jerusalem. He was raised by Mary and Joseph and perhaps other relatives in Nazareth and probably learned the carpentry trade. One relative specifically mentioned by Luke is Mary's cousin Elizabeth, who in her old age gave birth to *John the Baptist shortly before Jesus's birth. Some of the sources indicate that other children were born to Mary and Joseph after Jesus (e.g., *see* Brothers and Sisters of Jesus).

The gospel of Luke, the principal biblical source for Mary in the narratives of Jesus's infancy and childhood, also tells how, when Jesus was twelve years old, Mary and Joseph took him to the Jerusalem Temple—again, in fulfillment of Jewish law—for initiation into the faith. On the return journey, they lost him in the crowd and subsequently found him in the Temple impressing the religious leaders with his wisdom.

Joseph, probably considerably older than Mary, disappears from the sources at this time, and Mary's role becomes smaller as Jesus's becomes larger. She is mentioned in the context of the marriage feast at Cana (John 2.1–12), at Jesus's crucifixion (but only by John), and in Acts 1.14, the story of Pentecost. The accounts of Mary's later years, death, and assumption into heaven are found only in traditions outside the Bible, some as late as the fourth century CE. It is not known where she spent her final years, but it is generally believed that she lived with John the son of Zebedee in Jerusalem and died there. The date of her death is almost impossible to determine.

In addition to the gospel accounts, Mary is mentioned in the writings of some of the church fathers, including Justin Martyr, Ignatius, Tertullian, and Athanasius; in apocryphal works such as the Protevangelium of James (second century); and in the deliberations of the Council of Ephesus (431 CE), where she was proclaimed Theotokos, "God-bearer." A gnostic gospel of Mary and a Latin work from the Middle Ages called *The Gospel of the Birth of Mary* also exist.

It is through these and other sources that the powerful cult of Mary was born and grew, especially in the Roman Catholic, Anglo-Catholic, and Orthodox churches. Various feast days commemorate her importance for devotees: the Immaculate Conception (8 December), her purification in the Temple (2 February), the annunciation of the angel (25 March), her visit to Elizabeth when both were pregnant (2 July), and her assumption into heaven (15 August). Throughout the centuries, Mary has been revered not only as the Mother of God but also as a pure, ever-virgin woman, the perfect mother, the intercessor between human beings and God, and one who knows the deepest of human suffering, having borne witness to the agonizing and humiliating death of her firstborn son. She has been the object of pilgrimages and visions even to the present day, and the "Magnificat," attributed to her by Luke at the time of her visit to Elizabeth, has been part of Christian liturgy and music for centuries. Mary has been widely honored and even worshiped as representing inner strength and the exaltation of the oppressed over the oppressor.

Non-Christian sources are instructive in tracing parallels to the cult of Mary. Virgin Birth stories (e.g., Hera, Rhea Silvia, Brigid) were circulated in other cultures, as were tales of mothers mourning lost and deceased children (e.g., Demeter and Persephone; Isis and Horus). Iconographically, just as Mary was often portrayed holding or nursing the infant Jesus, so too was the Egyptian goddess Isis depicted suckling her infant son, Horus. Even as Mary was called Queen of Heaven and sometimes depicted surrounded by the zodiac and other symbols, so too were the deities Isis, Magna Mater, and Artemis.

Such parallels show that Mary's cult had roots in the cults of the female deities of the Greco-Roman pantheon, cults ultimately eradicated by Christianity. While Mary in some ways represents qualities impossible for human beings, especially women, to emulate—ever-virgin yet motherly; always gentle and obedient to God's will—her attributes nevertheless represent for many devotees important female properties not provided by the traditional all-male Trinity. For many, the adoration of a female figure is a vital psychological supplement to their faith.

*Valerie Abrahamsen*

**MATTHEW.** Matthew is named as one of the original disciples, and he has traditionally been identified as the author of the first (but not the oldest) Gospel in the New Testament. In the other Gospels and Acts, the name Matthew simply appears in a list of followers of Jesus, but in the Gospel that bears his name, Matthew is mentioned twice as a tax collector. This association has stuck through subsequent Christian history, although in the parallels to Matthew 9.9 in both Mark 2.14 and Luke 5.27, the tax collector is called Levi, not Matthew.

According to Papias (ca. 130 CE), "Matthew made an ordered arrangement of the sayings in the Hebrew dialect, and each one translated it as he was able" (quoted by Eusebius, the fourth-century bishop of Caesarea, *Hist. Eccl.*). This leads to the view that Matthew first wrote his Gospel in Hebrew, a view today rejected by almost all scholars. But Papias also gives us the earliest association of Matthew with the first canonical Gospel, an association that probably originated in his being mentioned twice within that Gospel, and continued in the manuscript traditions that add the superscript "according to Matthew."

Matthew is a gospel story in three parts, embedded with five great speeches of *Jesus. The story that is told is of the life and ministry of Jesus. It begins with his miraculous conception and birth and closes with his death and resurrection. The gospel proclaims the message that in Jesus, Son of God, God has drawn near with his eschatological rule to dwell to the end of time with his people, the church. The purpose of this message is to summon the reader or hearer to perceive that God is uniquely present in Jesus and to become Jesus's disciple. As Jesus's disciple, one becomes God's child, lives in the sphere of his end-time kingdom, and engages in his mission so that all people may find him in Jesus and also become Jesus's disciples.

It is commonly held that Matthew was written about 85 or 90 CE by an unknown *Christian who was at home in a church located in *Antioch of Syria. A date toward the end of the first century seems probable because the destruction of *Jerusalem, which occurred in 70 CE, appears to be an event that was rapidly receding into the past. Although the apostle Matthew may have been active in founding the church in which the gospel story attributed to him arose, it is unlikely that he was the story's author. On the contrary, the author exhibits a theological outlook, command of Greek, and rabbinic training that suggest he was a Jewish Christian of the second rather than the first generation. Also, Antioch of Syria commends itself as the place where he may have been at home, because the social conditions reflected in his story correspond with those that seem to have prevailed there: the city was Greek-speaking, urban, and prosperous, and it had a large population of both Jews and *gentiles.

Scholarly opinion holds that the church for which Matthew was written was made up of Christians of both Jewish and gentile origin. Socioculturally, this church was almost certainly living in an atmosphere of religious and social tension. Its mandate was to make disciples of all nations, and this was apparently provoking hostile reactions from both Jews and gentiles. As a body, the church of Matthew appears to have achieved organizational autonomy and to have been materially well off. Socio-economically, the way in which both monetary matters and ethical and religious questions associated with the topic of riches are treated in Matthew indicates that the church in which it arose was relatively prosperous. But Matthew's church was also rife with dissension. It was to meet the religious and moral needs of this multiracial, prosperous, yet divided and persecuted church that the author of Matthew told afresh the gospel story.

*Jack Dean Kingsbury, J. Andrew Overman*

**MEDES.** The Medes, like the *Persians, were a people of Aryan (Iranian) speech who probably entered the ancient Near East from the north. They were first encountered by the *Assyrians about 835 BCE; they occupied the north Zagros Mountain region and far eastward. The "strong Medes" bred excellent horses and suffered frequent Assyrian incursions. Sargon II in 713 BCE received the submission of some fifty of their chieftains, but in the 670s a leader named Kashtariti (Khshathrita) of Kar-Kashshi in Media was building a formidable power. With Ecbatana (Achmetha) as capital, the Medes soon rose to be rulers of an empire that reached from the central Zagros to Turkestan and included Persis and, by 600 BCE, Armenia and eastern Anatolia as well. Under the warrior king Cyaxares, after a period of Scythian dominance, they had captured *Nineveh in 612 BCE and shared the Assyrian kingdom with the *Babylonians, thus attracting the attention of Jeremiah. But in 550 BCE their elderly king Astyages was conquered by *Cyrus the Persian, whose mother was said to have been a Mede.

Under Cyrus the Medes were to some extent corulers of the empire; in fact, for several centuries the outside world continued to apply the name "Mede" to the imperial power (*see,* e.g., Esther 1.3). But after *Darius usurped the throne the Medes rose unsuccessfully in revolt (522–521 BCE) and lost such privileged status as they had enjoyed. There does, however, seem to have been a considerable Median legacy in the institutions and titulature of the Persian court, and the *Magi who formed the Iranian clergy were in origin a Median clan. The Medes are also mentioned as a nationality in Acts 2.9.

*J. M. Cook*

**MEGIDDO.** Situated southeast of Mount Carmel at the western approach to the Jezreel Valley, Megiddo assumed geopolitical significance throughout its long occupation (early fourth millennium to early fourth century BCE). The 13-acre (5.25-hectare) site thrived at the juncture of major international trade routes connecting the northeast (Hazor, Damascus), the northern Israelite and Phoenician coasts (Acco, Tyre, Sidon), and the south-central coast of Israel (Sharon Plain, Philistia, Egypt). Several archaeological expeditions have revealed significant remains from every period, including: Early-Middle Bronze Age Canaanite temple complexes with a circular altar; a Late Bronze Age treasury containing beautifully carved ivories; and multiphased gate structures, palaces, stables (or storerooms), a sophisticated water system, and grain storage facilities from the Israelite period. Besides archaeological data, Egyptian, Assyrian, and biblical records illuminate Megiddo's history. The latter mention the Israelites' inability to control this region during the settlement period; *Solomon's royal building activities here during the United Monarchy; and *Josiah's ill-fated attempt to intercept at Megiddo Egyptian military aid for *Assyria against *Babylon. Later eschatological references mention the valley around *Armageddon (Hill of Megiddo) as the site of the final battle between the forces of good and evil. *Ron Tappy*

**MELCHIZEDEK.** The king of Salem and priest of God Most High (El Elyon; *see* Names of God) who met Abram when the latter was returning victorious from battle. When Melchizedek met the patriarch, he gave Abram bread and wine, and he blessed him by God Most High. Abram in turn gave the priest a tenth of the spoils.

Later tradition identified Salem with *Jerusalem, the city that King *David conquered and transformed into his capital. Apparently David tried to unite royal and sacerdotal power by appropriating the order of Melchizedek, the king-priest.

The author of the letter to the *Hebrews, citing Psalm 110.4, argues that *Jesus is a priest forever after the order of Melchizedek. The fact that *Abraham paid him tithes shows how great Melchizedek was. The fact that Melchizedek blessed Abraham establishes Melchizedek's superiority, for the greater always blesses the inferior. Jesus, being in the same order, is therefore greater than Abraham, too.

One of the Dead Sea Scrolls portrays Melchizedek as a heavenly being who will bring salvation (in fulfillment of Isa) and judgment at the conclusion of the final jubilee.

In gnostic literature, Melchizedek is variously represented as the one who brings the baptismal waters and as one who gathers and emits light. One of the Nag Hammadi documents describes him as a prominent heavenly priest and warrior figure who, in being baptized, offered himself in sacrifice, in a way reminiscent of Jesus.

In the Slavonic version of 2 *Enoch, Melchizedek's old and sterile mother conceived him miraculously, apart from sexual intercourse. He was taken to paradise, where he was to be the head of all future priests. The text speaks of the last generation when a new Melchizedek will arise; greater than all his predecessors, he will work miracles and rule as king and priest. *William B. Nelson, Jr.*

**MESOPOTAMIA.** A Greek name meaning "between the rivers." As used by Greek writers from the second century BCE, it denotes the land between the Tigris and *Euphrates rivers from roughly the northern and western borders of present-day Iraq to where the two rivers came close together near present-day Baghdad.

"Mesopotamia" occurs eight times in the NRSV. Twice (Deut. 23.4; I Chron. 19.6) it renders *ʿărām nahărayim,* meaning "Aram of the two rivers"; the Hebrew transliterated as *Aram-naharaim* is used in the NRSV three times. The Septuagint has "Mesopotamia" at Genesis 24.10 and Deuteronomy 23.4, but "Syria of rivers" at Judges 3.8 and "Syria of Mesopotamia" at 1 Chronicles 19.6.

The phrase "Aram of the two rivers" is similar to "Aram of Bet-Rehov," "Aram of Damascus," and "Aram of Zobah"; strictly, it means Aramean territory between the two rivers, that is, northwest Iraq and northeast Syria. Where the Septuagint has "Mesopotamia," this is not a translation of the Hebrew but the use of an equivalent geographical name. Because of the difference in meaning between the modern use of "Mesopotamia" and the ancient use, translations are not consistent in the use of the term, and modern tendency is to avoid the word altogether or to modify it.

*For further treatment of the history and cultures of Mesopotamia, see* Assyria; Babylon; Sumer. *J. W. Rogerson*

**MESSIAH.** The term denotes an expected or longed-for savior, especially in *Jewish tradition, where some applied it to the revolutionary Simon Bar Kokhba (d. 135 CE), the mystic Shabbetai Zevi (1626–1676), and other "false messiahs," and in Christianity, where it is exclusively applied to *Jesus Christ.

The word is derived from the common biblical Hebrew word *māšîaḥ,* meaning "anointed." In Greek it is transcribed as *messias* and translated as *christos.* In the Hebrew Bible, the term is most often used of kings, whose investiture was marked especially by anointing with, and who were given the title "the Lord's anointed." It is even used of *Cyrus, king of the *Medes and *Persians. There is a possibility that some prophets may have been anointed, and according to some texts the investiture of priests includes anointing too, though this probably reflects political developments after the fall of the monarchy; the title is not normally given to priests or prophets. In Zechariah 4.14, a passage dated to 520 BCE, where king and priest are described as "the two anointed ones," the term *māšîaḥ* is avoided. By Maccabean times, however, it is used of the high priest.

In its primary biblical usage, then, "anointed" is virtually a synonym for "king," in particular *David and his descendants, and it should be understood in the context of the royal ideology documented in the books of *Samuel, Kings, and Psalms, even when it is applied secondarily to priests and others. The king was appointed by divine command, and he was adopted as son of God. His own person was sacrosanct, the future of his dynasty was divinely protected, and he was the unique instrument of God's justice on earth. As with the ideals and the realities of *Zion, the *Temple, the priesthood, and other institutions, the gap between the ideals of Davidic kingship and historical reality widened, and eventually royal language and imagery came to be applied primarily to a hoped-for future king, whose reign would be characterized by everlasting justice, security, and peace. Such a figure is popularly known as "the messiah," and biblical texts that describe him are known as "messianic," though the term "messiah" itself does not occur with this sense in the Hebrew Bible. At the heart of biblical messianism is the idea that God intervenes in history by sending a savior to deliver his people from suffering and injustice. Influenced by the Exodus tradition, the stories of *Joshua and *Judges, and established religious institutions, this messianic hope crystallized into several models. The first is that of a king like David who would conquer the powers of evil by force of arms and establish a reign of justice and peace. In some passages his wisdom is referred to, in others his gentleness and humility. Emphasis is on the divine initiative and on the result of the action, so that some visions of a "messianic" age make little or no mention of the messiah himself.

Belief in a priestly messiah, son of *Aaron, who would arise alongside the Davidic messiah to save Israel, appears in the Dead Sea Scrolls. The mysterious figure of *Melchizedek provides a title for one who is at the same time both king and priest. A third model is that of a prophet, anointed to "bring good news to the oppressed." The belief that a prophet like *Moses would arise, known as Taheb ("he who brings back"), is central to *Samaritan messianism.

Finally, the tradition that the divinely appointed savior should suffer has its roots in numerous psalms attributed to David, as well as in the traditional picture of Moses and the prophets as rejected and persecuted by their people. The notion that his suffering or self-sacrifice is in itself saving is given a unique emphasis in Christian messianism.

*John F. A. Sawyer*

**METHUSELAH.** One of the long-lived ancestors before the Flood. In the Sethite genealogy in Genesis 5.21–27, which lists one male for each of the ten generations from *Adam to *Noah, Methuselah is listed eighth, the son of *Enoch and the grandfather of Noah. Methuselah is the longest lived (969 years), but all ten live to remarkably high ages, as do the pre-Flood ancestors of Mesopotamian tradition. The name Methusaleh is very like Methushael, listed as Lamech's father and Enoch's great grandson in the similar genealogy in Genesis 4 (seven male ancestors from *Cain to Noah).

*Jo Ann Hackett*

**MICAH.** Micah was an eighth-century BCE prophet to whom the book of Micah is attributed.

Micah, a shortened form of Micaiah (which occurs in Jer. 26.18), means

"Who is like Yah(weh)?" He was a person of whom we know practically nothing other than his place of origin, which was Moresheth or Moresheth-gath, a tiny village in the Judean foothills. (Mic. 1.8–16, doubtless Micah's own words, confirms the information in the title of the book supplied late by an editor at 1.1, since here he seems to be speaking of the small part of the world that he knew best.) From other internal evidence it is likely too that the other data of the opening title are valid, namely, that he spoke "in the days of Kings Jotham, Ahaz, and Hezekiah of Judah." He was, in other words, a Judahite seer or prophet, roughly contemporary with the much better known *Isaiah.

Although Micah's comments on Judean society strongly parallel those of his presumed contemporary and supplement them to a large degree, there is a pronounced difference in tone between the prophecies of Isaiah and Micah. Micah's is the voice of the countryside, of one who has empirical knowledge of the result of the evil policies that Isaiah, an aristocrat of *Jerusalem, could only surmise, however much he wanted to empathize with the suffering of his compatriots. Micah was presumably from the common people, one who felt himself called on in that age of turmoil to speak in the name of Israel's God against evils that were no longer tolerable.

The nucleus of the book goes back to Micah of Moresheth, who, in the latter part of the eighth century BCE, was protesting the internal dissolution of his country and of its religious and national nerve. His prophetic career may have begun about 725 BCE when it had become evident that the northern kingdom of *Israel—where prophecy had begun and which had always been the "elder sister" of the kingdom of *Judah to the south (Ezek. 23.1–3)—was now doomed to disappear into the outreaches of the voracious *Assyrian empire. Judah, by a combination of cynical statecraft, collaborationism, and religiously unacceptable compromise, would still be able to hold off the inevitable for a time; indeed, it outlasted the Assyrians only to become prey to their Neo-Babylonian successors. But this was done by the sacrifice of national and religious integrity, and in the end the result was the same, as Ezekiel pointed out after the fact.

The words of the prophet were subsequently adapted to changed conditions, added to, and amplified in later generations. This process says nothing against the transmission of the biblical word but rather enhances its integrity. The biblical word, in the mind of those who preserved and developed biblical traditions, was not dead, said for one time, but a living word that could continue to inspire the faith community in which it had been engendered to further insights into the mind of God.

*Bruce Vawter, C.M.*

**MICHAEL.** One of the *archangels, whose name is a rhetorical question meaning "Who is like God?" (or, "Who is like El?"). In apocalyptic literature he is Israel's patron angel, who fights for Israel against the angels of other nations. As such later tradition identifies him as the nameless divine messenger called "the prince of the army of Yahweh" in Joshua 5.13–15 (note also the spiritual "Michael, Row the Boat Ashore"). Michael also becomes the surrogate of a now transcendent storm god, leading the heavenly armies in the fight against the forces of chaos, and thus is the adversary of *Satan. The battle between them becomes a favorite artistic theme and may occur in variant form in the legend of George and the dragon.

*Michael D. Coogan*

**MIDIAN.** The name of a tribal group that appears to have played a significant role in the premonarchic history of Israel. Very little is known of the Midianites, and even the location and extent of their homeland is a matter of scholarly debate. The only source of information about them is the Bible. No archaeological remains can yet be attributed to them, and, with the exception of references in the inscriptions of *Tiglath-pileser III and Sargon II to Ephah, one of the subtribes of Midian (referred to as a son of Midian), they do not appear in extrabiblical inscriptions.

The Midianites are generally portrayed in the Bible as seminomadic and nomadic shepherds and traders. Their eponymous ancestor is said to have been the son of *Abraham and Keturah and to have been sent by Abraham to the east, along with his brothers. In the narratives of Genesis, Numbers, Joshua, and Judges, groups of Midianites appear all across southern Palestine and Sinai, as well as in Transjordan. This is usually interpreted as an indication of the wide range of their regular migrations.

Although the Midianites are usually portrayed as enemies of Israel, Midian is presented in a more positive light in passages dealing with *Moses's sojourn with Jethro/Hobab, a priest of Midian and Moses's father-in-law. The tradition that Moses received his revelation of Yahweh while living with the Midianites and the influential role that Jethro plays in Exodus 18 have led to speculation that the worship of Yahweh may have been adopted by Israel from the Midianites. Such speculations, however, cannot be confirmed.

The battle led by *Gideon against the Midianites in Judges 6–8 appears to have been the last time that Midian was a significant political threat to Israel. No conflicts are reported between the two in the monarchic period. Midian, however, continued to survive and play a role in the spice and gold trade from *Arabia. In Isaiah 60:6, an early postexilic poem, reference is made to Midianite and Ephaite caravans along the Arabian trade routes. *Wayne T. Pitard*

**MIRIAM.** Sister of *Moses and *Aaron. Miriam is presumably the sister who watches over Moses in the bulrushes in the story in Exodus. She is called a prophet in Exodus 15.20, when she leads the women dancing with tambourines after the victory at the Sea of Reeds. Then in Exodus 15.21 she is said to sing the first verse of the song just attributed to Moses. Since both Moses and Miriam are connected in the text to this "Song of the Sea," it has been speculated that the song was originally attributed to Miriam. The process by which the name of a dominant figure like Moses could become attached to a piece of poetry and supplant the name of a less common figure like Miriam is more easily understood than the converse. The other major biblical story about Miriam is her and Aaron's criticism of Moses's leadership in Numbers 12. They complain for two reasons, that Moses has married a "Cushite" woman and that Yahweh has spoken through them as well as through Moses. The story in fact serves to affirm Moses's position as leader. Yahweh is greatly angered by their complaints and punishes Miriam (but not Aaron, despite v. 11) for speaking against Moses. She is afflicted with a skin disease that turns her skin white. Aaron asks Moses to intercede with Yahweh on her behalf, and when he does she is healed after spending seven days outside the camp. The reference to a father spitting in his daughter's face and the seven-day period of purification is obscure. If *Cush in this story is meant to refer to Ethiopia, as it often does in the Bible, then Miriam's white-as-snow skin is an ironic punishment for a complaint that would have included her objection to Moses's taking an African wife. More likely Cush here refers to *Midian and Moses's marriage to the Midianite woman Zipporah as the source of the criticism, although the reference could still also have suggested the dark skin color of Ethiopians in contrast to Miriam's disease.

Miriam died while the Israelites were at Kadesh, and she was buried there. She was remembered in Micah 6.4 as one of the leaders of the Exodus along with Moses and Aaron. *Jo Ann Hackett*

**MOAB.** A nation whose affiliation with Israel may have been the closest of all her neighbors. This is indicated by the affinity of the Moabite language and writing tradition to *Hebrew; by *David's ancestry from the Moabite *Ruth and his sending his parents for sanctuary in Moab; by the legend of Moab's birth through the incestuous union of *Lot and his elder daughter; and by religious affinities to Yahwism portrayed in the Moabite Stone.

Moab lay along the east side of the Dead Sea. North Moab, including the plains of Moab opposite *Jericho, covered an area from just north of the top of the sea to the Arnon 25 mi (40 km) south, which is mostly well-watered tableland, 2,000–2,800 ft (600–850 m) above mean sea level; here lay Heshbon, the peaks of *Nebo and Pisgah, Medeba, Beth-meon, Ataroth, and Dibon. South ("true") Moab, from the Arnon to the Zered, the boundary with *Edom, is tableland 1,000 ft (300 m) higher and more marginal agriculturally. A text of Pharaoh Ramesses II (early thirteenth century BCE) designates this region by the name Moab. Topographic survey, which at first seemed to display an occupation gap from roughly 2000 to 1300 BCE, has more recently contributed evidence of settlement throughout the second millennium, even in the south. Probably Moab was first a tribal society, then a monarchy.

Relations between Moab and Israel are complex and difficult to discern from the record—whether enmity or amity. The issue is bound up with whether north Moab was under Moabite control. Thus, Numbers 21 depicts the *Amorite king Sihon as having displaced Moab from north of the Arnon and makes Sihon, not Moab, Israel's foe. The Balak/*Balaam story in Numbers 22–24, on the other hand, portrays enmity and puts the action in north Moab. Deuteronomic tradition condemns Moab for inhospitality to Israel during the Transjordanian trek, but asserts that Yahweh granted Moab its (southern?) territory, so Israel is not to harass Moab. Judges 3.12–30 pictures enmity, showing Moab in possession of the north with a foothold at Jericho ("city of palms"); Judges 11, on the other hand, implies amity with Moab.

*Saul reportedly defeated Moab, but it is David who subjugated it, militarily and by vassal treaty. The next explicit information comes from the Moabite Stone about 830 BCE, where Mesha, king of Moab at Dibon, asserts he liberated north Moab from the control of the Israelite northern kingdom's Omri Dynasty, dispossessing the "men of Gad" during *Ahab's reign or more probably at Ahab's death about 850 BCE. Mesha's inscription implies that Omri had regained this control; had Moab escaped subjugation sometime between Solomon and Omri? The accounts in 2 Kings 3 (Jehoram of Israel) and 2 Chronicles 20 (Jehoshaphat of Judah) contribute contemporary episodes of conflict with Moab, further suggesting struggle for independence at the end of the Omri dynasty. And 2 Kings 10.32–33 places Hazael of Damascus in north Moab in this period; perhaps Moab gained freedom from Israel only to lose it to Syria.

Moab came under loose *Assyrian control, probably through vassal treaty, around 732 BCE. In the mid-seventh century, it functioned as loyal vassal by quelling Arab rebellion against Assyria. Moab appears as *Nebuchadrezzar's client, helping put down Jehoiakim's revolt around 600 BCE. This period of subservience to the great powers is the setting for Amos 2.1–3, Isaiah 15–16, and Jeremiah 48, which link Moab to Yahweh's international dominion. These oracles judge Moab, lament over it, and convey to it divine promises. After the Babylonian conquest of the region, Moab disappears from available records, though the *Ezra-*Nehemiah campaign against mixture with foreigners suggests that Moab still designates a people in the late fourth century BCE.

*Edward F. Campbell*

**MONEY CHANGERS.** Mentioned only in the account of *Jesus's attack on merchants in the *Temple, which according to the synoptic Gospels took place shortly before his arrest but is set by John at the beginning of Jesus's ministry. According to Exodus 30.11–16, every adult male Israelite was to pay half a shekel annually to the sanctuary. In the period of the Second Temple this tax was paid at Passover; to assist pilgrims to Jerusalem, money changers apparently functioned within the large open area known as the "Court of Gentiles" or in the porticoes that framed the Temple enclosure, converting to the proper payment different currencies or those that were religiously offensive because of portraits on coins. Although rabbinic sources provide some evidence for complaints about profiteering by the money changers, who charged as much as eight percent for their service, the reaction of Jesus seems exaggerated, especially in its fullest form in Mark 11.15–19. It is furthermore unlikely that one person could control all activity within the vast Temple courtyard; the Gospel narratives, written after the destruction of the Temple in 70 CE, are making a theological point about Jesus, depicting him as a prophet in the tradition of *Jeremiah and *Isaiah, both of whom are quoted directly.

*Michael D. Coogan*

**MOSES.** As primary leader of the Israelites in their Exodus from *Egypt and during their wanderings in the *wilderness, and as mediator of the Law, Moses dominates the biblical traditions from Exodus through Deuteronomy. In fact, Exodus–Deuteronomy appears to have been edited as a biography of Moses, reporting his birth at the beginning and his death at the end. Between these events the Bible relates many episodes about his life and work.

Born in secret during the oppression in Egypt as the younger of the two sons of a *Levite couple, Amram and Jochebed, Moses was hidden away for a time to avoid slaughter at the hands of the Egyptians and then placed in a basket amid the reeds of the *Nile. Discovered by a daughter of Pharaoh who had pity on the child, he was spared and, through the intervention of his older sister, was nursed by his own mother. Raised by Pharaoh's daughter as her son, the child received the name Moses (*mōšeh,* understood as a participle of the verb *māšâ,* "to draw out"; the name actually appears to be a form of the Egyptian verb *mśw,* "to be born," or the noun *mesu,* "child, son," appearing in such names as Thut-mose and Ah-mose). When grown up, Moses killed an Egyptian whom he saw beating a Hebrew and, when word of his deed spread, he fled the country to save his life. Taking refuge in *Midian, he married Zipporah, the daughter of a Midianite priest who is variously referred to as Reuel, Jethro, or Hobab. While in Midian, she bore him two sons, Gershom and Eliezer.

While Moses was tending his father-in-law's flocks near *Horeb, the mountain of God, God revealed himself in a burning bush and commissioned him to return to Egypt and, with the help of *Aaron, to lead the *Hebrews out of the land of oppression. Moses returned to Egypt, and he and Aaron produced signs and nine plagues to persuade Pharaoh to allow the Hebrews to depart Egypt, either to go on a three-day journey into the wilderness to offer sacrifice to God or to leave the land for good. The signs and plagues failed to convince Pharaoh, who repeatedly gave and withdrew his permission to leave. With the tenth plague, the slaughter of the firstborn, Pharaoh and his people urged the Hebrews to leave.

Moses and the people departed only to be pursued by Pharaoh, whose army was drowned in the returning waters of the *Red Sea after the waters had parted for the Israelites to cross.

During their long stay in the wilderness and on their journey to the *Promised Land, Moses endured the people's recurrent murmuring and complaining. He aided in securing good drinking water, oversaw the receipt of quails and manna, directed their war with the *Amalekites, and, at the suggestion of his father-in-law, established judges to hear and adjudicate the people's disputes.

At *Sinai, Moses committed the people to observe the commandments of God, communicated to him during a forty-day stay on the mountain and then addressed to the people and subsequently written down by either Moses or God. He received instructions for constructing the tabernacle and its accoutrements. The first tablets of the Law presented to Moses were smashed by him when he returned to the camp to discover that Aaron had supervised the construction of a golden calf around which the people were celebrating. Moses intervened with God not to destroy the people, and God or Moses again wrote the words of the commandments during a second forty-day period, which were again proclaimed to the people. Moses then supervised the construction and erection of the tabernacle, received further laws and instructions, and consecrated the tabernacle and ordained Aaron and his sons as priests.

After staying at Sinai for eleven months, a census was taken of the non-Levitical males above the military age of twenty, totaling 603,550, the Levites one month and older, totaling 22,000, and the firstborn males one month and older, totaling 22,273. After receiving further commandments from God, consecrating the Levites, supervising receipt and employment of the leaders' special offerings, Moses and the people observed the Passover and departed from Sinai on the twentieth day of the second month of the second year after leaving Egypt.

For the next thirty-nine years, Moses led the people in their journeys in the wilderness. Kadesh (-barnea), an oasis in the northern Sinai desert, and its vicinity are the scene of many of the episodes reported in Numbers 11.1–20.21. During this period the people continued their murmuring and complaining, were fed with manna and quails, and were supplied with water. Moses was confronted with complaints about his wife (whether Zipporah or not remains uncertain) by *Miriam and Aaron and with a rebellion led by Korah and his associates. Spies were sent out to make a reconnaissance of *Canaan but returned with a discouraging report about the strength of the inhabitants. A belated attempt to invade the region from the south, apparently without Moses's approval, led to disaster. During these episodes, Moses and Aaron received further ordinances from God to be communicated to the people. After the death and burial of Miriam at Kadesh, Moses sent messengers to the king of *Edom to request permission to pass through his country but was refused.

The last phase of Moses's life (thirty-eight years, according to Deut. 2.14) was concerned with the movement of the people into and their conquest of Transjordan. Journeying from Kadesh, they defeated the king of Arad and came to Mount Hor, where Aaron died. Leaving Mount Hor, Moses led the people southward to bypass the land of Edom. When God sent fiery serpents against the people because of their impatience, Moses constructed a bronze serpent as an instrument of healing. The people eventually arrived in the territory north of the land of *Moab, where they defeated kings Sihon of the *Amorites and Og of Bashan. While the Israelites encamped near the *Jordan across from *Jericho, King Balak of Moab hired *Balaam to curse Israel. After a plague ravaged the people because of their worship of the Baal of Peor, Moses ordered a census, which counted 601,730 males above the age of twenty fit for the military. After the census, Moses received instructions from God about dividing the land, about women's inheritance rights, the designation of Joshua as his successor, a calendar of sacrifices, and women's vows. A battle against the Midianites provided the occasion for divine instructions about the division of battle spoils. Moses allotted the captured territory in Transjordan to the *tribes of *Reuben and *Gad and half of *Manasseh and transmitted divine instructions about dividing the land west of the Jordan and setting aside cities for the Levites and *cities of refuge for those guilty of accidental homicide.

On the eve of his death, the first day of the eleventh month of the fortieth year after the Exodus, Moses delivered a series of farewell addresses to the people, expounding again the Law and its requirements for living in the land, offering a personal adieu, a song, and blessings on the tribes. With Joshua properly commissioned as his successor, and having inscribed his song and written and given directions for the reading and safekeeping of the book of the Law, at the command of God Moses went up Mount *Nebo, viewed the Promised Land, and died at the age of 120 years, full of life and vigor. He was buried by the Lord, "but no one knows his burial place to this day" (Deut. 34.1–8). God did not allow Moses to enter the land he viewed, either because of his own failure to provide proper recognition of God or because of the sins of the people.

Any critical attempt to assess the historicity of the portrait of Moses presented in Exodus to Deuteronomy must take into account a number of characteristics of this literature and its presentation. First, many of the stories are legendary in character and are built on folktale motifs found in various cultures.

The theme of the threatened child who eventually becomes a great figure, for example, was employed from Mesopotamia to Rome and appears in the stories about Sargon the Great, Heracles, Oedipus, Romulus and Remus, *Cyrus, and *Jesus. Second, Israel's theology located the giving of the Law and the formation of the national life outside the land it occupied and thus considered the wilderness period as its constitutional time. Hence, laws and institutions from diverse times and conditions are located in this formative era. Third, the duplications in the texts and the frequent lack of cohesion in the narratives and of consistency in details indicate that the material is composite and multilayered. Fourth, the lack of external frames of reference makes it impossible to connect any of the events depicted about Moses with the history of other cultures. The Egyptian Pharaoh of the oppression, for example, goes unnamed and no contemporary nonbiblical sources mention Moses. Finally, Moses is depicted as the archetype of several offices. Throughout he is representative not only of the good leader but also of the ideal judge and legal administrator, intercessor, cult founder, and prophet. In all of these he excelled and thus served as the standard by which others were judged.

In biblical literature outside the *Pentateuch, Moses is most often mentioned in the phrases "the book of Moses," "the law of Moses," and "the book of the law of Moses," indicating the development of the concept of the Torah as such and of its special authority and Mosaic authorship, themes that will become central for subsequent Jewish tradition. The same implication of the special scriptural authority of the first five books of the Bible, the books of Moses, is found in the New Testament, where there are repeated appeals to what Moses said as well as to the "law of Moses" and the "book of Moses."

Postbiblical tradition elaborated on Moses's biography from his birth to his death in such texts as the *Testament of Moses* and in haggadic literature. Details of these embellishments are also found in the New Testament in the reference to *Jannes and Jambres and in the account of the dispute between *Michael and the devil over Moses's body (Jude 9).

These haggadic legends were also known to such Hellenistic Jewish writers as *Philo and Josephus, who added to them the Hellenistic concept of the ideal man, so that the details of Moses's life reveal him to be the consummate human being and as such the appropriate founder of the theocratic state. This may be the background for the parallels drawn in the gospel of Matthew between the lives of Moses and Jesus. Yet for Matthew, as for the author of the letter to the Hebrews, Jesus is superior: Moses's presence at the transfiguration confirms Jesus's sonship, and that sonship is clearly superior to Moses's status as God's servant.

The artistic tradition of depicting Moses with horns on his forehead arose from the understanding by some ancient translators of the Hebrew verb *qāran* as related to the noun *qeren,* "horn"; an alternative is to understand the verb as meaning "to shine" (so NRSV, and most earlier English translations).

*John H. Hayes*

# N

## NABATEANS.

**Origins and Growth.** The consensus of modern scholarship no longer relates the Nabateans to the biblical Nebaioth, the firstborn son of *Ishmael, nor with the Nabatu/Nabaiati of Assyrian records. Rather, they are seen to have originated somewhere in the Arabian peninsula, emerging by at least the fourth century BCE and described by Diodorus Siculus as a sedentarized group of traders occupying the ancient *Edomite site known as Petra. Pliny adds some scant details of previous Red Sea island occupation and suggests an original tribal territory between those of the Qedar and Dedan tribes.

By the first century BCE, the group had become fully sedentary, urban, and monarchically organized, controlling the major north-south trade routes of Coele-*Syria and northern *Arabia. As a result of commerce, their sphere of influence extended far beyond their political borders, and their trading connections embraced the major luxury suppliers and markets of both east and west. Although frankincense and myrrh, along with Dead Sea balsams and bitumen, appear foremost in the list of their commercial products, such items as silk, gems, spices, and pharmaceuticals were probably also traded. With the trading routes went also other installations, resulting in more than a thousand sites known to have been established by Nabateans.

Their capital city, Petra, rapidly achieved a sophisticated urbanism, prompted by competition with surrounding people. A monarchic form of government (eleven kings have thus far been identified) further advanced their position as a true political state. The Nabateans seem to have reached their height under Aretas IV (9 BCE–40 CE), whose ethnarch attempted to arrest *Paul at *Damascus.

**Language.** Although the extant examples of Nabatean are basically Aramaic, they contain a large number of Arabisms. The script gradually developed into a semicursive, ligatured form, which ultimately served as the basis for the modern Arabic script.

Hundreds of Nabatean inscriptions have been found, including letters and contracts. No literary works, however, have as yet been recovered, leaving vast gaps in knowledge concerning the ideology, social structure, and even commercial history of the people.

**Technology.** Despite the lack of documentary data, the material remains of the Nabateans have furnished substantial evidence of high technological skill. Hydraulic engineering, architecture, ceramics, numismatics, metallurgy, along with sculpture and decorative art, are attested throughout Nabatene areas. Especially at Petra, such skills are seen at their best, for the capital city was embellished by succeeding rulers, in addition to being militarily secured and made more generally habitable. Likewise throughout the kingdom, different types of desert-adapted water systems for both agriculture and culinary purposes are found.

Architecturally, the Nabateans show an eclecticism to be attributed to their broad trading connections. Most obvious are the more than eight hundred funerary, cultic, and other architectural features at Petra, and the smaller number, mainly tomb façades, from Medain Selah. The vast majority of these installations are carved into cliff faces, but built structures are being uncovered by recent excavations at a variety of sites. At Petra these have included public secular and religious structures, along with private residential buildings.

Ceramics also reached an extremely high technical and decorative level by the first century CE. Most impressive was the development of a fine, thin red-painted pottery, generally used for open plates. This type has become the principal marker for identifying Nabatean sites throughout the area. Of equal importance, however, were more commercial ceramic vessels, such as *unguentaria* for oils and related products, which were developed for trade throughout the Roman empire; these have been identified as far west as Spain.

Coinage and other metal production are also noticeably represented at Petra. Coin production among the Nabateans possibly began as early as 90 BCE, and continued until the beginning of the second century CE.

Sculpture, in the round and in relief, along with castings of figurines, lamps, and other objects, appear in great quantities and types, some with marked artistic excellence, at Petra, Et-Tannur and elsewhere. Fresco, appliqué, and other decorative art examples, including the decoration of architectural orders, are also beginning to come to light.

Nabatene functioned as a virtually independent kingdom throughout the Roman period, until the need to consolidate the Near East led Trajan to incorporate the area formally into the empire. In 106 CE Roman forces entered Petra and the Nabatean kingdom ceased to exist. Nabatean life and culture were scarcely affected, however, and continued with little real evidence of Roman or Christian impact.

On the evening of May 19, 363 CE, Petra was struck by a disastrous earthquake and the city fell into ruins. With that calamity, the Nabateans, as such, disappeared from recorded history. Yet their cultural, linguistic, technological, and artistic influence continued, and permeated Near Eastern culture for generations to follow. *Philip C. Hammond*

**NAHUM.** A prophet to whom is attributed the book that bears his name. Nahum means "comfort," a name that stands in contrast with the violent vengeance portrayed in the book. He is identified as "the Elkoshite," but the location of Elkosh is unknown. We have no other information about this prophet.

The three chapters of the book of Nahum constitute a powerful poem that interprets events surrounding the fall of the *Assyrian capital of *Nineveh in 612 BCE in terms of the Lord's control of history on behalf of his people. The book contains some of the most powerful poetry in the Bible, a witness to its inspiration in another sense. The prophet-poet who wrote the book looked beyond the facts of Nineveh's destruction to discern and portray God's intentions in it.

Nahum's poem portrays the last days of Nineveh. This is seen as good news for Israel, a hope that is short-lived, since

*Egypt and *Babylon turned out to be worse masters than Assyria. But the poem is correct in marking the event as a turning point in history. In Nahum a historic event is presented as symbolic of the struggle between God and ultimate evil.

*John D. W. Watts*

## NAMES AND NAMEGIVING.

**Significance.** Throughout the Bible, names are full of meaning. Scholars have long recognized that both for ancient Israel and the ancient Near East as well as for early Judaism and Christianity, the name of a person, place, or thing was somehow connected to and descriptive of its essence and/or personality. Thus names of individuals expressed their personality and status or nature. This is reflected in those stories where an individual's name is changed in recognition of a changed nature, personality, or status. Examples include *Jacob's name being changed to Israel following his successful all-night wrestling match with an unnamed (!) divine being and Abram's name being changed to *Abraham after the institution of the covenant. The same phenomenon occurs in the name change or assumption of an additional name or throne name by kings in ancient Israel, as when Mattaniah is renamed *Zedekiah. The names of a newborn children seem normally to have been carefully chosen to reflect the circumstances of their birth as well as to indicate something of their personality or status.

**Types of Names.** Names may be divided into two categories: personal names and place names. Within these two categories we may also speak of simple names, consisting of one element, and compound names, consisting of two or more elements. Simple names for individuals may be taken from the names of plants and animals (Deborah = bee/hornet; Huldah = weasel). Compound names may be formed from nouns, but most compounds are sentence names that bring together a form of the divine name (Yo- [Jo-] or Yeho- [Jeho-] and -yah[u], all derived from "Yahweh"; or El; *see* Names of God in the Hebrew Bible) or a title of God (father, king, etc.) plus a verb, noun, or adjective descriptive of God (e.g., Elijah = Yah[weh] is God [ʾēl]). Names that incorporate a divine name, called theophoric names, can also occur in a short form in which the divine name is omitted; this short form is called a hypocoristicon (e.g., Jonathan/Nathan; Berechiah/Baruch).

**Process of Naming.** In the Hebrew Bible, children are regularly named by the mother shortly after birth), but the father or others could and frequently did also name the child. Genesis 30.6–24 preserves the stories of the births and namings of seven of the sons and one daughter of Jacob. In each case, punning or wordplay in the giving of the name is evident. Usually English translations supply the reader with notes that elucidate the wordplays found in the Hebrew text. Whether wordplay always played an important role is uncertain.

In the Hebrew Bible children were named shortly after birth, but in the New Testament the practice of waiting eight days to name a male child at his circumcision is attested. Luke's story of the naming of *John the Baptist also attests to the development within ancient Judaism of naming a newborn boy after either his father or grandfather. In the Second Temple period the latter practice is well attested in the family of the high priests.

From at least the Persian period onward, Jews often were given a non-Hebrew (Babylonian, Greek, Latin, etc.) name in addition to their Hebrew name. Biblical examples include Hadassah/Esther, Simon Peter, John Mark, and Saul/Paul. *Russell Fuller*

**NAMES FOR THE NAMELESS.** Although the Bible contains many named persons, it also refers to numerous individuals who are mentioned but not named. Through the ages, readers of the Bible have felt the need to identify these anonymous figures who play a part in scripture, and so names (at times more than one) have been provided for many of these unidentified persons.

**Hebrew Bible.** At the very beginning of the Bible, readers are prompted to ask: Who was Cain's wife? An answer is provided by the apocryphal Book of Jubilees, a Jewish text also known as "The Little Genesis" and thought to have been written in the second century BCE. According to Jubilees 4.9, after giving birth to *Cain and then *Abel, *Eve bore a daughter named Awan, who eventually became Cain's wife. After the birth of his son Seth, *Adam fathered another daughter and named her Azura; she later became Seth's wife.

The Book of Jubilees also identifies the wives of the other antediluvian males who appear in Genesis 5.6–31. *Noah, the last of this series, is said to have married Emzara, the daughter of Rakeel, who in turn was the daughter of Noah's father's brother. Other apocryphal texts give more names for Noah's wife—over a hundred different names are known!

Another imaginative source for names of unidentified women in the Hebrew scriptures are postbiblical Jewish legends. For example, the story of *Joseph recorded in Genesis does not include the name of Potiphar's wife, who tried to seduce the young Joseph. Later tradition supplies her name—Zuleika. Similarly, the book of Exodus details how the baby *Moses, abandoned in a basket and left floating among the reeds of the Nile, was found by Pharaoh's daughter, who was bathing in the river. The young woman adopted the child as her own. Different names have been ascribed to Moses's surrogate mother: one tradition calls her Thematis, while another names her Bithiah.

Postbiblical sources assign two wives to Job. His first wife, who died while Job was undergoing his trials, was named Sitis (or Sitidos), a name derived from the Greek transcription of Job's hometown, Uz. After Job regained his health, he married Jacob's daughter Dinah, with whom he had a second set of children.

The pseudo-Philonic text *Liber Antiquitatum Biblicarum* names the Ammonite ruler with whom Jephthah negotiated Getal. The daughter whom Jephthah presented as a sacrifice because of his regrettable oath was named Seila, and she lamented her virginity on a mountain called Stelac. The same book identifies the medium of Endor, who conjured up *Samuel's spirit for *Saul, as Sedecla, the daughter of Debin (or Adod) the Midianite.

**New Testament.** The New Testament has also been substantially embellished in later Christian tradition. The gospel of Matthew does not specify the number or the names of the *Magi who bring gifts to the infant Jesus. Since three gifts were offered, three wise men are assumed. Their names, Balthasar, Melchior, and Gaspar, were assigned in the *Excerpta Latina Barbari* by as early as the sixth century. Such traditions are expanded in the *Exposition of Matthew*, thought to have been written by the Venerable Bede, where it is recorded that each of the wise men came from one of the three main continents—Asia, Africa, and Europe. Furthermore, Bede also claims that the Magi were descendants respectively of Shem, Ham, and Japheth, the three sons of Noah. The East provides yet other traditions. In an Ethiopic text known as the *Book of Adam,* the Magi are named Hor, king of the Persians, Basanater, king of Saba, and Karsudan, king of the East. A dozen Magi journey to Bethlehem according to Armenian and Syrian traditions, and their names, as well as names for their fathers, are all recorded.

The anonymous shepherds to whom an angel comes to proclaim the news of Jesus's birth have also been a subject of traditional interest. A thirteenth-century Syriac compendium collected and edited by *bishop Shelemon and entitled *The Book of the Bee* declares there were seven shepherds and even lists their names: Asher, Zebulan, Justus, Nicodemus, Joseph, Barshabba, and Jose.

The twelve apostles are identified by the four Gospels, but the seventy (or seventy-two) disciples sent out by Jesus are unnamed. Yet, over the following centuries, many unfinished lists of their names were compiled. Of several somewhat varied lists of the full group, the first appears in the *Chronicon Paschale,* a lengthy chronological-historical text produced by about 650 CE. Matthias is the first disciple listed, followed by Sosthenes and Cephas, and then Linus and Cleopas. The list continues with the names of twenty-six people to whom Paul sends salutations at the end of his letter to the Romans (beginning with Aquila in Rom. 16.3 and ending with Quartus in 16.23). After these names come thirty-nine others, all compiled from the remaining Pauline letters and from Acts. Almost none of the names are Palestinian, but this did not seem to bother the compilers, who also allowed the duplication of several names on the list—the result of a somewhat mechanical combining of separate sources.

The *Book of the Bee* also names various children mentioned in the Gospels. The child whom Jesus sets in the midst of his disciples is identified as Ignatius, who later ruled as patriarch of *Antioch. Two of the children brought to Jesus so that he would lay his hands on them and bless them were *Timothy and *Titus, who later became bishops.

In Luke 16.19–31, Jesus does not name the rich man who asks for Lazarus's help. An Egyptian tradition of around 200 CE names the rich man *Nineveh, which is symbolic of haughty and indulgent luxury. Nineveh is also cited in an early manuscript of Luke. In the West, a different tradition is found in the pseudo-*Cyprianic treatise* De pascha computus (200 or 300 CE), with the identification of the rich man as Phineas. Later he is called *Dives.

Of the women in the New Testament, the one who was probably named earliest in Christian tradition was the Canaanite or Syrophoenician woman who sought out Jesus to help save her daughter who was possessed by a demon. The pseudo-Clementine *Homilies* of the third century calls the woman Justa, and her daughter Bernice. The apopcryphal *Acts of Pilate* also names Bernice as the woman who endured hemorrhages for twelve years. However, the later Arabic apocryphal gospel of John identifies her as Yusufiya (Josephia). The widow whose dead son Jesus resurrects as he was being carried by on his bier is named Lia (Leah) according to the Coptic text on Christ's Resurrection, ascribed to the apostle Bartholomew. Pilate's wife, who in Matthew 27.19 forewarns her husband to have nothing to do with Jesus, is variously identified as Claudia, Procla, and Perpetua.

Similarly, the robbers crucified on either side of Jesus were also given a variety of names. In the Western tradition, an Old Latin Gospel text names them Zoatham and Camma, while another refers to them as Joathas and Maggatras. In the East, they are called Dysmas and Gestas in the *Acts of Pilate,* which also identifies the Roman soldier who pierces Jesus's side with a spear as Longinus. The tenth-century Codex Egberti names the man who tried to ease Jesus's thirst with a sponge filled with sour wine as Stephaton.

In the second *Gospel of Peter,* after Jesus's burial the soldiers assigned to guard his tomb were supervised by a Roman centurion called Petronius. The *Book of the Bee,* produced much later, elaborates on the descriptions of the soldiers: "They were five in number, named Issachar, Gad, Matthias, Barnabas, and Simon; but others say they were fifteen, three centurions and their Roman and Jewish soldiers."

Many traditions name the individual who accompanies Cleopas to Emmaus on the afternoon of the first Easter (Luke 24.18); among the identifications are Nathanael, Nicodemus, someone named Simon (not Simon Peter), and the evangelist Luke.

Few if any of these traditions are based on accurate historical data. The readiness to give names to the biblical nameless is a witness to the fertile imaginations of Jewish and Christian writers and to their reluctance to accept unknown elements in biblical history.

*Bruce M. Metzger*

**NAMES OF GOD IN THE HEBREW BIBLE.** The Bible often refers to God by his proper name, which was probably pronounced Yahweh. In the Hebrew Bible, the consonants *yhwh* are usually to be read as Adonai *(ᵓădōnāy),* "my Lord," for the sake of reverence, and English versions represent the word by "Lord" or (less often) "God" in capital letters. The Hebrew word is a plural of majesty (with a singular meaning) of *ᵓādôn,* which is translated "Lord." The name Yahweh often appears in the phrase "Yahweh of hosts," as the Hebrew is probably to be translated (cf. "Yahweh of Teman" or "of Samaria" in the Kuntillet ᶜAjrud inscriptions of ca. 800 BCE), or the longer "Yahweh the God of hosts." Some have thought that the hosts, Sabaoth *(ṣĕbāᵓôt),* are the armies of Israel, but a reference to these human armies is inappropriate in, for instance, prophetic denunciations of Israel, and the word probably denotes heavenly or angelic armies. Some maintain that Sabaoth is an epithet in apposition to Yahweh and that it means something like "the Mighty One," but there is no evidence in Hebrew for such a meaning.

The usual Hebrew word for God is Elohim *(ᵓĕlōhîm),* another plural of majesty with a singular meaning when used of Yahweh. The singular form Eloah *(ᵓĕlōah)* appears, mainly in the book of Job, but the most common singular noun for God is El *(ᵓēl),* which has cognates in other Semitic languages and whose Ugaritic counterpart is used both for the chief god and as a general word for any god. The Israelites adopted this common Semitic word (El-Elohe-Israel, "El the God of Israel"), and some of the divine names compounded with El in the Hebrew Bible were probably originally used of non-Israelite deities. In Genesis 14.18–20, 22, we find El Elyon *(ᵓēl ᶜelyôn),* "God Most High," whose priest is *Melchizedek but who is identified by Abram with Yahweh. The word Elyon is used of Yahweh in other places in the Bible. In the fourth century CE, Philo of Byblos is cited by Eusebius of

Caesarea as referring to Elioun, the Most High (Greek *hupsistos*), as a *Phoenician god. The Aramaic cognate of Elyon is $^{c}$*lyn* (perhaps $^{c}$*elyān*), and a god with this name appears alongside El in a treaty of the eighth century BCE from Sefire in Syria.

The element El is found in divine names in Genesis, sometimes in connection with various places, such as Bethel, "the house of God," and we find El-Bethel, "God of Bethel." Thus, at a place in the desert there is El-roi ("a God of seeing"), and at Beer-sheba there is El Olam ("the Everlasting God," 21.33; cf. *špš*$^{c}$*lm* in a Ugaritic letter, and *šmš*$^{c}$*lm* in a Phoenician text of ca. 700 BCE, both of which mean "the eternal sun" god or goddess). Another name is El Shaddai, usually translated "God Almighty," and the Priestly writer in the *Pentateuch maintains that God first made himself known by that name before revealing his name Yahweh. The name is not restricted to P, for it is found in a number of places, and it is part of the names Zurishaddai and Ammishaddai. It is perhaps related to an Akkadian word for "mountain."

It is uncertain whether El-berith ("God of the covenant") in Judges 9.46 refers to Yahweh, for this deity seems to be the same as Baal-berith in 8.33; 9.4, and may be a Canaanite god. On the other hand, Baal, which means "lord," was sometimes used of Yahweh in early times without necessarily always identifying him with the Canaanite god *Baal. In 1 Chronicles 12.6, there is the personal name Bealiah, "Yah is Baal" (cf. *yhwb*$^{c}$*l* on an unpublished seal). *Saul and Jonathan, who were worshipers of Yahweh, had sons named, respectively, Esh-baal and Merib-baal, which were changed by editors to Ish-bosheth and Mephibosheth, in which "bosheth" ("shame") was substituted for "Baal." Jerubbaal (Jerubbesheth in 2 Sam. 11.21), *Gideon's other name, is probably to be explained similarly, notwithstanding the forced explanation in Judges 6.31–32. *David also had a son named Beeliada (*b*$^{c}$*lyd*$^{c}$), probably identical with Eliada in other lists. Hosea 2.16 says that Israel will call God "my husband" (lit. "my man") and no longer "my Baal" (i.e., "my lord," another word for husband), which may imply that some Israelites addressed God in the latter way.

Both God's holiness and his relation to his people are reflected in the phrase "the Holy One of Israel," which is characteristic of the book of *Isaiah. Although it is not strictly a name, it is relevant to mention this title here.

Yahweh is frequently described as melek, "king," "a great king over all the earth" or "above all gods," "my" or "our king," or "the King of glory." He "reigns" or "has become king," and he "will reign forever." Personal names include Malchiel and Malchiah, meaning "El" or "Yah is king." Isaiah sees a vision of "the King, Yahweh of hosts."

Various epithets and figures of speech are applied to God, but they cannot all be described as names or titles. In Genesis 15.1, Yahweh says to Abram "I am your shield," but that does not prove the theory that "the Shield of Abraham" was a title. On the other hand, God is described as "the Fear of Isaac"—the suggested alternative translation, "the Kinsman of Isaac," lacks sufficient evidence—and as "the Mighty One of Jacob"; these may be titles reflecting the special relationship of God with particular individuals. His relationship with people is also shown by names containing the element ʾ*āb*, "father," such as Abijah, Abiel, and *Abra(ha)m. Yet although God was viewed thus, and could be addressed as "my (or our) Father," it is doubtful whether the evidence suffices to justify the claim that "Father" was a title, let alone a name.

*See also* Jehovah.

*J. A. Emerton*

**NAPHTALI.** Son of Bilhah, *Rachel's maid, and *Jacob and one of the twelve *tribes of Israel. Rachel's reference to "mighty wrestlings" with her sister *Leah (Gen. 30.7) plays on the name Naphtali ("wrestler"). The tribe is allotted much territory west of the Sea of Galilee and the upper Jordan. The military prowess of Naphtali is praised in the blessings of Jacob and Moses. During the reign of *Solomon, Naphtali becomes an administrative district headed by Solomon's own son-in-law.

During the divided monarchy Naphtali undoubtedly suffered from the wars between Israel and Syria. "All the land of Naphtali" was captured by the *Assyrians in 732 BCE.

*Gary N. Knoppers*

**NATHAN.** The main *prophet in the court of King *David. As such, he set the pattern for the proper functioning of a royal prophet. He is introduced as the prophet through whom God establishes his covenant with David. Later, he pronounces God's judgment on David for David's sins against *Bathsheba and Uriah; but then he reports God's love for *Solomon, the son of David and *Bathsheba. This sets the stage for Nathan's role in helping Solomon succeed David to the throne. In Chronicles, Nathan is said to be partly responsible for recording the events of the reigns of David and Solomon. Though often dismissed as pious tradition, this is not an unreasonable claim. Many of the concerns that Solomon would have faced early in his reign (e.g., defending his claim to the throne)—when Nathan was still influential—are addressed by the stories about Nathan and David.

*Timothy M. Willis*

**NAZARETH.** A town in southern *Galilee about fifteen miles southwest of the Sea of Galilee and twenty miles from the Mediterranean westward. It was probably located at or near the site of the town by the same name in modern Israel. References to it occur in the Gospels and Acts, and all agree that Jesus was from Nazareth.

Although not situated on any main commercial roads, Nazareth was not far from them, and it was only several miles from Sepphoris, an important city near the road from Ptolemais to Tiberias. Its secluded position may explain the absence of references to it before Roman times, and this may indicate that it was an insignificant Jewish town. On the other hand, *Luke's references to it as a city rather than a village may indicate that it was not an insignificant place. Distinctions, however, between the two were not great, and they were sometimes used interchangeably; furthermore, Luke's knowledge of Palestine is not always correct.

Located on a hill in the Plain of Esdraelon, it was about 1,200 ft (365 m) above sea level. From its heights one could see mountains in three directions and view the Plain of Esdraelon on the south. The moderate climate, sufficient rainfall, and fertile soil were favorable for growing fruits, grains, and vegetables. The water supply of the town itself was restricted to one spring, supplemented by cisterns. If the spring is to be identified with the "Mary's Well" shown to tourists, it is the only shrine of the many in Nazareth that may go back to Jesus's time.

*Edwin D. Freed*

**NAZIRITE** (KJV: "Nazarite"). An individual who was dedicated (Hebr. *nāzîr*) to special sacred service through a vow made by the individual or by a parent. The dedication could last for a lifetime or for only a limited period.

A nazirite in Israel had to fulfill several conditions in order to remain consecrated. The man or woman had to abstain from the fruit of the vine and other intoxicants, avoid defilement by contact with a dead body (even that of a close relative), and not allow a razor to cut the hair. Rituals were specified to deal with a nazirite's unintentional contact with a corpse and to mark the completion of a period of dedication. Nazirites could drink wine when their term was completed, but some were tempted to do so before their vow was fulfilled.

The best-known nazirite is *Samson. His nazirite status was announced by a divine messenger while Samson was still in his mother's womb, and was later acknowledged by Samson himself. Part of the irony of the Samson story is that Samson appears not to keep any of his vows. He attended drinking feasts, touched the carcass of a dead lion, and allowed his hair to be cut by Delilah.

*Samuel is also called a nazirite; *Joseph is as well, but this may only be metaphorical in the sense of one separated from his brothers.

*Dennis T. Olson*

**NEBO.**

**1.** From Mount Nebo, perhaps modern Jebel Neba just west of Heshbon, *Moses viewed the *Promised Land across the Jordan before he died (*see* Pisgah). Later tradition tells of Jeremiah hiding the ark of the covenant on Mount Nebo.

**2.** Nebo is also the name of a town near Mount Nebo in territory allotted to the tribe of *Reuben. Israel's enemy *Moab often held this region; hence the prophetic oracles against Nebo. The *Moabite Stone hints at an important early Iron Age sanctuary of Yahweh here.

**3.** In Isaiah 46.1, Nebo refers to the *Babylonian god of writing, Nabu.

*Mary Joan Winn Leith*

**NEBUCHADNEZZAR.** *See* Nebuchadrezzar.

**NEBUCHADREZZAR.** The king of *Babylonia (605–562 BCE), frequently named in Jeremiah, Ezekiel, and Daniel, as well as by classical writers. The name is also rendered Nebuchadnezzar, a biblical variant; the form Nebuchadrezzar is closer to the Babylonian Nabû-kudurri-uṣur, "the (god) Nabu has protected the succession." He was renowned as the most distinguished ruler of the Neo-Babylonian (Chaldean) Dynasty founded by his father, Nabopolassar, in 627 BCE, and as the conqueror of *Jerusalem who took the Judeans into exile.

Nebuchadrezzar acted as commander in chief for his aging father when in 605 BCE he took Carchemish from the Egyptians and drove them back to their borders, thus freeing Syria and Palestine. According to the Babylonian Chronicle and Josephus, he broke off this campaign in order to return to take the throne of Babylon on hearing of his father's death. He campaigned frequently in the west, receiving tribute from many rulers and from Tyre, which he subsequently besieged for thirteen years. His vassals included Jehoiakim of Judah who, however, defected in 601, misinterpreting the fierce battle between the Babylonians and Egyptians that year as a victory for the latter. Nebuchadrezzar gained revenge by capturing Jerusalem on 16

March 597, when he set up a new king (Mattaniah/*Zedekiah) sympathetic to him. Jehoiachin, whom he called Yaukin, king of Judah, was taken prisoner to Babylon with the Temple vessels and many Judeans. Nebuchadrezzar also fought against Elam and the Arabs, and was present in the operations that led to the sack of Jerusalem in August 587/586 BCE as a reprisal for Zedekiah's activity as the focus of anti-Babylonian opposition. At that time, more Judeans were taken into exile, as they also were following a later raid, including one on Egypt attested in a fragmentary Babylonian text dated 568–567 BCE.

Little is known of the last thirty years of Nebuchadrezzar's rule. The tale of his madness may be a pejorative account of a period in the reign of his successor Nabonidus. Nebuchadrezzar's character may be reflected in his inscriptions, which do not emphasize his military exploits yet reflect his exercise of law, order, and justice as well as stressing moral qualities and religious devotion. He rightly claims to have rebuilt Babylon, its walls, palaces, temples, and defenses as a wonder to which all peoples came with tribute; the famous "hanging gardens" of Babylon are also attributed to him in some traditions. He died during a period that saw the seeds of economic decline resulting from the cost of his enterprises; he was succeeded by his son Amel-Marduk (Evil-Merodach).

*Donald J. Wiseman*

**NEGEB.** The Negeb is a mountainous desert south of Judah between the Arabah and the Mediterranean Sea. Its name means "dryness" but can also be synonymous with "the south." *Abraham and *Isaac sojourned there. The *Amalekites, Jerahmeelites, *Kenites (or Kenizzites), *Cherethites, and Calebites dwelt there. After the conquest of Canaan, it was allotted to *Simeon, but eventually incorporated into Judah ("Negeb of Judah at Beer-sheba"). The Bible depicts it as desolate although habitable. Archaeological evidence shows the Negeb was settled, at times surprisingly thickly, before, during, and after the biblical period.

*Joseph A. Greene*

**NEHEMIAH.** Son of Hacaliah, governor of the Persian province of Judah (Yehud) in the mid-fifth century BCE, and the main character in the book that bears his name.

It is generally accepted that Nehemiah came from Susa in *Persia to rebuild the walls of Jerusalem in 445/444 BCE. As the cupbearer of the Persian king Artaxerxes (probably Artaxerxes I, 465–424 BCE), Nehemiah held a high office of some influence at court. It is also probable that Nehemiah, serving in the presence of the queen, was a *eunuch; this may explain why he was unwilling to flee to the Temple of the Lord as protection against his enemies. It is clear that Shemaiah tried to lure him to the Temple in order to get him to transgress the stipulation forbidding eunuchs to enter the sanctuary. If he had done so, he could have lost his influence with the people and their trust.

After Nehemiah heard of the plight of his people in *Jerusalem and that the city was in ruins without a wall of defense against their enemies, he asked the Persian king's permission to go to Jerusalem in order to see what could be done. This was granted; Nehemiah was sent out as a governor of Judah with all the privileges pertaining to the post of governor of a province in the satrapy of Trans-Euphrates. To secure his safety he was granted an escort of soldiers to accompany him; this stands in contrast to the mission of *Ezra, in which no such escort was requested. It is, however, noteworthy that the mission of Nehemiah was of a political nature while that of Ezra was religious.

Artaxerxes's friendly gesture to Nehemiah was made just after a serious revolt broke out in the satrapy of the Trans-Euphrates. Megabyzus, the Persian general in Egypt, who put down the revolt in Egypt in 456 BCE, was also the satrap of the Trans-Euphrates. Megabyzus had generously promised the captured Egyptian king Inarus and certain Greek generals their release after the war. Artaxerxes, however, listened to his mother, the wife of Xerxes, the former king, and commanded their execution. This was a heavy blow to the pride of Megabyzus, and in 449 he fomented a rebellion against the Persian king, which Artaxerxes was unable to put down. Later, however, Megabyzus stopped the revolt and once again became a loyal subject of the king. It was thus politically expedient for Artaxerxes to send out Nehemiah, obviously one of his loyal officials, to Judah, one of the smaller but important provinces of the satrapy.

After Nehemiah arrived in Jerusalem he conducted a secret inspection of the walls of the city. It seems that he tried to hide his true intentions from the people so that news about his plans would not reach neighboring enemies. After the inspection Nehemiah decided to organize the Jews and to rebuild the walls. Nehemiah allotted sections of the walls to various persons and groups of persons to rebuild. Some scholars think the period of fifty-two days too brief to rebuild the walls, but if we keep in mind that a significant part of the wall needed only restoration, this time was not too short for such repairs. It has been pointed out that in similar circumstances the Athenians built a wall around Athens in just a month, and, in the face of an imminent attack on Constantinople by Attila after the wall was destroyed by an earthquake, the Eastern Romans restored it in sixty days.

With the building of the wall two serious problems developed for Nehemiah and the Jews. The first was a well-orchestrated attack of psychological warfare to stop building. This was done by neighboring nations, led by Sanballat I, governor of *Samaria, and assisted by Tobiah, probably a Persian official of the *Ammonites; somewhat later, these were joined by Geshem (Gashmu), chieftain of the *Nabateans or Arabs to the south and southeast of Judah, as well as by the Ashdodites of the old *Philistine territory to the west. With *Samaritans to the north and Ammonites to the east, Judah was nearly encircled by its enemies. They made use of rumors and threats to discourage Nehemiah and the Jews. But Nehemiah did not hesitate to take strong measures to ensure the safety of the workers on the walls. The last resort for his enemies was to try to divide the Jewish people by infiltrating their ranks with false rumors and to induce prophets to give false prophecies. But Nehemiah saw through all these attempts. In the end, the wall was completed and his enemies conceded that they had failed to achieve their goal.

The second problem was the poverty of the Jews. At that stage Judah had a weak economic infrastructure and the burden of taxes was heavy. The satrap collected taxes for the royal treasury, and both the satrap and his officials from the different provinces of the satrapy had to be paid. Furthermore, the governor and his officials collected taxes for their work. (Nehemiah, however, well aware of his subjects' poverty, did not collect taxes for himself and his officials.) Beyond these expenses, there were the tithes that the Jews were obliged to pay for the maintenance of the service in the Temple. It is thus not surprising that they had to go into debt and often were forced into debt-slavery in order to meet their obligations. After becoming aware of this problem, Nehemiah canceled all debts.

Nehemiah served for twelve years as governor of Judah and then returned to the royal court in Persia. After a few years, ca. 430 BCE, he went once more to Jerusalem, and was shocked by what he saw. The principles he had laid down during his previous service as governor had been neglected. Nehemiah was so dismayed that he took strong action. Having discovered that a place was furnished in the Temple for Tobiah the Ammonite by Eliashib the priest, Nehemiah threw the furniture of Tobiah out of the room and commanded that the place be purified. As a result of heavy taxes, the paying of tithes had been neglected; Nehemiah reinstituted the levy. Another problem was the desecration of the Sabbath by foreign traders in Jerusalem; he forbade them to do any business on the Sabbath within or outside the walls of Jerusalem. Finally, Nehemiah vehemently confronted the issue of marriages with foreigners. He even assaulted some of the men and pulled out their hair.

The book of Nehemiah ends abruptly without telling the reader what happened to either Nehemiah or Ezra. Nothing is said of the success of the measures taken against certain Jews described in Nehemiah 13. It is difficult to determine the precise relationship between the persons of Ezra and Nehemiah. It is understandable that Nehemiah is not mentioned in the memoir of Ezra in Ezra 7–10, because Nehemiah had not yet begun his mission. It is, however, difficult to understand why Ezra is not explicitly referred to in the memoir of Nehemiah, especially after his activities in teaching the Law, especially as it pertained to intermarriage. Because of the paucity of evidence this problem is hard to solve.

As with the book of Ezra, the great majority of modern scholars consider the book of Nehemiah to have been composed by the later Chronicler sometime in the fourth century BCE.

Because the book is for the most part derived from Nehemiah's memoir, one can form an excellent idea of his beliefs. The most important feature in the religion of Nehemiah is his sense of a living relationship with God. Despite his high regard for the Law, he did not regard it as the only form of mediation between humans and God. If we accept the authenticity of the prayers of Nehemiah, it becomes evident that he believed in immediate contact with God through prayer. As did other Jews in postexilic times, he believed in the dominant role of the Lord as the God of history: God could move the Persian king to give Nehemiah permission to go to Jerusalem; God determined every step that Nehemiah took after his arrival in Jerusalem. Although the work of Nehemiah was mainly political, a close relationship between politics and religion was presumed. Nehemiah never doubted that God was on his side and would finally grant him victory over his adversaries.

*F. Charles Fensham*

**NEPHILIM.** The Nephilim (from Hebr. *nāpal,* "to fall," hence probably "the fallen ones") are mentioned in Genesis 6.4 and Numbers 13.33. In Genesis, they are the children of the *sons of God and human women, and are called "heroes of old" and "men of renown." In Numbers, they are described as the giant aboriginal inhabitants of *Canaan, living at the time of Moses. It is not clear why or how the Nephilim survived the Flood to become the original *Canaanites; probably a duality of older oral traditions can be detected in the clash between these two texts. The Nephilim seem to share a common fate in Genesis and in Numbers, perhaps generated by their name—they exist only to die in a great destruction, either the Flood or the Israelite conquest. The Nephilim seem to be related to the *Rephaim, whose name is also connected with the dead, who are also giants, and who are also wiped out by the early Israelites.

*Ronald S. Hendel*

**NEW JERUSALEM.** *See* Jerusalem, *article on* Symbolism.

**NILE.** The exact etymology of the name of the great river of *Egypt derived from the Greek *neilos* is uncertain. The Egyptian name *yoteru* (later Coptic *eiōr*) is probably the basis of Hebrew *yĕʾōr.* The Nile, the longest river in the world (4,062 mi [6,540 km]), rises in a number of lakes in Central Africa and is joined by a tributary, the Blue Nile, near the city of Khartoum in the Sudan. The facts of its source were unknown to the Egyptians, who imagined that this was at Aswan, where the turbulent waters of the First Cataract were thought to well up from an underground cavern to flow north into Egypt and south into Nubia.

The Nile maintained the vegetation both in the extensive marshes in the north and on the agricultural lands bordering on its banks. From early times, a system of irrigation canals led from the main stream to assist cultivation. In mid-July each year the Nile began to rise, overflowing its banks and thus providing natural irrigation. This annual phenomenon, the inundation, also brought with it silt, a natural fertilizer composed of vegetable matter and red mud, largely carried down by the Blue Nile from Ethiopia. The rise of the waters and the deposit of silt accounted for the rich crops of Egypt. The actual height of the rise was important, for too small a rise was disastrous for the farmers, whereas too great a rise would lead to a breakdown of the irrigation system, the breaching of dikes, and the destruction of settlements. The levels of the inundation were carefully recorded by a series of Nilometers positioned along the course of the river. Identified with the inundation was the god Hapi, represented as a pot-bellied hybrid with pendulous breasts and colored green and blue like the flood waters and regarded as the guarantor of all life in Egypt.

In the Delta, the extensive marshes provided a natural habitat for numerous wild birds of all kinds, hunted both for food and for sport. It was in the marshes that the papyrus plant flourished, offering the essential material from which the Egyptians were able to manufacture a satisfactory and durable writing surface. A royal monopoly at one time, the product of the papyrus was exported throughout the ancient world until it was replaced in the ninth century CE by paper (a word that, while denoting a different substance, is derived from "papyrus").

Beyond maintaining ample moisture for successful crops in a land that, apart from the Delta, rarely experiences rain in any great measure, the Nile provided the main highway for travel and transport. Without the Nile it would have been impossible to convey the enormous quantity and weight of stone needed for the construction of the temples and the pyramids. Boats of all descriptions plied on the Nile: warships, cargo vessels, and seagoing ships capable of transporting cedar from Lebanon and copper from Cyprus. In addition, numerous small craft traveled the Nile, some to perform the business of ferries, for there were no bridges across the river, and others (scarcely more than bundles of papyrus plants tied together) to carry fishermen on their tasks. The normally prevailing north wind assisted the passage of sail-fitted boats upstream, while the flow of the river eased the labors of those paddling their crafts downstream.

Roads were unknown in ancient Egypt. There were, however, numerous pathways, mainly along the sides of the irrigation canals, suitable for passage by pedestrians and donkeys, the universal beasts of burden. Wheeled vehicles were almost unknown. Though the horse had been introduced during the period of the Hyksos, it was used only to draw the light war chariot. The camel arrived in the Nile valley only during the time of the Ptolemies. Hence the paramount importance of the Nile for communication and transport. *J. Martin Plumley*

**NIMROD.** Nimrod (literally, "we will rebel" or "let us rebel" in Hebrew) is described in Genesis 10.8–12 as a "mighty hunter before Yahweh." The list of the cities of his vast kingdom—Babel, Erech, and Akkad in *Babylon, followed by *Nineveh and Calah in *Assyria—seems to trace Mesopotamian history up to the beginnings of the Neo-Assyrian empire, when Nineveh and then Calah served as imperial capitals. Nimrod's name is likely a polemical distortion of the name of the Mesopotamian god Ninurta, who was a mighty hunter and warrior, a culture hero, and in some texts the ruler of the universe. Ninurta, who had cult centers in Babel, Calah, and other cities, was a divine patron of Neo-Assyrian kings (including Tukulti-Ninurta I, a less likely candidate for the original Nimrod). In Micah 5.5, the "land of Nimrod" is a synonym for Assyria. In postbiblical traditions, Nimrod, the inciter of "rebellion" who ruled Babel, was often identified as a giant (*see* Nephilim) and as the chief builder of the tower of *Babel. *Ronald S. Hendel*

**NINEVEH.** The capital of *Assyria in the seventh century BCE, when that empire had annexed the northern kingdom of Israel and forced Judah to pay tribute. Most biblical references reflect this time, when Nineveh was the center of the Assyria they knew. The book of *Jonah, even if written long afterward, remembers this period of Assyrian glory and Israelite humiliation. *Nahum prophesies the destruction of this enemy, as does *Zephaniah. *Sennacherib is said to have withdrawn to Nineveh after Yahweh inflicted a plague on his army besieging Jerusalem. Otherwise, Nineveh appears in the description of Assyria in Genesis 10.11–12, where its association with Calah reflects early-first-millennium geography, when Calah (Akkadian Kalḫu) was a major complement to Assur and Nineveh. Archaeological evidence shows that Nineveh already existed in the fifth millennium BCE, and contacts with Sumer and Akkad to the south are recorded in third-millennium texts. Nineveh remained an important Mesopotamian city for the next two thousand years, though it only became capital of Assyria under Sennacherib. *Daniel E. Fleming*

**NOAH.** The son of Lamech, and the father of Shem, Ham, and Japheth,

Noah was the hero of the biblical Flood narrative and the first vintner. After observing the corruption of all creation, God determined to cleanse and purify the earth through a flood. Noah, however, found favor with God, and he, together with his family and the seed of all living creatures, entered the ark and survived the deluge. From them the earth was then repopulated.

In many respects Noah was a second *Adam. The genealogy of Genesis 5 makes his birth the first after the death of the progenitor of humanity. Like Adam, all people are his descendants. God's first command to the primordial pair to "be fruitful, and multiply, and fill the earth" (Gen. 1.28) is echoed in God's first command to Noah and his sons after the Flood.

Other biblical figures in turn look back to Noah and are compared to him. *Moses also had to endure a water ordeal; in fact, the only other time that the Hebrew word for ark *(tēbâ)* is used in the Bible is for the basket in which Moses was saved. In Christian tradition, Noah is viewed as a precursor of Jesus, and the waters of the Flood are compared to the waters of baptism.

Noah has traditionally been viewed as an exemplary righteous person in extensive postbiblical Jewish, Christian, and Muslim literature. However, the phrase "righteous in his generation" has also been interpreted to mean that at any other time Noah's righteousness would not have been viewed as extraordinary (*b. Sanh.* 108a).

The legend of a hero who survives an inundation to repopulate the earth is one found in many cultures. Most closely related to the biblical account are the stories from ancient Mesopotamia. In the Sumerian flood story, the pious king Ziusudra survives two to three attempts, including a flood, to destroy humanity. After his ordeal, he offers a sacrifice to the gods, repopulates the earth, is granted immortality and sent to live in paradisiacal Dilmun. The eleventh tablet of the Gilgamesh Epic relates the story of Gilgamesh's ancestor Utnapishtim, who survived the flood to gain immortality through a capricious act of the god Ea/Enki. Many of the images and details of the story parallel the biblical account. Contextually closest to the biblical story is the Atrahasis Epic, which places the flood story in the context of a primeval history. In this version Atrahasis, the "exceedingly wise one" (also an epithet of Utnapishtim), survives three attempts to destroy humanity, the last of which is a flood. The great noise of humanity and the earth's overpopulation are given as reasons for the god Enlil's wish to bring destruction. After the flood, a divine compromise is reached on ways to limit the earth's population, an idea specifically rejected in the biblical account.

*See also* Ham.

*Carl S. Ehrlich*

**NOMADS.** When the Israelites came before God in *Canaan, the *Promised Land, bearing the first fruits of the harvest, they were to recall their origin with the words, "A wandering Aramean was my father" (Deut. 26.5)—a reference to *Jacob who, once he left his father-in-law in Haran, had no permanent home. He moved from a settled to a partly nomadic, herder's life; leaving Egypt, his descendants, after forty years in the wilderness, moved to a settled, agricultural life. Exchanging one way of life for the other was not an unusual act; there were always connections between the two, for nomads always need the town or village crafts and trade.

Nomadic life leaves little trace. The Bible and virtually all other ancient records were written by townsfolk, so our information is usually colored, somewhat hostile to nomads. The Egyptians thought their life-style uncivilized, and the Babylonians about 2000 BCE despised them as those who had no permanent homes, ate their meat raw, and did not bury their dead. At that time, tribes from central Syria moved into *Babylonia. The Babylonian scribes called them *Amorites, or "westerners." They overran the ancient cities and set up new states, at first on a tribal basis. King vied with king, and the famous Hammurapi briefly dominated them all. Babylonian urban culture overwhelmed the Amorites; apart from the language, no certain Amorite characteristics can be distinguished. Babylonian scribes marked as Amorite some names that have non-Babylonian features. Such names appear in Syria-Palestine, including some in Genesis. Israel's ancestors may be reckoned among these early second-millennium people. Like Israel, other states later traced their history back to nomads "who lived in tents." Interaction between townsfolk and nomads, "the desert and the sown," is illustrated by texts from Mari on the mid-Euphrates written about 1800 BCE. Mari's kings constantly tried to control neighboring tribes by force or diplomacy, lest they overrun the town. Israel faced the same problem with *Amalekites and *Midianites. Nomadic simplicity appealed to some, and the *wilderness period seemed to be an ideal state, unalloyed by the evils of Canaanite religion. Jehonadab son of Rechab began such a movement in Israel in the ninth century BCE lasting over two centuries, yet ending in the city's shelter (*see* Rechabites).

In the New Testament, nomadic life is taken as a figure of the spiritual life, and a reminder that the physical is transitory.

*Alan Millard*

# O

**OBADIAH.** Obadiah was a prophet to whom the book of Obadiah is attributed. The title gives us no information about the author except a name; Obadiah means "servant of the Lord." It gives no help in dating the book, though internal references imply that the destruction of *Jerusalem of 587/586 BCE had already occurred.

This book of twenty-one verses, the shortest in the Hebrew Bible, is formed of three distinct parts. Vv. 1–4 announce the Lord's decision to destroy *Edom because of its pride and its betrayal of *Judah. Vv. 15–18 announce the day of the Lord for all nations. And vv. 19–21 proclaim that the Lord's dominion will be demonstrated by the return of dispersed Israelites to live in *Canaan.

The central message of the book is found in v. 21: the dominion of God is sure and secure. The book should be read in the context of the Minor Prophets and of *Isaiah, for Obadiah's views are balanced by *Habakkuk and other books from *Micah through *Malachi. They put much more emphasis on the future Israel's worship of the Lord in Jerusalem than on political power over others. *John D. W. Watts*

**OLIVES, MOUNT OF.** The Mount of Olives is part of a ridge east of *Jerusalem directly across the Kidron Valley in the direction of Bethany and Jericho; the ridge's northern extension is called Mount Scopus, and its lower slopes *Gethsemane. With an elevation of approximately 2,800 ft (850 m), the ridge is higher than the Temple Mount across the Kidron Valley to the west.

In the Hebrew Bible the Mount of Olives is mentioned by name twice. In 2 Samuel 15.30–32 we are told of a sanctuary there. Zechariah 14:4 claims this is where the Lord's feet will stand on the apocalyptic day of the Lord.

In the Gospels, the Mount of Olives is the place where Jesus goes for rest or prayer when he is in or around Jerusalem. Jesus enters Jerusalem from the Mount of Olives, and it is there that the apocalyptic discourses in Mark and Matthew are set; Mark 13.3 may be an allusion to Zechariah 14.4. In Acts 1:12 the Mount is implied as the site of Jesus's ascension. These events in the narrative of the last days of Jesus in and around the Mount of Olives has made it a site for pilgrims to Jerusalem since the fourth century CE, when a small church was founded there; this may have been the basilica built by Constantine's mother Helena, mentioned by Eusebius. *J. Andrew Overman*

**ONAN.** The second son of Judah and his Canaanite wife Bath-shua (or "the daughter of Shua). After the death of his older brother Er without progeny, Judah ordered Onan to impregnate Er's wife Tamar. Although Onan did cohabit with Tamar, "he spilled his seed on the ground"; for this he was put to death by God. Onan's effort to avoid impregnating his sister-in-law has given rise to the term "onanism," a synonym for masturbation. This passage is then employed by some to indicate divine condemnation of autoeroticism. This interpretation, however, completely misses the point of the passage. Onan's sin was not sexual. Rather, it was his refusal to fulfill the obligation of levirate marriage, according to which a man was obligated to impregnate the wife of his brother if his brother had died without an heir, thus ensuring the continuation of his brother's line and inheritance. That fulfilling this obligation often raised additional questions regarding the apportioning of the familial inheritance is indicated by passages in Deuteronomy and Ruth. Thus Onan's sexual act, most probably coitus interruptus, was the means whereby he avoided his fraternal duty, in spite of the fact that he seemed to be fulfilling it by cohabiting with Tamar. For this deception he was punished.

*Carl S. Ehrlich*

**ORPHAN.** In biblical Israel, as in the ancient Near East in general, the socioeconomic well-being of a community depended primarily on the ability of adult males to provide financially for those around them, to protect them from physical harm, and, in general, to uphold their honor ("name"). Persons without a specific male to fulfill these obligations were at greatest risk in the community; therefore, there are many calls for the protection and proper treatment of the husbandless ("*widows") and the fatherless ("orphans"), as well as others at risk in an Israelite community. In the Hebrew Bible, widows are mentioned alongside orphans in thirty-four of the forty-two occurrences of the latter. This pairing continues into the Apocrypha, the New Testament, and early church writings. Other individuals at risk mentioned less frequently with orphans are *aliens, the weak, the needy, the *poor, the destitute, and *Levites. The greatest concerns of these individuals are that they will be unable to protect the property they have, unable to support themselves financially, and unable to maintain the "name" of their deceased husband or father. They are not, however, necessarily propertyless.

To provide care for these individuals is to "do justice" to them. Tragically, the males in a community often shirk this responsibility or even exploit their neighbors and relatives who are at risk. Those who perpetrate such injustices are called "fools" and "wicked." The failure or inability of orphans and others at risk to gain support forces them to turn to royal administrators for help. So, a primary responsibility of Israel's kings is to care for needy persons, like orphans. Unfortunately, this responsibility is mentioned most often in prophetic condemnations of the royal bureaucracy for failing to fulfill it. The theological foundation for these condemnations is important to recognize. God is the ultimate example of one who is concerned for the welfare of individuals like orphans; he is the ultimate "redeemer" for the orphan. The king and his officials are watched and criticized more than others because they have been designated as God's overseers of the people, including orphans. The failure of the king and his officials to do justice to orphans not only reflects badly on them but also on the God who established them.

In the New Testament, besides the exhortation to "care for orphans and widows in their distress," the only reference to orphans appears in John 14.18 ("I will not leave you orphaned"). The imagery suggests that Jesus's followers, by themselves, would not be able to maintain their "inheritance" from God; but Jesus is saying that he will act as their protector and provider. *Timothy M. Willis*

# P

**PALESTINE.** From the time of the Greek historian Herodotus (fifth century BCE), the term "Palestine" (derived from the word for *Philistine) designated the western tip of the Fertile Crescent, namely, the area on both sides of the *Jordan River, limited on the north by the Litani River and Mount *Hermon, on the east by the Syrian desert, on the south by the *Negeb desert, and on the west by the Mediterranean Sea. It falls into six broad geographical regions: the coastal plain, the Shephelah, the central mountain range, the Judean desert, the Jordan Valley, and the Transjordanian plateau. These can be visualized as north-south strips set side by side.

**The Coastal Plain.** This strip is divided into three unequal portions by the Ladder of Tyre (Rosh ha-Niqra/Ras en-Naqura) and Mount Carmel. Above Rosh ha-Niqra, the plain widens to the north reaching its greatest width at the *Phoenician city of Tyre, which in biblical times was an island. Between Rosh ha-Niqra and Mount Carmel, the plain averages 5 mi (8 km) in width. In addition to an annual rainfall of 24 in (600 mm), it is thoroughly watered, particularly south of Ptolemais (Akko), where the alluvium deposited by the Naaman and Kishon rivers has pushed the coastline forward into the Bay of Haifa. The two tips of the bay form natural harbors at Akko and Tell Abu Hawam.

South of Mount Carmel, the smooth coastline is devoid of natural harbors, but in antiquity there were lighterage stations at Dor, Strato's Tower, and Jaffa. In this area, the plain is much broader and runs all the way to Gaza. It is characterized by three parallel kurkar ridges, the remnants of prehistoric coastlines. The sand outside the first ridge gave way to swamps within, caused by the failure of rivers and wadis to drain completely. In biblical times, the third ridge was covered with oak, and the rich soil of the land reaching to the foothills was ideal for agriculture. The plain is divided in two by the Yarkon River, which begins at Aphek (Rosh ha-ᶜAyin). The plain of Sharon north of the Yarkon receives almost twice as much rain (12 in [300 mm]) as the plain of Philistia to the south. The great commercial highway, the Way of the Sea, had to pass through the 2 mi (3 km) gap between Aphek and the hills. This became a major crossroads when *Herod the Great built the first artificial harbor at Strato's Tower and named it Caesarea Maritima.

**The Shephelah.** As the biblical name ("lowlands") indicates, this is an area of low, rolling hills roughly 28 mi (45 km) long and 9 mi (15 km) broad, lying south of the Aijalon valley. The soft chalk and limestone hills are cut by wide valleys running both north-south and east-west. Even the driest part in the south receives about 10 in (250 mm) of rain, and in the biblical period it was intensely cultivated. Olives, sycamore figs, and vineyards are mentioned explicitly in the Bible. The key cities were *Gezer in the north, which dominated both the plain and the easiest access to the mountains, and *Lachish in the south, which controlled the main route through the center to Beth-shemesh and also the lateral route to *Hebron.

**The Central Mountain Range.** This region is by far the biggest, and can be divided into three areas, *Galilee, Carmel and *Samaria, and Judea.

***Galilee.*** This mountainous area is bordered on the north by the Litani River and on the south by the Jezreel Valley, which runs along the north side of the Carmel range and broadens out into the great plain of Esdraelon (140 $mi^2$ [365 $km^2$]) before sloping gently to join the Jordan Valley at Beth-shean. Because ancient settlements appear only on the edges, it must have been subject to flooding in biblical times. It was, nonetheless, a very important east-west route.

The classical division into Upper and Lower Galilee is based on the simple fact that the three highest peaks of the former are all over 3,300 ft (1,000 m), whereas the two highest of the latter barely attain 2,000 ft (600 m). Even though both benefit by an average rainfall of 30–20 in (800–500 mm), the terrain is generally unsuited to agriculture, and in the biblical period was covered by oak forests. The isolation of the perfectly rounded Mount Tabor (1,929 ft [588 m]) gave it a numinous quality. Beside it ran the Way of the Sea, angling out from Hazor to the coast through the Carmel range.

***Carmel and Samaria.*** Running southeast from the coast, the Carmel range is cut by two strategic passes, the Nahal Yoqneam and the Nahal ᶜIron, the latter with *Megiddo at its northern end. South of the Dothan Valley, the ridge coalesces with the mountains of Gilboa to create a much wider range with no Shephelah on the west and a steep drop into the Jordan Valley on the east. The central core of the area is constituted by Mount Gerizim (2,889 ft [881 m]) and Mount Ebal (3,083 ft [941 m]). The pass between them, controlled by *Shechem (Nablus), carried the major east-west route coming from the Jordan via the verdant Wadi el-Farᶜah, in which Tirzah (Tell el-Farᶜah) is located, and out to the coast just south of Samaria. This was the heartland of the northern kingdom of Israel, and the contrast between the closed site of Tirzah and the wide prospect to the west from Samaria is symbolic of the shift in policy that took place under Omri in the ninth century BCE (*see* Israel). In this period, the hills were heavily wooded, but the valleys, which are wider in the north, produced grain, olives, and grapes. North-south travel was difficult, except on the crest running south from Shechem. The first 12 mi (20 km) of the route lay in the fertile Michmethath Valley, but after the ascent of Lubban the road wound in narrow wadis past the sanctuaries of Shiloh and Bethel.

***Judea.*** Geographically, the Jerusalem hills are a saddle between Ramallah and *Bethlehem, which is some 650 ft (200 m) lower than the highest points of Samaria to the north and Hebron to the south. This facilitated east-west travel, and there have always been relatively easy routes to the coastal plain and the Jordan Valley. The forests that covered the hills when the Israelites first occupied the area gradually disappeared. The demands of a growing city were intensified by the insatiable appetite for firewood of a sacrificial cult that endured almost a thousand years. After the hills had been denuded, terraces began to be built on the slopes. The small fields thus developed supported mainly olive trees, but some grain crops as well. The average rainfall is 22 in (560 mm). Enveloped by higher hills with a poor water supply and a location off the natural routes, *Jerusalem would have been doomed to insignificance had *David not given it political weight by making it a religious center.

South of Bethlehem, the hills rise toward Hebron (3,300 ft [1,000 m]) and then descend to the great plain around Beer-sheba. The tree cover in the biblical period was oak with patches of pine, but Genesis 49.11 attests the intense cultivation of the vine in the valleys and on terraces. The only significant route ran north-south with only one good branch route to the coastal plain. The geographic homogeneity of the Hebron hills helps to explain why it was always the territory of a single tribe, *Judah.

**The Judean Desert.** This region borders the Hebron hills on the east. The rainfall decreases sharply some 3 mi (5 km) east of the watershed, and in 12 mi (20 km) the land drops 4,000 ft (1,200 m) to the Dead Sea. The vegetation is sufficient to support only sheep and goats. In biblical times, this was the grazing land of the settlements on the eastern edge of the hill country. There are few springs, but runoff can be collected in cisterns to water the flocks. The character of the terrain makes travel difficult. It descends to the east in a series of steps, the most important of which is the Valley of Achor at the northern end. These are cut by the deep gorges of the Wadi Murabbaᶜât and Wadi Ghiar, which drain into the Dead Sea; both had extensive prehistoric occupation. In the biblical period, the only significant route was that from Tekoa to En-gedi.

**The Jordan Valley.** From its principal source at Banyas (995 ft [303 m]) in the foothills of Mount Hermon, the Jordan River runs south in a great crack in the earth's surface where two tectonic plates meet. It continues down the Gulf of Aqaba/Eilat to become the Rift Valley in Africa. In biblical times, the area south of *Dan was an impassable swamp with Lake Huleh at its center. The Sea of *Galilee (12.5 by 7 mi [20 by 11 km]) at its longest and widest) is a freshwater lake 700 ft (210 m) below sea-level. It contains twenty-two species of fish, and fishing has always been essential to the local economy.

Shortly after the Jordan leaves the lake it is supplemented by the waters of the Yarmuk. In the 65 mi (105 km) to the Dead Sea the valley drops 540 ft (194 m) but the river meanders through 200 mi (322 km). The river bed with its tropical undergrowth that sheltered large wild animals is some 23 ft (7 m) below the valley, which widens to 14 mi (23 km) near *Jericho, where the rainfall averages only 6 in (150 mm).

The Jordan ends in the Dead Sea (1,285 ft [404 m] below sea level), which has no outlet. Water is lost only through evaporation (in the 105°F [40°C] heat of summer about 1 in [24 mm] each day), producing a high concentration of all the chlorides (26 percent as opposed to the 3.5 percent salinity of the oceans); in Hebrew it is called the "Sea of Salt" (Gen. 14.3; NRSV: "Dead Sea"). It averages 10 mi (16 km) wide, and its length was reduced to 30 mi (50 km) in 1976 when the area south of the Lynch Straits dried out. This may have been the size of the sea in the historical period, but some fifty thousand years ago the water level was 731 ft (225 m) higher, and the valley as far as Galilee was a long inlet of the Red Sea. The gradually rising continuation of the valley to the Gulf of Aqaba/Eilat is now called the Arabah, though in the Bible that term generally means other parts of the Rift Valley.

**The Transjordanian Plateau.** This region is a strip roughly 25 mi (40 km) wide starting at Mount Hermon and limited on the west by the escarpment of the Jordan Valley. On the east it gradually shades into the Syrian desert. The Golan, lying north of the Yarmuk river, was biblical Bashan and is a basalt plateau characterized by the small cones of extinct volcanoes. The fertile volcanic soil of the southern part gives way to wild pastureland in the north. The center of biblical Gilead is located between the rivers Yarmuk and Jabbok (Nahr ez-Zerqa), but the term is also employed to designate the area as far south as the Arnon River (Seil el-Mojib), which is also called *Ammon. The terrain and vegetation cover is very similar to that of the hill country of Samaria. At an average of 3,300 ft (1,000 m) above sea level, the plateau of *Moab lying between the Arnon and the Brook Zered (Wadi el-Hesa) is higher than the land to the north. In biblical times, it was proverbial for its fertility, and 2 Kings 3.4 highlights the productivity of its sheep farming. *Edom extends south of Moab as far as the Gulf of Aqaba/Eilat. Its average height parallels that of Moab, but the central peaks rise to 5,600 ft (1,700 m). Winters are very cold and the snows can last until March. Due to the altitude, the tree cover of this area extends much further south than the corresponding forests west of the Jordan. The great commercial route, the King's Highway, ran the length of the plateau linking *Damascus with the ports of Elath and Ezion-geber on the Gulf of Aqaba.

*Jerome Murphy-O'Connor*

**PATRIARCHS.** This term has been used in most scholarship to designate the ancestors of Israel, especially in Genesis 12–50, and its adjectival form is also generally employed, as in "patriarchal history," "patriarchal narratives," etc. These designations, however, are misleading, for in the traditions perserved in Genesis 12–50 and elsewhere in the Bible the "matriarchs" are also prominent. In this book the more inclusive terms ancestor(s) and ancestral are used for the biblical patriarchs and matriarchs, i.e., *Abraham, *Sarah, and *Hagar; *Isaac and *Rebekah; and *Jacob, *Leah, *Rachel, Bilhah, and Zilpah, and their children. For a discussion of the ancestral narratives, *see* Ancestors, The.

**PAUL.** Paul was born at Tarsus in Cilicia, at about the beginning of the common era. A member of a Hellenistic *Jewish family, which could trace its descent to the tribe of *Benjamin, he was given the Hebrew name Saul, as well as the name Paul. Unlike many Jews, he was also a Roman citizen.

As a child, Paul would learn of his Jewish heritage in the local *synagogue at Tarsus. He received at least the final stages of his education in Jerusalem, though, under the guidance of *rabbi *Gamaliel. He soon rose to a position of some eminence as a *Pharisee, perhaps even becoming a member of the *Sanhedrin.

When Christianity first came to prominence in *Jerusalem, he was strongly opposed to it and was prepared to take personal responsibility for ensuring its extermination. But while on his way to *Damascus in *Syria, chasing Jewish Christians who had fled there, he had a remarkable experience that changed the course of his life. Looking back on it twenty years later, he compared it to the appearances of *Jesus to the disciples after the Resurrection; as a result of that encounter, his fervent devotion to biblical faith as understood by the Pharisees was augmented by an unqualified commitment to the gospel.

From this point, his life took a new direction, as he threw himself into missionary work throughout Asia Minor and Greece. He established many churches, and saw himself as God's chosen agent to take the gospel to the gentiles. The New Testament nowhere mentions his death, but reliable traditions depict him as a martyr in Rome, beheaded during the persecution of Nero in the mid-60s CE.

**Sources.** We have two major sources of information about Paul: his letters and the book of Acts. There has been much debate concerning their relative worth. Paul's own writings must obviously have priority, though it is certainly not easy to reconstruct the story of someone's life on the basis of a miscellaneous and incomplete collection of occasional letters. Acts at least appears to provide a plausible framework, but is not always easy to correlate with what can be deduced from the letters.

Both sources must be treated with some caution, for neither was intended to be a biography. He features prominently in Acts, but the main focus there is on the rapid spread of Christianity from Jerusalem to Rome. The letters are mainly concerned with specific circumstances in the life of various churches, and inevitably reflect more of these than they do of Paul's own life. They contain limited personal details and report very few incidents.

Additionally, Acts and the letters deal with different aspects of Paul's life. Acts shows him as a great missionary pioneer, taking the gospel to far-flung corners of the empire. It therefore reports his initial preaching of the gospel to non-Christians and their reactions to it, but it never mentions the letters! But they were written to Christians, and show how Paul related to those already in the church. For this reason alone it is difficult to draw direct comparisons between the two sources of information.

Yet we have little alternative but to try to combine the two sources. Acts provides the one really useful clue to the chronology of Paul's life. The reference to his encounter with Gallio at *Corinth dates this incident somewhere between 1 July 51 and 1 July 52, and by judicious deductions from that it is possible to work out a general outline of Paul's life. But there are still problems. There is no agreement on the number and sequence of his early contacts with the Jerusalem Christians. There is also doubt over the number of times he was imprisoned, with Paul apparently implying an imprisonment at *Ephesus not mentioned in Acts.

**Background.** Tarsus was a typical Hellenistic city, with a cosmopolitan population and a variety of religious options for its people. Its citizens were well known for their interest in philosophy, and Tarsus was home to several prominent *Stoics, including Athenodorus, adviser to Augustus. No doubt, Paul had at least a passing acquaintance with their thinking, as well as some knowledge of the various mystery religions and of Greek philosophy in general. He occasionally makes specific reference to *Stoic writers, and some have thought his letters show influence from Stoic and Cynic debating styles. But it is unlikely that he had a formal education in such subjects. He did, however, enjoy and appreciate life in the Hellenistic cities, and his metaphors demonstrate close knowledge of urban activities.

Throughout his letters, Paul exhibits a passionate devotion to his Jewish heritage. He was always at pains to demonstrate that his understanding of the gospel was quite consistent with biblical faith, and that Christian believers were spiritual heirs to ancient Israel. Toward the end of his ministry, he invested much time and energy in maintaining good relations between gentile Christians and the church in Jerusalem. It was his insistence that gentile churches give financial aid to the church in Jerusalem that ultimately led to his arrest and transportation to Rome.

His thinking also owed a good deal to the beliefs of the original disciples. Admittedly, he could declare himself independent of the Jewish *apostles, but that was a tactical move in the face of strident opposition. When his presentation of the gospel is compared with other parts of the New Testament, it turns out to have the same basic structure as the preaching of Peter and other leading apostles. Moreover, the practical advice he gave his converts is surprisingly similar to that of other New Testament writers.

The nineteenth-century Tübingen school dismissed this picture as a harmonization produced by the writer of Acts in the interests of the later catholic church. They thought Paul radically different from Jerusalem and Jewish Christianity. More recently, things have turned full circle and some have argued that Paul was actually under the control of the Jewish church, and took his orders from Jerusalem; that too seems unlikely. Nevertheless, Paul was concerned for the unity of Jews and gentiles in the church, and we misunderstand him if we place his life and thinking outside the mainstream of first-generation Christianity.

**Missionary Activity.** Paul was convinced that on the Damascus road God had commissioned him to take the gospel to the gentiles. Both tactically and theologically he felt it was important that the gospel also be proclaimed to Jews, and, according to Acts, his usual practice was to go first to the local synagogue. Galatians 2.7–9, however, indicates that his activity was apparently directed exclusively to gentiles.

In his travels, Paul took advantage of the fine highway system built by the Romans, and in the course of three extended tours he visited most of the key centers in Greece and Asia Minor. Although he had a physical weakness, he must have been incredibly tough, judging from the list of hardships he survived.

Paul seems to have had a carefully designed strategy for evangelism. He aimed to establish churches in the largest population centers, which he could easily reach on the paved Roman roads. From there, local converts could take the message into more remote towns and villages. This was evidently successful. At least one of his letters (*Colossians) was written to a church founded in this way, and later in the first century most of the areas he visited had many flourishing congregations.

Paul's converts were a typical cross section of Roman society. Many Christians were *slaves, though the gospel also attracted cultured upper-class Romans. Some were clearly influential people, the kind who would take personal disputes to law courts and who could afford to make donations for good causes. Paul's coworkers also enjoyed the typically mobile lifestyle of the upper classes; in the absence of church buildings, the Christian community depended on the generosity of its richer members to provide facilities for corporate worship and hospitality for wandering preachers. At the same time, Paul was certain that the gospel transcended the barriers of race, sex, and class, and insisted on the equality of all believers.

**The Letters.** Literary epistles were common in the Roman world. Though

Paul followed the style of the day, in some ways his letters are not literary works. He was essentially a speaker, and his letters contain what he would have said had he been physically present. This no doubt explains his often uneven style. It also highlights some of the problems faced by the modern reader. At least one of Paul's letters was clearly written in answer to previous correspondence from the church at Corinth, and most of the others are a response to information that had reached him in one way or another. But of course we only have one side of the correspondence. And we may not even know that as well as we think, for ancient letter writers often entrusted significant parts of their message to the bearer of the letter to deliver orally. At best, therefore, reading Paul's letters is like overhearing one side of a telephone conversation: it is possible to pick up the general drift, but specific details are more elusive.

Not all of Paul's letters are like this. Some think *Romans a more considered statement of Paul's thinking. *Ephesians seems to have been a circular letter, sent to several churches. And in many letters, Paul shows that his writing can be sophisticated, while his detailed arguments must have been carefully worked out before they were written down.

Scholars disagree on whether all thirteen letters attributed to Paul are genuine. He regularly used a secretary, and wrote along with associates, so we may expect variations in style. But most doubt that the Pastoral letters come from Paul, while others have questioned Ephesians, Colossians, and 2 *Thessalonians, on a variety of theological, stylistic, and literary grounds.

The letters certainly give us an insight into Paul's character. He was a formidable opponent (*Galatians), but he also had a remarkable capacity for deep concern and true friendship. He had a realistic understanding of human relationships, and was sensitive to those less robust than himself. He also had an uninhibited sense of humor.

**Theology.** Paul did not become a Christian because he was disillusioned with Judaism. He was totally dedicated to biblical faith, and quite certain that it made sense. It was his conversion experience that changed his life and played a major part in the development of his theology.

He discovered that Jesus was no longer dead, but alive—and must be "the Son of God." He realized that the Law was not central to salvation, for on the Damascus road God had burst into his life not because of his obedience to the Law but in spite of it. All he could do was to respond to this demonstration of God's freely given love. As he did so, Paul became aware of a moral and spiritual transformation taking place within him, a process that would ultimately remake him to be like Jesus.

This challenged his preconceptions, especially his attitude to the Law. How could he reconcile his previous understanding of God's will with his new perspective? He did so most eloquently in the conflict with the judaizers of Galatia, arguing from the Bible itself that the Law had always been intended as merely a temporary word from God, and that faith had always been the true basis of salvation, as far back as the time of Abraham. This was why he was prepared to argue with such force that gentile converts did not need to become Jews in order to be proper Christians.

But this was not the only way Paul described his beliefs. Elsewhere he refers to the Christian life as "a new creation" (2 Cor. 5.17), in which men and women have been "rescued from the power of darkness and transferred to the kingdom of God's beloved son" (Col. 1.13–14). The "age to come" was not locked up in the future; it had burst into the present through the life, death, resurrection of Jesus, and the coming of the Holy Spirit.

Paul knew well enough that God's will was not yet fully effective on earth, and he expected a future divine intervention when the power of evil would finally be crushed, and when Jesus would return in glory. But he was certain that Christians were already a part of God's new order, and the church was to be an outpost of the kingdom in which God's will might become a reality in the lives of ordinary people. Through the work of God's Spirit, individuals, society, and the whole structure of human relationships, could be radically transformed, so that in the context of a physically renewed world system, God's people should grow to "the measure of the full stature of Christ" (eph. 4.14).

*John W. Drane*

**PELETHITES.** *See* Cherethites and Pelethites.

**PERSIA.** The home territory of the ancient Persians was the mainly mountainous terrain east of the head of the Persian Gulf. They called it Parsa (Grk. Persis); it was roughly equivalent to the modern Fars. The first appearance of this name (Parsua) in history, however, on the Black Obelisk of the Assyrian king Shalmaneser III (ca. 843 BCE) and followed eight years later by a mention of twenty-seven chiefs there, indicates a position somewhere in Iranian Kurdistan; but a similar name is recorded somewhere to the southeast a generation later. In 692–691 BCE, the name is cited in an alliance of peoples against *Sennacherib, which seems to have been centered in the Zagros further to the southeast.

By about 640 BCE, when a king named Kurash (Cyrus) appears in Assyrian annals, the Persians seem to have been established in Parsa; this ruling family was Achaemenid (descended from a semilegendary ancestor Achaemenes). It has been supposed that there were two Achaemenid royal lines, one (that of *Darius) in Parsa, the other (that of *Cyrus the Great) in a land called Anshan; but in 1972 it was discovered that Anshan lay in the middle of Parsa. These Persians were Indo-Iranian speakers like the *Medes (Darius spoke of himself as Ariya, i.e., Aryan or Iranian). They may perhaps have reached Parsa in stages from beyond the Caucasus; but some at least could have gradually infiltrated by way of northeastern Iran and Carmania. They were subject to the Medes before Cyrus the Great overthrew King Astyages in 550 BCE; according to Herodotus, they had been subject for the best part of a century.

Under Cyrus and his son Cambyses great conquests occurred in rapid succession: the Median empire in 550 BCE, western Asia Minor (the Lydian kingdom of Croesus) about 546 BCE, the *Babylonian empire with Elam and the Levant in 539 BCE, and (under Cambyses) *Egypt in 525 BCE. Darius I added Sind (Hindush) about 516 BCE. Thus the three great river lands of the Tigris and *Euphrates, the Indus, and (until 402 BCE) the *Nile were subject, and the resulting empire was the most extensive that the world had known.

Efficiency in military preparations and fighting skills had given the Medes and Persians a reputation for invincibility. But the failure to subdue the Scythians about 513 BCE and serious reverses in Greece between 492 and (under Xerxes) 480–479 BCE caused a collapse in confidence. After this, the sole successful major expedition in one hundred years was that in which the heroic marshal Megabyxos reconquered the Delta after a revolt (459–454 BCE). The later kings relied largely on Greek mercenaries and even fleets in their military operations in the west, with no great success, however, until the ruthless Artaxerxes III was able to bring his revolting satraps (governors) under control and in 345–343 BCE to reconquer *Phoenicia and Egypt. In the east of the empire and the Arabian fringes, however, peace seems to have generally been maintained with little exertion of force.

The system of imperial government set up by Darius I continued with little change until the end of Persian rule. In the Iranian and Anatolian satrapies noble Persian fief-holders kept household brigades and maintained order except in mountain regions where occasional punitive expeditions would be launched. Communication with the imperial chanceries was normally in Aramaic.

In Babylonia and Egypt, a developed administrative system was in existence and was taken over. The kings appointed fiscal overseers in the temples and normally enjoyed the cooperation of the priesthoods. Confiscation after conquest and revolts gave rise to great estates belonging to the king, royal relatives, and leading nobles or court officials. In Babylonia, many fiefs were related to obligations of military service. In what had once been *Solomon's kingdom west of the Euphrates, deportation in *Assyrian times had resulted in a mixed population with little nationalistic feeling except in Judah and Phoenicia; prompt acquiescence to Persian rule had saved the "people of the land" from confiscations after Cyrus's conquest of Babylon.

The Achaemenids worshiped Zoroaster's god Ahuramazda with his polarization of Justice (or Order) and the Lie; but this did not lead to religious intolerance. The deities Anahita and Mithra were hardly less revered by the Persians, and fire was worshiped as a god. The officiants were *Magi. Among gods of the subject peoples the Greek Apollo, the Syrian goddess Alilat, and Yahweh seem to have been specially favored. Thanks to Cyrus and Darius I, the new *Temple in Jerusalem was completed (515 BCE); subsequently *Nehemiah (445 BCE) and *Ezra (either 428 or 398 BCE) were sent there on special missions, and Darius II seems to have yielded to objections from the Jerusalem priesthood about the right of the Jewish garrison at Yeb (Elephantine, in Upper Egypt) to rebuild its temple and also to keep its own special feast of the Passover.

Persian rule thus allowed considerable cultural assimilation and religious syncretism, Babylon above all becoming a cosmopolitan center. Their art was a composite in which different traditions merged. The court style, which (like the Old Persian script) was devised by Darius I, exalted the grandeur of the king in a timeless setting; as seen in the Persepolis friezes it is impressive in its composure.

After the conquest by *Alexander the Great (334–323 BCE) the lands of the empire were ruled by Macedonian successor kings, Parthians, and Romans. Persia had no further importance in biblical history. *J. M. Cook*

**PETER.** *See* Simon Peter.

**PHARISEES.**

**Sources.** References to the Pharisees occur widely throughout Jewish and Christian literature of the first two centuries CE. Josephus lists them as one of the main Jewish parties emerging during the Hasmonean period. The

New Testament portrays them principally as opponents of Jesus and the early Christian movement, although it is from their ranks that Paul comes. Rabbinical literature contains many references to *pĕrûšîm,* partly as those who were opposed to the *Sadducees and partly as those opposed by the sages and the *rabbis.

**Name.** Greek *pharisaioi* and Hebrew *pĕrûšîm* can both be loosely transliterated as "Pharisees." The root *prš* in Hebrew can mean "to separate"; this may indicate that they were seen as sectarians (but by whom?) or that they sought holiness by the avoidance of what was unclean. Possibly the name was given to them by Sadducees, who thought of them as opposed to their ways.

**History.** The Pharisees' origin lie in the period of the *Maccabean revolt (166–159 BCE), where we hear of the emergence of a group of Jews zealous for the Law, the Hasideans, who opposed the way in which the high priests were accommodating to the intrusion of Hellenistic ways into Judaism. This renewal movement spawned not only the Pharisees but also the Essenes. It is likely that the Pharisees saw the establishment of the Hasmonean monarchy (140 BCE) as an opportunity for national renewal and the restoration of true observance of the Law. Certainly, unlike the Essenes, they remained in Jerusalem after the usurpation of the high priesthood by the Hasmoneans (152 BCE). They probably shared the popular enthusiasm for the successful campaign for Jewish independence, recorded in 1 Maccabees 14.27–49, when a great *synagogue of the Jews conferred the kingship and the high priesthood on Simon. Interestingly there is no sanction for such a synagogue, or assembly, in the Pentateuch, and this may have been justified by the oral tradition of the *elders that the Pharisees cultivated. The Pharisees thus have their origins in a popular movement based on scribal traditions for interpreting the Law. They legitimated the Hasmonean monarchy by allowing it to control the *Temple and subsequently sought to influence the monarchy both at court and in the *Sanhedrin, the council in Jerusalem that was the continuation of the great synagogue. In this they were by no means always successful, falling foul of John Hyrcanus (134–104) and Alexander Jannaeus (103–76) but being restored to favor by Salome Alexandra (76–67). As their authority at the royal court diminished they sought to influence the people through the local courts and synagogues where they enjoyed considerable success. They were not a uniform movement; over the years different schools of interpretation of the Law grew up around different teachers, notably Hillel and Shammai. After the First Jewish Revolt (66–70 CE) they emerged as the leaders, under Jonathan ben Zakkai, of the academy at Jamnia, which laid the foundation of rabbinic Judaism.

**Beliefs.** Central to their teaching is the belief in the twofold Law: the written and the oral Torah. What this in effect meant was the recognition of a continuing tradition of interpretation of the Law in the debates and sayings of the elders. Ultimately this would itself be written down in the Mishnah; but even then there was a continuing tradition of debate that found its documentation in the Talmud. Thus while some sources portray them as legalistic, it is perhaps fairer to say that they had a zeal for legal debate and for keeping alive the tradition of meditation and study of the Law. Importantly this also meant that they were able to relate the Laws to new areas of life not already dealt with, as well as to introduce new institutions such as the synagogues and schools.

They also seem to have been involved in the beginning of a concentration of purity rules and regulations that would subsequently play such an important part in the Mishnah and Talmud. In this way they began to relocate the center of holiness in the home and the local community. This prepared the way for the transition from a Temple state to a communal piety that could survive the destruction of the Temple.

The Pharisees also believed in the resurrection and in future rewards and punishments. They did not believe all received their just deserts in this age; only in a future age when God acted decisively to establish his rule would justice be done. This radical expectation of a new age indicates something of the revolutionary nature of the Pharisees that has often been overlooked. Once they themselves gained power, albeit in communities that were localized and that operated under the general protection of Rome, such radical hopes could be allowed to recede, although they would not disappear altogether.

*John Riches*

**PHILEMON.** Philemon was a Christian who lived in the Phrygian town of *Colossae in the middle of the first century CE and who is the addressee of Paul's letter to Philemon. The chief concern of the brief letter is the fate of Philemon's *slave Onesimus. That name meant "useful," and it was frequently given to slaves. It seems that this slave had at first been useful to his master, but had become useless because, having found conditions intolerable, he had fled from Colossae, probably taking with him certain valuables belonging to his owner.

The letter speaks of what followed that escape. Making his way to a larger city, Onesimus had been arrested and thrown into prison, where he met *Paul. Here the slave was converted and soon made himself useful to Paul. On his release, the new Christian had to decide what to do about the claims of his defrauded master. To return to him was to risk severe punishment, for escape from slavery was a capital offence and Philemon would have every right to select his own penalty. Encouraged by Paul, however, the slave decided to return and set out for Colossae, accompanied by Tychicus and bearing this letter from Paul. Such a decision must have been the result of intense inner struggle; on the one hand, there was the risk of punishment, at the very least the loss of freedom; on the other, the urging of Paul and the authority of his new master, Christ.

On the delivery of the letter, the master must also have faced a difficult decision. There would have been resentment over the violation of his property rights, supported as they were by Roman law and universal custom. Yet the letter was an appeal from an *apostle through whom Philemon, as well as his slave, had been converted. Paul asked the owner to welcome his slave as a brother, to accept restitution for former losses, and to treat him as if he were Paul himself. As master, Philemon must recognize the supreme authority of his own master, Christ. Even more than forgiveness was at stake, for Paul seems to have asked Philemon not only to free Onesimus but even to send him back to Paul to help in the mission work as a substitute for his onetime owner. Reading between the lines of the letter, we can see that each member of this triangle was taking a risk and making a sacrifice stemming from his allegiance to Christ.

In this letter, as in all ancient documents, many points remain uncertain. The hometown may have been Laodicea and not Colossae. The location of the prison is uncertain: Rome, or more likely *Ephesus. The slaveowner may have been Archippus and not Philemon. Nothing is known of the later history of the major characters, though it is barely possible that the one-time slave later became the *bishop in Ephesus. What is certain, however, is the radical character of conversion, not only of people but of their attitudes toward their own property, their rights, and their obligations. Brief as it is, the note gives a colorful vignette of life in a congregation in western Asia Minor.

*Paul S. Minear*

**PHILIPPI.** An important city in eastern Macedonia in Greece, home of the Christian community to which Paul's letter to the Philippians is addressed. After the decisive battle near Philippi of 42 BCE the emperor Octavian had made Philippi a Roman colony and gave to its citizens the rights and privileges of those born and living in Rome. According to the account in Acts, the church in Philippi began as follows: *Paul, on his second missionary journey, left Asia Minor for Macedonia, came to Philippi, preached the gospel; Lydia, a prominent woman from that area, and a few others became Christians. The church apparently was first housed in Lydia's home. In spite of its small beginnings, it grew and became an active Christian community, taking an important part in evangelism, readily sharing its own material possessions, even out of deep poverty, and generously sending one of its own people to assist Paul in his work and to aid him while he was in prison. Paul visited this church on at least three occasions.

Paul begins his letter with the typical greeting, and continues with thanksgiving to God and prayer for the Philippians' continued growth in love and good works. He makes known to them how the gospel has advanced even while he is in prison, and assures them that he will be released and will return to Philippi. He begs them to live worthily of the gospel in unity, harmony, and generosity without grumbling or complaining, keeping always before themselves Jesus Christ as the supreme model for any moral action; this section contains an exquisite example of an early Christian hymn, used and probably modified by Paul for his purposes here. He exhorts them further by describing the qualities of Timothy and Epaphroditus, and he promises to send both to Philippi. He warns them against evangelistic Jews or judaizers, whose teaching and practices are contrary to the gospel, and concludes the letter by making a final appeal for unity, offering suggestions as to how Christians should think and act and thanking the Philippians for their numerous gifts to him. He closes with salutations.

*Gerald F. Hawthorne*

**PHILISTINES.** A group of Aegean origin, the Philistines were one of the Sea Peoples who ravaged the eastern Mediterranean world subsequent to the collapse of Mycenean civilization at the end of the Late Bronze Age. Attempting to land in Egypt, they were repulsed in a great land and sea battle by Ramesses III (ca. 1190 BCE), after which they settled on the southwestern coastal strip of Canaan. There they established a confederation of five city-states, the pentapolis consisting of Ashdod, Ashkelon, and Gaza on the coast, and Ekron and Gath inland. Their expansion inland brought them into conflict with the Israelite tribes, who attempted to counter the threat by organizing themselves into a kingdom. Although the Philistines were able to prevail against *Saul, the first Israelite king, *David, Saul's successor and an erstwhile vassal of Achish, the Philistine king of Gath, decisively defeated them and halted their expansion. Over the next few centuries their relations with Israel were for the most part in the form of border skirmishes. In the tenth century Philistia came under loose Egyptian hegemony. As a consequence of the imperialistic ambitions of the Neo-Assyrian empire, the Philistines came under *Assyrian rule in 734 BCE. Despite occasional revolts against their overlords, they remained part of the Assyrian imperium, even prospering during the seventh century, until the fall of Assyria (612 BCE). Subsequently caught between Egypt and Babylonia, Philistia was conquered and ravaged by *Nebuchadrezzar in 604 BCE. This effectively ended the history of the Philistine people, although their name as handed down through Greek and Latin eventually became a name for the whole of the land they were never able to subdue, namely, Palestine. Archaeological activity focusing on recovering the material remains of the Philistines has been intense in recent years. Ashdod, Ashkelon, and Ekron (Tel Miqne), as well as smaller sites such as Tel Qasile on the coast and Tel Batash (ancient Timnah) inland, have been or are still being investigated. A picture has emerged of an extremely rich and highly developed civilization, putting a lie to the modern usage of the term "philistine." *Carl S. Ehrlich*

**PHOENICIA.** The Greek word *phoinix,* from which apparently the geographical region of Phoenicia is named, means, literally, "red purple." Thus, the name is derived from one product of the region, red dye, for which Phoenicia was famed throughout the ancient world. It was a shared interest in commerce and trade by the inhabitants of the region rather than any tightly knit political system that gave the Phoenicians their distinctive characteristics and ethos in the ancient world.

The territory inhabited by this people, Semitic in origin and Mediterranean in outlook and activity, was the narrow coastal plain extending from the Eleutherus river in the north to the Carmel range in the south, a distance of about 160 mi (260 km) in all, approximately the extent of modern *Lebanon with an extension to the south. From ancient times kings ruled the region centered in such cities as Byblos, Berytus (Beirut), Sidon, and Tyre. Physical features give the whole region a very distinctive character, as the coastal plain is narrow, and sometimes, as at the Ladder of Tyre, the mountains form a promontory into the sea. Elsewhere they rise sharply, separating the coast from the interior, even though at certain historical periods there was a natural tendency for the various city-states to include some of that hinterland in their territory. This was certainly true in the case of Tyre, whose territory at times included parts of Galilee. It was probably due to the peculiar physical layout of the region inhabited by the Phoenicians that the territory as a whole never attained a fully cohesive political structure but instead comprised a number of city-states, which left them vulnerable to the more centralized political powers in the region.

There were geographical advantages also. The coastline of the Phoenician territory had a number of excellent harbors, unlike Israel further to the south, and thus shipping was a significant aspect of the Phoenician way of life. In the ancient world, the Phoenicians were celebrated navigators; Herodotus also attributes to them the circumnavigation of Africa. A number of important Phoenician colonies were established in the western Mediterranean, Carthage in North Africa being the most famous. This westward orientation also led to the spread of the linear Phoenician alphabet to the west. In addition the climate, though warm, had good rainfall, and there was a rich vegetation with the famous cedars of Lebanon being particularly important as a supply of timber. *Solomon's building projects benefited from such a supply from King Hiram of Tyre, and there is even older evidence of Egyptian interest. Vitreous glass has been found in the region near Ptolemais, and there appears to have been a thriving fine-ware industry in Hellenistic times in the region.

Phoenician connections with the northern kingdom of Israel were generally close, as the marriage between *Ahab and *Jezebel, the daughter of the Tyrian king Ethbaal, illustrates. A distinctive Phoenician style of masonry is also characteristic of royal and public architecture at cities such as *Samaria and *Megiddo in the period. But like Israel and other states in the region, the Phoenician cities had strained relations with the *Assyrian and Neo-Babylonian rulers, and as they attempted to assert their independence, Sidon was destroyed and Tyre defeated after a thirteen-year siege by *Nebuchadrezzar. The *Persians adopted a more tolerant attitude toward their vassal states, and they utilized the navigational skills of the Phoenicians in their various campaigns to the west, most notably against the confederation of Greek city-states, until the Persian defeat at the famous naval battle of Salamis in 481 BCE.

It was during this period of relative autonomy that the various Phoenician states achieved a greater degree of harmony among themselves, and a confederation of Tyre, Sidon, and Arvad was formed, leading to a revolt against Persian rule and the consequent destruction of Sidon in 351 BCE. As *Alexander the Great began his conquest of the East, Tyre offered stout resistance to his advance on Egypt but was eventually destroyed in 332 BCE. In line with later Hellenistic policy, however, these cities, as well as Acco/Ptolemais closer to Jewish territory, were reestablished as Greek city-states and became important centers for the diffusion of Greek culture in Palestine and Syria. The games at Tyre in honor of Zeus Olympus were highly regarded, and some Jews, contrary to their religious beliefs, were tempted to participate. Nevertheless, inscriptions show that Phoenician as well as Greek was spoken in Tyre as late as the first century BCE.

In line with the process of hellenization elsewhere in the ancient world, the emerging culture was a mixture of the old and the new. Particularly in the sphere of religion, various deities that were worshiped in Hellenistic times, such as Zeus and Heracles, are the older Phoenician deities Baal Shamem (Lord of the Heavens) and Melqart in Greek dress. Both were closely associated with the older Canaanite deities such as El, known to us from discoveries at Ras Shamra, thus suggesting ancient and close links between the Phoenicians and the *Canaanites. Even prior to the Hellenistic age, Phoenician culture had been influenced by features from many quarters, including Greece, thus underlining the many contacts that had been established through trade and commerce. This can be seen both in their art and architecture, which apparently provided a blueprint for Solomon's *Temple.

Under the Romans, the various cities in Phoenician territory continued as they had been, but now as part of the network of urban centers that Rome utilized in controlling the east. Phoenicia is named as one of the regions to which the Christian movement spread from Jerusalem after the Hellenists had been forced out. It is doubtful, however, whether the old Phoenician culture had persisted to any great degree in the area. This combination of a memory of the ethnic background and recognition of the current cultural affiliation of the territory is found in Mark's description of the woman who came to Jesus requesting to have her daughter healed. She is described as being "Greek, Syrophoenician by birth" (Mark 7.26). The Tyrian shekel, because of its stability in a volatile currency market, remained the offering for the sanctuary in Jerusalem that every male Jew was expected to make throughout the Second Temple period, and recent archaeological evidence from Upper Galilee gives abundant evidence of the trading links that a religiously conservative Jewish population continued to have with Tyre in the early centuries CE. Thus, long-established patterns of religious diversity and commercial and trading links were maintained between the Jewish population and its Phoenician coastal neighbors—one example among many of human need transcending religious and cultural diversity. *Seán Freyne*

**PILATE, PONTIUS.** Governor of Judea under Tiberius Caesar, he ruled the province 26–36 CE. In addition to details about him occurring in the literary sources discussed below, he is also mentioned in an inscription found at Caesarea in 1961.

The first mention of Pilate, in Luke 13.1, concerns "the Galileans whose blood Pilate had mingled with their sacrifices," who were presumably visiting Jerusalem for Passover; this atrocity may explain the enmity between him and *Herod Antipas, ruler of Galilee. At the next Passover (3 April 33 CE, rather than 7 April 30 CE?), Pilate was again in Jerusalem to keep order, when the case of *Jesus was brought before him for review. Only now is he mentioned in the other three Gospels; since the last two do not even explain who he was, he must already have been fixed in the apostolic preaching as a historical anchor.

All four gospel accounts focus on Pilate's question, "Are you the King of the Jews?" In John (18.36), Jesus claims that his kingdom was "not of this world." In Luke the Jewish authorities assert that he was a rebel. According to John, *Caiaphas, as high priest, had long foreseen the need to act against Jesus in the political interest of the nation, but only Pilate could impose the death penalty. Pilate's skepticism about the political charge was neatly turned into a threat to his own status as "Caesar's friend" (John 19.12). Pilate washed his hands before the crowd to make clear where the moral onus lay and ironically retaliated against the authorities by identifying Jesus on the cross as "King of the Jews" (John 19.19).

The New Testament has Pilate maneuvered against his better judgment into authorizing what Jewish authorities had planned. Within two centuries he could be seen (by Tertullian) as in effect a Christian, and by the sixth century CE he had become a saint and martyr in the Coptic Church. Some modern analyses have attempted to shift responsibility back onto him: Jesus (or part of his following) was indeed revolutionary; it was a Roman detachment that arrested him; the *Sanhedrin was capable of carrying out a death penalty had it needed to and may not even have met formally on this occasion. The momentum of this argument arises partly from the monstrous price exacted in our age for the cry "His blood be on us and on our children," found only in Matthew (27.25) and to be understood in terms of that writer's own perspective as well as first-century politics.

The "procurator" of Judea was responsible for the estates of Tiberius Caesar there and for the Roman taxes. The Sanhedrin and other local authorities handled most other administration. In his military capacity, Pilate was also referred to as "prefect," that is, in command of the province, his powers including the supervision of justice. But being only of second (or equestrian) rank, he was subordinate to the senatorial legate of *Syria. Pilate's long term implies an understanding with the high priestly dynasty of Annas. He shares their success in keeping the peace, earning the oblique compliment of Tacitus (*Histories* 5.9), "under Tiberius nothing happened." His coinage, unlike Herod's and Caesar's, did not offend the second commandment by carrying a human likeness. He yielded to a suicidal protest by the Jews against the medallions on the military standards even though he had veiled them when brought into Jerusalem. But when they protested against the expenditure of Temple funds on an aqueduct for the city, he showed no mercy. When similarly brutal tactics were used against the *Samaritans in 36 CE, the latter appealed to Vitellius, the legate of Syria, who ordered Pilate to Rome to explain himself.

In 41 CE Philo published a "letter" of *Herod Agrippa to Gaius Caesar, successor of Tiberius, denouncing Pilate as "inflexible, stubborn, and cruel" (*Leg.* 299–305) and citing an episode when Tiberius had ordered him to remove from the palace in Jerusalem some shields that offended Jewish scruples. Clearly in the end Pilate lost the support of the Jewish leaders. Their threat to report him to Tiberius may imply that he was under suspicion as an appointee of Sejanus, the head of government whom Tiberius overturned in Rome in 31 CE. Certainly Philo's tirade would not have been possible if Pilate had been granted an honorable retirement.

*Edwin A. Judge*

**PISGAH.** A ridge or mountain in *Moab, at the northeast corner of the Dead Sea, from which *Balaam viewed Israel and *Moses viewed the *Promised Land before his death. It is in the vicinity of, if not identical with, Mount *Nebo. *Michael D. Coogan*

**POOR.** As the formulaic association of the poor with *widows and *orphans in ancient Near Eastern literature in general and in the Hebrew Bible in particular shows, poverty was an undesirable condition and not an ascetic discipline to be embraced for a higher goal. Protection and special care for these economically deprived members of society was a responsibility of kings, who demonstrated their power in part by their ability to help those unable to help themselves. This royal responsibility is found in Israel as well, as the interchange between *David and *Nathan in 2 Samuel 12.1–6 implies and the royal instruction in Proverbs 31.8–9 makes explicit.

In premonarchic Israel this obligation was incumbent on the nation as a whole. In some of its earliest legislation, Israel is instructed to ensure that the poor have both a fair hearing in judicial contexts and food from the harvest and sabbatical fallowness, and to lend money to the poor without interest. The prophets repeatedly reminded Israel of these obligations.

What was incumbent on the nation as a whole was also required of the individual. *Job's passionate declaration of innocence is a summary of the individual Israelite's moral code; as part of his assertion of complete righteousness, Job details his concern for the poor. This ethical obligation continues to be stressed in the New Testament and in the Qurʾān.

Those who oppressed the poor, then, were the wicked, and God was the protector of the poor. He would reward those who gave to the poor and would ultimately provide for them himself.

All of these texts make it clear that poverty was an unfortunate state. Its origins are explored only in wisdom literature, where it is often attributed to moral shortcomings or at least to a lack of industry, an example of the dominant biblical view that God rewards goodness and punishes wickedness. It must be noted, however, that this point of view is found in literature originating in well-to-do circles, mainly in Proverbs.

In the New Testament as well, poverty, especially self-impoverishment, is not an ideal in itself, but rather a condition temporarily assumed for the sake of some higher goal. *Paul illustrates this when he speaks of "the generous act of our Lord Jesus Christ, that though he was rich, yet for your sakes he became poor, so that by his poverty you might become rich" (2 Cor. 8.9). The context of the verse is the collection for the poor of the church in Jerusalem, an effort to which Paul was committed; Paul appeals to the Christians of *Corinth to imitate the selfless love of Jesus, out of concern for their more needy brothers and sisters. This idea of the "imitation of Christ," also present in Philippians 2.5–8, is made a general ideal in later, monastic Christianity, where poverty is embraced not just or not even primarily for the sake of others but as a means of freedom from material goods that enables one to attain a higher spiritual state in union with Jesus, who in an apparently hyperbolic proverb, said to one who would follow him: "Foxes have holes and birds of the air have nests, but the Son of man has nowhere to lay his head" (Matt. 8.20; Luke 9.58).

The advice of Jesus to the rich young man to "sell all and give to the poor" must be interpreted in the light of the eschatological urgency felt by early Christians and probably by Jesus himself, as well as the narrative context, despite later abstraction of that command into an ideal of "evangelical poverty." Following earlier biblical descriptions of divine judgment, Jesus is apparently anticipating a reversal of fortune when the kingdom of God appears: the undesirable conditions of the poor, hungry, mourning and persecuted will be altered. *Michael D. Coogan*

**PRIESTS AND HIGH PRIEST.** The major cultic persons in Israel. Through the centuries documented in the Bible, priestly duties and activities varied somewhat, but primary in the early period, and always basic, was the idea that a priest is a person attached to the service of God in a sanctuary, God's house. The original concept of the priest as server or minister of God in the sanctuary was analogous to that of a king's minister in the palace. As ministers in a palace set food on the table of an earthly king, early Israelite priests set holy bread on a table before God, a practice that underlay the provisions for the bread of the presence. As ministers of a king served as intermediaries for citizens wishing to ask the king what course of action to take, or what the king's mind might be, early Israelite priests, using the Urim and Thummim in the ephod, asked God the same sorts of questions for others, including the leaders of the people, a practice which evolved into the priestly giving of *tôrâ,* or law, as manifestation of the divine mind. It was as intermediary between God in his holy place and the people outside that a priest communicated God's blessing to the people.

**Priests and Sacrifice.** In early narratives, including J and E, it was perfectly right for someone who was not a priest to offer a sacrifice on an altar not attached to a sanctuary, without any priestly intervention. When sacrifice was offered at a sanctuary, however, the priests of that sanctuary were involved in it already in the premonarchic period, and their sacrificial prerogatives increased during the monarchic period. In Deuteronomy 33.10, bringing incense and burnt offerings before God is mentioned among the activities characteristic of priests, but it is in last place. In Ezekiel's prescriptions for priests as they are to function after the exile, their sacrificial activity is in first place, and in Jeremiah 33.18, within a postexilic addition to the book, priests are characterized entirely in terms of sacrificial work. This extension of the sacrificial role of priests can be correlated with an extension of the high degree of holiness proper to the interior of the sanctuary, the place where God's presence was focused, to the open-air altar in the courtyard in front of the sanctuary. The prerogatives of priests to perform all acts inside the house of God was extended to include any act entailing contact with the altar of sacrifice in the courtyard outside. In all of this the fundamental principle remained that the highest degree of holiness among human beings was that of priests, and that only they could rightly enter the spaces whose degree of spatial holiness was the highest.

**Priests and the Divine Will.** In early texts a priest is characterized not as a person engaged in sacrifice but as one who carries the oracular ephod containing the Urim and Thummim, which were manipulated in order to provide an expression of God's mind or will in answer to a question put to him. In the oldest part of the blessing of Moses for *Levi, the Urim and Thummim are still characteristic of a priest, but in Deut. 33.10, generally taken as part of a later expansion of the blessing for Levi added toward the middle of the monarchic period, God's ordinances and God's law (Hebr. *tôrâ*) are the primary objects of priestly responsibility, mentioned before incense and burnt offering. The word *tôrâ* may originally have been the word designating the divine response, communicated through a priest with his Urim and Thummim, to a question put to him; the Akkadian word *têrtu,* akin to Hebrew *tôrâ,* signified the response procured in certain types of Mesopotamian divination. If so, Israelite *tôrâ* evolved from a simple manifestation of God's will in the form of an answer "Yes" or "No" (through the Urim and Thummim) into a more complex pronouncement expressing the divine will in cultic matters based on such questions as the distinction of the holy from the profane, the pure from the impure, and in ethical matters too, because of the divine requirement of right behavior on the part of persons approaching what is holy, or, more profoundly, persons divinely expected to be holy. By the end of the monarchic period the meaning of *tôrâ* had been extended to include all divinely sanctioned law, of the types codified in the Pentateuch, and it was then as typically associated with a priest as the word of God was with a *prophet. In this expanded sense of "law," sacred because it was an expression of the divine will, *tôrâ,* something in which priests had always been the rightful experts, became something in which they were competent for deciding questions and settling disputes. Ultimately they became responsible not only for upholding all divine law but also for all casuistry and jurisprudence based on it. This is not to say that priests became teachers or preachers, unless by that, one has in mind their communicating law and legal decisions to the people. In the postexilic centuries priestly involvement with law weakened in the general consciousness, and priests increasingly came to be associated with sacrifice. The traditional idea of priests as persons making statutes and legal judgments known to the people (i.e., as persons with judiciary duties) was alive in the second century BCE, but as jurists learned in the law they were by then being supplanted by the *scribes. Membership of priests in commissions having judicial duties as well as administrative ones in the Roman period may have been due in large part to their social and political connections.

**Historical Evolution of Priesthood.** The historical roots of early Israelite priesthood probably lie, culturally, in the cultic systems of the Canaanites and other Northwest Semitic peoples, whose usual word for priest is essentially the same as the Hebrew word. Israelite settlements in Palestine had their Yahwist sanctuaries, and throughout the land there continued to be a multitude of such sanctuaries, each with one or more priests, until the ultimate suppression of all but the *Temple in *Jerusalem in the reign of *Josiah left Jerusalem the only place where anyone could actually function as a priest. In the period of the judges and in the early monarchic period one could be a priest without being a member of the tribe of Levi, and yet a *Levite was particularly desirable as a priest. If the unnamed ancestor of Eli in 1 Sam. 2.27–28 is Levi, as the context strongly suggests, then the priests of the sanctuary of the ark at Shiloh were Levites. Of the personal origins of *Zadok, the founding head of the priesthood of Jerusalem, nothing at all is said in the narratives in which he appears, or in any preexilic text. In some scholarly hypotheses concerning his undocumented origins he is held to have been a Levite, in others not.

By the time of Josiah's abolition of all sanctuaries except that of Jerusalem three centuries later, there was no longer any question of anyone's functioning as a priest unless he was a Levite, and the Levitical quality of the Jerusalemite "sons of Zadok" seems at that time not to have been called into question. Later still, when all priests were considered "sons of *Aaron," the postexilic Chronicler arranged things by presenting Zadok as an aide to an Aaronite commander in David's time, and by giving Zadok himself an Aaronite genealogy; the purpose of this is clearly that of giving the priests of Jerusalem Aaronite legitimacy, and its historicity is dubious. In any case, while any Levite, according to Deuteronomy, might in principle function as a priest if he were admitted to do so at the sole remaining sanctuary, in Ezekiel 40–48 only members of traditionally priestly families of Jerusalem (the "sons of Zadok") are admitted to the exclusively priestly service of the altar; all other Levites are relegated to a lower status with functions of Temple service that, except in 40.45, were not reckoned as priestly. The distinction between priests and subordinated Levites was firmly established in the postexilic restoration, but the fact that in P the priests are not called sons of the clearly Jerusalemite Zadok but "sons of Aaron" may indicate that some members of Levitical families not originally of Jerusalem, but of other cities in the south, were admitted to priestly service together with the "sons of Zadok" after the exile, as they had perhaps been admitted before the exile, before or after Josiah's reform. All of the cities assigned to the sons of Aaron in the final form of the lists of Levitical cities are indeed in the south.

In the actual division of duties between priests and Levites prescribed by P, the priests did everything that entailed contact with the altars and with the offerings after they had contracted holiness. They were responsible for rites of purification, because of the sacrifices and sacrificial blood involved. In the Persian, Hellenistic, and Roman periods each priest did his Temple service as a member of one of twenty-four divisions, each division functioning only during a short period of the year. When leadership in matters of piety passed largely to the *Pharisees around the second century BCE, priests retained respected and in many cases high social status. Some ordinary priests, in order to make ends meet, engaged in secular occupations, and many lived outside Jerusalem.

**The High Priest.** Priesthood in Jerusalem in the days of the monarchy had been hierarchically structured, under a head, usually called simply "the priest," or, if he needed to be distinguished from the "second priest," he might be called the "chief priest." The head of the priesthood of Jerusalem had always held a high place in the kingdom's administrative circles, but after the exile the high priest quickly became the head of the Jewish nation, both civilly and religiously. The presence of a Jewish civil administrator appointed by the Persian imperial government at certain times (ca. 520 BCE, and during the last half of the fifth century) did little to alter the high priest's position as far as the nation itself was concerned. Although Hasmonean rulers of the second and first centuries BCE assumed the title "king," they retained the high priesthood and its title, which was more important within the Jewish community itself. From this time on, the high priests and those close to them, rather worldly in their interests, were of the aristocratic party of the *Sadducees. With Herod the Great (37–4 BCE) ruling power in Judah passed completely out of priestly families, life tenure in high priesthood was abolished, and each appointment to the office of high priest was thereafter made by the Herodian ruler or, between 6–41 CE, by the Roman procurator. In the New Testament the plural "the high priests" refers to high priestly families as a group, or at times to the *Sanhedrin or some other group possessing official jurisdiction under the leadership or presidency of the high priest.

In the distribution of ritual responsibilities codified in P, on the basis of degrees of holiness, only the high priest, whose degree of holiness as a person was supreme, could enter the holy of holies, the innermost part of the Temple building and the place whose degree of spatial holiness was the highest, for the rites to be performed there on the annual Day of Atonement.

*Aelred Cody, O.S.B.*

**PRINCE OF THE POWER OF THE AIR.** Found only in Ephesians 2.2 (NRSV: "ruler of . . ."), this phrase reflects the common belief in the hierarchical organization of *angels and *demons. In the first century CE, "prince" generally refers to a political power, whether human or spirit. "Air" represents the region between earth and heaven, which is the traditional sphere of demonic activity. In this case, "power" refers to the realm within which power is exercised. Hence, the prince of the power of the air is the spiritual ruler over this hierarchical realm of demons, to which those who are not in Christ are also subject. *Patrick A. Tiller*

**PROMISED LAND.** When God called *Abraham, one of the things promised was land. Though the passage perhaps dates from the tenth century BCE, the promised territory specified in Genesis 15.18 is the land of *Canaan from the river of Egypt to the *Euphrates River; other boundaries given for the land are more modest. Genesis also records that the promise was subsequently reaffirmed to Abraham's descendants: *Isaac, *Jacob, *Joseph, and Jacob's other sons.

In biblical narrative, the promise was also renewed in the time of *Moses. According to Leviticus 25.23, however, the land belonged to God; the Israelites were merely tenants. Deuteronomy represents the land as a gift and describes it in somewhat hyperbolic terms, but continuance on the land was conditional upon obedience to the law. Both Leviticus and Deuteronomy offer the threat of exile and scattering among the nations if the Israelites break the law as well as the hope of restoration to the land should they subsequently repent. The Pentateuch thus contains different attitudes toward the land, reflecting the historical contexts of its authors, attitudes modeled in part at least on such ancient Near Eastern practices as royal grants of land as rewards to individual subjects.

*Joshua began the conquest of Canaan. While some passages indicate complete victory in his time followed by "rest from war" (Josh. 11.23), others make it clear that it was not that quick. When Joshua was an old man, there was still much territory left to seize. It was actually *David who completed the conquest in the tenth century BCE.

In about 921 BCE, the nation of Israel split into two kingdoms: *Israel in the north and *Judah in the south. Because of sin, prophets arose to warn the people of judgment. Amos addressed the northerners, threatening them with exile. Israel, the northern kingdom, fell to *Assyria in 721 BCE. Many were taken away to other parts of the Assyrian empire. Jeremiah, in the last days of the kingdom of Judah, predicted exile. Judah fell to Babylon in 587 BCE, with the result that many of the leaders were exiled to *Babylon. The book of Kings was written in the sixth century BCE to explain the two catastrophes: both kingdoms fell because of idolatry. Although the prophets pronounced the judgment of land loss, they also looked beyond the disasters to future times of healing and restoration.

During the exile, the Jews longed to return to their land but they learned to maintain their identity without it. While they could not offer animal sacrifice, since that could only be done in *Jerusalem, they could preserve their distinctive religion through prayer, Sabbath keeping, circumcision, and observing dietary laws.

In 538 BCE, King *Cyrus of Persia, having conquered Babylon a year earlier, allowed the Jews to return and rebuild their *Temple in Jerusalem, yet not all the Jews returned. Some became established in Babylon, giving rise to a community that thrived there for centuries. Those in the Dispersion contributed money to support the Temple. Land and sacrifice, now restored, were elevated in importance again, but Israelite religion was not exclusively tied to the land.

In 70 CE, the Temple was destroyed again, this time by the Romans, and the Jews were once more dispersed abroad. They survived this tragedy by maintaining their traditions wherever they went. It would be wrong to say that Judaism is indifferent to the land, however, for the devout Jew prays daily that Jerusalem will be rebuilt speedily, and part of the Passover celebration includes the hope that next year the feast will be eaten in Jerusalem.

In the late nineteenth century, Zionism developed. Largely a secular movement, its goal of the establishment of a homeland for the Jewish people was not primarily to fulfill biblical prophecy but to have a country where Jews could live in security, safe from persecution.

In the New Testament, there is little emphasis on geography, but the imagery of the promised land is symbolically used in the letter to the Hebrews. Abraham is a paradigm for Christians: just as he left his home country by faith, seeking a new one, so Christians should seek the heavenly country or city that God is preparing for them.

Hebrews also alludes to the wilderness wandering and the conquest. A whole generation was denied entrance into the land because of rebellion, disobedience, and unbelief. The admonition, then, is not to be apostate like them. Hebrews also suggests that Joshua did not really give the people rest; rather, God offers rest to those who are obedient and faithful. The author then encourages his audience to enter that rest, which refers not to conquering land and enjoying the ensuing peace, as it did earlier, but rather to trusting in God's works and ceasing from one's own.

Nationhood and land are not always spiritualized in the New Testament. Though Paul viewed those Jews who did not embrace Jesus as *Messiah to be outside of God's favor, he looked forward to a day when the Jewish people as a nation would turn back to God and be forgiven. Jesus also affirmed that the meek would inherit the earth. The book of Revelation tells of a thousand-year period when martyrs of the church would rule with Jesus. It also predicts the creation of a new heaven and a new earth.

Despite this spiritualization of the concept of the promised land, Christians too have on occasion seen themselves as "heirs according to the promise" in a territorial sense. Both the Boers of South Africa and the Puritan colonizers of New England saw themselves as a new Israel, led by God to a new Canaan, a "providence plantation."

*William B. Nelson, Jr.*

**PROPHETS.** *This entry consists of two articles, the first on prophets in* Ancient Israel, *and the second on the phenomenon of prophecy in* Early Christianity. *For discussion of individual prophets, see the entries under their names.*

### *Ancient Israel*

No comprehensive definition of an Israelite prophet is possible. The persons conventionally included in this category appear to have manifested great diversity of character and function. They are referred to by a number of terms that in some texts are used interchangeably, and some of these shed some light on their functions: "seer" implies a recipient of visions, and "man of God" suggests some kind of close relationship with the deity. But the most common designation, *nābîʾ*, usually translated as "prophet," is of uncertain derivation. The prophets of the eighth century BCE seem to have avoided terminological classification altogether.

In general, it may be said that prophets were men or women believed to be recipients through audition, vision, or dream of divine messages that they passed on to others by means of speech or symbolic action. The persons they addressed might be individuals, particular groups of Israelites, the whole nation, or foreign nations. The prophets, then, were divine messengers, as is indicated by the formula, "Thus Yahweh has said," which precedes many of their utterances. Frequently, these messages were unsolicited and were delivered under divine compulsion, though on some occasions a prophet was consulted by persons who inquired whether there was a message from God for them. Several of the prophetic books contain "call narratives" in which the prophets express their conviction that they have received a particular summons to prophesy. Several prophets, notably *Jeremiah, recorded their reluctance and even strong resistance to this divine constraint. These call narratives, however, belong to a literary genre, and may not be simply (auto)biographical.

Prophetic activity was not confined to Israel, nor were all prophets prophets of Yahweh. Although the term *nābîʾ* is not found elsewhere in the ancient Near East, activities comparable with those of the Israelite prophets are attested among other Semitic peoples, notably at Mari in the eighteenth century BCE. In Israel an early reference to prophets is found in a narrative that associates their activity with the founding of the Israelite kingdom by *Saul. For the next four centuries, both in northern Israel and in Judah, prophets are mainly found in close connection with the kings and with political events generally.

It is not possible to give a systematic account of this early prophecy—or indeed of much of the prophetic activity in the ensuing period—because the information available is so diverse. One can only note certain rather disparate scraps of information. There was the solitary prophet, liable to appear suddenly to confront the king, in contrast with the groups known as the "sons of the prophets" (NRSV: "company of prophets") who lived in isolated communities under a leader; these are in turn to be differentiated from groups of prophets maintained at the royal court. Other individuals appear to have been local seers or prophets (the explanatory note in 1 Sam. 9.9 does not throw much light on the distinction) who might be consulted in cases of lost property but might also serve in some local cultic capacity. While in some cases prophetic activity took the form of apparently insane behavior attributed to seizure by the spirit of God and prophets could simply be dismissed as "mad," others acted as military advisers to the king or confronted kings with their moral or religious misdeeds, condemning them in God's name; in some cases, they were even capable of fomenting a coup d'état, deposing one king and choosing and consecrating another. As miracle workers, they might make an ax head float but might also call down fire from heaven or raise a dead person to life.

Such examples of contrasting behavior and activity could be multiplied from the evidence of the books of *Samuel and Kings and, to some extent, from the prophetic books. These stories, which represent popular views of prophets, are to a large extent legendary in character; but they show clearly that Israelite prophecy was a many-sided phenomenon. Apart from some accounts of rather trivial miracle-working, however, they have one common characteristic: they represent the true prophet as the agent and defender of Yahweh in opposition both to religious apostasy and syncretism and to the authority of kings when these failed to uphold the cause of Yahweh or flouted his moral demands. This is especially true of the ninth-century prophets *Elijah and *Elisha.

The prophets of the eighth and seventh centuries BCE stood for the same principles as their predecessors. For this period, however, our sources of information are mainly of a different kind. The prophetic books (Isaiah, Jeremiah, Ezekiel, and the books of the twelve "minor" prophets) contain far fewer stories about prophets, and consist mainly of what purport to be records of words spoken by the prophets whose names they bear. The word of God received and transmitted by the prophet now assumes primary importance. It is, however, no easy matter to identify these words and to distinguish them from other material. In their present form, the prophetic books have all become repositories of other and later material, both prophetic and nonprophetic. This additional matter has its own importance and should not be regarded as in any way inferior to the words of the original prophet; but its presence makes it difficult to form a correct notion of his message.

The extent to which the prophecy of the eighth century BCE marks a decisive change in the character of Israelite prophecy is disputed. Two features, however, call for notice: first, the eighth- and seventh-century prophets addressed themselves not only to kings and other individuals and particular groups but also to the whole people; second, they were, as far as our information enables us to judge, the first to prophesy the destruction of the entire nation as a punishment for its sins. This prophecy of national disaster, sometimes presented as avoidable through repentance but sometimes not, was the main feature of the message of the prophets of the eighth century BCE (Hosea, Amos, Isaiah, and Micah) and also of Jeremiah and Ezekiel in the late seventh/early sixth. The latter, however, who survived the destruction of Judah and Jerusalem in 587/586 BCE, also offered hope for the future beyond the disaster. The prophets of the exile and the postexilic period were chiefly concerned with the hope of a restoration of the nation's fortunes and with current problems of the postexilic community.

The prophets were not primarily theologians; but some of them, in their attempt to present their message coherently and persuasively, achieved profound insights into divine and human natures and the relationship between God and his people Israel. (The theological teachings of the individual prophets are described in more detail in the articles on each prophet.)

The prophets whose words have been preserved were only a small and probably unrepresentative minority. Other prophets are frequently mentioned by them, usually unfavorably. It is clear that, especially in the time of Jeremiah, there were two groups of prophets opposed to one another. Jeremiah regarded his opponents, who offered the people a comforting message of national security based on the belief that God would protect them irrespective of their conduct, as false or lying prophets. Passages such as this reflect the problem faced by the people when two groups of prophets, each claiming to speak in Yahweh's name, proclaimed diametrically opposite messages. Attempts were made to establish criteria for identifying the genuine prophet, but these were unable to resolve the problem.

Prophets who delivered unpalatable messages not only encountered difficulties in gaining acceptance as authentic messengers of Yahweh but were liable to suffer humiliation and even threats to their lives. Yet insofar as they were believed to have an intimate relationship with God they were feared. Even kings were unable to ignore them. On the other hand, it is unlikely that prophets generally enjoyed an official status in either the religious or the political establishment. Recently, attempts have been made to define their role in sociological terms. Whatever results may eventually emerge from this kind of study, it can be safely asserted that the prophets about whom we have any detailed information came from a wide variety of social backgrounds, and functioned in a variety of ways. *R. N. Whybray*

### *Early Christianity*

Prophecy in the New Testament is the reception and subsequent communication of spontaneous and divinely given revelations; normally, those who were designated "prophets" in early Christianity were specialists in mediating divine revelation rather than those who prophesied occasionally or only once. The exhortation to desire earnestly to prophesy may be best explained as a call to all those who regarded themselves as gifted with inspired utterance (the "spiritual" ones) to aspire to prophesy rather than to speak in tongues: none are excluded a priori from the gift, but God will not in fact distribute any one gift to all. From what we can deduce about them from Acts and the Letters, as well as from the book of Revelation (a document that self-consciously presents itself as Christian prophecy in written form), prophets might conduct their ministry in one congregation or throughout a region, singly or more often in groups. In the lists of ministries they are mentioned next after *apostles; they are associated with teachers in the church at Antioch.

In the context of the church meeting the ministry of the prophet is spoken of as "revelation," and such an utterance is associated with the Spirit of God. This prophetic speech is not the same as speaking in tongues, nor is it the interpretation of tongues; it is some perception of the truth of God intelligibly communicated to the congregation. In Paul's view, it is an abuse of prophecy to pretend to an ecstatic frenzy so that prophets become, so to speak, out of hand; he insists that "the spirits of prophets are subject to the prophets" (1 Cor. 14.32), that is to say, each is in full possession of his or her faculties and is able to restrain the impulse to speak if the interests of order so require.

Most important, prophets were not to be given undiscerning credence. The utterances required "testing" or "evaluation" by other prophets (1 Cor. 14.29); only then were they to be received as the word of the Lord. This testing is not only to distinguish the Spirit's word from the speaker's natural impulses, but also to identify and exclude false prophecy. The most important criterion put forward by Paul for the evaluation of prophetic speech (or indeed for viewpoints expressed through a variety of oral and written forms of communication) was the content of the message, which should agree with the generally accepted beliefs and customs of the Christian community.

The gift of prophecy gradually fell into disuse and, in spite of occasional revivals, into a measure of disrepute because of the continuing presence of false prophecy and the difficulties or uncertainties involved in discerning it. Other factors contributing to the decline of prophecy were the increasing authority of an official ministry in a church becoming more institutionalized, and the tendency to rely more on rational and didactic forms of spiritual utterance; the latter led to the place of prophets being taken by teachers, catechists, scholars, and theologians, whose authority depended not on any revelation directly received but on the exposition of an existing authoritative tradition, especially the Bible. *David Hill*

**PROSELYTE.** An essentially religious term used to describe a convert from one form of belief to another. It is more appropriate to use the term only for the period when the Jews were a religious community rather than an independent nation-state, that is to say, from the postexilic period onward. The *Septuagint, the Greek translation of the Hebrew Bible, rendered the Hebrew word *gēr,* which means "sojourner" or "resident alien," as *prosēlytos;* in later Hebrew *gēr* came to have a religious rather than an ethnic meaning.

The word "proselyte" is found four times in the New Testament (Matt. 23.15; Acts 2.10; 6.5; 13.43; the first and last references are translated "convert" in the NRSV). The reference in Matthew makes it clear that some Jewish groups regarded missionary work as an important part of their practice, and the presence of proselytes at the Feast of Weeks (Pentecost) in Jerusalem (Acts 2) implies the success of such efforts. One of the basic requirements laid upon potential converts will have been circumcision, and some groups in the Hellenistic world condemned this as a form of mutilation incompatible with the ideal of bodily perfection. Nevertheless, the rite was almost certainly required as a means of entry to the covenant community. From roughly the first century CE (and possibly earlier) a form of water ceremony ("proselyte baptism") was also required. Our earliest descriptions of this come from rabbinic sources, though it is possible that *John the Baptist's practice was a related rite.

The references in Matthew and Acts support the likely hypothesis that the great majority of proselytes will have come from the *Diaspora, attracted by the lifestyle of Jewish communities in different parts of the Greek and later Roman world. *Synagogues, which first developed in the Diaspora, will have been the natural context for the beginning of an acquaintance with Judaism.

It has often been argued that alongside proselytes there existed a further group of sympathetic gentiles known as "God-fearers," who were attracted to Judaism but reluctant to be circumcised. It would probably be wrong, however, to see in this a technical term; "those who feared God" is simply a way of describing those pious people who were attracted to Judaism and subsequently to Christianity.

What kind of reception might proselytes expect among those already Jews? Rabbinic texts show that they were often regarded with suspicion, as is commonly the case with converts in many religions. It is in this light that varying traditions in the Hebrew Bible relating to converts can best be understood: the story of *Ruth, whatever its original point, clearly illustrates an open attitude to those who came to Judaism in adult life, whereas the concerns in the books of *Ezra and *Nehemiah for the dangers of mixed marriage (at least insofar as it involved non-Jewish women) show a more restrictive attitude.

*Richard Coggins*

**PROSTITUTES.** The granting of sexual access for payment is disparaged in the Bible and is associated linguistically with a variety of forms of sexual immorality. A metaphorical use of language related to prostitution dominates much of the Hebrew Bible, following *Hosea, who characterizes Israel's relations with foreign gods and nations as the actions of a promiscuous bride or a prostitute seeking lovers. This polemical usage often makes it impossible to determine the exact nature of the practices designated as "harlotry."

In its primary form, prostitution is an institution of patriarchal society that permits males to enjoy sexual relations outside of marriage while preserving exclusive right of access to their spouses. Hence the prostitute is normally female, and male (homosexual) prostitution is weakly, and differently, attested. While the prostitute was tolerated, she always bore a degree of opprobrium, even when praised for noble character or action. Men are warned against the wiles and waste of prostitutes, and wages from prostitution are prohibited as payment of vows. *Priests were forbidden to marry a prostitute or to force a daughter into prostitution.

The Hebrew term for prostitute, *zônâ* (a feminine participle with no masculine counterpart), is derived from the verb *zānâ,* which describes promiscuous sexual activity in general and more specifically fornication by an unmarried female, a crime punishable by death. What is tolerated for prostitutes, as a class set apart, is strictly proscribed for other *women.

It is widely assumed that some form of "sacred" or "cultic prostitution" characterized Canaanite religion; however, the language of prostitution is never used to describe cultic offices or activity in ancient Near Eastern texts outside the Bible's polemical usage. The Hebrew term sometimes rendered "sacred prostitute," *qĕdēšâ* (f.)/*qādēš* (m.), simply means "consecrated (person)." Association with prostitution, or sexual activity of any sort, is inferred from biblical contexts and has no parallel in extrabiblical texts.

New Testament texts group prostitutes (*pornē,* f.) with tax collectors as representing the lowest class in moral terms. The masculine form of the noun (*pornos,* meaning male prostitute in classical Greek) is used in the New Testament only in the general sense of "fornicator" or "one who practices sexual immorality" and may be extended to describe immorality in general. A similar sense is conveyed by the verb *porneuō* and the abstract noun *porneia* ("fornication"), which is frequent in ethical lists and is often associated with gentile cults and culture. The book of Revelation continues the figurative usage of the Hebrew Bible in characterizing *Babylon as the "great whore" and its offenses as "fornication." *Phyllis A. Bird*

**PUBLICANS.** The word "publicans" in some English versions of the New Testament comes from the Latin *publicani,* which is in a sense a mistranslation of the Greek *telōnai;* the NRSV translates the term as "tax collector." Both Greek states and Rome had only a rudimentary civil service and budgeting process. Hence minor taxes were regularly sold to a private company, which would pay the agreed price to the treasury and collect (in principle, at the fixed rate) from the taxpayers. These *telōnai* had long been known and disliked in the Greek East (an Alexandrian comic poet calls them "birds of prey"). Roman *publicani,* while they always performed this service, had an essentially different origin. They were state contractors who would buy at auction both performance contracts (e.g., building contracts or contracts for army supplies) and collection contracts (as for taxes or the revenues of mines or ponds or forests). During the age of Roman expansion and public building, in the Middle Republic, they made most of their money from the former and, as Polybius tells us, they widely distributed prosperity among Roman citizens. This changed when the reformer Gaius Gracchus in 123 BCE entrusted them with the collection of the principal tax (the tithe on produce) of the province of *Asia, which Rome had just acquired, and also with staffing the criminal courts, which tried senators for maladministration and, in due course, for other crimes. This vastly increased the scale of their undertakings, and made them a major power in the state, though they always narrowly defended their economic interests. Their power in the courts was temporarily removed by Sulla (81 BCE), but was soon essentially restored. As a result, governors and their staffs, instead of regulating their activities, tended to become their partners—often in collusion with the provincial upper class, which could pass the burden on to those below—in grossly exploiting the provinces, especially in the east, where Pompey introduced the Asian system to all the new provinces he organized, including Syria. On one occasion, a governor of Syria tried to take the system over for his own benefit, with some relief for the provincials, who had fewer appetities to satisfy. His enemy Cicero complains that he had handed the *publicani* over to Syrians and Jews, "nations born to be slaves." Although by no means the chief or only exploiters, they and their huge staffs were the most visible, at the point of collection, and caused most of the widespread anti-Roman feeling in the eastern provinces.

They were organized as companies of shareholders (in the late Republic shares were widely traded), under a board of directors *(magistri)* who were always equestrian in standing. In the provinces, a *promagister* (not a shareholder) was in charge of a large establishment, mostly of natives, and they were what provincials called *publicani,* the vastly better organized successors of the local *telōnai.*

In the civil wars they lost their power and their fortunes, as rival commanders freely confiscated their accumulated wealth in the provinces. Caesar removed the main tax of Asia from them, collecting it directly through state officials, and Augustus in due course extended this to other provinces. When the province of Judea was annexed, after the deposition of Archelaus in 6 CE (*see* Herodian Dynasty), the *publicani* were given only the minor taxes (chiefly tariffs, again) to collect. Such tariffs were traditionally imposed, purely for purposes of revenue, at various points along main roads, as well as in all ports, as import, export, and transit dues.

In the late Republic, the power of the *publicani* led to major abuses, which we know from Cicero's speeches. Illegal extra charges were widely added, and permitted by the governor, and violence was used to extort compliance. Although there was more control under Augustus, this is the background to what we find in Judea. The Jews soon hated the Roman occupation even more than they had hated Archelaus, whose deposition they had demanded. Native collectors of taxes were now seen as collaborators with the oppressor, using his backing for their illegal profits. The problem was apparently worse in Judea than elsewhere, presumably because of the religious element in the national resistance; it is interesting that the "publicans" appear only in the

Gospels, not in the rest of the New Testament, even though they were of course active in all the provinces. They are regularly coupled with sinners (note that where Matt. 5.46 has "publicans" Luke 6.32 has "sinners"), with *prostitutes, and with *gentiles. In the parable of the Pharisee and the publican, the latter knows his low place, whereas the former is the type of establishment respectability, despising him as an outcast. Talmudic literature continues this aversion, until it was forbidden even to accept alms from a tax collector. Yet wealth clearly conferred respectability. The chief tax collector *(architelōnēs)* at Jericho (perhaps a *promagister*) who followed *Jesus was treated by him like any other wealthy man, and in Josephus we find a *telōnēs* who is a notable of the Jewish community at Caesarea, working for the benefit of his community and trying to use his influence and his fortune on their behalf.

Most of the time we hear of the humble and despised publicans, whom Jesus made a point of treating, as he did other outcasts, like human beings who could be saved. This astonished and shocked (especially) the *Pharisees, which suggests a religious element in the aversion: dining with Levi was like dining with a gentile. It seems, however, that for ordinary people it was the exactions that were most disliked. Publicans who came to be baptized were told by *John the Baptist (just as soldiers were) to do what was their duty and not to abuse their power. This corresponds to the injunction to sin no more, which was all that Jesus required of humble people.

It is interesting that Matthew sets the story of the call of *Matthew (Levi) the tax collector at *Capernaum (the other accounts do not specify the location). If so, the *telōnēs* would be in the employ of Herod Antipas and would uniquely attest precisely similar aversion to *telōnai* who were not agents of Rome. But it must be suspected that Capernaum was wrongly introduced into the story, as one of Jesus's favorite towns.

*See also* Roman Empire

*E. Badian*

# Q

**QOHELETH.** *See* Ecclesiastes.

**QUEEN AND QUEEN MOTHER.** Although several Hebrew words are translated "queen," they denote different statuses or types of royal women. The two primary terms are *malkâ* and *gĕbîrâ*. *Malkâ* seems not to have been used, even as a descriptive title, for any Judean or Israelite ruler's wife. Instead, the Bible commonly refers to the "king's wife" or the "king's mother." *Malkâ* may connote foreignness; the queen of *Sheba, Vashti and *Esther (wives of the Persian king), and the abominated queen of heaven are all called *malkâ*. *Gĕbîrâ* seems to refer to the mother of the acknowledged heir to the throne or to the mother of the reigning king, hence "queen mother." She may also be the chief wife.

In a dynastic succession, heredity is the crucial factor. Almost every accession notice of a Judahite king includes not only his father's but also his mother's name. The queen mother's identity seems to have been relevant in establishing the legitimacy of the new Davidide. The *gĕbîrâ* frequently appears to come from a rich and well-connected Israelite family. It has been suggested that important provincial power groups ("the people of the land") had a vested interest in promoting a local woman to be the king's wife and subsequently pressuring the king to make her the *gĕbîrâ*.

With a power base of sorts behind her, a *gĕbîrâ* would have been able to exert some independent, if informal authority. Underlying Asa's removal of Maacah from being *gĕbîrâ* was probably a power struggle between court factions. The formal notice of the demotion suggests its unprecedented nature; it also implies that the *gĕbîrâ* enjoyed not only prestige but tangible privileges.

Several episodes have led scholars to conclude that the queen mother had official status. But recent studies have pointed out, on the basis of extrabiblical parallels, that the queen mothers involved in these episodes were unusual in having maneuvered their own sons into power even though the son had no legitimate claim to the throne. In such cases the new king owed a debt to his mother that he could scarcely ignore, and the queen mother's power might grow even greater.

Besides marrying women from local families, Israelite kings, like their ancient Near Eastern counterparts, had an eye to advantageous alliances and often chose wives from neighboring royalty. *Solomon's foreign wives are proverbial. *Jezebel was the daughter of the king of Tyre, and her daughter Athaliah married Jehoram of Judah.

Kings' daughters generally receive little mention, although a Hebrew seal inscribed "Maadanah, daughter of the king" has come to light. Michal, *Saul's daughter and *David's wife is exceptional, as is Athaliah's enterprising rebel daughter Jehosheba.

With their status and wealth, wives of rulers throughout the ancient Near East were often able to transcend the otherwise static boundaries determined by gender and society (*see* Women, *article on* Ancient Near East and Israel). In Mesopotamia, rulers' wives supervised their own households, administered palace industries, engaged in diplomacy, and participated in religious rituals apart from their husbands. This recalls the experience of the most documented biblical queen, Jezebel. She ran her own religious establishment and used her authority to initiate and execute policy. She sent official messages, counseled her husband, and, although 1 Kings 21.8 says that she arranged Naboth's death in *Ahab's name, elsewhere the wording may mean that the murder was committed on Jezebel's own authority.

Occasionally women ruled independently in the ancient Near East. The queen of *Sheba, who conducted economic negotiations with Solomon, may have belonged to a dynasty of queens who ruled in North Arabia, and during the Hasmonean period *Salome was for a brief time queen of Judea (76–67 BCE). Ancient records, however, tend to look with disfavor on women who ruled in their own name, whether it is the *Sumerian "king" KU.BAU (third millennium BCE), the Egyptian Pharaoh Hatshepsut (1486–1468 BCE), or Athaliah of Judah (843–837 BCE), whose six-year reign was the only break in the Davidic succession of Judahite kings.

In its attitude toward the historical queens of Israel and Judah, the Bible is either neutral (the royal accession notices), suspiciously laconic (e.g., Bathsheba and the wife of Jeroboam I), or decidedly negative (Maacah, Jezebel, Athaliah). Only Esther, in what is essentially a morale-raising fiction, merits an unequivocally favorable portrayal. From a literary point of view, however, *Sarah seems to be a positive paradigm for the *gĕbîrâ,* just as *Abraham is a paradigm for David. The narrative's insistence that Sarah, not *Hagar, will bear the son of the promise, is reminiscent of the attention paid to the identity of the king's mother in the royal accession notices. The gospels of Matthew and Luke may reflect this when they stress *Mary's role in bearing another son of the promise and future king. The later tradition of Mary as the heavenly queen, however, derives not from biblical but from imperial Roman political vocabulary.

*Mary Joan Winn Leith*

**QUEEN OF HEAVEN.** A goddess who, according to the prophet Jeremiah, was worshiped in Judah in the late seventh and early sixth centuries BCE. Jeremiah's remarks associate the goddess with fertility and, to some degree, with war; as her title "Queen of Heaven" indicates, she also has astral characteristics. Her cult is described as one that is particularly attractive to women, who bake offering cakes called *kawwānîm* in the goddess's image.

The Canaanite goddess who best fits this description is *Astarte, a goddess associated with both fertility and war and who has astral features. *Phoenician inscriptions also ascribe to Astarte the title "queen." Astarte's cult, however, is not known to be one in which women played a special role. Women on the other hand did have an important place in the cult of Astarte's Mesopotamian counterpart, Ishtar, whose female devotees ritually wept in imitation of the goddess's mourning over her dead lover, *Tammuz. Ishtar's cult also involved the offering of cakes called *kamānu,* a word cognate to Hebrew *kawwānîm.* The Queen of Heaven thus should be identified as a syncretism of Canaanite Astarte and Mesopotamian Ishtar. *Susan Ackerman*

**QUEEN OF SHEBA.** *See* Sheba, Queen of.

# R

**RABBI.** A term that arose in the first century CE for those ordained to be authoritative in their study, exposition, and practice of Jewish law. The rabbi could be found expounding the Torah in the *synagogue, much as Jesus did, although the application of the title to him was early and preserved its etymological meaning of "my master." The rabbi functioned as an interpreter of Torah and as a judge, most often of the claims of the *poor. By the third century, the rabbi was regarded as having magical powers such as the ability to communicate with the dead.

Rabbis generally worked part-time at a trade, as carpenters, cobblers, and the like. Not until the Middle Ages did the rabbinate become a profession. The rabbis were not a separate caste. They mixed with the common folk on a regular basis and usually came from the ranks of ordinary people, as in the case of the most eminent of all rabbis, Akiva. The rabbis believed that all Jews could live a holy life through observance of Torah, and they said that, if all Jews observed just two Sabbaths completely, salvation would come. Thus, common folk played an important part in the rabbinate's scheme. Rabbis could be entrusted with great responsibilities far removed from the world of Torah study in the rabbinical schools. There are instances of rabbis assuming public health responsibilities, including disaster prevention so that buildings would not collapse in a storm, and the rabbi would act to see that no one in his village lacked food to eat. Such was the central role of rabbis in late antiquity.

The earliest literary monument of the rabbis is the Mishnah. Completed around 200 CE, the Mishnah is basically a rambling legal compilation, striking in its ahistorical character as compared with earlier Jewish writings and in its lack of reference to scripture to support its rulings. Nevertheless, it was authoritative and became the basis for the Jerusalem Talmud (ca. 400 CE) and the Babylonian Talmud (ca. 500 CE), which comment on the Mishnah and supply its wants, ideological as well as scriptural (e.g., the Mishnah does not talk of the *Messiah).

The rabbis essentially shared the traditions and views of the *Pharisees. They embraced an all-knowing, all-wise, just, merciful, and loving God who supervised the lives of individuals and decreed the fates, even while giving room for free will to choose between good and evil. A world to come existed where recompense for the evils of this world could be expected. Both this world and the next revolved around Torah. The religion of the rabbis exalted the holy faith, the holy man, and the pursuit of a holy way of life. A part of that holy existence involved daily prayer, and the roots of the current Jewish prayerbook are to be found in the Mishnah. It was only by pursuing the holy on a daily basis that salvation could be achieved and the Messiah would come.

*Philip Stern*

**RACHEL.** Rachel, whose name means "ewe," was the younger daughter of Laban (brother of *Rebekah) and the wife of *Jacob. The account of the meeting and subsequent marriage of Rachel and Jacob is a love story, succinct in its narration. Jacob was charged by his father *Isaac to find a wife among his mother's people at Haran in *Mesopotamia. At the end of his journey, he came to a well where shepherds gathered to water their flocks. When he learned that they were from Haran, he asked them if they knew Laban; the shepherds pointed out to Jacob that Laban's daughter Rachel was approaching with her father's sheep. As soon as Jacob saw Rachel, he rolled the stone from the mouth of the well and watered the flock of Laban, his uncle. He kissed Rachel and made himself known to her as a relative. She then returned home and gave her father the news of the arrival of Jacob. Laban went to Jacob, greeted him, and brought him to his house, where he stayed a month helping with the daily chores. At the end of this time, his uncle suggested that even as a relative he should not serve for nothing. When he asked Jacob what his wages should be, Jacob, who loved Rachel, said, "I will serve you seven years for your younger daughter Rachel" (Gen. 29.18); this was agreed upon. At the end of the term, which passed quickly for him because of his love, he asked Laban for her hand in marriage.

A feast was prepared and Jacob received his wife who according to custom was veiled. In the morning he discovered that he had been deceived into accepting Rachel's elder sister, *Leah. When he confronted Laban, he was told that in that country the younger daughter was not given in marriage before the elder; disappointed but undaunted, Jacob worked another seven years for Rachel. Needless to say, she was his favorite wife and eventually became the mother of *Joseph and *Benjamin.

Some time later after a quarrel between Laban and Jacob, in which Rachel took her husband's part and then stole her father's household gods, the entire clan departed stealthily on the long journey to Canaan, where she died at Ephrath giving birth to her younger son Benjamin.

*See also* Ancestors, The.

*Isobel Mackay Metzger*

**RAHAB.**

**1.** The name (Hebr. *rāḥāb*) of the Canaanite *prostitute who saved the spies sent by Joshua to *Jericho, and who, along with her extended family, was subsequently incorporated into Israel. According to Matthew's genealogy of Jesus, she was the mother of Boaz, who married *Ruth, and thus the ancestor of *David.

**2.** A name (Hebr. *rahab*) for the primeval adversary of Yahweh in the battle prior to creation (*see* Israel), also known as the sea, the deep, the dragon, the serpent, and *Leviathan; this name, unlike the others, is not found in ancient Near Eastern sources outside the Bible. It is applied by extension to Egypt as the deity's quintessential historical.

*Michael D. Coogan*

**RAPHAEL.** An *archangel mentioned in the Bible only in the book of *Tobit, in which he is sent to cure the blindness of Tobit and to free the hapless Sarah from the power of a demon; to accomplish these tasks he acts as the companion and protector of Tobit's son Tobias on his journey. Raphael's name means "God has healed"; this explains his curative activity in Tobit and in postbiblical Jewish literature, such as 1 Enoch, in which he is sent to remove *Azazel and to heal the earth and is set over diseases and wounds. Later traditions identify Raphael as one of the divine messengers in Genesis 18.1–2, and as the angel who stirs the waters of the pool Beth-zatha (Bethesda). *Michael D. Coogan*

**REBEKAH.** A woman of insight and determination, Rebekah was the daughter of Bethuel and the sister of Laban the Aramean. She was brought from Haran to be the wife of *Isaac, the son of *Abraham, in the following way. After the death of *Sarah, Abraham commissioned his oldest servant to find a wife for Isaac from Abraham's kindred. The servant traveled to Haran in *Mesopotamia, the city of Abraham's brother, Nahor. On arrival outside the city in the evening about the time when the women usually came to draw water from the well, the servant made the ten camels he had brought with him kneel down nearby. He then prayed that God would guide him in making the right choice of a wife for Isaac. It so happened that Rebekah was the one thus identified. After she had given water to the camels, the servant introduced himself, gave her a gold ring and two bracelets, inquired whose daughter she was, and discovered that she was the daughter of Bethuel, son of Nahor (Abraham's brother). She immediately ran off to tell her mother's household about her encounter at the well. Her brother Laban, on hearing the news, went out to the servant and offered him hospitality. The servant would not accept any food until he had disclosed his mission. On hearing his words, Laban and Bethuel agreed that "the thing comes from the Lord" (Gen. 24.50), so they were willing to have Rebekah go back with the servant to become Isaac's wife.

Isaac and Rebekah were married and became the parents of twin sons, *Esau and *Jacob, who were later to vie for their father's blessing when he was old and blind. Rebekah favored Jacob and helped him through deceit to win the father's blessing. She died apparently while Jacob was in Mesopotamia and was buried in the cave of Machpelah.

*See also* Ancestors, The.

*Isobel Mackay Metzger*

**RECHABITES.** The Rechabites were an Israelite group known for their distinctive lifestyle. Drinking wine was proscribed. They refused houses, choosing instead to live in tents; they rejected agriculture, especially the cultivation of grapes. Jeremiah commended the Rechabites for obeying their strict rule, contrasting them with the other people of Judah who disobeyed God's laws.

Biblical tradition derives their name from Rechab, the father of Jonadab, although it was the latter who imposed the regulations. Possibly their lifestyle manifested an idealization of the *wilderness period when the Israelites lived in tents, worshiped God in a tent, and were faithful. But the Hebrew word for chariot comes from the same root as Rechab, and it may be that the Rechabites were a guild of chariot-makers. If so, their preference for tents might have resulted from their need to travel to the sources of metal ore.

In other references, we learn that the Rechabites may have been related to the seminomadic *Kenites. Malchijah, the son of Rechab, governed a district in the postexilic period. The Mishnah indicates that in the Second Temple period a special day was set aside for the Rechabites to bring the wood offering (*Ta*ᶜ*an.* 4.5). *William B. Nelson, Jr.*

**RED SEA.** The traditional translation (beginning with the Septuagint) of the Hebrew expression *yam sûf,* Red Sea is the name of the body of water crossed by the Israelites in their Exodus from Egypt. This translation, followed by later Greek biblical tradition and the Vulgate, would connect the miracle of the crossing with either the western (the Gulf of Suez) or the eastern (the Gulf of Aqaba/Eilat) branch of the Red Sea. But in Exodus 2.3–5 (and elsewhere in the Bible) *sûf* means "reed," and this is how the Septuagint and Vulgate translate it there; *yam sûf* refers to the eastern branch of the Red Sea in only two other texts. Most contemporary scholars, and a few modern translations (e.g., NJV), therefore prefer to translate the phrase "Reed Sea" or "Sea of Reeds."

The record of Israel's miraculous crossing is a complex one. According to what has been taken as the more ancient stratum of Exodus 14.21–22, perhaps from J, "The Lord drove the Sea back by a strong east wind all night, and turned the sea into dry land." Another stratum, possibly from P, reads: "Then Moses stretched out his hand over the sea . . . and the waters were divided. The Israelites went into the sea on dry ground, the waters forming a wall for them on their right and on their left," after which the waters enveloped the Egyptians. A third version, perhaps from E, reads, "At the morning watch the Lord in the pillar of fire and cloud looked down upon the Egyptian army, and threw the Egyptian army into panic. He clogged their chariot wheels so they turned with difficulty. The Egyptians said: 'Let us flee from the Israelites, for the Lord is fighting for them against Egypt.'" In the first case we have a natural event, where the miracle lies in the synchronism of natural forces; in the second we deal with a miracle in the absolute sense, so that any explanation is immaterial; in the third we have neither water nor a miracle proper; the Egyptians realize that something is going wrong and withdraw. A variant of the second version is found in chap.15. Any connection with volcanic or seismic phenomena should therefore be excluded.

The term "Sea of Reeds" or "Reed Sea" seems to mean a marshy area or a large body of water abundant in reeds in the eastern delta. One possible localization of the event, among the many that have been proposed, is Lake Sirbonis, where, depending on the tides, fresh water and saltwater can be found; another is the swampy region in the vicinity of the "Bitter Lakes." We must remember, however, that we are dealing here, as in the desert wanderings, with mythical, so with few exceptions, the localities mentioned cannot and perhaps should not be identified. *J. A. Soggin*

**REED SEA.** *See* Red Sea.

**REFUGE, CITIES OF.** *See* Cities of Refuge.

**REPHAIM.** In several biblical texts dead "shades" (NRSV) who inhabit the underworld; in other texts a race of fearsome giants who once lived in parts of Palestine and Transjordan. Scholars have in the past considered these two meanings distinct, but texts from Ugarit suggest they may be related. At Ugarit Rephaim most often refers to members of the aristocracy (military, political, or religious) who, as a result of their status while alive, attain some sort of superhuman, even semidivine, standing in the underworld. The probable etymology of Rephaim, from the verb meaning "to heal," also suggests that these dead Rephaim were thought to have power to help the living. The term Rephaim in the Bible likewise may refer to those among the deceased (e.g., the ancestral giants) who demonstrated extraordinary prowess during life and continue to exercise some sort of power after death. Notable in this regard is Isaiah 14.9, where the Rephaim of the underworld are described as those "who were leaders of the earth" and those "who were kings of the nations."

*See also* Nephilim.

*Susan Ackerman*

**REUBEN.** The firstborn son of *Jacob and *Leah and one of the twelve *tribes of Israel. Reuben's primogeniture indicates that in early Israel Reuben was a preëminent tribe. Reuben is guilty of incest with his mother's concubine Bilhah and is prominent in the rebellion against *Moses; the former is blamed for Reuben's later decline. The Reubenites, together with Gad, settle in the Transjordan. An early manuscript of the books of Samuel among the Dead Sea Scrolls mentions Reuben and *Gad's subjugation by Nahash, king of the *Ammonites, elucidating *Saul's deliverance of Jabesh-gilead. Scholars disagree whether Reuben was absorbed into Gad during the divided monarchy or retained its identity until the *Assyrian conquest (732 BCE). *Gary N. Knoppers*

**RIVER OF EGYPT.** The river of Egypt is the traditional southwestern boundary of the *Promised Land, generally identified with the Wadi el-ᶜArish ("Brook of Egypt"), ca. 48 mi (80 km) southeast of Gaza. This "river of Egypt" is not to be confused with the *Nile, for which the word *nāhār,* which properly means "river," is employed. The Hebrew phrase *naḥal miṣrayim* is normally used for this watercourse, and cognate wording is found in Assyrian records; it is translated by the NRSV as "the Wadi of Egypt." The only exception is Genesis 15.18, where *nāhār* is used, but this may be an error.

*Michael D. Coogan*

**ROMAN ARMY.** The most famous units in the Roman army were the legions or divisions stationed in the frontier provinces. They were supplemented by a (numerically equal) force of auxiliaries. In the city of Rome itself, there were several forces, especially the elite praetorian guard that protected the emperor.

The army carried out many duties in addition to those purely military; besides policing, there were bureaucratic functions. Officers, often assisted by small detachments of troops, performed many administrative and judicial tasks.

A legion was commanded by a senator called an imperial legate; under him were six military tribunes and sixty centurions. The full complement of a legion consisted of 5,500 to 6,000 men, who were Roman citizens. There were between twenty-five and thirty legions, but none was stationed in Judea until the Tenth Legion was sent there in 70 CE after the First Jewish Revolt. But there were four in Syria to the north, deployed in Judea when large-scale military intervention became necessary.

Legionaries were heavy infantry and were assisted by auxiliaries, especially cavalry, light-armed troops, and archers; it is not clear which of the latter the *dex-*

*iolaboi* of Acts 23.23 were. Auxiliaries were not Roman citizens, but it became customary to give them Roman citizenship after twenty-five years of service. The *auxilia,* as they were collectively known, were grouped into regiments of five hundred (in a few special cases a thousand) strong, called *alae* if cavalry, *cohortes* if infantry. Their commanders were prefects (tribunes in the case of regiments a thousand strong), usually drawn from the second order of the Roman nobility. Subordinate officers were called decurions in the *alae,* centurions in the cohorts.

The Romans also made use of the armed forces of semi-independent local kings (called "client" kings) within the Roman ambit, such as the *Herods. Soldiers from such armies are mentioned in Matthew 2.16 and Mark 6.17. Client kings often organized their armies on the Roman pattern.

The Roman forces mentioned in the New Testament were all auxiliaries. As Jews were excused from conscription into the Roman army for religious reasons, the soldiers at the crucifixion and in Acts were probably Syrian, *Samaritan, or Caesarean (from the non-Jewish population in Caesarea, the administrative capital of Judea): certainly, Herod the Great had Samaritans and Caesareans in his army, who were later incorporated into the Roman forces. Two regiments are named in the New Testament, the Italian and the Augustan Cohort. These can be compared or equated with the *Cohors II Italica Civium Romanorum* and the *Cohors Augusta I* of the eastern command at the time. Both were of higher status than other auxiliary regiments (like those of Syrians or Thracians) and were stationed in Judea, possibly because no legion was there. Claudius Lysias is called a *chiliarch* or tribune, implying that his cohort was a thousand strong (and part of it mounted, if the cavalry escorting Paul came from it). *Denis Bain Saddington*

**ROMAN EMPIRE.** Later Christian writers looked back to the origin of their faith and saw the work of divine providence in the coincidence of the birth of Jesus and the reign of Augustus, the first Roman emperor. Under Augustus and his successors, the empire stretched from the northwest corner of Europe to Egypt and from Mauritania to the Black Sea. It brought fifty million or more inhabitants under relatively stable rule—an ideal setting for the growth of a new religion.

**Rome Before the Emperors.** Roman imperial institutions and ideas of citizenship went back to the Republic and Rome's origin as a city-state. According to tradition, the city of Rome was founded by Romulus and Remus in 753 BCE at the northern edge of the plain of Latium in central peninsular Italy. Initially, the city-state was ruled by a king with the advice of the Senate, a council of elders from Rome's leading families who served for life. Important decisions, such as declarations of war, were ratified by an assembly of citizen-soldiers. The last king was expelled in 509 BCE, and his function was assumed by a pair of consuls elected annually by the citizen assembly from the body of senators. Later political thinkers interpreted these institutions as a mixed constitution with elements of monarchy (consuls), aristocracy (senate), and democracy (assembly), but in reality the senatorial aristocracy seems to have been most influential in making decisions.

Rome began its expansion in Latium as early as the regal period, but it was not until 338 BCE that Roman hegemony there was secured. From that base Rome came to dominate Italy by 270 BCE and the western Mediterranean following the two great wars against Carthage (264–241 BCE and 218–201 BCE); then the Romans moved quickly to establish hegemony over the whole Mediterranean basin with the defeat of Philip V of Macedonia (197 BCE) and Antiochus III of the Seleucid empire in Syria (189 BCE). Rome dominated from the early second century BCE but annexed these areas as provinces only slowly over the next century and a half. Syria and parts of Asia Minor came under direct Roman rule as a result of Pompey's eastern campaigns in the 60s BCE.

Rome's unparalleled victories yielded vast concentrations of wealth and power in the hands of some citizens. The world empire left the city-state constitution and idea of citizenship outdated. Roman citizenship, a status inherited from citizen parents, had formerly entailed privileges of participation in politics in the city and responsibility for military service. As Roman power spread, though, citizenship was diffused well beyond the city by the establishment of citizen colonies in Italy and abroad and by selective grant to the conquered (first to their Latin neighbors, then to all free Italians). Participation in voting assemblies in the city of Rome was impracticable for most of these new citizens, yet citizenship continued to bestow privileged status, legal rights to marry and make contracts under Roman law, and *provocatio* (protection of a citizen from arbitrary whipping or execution by magistrates through appeal to higher authorities).

The traditional Republican constitution was ultimately inadequate to the tasks of governing a vast empire abroad and of containing political competition at home. In striving with each other to attain the highest honors, senators resorted to escalating violence, culminating in two decades of civil war initiated by Julius Caesar in 49 BCE and finished by his adopted son, Augustus, who established himself as the first emperor.

**Roman Imperial Social Structure.** Augustus sought to legitimize his new regime by claiming to restore the *Respublica* and incorporating Republican institutions and aristocratic families. He styled himself *princeps* or first citizen, a traditional title for the leader of the Senate that avoided drawing attention to his autocracy. As part of his program of restoration, Augustus reaffirmed the traditional social order and strengthened its hierarchical divisions. It was a hierarchy based on wealth, respectable birth, and citizenship. High rank was marked by special clothing, the best seats at public spectacles, and various legal privileges.

At the top of the hierarchy were six hundred senators, propertied citizens of great wealth (at least one million sesterces or about one thousand times the annual salary of a legionary) who were chosen for the traditional senatorial offices at Rome. Equestrians or knights held second rank; they were citizens of free birth who possessed a census of at least four hundred thousand sesterces. Through the centuries of the empire they were recruited to serve in the imperial administration in increasing numbers. In addition to this imperial elite, each of the thousands of cities of the empire had its own local aristocracy from which was chosen a governing council consisting of a hundred or so of the town's wealthiest men (many of whom did not have Roman citizenship). These leisured elites became collectively known by the early second century CE as the *honestiores* or "more honorable men," in contrast to the humbler masses or *humiliores,* who constituted more than 90 percent of the population.

Several important distinctions of status divided ordinary working people. There were the citizens, concentrated mainly in Italy in Augustus's day but increasingly scattered throughout the provinces by the settlement of colonies and by imperial grant to favored individuals and communities. Noncitizen free provincials formed a huge amorphous group. The empire encompassed enormous cultural variation between city and countryside, and between regions. If Latin was spoken by the urban elites of the western empire and Greek was the primary tongue in the eastern cities, ordinary provincials continued to speak their native tongues, whether it be *Aramaic in Palestine or the Punic language around Carthage. They also continued to worship their own gods, which in some cases were assimilated to the Roman gods. Roman emperors and officials could be sensitive to the cultural diversity: the early governors of Judea tried to avoid affronts to Jewish monotheism, but later ones were less careful. When Florus attempted to take a large sum from the *Temple treasury in Jerusalem in 66 CE, he provoked a fierce rebellion that required seven years, the destruction of *Jerusalem, and widespread slaughter to suppress.

Beneath the free population in the social hierarchy were *slaves. Slavery as an institution was taken for granted; there were no serious abolitionist movements in antiquity. Slaves formed a substantial proportion of the population in Italy (perhaps one-third), where they were heavily involved in all aspects of economic production. In most of the provinces slaves were common only as domestic servants. By law, slaves were property who could be bought or sold, beaten or tortured at the owner's whim. As the attitudes of owners varied, so also did the living conditions of slaves.

**Imperial Political and Administrative Structures.** The emperor ruled the peoples of the empire from Rome with the help of men chosen from the elites; with the demise of Republican elections, the popular voice in politics was lost. The capital city had a population of about one million and encompassed extremes of wealth and poverty, lavish public monuments and filthy, cramped apartments. Much of the population, perhaps even a majority, was made up of slaves and freedmen from the eastern Mediterranean, Germany, and elsewhere. Rome was able to grow to be the largest city of pre-industrial Europe because of the privileges of conquest: provincial agriculture was taxed, and part of the grain was sent to Rome to feed the masses. To keep the urban plebs quiet, the emperor also put on various spectacles, including the gladiatorial fights and wild beast hunts, in which some Christians met their end. Despite the food distributions and public entertainment, violence occasionally broke out in the city, prompting emperors to expel foreigners or to find scapegoats. So Claudius expelled the Jews from Rome, and Nero began the official persecution of Christians when he needed scapegoats to blame for the great fire of 64 CE.

Italy was the land of citizens. As such, it was privileged with exemption from the land tax until the late third century CE. No governors were set over Italy; administration was largely left to the municipalities, with important matters referred to imperial officials in Rome.

Beyond Italy lay the Roman *imperium,* including client kings and directly ruled provinces. The Romans were slow to annex areas around the Mediterranean as provinces because they lacked a developed administrative apparatus. It was convenient to leave the governing of some peripheral areas to local kings in return for support of Rome in matters of foreign policy through occasional tribute and troops for Roman wars. Client kings paid heed to the authority of the emperor and the senior governors of nearby provinces. Accounts of the reign of *Herod the Great, the best-known client king, illustrate how dependent he was on the continuing goodwill of the emperor and his officials, which he curried by careful attention to their wishes as well as by gifts and bribes. Gradually, as in Palestine, the client kingdoms were added to the list of directly ruled provinces.

The several dozen provinces were administered by governors sent out from Rome. Their two principal concerns were the maintenance of law and order and the collection of taxes. Roman administration can be characterized as general oversight by a handful of imperial officials who relied on local leaders. The major provinces were governed by senators in different capacities. Provinces with legions were administered by imperial legates appointed by the emperor from among those senators he considered most reliable. *Syria, with the largest legionary army of the eastern empire, was a province of this type. Major provinces without armies, such as Achaea, where supervised by senatorial proconsuls chosen in the Senate. Judea from 6 CE was one of those lesser provinces administered by equestrians (initially army officers called prefects, then imperial agents with the title of procurator). All governors held broad authority, limited by their responsibility to the emperor, who issued some instructions for administration (*mandata*); equestrian procurators also occasionally received guidance from senatorial governors of neighboring provinces.

Governors were accompanied to their provinces by minimal staffs, including friends and relatives who acted as advisory councils. The meager staffs were supplemented by military officers and soldiers acting as major figures of authority in provincial administration. In their judicial capacity, governors heard the cases of Roman citizens who were subject to Roman law, and also adjudicated some other serious cases. For the most part, noncitizens were subject to local law and custom, and were left to local magistrates. Roman governors, reluctant to become entangled in squabbles among the natives, were often content to hold local leaders responsible for the preservation of order in their noncitizen communities. This tacit arrangement explains both the worry of *Caiaphas that disorder would provoke violent suppression from Rome and the aloofness of the Roman proconsul Gallio when Paul was brought before him. It also accounts for the slow and sporadic pattern of persecution of the Christians before 250 CE. Roman governors were instructed to punish with death anyone brought before them who persistently admitted to being a Christian, but they were not actively to seek out Christians. As a result, in the province of Africa the first execution on the charge of Christianity did not come until about 180 CE.

Most provincials encountered Roman government over the matter of taxes—taxes on the land, on the people who worked the land, on goods moving across provincial borders, on inheritances, on sales in the market, to name but a few. The Romans did not impose a uniform tax system on conquest, but usually took over local arrangements and contracted out the collection to private agents, the *publicani,* infamous for their rapacious methods of enrichment (*see* Publicans). Julius Caesar began to phase out these middlemen at the highest levels, but they continued into the Principate to collect indirect taxes, such as custom duties. In order to assess the main land and head taxes, imperial officials occasionally carried out censuses in which provincials were required to register themselves and their property. The imperial legate Quirinius oversaw such a census in Judea in 6 CE, which, on grounds of date and Roman administrative procedures, seems to be impossible to reconcile with the account in Luke 2.1–5.

In Augustus's day, the resources of the Roman empire were sufficient to fulfill the relatively light demands of the state, but they were limited by the agricultural base and the stagnant technology of the economy. Under the Christian emperors of the later empire, increasing demands for money and recruits to support the growing army and bureaucracy were met by more determined resistance. As the "barbarian" tribes pressed ever-harder against the frontiers, the limits left emperors unable to ward off the threats. In 410 CE, the Eternal City was sacked by Alaric and his Visigoths; the last Roman emperor of the west, Romulus Augustulus, was deposed by the German leader Odoacer in 476 CE.

*See also* Roman Army.

*Richard P. Saller*

**ROME.** *See* Roman Empire.

**RUTH.** Ruth is the heroine of the book of Ruth. The book is a gripping short story, incorporating folkloric features that make for ease of appreciation as common human experience, as well as distinctive cultural features commending Israel's theology and ethics.

The book begins with a background scenario of a Bethlehemite family, two parents and their two sons, sojourning in *Moab because of famine back home. The sons marry Moabites. Father and two sons die, leaving three *widows, Naomi, Orpah, and Ruth. Naomi, choosing to return home, urges her daughters-in-law to remain in Moab. Orpah does so, but Ruth cleaves to Naomi. Naomi, lamenting bitterly, arrives in *Bethlehem with Ruth accompanying her; she sees little prospect of fullness of life. Scene two has Ruth initiating efforts to support herself and Naomi by gleaning at the harvest, where she chances upon the field of Boaz, a worthy Bethlehemite. Boaz notices her, at first makes minimal provision, then moves to progressively greater care for this woman who has displayed such loyalty to her family. In scene three, Naomi, encouraged by the success of Ruth's first steps, directs her how to move things from a temporary to a long-term resolution: marriage and offspring for Ruth, redeemer care for Naomi. Ruth forces the matter with Boaz in a provocative scene at the threshing-floor, only to learn that the redeemer responsibility falls first upon a person other than Boaz. In the final scene, while Ruth and Naomi wait, Boaz maneuvers this other person to yield his role at a public forum in the town gate. The way is clear for Boaz to marry Ruth, provide an heir to Ruth's first husband, and provide a redeemer for Naomi. The redeemer is Obed, David's grandfather—this information is the striking climax of a chorus by the Bethlehem townspeople celebrating first Boaz, then Ruth and Naomi. The story closes with a genealogy connecting *David through Obed and Boaz to Perez, Judah's offspring.

The climax, which comes with the note about David in 4.17, suggests that blessing of Israel's royal line is an issue here. The blessing speeches in 4.13–17 are comparable to other Near Eastern royal blessings. If the David theme is intrinsic to the book, then it provides the historical datum that David had a Moabite ancestor. The book is quite probably part of a cycle of stories about David's ancestry, which would include Genesis 38 and other episodes now lost.

The universal appeal and the plausible presentation of typical Israelite life mask precise time and place, and release the story of Ruth for the pleasure and edification of all. A date for the book anywhere in the time of the Judean monarchy is plausible. The audience was probably village people and the storyteller a professional bard, quite possibly a wise woman. Alternatively, the story may be a self-conscious imitation of a folktale, written at the royal court.

*Edward F. Campbell*

# S

**SABEANS.** *See* Sheba, Queen of.

**SADDUCEES.** The Sadducees were one of the Jewish parties referred to by Josephus. Disputes between them and the *Pharisees are mentioned in later Jewish writings. They are depicted in the New Testament as opponents of *Jesus who, together with the Pharisees, tested him with questions. In Acts they feature as opponents of the early Christians.

The name (probably Hebr. *ṣaddūqîm*) is derived from *Zadok. The most likely association is with the high priest under David; although it is just possible, as one tradition suggests, that they were connected with a later Zadok, pupil of one of the Sages, Antigonus of Socho (early second century BCE), who, as they believed, rejected belief in the resurrection. There were of course Zadokites, descendants of the original high priest, who controlled the *Temple in Jerusalem for many centuries before the second century BCE, which is when Josephus introduces them. Possibly the emergence of Sadducees as a party is the result of a crisis occasioned by the usurpation of the high priesthood by Jonathan in 152 BCE; possibly this is also the point at which the Essenes broke away from the high-priestly group and moved out into the desert. In any case the Sadducees and the Pharisees both strove for influence at court and for control over the Temple, which would of course give them the power required to exercise an important role in national affairs. Fortunes changed not infrequently; doubtless the power of the Temple aristocracy was substantially limited under Roman rule, but the Sadducees were prepared to accept a measure of compromise with the Roman authorities and probably had influence with them. Once they lost their cultic function as a result of the destruction of the Temple (70 CE) they ceased to exist as a group. This may reflect the extent to which they had lost popular support.

We learn of their beliefs only from others' writings. Whereas the Pharisees accepted the authority of the Tradition of the *elders as a valuable tool for extending and interpreting the Law, the Sadducees did not. Nor did they, as the New Testament also attests, believe in the resurrection of the dead. Josephus also reports that they did not believe in fate but thought that men and women were in control of their actions. They are also said to have rejected belief in *angels and *demons.

The sense of all this is elusive. In their development of an oral tradition of legal interpretation, the Pharisees and Sages were in one way doing no more than what had been done throughout Jewish history, that is, adapting their legal traditions to changing circumstance. Why should the Sadducees oppose this? Possibly because the written Law reinforced their control over the Temple; possibly too because the Pharisees were attempting to undermine that position by transferring some of the priestly rituals and practices away from Jerusalem to the towns and villages outside. Certainly the Sadducees were concerned principally to uphold the Temple and its sacrifices: for them it was the proper observance of Temple ritual that maintained the covenant relationship between Israel and God.

Rejection of belief in the resurrection again indicates a traditionalist stance. Jews had long believed that so long as Israel obeyed the Law then God would rule over them and reward the righteous and punish the wicked in this life. Belief in the resurrection, on the other hand, was linked to beliefs that the present age was in the grip of dark powers, so that in this life the righteous would suffer, although God would ultimately vindicate them. Those who had died would be raised so that they too could receive their due rewards. To reject belief in the resurrection and, indeed, possibly also in demonic powers who controlled this world in the present age, was then also to reject the belief that this present age was radically corrupted; in fact, from the Sadducees' point of view, those who argued the contrary view may have appeared to deny the continued existence of the covenant between God and Israel. This may also explain their denial of fate. They believed that Jews were free to influence their destiny; if they obeyed the Law and repented and made due restitution when they sinned, then all would be well. The darker views of the world associated with belief in the resurrection also entailed beliefs in the pervasiveness of the power of sin (see Rom. 5.12–21, which may owe more than a little to Paul's Pharisaic background, although such beliefs should not be thought of as specifically Pharisaic), such that men and women were no longer in control of their fate. It is such views that the Sadducees rejected.

This may suggest a further reason why the Sadducees disappeared after 70 CE. Not only was their position as the Temple aristocracy fundamentally destroyed; their belief that the maintenance of the Temple cult would suffice to stave off real disaster for Israel had also been proven false. *John Riches*

**SAINT(S).** "Saint" most frequently translates some derivative of Hebrew *qādôš* and Greek *hagios.* Both words apply primarily to the gods as those beings who rightly deserved awe, or who were worthy of worship; their extended meaning includes those persons and things that had a unique relation to these gods. Because of this relationship, such persons and things were set apart from the unhallowed world about them so that they might be ceremonially clean, sufficiently pure to be of special service in the worship of the gods.

In the Hebrew Bible, the Lord God is holy, meaning that he is set apart from, different from, and transcendent over everything in the created order, and is therefore uniquely worthy of awe and worship. But because God stands in special relation to parts of his creation, certain things can be holy, such as *Jerusalem, the *Temple, the Sabbath, garments, water, and oil; and people can be holy, even an entire nation. Israel is called holy, elect, a people separated from all other peoples, set apart to the Lord God, that is, God's own people.

In the Bible, therefore, the word saints refers to "holy people"—holy, however, not primarily in the moral sense, but in the sense of being specially marked out as God's people. Thus, just as the people of Israel are "saints," "holy ones," a nation set apart by God for the worship and service of God, so in the New Testament those who comprise the church are also called holy, "saints," because they too are set apart to God, God's own people. The church is seen as the new Israel, the new community separated from the world around it and dedicated to God, the people of the end times to whom God will make good his promises. The term is also applied to dead members of the community, though this is not its primary biblical usage.

Moral or ethical ideas were never wholly absent from the word "saints," both in the Hebrew Bible and in the New Testament. Because God is holy, that is, because God is perfect in goodness and justice and love and purity, it is expected that his special people will pattern their lives accordingly. Hence, ethics belongs together with religion. Relationship with the God of the Bible demands a moral response in accord with the character of God.

*Gerald F. Hawthorne*

**SALOME.** The name of two women appearing in the New Testament:

**1.** The daughter of Herodias and Herod (Philip), and thus the granddaughter of *Herod the Great, famous as the performer of the dance for which, at her mother's instigation, she was rewarded with the head of *John the Baptist on a platter. She is not named in the Gospels, but Josephus identifies her and also reports her marriage to Herod's son, her uncle Philip. Salome's dance is a favorite theme in dance, art, and literature, as in Gustave Flaubert's story *Hérodias* and Richard Strauss's opera and Oscar Wilde's play, both called *Salome.*

**2.** A disciple of *Jesus, present at the crucifixion and at the tomb on the following Sunday. She is identified by Matthew as the mother of *James and *John and would therefore have been the wife of Zebedee as well as Jesus's aunt.

*Michael D. Coogan*

**SAMARIA.** Omri (885–873 BCE), the sixth king of the northern kingdom of *Israel, founded his new capital Samaria (Hebr. *šōmrôn*) on land purchased for the high price of two silver talents (7,200 shekels) from the family of Shemer. Archaeologists have found traces of a rural estate from the eleventh to the early ninth centuries on the hill of Samaria, on which Omri's new city was built; it was easily defended and located near important trade routes. Like the names Israel and Ephraim, Samaria may have become an alternate name for the northern kingdom as a whole.

Although the principal temple cities of the kingdom were Bethel and *Dan, an inscriptional reference (ca. 800 BCE) from Kuntillet ᶜAjrud (northern Sinai) to "Yahweh of Samaria and his Asherah" suggests that a shrine to Yahweh also stood in Samaria. Omri's son *Ahab built a temple to *Baal there, perhaps for his Phoenician queen *Jezebel. When *Jehu overthrew the Omride dynasty, he demolished Baal's temple and turned it into a latrine, but a shrine to the goddess *Asherah continued to exist.

Samaria flourished in the time of Omri and Ahab and again during the reign of Jeroboam II in the mid-eighth century. During the latter period Samaria symbolized the entire northern kingdom for the prophets *Amos and *Hosea, who condemned Israel's religious and social ills. The Samaria Ostraca, a cache of sixty-three inscribed potsherds recording what may be tax receipts, illustrates the concentration of wealth that the prophets criticized.

Kings of Samaria alternately allied themselves with or fought against *Damascus and *Judah. They enjoyed trade and diplomatic relations with the *Phoenicians, whose artistic influence is apparent in references to Ahab's ivory house and in the hundreds of eighth-century ivory furniture inlays excavated at Samaria. Splendid walls of local limestone cut in the precise Phoenician style surrounded Samaria's royal precinct. In later times pottery, bronzes, seal impressions, and locally minted coinage from the Persian period (sixth–fourth centuries) indicate that Samaria continued to be more open than Judea to foreign influences.

*Assyria conquered Samaria in 722 BCE, transforming it into the capital of the province of Samerina. The Assyrians deported Samaria's leading citizens and resettled conquered peoples from Syria and Mesopotamia there. Nevertheless, a large population of Israelites probably remained. The Judean kings *Hezekkiah and *Josiah made political overtures to these surviving, and prophets describe a future reunited Israel.

After the Babylonian exile, *Samaritans led by the governor Sanballat opposed *Nehemiah's attempts to rebuild Jerusalem. These Samaritans were probably Jews living both in Judea and in Samaria who had continued to worship and to administer the territory of ancient Israel in the exiles' absence; their quarrel with Nehemiah was political, not religious. It is notable that Samaritan women are not mentioned among those whom Jews have wrongfully married, although for priests such intermarriage was unacceptable.

From the many Yahwistic names on Wadi Daliyeh papyri (375–335 BCE), it seems that ruling-class Samaritans of the Persian period revered Yahweh. Late in the fifth century, Jews living in Egypt wrote for help in rebuilding their temple at Elephantine to leaders both in Jerusalem and in Samaria. Sometime after the arrival of *Alexander the Great (332 BCE), the Samaritans constructed on Mount Gerizim near *Shechem a temple of Yahweh to rival Jerusalem's, but evidence from the Dead Sea Scrolls suggests that the definitive religious break (the "Samaritan schism") between Samaria and Jerusalem, so apparent in the New Testament, did not occur before the Hasmonean period (second century BCE).

Alexander the Great's army destroyed Samaria in 331 after a rebellion. It was rebuilt to become a wealthy Hellenistic city surrounded by a massive wall with a series of monumental round watchtowers (one, ca. 63 ft [19 m] in diameter, still stands to a height of over 27 ft [8 m]). The Hasmonean John Hyrcanus destroyed the city in 108 BCE, but it began to revive after Rome took over Palestine (63 BCE). *Herod the Great embellished the city on a grand scale, renaming it Sebaste after the Greek title of the emperor Augustus. This magnificent city, with its colonnaded streets, stadium, theater, and temples, was demolished during the First Jewish Revolt (66–70 CE), but it soon revived and flourished until finally declining during the Byzantine period.

*Samaritans appear in key episodes in the Gospels and in Acts. Some reject Jesus, but he portrays a Samaritan as a good neighbor. Jesus's friendly meeting with the Samaritan woman demonstrates his openness to women; by her testimony she becomes one of the earliest missionaries. Philip's ministry to Samaria is the first by an apostle outside strictly Jewish territory; Samaria is a symbolically transitional place between

Judaism and the gentile world into which the Christian movement will travel. *Mary Joan Winn Leith*

**SAMARITANS.** The Samaritans are unique among the many religious groups described in the Bible apart from traditional Judaism and Christianity: the others have long passed into oblivion, but the Samaritans still survive in our own day, as a community preserving its ancient rites on its holy site, Mount Gerizim, near the ancient site of *Shechem and the modern city of Nablus.

The Samaritans are best understood as a conservative group within the total spectrum of Judaism. This rather clumsy definition is necessary because of the ambiguity of the word "Judaism." The word is sometimes used in a biblical context to denote the community owing allegiance to the Jerusalem authorities, with the Jerusalem *Temple its chief holy place; sometimes it refers to a broader complex of beliefs and practices, united mainly by reverence for the holy traditions enshrined in scripture. The Samaritans should be included in the Judaism of the second type but not of the first.

We can obtain some knowledge of the Samaritans from the Bible, but because these references are not free of polemic, it is best to begin by noting that our sources of knowledge include important material handed down by the Samaritans themselves. Chief among this is the Samaritan Pentateuch. The scroll preserved by the present-day Samaritan community is claimed by them to date back to Abishua, the great-grandson of *Aaron mentioned in 1 Chronicles 6.4; it is actually a medieval scroll, although it certainly preserves older traditions sometimes valued by textual critics (e.g., the reading "Gerizim" for "Ebal" is often preferred). The fact that the scroll contains only the Pentateuch is doubly significant: it reminds us that this is the extent of the writings regarded by the Samaritans as scripture; and it illustrates the conservative nature of the group, deeply distrustful of anything that smacked of innovation and modernizing.

Other features of their religious practice illustrate this point also. They have observed the Sabbath with great strictness, spurning those devices that Jews developed to facilitate ordinary life on the Sabbath. Ritual requirements, in particular those relating to food laws, have been understood and imposed with a greater degree of literalism than has been usual in Judaism as a whole. They claim that their holy mountain, Mount Gerizim, which is mentioned in the Pentateuch, has a greater claim to veneration than does Mount *Zion, for Jerusalem entered the people's history only relatively late, at the time of *David.

In these characteristic features it is possible to see the Samaritans as having a recognizable position within the spectrum of Judaism at the beginning of the common era. New Testament references, especially in *Luke and Acts, make it clear that by that time the Samaritans were an established group.

Unambiguous earlier references are few, the clearest being found in the Apocrypha. In Sirach 50.26, "the foolish people that dwell in Shechem" are condemned as if they were an *alien group; 2 Maccabees 6.2 makes a slighting reference to their willingness to compromise their ancestral traditions. Each of these statements is polemical, a hostile comment from a rival religious position. Much the same can be said of Josephus, who has frequent and almost invariably hostile references to the Samaritans, particularly in his *Antiquities.*

Although the historicity of his description of the building of the Samaritan temple on Mount Gerizim in the time of *Alexander the Great has been much doubted, its destruction by the Jewish king John Hyrcanus late in the second century BCE is beyond serious dispute.

Samaritan origins have often been described in terms of a schism, as if there were some specific event that separated them from the Jews. The Samaritans' own Chronicles date that event as early as the time of Eli, before the establishment of the monarchy. That is unlikely to be historical; equally improbable is the Jewish version, preserved in 2 Kings 17, which pictures the Samaritans as descended from aliens of non-Yahwistic origin, from which the true Israel was bound to distance itself. (This story gave rise to the later, contemptuous name for the Samaritans, "Kuthim" [from "Cuthah" in v. 24] and is also the only place in most English translations of the Hebrew Bible where the word "Samaritans" is found [v. 29].) This is religious polemic; nothing in Samaritan practice suggests any link with *Assyrian or other foreign origin. Nor should the Samaritans be identified, as is sometimes done, with those left in the land at the time of the Babylonian exile, or with the opponents of *Ezra and *Nehemiah. Their distinctive identity emerged later, and it is unlikely that any single event precipitated a schism.

How far they preserved characteristically northern traditions is difficult to decide. As the Hebrew Bible is a Jerusalem collection, hostile to the north, it is not easy to identify any distinctive northern traditions that the later Samaritans might have inherited. In any case, their characteristic features arise from the Judaism of the postexilic period, since all that we know of Samaritanism relates to religious rather than political or national characteristics: which books were holy, where might sacrifice properly be offered, which families might legitimately exercise the priesthood.

Some scholars have claimed to detect similarities between the Samaritans and the Dead Sea Scrolls community, but these are also widely questioned. More striking is the obvious sympathy toward the Samaritans shown by the author of Luke-Acts, who twice in the Gospel goes out of his way to praise a Samaritan. It has also been suggested, though this is less certain, that *Stephen, the central figure of Acts 6–7, was of Samaritan origin; certainly Simon Magus came to be associated with a heterodox form of Samaritanism. It is therefore clear that in the Roman period the Samaritans were an identifiable group, comparable with, but distinct from, the larger Jewish community; John 4.9, though the accuracy of the rendering has been questioned, expresses the situation clearly. There was a Samaritan diaspora, and the community maintained its existence, with a rebuilt temple, through the changing political circumstances that affected Palestine. The fourth century CE was a time of revival, with many of their theological and literary traditions reaching definitive form at that time. In the centuries since, their numbers have declined and they have suffered persecution, but they retain something of their distinctive identity and their ancestral home, despite all the political and religious turmoil that has affected Palestine.

*See also* Samaria.

*Richard Coggins*

**SAMSON.** Samson (whose name is derived from the word for "sun") was the twelfth and last judge of Israel before civil war threatened to tear the tribes apart. He harassed the *Philistines in the border country between his native *Dan, Judah, and Philistia. Besides killing thousands of Philistines, Samson ripped a lion apart with his bare hands and told a riddle about it, loved two women who betrayed him for very different reasons, burned Philistine crops, visited a Philistine *prostitute and carried off the city gates of Gaza on the same night, was blinded and enslaved by the Philistines, and caused his own death by toppling the pillars of the Philistines' temple upon himself and his foes.

With his powerful libido, Samson resembles other judges who fell outside the behavioral norms of Israelite society (left-handed Ehud, the woman *Deborah, young *Gideon, the bastard Jephthah). Unlike other judges, however, Samson was neither an adjudicator nor a "deliverer" of his people. Personal vengeance was the motive for his single-handed forays against the Philistines. Samson's obliviousness to the requirements of his *nazirite status suggests that it is not original to the Samson legend, although it is important in the literary framework of the biblical narrative.

The Samson story reflects an early stage of actual Philistine-Israelite confrontations, but it is rooted in Danite folktales and perhaps Philistine story traditions. It resembles tales of intertribal relations told in other areas where neighboring groups borrow story lines from each other. The Philistines were related to Homer's Mycenaean Greeks, and the Samson saga has motifs in common with Greek and other Indo-European literatures. Samson also resembles Gilgamesh, as well as tricksters like *Jacob.

Josephus is typical of early Jewish and Christian interpreters in his verdict that Samson's heroic death transcended the sins of his life. Samson's questionable morality could even be glossed over, or, as later for Milton in *Samson Agonistes,* superseded by his heroic death.

Judges 13–16 is one of the most artfully composed tales in the Bible. It is framed by a prediction of Samson's birth to his barren mother and his spectacular death, episodes that mirror each other (e.g., in the obtuseness of both Manoah and the Philistines, and the rituals for Yahweh and Dagon). There is an exuberance of wordplay, including etiologies, riddling couplets, and ring compositions. One finds foreshadowing, crisp characterizations (Samson, his mother and father), and clever inversions from episode to episode (compare the restraining of Samson by the men of Judah and by Delilah). Most of all, the narrative presents a subtle study of deception and betrayal, by humans and by God, for good and for ill.

*See also* Judges.

*Mary Joan Winn Leith*

**SAMUEL.** The son of Elkanah and Hannah, Samuel was Israel's leader in the transition from the premonarchic to the monarchic period. The books of Samuel preserve various traditions about him, and he is described in several roles. He was a *judge, in both the judicial and military senses of that office in the Bible; as the last of the judges, he was unable to defeat the *Philistines, and their threat to Israel's existence was the primary historical reason for the establishment of the monarchy. He was apparently a priest and probably a *nazirite. Most frequently, however, he is called a *prophet.

According to the Deuteronomic historians, for whom the prophets are key actors in their narrative, Samuel illustrates some of the key roles of later prophets. He was both king maker (for

*Saul and *David) and king breaker (Saul), like *Nathan, *Elijah, and *Elisha; he rebuked both kings and people for their violations of covenant (see especially 1 Sam 15.22, a saying that would fit well into the collections of the eighth-century prophets).

Because of this idealized portrait, drawn from Israel's later institutions and traditions and shaped by the Deuteronomic historians, it is difficult to say much about Samuel historically, especially on the key issue of the monarchy: was he for or against it? Our sources give both perspectives. But of his importance in the crucial period of the mid-eleventh century BCE there can be no doubt, and he is linked with *Moses as one of Israel's preeminent leaders.

The two books of Samuel are in reality one: in the Hebrew text, they run continuously, with the counting of words and sections characteristic of the Hebrew tradition coming only at the end. The division into two appears first in the Greek translation (the Septuagint) and then in the Latin Vulgate: from there it came to be used in other translations, and by the sixteenth century also in printed Hebrew Bibles. The traditional title "Samuel" reflects the fact that he dominates much of the material, particularly in the establishing of the monarchy; hence he came to be seen as the author. The Greek and Latin texts use titles that cover also the following books of Kings—thus either "four books of kingdoms" or "four books of kings." Since these four books together cover the whole period of the monarchy, these latter titles are really more appropriate.

*Peter R. Ackroyd, Michael D. Coogan*

**SANHEDRIN.** The Gospels and Acts utilize this Greek term for council, which literally means "sitting together," both for the locus of opposition to Jesus and his movement, often in combination with *elders and chief priests, and for the venue where both Jesus and his followers make their defense.

This term for a kind of judicial and administrative body goes back in Roman Palestine at least to Pompey the Great. When Pompey was pulled into a domestic dispute between two quarreling Hasmonean brothers in 66 BCE, the Romans decided to run Palestine directly. Pompey reorganized Palestine as part of his larger project of subduing and organizing the entire Greek East for the Roman Senate, dividing it into five councils (*synedria*).

The fact that this neutral administrative term becomes firmly imbedded in the Gospel tradition as a place of local officials hostile to the Jesus movement and with the power to do something about it highlights the utilization of local elites by Rome in their ever-expanding colonial rule. The Sanhedrin was a court made up of local elite, probably with some sort of Roman oversight, that handled census, tax, and other administrative and military responsibilities. In the divided socioeconomic context of Roman imperial rule, as time went on the Sanhedrin had a negative connotation for many who had to pay an increasing amount in taxes, stood a good chance of losing their land, and had to contend regularly with the reality of foreign occupation.

In the rabbinic period (ca. 200 CE) Sanhedrin became a technical term for the rabbinic court. This court and its leaders adjudicated many of the rulings that made their way into the Mishnah, the first codification of rabbinic law and debate. There is an entire tractate in the Mishnah devoted to Sanhedrin.

*J. Andrew Overman*

**SARAH.** The wife of *Abraham and mother of *Isaac. Before Genesis 17.15 she is called Sarai; the two forms of the name are linguistic variants, both meaning "princess." The book of Genesis describes her as a beautiful woman, a theme elaborated by later tradition, especially the *Genesis Apocryphon* from Qumran. According to the biblical narrators, Abraham was so conscious of her beauty that before they entered Egypt at the time of a severe famine in their own land, he begged her not to reveal to the Egyptians that she was his wife but rather his sister, lest he be killed. Indeed, as it turned out, the Egyptians thought her so beautiful that she was taken into Pharaoh's house to be his wife, and for her sake Abraham prospered. In time, however, after great plagues had afflicted Pharaoh and his household, the true identity of Sarah was revealed to Pharaoh, who ordered Abraham to be gone with his wife and all his possessions. A variant of this story is found in Genesis 20.1–14.

During their years of wandering, Sarah was childless, and so God's promise that she would be the ancestor of nations was unfulfilled. Accordingly she persuaded Abraham to take her Egyptian *slave, *Hagar, as his wife. He did so, and she bore him *Ishmael. At the age of ninety, however, Sarah bore *Isaac, thus fulfilling the divine promise. Sarah lived to be 127 years old, died in the land of Canaan, and was buried at Machpelah.

In Isaiah 51.2 Sarah is referred to as the great mother of the nation; in the New Testament she is held up as an example of a wife's proper respect for her husband. Paul uses the account of the birth of a son to Sarah by divine promise to develop an allegory of the new covenant in Christ and the heavenly Jerusalem (Gal. 4.22–31).

*See also* Ancestors, The.

*Isobel Mackay Metzger*

**SATAN.** The name of the archenemy of God and the personification of evil, particularly in Christian tradition. The name may derive from a Semitic root *śṭn,* but the primitive meaning is still debated, the most popular suggestions being "to be remote" and "to obstruct." Some alternative roots include *śwṭ* (cf. Hebr. "to rove") and *šṭn* (cf. Arabic "to burn," especially of food).

In the Hebrew Bible *śāṭān* could refer to any human being who played the role of an accuser or enemy. In Numbers 22.32 *śāṭān* refers to a divine messenger who was sent to obstruct *Balaam's rash journey.

Job 1–2, Zechariah 3, and 1 Chronicles 21.1 have been central in past efforts to chart an evolution of the concept of *śāṭān* that culminates in a single archenemy of God. However, such evolutionary views have not gained general acceptance because *śāṭān* in these passages does not necessarily refer to a single archenemy of God and because the relative dating of the texts remains problematic. In Job 1–2, the *śāṭān* seems to be a legitimate member of God's council. In Zechariah 3.1–7 *śāṭān* may refer to a member of God's council who objected to the appointment of Joshua as chief priest. The mention of *śāṭān* without the definite article in 1 Chronicles 21.1 has led some scholars to interpret it as a proper name, but one could also interpret it as "an adversary" or "an accuser" acting on God's behalf.

Most scholars agree that in the writings of the third/second centuries BCE are the first examples of a character who is the archenemy of Yahweh and humankind. Nonetheless, the flexibility of the tradition is still apparent in the variety of figures who, although not necessarily identical with each other, are each apparently regarded as the principal archenemy of God and humankind in Second Temple literature. Such figures include Mastemah, Semyaz, and *Belial at Qumran. Still undetermined is the extent to which the concept of the Hebrew *śāṭān* was influenced by *Persian dualism, which posited the existence of two primal and independent personifications of good and evil.

Although it shares with contemporaneous Jewish literature many of its ideas about demonology, the New Testament is probably more responsible for standardizing "Satan" (Greek *satanas*) as the name for the archenemy of God in Western culture. However, the devil (the usual translation of "Satan" in the Septuagint), Beelzebul ("the prince of demons"; *see* Baal-zebub), "the tempter," Beliar, "the evil one," and Apollyon are other names for Satan in the New Testament. Lucifer, a name for Satan popularized in the Middle Ages, derives ultimately from the merging of the New Testament tradition of the fall of Satan from heaven with an originally separate biblical tradition concerning the Morning Star (cf. Isa. 14.12).

According to the New Testament, Satan and his *demons may enter human beings in order to incite evil deeds and to cause illness. Satan can imitate "an angel of light" (2 Cor. 11.14), has command of the air, and accuses the faithful day and night before God. Jude 9 mentions the struggle between Satan and the archangel *Michael for the body of *Moses. Revelation 20.2, among other texts, equates "the Devil and Satan" with "the dragon," thus reflecting the merging of ancient myths concerning gigantic primordial beasts that wreak havoc on God's creation with the traditions concerning Satan. Satan's destiny is to be cast into a lake of fire.

In 563 CE the Council of Braga helped to define the official Christian view of Satan that, in contrast to dualism, denied his independent origin and his creation of the material universe. As J. B. Russell (*Lucifer: The Devil in the Middle Ages,* 1984) notes, writers and theologians of the medieval period popularized many of the characteristics of Satan that remain standard today and that have roots in, among other sources, Greek, Roman, and Teutonic mythology. Although the Enlightenment produced explanations of evil that do not refer to a mythological being, the imagery and concept of Satan continues to thrive within many religious traditions.

*Hector Ignacio Avalos*

**SAUL.** The first king of Israel, who ruled ca. 1020–1000 BCE. His story is part of the larger account, in the books of *Samuel, of how Israel became a nation-state. Saul is one of the few biblical characters of whom the term "tragic" has often been used. Glimpsing this dimension, D. H. Lawrence in his play *David* has Saul say of himself, "I am a man given over to trouble and tossed between two winds."

His story begins in 1 Samuel 8 with the *elders of Israel asking *Samuel, priestly prophet and judge, to appoint a king to judge (govern) them "like all the nations." For the people, the theocratic rule that Samuel delegates to his corrupt sons portends disaster. Only a generation earlier such corruption in the house of Eli had incurred Yahweh's anger and brought Israel defeat. For the deity, however, the request spells yet again the people's failure to see Yahweh's sovereignty and providential care. To an equally affronted Samuel, Yahweh observes that it is "not you they have rejected, but me they have rejected from being king over them." Yet, surprisingly, Yahweh decrees that the prophet obey the people and appoint for them a king. And so it transpires, much against Samuel's better judgment, which he expresses in mighty counterblasts against both king and people. Thus, the kingship is grounded in conflict between deity, prophet, and people.

Saul (whose name means "asked for"), the handsome son of a wealthy Benjaminite, is Yahweh's "designate" (Hebr. *nāgîd;* NRSV: "ruler"). He goes looking for his father's livestock and finds kingship instead.

Saul is made king before Yahweh at the cult center in Gilgal, and in Gilgal his kingship begins to unravel. Pressed to act decisively when a great host of *Philistines threatens his fearful and deserting army, he refuses to wait for Samuel beyond a time previously appointed by the prophet, and he offers a sacrifice. Samuel, as though waiting in the wings, immediately appears and, ignoring the king's explanation, condemns him outright. Saul, asserts the prophet, has not kept Yahweh's commandment, and his kingdom will not continue. Yahweh has sought out another "designate," a man sought out according to the divinity's own intention ("heart").

Commentators have long debated the reason for the condemnation. Other texts in Samuel and Kings make it unlikely that it is simply a matter of cultic law, involving the king's intrusion upon a priestly or prophetic office. Rather, the immediate cause appears to be Saul's breaking of Samuel's ambiguous instruction to wait—as interpreted by Samuel. But lying behind Samuel's readiness to condemn lurks perhaps a more pertinent reason rooted in the origins of Saul's kingship. Saul, asked for by the people, represents rejection for both prophet and deity. For the sake of theocracy this king must, in turn, be rejected.

In Gilgal comes final rejection (1 Sam. 15). Returning from a campaign against the *Amalekites with the captured king, Agag, and the best of the livestock, Saul once again meets a vehement Samuel. Why, demands the prophet, has Saul not done as instructed and "devoted [by destruction]" to Yahweh all living things? Saul responds that he has done what he was commanded to do, and that the animals have been brought to Gilgal for sacrifice. The issue turns on the difference between "devotion" and "sacrifice." Samuel, however, ignores Saul's explanation and invokes Yahweh's judgment upon him. Before such unrelenting opposition Saul acquiesces and asks pardon. But spurning him, Samuel declares that he is rejected as king—Yahweh has chosen "a neighbor" who is "better" than he. The reader soon learns that this man is *David, son of Jesse.

The remainder of the king's story is played out against this backdrop. Saul knows that the deity has rejected him, but he does not know his successor's identity. Yahweh, soon to be so eloquent for David, remains silent before Saul. That silence produces the irony of the young David being introduced into Saul's court in order to make him well. It also feeds the king's growing suspicion and jealousy of the successful and admired young captain. Yet, as if that corrosive silence were not enough, the deity provokes Saul directly: an "evil spirit from God" goads him to violence and disrupts his son Jonathan's attempt at reconciliation.

David's fortune is Saul's fate: whatever Saul attempts to turn against David rebounds against Saul. Using as bait his own daughter, Michal, Saul seeks to entice David into a suicide mission; instead, he gains two hundred Philistine foreskins and loses his daughter, who will herself later betray her father to save the husband she loves; her subsequent story is poignant. Likewise, Saul's savage revenge upon the priests of Nob for having helped the fleeing David only displaces into the fugitive's hand the oracular ephod.

Both Jonathan with goodwill and Saul with resentment come to see David's succession as inevitable. Saul, moreover, spared twice by his elusive rival, confesses publicly the superior justice of David's actions. King and competitor each forswear all hostile intent toward the other, but they keep their distance and go their own way. As David works for the Philistines and accumulates power, Saul faces them in battle. He seeks again a word from the silent Yahweh and, in desperation, has a medium conjure up the spirit of Samuel. The word he receives is a reiteration of rejection, but with one addition: on the next day he and his sons will die. So it happens that as David carries off booty from the Amalekites, Saul and his sons fall to the Philistines on Mount Gilboa among the slain men of Israel.

The king asked for by the people has failed: the way is now open for the king offered by Yahweh. Yet the people's king never forfeits their loyalty. The book ends with a moving epilogue. The inhabitants of Jabesh-gilead, delivered by Saul as his reign began, now risk their lives to close his reign with dignity. Retrieving his body from the walls of Philistine Beth-shan, they claim him as their own and honor him with burial in Jabesh. David, too, pays his own homage in a poem of beauty and irony, a poem perhaps more beautiful than honest.

*See also* Israel; Judah, The Kingdom of.

*David M. Gunn*

**SCRIBES.** Scribes were distinguished professional people throughout the ancient world. Although they were called scribes because they could read and write, they were not only copyists. In Israel, some were officials who had authority to draw up legal documents. Some held special positions in the royal palace and functioned as ministers of finance or secretaries of state. Some were academic advisers to the king. During the *diaspora in *Babylon, scribes became responsible for preserving and interpreting scripture. Later, scribes were also called "the wise" and described as those with special knowledge of the Law. Early in the conflict with Antiochus Epiphanes (ca. 168 BCE), a group of Jewish scribes met with Antiochus's agents to negotiate justice. They were probably local politicians with legal training.

In the New Testament, scribes are described functioning as *lawyers and judges, and they are shown arguing with *Jesus over legal matters—authority to forgive, traditions of the elders, dietary laws, purity laws, interpretation of scripture, and Sabbath observance. Scribes were often associated with *Pharisees, but the two were not identical. The "scribes of the Pharisees" were probably legal counselors employed by the Pharisees. Chief priests also employed scribes as their legal counselors.

Scribes were associated with the *Sanhedrin, probably as clerks, legal counselors for participants in trials, and judges. The fact that Jesus was reported arguing with the scribes at the same time that he was refuting the Pharisees does not prove that scribes were Pharisaic. Since the scribes whom Jesus attacked were defending the Pharisees, Jesus opposed them as well as the clients they represented.

The authority of scribes was delegated. They interpreted existing law; they did not create it. Well-trained scribes were acquainted with all kinds of law, both ancient and contemporary. When Jesus was distinguished from the scribes as one who had authority, the implication was that, as the *Messiah, he had authority to make law, just as *David and other kings did. This gave him authority over the Sabbath and all other national laws. He also had authority to pardon, as other kings did.

Some scribes also copied biblical texts. The care with which this was done has been recognized with the discovery of the Dead Sea Scrolls, which allow scholars to compare medieval texts with examples copied a thousand years earlier. The relatively few differences disclosed are not so often scribal errors as variant texts. At the ends of some books, the scribe gave the total number of words in the book and told which word was the exact middle, so that later scribes could count both ways to be sure they had not omitted a single letter; this tradition was continued by the Masoretes.

*George Wesley Buchanan*

**SEBA.** A part of the kingdom of *Sheba, perhaps a colony in northeast Africa.

**SENNACHERIB** (Sin-aḫḫe-eriba). King of *Assyria (705–681 BCE). Sennacherib, as crown prince under his father Sargon II (722–705 BCE), served as administrator in the Assyrian heartland while his father was on campaign. After Sargon had been killed in battle, Sennacherib viewed this as a sign of divine disfavor and dissociated himself from his father. He abandoned Sargon's newly built capital and, contrary to Assyrian custom, omitted his genealogy in official inscriptions. Sennacherib chose as his capital the old city of *Nineveh, which he embellished by installing wide boulevards, bringing in mountain water by aqueduct, planting trees, and laying out parks. Sennacherib campaigned actively in foreign lands, chiefly against *Babylon (dominated at this time by Chaldeans) and Elam. His struggles with Babylon reached a crisis after the Babylonians had handed over his crown prince, Ashur-nadin-shumi, to the Elamites; Sennacherib eventually besieged, captured, and ruthlessly destroyed the city, diverting a watercourse through the ruins so that the site would be permanently obliterated.

In 701 BCE, Sennacherib led an expedition into Palestine to reinstate his ally Padi of Ekron, who had been deposed by his subjects. The siege of *Lachish during this campaign is vividly illustrated in the reliefs from the royal palace at Nineveh. After the fall of Lachish, Sennacherib besieged *Hezekiah in *Jerusalem, imprisoning him, as the Assyrian annals report, "like a bird in a cage"; Hezekiah made peace only by paying extensive tribute. Because of apparent discrepancies in the biblical and extrabiblical accounts of Sennacherib's activities in Palestine, it has sometimes been proposed that Sennacherib mounted another, less successful expedition—not recorded in the cuneiform records—against the area at some time after 689 BCE; but this is unlikely. Nevertheless, the survival of Jerusalem was viewed as the equivalent of a victory by some biblical writers, and this led to the narrative of the city's miraculous deliverance, celebrated in Byron's "The Destruction of Sennacherib." Sennacherib was assassinated in 681 BCE by his son Arda-Mulishshi.

*John A. Brinkman*

**SERAPH, SERAPHIM.** Hebrew singular and plural for supernatural beings associated with the presence of God, and in postbiblical tradition identified as one of the choirs of *angels. They appear only once in the Bible, in the call-vision of Isaiah 6, where they sing praise to God in the now-famous words of the "Thrice Holy" hymn. Isaiah saw the Lord on his throne, surrounded by seraphim in the same way that early rulers were surrounded by a courtly retinue. Like the derivative four living creatures of Revelation 4.8, the seraphim had three pairs of wings, one for flying, one for covering their eyes (for apparently not even these beings could look directly on God), and one to cover their feet (almost certainly a euphemism for genitalia).

The noun *śārāp* is usually related to the verb *śārāp,* "to burn." Because the term appears several times with reference to the serpents encountered in the wilderness, it has often been understood to refer to "fiery serpents." From this it has also often been proposed that the seraphim were serpentine in form and in some sense "fiery" creatures or associated with fire. In Isaiah 6.6 one of the seraphs brings the prophet a live coal from the fire on the altar; note, however, that the seraph uses tongs.

*David G. Burke*

**SEVEN CHURCHES, THE.** The Revelation to John was addressed to seven churches in the Roman province of *Asia. There were other churches in the province (*Colossae and Troas), but seven were chosen to represent the entire church. The letters to these churches present a picture of diversity in Christianity. The church of *Ephesus, which had been founded by *Paul, and remained for many centuries one of the chief centers of the eastern church, was zealous in guarding against heresy (that of the Nicolaitans), but lacking in Christian love. The church of Smyrna appears to have stood up well under harassment and, sometimes, the imprisonment of its members. Pergamum was an important religious center, with a famous shrine of Zeus, a temple of Asklepios with a renowned medical school, and a temple of Augustus; "Satan's throne" may mean any of these, but probably refers to emperor worship. The church had suffered some persecution but it had remained faithful, though there was some laxity with regard to the Nicolaitans. The church of Thyatira abounded in love and faith, service and patient endurance, but allowed the evil teachings of a prophetess *Jezebel. The church of Sardis was outwardly flourishing, but not without serious damage to its spiritual life. Philadelphia, on the other hand, was a city where Christians were isolated in the community; but the church had remained faithful. At Laodicea the church seemed to be flourishing, but was spiritually poor.

Each letter is specific and contains praise and criticism, warning and encouragement as appropriate. But the plural "churches" at the end of each letter shows that they were meant to be read by every church. They are part of the opening vision of Revelation, where John saw the heavenly Son of man surrounded by seven lampstands, which were the seven churches. The letters show that this was not meant as a picture of an ideal church, but as a means of showing the churches as they really are, with their heresies, quarrels, and weak faith, but also with their faith and hope and love. This introduction to the Revelation plays an essential part in the book's purpose of warning and comfort.

*David H. van Daalen*

**SEVEN, THE.** According to Acts 6.1–6, a dispute arose between "Hellenists" and "Hebrews" over the distribution of food to *widows. The *twelve decided that "seven men of good standing" be chosen to oversee the task. In some later Christian traditions this decision is understood as the institution of the office of deacon, though that title does not occur in the passage. This passage has traditionally been interpreted as reflecting tension between Jewish and gentile Christians. But recent scholarship has shown the fine line that existed between Jews and Greeks in this part of the world in the Roman period. Even Acts itself warns against too glib an approach to ethnic and religious identities. The "God-fearers" in Acts are just such a group who stand on the border between putative Greek and Jewish culture. It is more likely then, that both groups are Jewish Christians, the Hebrews being Aramaic-speakers and the Hellenists perhaps originally from the Dispersion but now living in Jerusalem. The episode would thus reflect tension between them, a tension resolved by the establishment of a new form of leadership in some ways parallel to the twelve; two of the seven, *Stephen and Philip, are active preachers just like the twelve. The narrative may also be inspired by the accounts of Moses's sharing of leadership. *J. Andrew Overman*

**SHALMANESER V.** Shulmanu-ashared, King of *Assyria (727–722 BCE); otherwise known as Ululayu ("born in the month Ululu"). As son of his predecessor, *Tiglath-pileser III (745–727 BCE), Shalmaneser served as administrator in Calah, the Assyrian capital, while his father campaigned in foreign lands. After Tiglath-pileser's death, Shalmaneser inherited the dual monarchy of Assyria and *Babylonia and ruled for almost five years. Because Shalmaneser's reign was unexpectedly brief, court scribes had not drafted an official account of his campaigns and building achievements before his death; accordingly, his known royal inscriptions consist chiefly of eight Assyrian-Aramaic bilingual texts on lion weights from Calah. Thus, the events of his reign must be reconstructed at present principally from later cuneiform inscriptions, the Assur Ostracon, brief references in 2 Kings, and Hellenistic texts such as Josephus's *Antiquities.* Shalmaneser was on the throne when *Samaria fell to the Assyrians in 722 after a three-year siege (Babylonian Chronicle); but the subsequent deportation of the Israelites probably took place in 720 under his successor, Sargon II (722–705 BCE).

*John A. Brinkman*

**SHEBA, QUEEN OF.** A ruler of a people called the Sabeans, who occupied a territory in southwest Arabia, approximately where Yemen is today. The Semitic inhabitants of Sheba built up a far-reaching trade, especially in spices and precious metals and stones; they colonized nearby parts of Africa, including the Ethiopian coast. Sheba was a prosperous land and thus a symbol of wealth.

In the tenth century BCE, Sheba's queen is said to have visited *Solomon, the king of Israel. She arrived with extravagant gifts and with questions to test Solomon's wisdom. Her visit reflects several important and interrelated features of Solomonic rule: internationalism, diplomacy, and sagacity. Solomon's peaceful domination of far-flung territories was sustained through his skill as a diplomat rather than through the repeated show of military force, and his close ties with foreign nations is evident in the numerous relationships he is said to have established with women from outside his native land. Such diplomatic skill, particularly on the international level, is associated throughout the ancient Near East with wisdom. The Queen of Sheba's interaction with Solomon exemplifies that connection. The report of her visit to *Jerusalem is a vehicle for the biblical author to extol Solomon's wealth and wisdom. Furthermore, the Queen of Sheba, by transporting some of her nation's wealth to Jerusalem, thus aggrandizes the capital of Solomon's empire and contributes to the assertion of Jerusalem's prominence in the Near East at that time.

According to later legend, the relationship between Solomon and the queen was more intimate, and their son was the founder of the (former) royal house of Ethiopia. *Carol L. Meyers*

**SHECHEM.** A major Canaanite and Israelite city in the hill country of Ephraim, Shechem first appears in the historical record as an enemy of *Egypt in an execration text and on a stele of the nineteenth century BCE. During the Amarna period (fourteenth century), Shechem, under its ruler, Labayu, and his sons, asserted itself against the other Canaanite city-states and, hence, against the weakening Egyptian hegemony in Canaan.

Shechem appears prominently in the ancestral narratives. *Abraham had a theophany near Shechem and built an altar there, as did *Jacob. In Genesis 34, *Simeon and *Levi kill the inhabitants of Shechem and plunder it in retaliation for the rape of their sister Dinah by Shechem, son of Hamor. *Joseph's body was brought back from Egypt and buried at Shechem (see also the somewhat erroneous), and *Joshua's great covenant renewal ceremony took place there. The first abortive Israelite attempt at kingship under Abimelech was centered at Shechem, but Abimelech exacted a terrible revenge in the city after a mutual falling out. It was to Shechem that Jeroboam I went to be crowned first king of *Israel, and it served as his first capital.

Shechem has been located at the site of Tell Balatah, guarding the pass between Mount Ebal to the north and Mount Gerezim to the south, near modern Nablus. After earlier village occupation of the site in the Chalcolithic period, a large and well-fortified urban center developed at Shechem in the Middle Bronze Age (ca. 1850–1550 BCE). Of particular interest are the temples found at the site, including one designated the "fortress temple" because of its massive walls. After a violent destruction at the end of the Middle Bronze Age, presumably by one of the early pharaohs of Dynasty XVIII, Shechem lay uninhabited for close to a century. Completely rebuilt, probably with Egyptian consent, the city prospered during the first part of the Late Bronze Age, only to suffer destruction at the hands of Labayu's enemies, whether Egyptian or Canaanite or both. The subsequent Late Bronze Age city was not as prosperous, yet it managed to survive into the early Iron Age, when it probably passed peacefully into Israelite hands. The destruction of Shechem in the late twelfth century is generally attributed to Abimelech. Shechem recovered to some extent during the following centuries, becoming a town of some importance, until it was once again destroyed, this time by the *Assyrians in their campaign of conquest ofthe northern kingdom Israel (724–722 BCE). The habitation of Shechem remained poor and sparse throughout the remainder of the Iron Age and the first part of the Persian period. During the Hellenistic period (as of ca. 330 BCE) Shechem regained some of its ancient importance and glory as the *Samaritan rival of Jerusalem. The city was finally destroyed in 107 BCE by the Hasmonean John Hyrcanus. *Carl S. Ehrlich*

**SILAS.** As representatives of the church in Jerusalem, Silas and Judas/Barsabbas are sent to Antioch to report on the decree of the Apostolic Council. They are then said to return to Jerusalem, but several verses later, Silas is chosen to accompany *Paul on a new missionary journey. Silas is described as a *prophet, but in Acts he follows Paul silently through Macedonia until Beroea, and rejoins him in Corinth, after which he is not mentioned again. Paul refers to a coworker named Silvanus in some of his letters, leading to the common assumption that the Silvanus named in the letters is identical with the Silas described in Acts. *Daniel N. Schowalter*

**SILVANUS.** *See* Silas.

**SIMEON.**

**1.** The name given to *Jacob's second oldest son, born to *Leah. After the conquest, the tribe descended from Simeon was given territory in the south of *Canaan, within the land later controlled by Judah.

**2.** In the New Testament, Simeon is the name of a devout man, said to be waiting for the "consolation of Israel," introduced by Luke. When he sees the infant Jesus being brought into the Temple, he gives praise for having seen God's salvation; his brief words are traditionally known by the first two words of the Latin translation, *Nunc Dimittis.* Simeon also informs *Mary that Jesus's coming would have an impact on all of Israel and that she would suffer as well.
*Daniel N. Schowalter*

**SIMON PETER.** The son of *Jonah or *John; originally he was known as Simon. According to the Gospels, *Jesus gave him the name Peter, the Greek translation of an Aramaic word "Cepha(s)" meaning "stone, rock." He and his brother Andrew were fishermen of the poorer class, since apparently they did not own a boat. He was among the first disciples whom Jesus called. Married, his wife later traveled with him on some of his missionary journeys.

An *apostle and one of the *twelve, he was prominent among them, belonging to a small inner group. He often acted as their spokesperson, especially in acknowledging Jesus as the *Messiah, though he did not understand Jesus would have to suffer. On several other occasions he is presented in a poor light, particularly in the gospel of *Mark and especially in his denial of Jesus. We should, however, remember that the purpose of the Gospels is to inform us about Jesus, not to give a biography of Peter. Peter's failures serve to highlight Jesus's courage and compassion.

After the resurrection, Peter was the first male disciple to see the risen Jesus, and he quickly took a leading position in the young church. According to Luke's account in Acts, he preached, healed the sick, went as envoy from Jerusalem to oversee the work of other missionaries, and suffered for his faith. Guided by a vision, he was the first to preach to and convert gentiles, and he supported *Paul on this matter in the council of Acts 15. Paul's own account of Peter's position in the controversy differs somewhat; in *Galatians we are told that on a visit to Antioch, Peter refused to have full fellowship with gentile Christians. At either the council of Acts 15 or another, Paul was allotted the gentiles as his missionary concern and Peter the Jews. After this Peter disappears from the New Testament story. *James, the brother of Jesus, apparently became the sole leader of the Jerusalem church, and Peter went traveling. He may have visited *Corinth and/or the areas mentioned in 1 Peter 1.1 and came to Rome shortly before his death. Extrabiblical tradition says that he was martyred when Nero persecuted the Christians there (64 CE). Yet later tradition claims that St. Peter's in Rome was built over his burial place.

The meaning of Jesus's words to Peter in Matthew 16.17–19 have been disputed. Is the rock Peter himself, his confession, or Peter as confessor? Is the power of the keys that of ecclesiastical discipline or of admitting to the church through preaching? Is binding and loosing the determination of what is correct and orthodox or the power to excommunicate? Is this power restricted to Peter alone or given to the whole church? Were the words of 16.17–19 spoken by the incarnate Jesus, the risen Jesus, or did they come into being later to represent the position Peter actually attained?

Early tradition associates Peter with the gospel of *Mark. Some later apocryphal writings were written in his name, a gospel of Peter and at least two apocalypses. There was also an Acts of Peter. Their appearance indicates his importance for the second-century church. In the first century, there was a group that strongly supported him.

Two of the writings of the New Testament are attributed to him, 1 and 2 Peter.

**1 Peter.** Although it is structured like other letters of the period, 1 Peter contains little of a personal nature; addressed to Christians in a wide area, it reads more like an address than a letter. Some scholars have therefore viewed it as a baptismal sermon or as a letter that includes, or was derived from, such a sermon or baptismal liturgy. It is preferable to regard it as a letter of a general nature, directed to readers far distant from the writer, who is unfamiliar with the details of their situation. In writing it, he makes considerable use of existing Christian tradition in the way of creedal and catechetical material, as well as of the Septuagint and the traditions about Jesus.

Three views have been held on its authorship. According to the first, the letter was written by the apostle Peter because his name appears on it, it has reminiscences of the teaching of Jesus that he could have provided, and 5.1 may suggest the writer was an eyewitness to the death of Jesus. But the Greek in which the letter is written suggests an educated author rather than a simple fisherman; the Septuagint, to which Peter would not have been accustomed, is used in biblical quotations in the way someone brought up with it would use it; the account of the death of Jesus is not that of an eyewitness but is drawn from Isaiah 53. So it has been suggested that *Silvanus acted as secretary to Peter; the general thought in the letter would have been that of Peter, but its actual expression that of Silvanus. Since, however, the main support for Peter's authorship comes from the detail of the letter and not its general thought, this makes difficult the idea of Silvanus as secretary. If he had been secretary, we might expect him to add his own greetings. It has been suggested that he wrote it after the death of Peter to preserve Peter's teaching, but it is hardly likely that he would then have introduced the self-praise of 5.12. Increasingly, therefore, scholars have come to believe that the letter is pseudonymous (writing in the name of another person was not unknown in the ancient world). Disciples of Peter after his death may have continued to expound the special themes of his teaching, believing it should be made known to a wider circle. Each of these theories fits with the belief that the letter was written from Rome (Babylon in 5.13 is probably a code name for Rome), where Peter died.

The letter must have been written prior to 120–130 CE, for by then other writers know it. It shows the influence of Pauline ideas and terms, and this suggests it must be later than 60 CE, for it was about this time that *Paul came to Rome. If Peter himself wrote it from Rome, it was also about this time that he arrived there. The sporadic and local nature of the persecutions means they cannot help in determining the date. Their strength together with the areas to which the letter was written, most of which do not appear to have been evangelized early, suggest a period later than the death of Peter, perhaps around 80 CE.

**2 Peter.** This book presents itself as a testament or farewell discourse of the apostle Peter, written in the form of a letter shortly before his death. Its object is to remind readers of Peter's teaching and to defend it against false teachers, who were casting doubt on the Lord's coming to judgment (the parousia) and advocating ethical libertinism.

Work belonging to the literary genre of "testament" were generally pseudepigraphal, attributed to biblical figures long dead, and probably understood as exercises in historical imagination. The use of the genre suggests that 2 Peter is a work written in Peter's name by someone else after his death, though it is possible that the testament genre could have been used by Peter to write his own, real testament. But it should also be noticed how the predictive character of the testament is used in 2 Peter. Nothing in the letter reflects the situation in which Peter is said to be writing; the whole work is addressed to a situation after Peter's death. The predictions of false teachers function as pegs on which is hung the apologetic debate about the validity of Peter's message. Moreover, whereas the testamentary passages speak of the false teachers in the future tense, predicting their rise after Peter's death, the apologetic sections and the denunciation of the false teachers refer to them in the present tense. It is scarcely possible to read 2 Peter without supposing the false teachers to be contemporaries of the author. The alternation of predictive and present-tense references to them is therefore best understood as a deliberate stylistic device to convey the message that these apostolic prophecies are now being fulfilled. In other words, Petrine authorship is a fiction, but one that the author does not feel obliged to maintain throughout his work. In that case, it must be a transparent fiction, a literary convention that the author expected his readers to recognize as such.

For these and other reasons, most modern scholars consider 2 Peter to be pseudepigraphal, though some still defend Petrine authorship. The most cogent additional reasons for denying Peter's authorship are the Hellenistic religious language and ideas, and the evidence for dating the work after Peter's death in the mid-60s CE. Scholars differ widely on the date of 2 Peter, which many consider to be the latest New Testament writing, written well into the second century CE. But the clearest evidence for a postapostolic date is 3.4, which indicates that the first Christian generation has died, and this passage may well suggest that the letter was written at the time when this had only just become true, around 80–90 CE. This was the time when those who had expected the parousia during the lifetime of the apostolic generation would face the problem of the nonfulfillment of that expectation, but there is no evidence that this continued to be felt as a problem in the second century.

The literary relationship between 2 Peter and *Jude is another consideration relevant to the date of 2 Peter. There are such close resemblances that some kind of literary relationship seems certain. Some scholars have held that Jude is dependent on 2 Peter or that both depend on a common source, but most conclude that 2 Peter has used Jude as a source. Of course, this requires a late date for 2 Peter only if Jude is dated late.

If 2 Peter was written not by Peter, but after his death, why did the author present his work in the form of Peter's testament? Probably because his intention was to defend the apostolic message in the period after the death of the apostles against teachers who held that, in important respects, the teaching of the apostles was now discredited. By writing in Peter's name he claims no authority of his own, except as a faithful mediator of the apostolic message, which he defends against attacks. The form of the letter as an apostolic testament is therefore closely connected with its apologetic purpose as a vindication of the normative authority of the apostolic teaching. That the author chose to write *Peter's* testament is probably best explained if he was a leader of the Roman church, which had counted Peter as the most prestigious of its leaders in the previous generation.

*Richard J. Bauckham, Ernest Best*

**SINAI.** A triangular peninsula, bordered on the north by the Mediterranean Sea, on the west by the Gulf of Suez and the Suez Canal, and on the east by the Gulf of Aqaba/Eilat. Moving from the coastland south, the terrain gradually rises to the Ijma Plateau, near the center of the peninsula. The region south of the plateau becomes mountainous before the terrain descends to a narrow coastland between the mountains and the gulfs. From the fourth millennium BCE the mountains have been mined for copper, which was exported to both Egypt and Canaan.

It is generally assumed that somewhere on this peninsula is Mount Sinai, the mountain from which Moses reputedly delivered the Ten Commandments to the Israelites, but evidence is scant for determining which of the many mountains was called Mount Sinai during the time of the wilderness wanderings. Since Sinai is the wilderness nearest Egypt, this seems the most likely place for Mount Sinai, but there are problems. The mountain from which Moses received the commandments is sometimes called Sinai and sometimes *Horeb. It is also labeled "the mountain of God" and simply "the mountain." It is not certain whether these were different names for the same place or different mountains. Some have thought it was initially Horeb but was renamed Sinai after the peninsula, but no one knows when the peninsula was named "Sinai"; neither Josephus nor Paul calls it by that name.

One of the ways scholars have tried to identify Mount Sinai has been to conjecture the route the Israelites traveled on their way to Canaan. Since the most direct route from Egypt follows the Mediterranean coastline, some have assumed that the Israelites took this route, and that one of the nearby mountains in the northern lowland or southern Canaan was Mount Sinai, but archaeological remains show that the Egyptians had this well-traveled route fortified; consequently, refugees probably avoided such confrontation. It is more likely that they turned south. Since they reportedly lived in this wilderness for about forty years, they may not have planned originally to settle in Canaan.

The most popular candidate for Mount Sinai is Jebel Musa ("the mountain of Moses") near Saint Catherine's Monastery. This identification was apparently first made by Byzantine monks in the fourth century CE, and there is no evidence to show that they had any local data that are not known today for choosing the site. Most of the modern sites are named after plants, trees, and topographical features, and they provide no clues to ancient Israelite history. Other possible sites include several mountains in northwestern Arabia, and Mount Karkom in Machtesh Ramon just west of the Arabah; the latter conjecture, made in 1985, was based on art and architecture found on and around Karkom, but it depends on a date for the Exodus in the third millennium BCE.

When Byzantine monks settled in Sinai (300–600 CE) they were able to dig wells, make terraces and direct rainfall, and raise gardens and orchards in valleys. The Emperor Justinian had a church constructed and a monastery fortified (527 CE); this was later called Saint Catherine's Convent. Within an area of two square miles is the Byzantine identification of the site of the burning bush, the place where Moses struck the rock, the mountain where God spoke to Moses, and the hill where Aaron made the golden calf. The monks apparently found an isolated location in this historic peninsula where they could survive. They then identified biblical sites with places in their immediate surroundings.

*George Wesley Buchanan*

**SIRACH** (Ecclesiasticus). Sirach is the author of the book named for him. One of the earliest of the deuterocanonical/apocryphal books, Sirach is the most extensive portion of Israelite wisdom literature preserved in the Bible. Modeled in great part on Proverbs, Sirach is a compilation of materials that include moral and ethical maxims, folk proverbs, psalms of praise and lament, theological reflections, homiletic exhortations, and pointed observations about Jewish life and religious mores in the second century BCE. It is one of the longest books of the Bible.

Sirach is one of the rare books of the Hebrew Bible that was actually written by the author to whom the book is ascribed. In 50.27, he identifies himself as "Jesus (Hebr. *yēšûaᶜ*), son of Eleazar, son of (Hebr. *ben*) Sira (Grk. *S[e]irach*)"; hence, the name Ben Sira, or Sirach, which is found in the title of the book in Greek. Since the extant Hebrew manuscripts begin with 3.6b, we do not know what title the book had in Hebrew. The Latin title, Ecclesiasticus, probably means "the ecclesiastical (or church) [book]," because it was used so widely in the Christian liturgy.

The book was written originally in Hebrew, as Ben Sira's grandson states explicitly in the foreword to his Greek translation. The date when Ben Sira composed the book can be calculated on the basis of information provided in the foreword. The grandson writes that he "came to Egypt in the thirty-eighth year of the reign of Euergetes and stayed for some time." The year would be 132 BCE, in the reign of Ptolemy VII Physcon Euergetes, who began his rule in 170 BCE as co-regent with his brother Ptolemy VI. If we allow sufficient time between grandson and grandfather, we arrive at a date ca. 180 BCE for the composition of the book. This date receives support from the book itself. In 50.1–21, Ben Sira writes a lengthy panegyric on Simeon II, who was high priest from 219–196 BCE. This poem gives the impression that Simeon had been dead for several years. The Greek translation was published in Egypt some time after 117 BCE. The Greek is the most important witness to the text whenever the Hebrew is not extant.

The theology of Sirach is essentially Deuteronomic; hence, it is traditional and conservative. He reflects the teachings of earlier biblical books on such subjects as God, the election of Israel, retribution, morality, kindness to the *poor and disadvantaged, the centrality of fear of the Lord. The expression "fear of the Lord/God" occurs about sixty times in Sirach, and the term "wisdom" about fifty-five times. In 1.1–2.18 there is a detailed treatise on wisdom as fear of the Lord. The fundamental thesis of Sirach is that wisdom, which is identified with the Law, is bestowed only on one who fears the Lord. God grants wisdom to those who love him, that is, those who "keep the commandments" (1.26). Fear of the Lord, which is "the beginning of wisdom" (1.14; cf. Prov. 9.10), "gives gladness and joy and long life" (1.12). Fear of the Lord and wisdom make life meaningful and worthwhile. Sinners or fools—the terms are synonyms for Ben Sira—can never attain wisdom.

The doctrine of God reflects earlier biblical traditions. God is one and the same from all eternity. He created all things by simply uttering his almighty word. He knows all things, even the deepest mysteries of the universe, and sees all things even before they occur. God is merciful not only to his chosen people but to other nations as well. Believers may address God as Father, confident that he will listen to their prayer. Ben Sira denies that God is responsible in any way for human sin. Virtue and vice result from human free choice. But the origin of sin according to Genesis 3.1–6 is also alluded to in Sirach (25.24). Since human beings are free, there is hope even for sinners, for they can turn away from sin and repent.

Ben Sira teaches the traditional doctrine of retribution: reward for fidelity to the Law or punishment for infidelity takes place in one's lifetime here on earth; after death *saint and sinner alike are thought to go to Sheol, the nether world, where they share a dark, listless, dismal survival separated from the Lord. The grandson's Greek translation, however, makes definite allusions to retribution in the afterlife, and a later recension, called Greek II, makes even more allusions, as do the still later Latin and Syriac versions. One survives in one's children and in one's good name. Prayer, being the language of faith, is found in several places in Sirach. Respect for the priests and the offering of sacrifices are enjoined, but these are useless if one is guilty of injustice. Observance of the Law, especially with regard to charity, is the best form of sacrifice and worship. The sacrifices of the wicked who oppress the poor are not acceptable to God; Ben Sira speaks emphatically of the need to practice social justice and to assist the weak and the defenseless.

*Alexander A. DiLella, O.F.M.*

**SLAVES.** The socioeconomic institution of slavery was present in both Israel and early Christianity. Slavery among the Israelites shared many of the features present in other ancient Near Eastern cultures, just as slavery among Christians was similar to the practices prevailing in the *Roman empire. Throughout the Bible, however, distinctive humanitarian impulses regulate the treatment of slaves.

Exodus 21.1–11, Leviticus 25.39–55, and Deuteronomy 15.12–18 define the status and regulate the treatment of slaves. Each text is literarily framed by Israel's moral obligations to God's order for their lives: Exodus 21 by the Ten Commandments, which put the Covenant Code laws under sole allegiance to Yahweh (note that the rights of the slave's release are guaranteed as the code's first stipulation); Leviticus 25 and Deuteronomy 15 by Sabbath and sabbatical regulations, which include the obligation to treat the *poor generously. Rather than viewing slavery as a divinely sanctioned institution, as proslavery writers argued over a century ago, the biblical texts accent how God's commands protect slaves from cruel and capricious treatment.

Three types of servile status are identifiable in Israel's practice: an Israelite became a servant to a fellow Israelite voluntarily as security against poverty, or by birth or purchase (Exod. 21.32 sets the compensation for a slave's death at thirty shekels); Israelites took non-Israelites as slaves through capture in war or purchase; Israelites sold themselves to non-Israelites as security against debt. In the first category, servants were guaranteed both the seventh-year sabbatical and fiftieth year jubilee releases. In the second category, slaves, though circumcised and sworn into covenant membership, did not receive the benefit of these releases, but were protected against oppression. In the third category, slaves were eligible for redemption by a relative at any time, and were mandatorily freed in the jubilee year. Slaves in all categories enjoyed Sabbath rest and participated in Israel's religious festivals. (*See* Hebrews.)

The moral imperative that mercy and kindness be shown toward slaves was based upon God's deliverance of Israel from slavery in Egypt: "Remember that you were a slave in the land of Egypt, and the Lord your God redeemed you; for this reason I lay this command upon you today" (Deut. 15.15; see also Lev. 25.42–43). The prophets also criticized injustices in Israel's slavery: forbidding King Ahaz to enslave captives from Judah, attributing Israel's exile to failure to give sabbatical release to the slaves, calling Israel to "let the oppressed go free and to break every yoke" (Isa. 58.6). In the eschatological vision of Joel, God's spirit would be poured out also on slaves.

Jesus's ministry and the writing of the New Testament literature occurred within the cultural practice of slavery, both Jewish and Roman. The Talmud indicates that various types of servile status continued among Jews from around 200 BCE to 400 CE. Many events and teachings in the Gospels reflect the presence of slaves, especially in the household.

The New Testament letters frequently regulate the conduct of masters and slaves. Although the gospel of Jesus Christ abolished distinctions between slave and free, slaves were instructed not to presume upon their new standing to legitimate careless work or disrespect toward masters. Slaves were called to direct accountability to God for proper conduct within the existing social institution. Masters similarly were told to treat their slaves justly and kindly. *Paul sent the runaway slave, Onesimus, back to his owner *Philemon, instructing Philemon to receive Onesimus as a brother "both in the flesh and in the Lord" even "as you would welcome me" (Philem. 16–17).

The biblical vocabulary for slavery, in both its noun (Hebr. $^{c}$*ebed,* Grk. *doulos*) and verb forms *($^{c}$ābad; douloō),* carries a wide range of meaning, from domestic service to enforced labor (1 Kings

9.15–22), and is metaphorically extended to the relationship of humans to God. Thus, both *Moses (Deut 34.5; etc.) and *David (Ps. 18.1) are called the "servant [Hebr. *ᶜebed*] of the Lord," and Israel and others are instructed to "serve" *(ᶜābad)* the Lord (Deut. 11.12; Ps. 2.11; etc.). The same imagery is found in the New Testament. Just as Jesus took upon himself "the form of a slave" (Phil. 2.7), so Jesus's followers are also to think and do; thus, Paul identified himself as a slave of Christ.

*Willard M. Swartley*

**SODOM AND GOMORRAH.** Two cities, legendary for their incorrigible wickedness and for their ultimate annihilation by God in a cataclysm of "brimstone and fire." In the story of *Abraham's war against the kings of the east, Sodom and Gomorrah are numbered among the "five cities" in the "Valley of Siddim," along with Admah, Zeboiim, and Zoar. Abraham's nephew *Lot sojourned for a time in Sodom but fled at divine instigation before the city's final devastation. Passages mentioning Sodom and Gomorrah generally agree in locating them along the southern shore of the Dead Sea, but so far no archaeological evidence for their existence has been found there. Suppositions that their remains may yet be discovered beneath the shallow waters of the southern Dead Sea are unlikely ever to be proved. Early Bronze Age (third millennium BCE) settlements and cemeteries at Bab edh-Dhra and Numeira on the southeastern edge of the Dead Sea do, however, provide evidence for very early pre-Israelite occupation in the region. The presence of these ruins, abandoned long before the advent of the Israelites in Canaan, may have given rise much later to local legends that their destruction resulted from divine wrath. At a subsequent stage these legends may have become attached to stories of the wanderings of Abraham and Lot in Canaan.

Whatever the origin of these legends, Sodom and Gomorrah become powerful symbols of human wickedness and divine retribution. Sodom and Gomorrah together (or more frequently, Sodom alone) are held up as archetypes of sinfulness, justly deserving and finally receiving God's punishment. This theme is prominent in prophetic writings and in the New Testament.

*Joseph A. Greene*

**SOLOMON.** The son of *David and *Bathsheba, Solomon ruled over Israel ca. 962–922 BCE. His exploits are detailed in 1 Kings 1–11 and 1 Chronicles 28–2 Chronicles 9. Supported by Bathsheba, *Nathan, and Benaiah, he came to power in a coup d'état that sidetracked his older brother, Adonijah, and Joab. His reign was marked by prosperity and prestige, grandiose building projects, and a cultural transformation.

The prosperity is portrayed in the fulsome description given in 1 Kings 4.20–28 and 10.14–29, in the marriage with Pharaoh's daughter (and there was a considerable harem), in the international role indicated by his dealings with Hiram of Tyre and the visit of the Queen of *Sheba, as well as the extensive international trade (a fleet at Ezion-geber; "Tarshish" ships; trading in horses and chariots).

Solomon's building program consisted principally in the *Temple as well as the palace complex (the palace, the "House of the Forest of Lebanon"—a kind of armory—and even a palace for his Egyptian wife). In addition, he built up a corps of chariots and cavalry that functioned out of chariot cities in the realm. Such opulence was sustained by a revision of the administrative areas in the kingdom, which led to increased revenue for the crown, as well as to a weakening of the old tribal ties and to further assimilation of the Canaanite population. All this was obtained at a price, as is suggested by Solomon's having to cede land to Hiram of Tyre and by the *corvée.* Despite 1 Kings 9.20–22, it appears that Israelites as well as Canaanites were involved in forced labor, and this became a major complaint against Solomon.

The cultural transformation of the population must have been considerable, though it is largely a matter of historical inference. But political centralization won out over the old tribalization; a new wealthy class emerged, and cleavage between rich and poor increased. This aspect of Solomon's reign is not reflected in the tradition. Rather, his reign is acclaimed, and his personal wisdom is underlined. His wisdom is compared to that of the Egyptians, and is illustrated by the famous incident of the two *prostitutes. Hence he has come down in the tradition as the wise man par excellence, to whom several works were eventually attributed: Psalms 72 and 127, the book of Proverbs, the Song of Solomon, and *Ecclesiastes within the Hebrew Bible; Wisdom of Solomon among the apocrypha; Psalms and Odes among the pseudepigrapha. Scholars have inferred that such compositions as the Yahwist history (J) probably date to the Solomonic period.

The theological judgment passed upon Solomon is mixed. The name Jedidiah (beloved of Yah or the Lord) was given him by the prophet Nathan. The description of his sincerity and simplicity is highlighted in the sacrifice at Gibeon. He asks for a "listening heart" (1 Kings 3.9; NRSV: "understanding mind") whereby to rule the people, and the Lord assures him of this as well as of riches and glory. On the other hand, the typical Deuteronomic judgment on royalty is also passed upon Solomon, and notice is taken of the "adversaries" whom the Lord raised up: Hadad the Edomite, Rezon of Damascus, and especially Jeroboam, who was to lead the rebellion against Rehoboam, Solomon's son.

Nothing is known of "the Book of the Acts of Solomon" (1 Kings 11.41), which might have cast a fuller light on the reign of the fabled monarch. But the immediate dissolution of the united monarchy in the lifetime of his son is surely suggestive of the inadequacies of Solomon's reign.

**The Song of Solomon.** The Song of Solomon follows the book of *Ruth in the Hebrew Bible and Ecclesiastes in the Septuagint. Also called the Song of Songs (i.e., the most excellent song) and the Canticle (of Canticles), it was divided in the Middle Ages arbitrarily into eight chapters, which do not correspond to significant units of content. This brief composition of fewer than two hundred poetic verses has always been an enigma, and little agreement exists concerning such questions as origin, date of composition, structure, and unity.

The attribution "to Solomon" affixed to the Song is an editorial superscription that links this poetry to Israel's famous poet and sage rather than a declaration of authorship. No hint of actual author or authors appears in the text. The intense style of poetry belongs to the genre of love lyrics found in ancient Egyptian collections. Lush, extravagant imagery appealing to the senses of smell, taste, and touch, detailed descriptions of the human body, male and female, and highly stylized terms of endearment like dove, sister, and king link the Song to other ancient Near Eastern cultures.

The Song of Solomon displays striking metaphors from a variety of flora and fauna, some twenty-five species of plants and ten of animals, mentioned not as a display of learning but for the images they invoke. It also exploits the evocative power of place names like *Lebanon, home of fragrant cedars, Gilead, famous for its balm, snow-covered Amana, and Tirzah, ancient capital of the northern kingdom of Israel.

Nothing in the Song itself proves its date of composition. It seems to be made up of lyrics that came down in oral tradition long before they were gathered into their canonical form. The appealing subject matter and vivid imagery, like the woman being compared to a mare that throws the war stallions of the pharaoh's chariots into disorder, explain why these lyrics were preserved in the schools of the Temple of Jerusalem. They proved to be a useful teaching tool. Boldness of imagery, repetitions, and variations on erotic themes point to frequent recital before they were edited in the final form, possibly between 450–400 BCE. This date is plausible because of widespread scribal activity at that time, because the syntax exhibits Aramaic constructions, and because the *Persian loan word for paradise is found in 4.13.

**The Wisdom of Solomon.** This Greek work of a Hellenistic Jewish author is not found in the Hebrew Bible. In the Septuagint it follows the book of *Job; in the Vulgate it follows the Song of Solomon. The book is thus considered one of the Apocrypha by Jews and Protestants but is accepted as canonical by the Roman Catholic and most Orthodox churches.

Scholars have dated the work from 100 BCE to 100 CE on the basis of links to Hellenistic philosophy, literature, and science. Cultured readers of that period would have been familiar with its terminology, such as "intelligent spirit" that "pervades" and "penetrates" all (7.22, 24), "living spirit" (15.11), with its description of the human body as an "earthly tent" (9.15), and with references to the cosmic god Aeon. They would applaud the use of compound terms, including over seventy beginning with the negative prefix equivalent to the English "non-."

The book is pseudonymous: its author's identity is hidden by the literary technique of writing in the person of Israel's great wisdom-figure, Solomon. This approach fit the author's purpose: to compose an apologia for Israel's traditional religious beliefs in a cosmopolitan setting. Such a procedure would not have misled the cultured audience to whom this sophisticated composition was directed. Omission of proper names assumes that readers were familiar with Israelite tradition. The style and religious intensity identify its author as a pious teacher.

The "autobiography" of the idealized Solomon, whose life was a search for Lady *Wisdom, describes the plan of action necessary for Israel's future leaders. Wisdom's gifts to the devout include qualities and skills valued in Hellenistic Alexandria. Enthusiasm for Israel's tradition is no barrier to cultural progress. The author believed that Israel's role as God's chosen people was as important as ever and guaranteed by constant divine protection. The Wisdom of Solomon preserves the carefully planned appeal of a learned and imaginative Jewish teacher to his cultured students to cultivate loyalty to their revealed faith in an environment threatening their religious identity.

Only fidelity to their received revelation wins eternal life with God.

*Roland E. Murphy, O. Carm.; James M. Reese, O.S.F.S.*

**SONS OF GOD.** The sons of God (or children of God; Hebr. *bĕnê ʾĕlōhîm,* and variants) are divine members of God's heavenly assembly. They are depicted in many roles: praising God at the dawn of creation; praising God in heaven; meeting in the heavenly assembly before God; representing the foreign nations (following a text from Qumran and the LXX); and, most curiously, marrying and having offspring with human women. Other terms, such as *seraphim, *angels (i.e., "messengers"), and hosts of heaven also refer to these members of God's heavenly assembly. The sons of God are also identified with the stars in heaven. The title "sons/children of God" is familiar from Ugaritic mythology, in which the gods collectively are called the "children of El (literally, God)" *(bn ʾil).* One of El's titles is "Father of the Children of God," indicating that the term refers to the gods as his physical offspring, with *Asherah (called "Creatress of the Gods") as their mother. The sons/children of God are also found in Phoenician and Ammonite inscriptions, referring to the pantheon of subordinate deities, indicating that the term was widespread in West Semitic religions. Beginning in the seventh and sixth centuries BCE, several Israelite writers (especially Jeremiah, the Deuteronomist, and Second Isaiah) explicitly rejected the notion that there were gods other than Yahweh, and depicted the "hosts of heaven" as a foreign intrusion in Israelite monotheism.

*Ronald S. Hendel*

**STEPHEN.** The first Christian martyr, Stephen appears only in Acts. He is first mentioned as one of the *seven appointed to ensure equitable distribution of food between "Hebrews" and "Hellenists." The seven were probably leaders of the Hellenistic group in the Jerusalem church.

According to Acts 6, in an explicit literary parallel to Luke's story of Jesus, Stephen was charged with blasphemy and summoned to defend himself before the supreme *Sanhedrin.

His defense is a detailed exposition of the teaching that had provoked the charges against him. The speech may be regarded as a manifesto of early Hellenistic Christianity or at least of one phase of it. It does not represent Luke's point of view: for most of Luke's narrative, his appraisal of the *Temple is much more positive than Stephen's. Quoting the scriptures in support of his position, Stephen argues that to speak of the Temple as an institution to be destroyed or superseded was not to commit blasphemy, because God is independent of any building. It was commonly held by many early Christians that in Christ the Temple order had given way to something better, but Stephen's assertion that the Temple was a mistake from the beginning is without parallel in the New Testament. The position nearest to it is in the letter to the Hebrews, but its author simply ignores the Temple and bases his exposition of the high-priestly ministry of Christ on the biblical account of the wilderness tabernacle.

Stephen was apparently found guilty of blasphemy and sentenced to death. His execution took the form of a judicial stoning, carried out in accordance with the Law. Those who bore witness against him had the duty of throwing the first stones; on this occasion "a young man named Saul" guarded their cloaks as they did so, and thus *Paul makes his first appearance.

Analogies have been found to Stephen's position among the *Samaritans, the Qumran community, and the Ebionites. These groups, for various reasons, expressed a negative attitude to the Jerusalem Temple and its ceremonial. But Stephen's critique is distinctive; not only is it rooted in the preexilic prophets but it has a new basis in the Christ event. The radical Hellenistic theology represented by his speech survived particularly in Alexandrian Christianity, where its best-known expression is the letter of Barnabas (late first/early second century CE).

Stephen's impeachment and execution are said to have precipitated a persecution of the Jerusalem church, especially its Hellenistic members, who were forced to leave Jerusalem and Judea. But they preached the gospel wherever they went. Stephen's fellow-almoner Philip preached it in *Samaria; others, unnamed, preached it to the Greeks of *Antioch. Stephen's blood proved to be the seed of gentile Christianity.

*F. F. Bruce*

**STOICS.** A philosophical school founded in Athens by Zeno of Citium (335–263 BCE) which became the most influential philosophic sect in the Greco-Roman world. Stoics conceived of philosophy as the knowledge of things divine and human, and its goal as a life in harmony with nature. They thought that the universe was permeated by the Logos or Reason, also referred to as God or Providence. Human beings, they held, are particles of God, for divine Reason is manifested in a special way in human reason. As one rationally develops those conceptions of the divine that are innate in all people, one more clearly discerns the nature of things, including oneself. Stoics who make progress in this manner advance from ignorance, which is responsible for vice, to knowledge of reality, which makes virtue possible. Virtue and vice they delineated in extensive lists. Stoics disregarded all matters external to themselves, and cultivated an impassivity which made them self-sufficient or content *(autarkēs)*. Hardships that befell them therefore did not affect their true selves, but merely showed their true character. Their view of divine kinship gave a devotional cast to their language, and their doctrine that all things in the universe are in harmonious relationship to each other accommodated much of popular religion, including the veneration of religious images. As a messenger of the divine, the Stoic sage sought to show others their error and to lead them to the good. This included instruction in civic responsibility, which Stoics, as did other philosophers, summarized in lists of duties of members of a household.

In Jewish thought, wisdom was personified and increasingly related to the doctrine of creation. Stoic echoes of the cosmic wisdom are present in the Septuagint translation of Proverbs 8.22–31, and other Stoic elements begin to appear in Jewish literature, partly, perhaps, in reaction to Epicurean tendencies in such works as *Ecclesiastes. *Sirach advances a Stoic-like view of God as "the all" (43.27) who is responsible for every human experience, yet differs from Stoic pantheism in deeming God greater than his works. Wisdom, like the Stoic Logos, permeates the universe, but is identified with the Law of Moses, which is thus elevated to something suprahistorical and rational. The Wisdom of Solomon similarly describes all-pervading Wisdom as the agent of creation, which is directed by divine providence. Using the Stoic notion of natural theology, Wisdom of Solomon argues that, while knowledge of God is possible by observing creation, human failure to attain this knowledge resulted in an unpardonable ignorance that plunged humanity into idolatry and immorality. Stoic influence is also clearly discernible in 4 *Maccabees, which defines wisdom as the knowledge of divine and human things and sets out to determine whether devout reason is master of the passions. Unlike the Stoics, however, the author advocates the mastery, not eradication, of the passions.

Stoics are mentioned explicitly in the Bible only in Acts 17.18, where, according to Luke, in company with their opponents the *Epicureans they encounter *Paul. The sermon that follows has Paul making extensive use of popular Stoicism: the veneration of images as an expression of human religiosity, providence, kinship with the creator God, and the quotation of writers who represent Stoic views. Since Stoics focused on the material world, Paul's reference to the resurrection is mocked by his audience. Similar Stoic thought, perhaps mediated by Jewish wisdom traditions, is used in Romans 1.18–32. But, where in Acts 17 Paul is represented as using Stoicism positively, excusing former ignorance, in Romans he uses it to indict, as Wisdom 13 does: God had granted knowledge of himself in creation, but that knowledge was rejected and humanity was therefore given over to immorality. The Stoic interpretation of Wisdom as the agent of creation may also have influenced the view of the Logos in John 1.1–2. Paul further uses Stoic lists, many of which may have come to him by way of Hellenistic Judaism, such as lists of virtues and vices and of hardships. Paul christianizes such lists, as he does the Stoic view of self-sufficiency. In Philippians 4.11–13, he claims to be content *(autarkēs)*, which does not mean that he is impassive or had attained self-sufficiency on his own; on the contrary, he is able to experience all things fully because God empowers him. The Stoic lists of social responsibilities are similarly christianized. God's initiative and the eschatological perspective also place the Stoic-sounding language of 2 Peter 1.3–4 in a different Christian perspective. *Abraham J. Malherbe*

**SUSANNA.** A devout and beautiful Jewish woman, whose name means "lily." She was falsely accused of adultery, but saved from sentence of death by the young Daniel, who presented in court an unorthodox but clever defense; and she is the heroine of the small book of the Apocrypha that goes by her name.

In Theodotion's edition of the Greek and in several ancient versions based upon it, Susanna appears as a prefix to chap. 1 of the book of *Daniel, but in the older Greek Septuagint and the Latin Vulgate it is placed in an appendix after chap. 12 along with the story of Bel and the Dragon. It seems almost certain that it was originally an independent work, since neither the style and setting of the story nor the character of Daniel, its hero, seem to harmonize with the rest of the book. Other independent stories about Daniel were current in antiquity, as is evidenced by the discovery of fragments of Daniel legends among the Dead Sea Scrolls.

The story is interesting and well told. Susanna, the wife of Joakim, a wealthy and highly respected Jew who lived in Babylonia during the exile, used to walk every afternoon in the garden of her house, and attracted the lecherous interest of two *elders of the community who had been appointed judges and were frequent visitors to Joakim's home. Separately bent on seducing her, they met by chance in the hiding place where each had her under observation, and concocted a plot against her virtue. One day when she was bathing in the garden and the doors to the house had been shut by her two maids, the elders rushed out of their place of concealment and demanded that she lie with them; otherwise they would publicly accuse her of committing adultery with a young man, and would declare that they had witnessed the act. Susanna, true to her principles, refused their request and said she was willing to accept the consequences. When the inevitable trial began, they carried out their threat and, as a result, she was condemned to die. But at the critical moment God inspired the youthful Daniel to protest against the sentence and to undertake to cross-examine the two elders separately. In an anticipation of the technique of the classic detective story, he caught them in a clear contradiction about the kind of tree under which the alleged crime was committed, with the result that Susanna was acquitted and the accusers suffered the fate they had intended for her (cf. the similar ironic reversal in *Esther).

The tale is commonly accepted as fiction, but there has been no general agreement on its purpose. Some scholars have thought the story a kind of midrash dealing with the fate of the two false prophets, Ahab and Zedekiah, who were the objects of a curse by Jeremiah, and were accused by him, incidentally, of adulterous conduct. Others regard it as a partisan polemic calling for an improvement in the commonly accepted procedures of the rabbinic courts. The prevailing view, however, sees it as simply a popular tale, probably secular, and perhaps even non-Jewish in origin, which has been provided with edifying religious motifs and adapted for Jewish readers. Some scholars who assert that specific elements in the story have been taken from traditional folklore, notably the theme of the "wise child"—the youth who displays more insight than his elders and is able to correct some flagrant injustice—but the evidence is vague and indecisive.

Until comparatively recent times, it was the common view that the original language was Greek; this seems especially persuasive because of the puns on the names of the two trees in vv. 54–55 and 58–59, which make sense only in Greek. Recently, however, the book has increasingly been thought a translation from an original Semitic text, probably Hebrew but possibly Aramaic, though there is no supporting external evidence. The book does, however, contain a number of apparent Hebraisms, and the social ambience suggests a Palestinian origin. The puns could have been introduced by the Greek translator. The date could be as early as the Persian period and certainly no later than ca. 100 BCE, when the Septuagint translation was completed. The story of Susanna was a popular subject of later Christian art and literature, and poetic versions of the tale are known in several European languages. *Robert C. Dentan*

**SYNAGOGUE.** The emergence of the synagogue constituted a revolutionary development in the history of Judaism. The synagogue represented not only a wholly new concept of religious observance but also a new form of communal institution. With the synagogue the nature of official worship shifted dramatically, with prayer, study, and exhortation replacing sacrifice as the way to serve God. Officiating on behalf of the community was no longer confined to a small coterie of *priests but was open to all. Ceremonies were conducted in full view of the participants, with the masses of people no longer being relegated to outer courtyards, as was the case in the Jerusalem *Temple. Moreover, the synagogue was a universal institution and not confined to any one specific locale.

Despite its importance in Jewish history, the origins of the synagogue and its early development are shrouded in mystery. Only during and after the first century CE does literary and archaeological evidence appear for Palestine. As for the Roman Diaspora, references before then are practically nonexistent (and what does exist refers to the Diaspora). Synagogue inscriptions from third- and second-century BCE Egypt have been preserved, as have remains of a Delos synagogue building dating from the first century BCE.

Owing to the paucity of sources, opinions have varied widely as to when, where, and why the synagogue developed. Theories have ranged from the late First Temple period (eighth-seventh century BCE), through the exilic (sixth century) and postexilic (fifth century) eras, and down to the late Persian (fourth century) and Hellenistic times (third or second century). Most scholars have assumed a midway position, one that posits the emergence of the synagogue closely following the destruction of the First Temple in 587/586 BCE, either during the Babylonian exile or soon after, when the Jews returned to Judea during the era of restoration.

Over the centuries the synagogue became a fully developed communal institution and apparently the central one in most communities. It served as a place for study, sacred meals, court proceedings, depositing communal funds, and political and social meetings, as a hostel, and as a residence for certain synagogue officials. Of central importance, of course, were the religious services. At first these consisted primarily of the Torah-reading ceremony and its accompanying activities: translation of the Torah into the vernacular, be it Aramaic (Targums) or Greek, the *haftarah* or a selected reading from the prophets, and a sermon. The sources from the Second Temple period—Josephus, Philo, rabbinic writings, and the Theodotus inscription—point to this centrality. The existence of regular communal prayers at this time is unclear. While prayer appears to have been an integral part of the religious service in the *diaspora, its presence in Palestinian synagogue settings before 70 CE is unattested. Only after this date are we on firm ground in assuming the importance and centrality of public prayer in all synagogue settings.

These two components of the religious service—Torah reading and prayer—were characterized in antiquity by their fluidity no less than their uniformity. While Torah reading was accepted as normative on Sabbaths and holidays and later on Mondays and Thursdays as well, the division into weekly portions varied considerably. In Palestine the Torah was read over a three- or three-and-a-half-year period with a plethora of local traditions on the precise divisions of the weekly portions. Moreover, the practice in Babylonian communities living in late Roman and Byzantine Palestine only added to this diversity: They concluded the Torah reading in one year. How widespread the custom was of translating the Torah portion into the vernacular is unknown, but the use of Greek in addition to Aramaic cannot be denied. The place of the sermon in the synagogue service was likewise diverse. The content, of course, might have varied considerably from one of an expository nature to one of ethical, political, halakhic, or even eschatological dimensions. When sermons were delivered on the Sabbath (Friday evening, Saturday morning, or Saturday afternoon), or when during the service (before or after the Torah reading), might differ widely from one congregation to another.

The diversity is found also with regard to prayer. Undoubtedly by the post-70 era the two main foci of the prayer service had crystallized. The Shema prayer with its accompanying paragraphs had been adopted from Temple practice and was now supplemented by three blessings, each focusing on a central theme, respectively—creation, revelation, and redemption. Together this unit provided the central ideational portion of the prayer experience and was recited in the synagogue twice daily, during the morning and evening services. The second focus of the prayer service was the Shemoneh Esreh (literally, "eighteen" blessings, although a nineteenth was added some time in late antiquity) or the Amidah (standing prayer). When precisely this prayer came into usage is unknown, but by the second century CE it held a central position. Recited three times daily, no special prayer service, be it on the Sabbath, Holiday, or High Holiday, was complete without it. The Amidah consisted of three parts: the first three benedictions were in praise of God, the last three were expressions of thanks, while the middle section changed each day. On a weekday, twelve (later thirteen) petionary blessings were recited; on Sabbaths and holidays this section expressed the unique message of that particular day. During the early centuries CE prayers were added to the morning service, such as prayers of supplication, morning blessings, psalms of praise, and others.

During the Byzantine period, the recitation of liturgical poems—*pîyyûṭîm*—was added to the service, particularly those for the Sabbath and holidays. When and from where the *pîyyûṭ* developed has been a subject of scholarly debate. Some claim it evolved from earlier midrashim, prayers, or songs recited in the Temple and synagogue, others see it as the adoption and adaptation of liturgical poems recited in Byzantine churches, and still others as a protest against organized, fixed prayers. Whatever the explanation, the *pîyyûṭ* made its appearance in fourth- and fifth-century Palestine, and today we know of at least twenty poets who functioned in the pre-Muslim era. These *pîyyûṭîm* were recited during the morning service, either in addition to or in place of the fixed liturgy.

Archaeological remains of the ancient synagogue abound. In Palestine alone traces of over a hundred structures have been identified, and in the Diaspora some fifteen. The latter stretch from Dura Europos on the Euphrates River in the east, to Tunisia on the North African coast in the west. The overwhelming majority of synagogue remains in Palestine are located in the *Galilee and Golan regions; others are to be found in Beth-shean, coastal areas, and Judea. Architecturally, these synagogues can be divided into three types. The Galilean type, characterized by a monumental and richly decorated facade, was oriented towards Jerusalem, often with three entrances. Fine ashlar masonry of either limestone or basalt was characteristic of these buildings, and their rectangular interiors were simple, with two or three colonnades dividing the hall into a central nave with two or three aisles. Entablatures, pilasters, and friezes typical of Roman art of late antiquity decorated the buildings, along with molded stucco and painted plaster. With but few exceptions, no permanent shrines for the Torah scrolls have been found.

The second type of synagogue modelled itself after the basilical plan used extensively in Byzantine churches, and was modest on the exterior, reserving its splendor for the interior. In contrast to the Galilean type with its splendid entrance on the facade facing Jerusalem, the entrance in the basilica type shifted to the wall opposite the direction of prayer. A round or square apse was set in the wall facing Jerusalem in which the Torah ark rested on a raised platform *(bîmâ).* Only two rows of columns lined the elongated character of the prayer hall. Most notable in the basilica type of synagogue was its richly decorated mosaic floor, often in clear imitation of regnant Byzantine patterns and not infrequently with unique Jewish symbols, such as a menorah, Torah ark, lulav, ethrog, and shofar. Such symbols were practically nonexistent in buildings of the Galilean type. Finally, a third type of building which appears in but a few locales of Palestine and the Diaspora is the broadhouse synagogue. The uniqueness of these buildings is that their focus of worship, either an apse, *bîmâ,* or shrine—which is located along the long wall of the synagogue. These buildings share features common to the other types in most other respects.

Aside from the Jewish symbols mentioned above, Jewish figural art is represented in only a few synagogues: the Aqedah at Beth Alpha, *Noah at Gerasa, *David at Gaza, and *Daniel at Na$^{c}$aran and Susiya. Of an entirely different order is the third-century CE synagogue of Dura Europos, whose walls are covered from floor to ceiling with decorated panels. These panels depict scenes from the Bible, using Greek and Persian artistic motifs and incorporating a significant amount of *midrash* (rabbinic or otherwise) in their interpretations and representations. One of the most striking examples of synagogue art, at Hammath Tiberias and elsewhere, represents Helios, the zodiac signs, and the four seasons. Interpretations of these motifs vary considerably. The first reaction was to interpret them as the gift of the emperor or as an expression of some fringe group in Judaism. With the discovery, however, of such pavements all over Israel, it became clear that this was a popular and accepted form of artistic expression. Among the interpretations proposed of the zodiac motif are: it was simply a decorative motif; it reflects the importance of the Jewish calendar; it represents the power of God in creating the world each day; it stands for the Divine himself; it reflects belief in *angels, especially Helios, who was well known within certain Jewish circles of the period. Of these several explanations, none has won general acceptance.

Owing to the centrality of the synagogue as the primary Jewish communal institution and to the extensive remains that have survived, the study of this institution is of paramount importance for those wishing to gain as complete a picture of ancient Judaism as possible. Patterns of Jewish settlements, the diversity of religious practices, the influence of surrounding cultures, Jewish artistic expression, Jewish prosography, titles and professions among synagogue donors are areas well attested in synagogue remains. *Lee Levine*

**SYRIA.** Syria is a geographical area bounded by the *Euphrates River on the east, Palestine on the south, and the Mediterranean Sea on the west. It has been assumed that the name Syria derived from Tyre, which was the port of entry for Romans, Greeks, and others who explored or expanded eastward.

Syria's major centers were *Damascus, *Antioch on the Orontes, and the region of the two rivers, the Tigris and the Euphrates.

In the Hebrew Bible, *David extends his kingdom up to Damascus in Syria. Syria, generally called *Aram, is clearly a foreign country, but close enough to go in and out of, know quite a lot about, and seriously compete with, both religiously and economically. Syrian gods are criticized, and there are wars with numerous Syrian kings and cities.

The region was captured by *Tiglath-pileser III in the eighth century BCE, conquered by *Alexander the Great, and later became a center for the Seleucid dynasty that ultimately provoked the Maccabean revolt in Palestine in 165 BCE. Roman writers could frequently lump Palestine and Syria together without distinction under the name Coele-Syria. Pompey and leaders after him, including *Herod the Great, used Damascus as a center for military and bureaucratic expansion. It was from Damascus that Pompey launched his pacification of Palestine in 66 BCE in the wake of the Hasmonean civil war. Both cities were among the leading cultural, religious, and economic centers of the entire Roman empire.

Syria is rarely mentioned by name in the New Testament. On several occasions, Syria is referred to as proof that Jesus's fame is spreading; in Acts, Syria is mentioned in the context of the spread of Christianity.

There were numerous and sizable Jewish communities in Syria. The Jews of Antioch are singled out by Josephus as a vibrant community who were constantly attracting gentiles to their religious ceremonies. In the fourth century CE, the sermons delivered by John Chrysostom against the Jews make it clear that the Jewish community in Antioch was still large, popular, and a threat to Christians like Chrysostom.

Similarly Syria and its larger cities became centers for early Christianity. The early second-century writer Ignatius of Antioch emerged as an important figure in the early church, as did Chrysostom, and many early Christian texts, including some of the Gospels, have been associated with Syria.

Syria in history and today remains an intriguing if enigmatic country and culture, which represents and joins city and village, east and west, Jew, Christian, and Muslim. It has played a pivotal role in the development and definition of Jewish and Christian belief and identity.

*J. Andrew Overman*

# T

**TAMMUZ.** Tammuz corresponds to the *Sumerian deity Dumuzi, who figures prominently in myths, sacred marriage texts, and laments. Largely a tragic figure, he is the lover of the goddess Inanna who consigned him to the netherworld. The presence of two kings named Dumuzi in the Sumerian King List, one before the flood and one after, suggests that there may have been a historical person with that name.

Much of the early scholarly attention concerning Tammuz focused on James G. Frazier's interpretation *(The Golden Bough),* in which Tammuz was connected to the motif of the dying god. In this understanding, now largely abandoned, the death and resurrection of the god corresponds to the seasonal cycle with its alternation of decay and revival of plant life.

In the single biblical occurrence of Tammuz, the prophet sees women at the Temple court weeping for Tammuz. The ample first-millennium BCE cuneiform documentation pertaining to mourning rites for Dumuzi provides a suitable backdrop for the passage in Ezekiel.

In Judaism, the fourth month of the year (June/July) is called Tammuz.

*James H. Platt*

**TAX COLLECTORS.** *See* Publicans.

**TEMPLE.** A building or place symbolizing the presence of a deity or deities, intended for the purpose of worship. In the Bible, "temple" usually refers to the Temple erected by *Solomon or the Temple of *Zerubbabel that was enlarged and refurbished by *Herod.

**Terminology.** Hebrew *hêkāl* comes from Akkadian *ekallu,* which in turn is derived from *Sumerian *É.GAL,* "great house." The term is generic, and can apply to the house of a god (a temple) or to the house of a king (a palace). It is used of Ahab's palace and that of the king of Babylon. As Israel's king, Yahweh dwelt in a palace, seated on a throne. The word is also used of the house of Yahweh at Shiloh; of Solomon's Temple; of the Second Temple, built by Zerubbabel; of the Temple of Ezekiel's vision; and of God's heavenly dwelling place.

Hebrew *bayit,* "house," by itself, is used very often of the Temple, or in combination, "house of God," and especially "house of Yahweh." This word was also used of the tent of worship, of a local shrine, and of temples of other gods. The term "house," referring to the Temple at Jerusalem, is a broader term, including the nave (strictly speaking, the *hêkāl*) and the inner sanctuary (the holy of holies). The Temple mount is known as "the mountain of the Lord's house" or even "the mountain of the house."

Greek *hieron,* "sanctuary, temple," in the New Testament is used once of the temple of Artemis, but otherwise of the Temple at Jerusalem. The term includes the whole Temple complex. Unfortunately, both this and the next term *(naos)* are translated "temple," which leads to confusion. Jesus, who was not a priest, could not enter the "temple" *(naos),* nor could the *money changers, nor could Paul. The word used in each instance is *hieron,* which might be more accurately translated "temple mount."

Greek *naos,* "temple," is used in the New Testament of Herod's Temple, that is, the sanctuary itself and not the entire Temple area, and of the heavenly sanctuary (but there is no temple in the New Jerusalem, for the Lord God himself is the temple). The word is also used of sanctuaries of other gods (translated "shrines"; *hieron*). Used figuratively, *naos* refers to the human body and to the church.

Greek *oikos,* "house" (referring to the Temple), except for Luke 11.51 and Hebrews 10.21, occurs only in quotations in the New Testament of passages in the Hebrew Bible where *bayit* is used.

**Solomon's Temple.** The tabernacle had served as the center of worship from the time of *Moses to *David. David wanted to build a more permanent structure, but the Lord forbade it. David set about collecting materials and making plans for the building to be built by his son, Solomon.

The Temple was located on the eastern hill, north of the city of David, where the Dome of the Rock is located today. (*See* Jerusalem.) At that time the Temple mount was considerably smaller, Solomon having enlarged it somewhat and Herod having enlarged it still more to the present size of the platform known as Haram esh-Sharif. This is "the threshing floor of Araunah the Jebusite" (2 Sam. 24.18), "Mount Moriah" (2 Chron. 3.1), and probably the *Zion of the Psalms and the prophets although the term belonged to the city of David.

The general plan of the Temple was similar to that given for the tabernacle: rectangular, with a porch or vestibule (*ʾûlām,*) facing east, a nave *(hêkāl),* and an inner sanctuary (*dĕbîr*) or holy of holies. The dimensions were double those of the tabernacle: 60 cubits by 20 (1 cubit = 19.7 in [0.5 m]), but triple its height (30 cubits). The building was of hewn stone, dressed at the quarry. The porch was 10 cubits deep and 120 cubits high—a numeral that may have suffered textual corruption. Two columns, Jachin and Boaz, made of hollow bronze, 35 or 40 cubits high, stood at each side of the entrance. The inner walls of the *hêkāl* were lined with cedar brought from *Lebanon, and the entire structure was lined with gold. The holy of holies was overlaid with "pure" gold. The skilled work was done by Tyrian artisans supplied by King Hiram and under the supervision of a person also named Hiram or Huram-Abi.

The holiest place contained the ark of the covenant and two winged figures (*cherubim) of olive wood overlaid with gold that stretched from wall to wall. Doors of olive wood, covered with gold, separated the holy of holies from the nave, and similar doors separated the nave from the porch. The nave contained the golden altar (to distinguish it from the bronze altar in the courtyard) made of cedar or the "altar of incense," which stood before the holy of holies; the golden table for the bread of the Presence ("showbread"); the golden lampstands and other items.

The building was surrounded by two courts, the inner one constructed of three courses of stone and one of cedar beams (also called the court of the priests), and the great court, which probably also enclosed the royal buildings. The size of the inner court is not given, but if it was double the size of the court of the tabernacle, it would have been 200 by 100 cubits. The inner court contained the bronze altar where sacrifices were offered, the ten bronze basins on ten stands, five on each side of the house, and the great sea (the molten or bronze sea) on the southeast corner of the house. The bronze work was cast in the Jordan valley, the most impressive being the great sea, 10 cubits in diameter and 5 cubits high, with a capacity of 2,000 baths (approximately 10,000 gal [40,000 liters]). The water was used for supplying the lavers for washing the parts of the sacrificial victims and for the priests' ablutions.

The First Temple, having been plundered several times, was finally destroyed by *Nebuchadrezzar in 587/586 BCE.

**Ezekiel's Temple.** The Temple in Ezekiel 40–48 is presented as a vision, and so the details may be assumed to be symbolic rather than material. The plan in general follows closely that of Solomon's Temple, although it is markedly symmetrical. Some of the description is more detailed than that given in Kings or Chronicles, and such details as the plan and dimensions of the gates have been indirectly confirmed by archaeological discoveries at *Gezer, *Hazor, and *Megiddo.

**Zerubbabel's Temple.** When the Jews returned from exile (538 BCE) there was an effort to rebuild the Temple. The work was begun but languished until 520, when as a result of the encouragement of *Haggai and *Zechariah, it was resumed and the Temple was finished on the third day of Adar in the sixth year of *Darius (12 March 515). It was comparable in size to Solomon's Temple and probably also in its ground plan, with the holy of holies and the sanctuary with the golden altar, table lampstand, and other furnishings. It was surrounded by an inner court with the altar of burnt offering and an outer court. According to Josephus, reporting Hecateus, the outer court was approximately 500 by 150 ft (150 by 45 m), and the altar of unhewn stones was 20 cubits square and 10 cubits in height. According to the Talmud, five things were missing from the Second Temple: the ark, the sacred fire, the *shekinah,* the holy spirit, and the Urim and Thummim.

**Herod's Temple.** Herod did not tear down the Second Temple—that would surely have instigated a revolt, as Herod recognized. He rebuilt and refurbished it by preparing materials for parts, using priests as carpenters and masons in the sacred areas, and doing the work by sections. The building was made new without ever destroying the old and without interrupting the sacred offerings and sacrifices. Begun in Herod's twentieth year (20 BCE), it was finished in a year and a half.

Work on the Temple platform may have begun in Herod's fifteenth year, and it continued until ca. 64 CE. The Kidron valley was partially filled, shifting its bed eastward; likewise the central (Tyropoeon) valley was partially filled, shifting it several hundred feet to the west. Using huge ashlars ("Herodian" stones, ca. 40 in [1 m] high, 3 to 10 ft [1–3 m] long [one measures 39 ft (12 m) in length!], and 13 ft [4 m] wide), the western, southern, and eastern walls were built, and the Temple mount was extended to a width of 915 ft (280 m) across the southern end, 1, 017 ft (310 m) across the northern, and approximately 1,500 ft (450 m) north to south. At the southeastern corner, the wall rose 158 ft (48 m) above the Kidron valley. A stoa or portico was built along all four sides, with marble columns 25 cubits high, and ceiled with cedar panels; the royal stoa at the south had four rows of columns, the others had double rows of columns. The stoa along the eastern side was attributed by Josephus to Solomon.

The Temple itself was surrounded by a wall or balustrade, 3 cubits high, separating the holy place from the court of the gentiles. It was 322 cubits east to west by 135 cubits north to south, raised by 14 and 5 steps (all steps were 1/2 cubit). The holy place was not in the center of the Temple mount, but more to the north and west. On the surrounding wall were warnings, some in Greek, others in Latin, forbidding the entry of any gentile under penalty of death; two of these have been found. Ten cubits inside the balustrade a wall of 25 cubits high surrounded the sacred area, with seven gates: three each on the north and south sides, one on the east.

Within this holy place, there were increasingly sacred areas: the court of the women at the east, the court of the Israelites (i.e., males only), the court of the priests, then the Temple *(naos).* This area was separated from the Women's Court, being 15 steps higher, and could be entered through the Nicanor Gate. The Temple was still higher by another 12 steps; it consisted of the porch (100 by 100 cubits, 11 cubits wide), the nave (40 by 20 cubits) containing the table of the Presence, the lampstand or menorah (taken to Rome by Titus and portrayed on the Arch of Titus), and the altar of incense, and behind that the holy of holies (20 by 20 cubits), which was empty except for a sacred stone. Built into the wall around the Temple were rooms or chambers, increasing the size of the Temple by 70 to 100 cubits. To the east and south of the Temple was the altar, 32 cubits square, and north of the altar the place of slaughtering.

Only the priests could enter the Temple, and only the high priest could enter the holy of holies, and that only on the Day of Atonement. The priests were divided into twenty-four "courses," each course serving twice a year for a week. A veil of Babylonian tapestry hung in the opening to the nave; a second veil separated the nave from the holy of holies. It would seem that it was the outer veil that was torn at the time of the death of Jesus, since the inner veil would not be seen by bystanders.

There were eight gates leading into the Temple mount: one on the north, four on the west, two on the south, and one on the east; the Mishnah says five, naming only one on the west. Along the western wall was the deep central valley, with a paved walk that continued around the southern end of the Temple. A great staircase led up to the triple Huldah gate, and next to the stairs was a structure containing a large number of immersion pools for ceremonial cleansing (Hebr. *miqwāʾôt*). The worshiper, after his or her purification, entered the right of the two double gates and passed through a tunnel leading upward into the Temple area. A second entrance could be made by a large staircase that led to the royal stoa ("Robinson's Arch" marks this entrance), but no purification was available here. Leading from the western hill to the Temple mount was a bridge ("Wilson's Arch" marks this). Details of the other entrances are not clear; they were possibly located where Barclay's and Warren's Gates are now. The Tadi Gate was in the northern wall; possibly the sacrificial animals were brought in by this entrance, since it was near the Sheep Pool and Market. The Susa gate in the eastern wall was used only by the high priest and priests in connection with the ceremony of burning the red cow at a location on the Mount of Olives from which the high priest could look directly into the entrance of the sanctuary.

**Destruction of the Temple.** There is a full account of the capture of Jerusalem in *War* 5–6, according to which Titus commissioned Josephus to urge the Jews to surrender in order to spare the Temple, but to no avail. The Antonia was razed to the ground in August 70 CE, and the continual sacrifice ceased to be offered. Josephus made a second appeal. Titus then decided to destroy the Temple. This occurred on the tenth day of the fifth month (Ab; according to Jewish tradition, the ninth of Ab), the same day on which the First Temple had been burned by the king of Babylon. Josephus portrays the Romans as trying to extinguish the fire that had been started by the insurgents. Widespread plundering, murder, and finally the burning of all structures on the Temple mount ended the history of the Temple.

*William Sanford LaSor*

**TETRARCH.** A title originating in Greece, the only place where its literal meaning of "ruler of a fourth (part)" applied, and used throughout the Near East in the Hellenistic and Roman periods for subordinate rulers. In the *Roman empire a tetrarch was of lower rank than an ethnarch ("ruler of a people"), who in turn was lower than a king. According to Josephus, Herod the Great was first appointed tetrarch over Judea in 42 BCE by Mark Antony and shortly thereafter named king. On Herod's death, his sons Philip and Antipas were named tetrarchs over *Galilee and Perea, and Gaulanitis (the modern Golan), respectively, while Archelaus was promised that his rank of ethnarch over Judea would be elevated to king if he proved worthy.

Both the New Testament and other ancient sources use these titles inconsistently; for example, Herod Antipas is called tetrarch in Matthew 14.1 but king in 14.9 and in the parallels in Mark 6. The NRSV uses "ethnarch" in 1 Maccabees but "governor" for the same term in 2 Corinthians 11.32, and it always translates "tetrarch" by the generic "ruler."

*Michael D. Coogan*

**THESSALONICA.** A coastal city (Thessaloníki) in eastern Macedonia in Greece, home to the *Christian community to which the two letters of *Paul to the Thessalonians are addressed.

Thessalonica was one of the towns in Macedonia that was visited by Paul, *Silas, and *Timothy during the second of the missionary tours described by Luke in Acts 16–18. It was in fact the capital of the Roman province of Macedon, an important commercial center situated on the major highway, the Via Egnatia. Not surprisingly, its population included Jews. Paul and his companions spent a brief time here after leaving Philippi, but sufficiently long to gain a number of converts from Jewish and Greek attenders at the *synagogue and so to establish a church. According to Luke, Jewish opposition forced the missionaries to leave precipitately. They moved into Achaia and worked briefly at *Athens and then for a longer period at *Corinth. It was during this period that Timothy paid the visit mentioned in 1 Thessalonians 3.1–6, and that Paul wrote the first letter, doubtless from Corinth.

The history of the church between its foundation and the composition of the letter is known only from allusions in the letter. The picture that emerges is of a church free from groups opposed to Paul, and developing in faith and love. Certainly, Paul was worried about whether the church could stand up to attacks from outside, but this concern arose more from the recent foundation of the congregation than because of any inherent defects.

The major point where Paul felt the need to give instructions was the future advent (or parousia) of the Lord Jesus. It is unlikely that there were any false teachings; it appears rather that the Thessalonian Christians had not fully understood Paul's teaching about the parousia and the resurrection of the dead. The second coming of the Lord played a prominent part in Paul's preaching, for he refers to it with remarkable frequency in the letter. Otherwise, the letter reflects the typical characteristics of Paul's thought, including the distinctive use of the phrase "in Christ" to characterize the nature of the Christian life. There is no doubt that Paul was the author of this letter.

The second letter raises problems to which there are no generally agreed answers. Its language and content are sufficiently similar to those of 1 Thessalonians to indicate that, if authentic, it was probably written not long after the first letter. Yet it lacks concrete references to the situation of the readers or of the writer. From chap. 1, it appears that attack from outside must have worsened. The pungency of Paul's language may also suggest that he himself was the object of particular attack from people outside the church.

The situation behind chap. 2 is difficult to reconstruct. There must have been a group in the church who believed that they were living in the very last days. They appear to have been encouraged in this view by some statement that was alleged to have come from Paul himself. Paul, however, stopped short of affirming that the end had actually arrived, and he referred to other events that must happen before the return of the Lord.

In the final part of the letter we find evidence that some members of the church were living in idleness at others' expense. Although no explicit connection is made, it is hard not to believe that the apocalyptic excitement reflected in chap. 2 contributed to this situation. It called forth strong censure from Paul, who firmly believed that Christians should work for their living. Apparently, discipline in the church consisted of exclusion from the privileges of fellowship.

It is argued that 2 Thessalonians is a later composition by another writer who wished to use Paul's name to correct his teaching or false inferences from it, perhaps even to claim that this letter alone was authentic and that 1 Thessalonians was to be rejected. Although it must be granted that there are some oddities in the language, structure, and thought of the letter, the difficulties in considering it pseudonymous are greater.

*I. Howard Marshall*

**THOMAS.** An *apostle, named in all lists of the *twelve, but a major character only in the gospel of John. Mentioned in John 11.16 and 14.5, Thomas is prominent in John 20.24–29, where his insistence on physical proofs for Jesus's resurrection has led to the phrase "doubting Thomas." Several apocryphal works are ascribed to or are about Thomas, including the gnostic gospel of Thomas and the Acts of Thomas. In the latter, his name, which means "twin" in Aramaic, is the basis for his identification as Jesus's twin brother. He is also said to have preached the gospel as far east as India. *Michael D. Coogan*

**THREE YOUNG MEN.** *See* Azariah (The Three Young Men).

**TIGLATH-PILESER III.** Tukulti-apil-Esharra, King of *Assyria 745–727

BCE, sometimes known by the hypocoristic Pul or Pulu. Having risen to power after a revolt against Ashur-nirari V (755–745 BCE), Tiglath-pileser reversed decades of Assyrian political decline and ousted Urartu as the principal power in Western Asia. He laid the foundations for the most expansive phase of the Neo-Assyrian empire by a prolonged series of annual campaigns, by reorganizing and geographically extending the Assyrian provincial system, and by massive deportations of troublesome subject populations.

After early campaigns against Arameans in *Babylonia and against western Iran (745–744 BCE), Tiglath-pileser turned his attention to the more crucial northern and western fronts. He defeated Urartu in 743 and 735 BCE and crushed its Syrian allies, particularly Arpad (742–740 BCE). He invaded Syria and Palestine in 738 and 734 BCE, reaching almost to the border of Egypt and receiving the submission of Zabibe, queen of Arabia. Menahem of Israel paid tribute to Tiglath-pileser, who withdrew from his kingdom. When Pekah had succeeded to the throne, Tiglath-pileser captured part of the northern section of Israel and later deported some of the population to Assyria. On behalf of Ahaz of Judah, who had sent him munificent gifts, Tiglath-pileser campaigned against *Damascus and Israel. After Tiglath-pileser had captured Damascus, Ahaz met him there; Ahaz was subsequently accused of changing cult paraphernalia because of the Assyrian king.

Tiglath-pileser campaigned in Babylonia in 731 and 729 BCE and then himself became king of Babylonia in 728. After his death in 727 BCE, he was succeeded by his son, *Shalmaneser V.

*John A. Brinkman*

**TIMOTHY.** An important associate of *Paul. Born in Asia Minor of a Jewish mother and a *Gentile father, he became Paul's companion and, according to Acts, accompanied him on his first journey to Greece and later served as his emissary to Christian communities there, including *Corinth. Paul calls Timothy his "brother and co-worker" (1 Thess. 3.2; 2 Cor 1.1; Rom. 16.21).

Timothy is the addressee of the two letters to Timothy, which, along with the letter to *Titus, are called the pastoral epistles. The three are closely related in both content and form and offer advice about the exercise of the pastoral office in the care and oversight of congregations.

The goal of the Pastoral Letters is to provide instructions on how the household of God should live in Paul's spirit during the post-Pauline era, when the expectation of the Lord's imminent coming has receded and teachers are propounding false doctrine in the apostle's name. In this situation the author writes to two of Paul's most trusted collaborators with a message that is actually addressed to an entire church, be it a long-standing gentile church like that of *Ephesus addressed in 1 Timothy or a new Jewish Christian church like that of Crete addressed in Titus. The instructions that are to govern the churches addressed in 1 Timothy and Titus have Paul's apostolic authority behind them. Paul's last will and testament in 2 Timothy requires that the entire church, but especially its leaders, imitate Paul's example (especially his willingness to suffer for the faith), follow his instructions, hold on faithfully to the deposit of faith, and be guided by his predictions. In doing so, they will be able to combat false teaching.

The authorship of these letters is contested. While the Pastoral Letters have a noticeable Pauline character, there are five major areas in which they differ from the indisputably genuine Pauline letters. First, the vocabulary and style vary greatly from those of the letters to the Romans and Corinthians and are closer to those of the apostolic fathers such as Polycarp. Second, the theological concepts and the stress on public respectability differ markedly from emphases in the undisputed Pauline letters. Third, church order does not correspond to that found in the genuine Pauline letters but is more like that in evidence toward the end of the first century CE. Fourth, the author relies much more heavily on traditions, both creedal and hortatory, than the Paul of the authentic letters; unlike Paul in Galatians, for example, he rarely argues theologically with opponents but merely upbraids them. Finally, the Pastoral Letters do not fit into the career of Paul as detailed in Acts and Romans.

Theories that attempt to account for these differences are as follows. First, accepting the Pastoral Letters as fully authentic, it is felt that Paul was indeed freed from his first imprisonment and returned to the East for further missionary work. 1 Timothy and Titus reflect this mission. Arrested again, Paul was imprisoned, tried, and executed in Rome. 2 Timothy issues from the time of this second imprisonment. Paul's need to establish church order in communities and to counteract false teachers accounts for the different vocabulary of the Pastoral Letters. These last letters date to ca. 65 CE, and because they stem from an aged Paul, they lack the theological acumen of a vibrant and young Paul.

Another theory also presupposes further missionary work by Paul in the East, but accounts for the high incidence of uncharacteristic Pauline elements in the Pastoral Letters by postulating that Paul employed a secretary to whom he gave greater responsibility in creating these letters ca. 65 CE.

A third theory holds that the Pastoral Letters contain so many un-Pauline words and concepts because they were written by a later author, who, ca. 85 CE, desired to apply the teaching of Paul to new situations in the Pauline missionary territory. This author worked into his letters fragments of genuine Pauline letters, and this accounts for the personal notes, which a later author presumably would not have invented.

A fourth theory is more radical and maintains that the letters are completely pseudonymous and are in this regard like the contemporary pseudonymous Socratic letters, which are written under Socrates's name and apply his teaching to a later time. In writing three letters, the author was influenced by the trend in evidence in Cicero, Seneca, and Pliny of publishing a collection of letters. Writing ca. 100 CE, the author uses personal notes to add verisimilitude to the letters and to present Paul as an example to be imitated. Thus, the personal note of 2 Timothy 4.13, which depicts the imprisoned Paul asking that the cloak he left behind in Troas be brought to him, adds local color to the letter and also shows how Paul embodies his teaching of contentment with the basic necessities of life. The view adopted here is a modification of this fourth position and dates the Pastoral Letters ca. 85 CE.

*Michael D. Coogan*
*Robert J. Karris, O.F.M.*

**TITUS.** An important associate of *Paul. He accompanied Paul on his second journey to *Jerusalem, served as his emissary to *Corinth, and was designated by him to oversee the collection of contributions for the church in Jerusalem. Paul refers to Titus as his "partner and co-worker" (2 Cor. 8.23). Although Titus was a *Gentile, he was not required to be circumcised, despite the opinions of some Jewish Christian leaders. Titus thus symbolizes the growing separation of Christianity from Judaism, as Gentile Christians like Titus were not bound to observe many aspects of Jewish Law.

Titus is the addressee of the letter to Titus, one of the Pastoral Letters; for further discussion, *see* Timothy.

*Michael D. Coogan*

**TOBIT.** The book of Tobit, regarded by Jews and Protestants as apocryphal and by Roman Catholics and some Orthodox churches as deuterocanonical, is named after its alleged author, Tobit, a generous and God-fearing Jew whose blindness and poverty in *Nineveh are the direct result of his performing one of his most characteristic good deeds, namely, burying an executed compatriot. But thanks to the courageous efforts of his devoted son, Tobias (who unknown to both of them was assisted by the angel *Raphael masquerading as Azariah), Tobit ultimately recovers his sight and fortune and also gains a virtuous daughter-in-law, Sarah, a Median relative from whom Tobias has exorcised Asmodeus, the demon who had claimed the lives of each of her seven previous husbands on their wedding night. Shortly before his death as a very old man, Tobit has Tobias and his large family move from Nineveh to Ecbatana, where Tobias lives to a very rich old age.

Although the book has all the outer trappings of a historical account, including mention of well-known historical personages (e.g., *Shalmaneser V and *Sennacherib) and places (e.g., *Nineveh, Ecbatana, and Rages), the narrative is best understood as a novella or, more specifically, a *diaspora romance, centering on a successful quest. The story is intended to edify and to inspire faith in God and human effort; for without Tobias's own devotion and courage, neither his father nor his wife would have been delivered, the help of the angel Raphael notwithstanding.

In creating this charming pastiche about everyday Jewish "saints" in the Dispersion, the ancient narrator utilized as his basic fabrics three well-known folktales: the ubiquitous story of the Grateful Dead, the tale about a man who was at first impoverished but ultimately was rewarded for burying an abused corpse; the Monster in the Bridal Chamber, a widespread tale featuring an evil creature who is in love with a beautiful maiden and kills her husband on their wedding night; and the Ahiqar Story, the last-named being a wise courtier who, though betrayed by his adopted son, is ultimately vindicated.

Even though the basic fabrics of the book are secular folktales, their designs and colors are distinctly biblical, being patterned after stories in Genesis (e.g., the story of Joseph and the betrothal stories of Isaac and Jacob) and colored by the theology of the book of Deuteronomy in general, and its doctrine of just deserts in particular. The author of Tobit also used the biblical *Job as the model for Tobit; the two characters are both men of outstandingly good deeds and piety who, though they suffered and were tested, did not lose their faith and ultimately were rewarded with even greater blessings.

The book of Tobit, like the meaning of his name ("[God] is my good"), is essentially ironic. Although Tobit fed the hungry, clothed the naked, and buried exposed corpses—all of which he insisted delivers one from death and keeps one "from going into the Darkness" (Tob. 4.10)—he lost both his wealth *and* his sight. Sarah, too, is an ironic figure: a virtuous, loving, and level-headed young maiden, she was plagued by an evil that almost drove her to suicide.

Converging lines of evidence suggest that the book was composed in Aramaic sometime ca. 225–175 BCE. The book's presence among the Dead Sea Scrolls at Qumran virtually rules out a first-century BCE date. *Carey A. Moore*

**TOPHETH.** A site southwest of *Jerusalem in the Valley of Hinnom (*see* Gehenna) where, according to Jeremiah, worshipers burned their sons and daughters as offerings. Jeremiah associates this ritual of child sacrifice with the god *Baal; elsewhere the god to whom children are sacrificed at the Topheth is called Molech. Inscriptional evidence from cemeteries of infants and young children found at Carthage and elsewhere in the Phoenician world, however, suggests that Molech may be a common noun meaning "sacrificial offering"; also, Jeremiah's prophecies associating the cult with Baal may not be historically accurate. At least some people apparently sacrificed their children to Yahweh, including Kings Ahaz and *Manasseh. The great reformer king of Judah, *Josiah (ca. 640–609 BCE), is said to have destroyed the Topheth as part of his purification of the Yahwistic cult.

*Susan Ackerman*

**TOWER OF BABEL.** *See* Babel, Tower of.

**TRIBES OF ISRAEL.** The Hebrew Bible in its final form takes it for granted that the Israelite people is descended from the twelve sons of *Jacob, each being the ancestor of the tribe named after him. This tradition has persisted into later times. The book of Genesis records the births of Jacob's twelve sons, and then provides a list of them arranged under the names of their mothers: *Reuben, *Simeon, *Levi, *Judah, *Issachar, and *Zebulun were the sons of *Leah; *Joseph and *Benjamin the sons of *Rachel; *Dan and *Naphtali the sons of Jacob's concubine Bilhah; *Gad and *Asher the sons of his concubine Zilpah. After Joseph, in Egypt, brought his family from Canaan, the twelve brothers and their families continued to reside in Egypt and there increased in numbers, becoming the people of Israel, literally the "sons of Israel," Jacob's name having been changed by God to *Israel. This united people, after many vicissitudes, took possession of the land of Canaan and established their home there, with each tribe assigned its own territory.

The Bible is, however, not consistent with regard to either the number or the names of the tribes. In the numerous tribal lists found in the various books of the Bible, the number varies from eleven to thirteen. These variations are mainly due to the appearance in some lists of the two sons of Joseph, *Ephraim and *Manasseh as separate tribes, and to the omission of Simeon or Levi from others. In the Song of Deborah, which is not necessarily a complete roll call of the tribes, Judah and Gad are missing, while Machir, the son of Manasseh appears to take the place of his "father." The variations are presumed to reflect fluctuations in the constitution and history of the tribes and their relative size and importance.

Very little is known of the early history of the tribes. The "blessing of Jacob" and the "blessing of Moses" contain some very ancient, but also very cryptic, allusions to early tribal events and characteristics, but these passages have also undergone later expansions and editing, especially in the blessing of Judah, which is a "prophecy" of the kingdom of *David, and that of Joseph, which reflects the special prominence at some time of the tribes of Ephraim and Manasseh. Parts of the books of Joshua and Judges preserve traditions of the early history of some of the tribes during and after their settlement in Canaan. Some of these passages suggest that the tribes, rather than conquering and settling the entire country as a united people (the impression given by the book of Joshua in its present form), possessed no military or political unity at the time of the settlement, but were independent units each making its way into the country, in some cases encountering opposition from the local population.

There can be little doubt that the concept of Israel as a close-knit family of twelve tribes acting in concert before, during, and after the settlement in Canaan is an elaboration of a later period. Although the tribes probably entered the country from outside, they did so for the most part in a piecemeal way, over a long period of time; the people of Israel was in fact constituted for the first time on Canaanite soil. Indeed, some of the tribes, such as Ephraim and Judah, appear to have acquired their names after their arrival in Canaan.

Little is known of the lives of the tribes after their arrival in Canaan, and of the process by which they may have moved toward some kind of national consciousness before the institution of the monarchy; scholarly opinions differ widely. Two groups, Judah (which seems to have been composed of several originally distinct elements) in the south, and the "house of Joseph" (which at some point constituted two distinct tribes, Ephraim and Manasseh) in the central highlands, seem to have been especially prominent. Less is known of the history of the other tribes further north and to the east of the Jordan, with the exception of Dan, which moved, probably under *Philistine pressure, from its original territory to the extreme north of the country. The tribe of Levi is an enigma. According to some traditions it was distinguished from all other tribes in that it was given no territorial rights but had special sacerdotal functions that entitled it to material support from the other tribes, among whom its members moved. In other passages, however, it is portrayed as being on the same footing as the other tribes. (*See* Levites.)

It is important to realize that the word "tribe" does not necessarily suggest a nomadic or seminomadic existence or origin: in the ancient Near East and elsewhere, it frequently denotes a territorial group of settled agricultural or even urban people who claim a common ancestry. Moreover, despite the impression given by many passages in the Bible, the tribe was not the basic social or economic unit in Israel in either premonarchic or later times; the basic units were the family and the village, which were bound together by local agricultural and other common concerns. The larger body, the tribe, was a much looser unit whose main function was apparently, in the period before the monarchy, to provide a militia in times of danger. With the advent of the monarchy, the tribes lost this function and were henceforth little more than a means of genealogical identification. The division of the kingdom after the death of *Solomon was a political rather than a tribal matter.

*See* Israel, History of.

*R. N. Whybray*

**TWELVE, THE.** "The twelve" is an expression employed by all the Gospel writers, and once by Paul, to denote an inner, more intimate circle of followers of Jesus. They are listed by name in Matthew 10.2–4, Mark 3.16–19, Luke 6.14–16, and Acts 1.13, and although these lists do not always agree in either the names or their order, the reader is always told that Jesus chose twelve disciples in particular. While these twelve are *disciples, they are further distinguished by the designation "the twelve." This is especially the case in Acts 6.1–2, where the disciples and the twelve are juxtaposed; the latter are clearly the authorities in the story. As readers, we know who the twelve are, including *Judas Iscariot—a point stressed by all the authors, and we see that they are the recipients of special instruction, have certain expectations from Jesus, and bear the burden of gathering the community of his followers together after the upheaval of the crucifixion and resurrection.

Whether the names and the widespread agreement among the Gospel writers about the number twelve are historical facts is difficult to say. Did Jesus really call twelve followers initially who then called others? This is possible. Did Jesus consciously act as if he were establishing the new Israel by selecting twelve representatives? The symbolic significance of the number twelve is difficult to miss. But there are others in the story who are just as close or closer to him than the twelve, such as some women and others who are called disciples. The twelve do get special teaching; perhaps Jesus was training leaders to carry on in his stead. In Mark, however, the twelve hardly understand anything; the special teaching apparently does not pay off. The roles of the disciples and the twelve are so important in the stories, and they have received so much attention from both the authors and the interpreters, that what actually transpired historically is impossible to retrieve. Matthew himself, for example, uses the terms disciple, *apostle, and the twelve interchangeably in chap. 10, as if these were all equivalent or the distinctions were needless.

The symbolism of the number twelve was certainly clear to the authors, and it has not been lost on subsequent interpreters. A program of the renewal if not the reconstitution of Israel by the Jesus movement is strongly suggested by the number itself, as well as the collection of twelve baskets at the multiplication of the loaves and fishes, the portrayal of the disciples sitting on twelve thrones judging Israel, and the repeated use of the number twelve in the book of Revelation. The usurpation of Israel's symbols and heroic figures (*see* Tribes of Israel) along with Israel's scriptures and myths, and in particular use of the potent symbol twelve, points in this direction for early Christianity. Ultimately, however, the church claimed through Melito, Justin, and others to be a "third race" and not the renewed Israel the number twelve suggested.

*J. Andrew Overman*

# U

**UR OF THE CHALDEANS.** The homeland of *Abraham and the starting point of his migration to Canaan, Ur of the Chaldeans (AV: Chaldees) is traditionally identified with the southern Mesopotamian site Tell el-Muqayyar, on the *Euphrates river. The site was systematically excavated from 1922 to 1934 by Sir Leonard Woolley. Among his discoveries were the ziggurat constructed by Ur-nammu, the founder of the Ur III Dynasty, in the late third millennium BCE and, in the royal cemetery, the burial of queen Pu-abi, whose grave had never been robbed.

The identification of "Ur of the Chaldees" with Tell el-Muqayyar is not universally accepted. Some scholars have suggested that it is Urfa (Edessa), while others have proposed a connection with a city named Ura. It has also been suggested that Ur in this context may reflect the generic Sumerian word for city, URU; note that in the Septuagint "Ur of the Chaldeans" is translated "land of the Chaldeans."

The Chaldeans were a group of five tribes who became dominant in *Babylonia during the late sixth century BCE. They are not mentioned by name in any source before the ninth century, which makes the biblical phrase "Ur of the Chaldeans" relatively late.

*James H. Platt*

# W

**WIDOWS.** The term "widow," the usual translation of Hebrew *ʾalmānâ* and Greek *chēra,* has a more specific meaning in the biblical texts than the English word conveys. The woman designated by these terms was not merely someone whose husband had died; she lived outside of the normal social structure in which every female lived under the authority of some male; she was responsible to and for herself.

The structure of ancient society was kinship-based and patriarchal. Marriage within this society represented a contract made between two families rather than between two individuals. When a woman married, she passed from the authority of her father's household to the authority of her husband's household. When her husband died, her status was determined in relation to the surviving members of his household.

Biblical law provided for a woman of childbearing age whose husband had died without male issue. By means of a levirate marriage the dead man's wife was given to a relative of the husband's family in order that a child be produced to inherit the dead husband's estate. This practice not only provided for inheritance rights but also secured the well-being of the woman. However, a man could legally refuse to carry out this obligation. For example, concern for the diminution of his own inheritance might prompt the dead husband's relative to forgo a levirate marriage. The stories of Tamar, Judah's daughter-in-law who was temporarily an *'almānâ,* and *Ruth illustrate the implementation of levirate marriage.

While the Hebrew Bible identifies certain women as *ʾalmānôt* (plural of *ʾalmānâ*) and specifies their distinctive clothing, its depiction of them is sketchy. Laws from ancient Mesopotamia provide some details. In the Middle Assyrian Laws, the *almattu* (cognate with *ʾalmānâ*) emerges as a woman whose husband and father-in-law were deceased, and who had no son capable of providing for her. A woman in this state was issued a document verifying her new status, and henceforth could act on her own. Presumably, the document gave her access to a society that normally excluded women from the public sphere.

There is evidence that the biblical *ʾalmānâ* may have been similar to the Mesopotamian *almattu.* That she was a woman living beyond male authority is illustrated by the law regarding women's vows: while the validity of a vow made by a woman depended ordinarily upon the approval of either her father or her husband, the validity of an *ʾalmānâ*'s vow stood on its own.

The *ʾalmānâ*'s independence from male authority was at the same time a sign of her precarious social position. In more than half of its occurrences, the *ʾalmānâ* is linked with the *orphan or with the orphan and the client. Existing outside of the normal social structure, these three groups were susceptible to oppression, injustice, and exploitation. Because the ᵓ*almānâ* had no male protector, Yahweh was pictured as her primary defender and every Israelite was supposed to treat her justly. The Bible legislates the protection and support of the ᵓ*almānâ* and exhorts against oppressing her. Prophetic texts claim that the welfare of the defenseless ᵓ*almānâ,* orphan, and *alien was the measure by which Yahweh determined the moral fiber of his people. The vulnerability and isolation of the ᵓ*almānâ* suggested a metaphorical use of the term, and prophetic texts describe a vulnerable city (Babylon, Jerusalem) or land (Israel, Judah) as an ᵓ*almānâ.*

The vulnerable and unconventional social position of the ᵓ*almānâ* is also evident in laws regulating the priesthood. The affiliation of a *priest with such a woman was a source of concern. While Leviticus 21.14 implicitly permits a priest to marry an ᵓ*almānâ* but forbids a high priest from doing so, in Ezekiel 44.22 no priest is allowed to marry an ᵓ*almānâ* unless her husband had been a priest. Other legislation permits a priest's daughter who is an ᵓ*almānâ* to eat at his table.

From the mention of the widow (Grk. *chēra*) in the Gospels, it is evident that the Hebrew ᵓ*almānâ*'s precarious and threatened existence persisted into the first century CE. Early Christianity singled out widows as recipients of social welfare, establishing an organized means of caring for this group of women. In the Jerusalem church, a food distribution program is specified. 1 Timothy 5 mentions an official list of widows with eligibility requirements that included age and certain religious and moral behavior in addition to the absence of a responsible family member.

*See also* Poor; Women.

*Paula S. Hiebert*

**WILDERNESS.** Hebrew *midbāar,* "wilderness, desert," originally meant "place of herding." Since many wilderness areas of Palestine were sparsely vegetated, in contrast to the barren Syro-Arabian desert, nomads could traverse them with asses and flocks. Oases sustained concentrated settlements of pastoralists and agriculturalists.

The wilderness has mostly negative associations in the Bible. It is a bad place of hunger, thirst, and deprivation; it is unsettled, nonarable, windswept, haunted by noxious beasts and demons, and echoing with frightful noises. It is the domain of *Cain, *Ishmael, *Esau, and raiders such as the *Arabs, *Midianites, and *Amalekites. Apart from nomads and the lawless, only the mad inhabit the wilderness, or those with no other recourse. The wilderness is figuratively dark, recalling the primordial state of the universe. To punish a people God may "uncreate" a country, converting arable land to wilderness.

On the other hand, there is nostalgia for aspects of the seminomadic lifestyle of the ancestral and Exodus periods. The *Rechabites continue to build no houses, plant no fields, and live in tents. The tent in particular remains a powerful symbol: God's proper dwelling is a tent; the cry of secession from the Davidic kingdom is "To your tents, O Israel," and Hosea predicts a return to tents. Pastoralism, too, has positive associations. Both God are shepherds, a common royal epithet in antiquity. As divine king, *Jesus, too, is shepherd.

The wilderness is also a place for spiritual renewal. *Hagar, *Moses, and

*Elijah flee there and meet God. Jesus similarly seeks solitude in the desert. The wilderness is above all associated with the wanderings of Israel narrated in Exodus-Deuteronomy. Most texts recall this as a time of tension between God and his people, but Jeremiah 2.2–3 and Hosea 2.15 idealize it as a time of piety. Some sources maintain that God simply found Israel in the desert and brought them to the land, apparently ignoring the Exodus proper. It was in this wilderness, at Mount *Sinai/Horeb, that God entered into a covenant with Israel, a covenant reaffirmed on the wilderness borders of the *Promised Land (Deuteronomy).

Nostalgia for desert life and the negative associations of the wilderness are, ironically, compatible. Israel is forced to rely upon God in the most inhospitable of climates, and God shows his power to sustain them, just as *Jesus feeds the multitudes in the desert. The desert is also God's crucible, in which he tests Israel and eliminates the unwanted.

Some prophets believe that Israel must return to the desert for renewal and purification. Second *Isaiah, encouraging Babylonian Jews to cross the desert and rebuild Judah, envisions the desert negated, turned into a paradise.

The Qumran community conceived of itself as fulfilling the call of Isaiah 40.3, to make a way in the desert in preparation for a national rebirth. *John the Baptist was viewed in the same light. The tradition of desert monasteries continues to this day. *William H. Propp*

**WISDOM.** Biblical wisdom literature emphasizes the desirability and the elusiveness of true wisdom (Hebr. *hokmâ,* a feminine noun). Job 28.25–27 even locates wisdom with God at *creation. Thus it is of interest that a series of poems in Proverbs 1–9 metaphorically personifies wisdom as a woman in a variety of positive female roles; *see* Women, *article on* Ancient Near East and Israel.

The female figure of Wisdom first appears in Proverbs speaking as a *prophet, a profession to which both men and women were called. In Proverbs 9.1–6, Wisdom is a high-ranking woman who can employ a messenger; on her own initiative she invites the "simple" to a banquet in her substantial seven-pillared house.

Wisdom is also a "sister" (Prov. 7.4), a word with two connotations: a literal sister with whom a man may associate on the intimate level of family, or alternately a wife or lover (as in the Song of *Solomon). In the book of Proverbs, both the ideal wife and the woman Wisdom are "more precious than jewels," and Proverbs 4.6 enjoins the listener not to forsake Wisdom just as Proverbs 5.15–17 demands marital fidelity. Like wives and mothers in ancient Israel, Wisdom is a counsellor and teacher. Interestingly, she is not a child-bearer, although she is regularly described as a life-giver or life-preserver.

The dividing line between Wisdom the woman and God can grow hazy. Without the introductory verses to Proverbs 1.22–33 one might easily assume that the speaker is not Wisdom but God! Theologians have observed that Wisdom functions as a mediator between God and humanity. She is God's companion before the beginning of creation; yet God offers her, as she offers herself, to God's human subjects. If they accept her, they will find that God is protecting and guiding them. Scholarly consensus places the book of Proverbs in the postexilic period (fifth–fourth centuries BCE), although it is generally agreed that Proverbs contains motifs and themes that were part of preexilic Israelite culture. Wisdom's mediating role may have answered a spiritual need earlier fulfilled by the king.

Scholars have pursued the theory that Wisdom the woman is in some way related to an ancient Near Eastern goddess or goddesses. Evidence is lacking for the suggestion that a goddess, Wisdom, was worshiped in preexilic times in Israelite scribal schools. She does however share some attributes with the Egyptian goddess Maat, "Truth," and with certain ancient Near Eastern goddesses who protected the king and his officials.

Wisdom the woman's most striking affinities, however, are with *Asherah, the Canaanite fertility goddess. Wisdom is the tree of life, and Asherah's primary symbol was a tree of life. Wisdom's banquet invitation recalls Asherah's banquet in the Ugaritic myth of *Baal. Proverbs 9 may consciously play on the ambiguities of the word "house," which can also mean temple; in ancient Near Eastern mythology, the construction of a house/temple for the gods is often the climax of cosmogony, notably also the theme of Wisdom's preceding address in Proverbs 8.22–31.

At the same time, there are clearly similarities between Wisdom's corrupt counterpart, the "foolish woman" of Proverbs 9.13–18, and several goddesses in ancient Near Eastern myths whose seductive blandishments and promises of life to the young male hero can lead to death. It has been suggested that throughout Proverbs 1–9, in a particularly Israelite twist, the description of the evil seductive/adulterous woman may deliberately employ Canaanite goddess imagery in order to undercut it.

It is not impossible that Lady Wisdom represents an irruption in the Bible of the persistent but biblically suppressed Israelite worship of a female counterpart to Yahweh. In the book of Proverbs, however, both Wisdom the woman and the "foolish woman" seem to be literary creations in which goddess language has been artfully transformed and recombined with imagery from other elements of Israelite female experience.

The motif of Wisdom the woman subsequently played a notable part in Jewish and Christian thought. She appears, for example, in the Wisdom of Solomon, in *Sirach, in *Baruch 3:9—4:4, and in the nonbiblical texts from Qumran, and her words are echoed in the New Testament. Perhaps most resonant of all was Wisdom's speech in Proverbs 8.22–31, stressing her presence at the beginning of creation. Sirach equates Wisdom with the creative word of God and with Torah. Readers of the Jewish philosopher Philo of Alexandria (first century CE) have found it difficult to disentangle the properties of God's word (*logos*) from wisdom (*sophia*). *Paul calls Christ the wisdom (*sophia*) of God. The mini-creation story in John 1.1–3 consciously evokes Proverbs 8. And for gnostic Jews and Christians, the female principle Sophia was a figure of great complexity and primary importance.

*Mary Joan Winn Leith*

**WISE MEN, THE THREE.** *See* Magi.

**WITCH.** Biblical references to witches reflect a category of ritual specialist whose status and function are now virtually unknown. Texts from other ancient Near Eastern cultures provide evidence of a variety of both male and female cultic functionaries, and there is evidence of ritual practitioners, such as oracular speakers, who were not part of a temple cult. The Hebrew Bible, by contrast, accords official cultic status to only two related categories of males, *Levites (temple functionaries) and sacrificial priests, while portraying all other ritual experts pejoratively.

Several Hebrew terms are associated with the English word "witch." These can also be translated "sorcerer," "sorceress," "medium," or "necromancer." Most appear in references to prohibited practices and seem to be concerned with divination or necromancy. Women may have been especially involved in such activities since they were excluded from those of the official cult. Specific association with women is found in Exodus 22.18, Leviticus 20.27, and 2 Kings 9.22. A phrase meaning "a woman proficient in necromancy" is used in 1 Samuel 28.7; commonly known as "the witch of Endor" (wording not found in the Bible), this woman is able to make the dead prophet *Samuel appear before *Saul, even though he had prohibited the practice.

The strong condemnation of witches and other ritual specialists with whom they are often grouped may be the result of an attempt by ancient Israelites to distinguish their religious practices and beliefs from those of surrounding cultures, as well as to provide central state control of all forms of religious observance. But both the legal prohibitions and the prophetic attacks on various forms of magic, sorcery, divination, and necromancy indicate that they were a perennial aspect of popular religion in ancient Israel, as they have been in postbiblical Jewish and Christian traditions.

The injunction "Thou shalt not suffer a witch to live" (KJV) was invoked in enforcing the death penalty against women accused of witchcraft in Europe and England from the sixteenth to the eighteenth centuries, and in Salem, Massachusetts, in 1692.

*See also* Israel.

*Drorah O'Donnell Setel*

**WOMEN.** *This entry on the roles and status of women consists of four articles:*

*An Overview*
*Ancient Near East and Israel*
*Second Temple Period*
*Early Christianity*

*The introductory article is an overview of the status of women in biblical times, and the remaining articles are more detailed discussions of women in the* Ancient Near East and Israel, *in Judaism of the* Second Temple Period, *and in* Early Christianity. *Related discussion is found in entries on individual women named in the Bible.*

### *An Overview*

Before the Babylonian exile in 587/586 BCE, women in Israel enjoyed a status and freedom comparable to that of men. Israel lived in a patriarchal world, but her society was always informed by a faith that gave equality to women in the eyes of God. Thus, the woman is understood in the tenth-century BCE story of Genesis 2.18 as the necessary complement of the man and as his helper in a relationship of mutual companionship and assistance, just as male and female both are necessary to the image of God in the sixth-century BCE account of Genesis 1.27. The subordination of women to men is considered to be the result of human sin, and the subsequent practice of polygamy is a manifestation of the spread of sin.

Women are found serving as *prophets, *judges, and *queens in preexilic Israel. They are never excluded from the worship of God. They are sometimes honored as models of wisdom. The honor of mothers ranks with that of fathers in Israel's basic law, the Ten Commandments. The family rights of wives and mothers are protected by law. The woman who engages in profitable commercial enterprises, who teaches with wisdom, and who serves the community through deeds of charity is honored as an ideal.

Though single females lived under the authority of their fathers in Israel, love and choice in marriage were known, and the woman was never considered a piece of property to be bartered. Sexual love was celebrated as a gift of God, and the marital relationship was so prized that it could serve as a metaphor of the love between God and his covenant people—an impossibility if marriage had been a repressive relationship for the woman.

Those preexilic stories in the Bible that exhibit cruelty toward women and treat them as objects of degradation reflect the environment in which Israel lived and are intended as protests against it.

When Israel was carried into Babylonian exile, her priests in exile determined that they would draw up a plan for Israel's life that would ensure that she would never again be judged by God. They therefore collected together and wrote priestly legislation that would ensure Israel's ritual and social purity. At the same time, they emphasized the importance of circumcision as a sign of the covenant. This emphasis brought sexuality into the realm of the cult and related females to the covenant community only through their males. The blood of the sacrifice on the altar became the means of atonement for sin, and blood outside of the cult became ritually unclean. Thus, women were excluded from the cult during their menstruation and childbirth. Indeed, they were increasingly segregated in worship and society. They had access to the holy only through their males. A woman's court was added to the *Temple to distance them from the sanctuary. Their vows to God were no longer considered as valuable as those of males, and a husband could annul the vow of his wife. In the Second Temple period, women were excluded from testifying in a court trial; they were not to be seen in public or to speak with strangers, and outside their homes they were to be doubly veiled. They could not even teach or be taught the Torah in their homes—a far cry from that time when Huldah the prophet interpreted Deuteronomy for King *Josiah—and they were not to be educated. They had become second-class Jews, excluded from the worship and teaching of God, with status scarcely above that of *slaves.

The actions of *Jesus of Nazareth toward women were therefore revolutionary. He did not hesitate to engage even unclean foreign women in public conversation. He ignored all strictures of ritual impurity. He himself taught women, gave them an equal rank with men as daughters of *Abraham, openly ministered to them as "children of wisdom," and afforded them the highest respect as persons. Women belonged to the inner circle of the disciples, and they are attested as the first witnesses of the resurrection. The Fourth Gospel begins and ends with the testimony of a woman to the Christ.

Women therefore played a leading role in earliest Christianity, being baptized and receiving the Spirit, doing acts of charity, suffering imprisonment for their faith, and serving as ministers of the church. They were allowed to preach and to pray in worship, as well as to prophesy and to teach. Their equal status in Christ was strongly affirmed by Paul, who considered the ancient subordination of women in Genesis 3.16 to have been overcome by Christ. When Paul was faced with the misuse of Christian freedom in his churches, however, he could revert to his Pharisaic background to silence both contentious men and women in his congregations.

As Christianity spread through the Roman world of the late first and early second centuries CE, it faced the necessity of consolidating its doctrine and regularizing its polity, over against judaizers and gnostics. Unfortunately, in an alien environment, the church bought these developments at the price of the freedom of females. Because some women fell prey to gnostic teachings, they were forbidden leadership in some churches, on the basis of rabbinic interpretations of the scriptures. Patriarchal patterns of marriage reasserted themselves, though these were often tempered by a high view of marriage and of the mutual subjection of both husband and wife to Christ. Most importantly, political power struggles for control of ecclesiastical districts led to the formation of a male hierarchy in the church that often continues to this day, in opposition to the witness of much of the Bible. *Elizabeth Achtemeier*

### *Ancient Near East and Israel*

The images of women in the Bible were shaped by literary genres and colored by historical circumstances and political ideologies. Furthermore, over the last two and a half millennia the Bible has accumulated additional resonances from the religious traditions that take it as a foundation. In essence, however, the Bible is an ancient Near Eastern document and can best be studied and understood in that context.

**Women and the Family.** Family and family ties determined the status and fate of women as well as men. An Israelite man or woman's formal name customarily included the name of the father; alternatively, a woman might be referred to as "PN (personal name) the wife of PN." Children were subject to their father until the parents arranged for their marriage. Nevertheless, love poetry from Mesopotamia, Egypt, and Israel (the Song of Solomon) implies that children may have had some influence on their parents' selection. At her marriage the Israelite bride moved to her husband's household and was thenceforth subject to him.

The strains in a society so rooted in the family are occasionally apparent in the Bible. The outrages against *Hagar, *Dinah, and the two Tamars arise partly out of the sexual dynamics of the family. A childless *widow had little autonomy and was supposed to return to her father's house. Widows with sons, divorced women, and *prostitutes were probably less dependent on male authority, but if they were poor, their lives could become precarious in the absence of a related male protector.

The Bible reflects Israel's double standard in its attitude toward male and female sexuality. Virginity was required of the bride but not of the groom; by contrast, in Babylon before the sixth century BCE the bride's virginity was not an important part of marriage agreements. Husbands were free to visit prostitutes even as they enjoyed exclusive rights to their wives' sexuality. In Israel adultery with a married woman meant death for both offenders, but a man who raped an unbetrothed virgin was simply compelled to marry her. Deuteronomy 24.1–4 implies that only men initiated divorces. In only one book of the Bible, the Song of Solomon, are male and female sexuality described in an equally positive manner.

The limitations placed on ancient Near Eastern women can be regarded in part as a function of patrilineal systems that try to keep children and property within the family, rather than as an example of low female status. Families usually traced their genealogies through the male line, with sons inheriting the bulk of the father's property. The biblical term for the family household, "the father's house," reflects the priority of the paternal family line. A wife suspected of infidelity thus threatened more than just the husband's honor; the identity of her children could no longer be securely tied to the husband and his lineage.

When there were no sons, daughters could play a role in preserving the integrity of the family property. At Nuzi in eastern Assyria and at Emar in Syria, a father without sons could declare his daughter legally a son and heir. Similarly, Numbers 36 provides for the daughters of Zelophehad to inherit their father's estate, but with the qualification that they must marry within their father's clan. The fact that the patriarchs were related to their spouses may be a reflex of these sorts of concerns.

It is not surprising that most biblical references to women concern mothers. Whereas *Abraham's servant enumerates his master's greatness in terms of property, *Sarah's prominence comes from being potentially, then actually, *Isaac's mother. Rachel and Hannah suffer for their apparent sterility. The only stipulation in the Ten Commandments that treats women and men equally is the command to honor both father and mother.

The Bible's focus on male-dominated institutions and values ignores the details of a woman's everyday life in the home. Although the Bible portrays men and women preparing food, it assumes that women did the cooking for their families. Mothers provided the primary care and nurture for children until they were weaned at about three years old. From Proverbs 1.8 and 31.1 and by ethnographic analogy, it appears that mothers were also responsible for the socialization and much of the moral education of their small children.

Mothers are particularly prominent in one of the most familiar biblical stories, that of the miraculous birth of a son to a sterile mother. Despite its primary focus on God and the child, the genre is careful to mark the mother as special. For example, Pharaoh, the most powerful man in the world, cannot resist Sarah's beauty (cf. the similar stories of Rachel, *Samson's mother, and Hannah). This theme reappears in the Gospel accounts of Elizabeth and of *Mary, whose virginity, rather than sterility, serves to imply that *Jesus's birth is the most miraculous of all.

**Social Patterns and Female Power.** By combining ethnography and archaeology, scholars are reassessing the nature of the premonarchic Israelite community (1200–1000 BCE) and of women's roles in this period. The pattern of complex households in small villages was probably a response to the labor needs generated by early Israel's agrarian environment. Micah's household, with living units occupied by Micah, his mother, his sons (and perhaps their wives), a hired priest, and servants, mirrors the archaeological evidence. Because each household member made a crucial contribution to the household, there was greater scope for women to exercise informal authority. Indeed, the Bible accepts as normative the phenomenon of wives counseling and influencing their husbands (e.g., *Eve; Samson's mother; Abigail; the Shunammite woman; Job's wife).

*Samuel is reported to have predicted in the late eleventh century BCE that kingship would break up the rural family and disrupt old patterns of formal and informal family authority. And, in fact, small freeholds did give way to landed estates, although Israel's economy remained agriculturally based, and rural women probably influenced their families more than their urban counterparts. Urban male-dominated royal, military, economic, and religious institutions took the lead in shaping Israelite culture and defining its norms and values. The Bible is rooted in these institutions; this explains why so much of Israelite women's lives, experiences, and values have remained hidden and inaccessible.

**Women's Legal Status.** Cuneiform tablets show that wealthy Mesopotamian wives and widows throughout history made business contracts and appeared in court as plaintiffs, defendants, and witnesses. They borrowed and lent money, and bought and sold property. Almost always, however, the woman is acting in concert with or on behalf of her husband or another male family member. In Egypt, women from different social strata engaged in litigation and owned houses and fields, which they seem to have been able to bequeath as they liked (but usually within the family).

Israelite seals and seal impressions with women's names provide important evidence that in Israel, as in Mesopotamia and Egypt, women had the right to sign documents, a fact that the Bible never hints at. Relatively egalitarian ideals underlie the old laws of Exodus 21.26–32, where a value is placed on an injury irrespective of the sex of the injured party. But casuistic laws that begin "If a man . . ." usually refer to the man with the Hebrew word *ʾîš* ("a male") rather than with the generic *ʾādām* ("human being"). When an occasional law clearly applies to both men and women, *ʾiššâ* ("woman") may be added. Apodictic laws are declared in second person masculine verb forms and may implicitly exclude women, as do many collective social terms. For example, in Exodus 19.14 Moses returns to "the people," who in the next verse are ordered to stay away from women.

**Women's Activities Outside the Home.** Besides being wives, concubines, and mothers, the Bible shows women working in the fields, fetching water, and tending flocks. They were midwives and nurses. Royal establishments employed women as perfumers, bakers, cooks, and singers. Although only men are mentioned as potters in the Bible, ethnographic analogies suggest that women were skilled in this important craft, and in weaving as well. There are references to enslaved women, some of whom would have been debt-slaves or war-captives. Prostitutes were tolerated but, as in Mesopotamia, they were relegated to the margins of society (Deut. 23.17 outlaws only prostitutes associated with non-Yahwistic cults).

Wives of rulers, queens, and women of the nobility were able to act with a relative degree of autonomy. The queen of *Sheba, who may have belonged to a dynasty of Arabian queens, negotiated with King *Solomon. Biblical accession formulas in 1 and 2 Kings are careful to note the name of each new Judahite king's mother, and the queen mother may have had quasi-official status.

**Women's Religious Practice and Experience.** All biblical evidence for women's religious experience has been filtered through male eyes; thus much remains hidden. The description of the ideal wife, for example, mentions her wise advice, but is mute about religious activity. Men and women incurred temporary ritual impurity, and thus exclusion from the cult, for genital emissions, but menstruation especially penalized women. A woman after the birth of a son was impure for seven days, but for fourteen after a daughter's birth.

Biblical laws obliged only men to attend the three primary pilgrimage feasts, but women such as Hannah clearly participated as well. During the festival she prays and makes a vow, and when Samuel is born she praises God with a song of thanksgiving. The detailed legislation regarding women's vows suggests that this was a significant form of female piety. The personal piety of several women appears in accounts of wives or widows consulting or helping prophets. The motif in the Gospels of women appealing to and following Jesus derives in part from these stories.

Monotheistic Israel differed from Mesopotamia and Egypt, where women served many deities as priestesses and even as high priestesses. The Israelite priesthood consisted of men who inherited the office from their fathers. Some women in Israel, called *qedēšôt* (formerly translated as "sacred prostitutes") were apparently consecrated to non-Yahwistic cults, but their function is unclear. Women served in some unexplained capacity at the tent shrine, and after the exile the *Temple employed female singers.

What Israelite women did at the pilgrim feasts and how their worship differed from that of men is unclear, but it is an instructive question. Recognizing that gender differentiation—in tandem with the preconceptions of the observer—plays a role in determining what is considered "religious," scholars are beginning to reassess the ancient forms of women's piety. For example, Hannah stays home from the feast to nurse Samuel, which might suggest that women's spirituality was contingent upon and secondary to men's. Is she temporarily cutting herself off from God, or were there compensatory home-centered rituals?

Besides the preparation of the corpse and funerary lamentations, Israelite women no doubt participated in additional rituals related to the lifecycle. One suspects that midwives performed birth rituals. The tradition of mourning for Jephthah's daughter may have been a rite of passage for adolescent girls. Zipporah performs a marriage-related circumcision. The prophets *Deborah and Huldah were married women; perhaps they should be compared to postmenopausal women in other societies who become religious practitioners.

*Miriam, Deborah, Huldah, and Noadiah are called *prophets. Deborah's and Huldah's prophecy seems to differ in no way from male prophecy. Contemporaneously with Huldah (seventh century BCE), the *Assyrians were very interested in and influenced by prophecy; texts mention female prophets, many of whom apparently operated independently of any temple cult.

Power struggles among priestly families may underlie the account in Numbers 12 of Miriam's and *Aaron's revolt. Micah 6.4 is mute on the subject of any wrongdoing, and equally commends Miriam, *Moses, and Aaron as deliverers. Miriam's very presence in the account of the *Exodus and wilderness wanderings, complete with death notice in Numbers 20.1, suggests that she was an important cultic leader in Israelite memory.

Certain practices that the Bible considers abhorrent may at times have constituted mainstream Israelite religious activity. Significant female participation may be sought in lost, hidden, or forbidden categories of worship. The Bible condemns *Saul for consulting Samuel's ghost through the female medium at

Endor (*see* Witch), and disapproves of what seems to be a cult of the dead; yet recent research has shown that the cult of dead ancestors was important to many Israelites. In the two biblical episodes involving teraphim (household gods related to the cult of dead ancestors), the persons handling them are women.

The numerous female clay figurines (often called Asherah figurines) found in Israelite domestic and tomb contexts must have had a religious function, perhaps related to a mother-goddess cult. Evidence from Kuntillet ᶜAjrud in the Sinai and elsewhere, in combination with reassessments of the biblical text, suggests that many Israelites during the monarchy worshiped the Canaanite goddess *Asherah, possibly even as a consort of Yahweh.

It is worth noting two exceptions to the Bible's tendency to treat women as lesser members of the religious congregation; both mark the inauguration in *Jerusalem of a new religious era. When *David installs the ark in Jerusalem, women and men share in the ritual meal, and when *Ezra conducts his public reading of the Torah, the text stresses that his audience consists of understanding men and women. Reminiscent of the latter passage is Genesis 1's assumption of the equal status of male and female; the gender-inclusiveness of this text (generally dated to the exilic period) may reflect the importance of women among the exiles in maintaining the cohesion of family, community, and religion in the absence of male-dominated institutions such as the kingship and the Temple priesthood, which could no longer be regarded as keepers of the national identity.

**Female Symbolism.** Women play an important role in the Bible's symbolic repertory. One of the most striking and influential metaphors in the Bible is the personification of *Wisdom as a woman. Jeremiah 31.15 describes war-ravaged Israel as a mother, Rachel, weeping for her dead children. In a familiar biblical metaphor, God too becomes a parent who feels exasperation but also compassion—literally "womb-feeling"—for the child Israel. Israel, Jerusalem, and even foreign nations and cities may be personified as daughters. Marriage becomes a central metaphor to describe the past and future intimacy of God the husband and Israel the wife, who all too often turns into an adulteress ("playing the harlot") with other gods. Political considerations help to explain the function of some women in the Bible. Abishag is actually a symbolic pawn, first of the northern tribes, then of Adonijah. The story of *Rahab and the presence of women in genealogies served to imply that the descendants of these women belonged to kinship groups considered subordinate by more dominant Israelite tribes.

Biblical laws against a man lying "with a male as with a woman" and against cross-dressing suggest that the borders between male and female realms are not to be crossed. Women are not warriors; thus it is ultimate humiliation for Sisera and Abimelech to die at the hands of a woman (cf. Judith). Jeremiah's oracle against Babylon even threatens Babylonian mercenaries with becoming women. At the same time, in the deliberately shocking imagery that characterizes prophetic discourse, Jeremiah epitomizes the newness of the era when Jerusalem will be restored by suggesting some sort of gender reversal.

**Negative Views of Women.** Women in the Bible are generally less important than men and subject to male authority, but paradoxically women are also very powerful in one respect, their seductive persuasiveness. The Bible singles out foreign women as dangerous, liable to lead their partners away from exclusive Yahwism. The Bible condemns Phoenician *Jezebel for persuading Ahab to neglect the Israelite covenant with Yahweh. Canaanite *Rahab and *Ruth the Moabite are exceptions as good foreign women who take Yahweh as their God. The opposite phenomenon—Israelite women led to apostasy by foreign men—is addressed only metaphorically, when Israel is personified as a adulterous wife who has been unfaithful to her husband, Yahweh.

The prophets denounce vain and selfish women, and Proverbs scorns contentious and headstrong women. The "strange" woman of Proverbs 1–9, a combination of every possible negative female type (an adulteress, a cult-related prostitute, a goddess, a foreign woman), is a literary creation who functions rhetorically as the exact opposite of a positive female figure, Lady *Wisdom.

The Bible's negative assessment of several women may arise from an unspoken political or rhetorical subtext (e.g., Michal, Jezebel, Athaliah, Gomer). Potiphar's wife and Delilah are bad women indeed, but folklorists recognize that these "evil" women play a crucial role in propelling the central character toward hero status, a story pattern repeated in countless folktales.

Genesis never refers to a woman as the cause of the human condition (*see* Eve). The earliest biblical reference to this concept occurs in Sirach 25.24 (early second century BCE). It is a doctrine, like the related ones of original sin and *Satan, that developed during the Second Temple Period (ca. 500 BCE–70 CE), to be taken up in turn by early Christianity.

**Social Reality and Narrative Patterns.** Investigators of women's history view with interest the intersection between religious symbols and narrative patterns on the one hand and social reality on the other. The fact that Ishtar or Hathor is an authoritative female deity does not mean that real-life women could achieve comparable power in Mesopotamian or Egyptian society.

Nevertheless, in actual society and in literature, women who function on the upper or lower margins of normative society—queens, wealthy widows, priestesses, prostitutes—may transcend otherwise static boundaries determined by gender. As high priestess of the Sumerian mood god, the princess Enheduanna (twenty-third century BCE) composed hymns which may have provided a model for later hymnists. The prostitute Rahab negotiates successfully for the common good of her family and Israel. In the Gilgamesh Epic, the prostitute Shamhat is pivotal in bringing Enkidu from bestiality to civilization; her role may usefully be compared to that of Eve in Genesis 3. Anthropologists have observed that this mediating quality is often a distinctive aspect of femaleness.

A recurrent pattern in biblical stories about women is their use of indirection, even subterfuge, to achieve divinely sanctioned ends. By seemingly devious actions which invert or overthrow established but restrictive social hierarchies, women often bring about a new order of life and freedom.

*Mary Joan Winn Leith*

### *Second Temple Period*

Interest in the role and status of women in Second Temple Judaism (and generally in Judaism and Christianity) has increased exponentially in the past twenty-five years. As research has progressed, however, the difficulty of reclaiming women's voices from a largely silent patriarchal textual tradition has been acknowledged. The major groups of texts of the Second Temple period are androcentric in focus, written by male authors for a male audience, and they mention women only rarely and usually in peripheral contexts. A second body of evidence that can be utilized in the search for women's lives is archaeological, the material remains of society both in Palestine and in the *Diaspora. But material remains are generally silent as to the gender of their owners, and so are subject to the potentially biased interpretation of the excavator. These limitations make the recovery of women's lives from the Second Temple period fraught with difficulty.

**Women's Daily Lives.** The beginning of the Second Temple period was the era of *Persian domination of the ancient Near East (538–332 BCE). During this time Jewish settlement was concentrated in Babylon, Judea, and to a more limited extent in Egypt. Judea in this period was poor, with a rural, agrarian economy. Extended families (the "father's house") worked their own fields and were self-reliant in most matters of daily existence. Both women's and men's work was essential to the survival of the family unit. Women's tasks included agricultural labor, food processing, textile manufacture, and child care (women would often have ten or more pregnancies to insure that a minimum number of children survived to adulthood). Because of the interdependent nature of the family unit, gender roles were not sharply defined except for biological function.

As Greek culture spread over the ancient Near East, especially in the Hellenistic period (332–ca. 200 BCE), the mingling of the two worlds produced the unique blend of culture called Hellenism. Hellenism created a more urban, mobile society, and also saw the rise of an extensive Diaspora community, particularly in Alexandria in Egypt and in Asia Minor. Urban life brought with it smaller families and specialized economic roles, so that women's roles became more circumscribed. While men performed their tasks in the public sphere, women became more confined to the home, limited to their maternal and housekeeping roles (this is primarily true for upper- and middle-class women). Spinning and weaving continued to be women's work. Upper-class women evidently could and did play active roles in the Greco-Roman Jewish Diaspora, but for the vast majority of women such occasions were limited. Educational opportunities expanded for women in this period, but a good part of the population remained illiterate. The visual arts reveal a new interest in the eroticism of women. So women as women are both more visible, in art and literature, and less visible, being more and more confined to the home. This created a tension in Hellenistic society's view of women, reflected in Jewish literature of the period.

**Women in Postexilic Biblical Literature.** The group of canonical works from the Persian period is small, and few of those are concerned with women; notable exceptions are the books of Esther, Ruth, and the Song of Solomon, all of which contain positive portrayals of women.

The book of *Esther, written in the late Persian-early Hellenistic period, is a fictional account of events leading up to the Jewish festival of Purim. Set in the eastern Diaspora, the book describes how a young Jewish girl named Esther became the consort of the Persian king and saved her people from destruction by her resourcefulness and courage. Notorious for its lack of interest in religious matters (it never mentions God, although the author clearly believes in a divine providence at work in human affairs), the book focuses on the Jews as an ethnic group and on Esther as a human heroine who saves her people by her own actions and thus as a role model for Jews in the *Diaspora.

The date of the book of *Ruth is disputed, but sometime in the fifth century BCE is reasonable, understanding the book as a response to the postexilic decrees by Ezra and Nehemiah against intermarriage. The main character is Ruth the Moabite, who accompanies her Israelite mother-in-law Naomi back to Judea after the death of their husbands, and eventually, through her own praiseworthy actions, becomes the ancestress of king *David. The book concerns itself with the mundane things of life: food, marriage, offspring, and particularly the covenant-loyalty of one (foreign) woman for another. Ruth becomes the paradigm of loyalty for all women and men, and her attachment to Naomi resembles the marriage vow: "Where you go, I will go; where you lodge, I will lodge; your people shall be my people, and your God my God. Where you die, I will die—there will I be buried. May the Lord do thus and so to me, and more as well, if even death parts me from you!" (1.16–17).

The Song of *Solomon (of uncertain date, but with final redaction in the Second Temple period), is the only book in the Bible partly written in a woman's voice. It is a series of love songs that are frankly erotic in character, celebrating the sexual life between an unnamed woman and a man, with the woman acting as a free agent, pursuing her lover, initiating their encounters, and glorying in their physical love. Conspicuously absent are the usual biblical roles for women, those of wife and mother. The couple functions as equals in their erotic union, resulting in an unusual and compelling portrayal of the woman.

**Women in the Apocrypha.** The Apocrypha are writings considered canonical by the Roman Catholic and Eastern Orthodox churches, but not by Judaism and the Protestant churches. Like the Hebrew Bible, the Apocrypha comprise various types of literature, and also like the Hebrew Bible, they are androcentric, mentioning women only occasionally, when their lives impinge on the activities of men. Two important portraits of women are found in the Additions to *Esther and the book of *Judith.

The Additions to Esther are six major blocks of material added to the Hebrew book of Esther, along with minor changes in the text, when it was translated into Greek, probably in 78 BCE. The Additions attempt to remedy problems perceived in the Hebrew book: the lack of mention of God and Esther's non-Jewish lifestyle. The changes make Esther a pious but passive girl, relying on God instead of herself, so that God becomes the true hero of the story. Esther's beauty is emphasized and her brains and skill downplayed. The changes may have rendered Esther more palatable as a heroine to a Hellenistic audience accustomed to passive romantic heroines. This, then, is an example of conscious downgrading of the role of a woman.

The book of Judith, probably composed in the second century BCE, presents an unambiguous female hero. In this fictitious narrative, Judith (whose name is a feminine form of the word for "Jew"), a beautiful, wealthy, and pious widow, leaves her quiet existence to save her town of Bethulia from the besieging Assyrians. She does this by pretending to desert to the enemy and then seducing the Assyrian general Holofernes; when he is drunk, she cuts off his head and returns to Bethulia in triumph. Thus "one Hebrew woman has brought disgrace on the house of King Nebuchadnezzar." However, this behavior by a woman is acceptable only in national emergencies; after the Assyrians are defeated, Judith returns to her quiet existence, remaining a widow until her death. Women's power is expressed in Judith, but only within the confines of patriarchy.

**Women in the Pseudepigrapha.** Similarly ambivalent attitudes toward women also exists in the eclectic collection of Jewish writings known as the Pseudepigrapha. The Conversion of Asenath and The Testaments of the Twelve Patriarchs are two examples of the wide variety of portraits of women in this literature.

The Conversion of Asenath was written to answer the question of how *Joseph, the quintessential man of God, could have married an Egyptian, "Asenath daughter of Potiphera, priest of On" (Gen. 41.45). According to the story, Joseph does indeed refuse to marry Asenath at first, because she is an idol worshipper. But Asenath, who the text emphasizes is a virgin, is so stricken by Joseph's refusal that she repents and converts to the worship of Joseph's God. The bulk of the story is the account of Asenath's conversion. She retires to her chamber, puts on mourning garments, and laments and fasts for seven days. On the eighth day she repents her idolatry and confesses to God. In response an archangel appears to her, declares that her repentance has been accepted, and gives her a mysterious honeycomb to eat. Her marriage to Joseph follows, and she lives (basically) happily ever after. Asenath is the prototype for all future *proselytes, an important role for a woman. However, once again her prominence is within the context of patriarchy, for the purpose of her conversion is to enable her to marry Joseph.

The Testaments of the Twelve Patriarchs are part of the genre of pseudepigraphical literature known as testaments, which are the deathbed words of prominent figures from Israel's past, in this case the eponymous ancestors of the twelve *tribes. Each testament is concerned with particular virtues or vices, which the patriarch instructs his offspring to practice or ignore. The theme of chastity enjoys special prominence in the Testaments. Therefore in the Testaments women exist chiefly as temptations for pious men, their lewdness often coupled with drunkenness as an aid to fornication. For example, Judah, telling of his intercourse with his daughter-in-law Tamar, says, "Since I was drunk with wine, I did not recognize her and her beauty enticed me because of her manner of tricking herself out" (12.3; *The Old Testament Pseudepigrapha* [ed. James H. Charlesworth, Doubleday, 1983] 1, 798). *Reuben, while discussing his sin with his father's concubine Bilhah, says, "Do not devote your attention to a woman's looks, nor live with a woman who is already married, nor become involved in affairs with women" (3.1; ibid., 783). In the Testaments, women exist only as objects to trip up heedless men.

All of the above examples are from literature that in some way features women prominently. But we know almost nothing about the communities that produced this literature and their relation to one another. With classical sources, we are on firmer ground, for we know more about the authors and their audiences.

**Women in the Classical Sources.** Josephus and Philo are the main sources for Jewish thought about women in classical literature. Josephus, who wrote in Rome under the patronage of the Flavian emperors after the First Jewish Revolt (66–70 CE), wrote several works, including *The Antiquities of the Jews,* which is essentially a rewriting of the biblical text for apologetic purposes. In attempting to present Jews and Judaism in a favorable light to his Greco-Roman audience, Josephus makes many changes in the presentation of biblical narratives, including their portrayals of women. One example will suffice. When Josephus rewrites the story of Esther, he has before him both the Hebrew and the Septuagint versions of the book. He chooses to retain most of the changes introduced by the latter, heightening the erotic aspect even more, and downplaying Esther's active role in the story. Thus, the Jewish people are saved, but mainly because Esther is beautiful and the king desires her sexually, not because of her intelligence and resourcefulness.

Philo, a first-century CE Alexandrian Jew with an extensive knowledge of Greek philosophy and literature, undertakes an allegorical interpretation of the biblical text that is a fusion of Jewish thought and Greek philosophy. Therefore, the women and men in the biblical stories become symbols for higher philosophical realities. In the process the women are completely denigrated. Philo draws his dichotomy of male/female from Pythagorean and Aristotelian schemes. Man is *nous* or "mind," the higher intellectual capacity; woman, on the other hand, is *aisthēsis* or "sense-impression," the lower form of perception. Man *(nous)* is immortal, in the image of God, while woman is mortal, closely connected with *sōma,* "body." Since the goal of *nous* is to be free of the troubles of the body, woman is automatically placed in the category of undesirable and wrong. Philo's are the most systematically misogynist of all the writings we have surveyed.

**Conclusion.** A pattern has emerged in this survey. The earlier literature, stemming from a period when gender roles were more egalitarian and both men and women had essential economic and social roles to play, allows women greater freedom of action and a louder voice (Esther, Ruth, Song of Solomon). The later literature, influenced by Hellenistic culture with its more restricted view of women's roles, allows women to act only in relation to men, or in situations of crisis (Asenath, Judith). Finally, in literature written by men on whom the influence of Greek thought is clear, women are more thoroughly denigrated and swept from the stage of an all-male world (Josephus, Philo). *Sidnie Ann White*

### *Early Christianity*

Information on early Christian women is found in the New Testament, writings of the early church fathers, apocryphal and gnostic literature, and archaeological finds such as inscriptions and papyri. In recent years, these sources, historically overlooked for data on women, have been exploited by scholars, resulting in dozens of important secondary works. While the evidence must be treated carefully by the historian and theologian, it furnishes proof that data on the women of antiquity do exist; in fact, the study of women in the New Testament and early church constitutes one of the liveliest and most fruitful areas of biblical scholarship today.

**The Greco-Roman and Jewish Heritage.** Like Christians in general, women in the early church were products of the wider culture. In general, women were dependent both financially and legally on the men in their lives—fathers, husbands, uncles, brothers, and sons. Women generally married while still teenagers, bore one or more children, and died young (the average life expectancy was thirty-four years), often in childbirth. If a girl survived childhood (i.e., was not exposed), and a woman survived childbirth, she might live a long life and bury her husband: women were the primary caretakers of the graves of family members, including those of in-laws. It was also women who passed on the household (usually the men's) religious practices such as ancestor worship to their descendants.

Except in the most outlying rural areas, women were not isolated from each other or from other men. Middle- and upper-class women living in villas or in urban areas often functioned as chief household managers, especially when their husbands were absent for long periods of time on commerce or at war. While there is considerable evidence for independent and wealthy women, most women lived in slavery, near poverty, or middle-class stability; therefore, most worked for wages for their own economic survival and that of their families, even if they were married to a merchant or freedman. In some cases, women may have been secluded in their homes, but for the most part they moved freely in many spheres of the Greco-Roman world—the agora, baths, businesses, and religious associations.

With regard to religious background, some early Christian women were Jewish, since Christianity was a sect of Judaism for a time. Other women converted from Greco-Roman cults, while still others, often in the same family or neighborhood, remained non-Christian. This coexistence of adherents of different religions systems was often peaceful but could lead to conflict, often over the issue of appropriate roles of women in the various groups.

Evidence from both Jewish and Greco-Roman circles shows that women held leadership roles in these groups. In Judaism, archaeological and other evidence demonstrates that some women in the first few centuries CE held positions such as head of a *synagogue *(archisynagōgis),* leader *(archēgissa),* *elder *(presbytis),* "mother of the synagogue" (*mater synagogae*), and priest (*hiereia*). The exact functions of these women are difficult to ascertain, but they were probably equivalent to the functions of men bearing parallel titles. The evidence further demonstrates that women were integrated into regular services, not segregated in "women's galleries" or separate rooms, and that some were major financial contributors to local synagogues.

Similarly, women held leadership roles in many, if not most, of the myriad Greco-Roman cults that allowed women members. Some of their functions included priest, musician, stolist, prophet, torchbearer, dancer, and mourner. Outside of religion, women worked as midwives, lawyers, merchants, artists, teachers, physicians, *prostitutes, and laborers and professionals of all sorts.

Women in positions of authority in religion and society did not constitute a majority: the culture was still patriarchal, that is, controlled primarily by men. However, the fact that women did play some leadership roles in both Judaism and the larger society became significant for the growth of Christianity: women who were drawn to it undoubtedly would have expected to be active participants in the new cult if not leaders. Their presence had a definite effect on the development of the canon, the emerging role of the priest and *bishop, as well as liturgy, theology, and battles with heresy and gnosticism.

**Women in the Early Christian Movement.** The New Testament and early church fathers provide preliminary data on women. The earliest evidence, from *Paul's letters, suggests that women functioned as dynamic leaders of the movement, *deacons, *apostles, and missionaries. The Gospels relate that Jesus had women followers as well as men and treated women as equals; it was also women who were the first to bear witness to his resurrection. The Acts of the Apostles mention the four daughters of Philip who prophesied; Lydia from Thyatira, a merchant and the head of her household; the missionary couple, Priscilla and Aquila; house-church leaders; and prominent converts.

Thus, in pre-Pauline and Pauline Christian communities, women appear to have functioned almost identically to men. In fact, it is possible that more women than men were house-church leaders, hosting vital prayer meetings that became the kernel of the movement. At least one woman deacon, Phoebe, is recorded in the New Testament, and she functioned as an official teacher and missionary in the church of Cenchreae. Euodia and Syntyche from Philippi were prominent leaders of that community, and *Junia served the church at Rome as an apostle. The most prominent woman in the New Testament is Prisca/Priscilla, who worked alongside her husband and was probably the more renowned of the pair. The women Mary, Tryphaena, Tryphosa, and Persis in Romans 16 are described as having labored *(kopian)* for the Lord, the same term Paul used to describe his own evangelizing and teaching activities. (See Elizabeth Schüssler Fiorenza, *In Memory of Her,* New York, 1983.)

Celibacy became a major life-style choice for both men and women early in the Christian movement, and by the third and fourth centuries men and women were living in houses and monasteries (a term that includes convents) segregated by gender. Renunciation by men was not deemed problematic, but the popularity of female celibacy led to fears that women's independence would undermine the very fabric of home and society. Early attestations of this popularity and the subsequent social tensions it created are found in many of the apocryphal Acts of the second and third centuries, including the Acts of Paul and Thecla, the Acts of Andrew, the Acts of Peter, and the Acts of Thomas. In the stories in these Acts, celibacy was idealized, and many women were portrayed as heroines for breaking off engagements and leaving husbands and traditional home situations for the sake of the gospel. While many of the stories in the Acts may be fictitious, they probably originated in oral form in circles of independent women and reflect actual people, events, and trends.

Other threats to the survival of the young church in the eyes of male leaders included the leadership of independent women in gnostic and heretical groups. Two prophets, Priscilla and Maximilla, were prominent in the Montanist sect of the second century, and women in those groups may have baptized and celebrated the Eucharist. Some gnostic sects also allowed women to serve as priests and to baptize. Bishop Atto of Vercelli (ca. 885–961) wrote in several tracts that women were ordained just like men in the ancient church, were leaders of communities, were called elders *(presbyterae),* and fulfilled the duties of preaching, directing, and teaching.

Female celibacy and other acts of independence led male leaders to disseminate countertreatises in which they prescribed strict behavior for all women and attempted to bring the entire Christian movement more in line with the overall culture's ideal of the patriarchal family and household. The New Testament "household codes," written by followers of Paul, not Paul himself, clearly urged women's subordination to men. The so-called Pastoral letters (1 and 2 Timothy and Titus) are also early works accepted into the New Testament canon. 1 Timothy 2.11–12 forbade women from speaking in church, and Titus 1.7–9 assumed that only men would be bishops.

**Retrenchment and Later Trends.** The church fathers of the second through fourth centuries, being among those who agitated against women's independence, decreed that women could only minister to other women as deacons or be enrolled as virgins or widows. Women deacons as described in third- and fourth-century documents were at least fifty or sixty years of age, ministered to sick and *poor women, were present at interviews of women with (male) bishops, priests, or deacons, and instructed women catechumens. Before the decline of adult baptism, women deacons assisted at the baptisms of women, probably their most important role. Women deacons may have been the only women admitted into ministry in the orthodox church by the laying-on of hands by the bishop. In the earliest church, however, female deacons may have functioned much more similarly to male deacons, since the sources are not always clear.

Widows and virgins, while not ordained, had recognized status and privileges in the early church. However, there were restrictions placed on them. Widows in New Testament times had to be at least sixty years of age and married only once; younger widows were expected to remarry. The references to virgins in the New Testament are more vague, but the order seems to be closely linked to that of widows.

Meanwhile, the male leaders reserved for themselves the right to serve the whole church in the more important and powerful roles such as elder *(presbyteros)* and bishop *(episkopos)* and adhered to the ideal of the monarchical episcopate: the high reverence due the bishop and the subordination of others to that office. Bishops in these fathers' minds could, of course, only be fellow men, and the directives they set down toward women could be stringent.

Polycarp, bishop of Smyrna, writing to the Philippians around 110 CE, attempted to limit women's behavior by clearly delineating their roles as virgins, widows, and ever-faithful wives. Ignatius of Antioch urged Polycarp to be the "protector" of widows and exhorted women to be "altogether contented with their husbands" (*Ep. Polycarp* 4,5). Libanius (314–95) complained that women distract men from their religious duties. Canons from the Council of Gangra in 340 declare anathema women who wear male attire, who leave their husbands, and who cut off their hair, a sign of their subjection.

Tertullian, perhaps the most misogynist of all the early fathers, wrote four lengthy treatises dealing with women: *On the Apparel of Women* (ca. 202), *On the Veiling of Virgins* (ca. 204), *To His Wife* (ca. 207), and *On Monogamy* (ca. 208). In *On the Apparel of Women* 1.1, he described women as "the gateway of the devil" and blamed them for leading men astray through their sexual wiles. In chap. 9 of *On the Veiling of Women,* he wrote, "It is not permitted to a woman to speak in the church; but neither is it permitted her to teach, nor to baptize, nor to offer, nor to claim to herself a lot in any manly function, not to say in any sacerdotal office." To Tertullian's way of thinking, the ideal woman was a totally subservient being, completely regulated by strict rules governing every facet of her life—a far cry from the autonomous woman of many of the nascent Christian communities.

One early church leader who was more positive toward women in some ways was Jerome (342–420). In a number of letters between him and the many women of his social circle, Jerome appears as a sort of mentor and father figure to upper-class women who had chosen the celibate life-style. One of his Roman disciples, Paula, founded a monastery near *Bethlehem.

However, even some of Jerome's saintly women were admired for leading lives that followed strict rules of behavior, rules not generally applied to men. Fabiola, a young Christian woman from Rome, divorced her husband because he was a sinner; this was applauded by other Christians. However, these same Christians, including Jerome, condemned her for subsequently remarrying: "She did not know that the rigor of the gospel takes away from women all pretext for remarriage, so long as their former husbands are alive." When she finally realized her "mistake," she publically confessed and was restored to communion. Then, being wealthy, she sold her property and, with the money, founded a hospital to nurse the poor and sick.

Monasticism became increasingly important for women in the face of these restrictions and the eradication of heretical and gnostic groups that had promoted women's independence. A number of women besides Paula, mostly from the upper strata of society, founded or cofounded all-women houses, communities, and nunneries where young women learned to read, write, paint, and draw. Such houses, like those of men, followed rules of order and were self-supporting and devoted to prayer and good works. At first the houses were independent of local church authorities, but over time they were brought under the jurisdiction of the bishop.

While female monasteries may have been centers of opportunity primarily for members of the upper classes, thereby restricting most other women to marriage in patriarchal households or to lives as virgins and widows dependent on men, these communities nevertheless made important contributions to the entire church that have historically been overlooked. While the evidence is meager, especially compared with evidence from all-male enclaves, it suggests that all-women groups produced high-quality illuminated manuscripts; wove many of the tapestries that adorned the great basilicas, as well as the ornate robes worn by clergy; crafted at least some of the silver Communion ware and jewelry used in the liturgy; and contributed to sketch books that served imperial architects as blueprints for exquisite mosaics that decorated many basilicas. Also, women in some communities taught men reading, writing, and drawing; dispensed wisdom to male leaders; and became renowned as leaders of centers of learning.

Significantly, despite attempts by the hierarchy through the ages to conceal the evidence, there is attestation for women priests into the Byzantine era. An epistle of Pope Gelasius I (492–96) to bishops in Italy and Sicily mentions in annoyance that women were officiating at the sacred altars and taking part in ecclesiastical affairs imputed only to men. An inscription from Bruttium dating to the end of the fifth century mentions the presbytera Leta (*Corpus incriptionum latinarum* 10.8079), and another from Salona in Dalmatia (425 CE) mentions the presbytera Flavia Vitalia. While these attestations are rare, they confirm that women functioned sacerdotally—and that male bishops occasionally ordained them. *Valerie Abrahamsen*

# Y

**YAHWEH.** *See* Names of God in the Hebrew Bible.

**YAM SUF.** *See* Red Sea.

# Z

**ZADOK, ZADOKITES.** Zadok was one of *David's two priests. He sided with *Solomon against Adonijah in the succession struggle late in David's life and anointed Solomon king at David's request. As a result, he was the sole chief priest under Solomon, while Abiathar was banished to Anathoth. Zadok's descendants controlled the priesthood in *Jerusalem from this time on until the exile (the chief priest in *Hezekiah's time is said to be from the house of Zadok), and in *Ezekiel's vision of the restoration, all the priests in charge of the altar are Zadokites; and especially 48.11, where Zadokites are separated from other Levites). While there is some controversy about Zadok's origins, his lineage in 1 Chronicles 6.1 8, 49 53 ties him to *Aaron through Eleazar, and there is a Zadok from the house of Aaron mentioned as part of David's army at *Hebron, so it would seem that he was an Aaronite priest.

After the exile, the Zadokites apparently controlled the high priesthood until the time of Antiochus IV Epiphanes in the second century BCE. The Qumran sect was dedicated to the Zadokite priesthood, as well, and it has been suggested that the name of the priestly *Sadducees is derived from Zadok. *Jo Ann Hackett*

**ZAPHON.** The Hebrew word *ṣāpôn* is one of the ordinary words for "north"; this is its most frequent meaning in the Bible, but it is derived from its primary sense. Zaphon was the name (meaning "lookout") of a mountain on the Mediterranean coast ca. 6 mi (10 km) north of Ugarit, later called Mount Casius and now Jebel el-ᵓAqraᶜ. As a prominent peak in the northern part of the *Canaanite world, its name was used as a synonym for the direction north, just as one of the words for "west" literally means the (Mediterranean) Sea. It is primarily identified with *Baal, as widespread references to Baal-zephon indicate; it was his home and as such could also be deified.

There are several passages in the Bible in which the original sense of *ṣāpôn* as the mountain home of the storm god is meant. Job 26.7 and Isaiah 14.13 are both in contexts permeated with references to Canaanite mythology. Psalm 89.12 may refer to Zaphon and Amanus, rather than north and south, as parallel to Tabor and *Hermon. The usual translation "Mount Zion in the far north" in Psalm 48.2 is a geographical absurdity; but the identification of Yahweh's home, *Zion, with Baal's home, Zaphon, makes sense in light of the Canaanite origins of the Jerusalem *Temple and its ideology. The verse should therefore be rendered: "Mount Zion, the heights of Zaphon, is the city of the great king." The name of the prophet *Zephaniah is probably also derived from this meaning.

Zaphon is also the name of an important town in the Jordan Valley.

*Michael D. Coogan*

**ZEALOT.** Zealot is a term that has been associated with a movement of revolutionaries active throughout the first century CE in Roman Palestine and thus during the time of Jesus's ministry. These Zealots supposedly played the major role in the social unrest which ultimately erupted in the First Jewish Revolt against Rome in 66 CE. Jesus's teaching, and in particular speeches such as the Sermon on the Mount, have been read against the Zealots' advocacy of armed resistance against and the overthrow of the Roman occupational forces and administrators. In fact, one of Jesus's followers, Simon, was called "zealot," but this may simply be a descriptive epithet rather than meaning a member of an organized group.

However, this older and disturbingly tidy scholarly reconstruction concerning the Zealots has recently been overturned. The Jewish revolt in 66–70 is not now viewed as the work of a longstanding group called the Zealots. A much closer reading of Josephus reveals that such an organized group did not exist for the six decades before the revolt. The Zealots only emerge at the outset of the revolt, and then only as a coalition of popular groups seeking the overthrow of Rome, including numerous bandit groups (Grk. *lastai*), Sicarii or dagger people (urban terrorists), as well as groups lead by messianic figures and popular kings. The pioneering work of Richard A. Horsley, particularly in his work, *Bandits, Prophets, and Messiahs: Popular Movements at the Time of Jesus* (New York, 1985) has demonstrated this with great clarity. During the first century the colonial situation brought on by Roman domination and exacerbated by the ruling *Herodian dynasty escalated into a socioeconomic malaise characterized by great debt, unemployment, social division, crime, banditry, and finally revolt; the Jesus movement developed in this context, and many of Jesus's sayings are only understandable when placed in it. Josephus describes these social ills and the movements which arose in *Galilee and Judea with disdain. "Zealot" became one term to describe the brief coalition of such movements. As the coalition fragmented, some groups went to Masada in the south to await the outcome of the struggle, some killed each other, and others fought the Romans to the death. There was thus no single, monolithic group called the Zealots against whom other perspectives can be easily measured.

*J. Andrew Overman*

**ZEBULUN.** Son of *Jacob and *Leah and one of the twelve *tribes of Israel. The tribe settled in the region of Galilee between *Asher and *Naphtali to the north and *Manasseh and *Issachar to the south. Zebulun figures prominently in the wars of Judges. According to the Chronicler, Zebulun continues to play a major role during *David's reign. Members of this tribe seem to have survived the *Assyrian conquest. King Josiah's wife, Zebidah, came from Rumah in Zebulun.

The Jewish community of *Galilee in the Second Temple period perhaps stemmed in part from Zebulun. After the destruction of the Second Temple, the Jewish academic centers of learning located in this area were pivotal to the survival of Jewish tradition.

*Gary N. Knoppers*

**ZECHARIAH.** The late sixth-century BCE prophet to whom is attributed the book of Zechariah.

**Zechariah 1–8.** The first eight chapters of the book contain the teaching of Zechariah in a series of eight visions of the night together with accompanying oracles. These are sandwiched between accounts of his preaching in 1.1–6 and chaps. 7–8. Like *Haggai, Zechariah is said to have prophesied in the second year of *Darius the Persian (520 BCE), but his ministry extended to the fourth year (518 BCE). Like Haggai, therefore, he is addressing and seeking to encourage the postexilic community in Judah in all their frustrations and difficulties.

Several visions and oracles assure the people of God's imminent action on their behalf. While the first vision, that of the horsemen, shows that nothing can yet be seen to be happening, the oracle brings assurance that God is deeply concerned for the welfare of *Jerusalem, which he is about to "choose" again and to which he will come to resume his dwelling. He will punish the nations that have destroyed the city and taken its citizens into exile, the theme also of the second vision of the "horns" and "smiths." The third takes up Second *Isaiah's picture of the unlimited size of the restored city and assures them that God's glory (his presence) will be in the city. God will protect them as he did when he led the Israelites in the wilderness by a pillar of fire. The oracle that follows calls on the exiles to return, for Yahweh is about to dwell in the city to which not only Jews, but all nations, will come. The fourth vision shows the cleansing of Joshua, the high priest (called Jeshua in Ezra and Nehemiah), a sign that God is now determined to forgive and cleanse the community. The fifth suggests a joint leadership of *Zerubbabel as civil governor and Joshua, and contains a promise that Zerubbabel will complete the rebuilding of the *Temple, but also a warning that he must do so only in complete reliance on God's spirit. The two visions in chap. 5 announce the cleansing of the restored community, while a final vision, echoing the first, pictures horsemen and chariots patrolling the earth, reporting that God's spirit is now at rest in the north country (traditionally the direction from which Israel's enemies have come in judgment from God). Now, however, this is the peace, not of inaction, as in the first vision, but of the resolution of the people's problems by God's saving actions. The passage 6.9–15, along with 3.6–10, seems to describe a situation in which the priestly line has assumed preeminence, while messianic hope now attaches to an unnamed and future figure called the Branch.

The surrounding oracles contain warnings against repeating the sins of preexilic generations who ignored the teaching of the prophets. They reinforce the promises of the visions of an imminent new age by assuring questioners that all mourning fasts for the fall of Jerusalem are about to be replaced by joyful festivals of celebration.

The fact that 1.1–6 and chaps. 7–8 contain echoes of some of the "sermons" in the books of Chronicles may suggest that the teaching of Zechariah was handed down by preaching and teaching personnel of the postexilic Temple. This is strengthened by the presence of teaching on such subjects as true fasting, found elsewhere in postexilic literature. Again, oracles of Zechariah are taken up and expounded afresh in 8.1–8, while 8.9–13 appears to be exposition of Haggai 2.15–19. The universalist tone in Zechariah's teaching is strongly and splendidly renewed in 8.20–23.

Zechariah, like Haggai, was thus remembered as a prophet who encouraged the immediate postexilic community by assuring them of God's imminent action in terms that echoed the preaching of *Ezekiel and Second Isaiah and took up themes of the preexilic *Zion/David theology expressed in many psalms. His picture of a joint messiahship of civil and religious leaders was to reappear in the teaching of the Qumran community. The form of the teaching in a series of visions is reminiscent of one test of a true *prophet in some of the earlier literature, namely, that he had been admitted to the council of heaven. The stronger sense here, however, that what is happening on earth is a projection of what is happening in heaven, has suggested to some that in Zechariah 1–8 we have an early hint of apocalyptic.

**Zechariah 9–14.** In Zechariah 9–14 no mention is made of the building of the Temple that now is standing, nor of the time of Darius I, while there is a reference to "Yawan" (literally, Ionia; NRSV: "Greece") in 9.13. There is nothing corresponding to the visions of chaps. 1–8 or to the ethical teaching of 1.1–6 and chaps. 7–8. For these reasons most scholars assign these chapters to a later time and another hand or hands. Broad thematic features are, however, common to both parts of the book, such as a strongly Zion-centered interest, God's cleansing of the community in preparation for his final act of salvation, a marked universalism, dependence on earlier prophecy, and a concern for a true and proper leadership as one sign of the new age. These suggest that the later parts of the book came from circles that maintained the traditions of Zechariah's teaching.

The material is broadly of two kinds: eschatological passages that look forward to the triumph of God over evil and controversy passages in which strong attacks are made on those who are seen as false leaders of the community, in the manner of some earlier prophetic books.

So much is obscure in these chapters that interpretation of them can be only tentative. The view that they came from a sharply eschatological party that found itself increasingly at odds with the official priesthood and Temple, and so looked for a more and more radical intervention of God, would account for much that is here. If that were so, it would mean that some of the factors that later gave rise to the Qumran community were already being felt by those from whom chaps. 9–14 came, perhaps in the third century BCE. *Rex Mason*

**ZEDEKIAH.** Last king of *Judah (597–587/586 BCE). A younger son of *Josiah, he was placed on the throne by *Nebuchadrezzar of *Babylon to replace his uncle, Jehoiachin, whom Nebuchadrezzar had deposed. Nine years later, Zedekiah rebelled against Nebuchadrezzar, prompting him to besiege and destroy *Jerusalem.

In the book of *Jeremiah, Zedekiah's reign is described in fatalistic tones: destruction by Babylon is inevitable; submission to Nebuchadnezzar is Zedekiah's only option; he and the people refuse to heed Jeremiah's warnings and should expect punishment; the insincerity of repentance is exposed. On one occasion, Zedekiah reveals his belief in the truth of Jeremiah's warnings, yet he fears certain Judahites more than God's wrath. In the end, he attempts to escape under cover of darkness, but is captured by the Babylonians and led away in shame. *Timothy M. Willis*

**ZEPHANIAH.** The late seventh-century BCE prophet to whom is attributed the book of Zephaniah. This ninth book of the Minor Prophets proclaims the coming day of the Lord, with its judgment on Israel and the nations, to be the best hope for salvation.

The prophet's name means "Yah(weh) protects"; in an earlier form it may have been a confession, "Zaphon is Yahweh," *Zaphon being the deified Canaanite mountain who is thus identified with Israel's Yahweh. The superscription goes to unusual lengths in giving the prophet's ancestry, which is traced back to *Hezekiah, the great Judean king.

The prophecy is dated to the reign of King *Josiah (640–609 BCE), who was responsible for major reforms in Judah's worship. Josiah was the "son of Ammon," who was murdered by revolutionaries. But a group called "the people of the land" rose up to quell the revolution and put his son Josiah on the throne. This group supported Josiah in his reforms and *Jeremiah in his preaching. Zephaniah seems to be very close to their goals and aims.

Zephaniah fought against foreign influences and against the worship of other gods. His message is close to that of the great eighth-century prophets, especially *Isaiah. He taught that pride was the major sin of humankind, and that it leads to rebellion against divine authority. He understood God's judgment to be universal. Hope for him lay beyond the great day of judgment. The book serves as a bridge between the eighth-century prophets of judgment such as *Hosea and *Amos, and the prophets after the exile, such as *Haggai and *Zechariah, who proclaimed a coming salvation of God.

The book is composed as a dramatic dialogue between Yahweh and someone else, possibly the prophet. It seems to promise only doom for all creation, including Israel. Such a fate is thoroughly deserved. Then a slight hope is raised for some to survive when specifically identified peoples are marked for the judgment; some hope for the "humble of the land" is disclosed. Finally the Lord's mercy offers a way of escape for the nations and for Israel.

Zephaniah makes a strong contribution to the understanding of the day of the Lord. In the Minor Prophets, this day is understood as a decisive turning point in which the Lord's judgment falls upon Israel and the nations for their idolatry and pride. The events that lead up to *Jerusalem's final destruction in 587/586 BCE are clearly in mind. Zephaniah shows that this terrible moment can bring the opportunity for a new beginning, for both Israel and the nations. The true opportunity is for those who are "humble and lowly" (3.12). The book opens the door to the messages that the following three books of the collection will bring. In Haggai and Zechariah, God leads in rebuilding the *Temple a full century after Zephaniah's time, and the final chapters of Zechariah as well as *Malachi look to the opportunities and responsibilities of the people of God in the postexilic age.

*John D. W. Watts*

**ZERUBBABEL.** The name, meaning "offspring of Babylon," of a descendant of *David who returned from the Babylonian exile (Ezra 2.2) to become governor of the Persian province of Yehud (Judah) under *Darius I (522–486 BCE). He was a grandson of Jehoiachin (Jeconiah), the exiled king of Judah. Zerubbabel and Joshua the high priest were responsible for the completion of the rebuilding of the *Temple. Hopes for the restoration of the nation were probably attached to him because of his ancestry. Haggai 2.23 calls him the "servant of Yahweh" and the one he has "chosen." The prophet Zechariah mentions a "branch," which also may refer to

Zerubbabel. Although the Temple was only begun in 520 BCE and was finished in 515 BCE, there is no mention of Zerubbabel at its dedication. It may be that he was removed from power by the Persian authorities because of the threat of rebellion in Yehud. Zerubbabel appears in the genealogies of Jesus in Matthew 1 and Luke 3. *Russell Fuller*

**ZION.** A name of *Jerusalem. The etymology of the Hebrew term is unknown. Perhaps the earliest reference to Zion is the account in 2 Samuel 5 of *David's conquest of Jerusalem, then under the control of the *Jebusites; v. 7 speaks of "the stronghold of Zion." This and other texts, as well as recent archaeological research, suggest that Zion was limited originally to the Jebusite fortress located on the crest of a hill at the southeast corner of Jerusalem, also called the Ophel. After his victory, David renamed the stronghold "the city of David." With its physical features and the presence of the fresh-water spring of Gihon nearby, the site was of strategic importance. The city of Jerusalem soon expanded north along the eastern ridge to include what became the Temple mount, but even then the name Zion could be restricted to the city of David to the south. According to 1 Kings 8.1, at the dedication of the *Temple *Solomon had the ark of the covenant brought up to the Temple from "the city of David, which is Zion."

Later, poetry recalled that it was David who had found the ark and brought it to Zion, the place Yahweh desired for "his habitation." Already in early texts from the book of Psalms, however, Zion refers not to David's city but preeminently to Yahweh's dwelling place, Yahweh's "holy hill." This extension of the term is probably connected with the transfer of the ark from the city of David to the Temple newly constructed by Solomon. The ark represented the footstool of Yahweh's royal throne, and the Temple enshrining it symbolized the presence of Yahweh as king. In this way the term Zion lost its originally precise geographic designation and came to refer to the Temple area and even to the entire city of Jerusalem. In later times the name Zion was erroneously restricted to the western hill, still called Mount Zion, but this was uninhabited until the eighth century BCE (*see* Jerusalem). But what it lost in geographic precision Zion more than regained in the rich symbolism associated with it.

That symbolism centered on Zion as the dwelling place of Yahweh as king. Since it was viewed as the site of Yahweh's throne, Zion was portrayed as a lofty peak extending into heaven, the point at which heaven and earth meet. Thus, Psalm 48.1–2 depicts Zion as Yahweh's holy mountain "on the heights of Zaphon" (NRSV: "in the far north"). *Zaphon was the mountain home of the Canaanite god *Baal, and imagery from Canaanite religion is applied to Zion in Psalm 48 and elsewhere. True to its original designation of "stronghold," but especially because Yahweh reigned there as king, Zion was also a symbol of security. Yahweh was Zion's defender against the threats of kings and nations. For that reason Zion was also portrayed as the place of refuge, especially for the *poor.

All of this seems to have given rise to a notion of Zion's inviolability, as reflected in Micah 3.9–12 and Jeremiah 7.1–15. According to these prophets, the people of Jerusalem believed the city's security against *Assyrian and *Babylonian threats to be guaranteed. The book of *Isaiah accepts the notion of Zion's inviolability but distinguishes between the security promised to Zion and the destruction with which Yahweh threatens Jerusalem. Zion will endure even beyond Jerusalem's destruction.

After Jerusalem and the Temple were destroyed in 587/586 BCE, hopes for the future were often expressed in terms of the restoration of Zion; because of this hope, the modern Zionist movement took the ancient designation as its own. In some texts from the exilic and postexilic periods, Zion/Jerusalem is addressed in royal language common to the Near East; in others, Zion is portrayed as a mother. Occasionally, Zion is identified with the community itself: "saying to Zion, 'You are my people'" (Isa. 51.16). 2 Esdras speaks of Zion in referring to the heavenly Jerusalem that would ultimately replace the earthly one. In Hebrews 12.22, Zion refers to the "new covenant" of Jesus. In all of these diverse ways, Zion is the "city of God."

*Ben C. Ollenburger*

# BIBLIOGRAPHY

*To assist readers, the editors have prepared this bibliography of some important and useful books available in English about the Bible.*

**Critical Introductions.** These provide summaries of modern scholarly research on the formation of the Bible from the smallest literary units to the final canonical arrangement, as well as a bibliographic starting point.

Childs, Brevard S. *Introduction to the Old Testament as Scripture.* Philadelphia: Fortress, 1979.

———. *The New Testament as Canon: An Introduction.* Philadelphia: Fortress, 1985.

Collins, Raymond F. *Introduction to the New Testament.* Garden City, N.Y.: Doubleday, 1983.

Hayes, John H. *An Introduction to Old Testament Study.* Nashville, Tenn.: Abingdon, 1979.

Koester, Helmut. *Introduction to the New Testament,* vol. 2: *History and Literature of Early Christianity.* 2d ed. New York: de Gruyter, 2000.

Kümmel, Werner G. *Introduction to the New Testament.* Rev. and enl. ed. Nashville, Tenn.: Abingdon, 1996.

**Popular Introductions.** These are frequently used as texts in undergraduate courses, and provide readable surveys of the development of the Bible and of the history of the biblical world.

Alter, Robert, and Frank Kermode. *The Literary Guide to the Bible.* Cambridge, Mass.: Belknap, 1987.

Anderson, Bernard W. *Understanding the Old Testament.* Abr. 4th ed. Englewood Cliffs, N.J.: Prentice-Hall, 1998.

Barr, David L. *New Testament Story: An Introduction.* 2d ed. Belmont, Calif.: Wadsworth, 1995.

Court, John M., and Kathleen M. Court. *The New Testament World.* Englewood Cliffs, N.J.: Prentice-Hall, 1990.

Crenshaw, James L. *Old Testament Story and Faith: A Literary and Theological Introduction.* Peabody, Mass.: Hendrickson, 1992 (repr. of 1986 ed.).

Duling, Dennis C., and Norman Perrin. *The New Testament: Proclamation and Parenesis, Myth and History.* 3d ed. Fort Worth, Tex.: Harcourt Brace, 1994.

Ehrman, Bart D. *The New Testament: A Historical Introduction to the Early Christian Writings.* 2d ed. New York: Oxford University Press, 1999.

Freed, Edwin D. *The New Testament: A Critical Introduction.* 3d ed. Belmont, Calif.: Wadsworth, 2000.

Gottwald, Norman K. *The Hebrew Bible: A Socio-Literary Introduction.* Philadelphia: Fortress, 1985.

Harrington, Daniel J. *Interpreting the New Testament: A Practical Guide.* Collegeville, Minn.: Liturgical, 1990.

Harris, Stephen L. *The New Testament: A Student's Introduction.* 3d ed. Mountain View, Calif.: Mayfield, 1998.

Johnson, Luke T. *The Writings of the New Testament: An Interpretation.* Rev. ed. Minneapolis, Minn.: Fortress, 1999.

Kee, Howard C. *Understanding the New Testament.* 5th ed. Englewood Cliffs, N.J.: Prentice-Hall, 1993.

Metzger, Bruce M. *The New Testament: Its Background, Growth, and Content*. 2d. ed., enlarged. Nashville, Tenn.: Abingdon, 1983.

Rendtorff, Rolf. *The Old Testament: An Introduction*. Philadelphia: Fortress, 1986.

Rogerson, John W., and Philip Davies. *The Old Testament World*. Englewood Cliffs, N.J.: Prentice-Hall, 1989.

Sandmel, Samuel. *The Hebrew Scriptures: An Introduction to their Literature and Religious Ideas*. New York: Oxford University, 1978.

### History

Bickerman, Elias J. *The Jews in the Greek Age*. Cambridge, Mass.: Harvard University, 1988.

Bright, John. *A History of Israel*. 4th ed. Louisville, Ky: Westminster John Knox, 2000.

Cohen, Shaye J. D. *From the Maccabees to the Mishnah*. Philadelphia: Westminster, 1987.

Coogan, Michael D., ed. *The Oxford History of the Biblical World*. New York: Oxford University, 1998.

Edwards, I. E. S., ed. *The Cambridge Ancient History*. 3d ed. London: Cambridge University, 1970– .

Herrmann, Siegfried. *A History of Israel in Old Testament Times*. 2d ed. Philadelphia: Fortress, 1981.

Jagersma, Henk. *A History of Israel in the Old Testament Period*. Philadelphia: Trinity, 1983.

———. *A History of Israel from Alexander the Great to Bar Kochba*. Philadelphia: Fortress, 1986.

Koester, Helmut. *Introduction to the New Testament*, vol. 1: *History, Culture, and Religion of the Hellenistic Age*. 2d ed. New York: de Gruyter, 1995.

Miller, J. Maxwell, and John H. Hayes. *A History of Ancient Israel and Judah*. Philadelphia: Westminster, 1986.

Safrai, Shmuel, and Menahem Stern, eds. *The Jewish People in the First Century: Historical Geography, Political History, Social, Cultural and Religious Life and Institutions*. 2 vols. Philadelphia: Fortress, 1974, 1976.

Schürer, Emil. *The History of the Jewish People in the Age of Jesus Christ*. 4 vols. Rev. and ed. by Geza Vermes and Fergus Millar. Edinburgh: T. and T. Clark, 1973–87.

Shanks, Hershel, ed. *Ancient Israel: A Short History from Abraham to the Roman Destruction of the Temple*. Rev. ed. Washington, D.C.: Biblical Archaeology Society, 1999.

———, ed. *Christianity and Rabbinic Judaism: A Parallel History of Their Origins and Early Development*. Washington, D.C.: Biblical Archaeology Society, 1992.

Soggin, J. Alberto. *An Introduction to the History of Israel and Judah*. 2d ed. Valley Forge, Penn.: Trinity, 1993.

de Vaux, Roland. *The Early History of Israel*. Philadelphia: Westminster, 1978.

**Nonbiblical Texts.** These standard anthologies and surveys provide introductions to the literatures of the ancient Near Eastern and Greco-Roman neighbors of ancient Israel and earliest Christianity, as well as to early Jewish and early Christian writings not included in the canon.

Barrett, C. K., ed. *The New Testament Background: Selected Documents*. Rev. ed. San Francisco: Harper and Row, 1989.

Cameron, Ron, ed. *The Other Gospels: Non-Canonical Gospel Texts*. Philadelphia: Westminster, 1982.

Charlesworth, James H., ed. *The Old Testament Pseudepigrapha*. 2 vols. Garden City, N.Y.: Doubleday, 1983, 1985.

Coogan, Michael D. *Stories from Ancient Canaan*. Philadelphia: Westminster, 1978.

Hallo, William W., and K. Lawson Younger, eds. *The Context of Scripture*. 2 vols. Leiden, Neth.: Brill, 1997, 1999.

Miller, Robert J., ed. *The Complete Gospels: Annotated Scholars Version*, Rev. ed. Sonoma, Calif.: Polebridge, 1995.

Nickelsburg, George W. E. *Jewish Literature between the Bible and the Mishnah: A Historical and Literary Introduction*. Philadelphia: Fortress, 1981.

Pritchard, James B., ed. *Ancient Near Eastern Texts Relating to the Old Testament*

*[ANET]; The Ancient Near East in Pictures Relating to the Old Testament [ANEP].* Rev. ed. Princeton: Princeton University, 1969. (There is an abridged version of both: *The Ancient Near East: An Anthology of Texts and Pictures [ANETP],* 2 vols., 1958, 1975.)

Robinson, James M., ed. *The Nag Hammadi Library in English.* Rev. ed. San Francisco: HarperCollins, 1988.

Schneemelcher, Wilhelm, ed. *New Testament Apocrypha.* Ed. Robert McL. Wilson. 2 vols. Nashville: Westminster/John Knox, 1991 (1965).

Sparks, H. F. D., ed. *The Apocryphal Old Testament.* Oxford: Clarendon, 1984.

Stone, Michael E., ed. *Jewish Writings of the Second Temple Period: Apocrypha, Pseudepigrapha, Qumran, Sectarian Writings, Philo, Josephus.* Philadelphia: Fortress, 1984.

Vermes, Geza. *The Complete Dead Sea Scrolls in English.* New York: Allen Lane, 1997.

**Archaeology**

Aharoni, Yohanan. *The Archaeology of the Land of Israel.* Philadelphia: Westminster, 1982.

Ben-Tor, Amnon, ed. *The Archaeology of Ancient Israel.* New Haven: Yale University, 1991.

Kenyon, Kathleen M. *The Bible and Recent Archaeology.* Rev. ed. by P. R. S. Moorey. Atlanta: John Knox, 1987.

Mazar, Amihai. *Archaeology of the Land of the Bible: 10,000–586 B.C.E.* New York: Doubleday, 1990.

Meyers, Eric M., ed. *The Oxford Encyclopedia of Archaeology in the Near East.* 5 vols. New York: Oxford University, 1997.

Stern, Ephraim, ed. *The New Encyclopedia of Archaeological Excavations in the Holy Land.* 4 vols. New York: Simon and Schuster, 1993.

Stillwell, Richard et al., eds. *The Princeton Encyclopedia of Classical Sites.* Princeton: Princeton University, 1976.

Wilkinson, John. *The Jerusalem Jesus Knew: An Archaeological Guide to the Gospels.* New York: Thomas Nelson, 1983.

**Geography**

Aharoni, Yohanan. *The Land of the Bible: A Historical Geography.* Rev. ed. Philadelphia: Westminster, 1979.

Aharoni, Yohanan, and Michael Avi-Yonah. *The Macmillan Bible Atlas.* 3d ed. New York: Macmillan, 1992.

Baly, Denis. *The Geography of the Bible.* Rev. ed. New York: Harper and Row, 1974.

May, Herbert G. *Oxford Bible Atlas.* 3rd ed. rev. by John Day. New York: Oxford University, 1984.

Orni, Ephraim, and E. Ephrat. *Geography of Israel.* 4th ed. Jerusalem: Israel Universities, 1980.

Pritchard, James B. *The Harper Atlas of the Bible.* New York: Harper and Row, 1987.

**Religion and Society.** All of the following are major contributions to the study of Israelite, early Jewish, and early Christian religion, literature, and culture. While the discussion is frequently technical, they will repay serious reading.

Albertz, Rainer. *A History of Israelite Religion in the Old Testament Period.* 2 vols. Louisville: Westminster John Knox, 1994.

Cross, Frank Moore. *Canaanite Myth and Hebrew Epic: Essays in the History of the Religion of Israel.* Cambridge, Mass.: Harvard University, 1973.

Kaufmann, Yehezkel. *The Religion of Israel from Its Beginnings to the Babylonian Exile.* Chicago: University of Chicago, 1960.

Kraemer, Ross Shepard. *Her Share of the Blessings: Women's Religions among Pagans, Jews, and Christians in the Greco-Roman World.* New York: Oxford University, 1992.

Kraus, Hans-Joachim. *Worship in Israel: A Cultic History of the Old Testament.* Richmond, Va.: John Knox, 1966.

Noth, Martin. *A History of Pentateuchal Traditions.* Trans. Bernhard W. Anderson. Englewood Cliffs, N.J.: Prentice-Hall, 1972.

Sandmel, Samuel. *Judaism and Christian Beginnings.* New York: Oxford University, 1978.

Segal, Alan F. *Rebecca's Children: Judaism and Christianity in the Roman World.* Cambridge, Mass.: Harvard University, 1986.

Schiffman, Lawrence H. *From Text to Tradition: A History of Second Temple and Rabbinic Judaism.* Hoboken, N.J.: Ktav, 1991.

Stambaugh, John E., and David L. Balch. *The New Testament in Its Social Environment.* Philadelphia: Westminster, 1986.

de Vaux, Roland. *Ancient Israel: Its Life and Institutions.* New York: McGraw-Hill, 1965.

Weber, Max. *Ancient Judaism.* New York: Free Press, 1952.

### Biblical Theology

Botterweck, G. Johannes, and Helmer Ringgren, eds. *Theological Dictionary of the New Testament.* Grand Rapids, Mich.: Eerdmans, 1977–.

Bultmann, Rudolf. *Theology of the New Testament.* New York: Scribner's, 1955.

Childs, Brevard S. *Biblical Theology of the Old and the New Testaments: Theological Reflection on the Christian Bible.* Minneapolis: Fortress, 1993.

Conzelmann, Hans. *An Outline of the Theology of the New Testament.* New York: Harper and Row, 1969.

Eichrodt, Walther. *Theology of the Old Testament.* 2 vols. Philadelphia: Westminster, 1961–1967.

Fredriksen, Paula. *From Jesus to Christ: The Origins of New Testament Images of Jesus.* New Haven: Yale University, 1988.

Fuller, Reginald H. *The Foundations of New Testament Christology.* New York: Scribner's, 1965.

Hanson, Paul D. *The People Called: The Growth of Community in the Bible.* San Francisco: Harper and Row, 1986.

Kittel, Gerhard, and Gerhard Friedrich, eds. *Theological Dictionary of the New Testament.* Grand Rapids, Mich.: Eerdmans, 1985.

Levenson, Jon D. *The Hebrew Bible, the Old Testament, and Historical Criticism.* Louisville, Ky.: Westminster/John Knox, 1993.

von Rad, Gerhard. *Old Testament Theology.* 2 vols. New York: Harper and Row, 1962–1965.

Wright, G. Ernest. *God Who Acts: Biblical Theology as Recital.* Chicago, Ill.: Regnery, 1952.

**Methodology.** A series of useful "Guides to Biblical Scholarship" is published by Fortress Press (Minneapolis). More detailed surveys are found in three volumes on "The Bible and Its Modern Interpreters," published by the Society of Biblical Literature and Scholars Press (Atlanta); they are:

Knight, Douglas A., and Gene M. Tucker, eds. *The Hebrew Bible and Its Modern Interpreters.* 1985.

Kraft, Robert A., and George W. E. Nickelsburg, eds. *Early Judaism and Its Modern Interpreters.* 1986.

Epp, Eldon Jay, and George W. MacRae, eds. *The New Testament and Its Modern Interpreters.* 1989.

### Textual Criticism

Aland, Kurt, and Barbara Aland. *The Text of the New Testament: An Introduction to the Critical Editions and to the Theory and Practice of Modern Textual Criticism.* 2d ed. Grand Rapids, Mich.: Eerdmans, 1989.

Metzger, Bruce M. *The Text of the New Testament: Its Transmission, Corruption, and Restoration.* 3d ed. New York: Oxford University, 1992.

Tov, Emanuel. *Textual Criticism of the Hebrew Bible.* Minneapolis: Fortress, 1992.

**History of Interpretation.** In addition to articles in *ABD* and *IDB* and *IDBSup* (see next heading), good starting points are:

Baird, William. *History of New Testament Research,* vol. 1: *From Deism to Tübingen.* Minneapolis: Fortress, 1992.

Coggins, R. J., and J. L. Houlden. *A Dictionary of Biblical Interpretation.* Philadelphia: Trinity, 1990.

Greenslade, S. L., et al. *The Cambridge History of the Bible.* 3 vols. Cambridge University, 1963–1970.

Hayes, John H. *Dictionary of Biblical Interpretation.* 2 vols. Nashville, Tenn.: Abingdon, 1999.

Kümmel, Werner Georg. *The New Testament: The History of the Investigation of Its Problems.* Nashville: Abingdon, 1972.

Kugel, James L., and Rowan A. Greer. *Early Biblical Interpretation.* Philadelphia: Westminster, 1986.

Morgan, Robert, and John Barton. *Biblical Interpretation.* New York: Oxford University, 1988.

Neill, Stephen, and N. T. Wright. *The Interpretation of the New Testament, 1861–1986.* 2d ed. New York: Oxford University, 1988.

Orlinsky, Harry M., and Robert G. Bratcher. *A History of Bible Translation and the North American Contribution.* Atlanta: Scholars, 1991.

**Reference**

***Encyclopedic Dictionaries.*** Of the many Bible dictionaries available, these are some of the better and most recent. All provide extensive bibliography for further reading.

Achtemeier, Paul J., ed. *The HarperCollins Bible Dictionary.* San Francisco: HarperSanFrancisco, 1996.

Buttrick, George A., ed. *The Interpreter's Dictionary of the Bible [IDB],* 4 vols., with *Supplementary Volume [IDBSup]* (ed. K. Crim). Nashville: Abingdon, 1963, 1976.

Freedman, David Noel et al., eds. *The Anchor Bible Dictionary [ABD].* New York: Doubleday, 1992.

———, ed. *Eerdmans Dictionary of the Bible.* Grand Rapids, Mich.: Eerdmans, 2000.

Mills, Watson E., ed. *Mercer Dictionary of the Bible.* Macon, Ga.: Mercer University, 1990.

***Concise Commentaries***

Anderson, Bernhard W., ed. *The Books of the Bible.* 2 vols. New York: Scribner's, 1989.

Brown, Raymond E., et al., eds. *The New Jerome Biblical Commentary.* Englewood Cliffs, N.J.: Prentice Hall, 1990.

Laymon, Charles M., ed. *The Interpreter's One Volume Commentary on the Bible.* Nashville: Abingdon, 1971.

Mays, James L., ed. *The HarperCollins Bible Commentary.* San Francisco: HarperSanFrancisco, 2000.

Newsom, Carol A., and Sharon H. Ringe, eds. *The Women's Bible Commentary.* Exp. ed. Louisville: Westminster John Knox, 1998.

***Other Useful Reference Works.*** These more general encyclopedias have a large number of articles on the Bible and related topics.

Eliade, Mircea et al., eds. *The Encyclopedia of Religion.* New York: Macmillan, 1987.

Roth, Cecil, ed. *Encyclopaedia Judaica.* New York: Macmillan, 1972.

***Bibliographies***

Fitzmyer, Joseph A. *An Introductory Bibliography for the Study of Scripture.* 3d ed. Rome: Pontifical Biblical Institute, 1990.

Harrington, Daniel J. *The New Testament: A Bibliography.* Wilmington, Del.: Michael Glazier, 1985.

Stuart, Douglas. *Old Testament Exegesis: A Primer for Students and Pastors.* 2d ed. Philadelphia: Westminster, 1984.

Zannoni, Arthur E. *The Old Testament: A Bibliography.* Collegeville, Minn.: Liturgical, 1992.

# INDEX

* Note—In entries with multiple page references, page numbers in **bold** refer to the main entry.

THE NEW OXFORD

# BIBLE MAPS




*Prepared by Oxford Cartographers*
*and based on the Oxford Bible Atlas.*

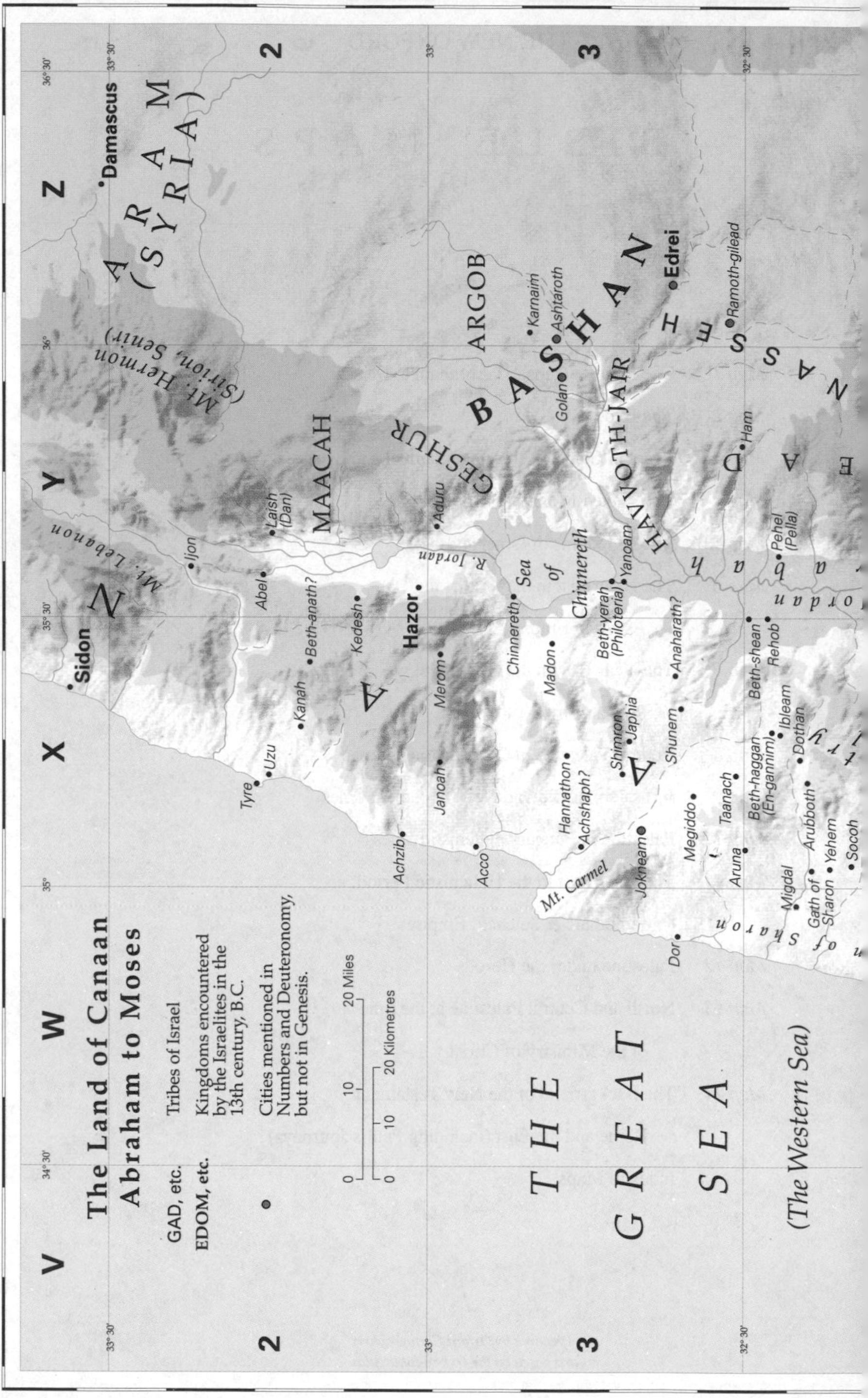
The Land of Canaan
Abraham to Moses
GAD, etc. Tribes of Israel
EDOM, etc. Kingdoms encountered by the Israelites in the 13th century, B.C.
Cities mentioned in Numbers and Deuteronomy, but not in Genesis.
0 10 20 Miles
0 10 20 Kilometres
THE GREAT SEA
(The Western Sea)
V
W
X
Y
Z
2
3
34° 30'
35°
35° 30'
36°
36° 30'
33° 30'
33°
32° 30'
Sidon
Tyre
Uzu
Achzib
Acco
Mt. Carmel
Dor
Mt. Lebanon
Ijon
Abel
Laish (Dan)
Kanah
Beth-anath?
Kedesh
Hazor
Merom
Janoah
Hannathon
Achshaph?
Jokneam
Shimron
Japhia
Madon
Chinnereth
Sea of Chinnereth
R. Jordan
Beth-yerah (Philoteria)
Yanoam
Anaharath?
Shunem
Megiddo
Taanach
Aruna
Beth-haggan (En-gannim)
Ibleam
Dothan
Arubboth
Migdal
Gath of Sharon
Yehem
Socoh
Beth-shean
Rehob
Pehel (Pella)
Ham
Aduru
MAACAH
GESHUR
Mt. Hermon (Sirion, Senir)
ARAM (SYRIA)
Damascus
ARGOB
BASHAN
HAVVOTH-JAIR
Golan
Karnaim
Ashtaroth
Edrei
Ramoth-gilead

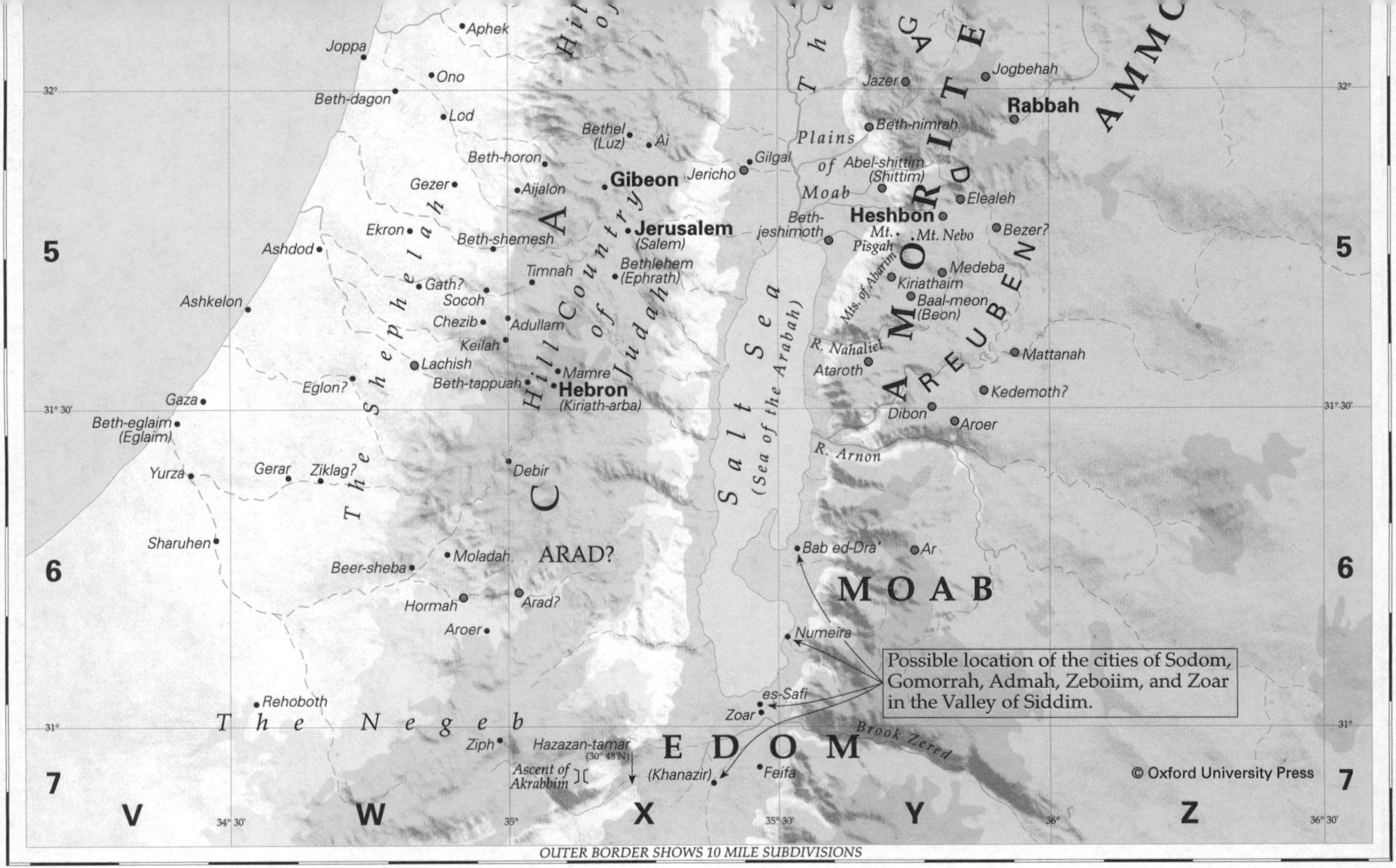
Aphek
Joppa
Ono
Beth-dagon
Lod
Bethel
(Luz)
Ai
Beth-horon
Gezer
Aijalon
Gibeon
Jericho
Gilgal
Ekron
Ashdod
Beth-shemesh
Jerusalem
(Salem)
Timnah
Bethlehem
(Ephrath)
Gath?
Socoh
Ashkelon
Chezib
Adullam
Keilah
Lachish
Mamre
Eglon?
Beth-tappuah
Hebron
(Kiriath-arba)
Gaza
Beth-eglaim
(Eglaim)
Yurza
Gerar
Ziklag?
Debir
Sharuhen
Moladah
ARAD?
Beer-sheba
Hormah
Arad?
Aroer
Rehoboth
The Negeb
Ziph
Hazazan-tamar
(30° 48'N)
Ascent of Akrabbim
(Khanazir)
EDOM
Feifa
Zoar
es-Safi
Numeira
Bab ed-Dra'
Ar
MOAB
Possible location of the cities of Sodom, Gomorrah, Admah, Zeboiim, and Zoar in the Valley of Siddim.
Brook Zered
© Oxford University Press
The Shephelah
Hill Country of Judah
CANAAN
Salt Sea
(Sea of the Arabah)
R. Nahaliel
Ataroth
R. Arnon
Dibon
Aroer
Kedemoth?
Mattanah
REUBEN
AMORITES
Mts. of Abarim
Kiriathaim
Baal-meon
(Beon)
Medeba
Mt. Pisgah
Mt. Nebo
Bezer?
Beth-jeshimoth
Heshbon
Elealeh
Plains of Moab
Abel-shittim
(Shittim)
Beth-nimrah
Jazer
Jogbehah
Rabbah
GAD
AMMON
5
6
7
V
W
X
Y
Z
32°
31° 30'
31°
34° 30'
35°
35° 30'
36°
36° 30'
OUTER BORDER SHOWS 10 MILE SUBDIVISIONS

# MAP 2

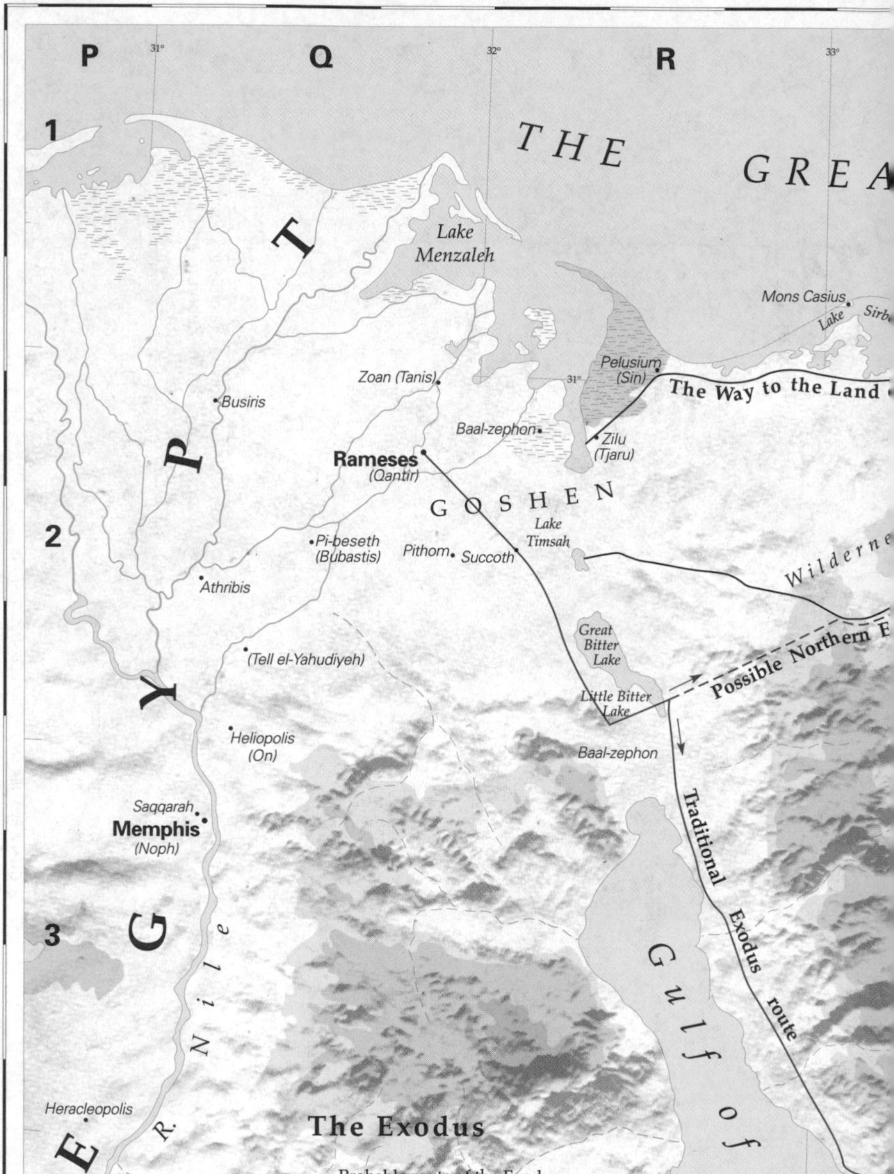

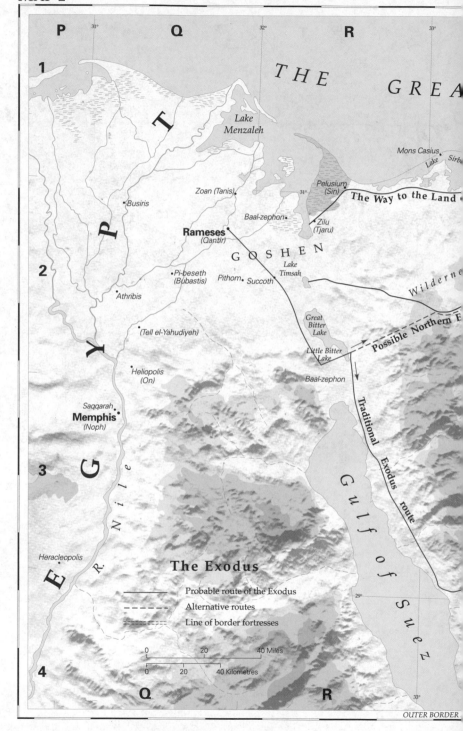

P
Q
R
31°
32°
33°
1
2
3
4
THE GREA
EGYPT
Lake Menzaleh
Mons Casius
Lake Sirb
Pelusium (Sin)
The Way to the Land
Zoan (Tanis)
31°
Busiris
Baal-zephon
Zilu (Tjaru)
Rameses (Qantir)
GOSHEN
Lake Timsah
Pi-beseth (Bubastis)
Pithom
Succoth
Wilderne
Athribis
Great Bitter Lake
Possible Northern E
(Tell el-Yahudiyeh)
Little Bitter Lake
Heliopolis (On)
Baal-zephon
Saqqarah
Memphis (Noph)
Traditional Exodus route
R. Nile
Gulf of Suez
Heracleopolis
The Exodus
Probable route of the Exodus
Alternative routes
Line of border fortresses
0
20
40 Miles
0
20
40 Kilometres
29°
Q
R
33°
OUTER BORDER

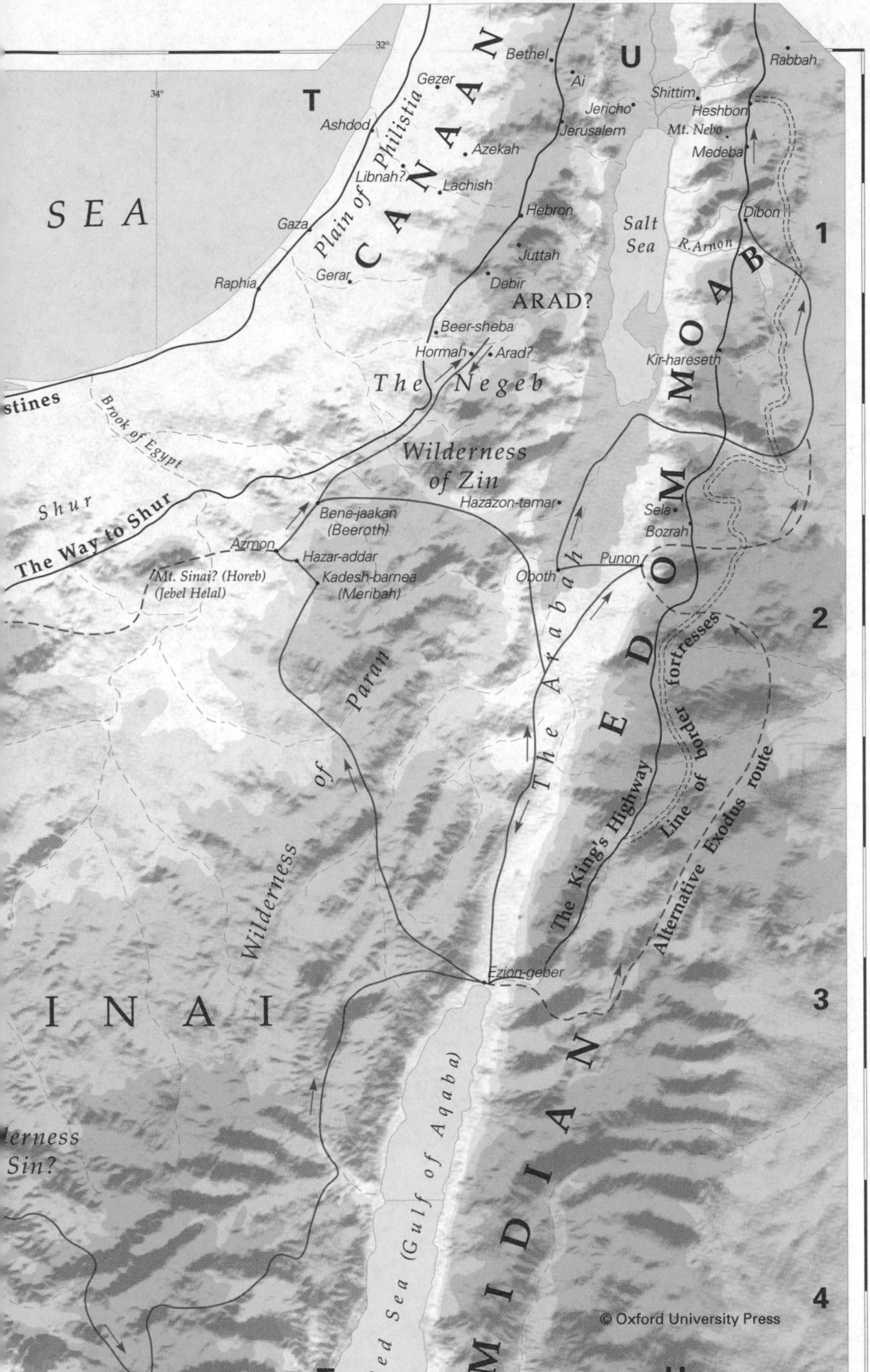


E SUBDIVISIONS

MAP 3

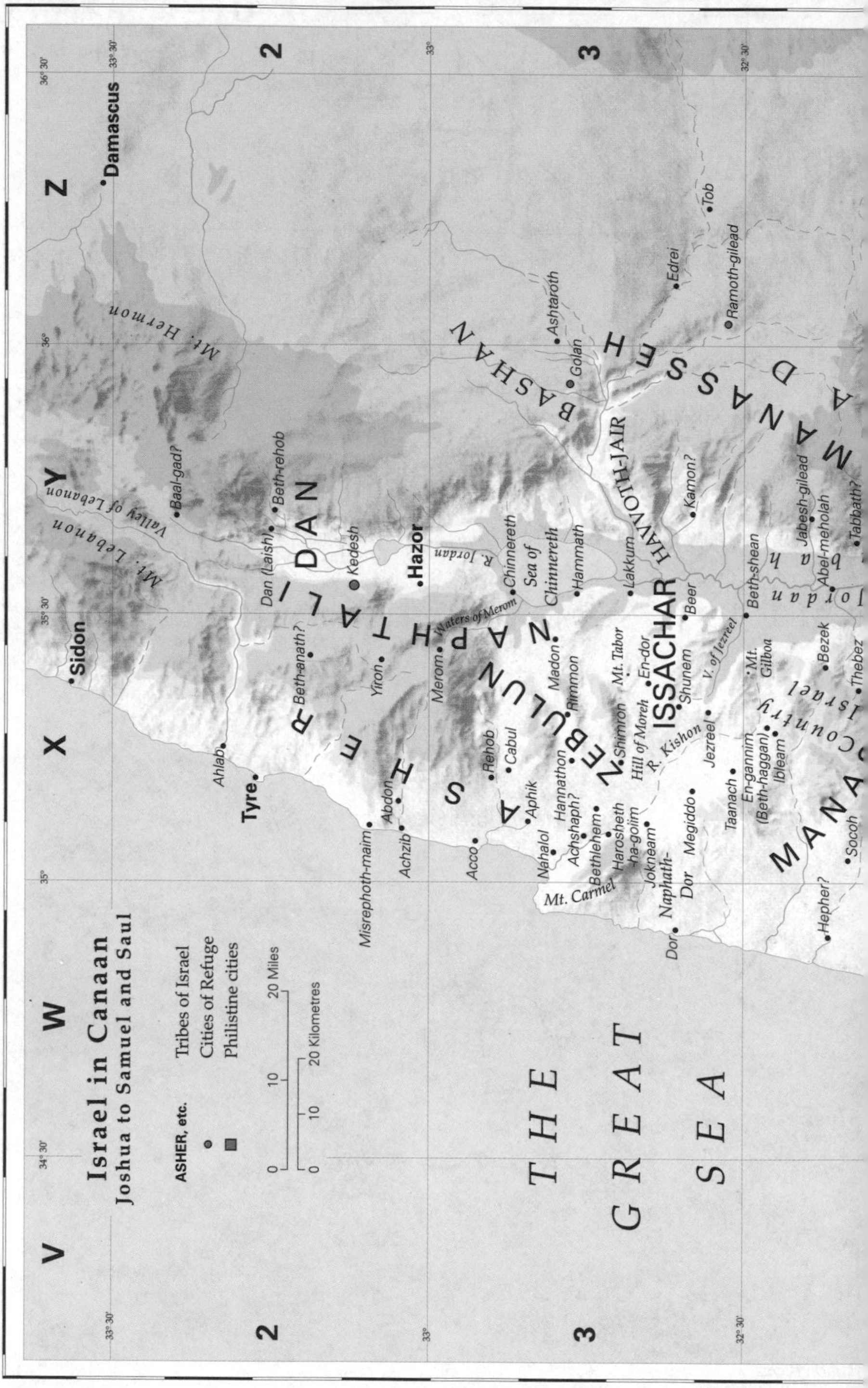
Israel in Canaan
Joshua to Samuel and Saul
ASHER, etc.
Tribes of Israel
Cities of Refuge
Philistine cities
0
10
20 Miles
0
10
20 Kilometres
THE GREAT SEA
V
W
X
Y
Z
2
3
Damascus
Sidon
Tyre
Ahlab
Mt. Hermon
Mt. Lebanon
Valley of Lebanon
Baal-gad?
Beth-rehob
Dan (Laish)
DAN
Kedesh
Hazor
R. Jordan
Beth-anath?
Yiron
Waters of Merom
Merom
NAPHTALI
Chinnereth
Sea of Chinnereth
Hammath
BASHAN
Ashtaroth
Golan
Edrei
Tob
Ramoth-gilead
HAVVOTH-JAIR
MANASSEH
Lakkum
Kamon?
ASHER
ZEBULUN
Madon
Rimmon
Mt. Tabor
En-dor
ISSACHAR
Beer
Shunem
V. of Jezreel
Beth-shean
Jabesh-gilead
Abel-meholah
Tabbath?
Jordan
Misrephoth-maim
Abdon
Achzib
Rehob
Cabul
Aphik
Acco
Hannathon
Achshaph?
Nahalol
Bethlehem
Harosheth-ha-goiim
Shimron
Hill of Moreh
R. Kishon
Jokneam
Mt. Carmel
Naphath-Dor
Dor
Megiddo
Jezreel
Taanach
En-gannim (Beth-haggan)
Ibleam
Mt. Gilboa
Bezek
Thebez
Country of Israel
Socoh
Hepher?

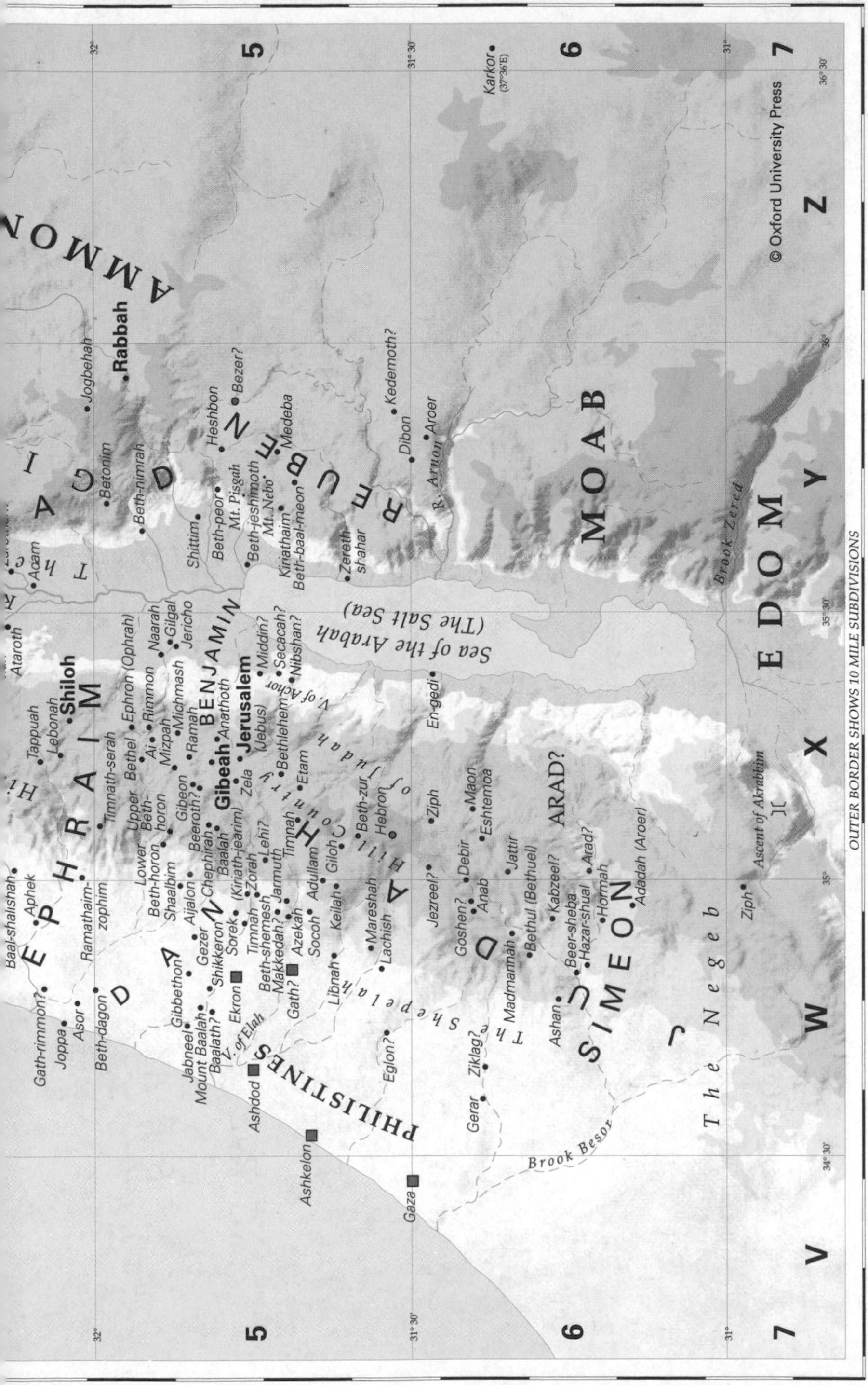
AMMON
Rabbah
Jogbehah
Betonim
Beth-nimrah
GAD
Adam
Ataroth
EPHRAIM
Shiloh
Tappuah
Lebonah
Baal-shalishah
Aphek
Ramathaim-zophim
Timnath-serah
Upper Beth-horon
Lower Beth-horon
Bethel
Ephron (Ophrah)
Ai
Rimmon
Mizpah
Michmash
Naarah
Gilgal
Jericho
BENJAMIN
Anathoth
Ramah
Gibeon
Beeroth?
Gibeah
Jerusalem
(Jebus)
Zela
Baalah
(Kiriath-jearim)
Chephirah
Shaalbim
Aijalon
Gezer
DAN
Gibbethon
Shikkeron
Sorek
Zorah
Ekron
Timnah
Beth-shemesh
Jarmuth
Lehi?
Makkedah?
Azekah
Gath?
Socoh
Adullam
Keilah
Libnah
Mareshah
Lachish
Eglon?
Giloh
Timnah
Etam
Bethlehem
Beth-zur
Hebron
Hill Country of Judah
JUDAH
V. of Achor
Middin?
Secacah?
Nibshan?
En-gedi
Ziph
Maon
Eshtemoa
Carmel
Jattir
Debir
Anab
Goshen?
Jezreel?
Madmannah
Bethul (Bethuel)
Kabzeel?
ARAD?
Arad?
Hormah
Adadah (Aroer)
Beer-sheba
Hazar-shual
Ashan
SIMEON
The Negeb
Ziklag?
Gerar
Brook Besor
The Shephelah
PHILISTINES
Ashdod
Ashkelon
Gaza
Jabneel
Mount Baalah
Baalath?
V. of Elah
Joppa
Asor
Beth-dagon
Gath-rimmon?
Sea of the Arabah
(The Salt Sea)
Shittim
Beth-peor
Mt. Pisgah
Beth-jeshimoth
Mt. Nebo
Kiriathaim
Beth-baal-meon
Zereth-shahar
Heshbon
Bezer?
Medeba
REUBEN
Kedemoth?
Dibon
Aroer
R. Arnon
MOAB
Brook Zered
EDOM
Ziph
Ascent of Akrabbim
Karkor
(37°36'E)
© Oxford University Press
V
W
X
Y
Z
5
6
7
32°
31° 30'
31°
34° 30'
35°
35° 30'
36°
36° 30'
OUTER BORDER SHOWS 10 MILE SUBDIVISIONS

MAP 4

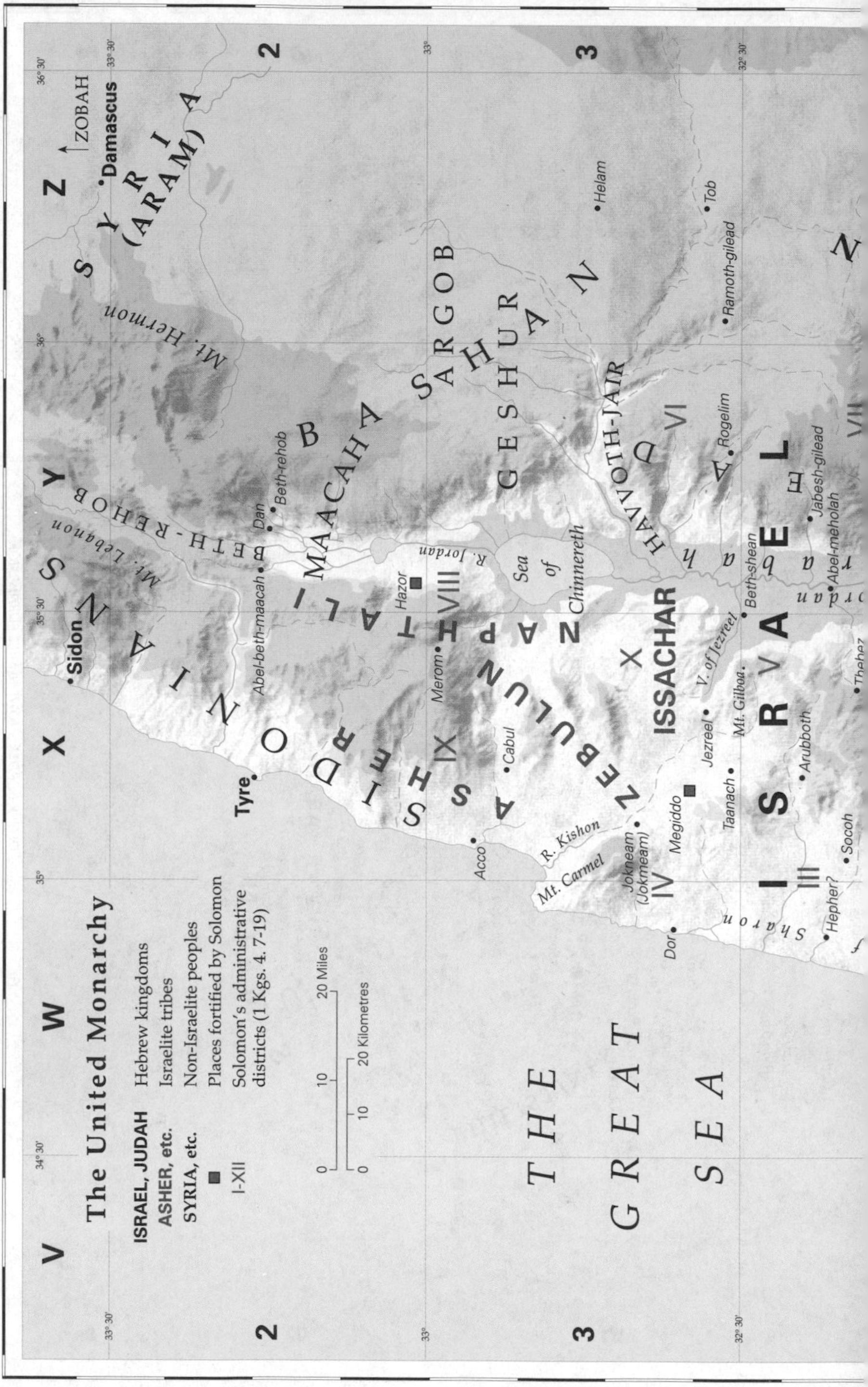

The United Monarchy
ISRAEL, JUDAH Hebrew kingdoms
ASHER, etc. Israelite tribes
SYRIA, etc. Non-Israelite peoples
Places fortified by Solomon
I-XII Solomon's administrative districts (1 Kgs. 4. 7-19)
0 10 20 Miles
0 10 20 Kilometres
THE GREAT SEA
V
W
X
Y
Z
2
3
34° 30'
35°
35° 30'
36°
36° 30'
33° 30'
33°
32° 30'
SIDONIANS
SYRIA (ARAM)
ZOBAH
Damascus
Mt. Hermon
Mt. Lebanon
BETH-REHOB
ARGOB
MAACAH
GESHUR
BASHAN
HAVVOTH-JAIR
NAPHTALI
ASHER
ZEBULUN
ISSACHAR
ISRAEL
GAD
Sidon
Tyre
Acco
Cabul
Merom
Hazor
Abel-beth-maacah
Dan
Beth-rehob
R. Jordan
Sea of Chinnereth
Helam
Tob
Ramoth-gilead
Rogelim
Jabesh-gilead
Abel-meholah
Beth-shean
V. of Jezreel
Jezreel
Mt. Gilboa
Taanach
Megiddo
Jokneam (Jokmeam)
R. Kishon
Mt. Carmel
Dor
Sharon
Arubboth
Socoh
Hepher?
Thebez
I
III
IV
V
VI
VII
VIII
IX
X

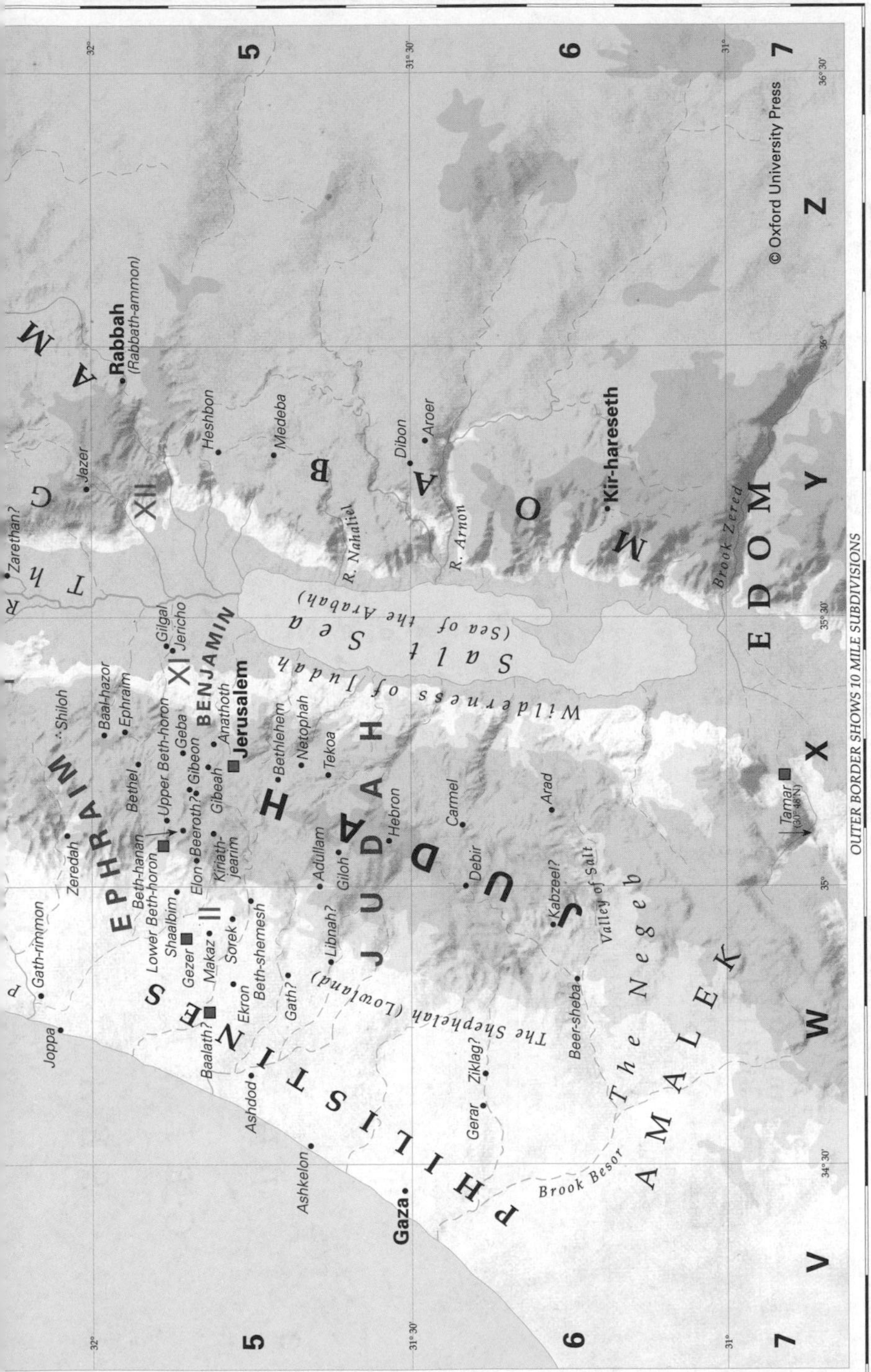

5
6
7
V
W
X
Y
Z
32°
31° 30'
31°
34° 30'
35°
35° 30'
36°
36° 30'
PHILISTINES
EPHRAIM
JUDAH
BENJAMIN
AMALEK
EDOM
MOAB
AMMON
The Negeb
The Shephelah (Lowland)
Wilderness of Judah
Salt Sea
(Sea of the Arabah)
Brook Besor
Valley of Salt
Brook Zered
R. Arnon
R. Nahaliel
Gaza
Ashkelon
Ashdod
Joppa
Gath-rimmon
Zeredah
Shiloh
Baal-hazor
Ephraim
Bethel
Beth-hanan
Lower Beth-horon
Upper Beth-horon
Shaalbim
Gezer
Makaz
Baalath?
Ekron
Elon
Beeroth?
Gibeon
Geba
Gibeah
Anathoth
Kiriath-jearim
Sorek
Beth-shemesh
Jerusalem
Bethlehem
Netophah
Tekoa
Gath?
Libnah?
Giloh
Adullam
Hebron
Carmel
Debir
Arad
Kabzeel?
Beer-sheba
Ziklag?
Gerar
Tamar
(30° 48' N)
Gilgal
Jericho
Zarethan?
Jazer
Heshbon
Medeba
Rabbah
(Rabbath-ammon)
Dibon
Aroer
Kir-hareseth
II
XI
XII
© Oxford University Press
OUTER BORDER SHOWS 10 MILE SUBDIVISIONS

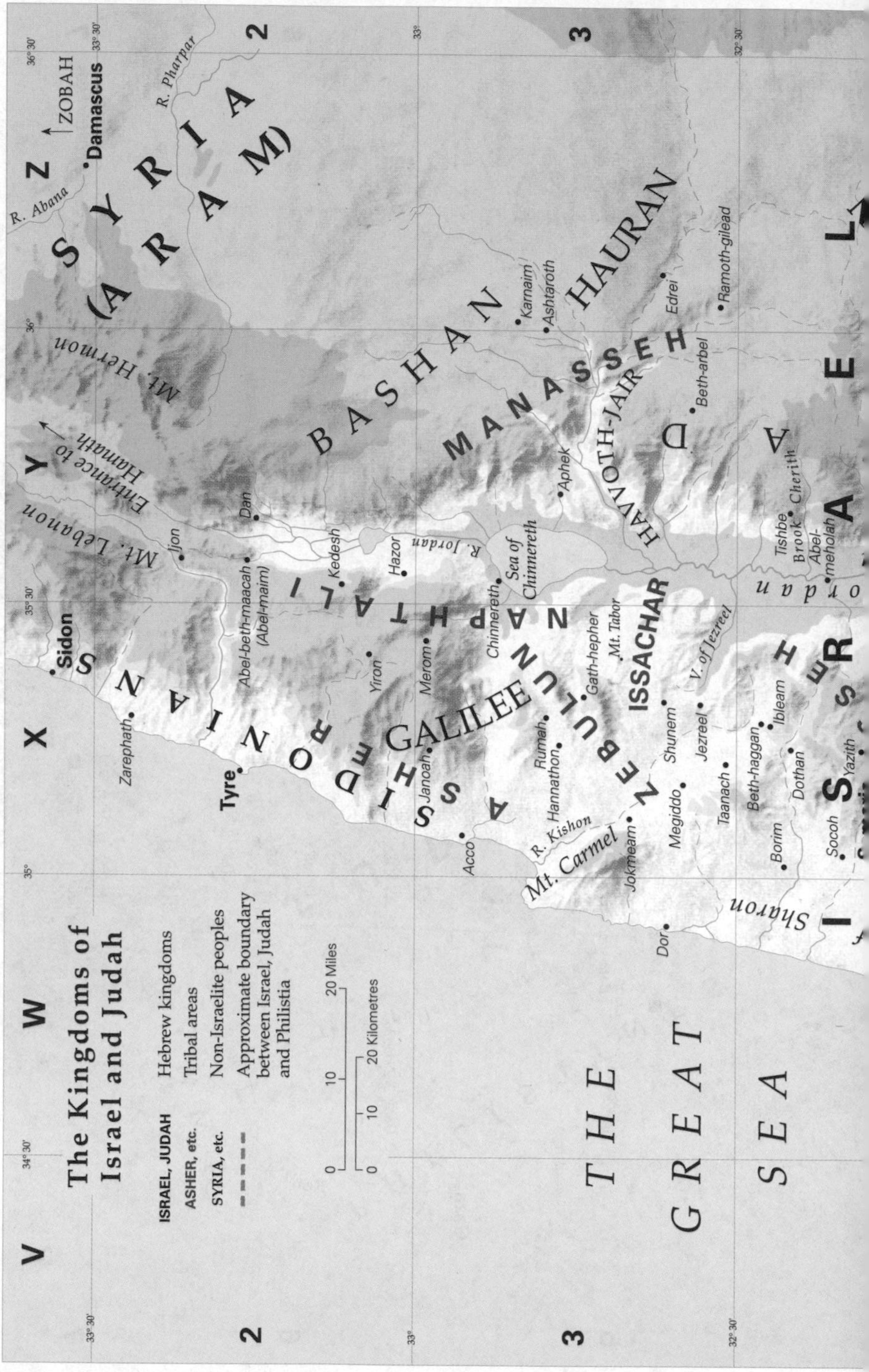
The Kingdoms of Israel and Judah
ISRAEL, JUDAH Hebrew kingdoms
ASHER, etc. Tribal areas
SYRIA, etc. Non-Israelite peoples
Approximate boundary between Israel, Judah and Philistia
0 10 20 Miles
0 10 20 Kilometres
THE GREAT SEA
V
W
X
Y
Z
2
3
34° 30'
35°
35° 30'
36°
36° 30'
33° 30'
33°
32° 30'
ZOBAH
Damascus
R. Abana
R. Pharpar
SYRIA (ARAM)
Mt. Hermon
Entrance to Hamath
Mt. Lebanon
Sidon
SIDONIANS
Zarephath
Tyre
Ijon
Dan
Abel-beth-maacah (Abel-maim)
Kedesh
Hazor
Yiron
Merom
Janoah
NAPHTALI
ASHER
GALILEE
R. Jordan
Sea of Chinnereth
Chinnereth
BASHAN
Karnaim
Ashtaroth
HAURAN
Edrei
Ramoth-gilead
MANASSEH
HAVOTH-JAIR
Aphek
Beth-arbel
GAD
ZEBULUN
Gath-hepher
Mt. Tabor
ISSACHAR
Rumah
Hannathon
R. Kishon
Acco
Mt. Carmel
Jokmeam
Megiddo
Shunem
Jezreel
V. of Jezreel
Taanach
Beth-haggan
Ibleam
Dothan
Tishbe
Brook Cherith
Abel-meholah
Jordan
Borim
Socoh
Yazith
Dor
Sharon
ISRAEL

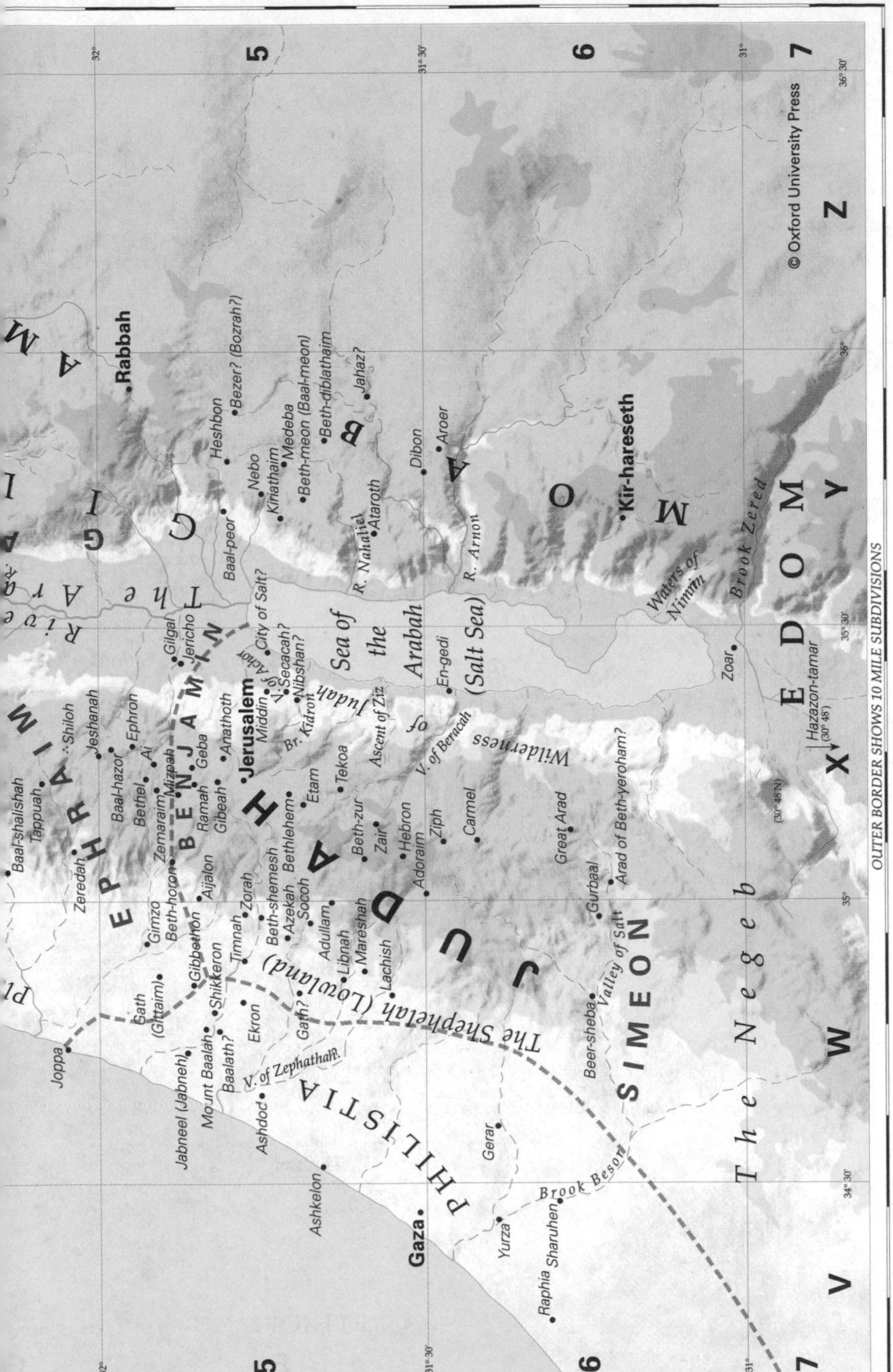
PHILISTIA
JUDAH
BENJAMIN
EPHRAIM
SIMEON
MOAB
EDOM
GILEAD
AMMON
The Negeb
The Shephelah (Lowland)
Wilderness of Judah
Sea of the Arabah (Salt Sea)
The Arabah
River
Joppa
Jabneel (Jabneh)
Mount Baalah
Baalath?
Ashdod
Ashkelon
Gaza
Raphia
Sharuhen
Yurza
Brook Besor
Gerar
Beer-sheba
Valley of Salt
Gurbaal
Arad of Beth-yeroham?
Great Arad
Carmel
Ziph
Hebron
Zair
Adoraim
Beth-zur
Lachish
Mareshah
Libnah
Adullam
Socoh
Azekah
Beth-shemesh
Timnah
Zorah
Ekron
Gath?
Shikkeron
Gath (Gittaim)
Gibbethon
Gimzo
Beth-horon
Aijalon
Zeredah
Baal-shalishah
Tappuah
Zemaraim
Bethel
Baal-hazor
Ai
Ephron
Jeshanah
Shiloh
Mizpah
Ramah
Geba
Gibeah
Anathoth
Jerusalem
Bethlehem
Etam
Tekoa
Middin
V. of Achor
Secacah?
Nibshan?
Br. Kidron
Ascent of Ziz
V. of Beracah
En-gedi
City of Salt?
Jericho
Gilgal
V. of Zephathah
Baal-peor
Heshbon
Nebo
Kiriathaim
Medeba
Beth-meon (Baal-meon)
Beth-diblathaim
Bezer? (Bozrah?)
Jahaz?
Rabbah
Ataroth
R. Nahaliel
Dibon
Aroer
R. Arnon
Kir-hareseth
Waters of Nimrim
Brook Zered
Zoar
Hazazon-tamar (30° 48')
(30° 48' N)
V
W
X
Y
Z
5
6
7
32°
31° 30'
31°
34° 30'
35°
35° 30'
36°
36° 30'
© Oxford University Press
OUTER BORDER SHOWS 10 MILE SUBDIVISIONS

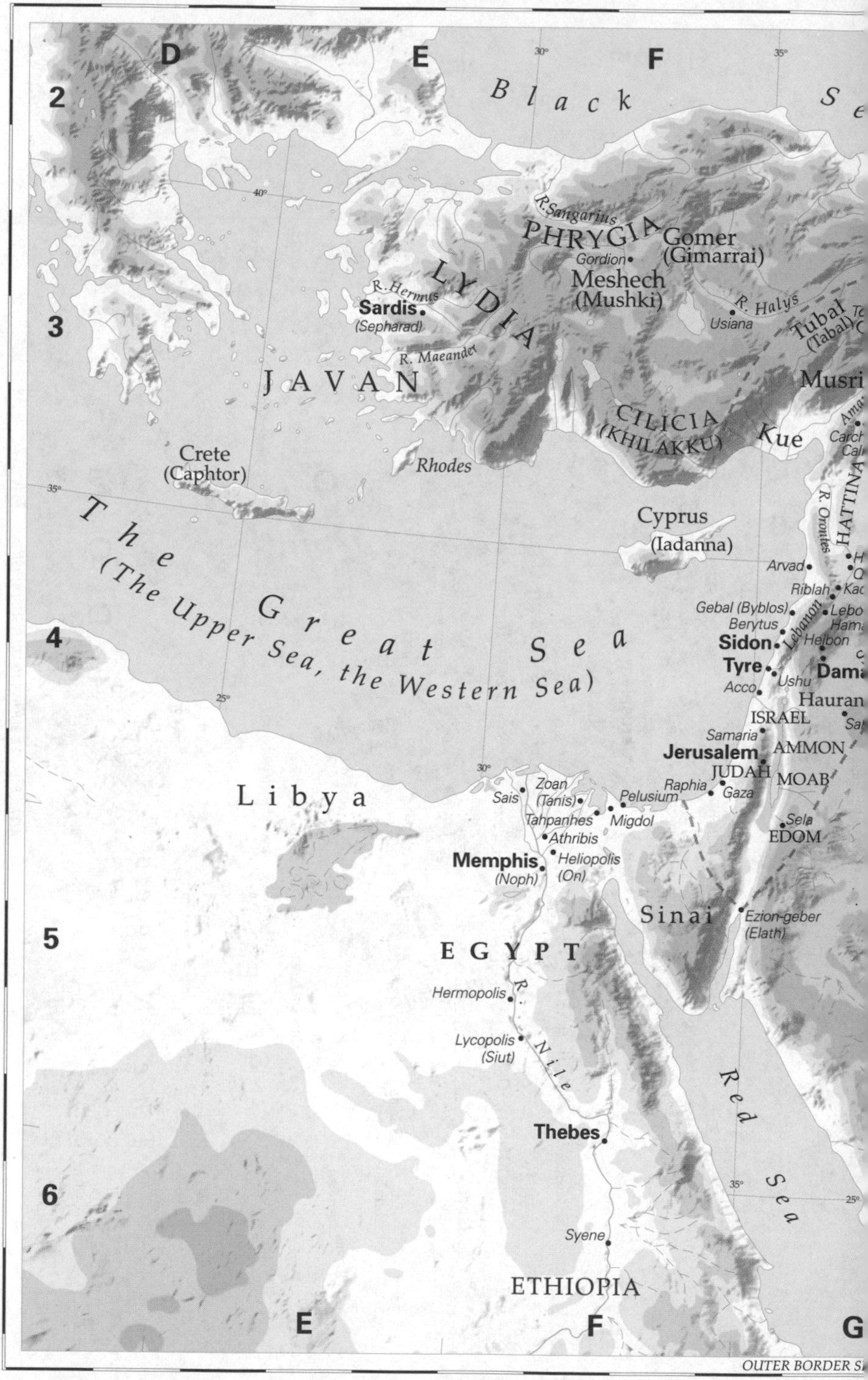
D
E
F
2
3
4
5
6
30°
35°
40°
25°
Black
PHRYGIA
R. Sangarius
Gomer
(Gimarrai)
Gordion
Meshech
(Mushki)
LYDIA
R. Hermus
Sardis
(Sepharad)
R. Maeander
R. Halys
Usiana
Tubal
(Tabal)
Musri
JAVAN
CILICIA
(KHILAKKU)
Kue
HATTINA
R. Orontes
Crete
(Caphtor)
Rhodes
Cyprus
(Iadanna)
The Great Sea
(The Upper Sea, the Western Sea)
Arvad
Riblah
Gebal (Byblos)
Berytus
Lebanon
Sidon
Helbon
Tyre
Ushu
Acco
Hauran
ISRAEL
Samaria
AMMON
Jerusalem
JUDAH
MOAB
Raphia
Gaza
Libya
Zoan
(Tanis)
Sais
Pelusium
Tahpanhes
Migdol
Athribis
Memphis
(Noph)
Heliopolis
(On)
Sela
EDOM
Sinai
Ezion-geber
(Elath)
EGYPT
Hermopolis
R. Nile
Lycopolis
(Siut)
Red Sea
Thebes
Syene
ETHIOPIA
E
F
G

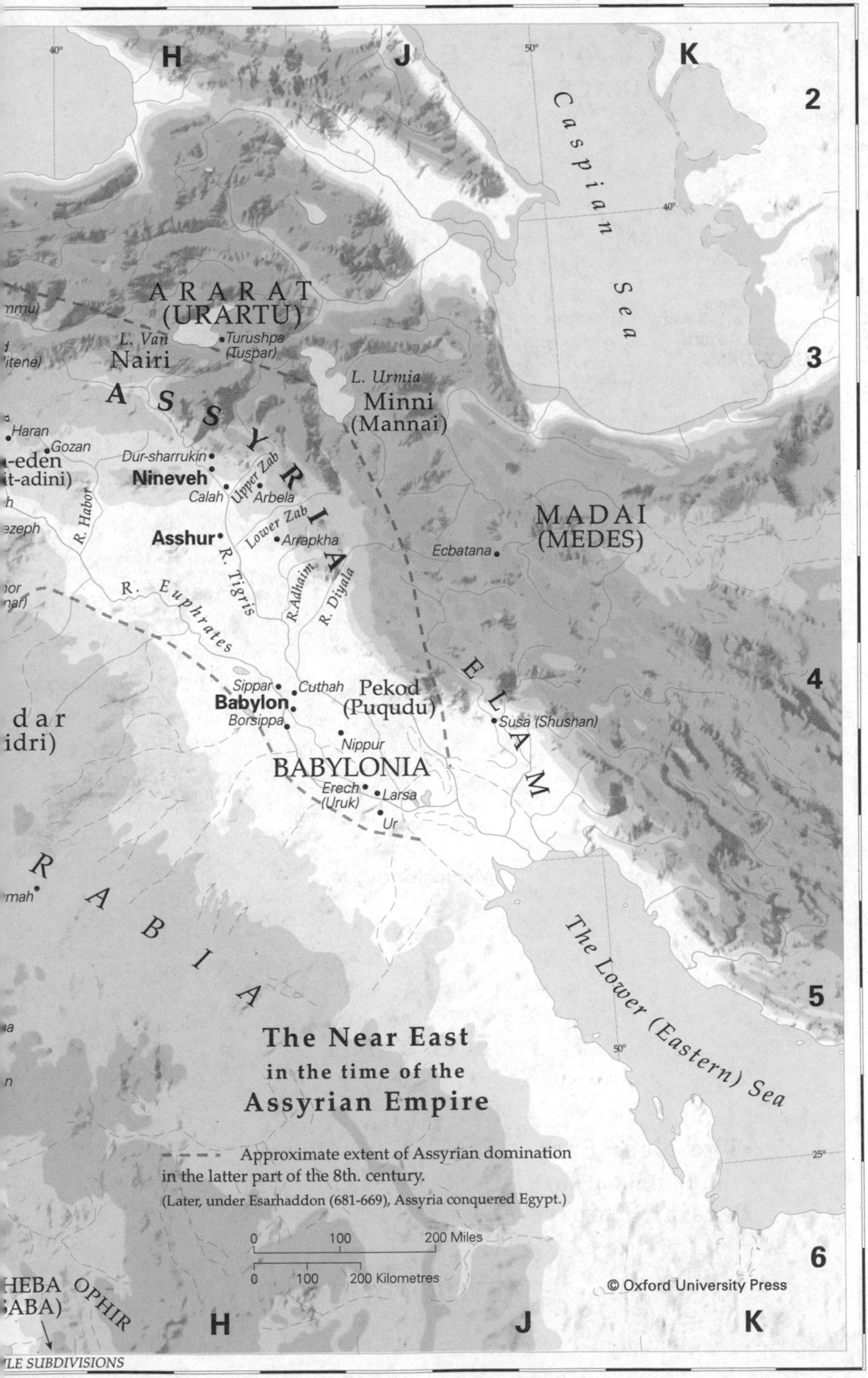
H
J
K
2
3
4
5
6
Caspian Sea
ARARAT (URARTU)
L. Van
Turushpa (Tuspar)
Nairi
ASSYRIA
L. Urmia
Minni (Mannai)
Haran
Gozan
Dur-sharrukin
Nineveh
Calah
Upper Zab
Arbela
R. Habor
Asshur
Lower Zab
Arrapkha
MADAI (MEDES)
Ecbatana
R. Tigris
R. Adhaim
R. Diyala
R. Euphrates
ELAM
Sippar
Cuthah
Pekod (Puqudu)
Babylon
Borsippa
Susa (Shushan)
Nippur
BABYLONIA
Erech (Uruk)
Larsa
Ur
ARABIA
The Lower (Eastern) Sea
The Near East in the time of the Assyrian Empire
Approximate extent of Assyrian domination in the latter part of the 8th. century.
(Later, under Esarhaddon (681-669), Assyria conquered Egypt.)
0 100 200 Miles
0 100 200 Kilometres
OPHIR
© Oxford University Press

# MAP 7

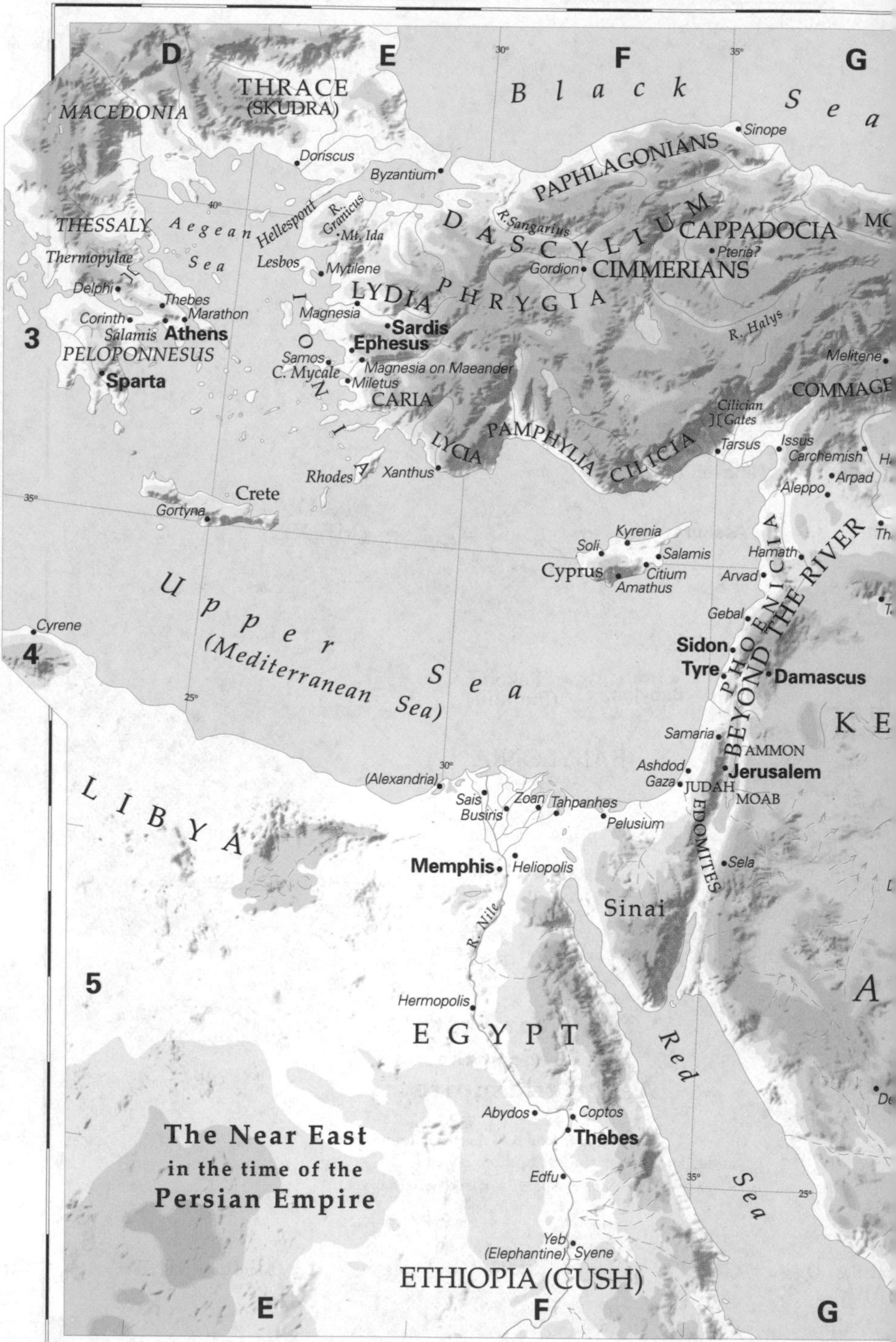
The Near East
in the time of the
Persian Empire
D
E
F
G
3
4
5
30°
35°
40°
25°
Black Sea
MACEDONIA
THRACE
(SKUDRA)
Doriscus
Byzantium
Sinope
PAPHLAGONIANS
THESSALY
Aegean
Sea
Hellespont
R. Granicus
Mt. Ida
DASCYLIUM
R. Sangarius
CAPPADOCIA
Pteria?
Thermopylae
Lesbos
Mytilene
Gordion
CIMMERIANS
Delphi
Thebes
Marathon
LYDIA
PHRYGIA
Corinth
Salamis
Athens
Magnesia
Sardis
R. Halys
PELOPONNESUS
Sparta
Samos
C. Mycale
Ephesus
Magnesia on Maeander
Miletus
IONIA
CARIA
Melitene
COMMAGE
Cilician Gates
Tarsus
Issus
Carchemish
Arpad
Aleppo
PAMPHYLIA
CILICIA
LYCIA
Rhodes
Xanthus
Crete
Gortyna
Kyrenia
Soli
Salamis
Cyprus
Citium
Amathus
Hamath
Arvad
PHOENICIA
BEYOND THE RIVER
Upper Sea
(Mediterranean Sea)
Cyrene
Gebal
Sidon
Tyre
Damascus
Samaria
AMMON
Ashdod
Gaza
Jerusalem
JUDAH
MOAB
EDOMITES
Sela
(Alexandria)
Sais
Zoan
Tahpanhes
Busiris
Pelusium
LIBYA
Memphis
Heliopolis
Sinai
R. Nile
Hermopolis
EGYPT
Red Sea
Abydos
Coptos
Thebes
Edfu
Yeb
(Elephantine)
Syene
ETHIOPIA (CUSH)
OUTER BORDER S

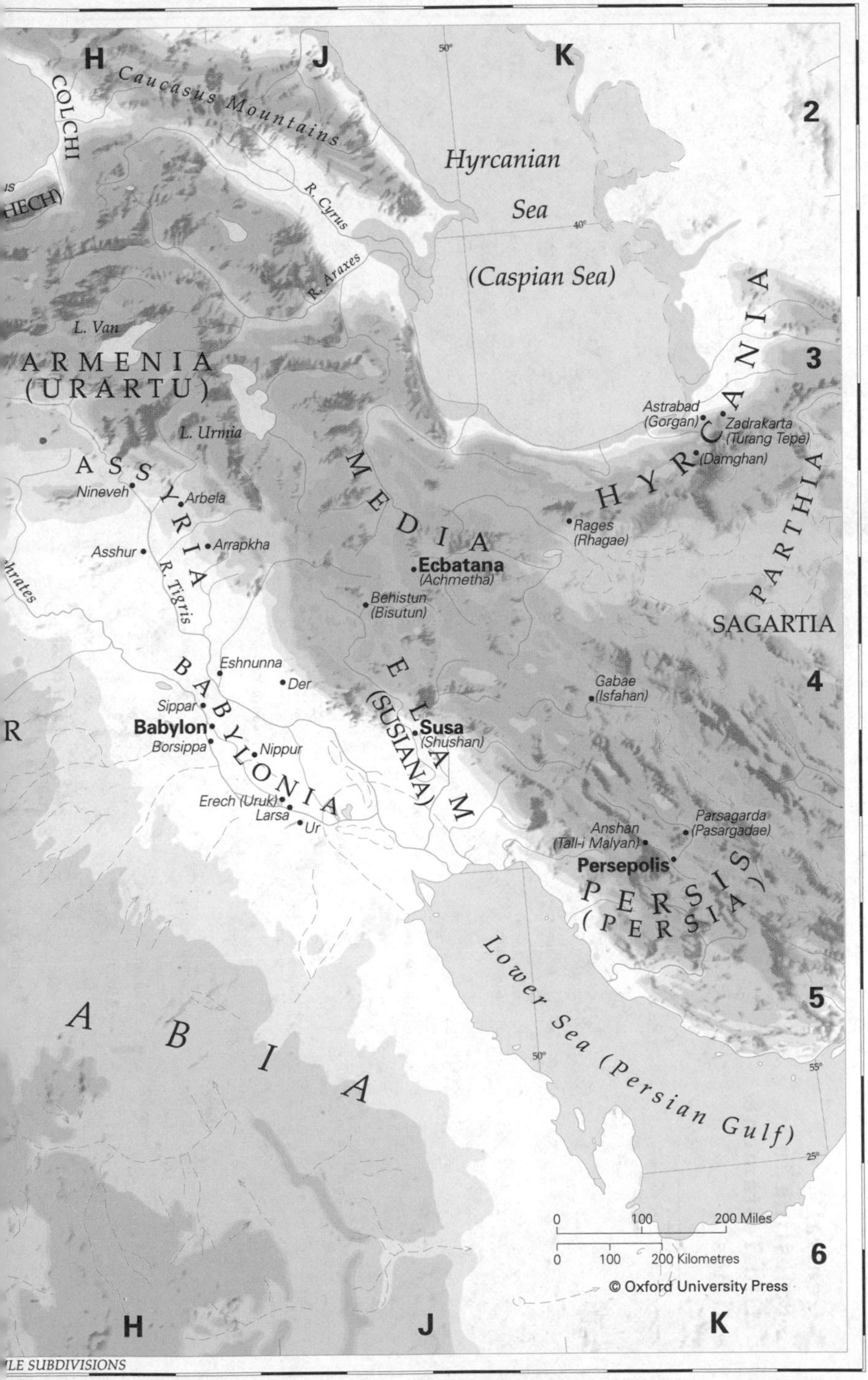
H
J
K
Caucasus Mountains
COLCHI
Hyrcanian
Sea
(Caspian Sea)
R. Cyrus
R. Araxes
L. Van
ARMENIA
(URARTU)
L. Urmia
ASSYRIA
Nineveh
Arbela
Asshur
Arrapkha
R. Tigris
MEDIA
Ecbatana
(Achmetha)
Behistun
(Bisutun)
Rages
(Rhagae)
HYRCANIA
Astrabad
(Gorgan)
Zadrakarta
(Turang Tepe)
(Damghan)
PARTHIA
SAGARTIA
Gabae
(Isfahan)
BABYLONIA
Eshnunna
Der
Sippar
Babylon
Borsippa
Nippur
Erech (Uruk)
Larsa
Ur
ELAM
(SUSIANA)
Susa
(Shushan)
Anshan
(Tall-i Malyan)
Parsagarda
(Pasargadae)
Persepolis
PERSIS
(PERSIA)
Lower Sea (Persian Gulf)
ABIA
2
3
4
5
6
50°
40°
55°
25°
0 100 200 Miles
0 100 200 Kilometres
© Oxford University Press

# MAP 8

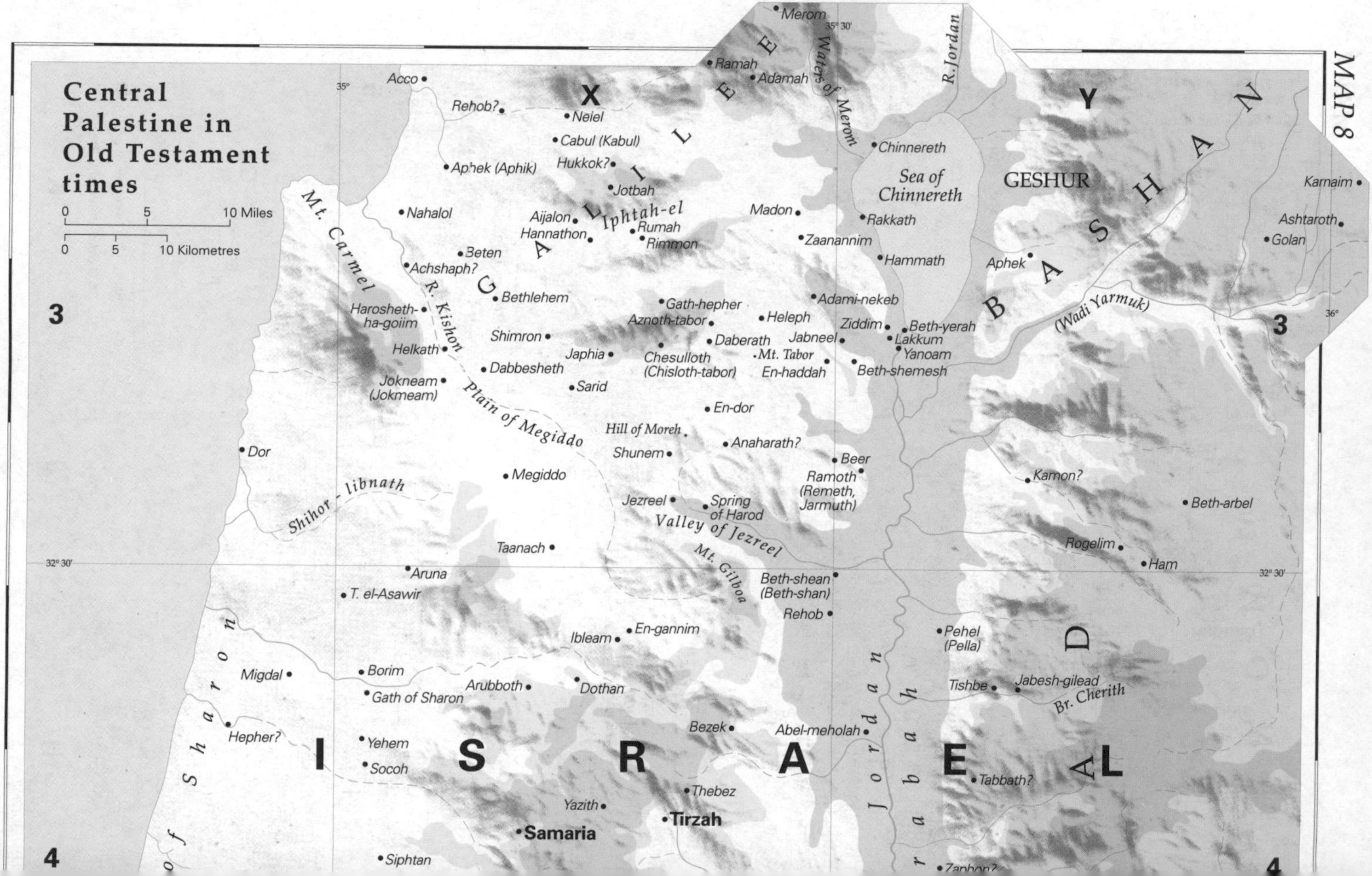

Central Palestine in Old Testament times
0 5 10 Miles
0 5 10 Kilometres
3
4
35°
36°
35° 30'
32° 30'
GALILEE
ISRAEL
BASHAN
GILEAD
GESHUR
Acco
Rehob?
Neiel
Cabul (Kabul)
Aphek (Aphik)
Hukkok?
Jotbah
Nahalol
Aijalon
Hannathon
Iphtah-el
Rumah
Rimmon
Beten
Achshaph?
Mt. Carmel
R. Kishon
Bethlehem
Harosheth-ha-goiim
Helkath
Shimron
Japhia
Dabbesheth
Jokneam (Jokmeam)
Sarid
Plain of Megiddo
Dor
Megiddo
Shihor-libnath
Taanach
Aruna
T. el-Asawir
Migdal
Borim
Gath of Sharon
Arubboth
Hepher?
Yehem
Socoh
Sharon
Plain of Sharon
Siphtan
Samaria
Tirzah
Yazith
Thebez
Bezek
Dothan
Ibleam
En-gannim
Jezreel
Spring of Harod
Valley of Jezreel
Mt. Gilboa
Shunem
Hill of Moreh
Anaharath?
En-dor
Gath-hepher
Aznoth-tabor
Chesulloth (Chisloth-tabor)
Daberath
Mt. Tabor
En-haddah
Heleph
Jabneel
Adami-nekeb
Zaanannim
Madon
Ramah
Adamah
Merom
Waters of Merom
R. Jordan
Chinnereth
Sea of Chinnereth
Rakkath
Hammath
Ziddim
Beth-yerah
Lakkum
Yanoam
Beth-shemesh
Beer
Ramoth (Remeth, Jarmuth)
Beth-shean (Beth-shan)
Rehob
Abel-meholah
Jordan
Jabbok
Pehel (Pella)
Tishbe
Jabesh-gilead
Br. Cherith
Tabbath?
Zaphon?
Aphek
(Wadi Yarmuk)
Kamon?
Beth-arbel
Rogelim
Ham
Karnaim
Ashtaroth
Golan

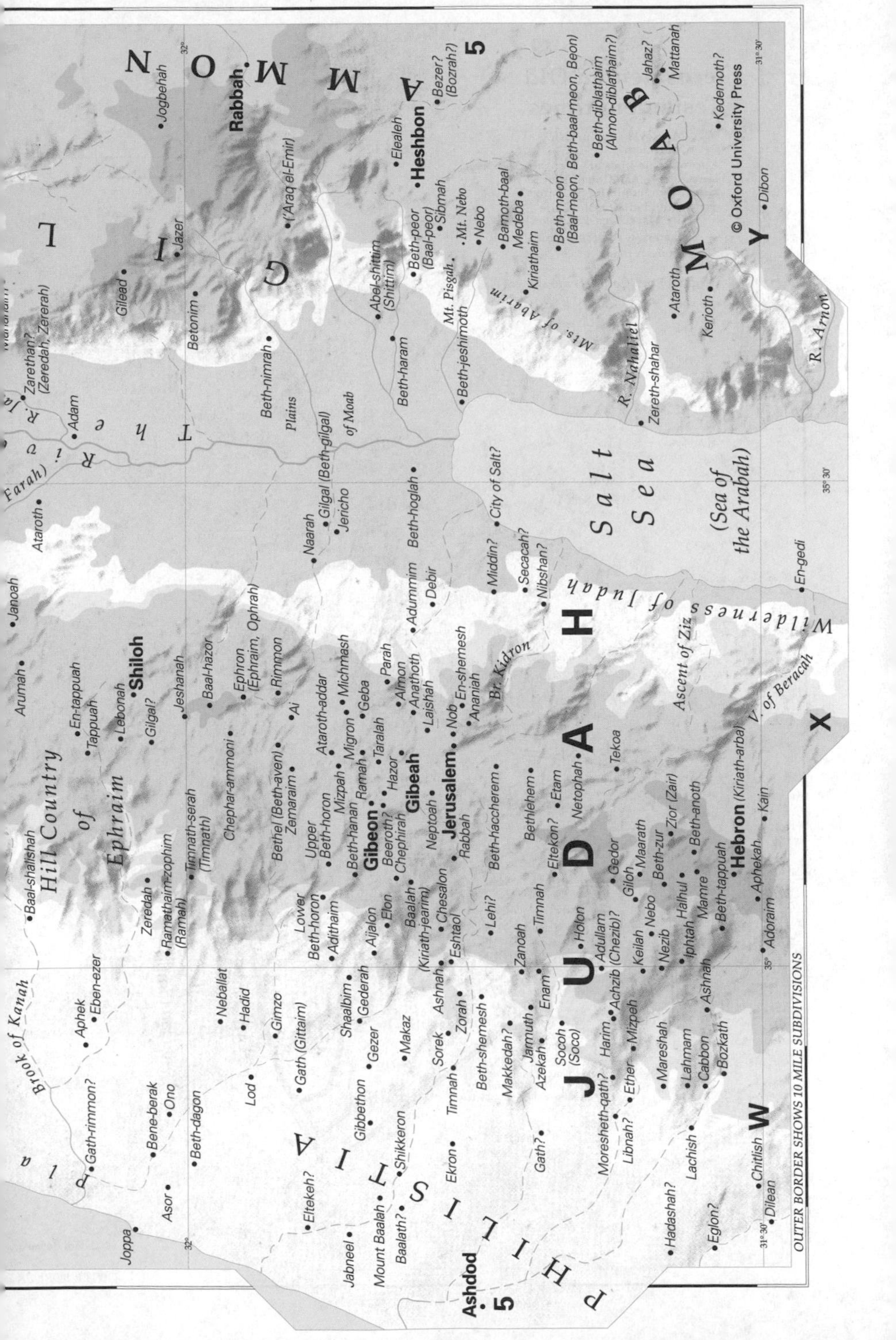

GILEAD
AMMON
MOAB
JUDAH
PHILISTIA
Hill Country of Ephraim
Plains of Moab
Salt Sea
(Sea of the Arabah)
Wilderness of Judah
Mts. of Abarim
R. Jabbok
R. Nahaliel
R. Arnon
Brook of Kanah
Br. Kidron
Ascent of Ziz
V. of Beracah
Mt. Pisgah
Mt. Nebo
Rabbah
Heshbon
Jerusalem
Gibeon
Gibeah
Shiloh
Hebron (Kiriath-arba)
Ashdod
Joppa
Jogbehah
Jazer
Gilead
Zarethan? (Zeredah, Zererah)
Adam
Betonim
Beth-nimrah
('Araq el-Emir)
Elealeh
Bezer? (Bozrah?)
Beth-peor (Baal-peor)
Sibmah
Abel-shittim (Shittim)
Beth-haram
Beth-jeshimoth
Nebo
Bamoth-baal
Medeba
Kiriathaim
Beth-meon (Baal-meon, Beth-baal-meon, Beon)
Beth-diblathaim (Almon-diblathaim?)
Jahaz?
Mattanah
Kedemoth?
Dibon
Ataroth
Kerioth
Zereth-shahar
Ataroth
Janoah
Arumah
En-tappuah
Tappuah
Lebonah
Gilgal?
Jeshanah
Baal-hazor
Ephron (Ephraim, Ophrah)
Rimmon
Ai
Naarah
Gilgal (Beth-gilgal)
Jericho
Beth-hoglah
City of Salt?
Middin?
Secacah?
Nibshan?
Adummim
Debir
En-gedi
Baal-shalishah
Zeredah
Ramathaim-zophim (Ramah)
Timnath-serah (Timnath)
Chephar-ammoni
Bethel (Beth-aven)
Zemaraim
Ataroth-addar
Michmash
Geba
Migron
Taralah
Parah
Almon
Anathoth
Laishah
Nob
En-shemesh
Ananiah
Upper Beth-horon
Lower Beth-horon
Mizpah
Ramah
Hazor
Beth-hanan
Beeroth?
Chephirah
Neptoah
Rabbah
Beth-haccherem
Bethlehem
Etam
Netophah
Tekoa
Eltekon?
Gedor
Maarath
Beth-zur
Zior (Zair)
Beth-anoth
Halhul
Mamre
Beth-tappuah
Aphekah
Kain
Adoraim
Aijalon
Elon
Baalah (Kiriath-jearim)
Chesalon
Eshtaol
Adithaim
Lehi?
Timnah
Holon
Adullam
Achzib (Chezib)?
Giloh
Nebo
Keilah
Nezib
Iphtah
Ashnah
Zanoah
Enam
Jarmuth
Socoh (Soco)
Azekah
Harim
Mizpeh
Ether
Mareshah
Lahmam
Cabbon
Bozkath
Aphek
Eben-ezer
Neballat
Hadid
Gimzo
Lod
Gath (Gittaim)
Shaalbim
Gederah
Gezer
Makaz
Sorek
Zorah
Beth-shemesh
Makkedah?
Gath-rimmon?
Bene-berak
Ono
Beth-dagon
Asor
Gibbethon
Shikkeron
Ekron
Timnah
Gath?
Moresheth-gath?
Libnah?
Lachish
Chitlish
Dilean
Hadashah?
Eglon?
Eltekeh?
Jabneel
Mount Baalah
Baalath?
32°
31° 30'
35°
35° 30'
5
W
X
Y
OUTER BORDER SHOWS 10 MILE SUBDIVISIONS
© Oxford University Press

MAP 9

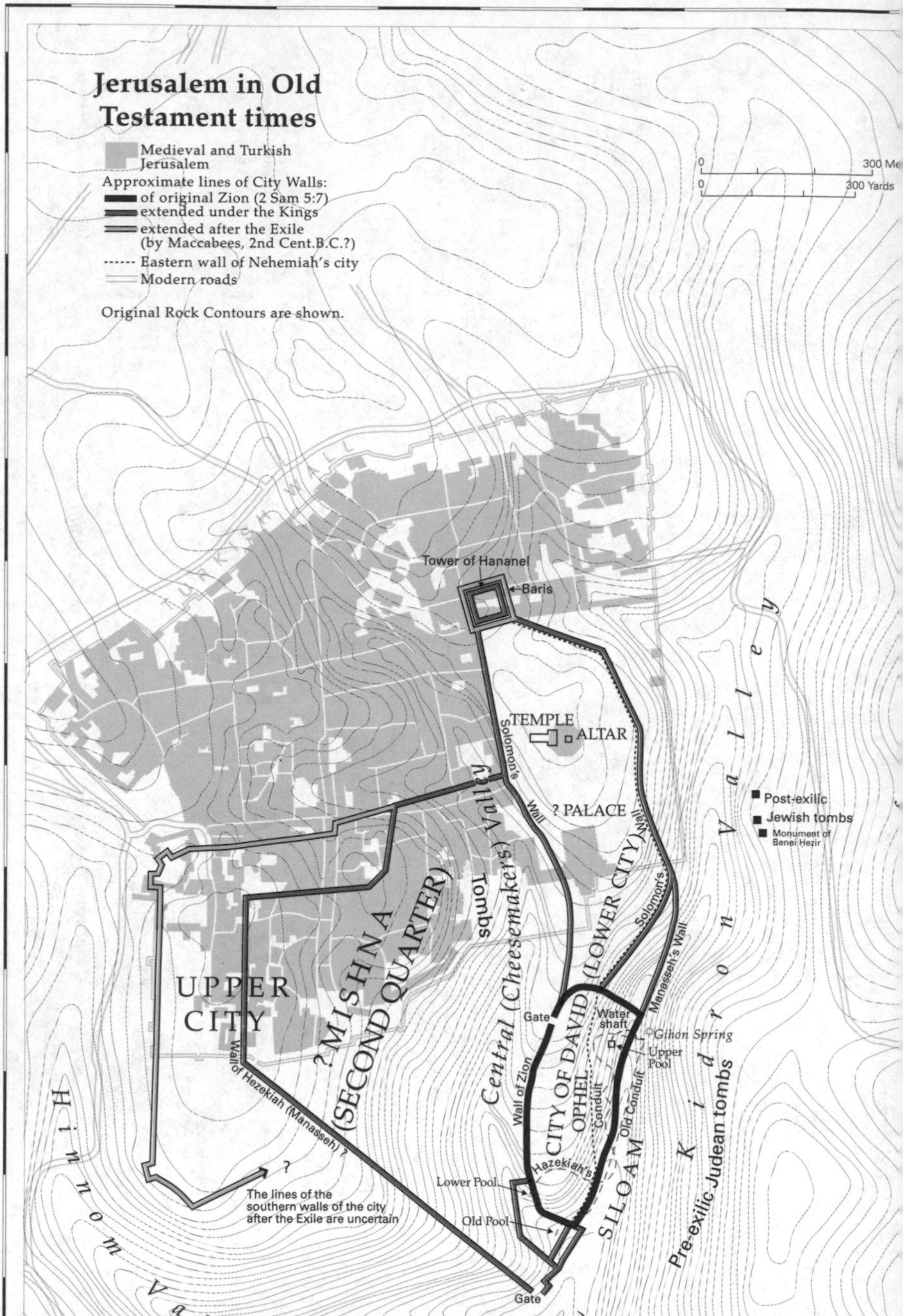
Jerusalem in Old Testament times
Medieval and Turkish Jerusalem
Approximate lines of City Walls:
of original Zion (2 Sam 5:7)
extended under the Kings
extended after the Exile (by Maccabees, 2nd Cent.B.C.?)
Eastern wall of Nehemiah's city
Modern roads
Original Rock Contours are shown.
0
300 Me
0
300 Yards
TURKISH WALL
Tower of Hananel
Baris
TEMPLE
ALTAR
Solomon's Wall
? PALACE
Post-exilic
Jewish tombs
Monument of Benei Hezir
Kidron Valley
Central (Cheesemakers') Valley
Tombs
?MISHNA (SECOND QUARTER)
UPPER CITY
CITY OF DAVID (LOWER CITY)
OPHEL
Solomon's Wall
Manasseh's Wall
Gate
Water shaft
Gihon Spring
Upper Pool
Wall of Zion
Conduit
Old Conduit
Hazekiah's
Wall of Hezekiah (Manasseh) ?
SILOAM
Pre-exilic Judean tombs
Lower Pool
Old Pool
The lines of the southern walls of the city after the Exile are uncertain
Gate
Hinnom Valley (?Topheth)
En-rogel Spring
© Oxford University

OUTER BORDER S

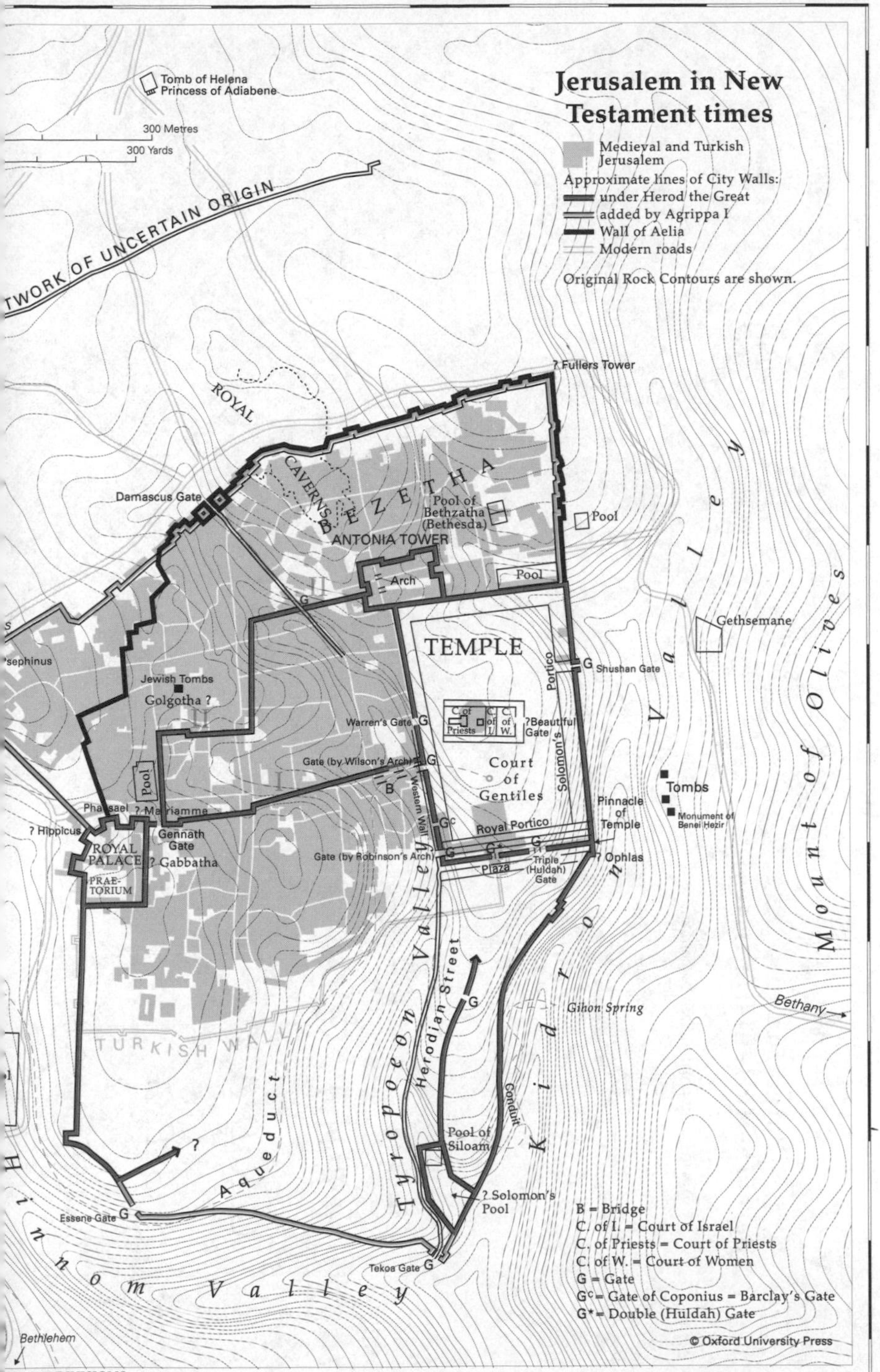
Jerusalem in New Testament times
Medieval and Turkish Jerusalem
Approximate lines of City Walls:
under Herod the Great
added by Agrippa I
Wall of Aelia
Modern roads
Original Rock Contours are shown.
Tomb of Helena Princess of Adiabene
300 Metres
300 Yards
TWORK OF UNCERTAIN ORIGIN
ROYAL
CAVERNS
BEZETHA
? Fullers Tower
Damascus Gate
Pool of Bethzatha (Bethesda)
ANTONIA TOWER
Pool
Arch
Pool
G
TEMPLE
Portico
G Shushan Gate
Gethsemane
'sephinus
Jewish Tombs
Golgotha ?
Warren's Gate
C. of Priests
C. of I.
C. of W.
?Beautiful Gate
Solomon's
Gate (by Wilson's Arch)
Court of Gentiles
Western Wall
B
Pool
Phasael
? Mariamme
? Hippicus
Gennath Gate
ROYAL PALACE
? Gabbatha
PRAE-TORIUM
Royal Portico
Pinnacle of Temple
Tombs
Monument of Benei Hezir
Gate (by Robinson's Arch)
Plaza
Triple (Huldah) Gate
? Ophlas
Kidron Valley
Mount of Olives
Tyropoeon Valley
Herodian Street
G
Gihon Spring
Bethany
TURKISH WALL
Aqueduct
Conduit
Pool of Siloam
?
? Solomon's Pool
Essene Gate G
Tekoa Gate G
Hinnom Valley
Bethlehem
B = Bridge
C. of I. = Court of Israel
C. of Priests = Court of Priests
C. of W. = Court of Women
G = Gate
Gc = Gate of Coponius = Barclay's Gate
G* = Double (Huldah) Gate
© Oxford University Press
RD SUBDIVISIONS

MAP 10

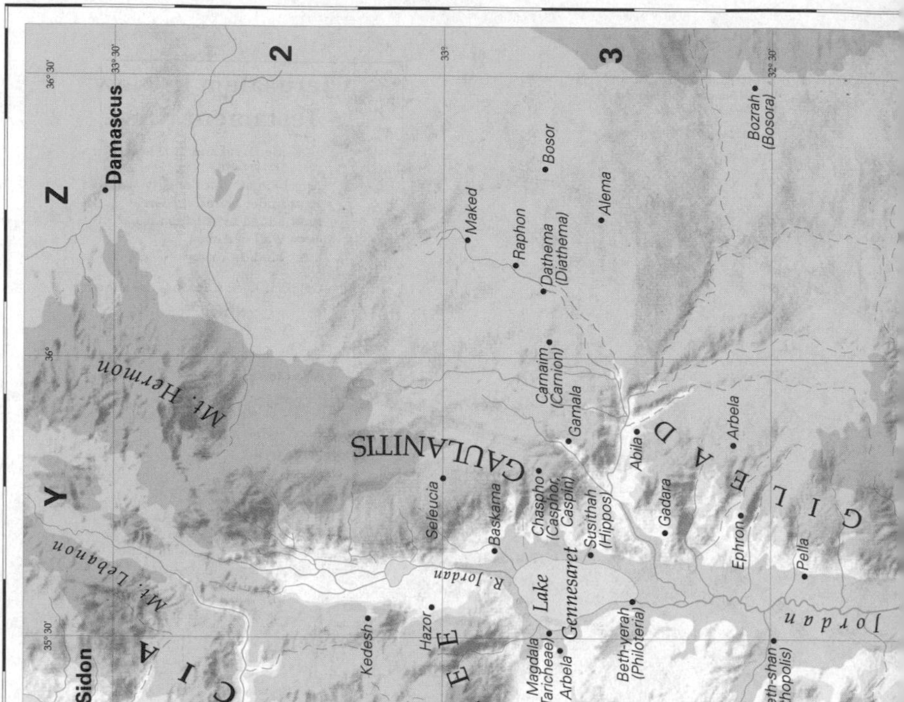

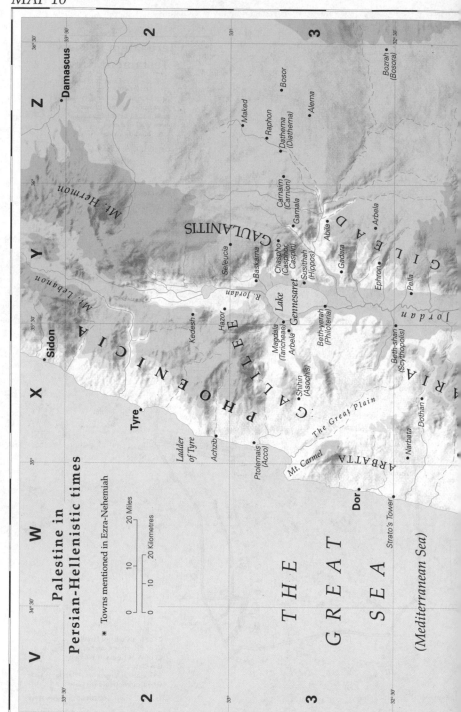

Palestine in
Persian-Hellenistic times
Towns mentioned in Ezra-Nehemiah
0 10 20 Miles
0 10 20 Kilometres
V
W
X
Y
Z
2
3
34° 30'
35°
35° 30'
36°
36° 30'
33° 30'
33°
32° 30'
THE
GREAT
SEA
(Mediterranean Sea)
Damascus
Sidon
Tyre
Dor
Strato's Tower
Ladder
of Tyre
Achzib
Ptolemais
(Acco)
Mt. Carmel
ARBATTA
The Great Plain
Narbata
Dothan
Shihin
(Asochis)
Beth-shan
(Scythopolis)
Magdala
(Taricheae)
Arbela
Beth-yerah
(Philoteria)
Lake
Gennesaret
Kedesh
Hazor
Seleucia
Baskama
R. Jordan
Jordan
Chaspho
(Casphor,
Caspin)
Susithah
(Hippos)
Gamala
Carnaim
(Carnion)
Abila
Gadara
Ephron
Pella
Arbela
Dathema
(Diathema)
Raphon
Maked
Alema
Bosor
Bozrah
(Bosora)
Mt. Hermon
Mt. Lebanon
PHOENICIA
GALILEE
GAULANITIS
GILEAD

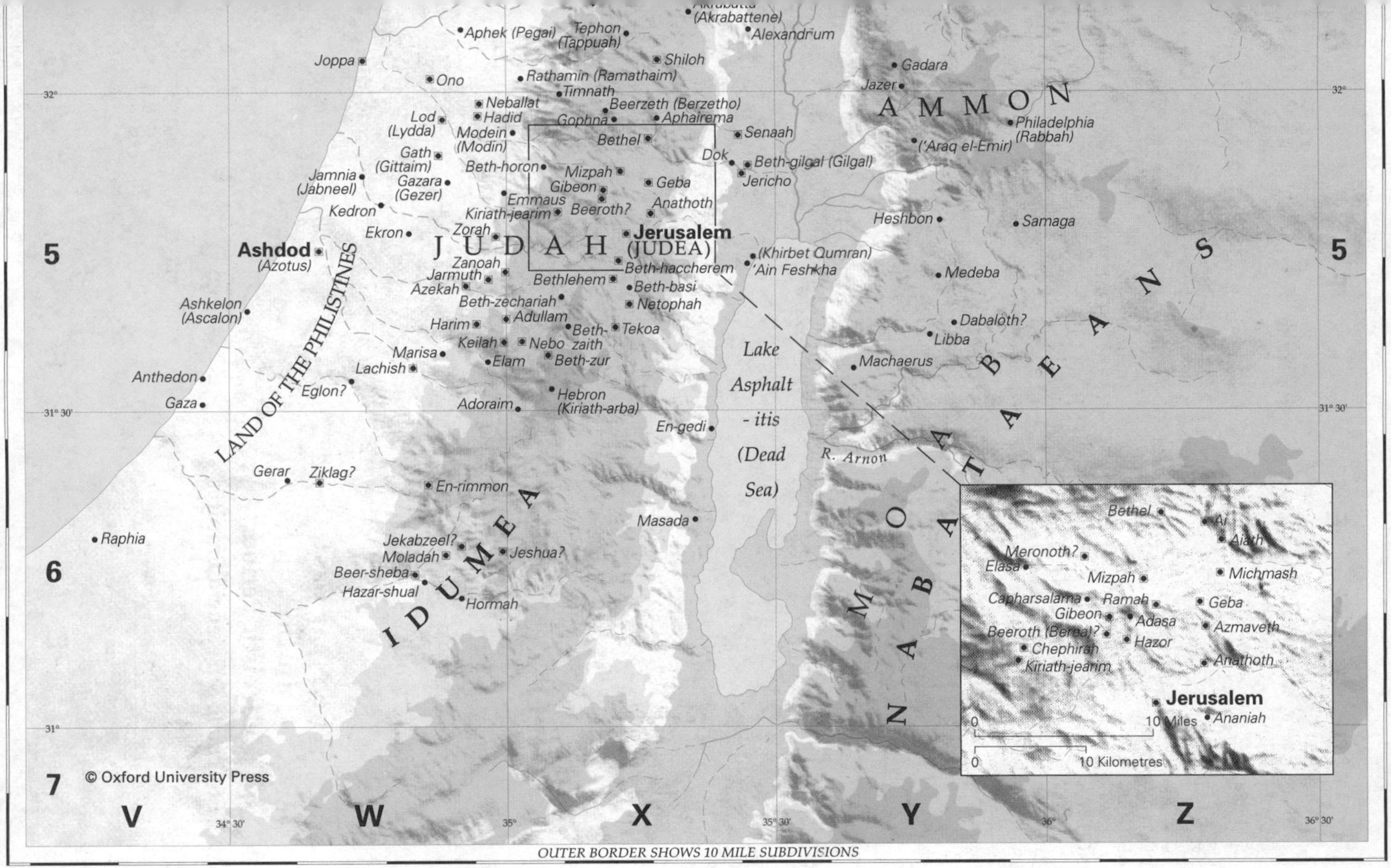
AMMON
NABATAEANS
MOAB
NABATAEA
JUDAH
(JUDEA)
IDUMEA
LAND OF THE PHILISTINES
Lake Asphalt-itis (Dead Sea)
R. Arnon
(Akrabattene)
Aphek (Pegai)
Tephon (Tappuah)
Alexandrum
Joppa
Shiloh
Gadara
Ono
Rathamin (Ramathaim)
Jazer
Timnath
Neballat
Beerzeth (Berzetho)
Lod (Lydda)
Hadid
Gophna
Aphairema
Philadelphia (Rabbah)
Modein (Modin)
Bethel
Senaah
('Araq el-Emir)
Gath (Gittaim)
Dok
Beth-gilgal (Gilgal)
Beth-horon
Mizpah
Jamnia (Jabneel)
Geba
Jericho
Gazara (Gezer)
Gibeon
Emmaus
Anathoth
Kedron
Kiriath-jearim
Beeroth?
Heshbon
Samaga
Ekron
Zorah
Jerusalem
Ashdod (Azotus)
(Khirbet Qumran)
'Ain Feshkha
Zanoah
Beth-haccherem
Medeba
Jarmuth
Bethlehem
Beth-basi
Azekah
Ashkelon (Ascalon)
Beth-zechariah
Netophah
Dabaloth?
Adullam
Harim
Beth-zaith
Tekoa
Libba
Keilah
Nebo
Marisa
Machaerus
Elam
Beth-zur
Lachish
Anthedon
Hebron (Kiriath-arba)
Eglon?
Gaza
Adoraim
En-gedi
Gerar
Ziklag?
En-rimmon
Masada
Raphia
Jekabzeel?
Jeshua?
Moladah
Beer-sheba
Hazar-shual
Hormah
Bethel
Ai
Aiath
Meronoth?
Elasa
Mizpah
Michmash
Capharsalama
Ramah
Geba
Gibeon
Adasa
Beeroth (Berea)?
Azmaveth
Hazor
Chephirah
Anathoth
Kiriath-jearim
Jerusalem
Ananiah
0
10 Miles
0
10 Kilometres
32°
31° 30'
31°
34° 30'
35°
35° 30'
36°
36° 30'
5
6
7
V
W
X
Y
Z
© Oxford University Press
OUTER BORDER SHOWS 10 MILE SUBDIVISIONS

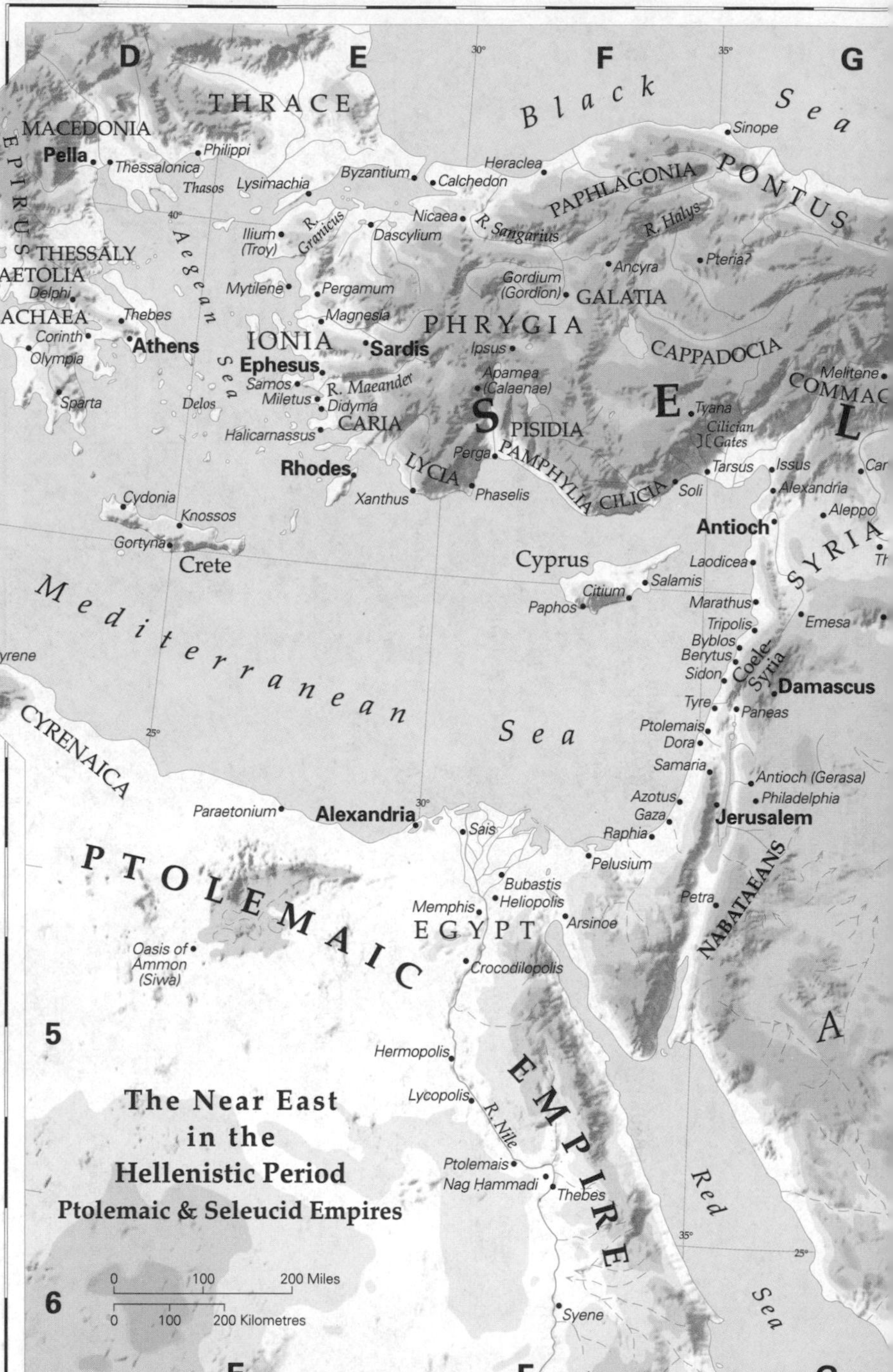
The Near East
in the
Hellenistic Period
Ptolemaic & Seleucid Empires
D
E
F
G
3
4
5
6
30°
35°
40°
25°
THRACE
MACEDONIA
EPIRUS
Pella
Philippi
Thessalonica
Thasos
Lysimachia
Byzantium
Calchedon
Heraclea
Black Sea
Sinope
PAPHLAGONIA
PONTUS
R. Halys
R. Sangarius
Nicaea
Dascylium
Ilium (Troy)
R. Granicus
THESSALY
AETOLIA
Delphi
ACHAEA
Thebes
Corinth
Athens
Olympia
Sparta
Aegean Sea
Delos
Mytilene
Pergamum
Magnesia
IONIA
Sardis
Ephesus
Samos
Miletus
Didyma
R. Maeander
CARIA
Halicarnassus
Rhodes
LYCIA
Xanthus
Phaselis
Perga
PAMPHYLIA
PISIDIA
Apamea (Calaenae)
Ipsus
PHRYGIA
Gordium (Gordion)
GALATIA
Ancyra
Pteria?
CAPPADOCIA
Tyana
Cilician Gates
Tarsus
Soli
CILICIA
Issus
Alexandria
Melitene
COMMAG
S E L
Car
Aleppo
Antioch
SYRIA
Laodicea
Marathus
Tripolis
Byblos
Berytus
Sidon
Coele-Syria
Damascus
Emesa
Tyre
Paneas
Ptolemais
Dora
Samaria
Antioch (Gerasa)
Philadelphia
Azotus
Gaza
Raphia
Jerusalem
NABATAEANS
Petra
A
Cyprus
Salamis
Citium
Paphos
Cydonia
Knossos
Gortyna
Crete
Mediterranean Sea
Cyrene
CYRENAICA
Paraetonium
Alexandria
Sais
Pelusium
Bubastis
Heliopolis
Memphis
Arsinoe
EGYPT
PTOLEMAIC EMPIRE
Oasis of Ammon (Siwa)
Crocodilopolis
Hermopolis
Lycopolis
R. Nile
Ptolemais
Nag Hammadi
Thebes
Syene
Red Sea
0 100 200 Miles
0 100 200 Kilometres
OUTER BORDER

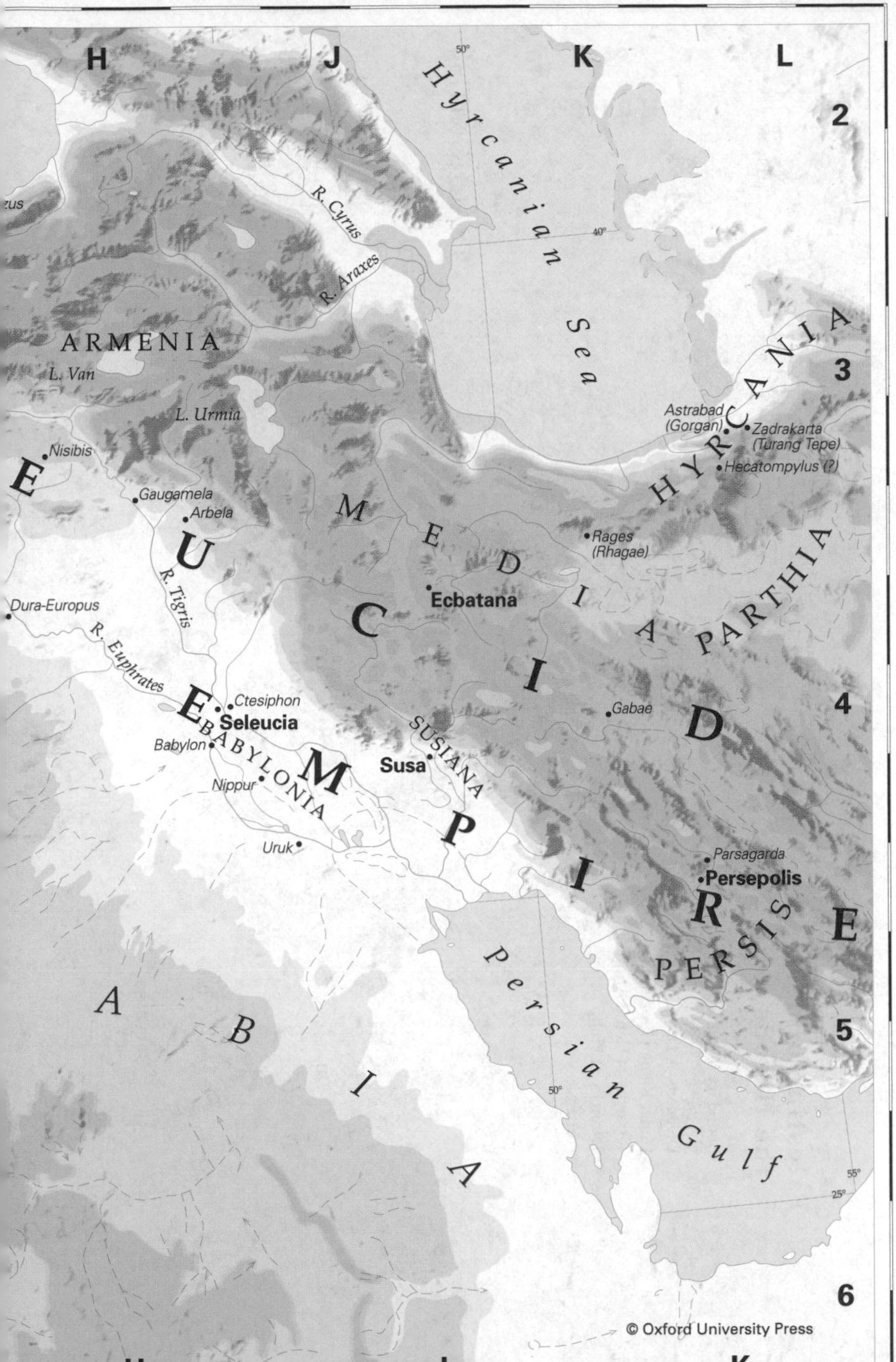


LE SUBDIVISIONS

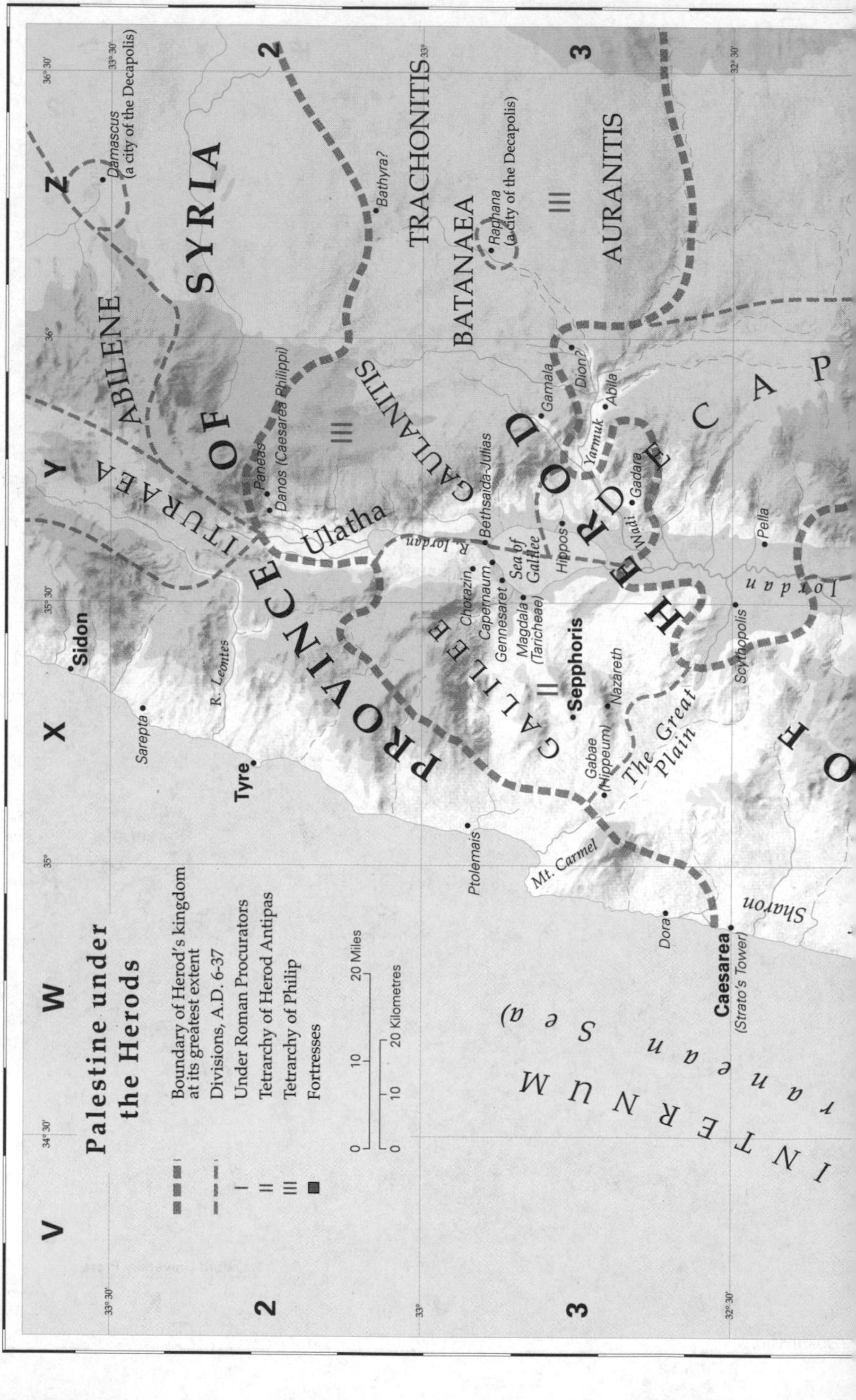
Palestine under the Herods
Boundary of Herod's kingdom at its greatest extent
Divisions, A.D. 6-37
I Under Roman Procurators
II Tetrarchy of Herod Antipas
III Tetrarchy of Philip
Fortresses
0 10 20 Miles
0 10 20 Kilometres
V
W
X
Y
Z
2
3
34° 30'
35°
35° 30'
36°
36° 30'
33° 30'
33°
32° 30'
PROVINCE OF SYRIA
ABILENE
ITURAEA
TRACHONITIS
BATANAEA
AURANITIS
GAULANITIS
GALILEE
DECAP
HEROD
Damascus (a city of the Decapolis)
Bathyra?
Raphana (a city of the Decapolis)
Sidon
Sarepta
Tyre
R. Leontes
Paneas
Danos (Caesarea Philippi)
Ulatha
Bethsaida-Julias
R. Iordan
Chorazin
Capernaum
Gennesaret
Magdala (Taricheae)
Sea of Galilee
Hippos
Gamala
Dion?
Abila
Yarmuk
Gadara
Wadi
Pella
Iordan
Sepphoris
Nazareth
Scythopolis
Gabae (Hippeum)
The Great Plain
Ptolemais
Mt. Carmel
Dora
Caesarea (Strato's Tower)
Sharon
INTERNUM Mare (Mediterranean Sea)

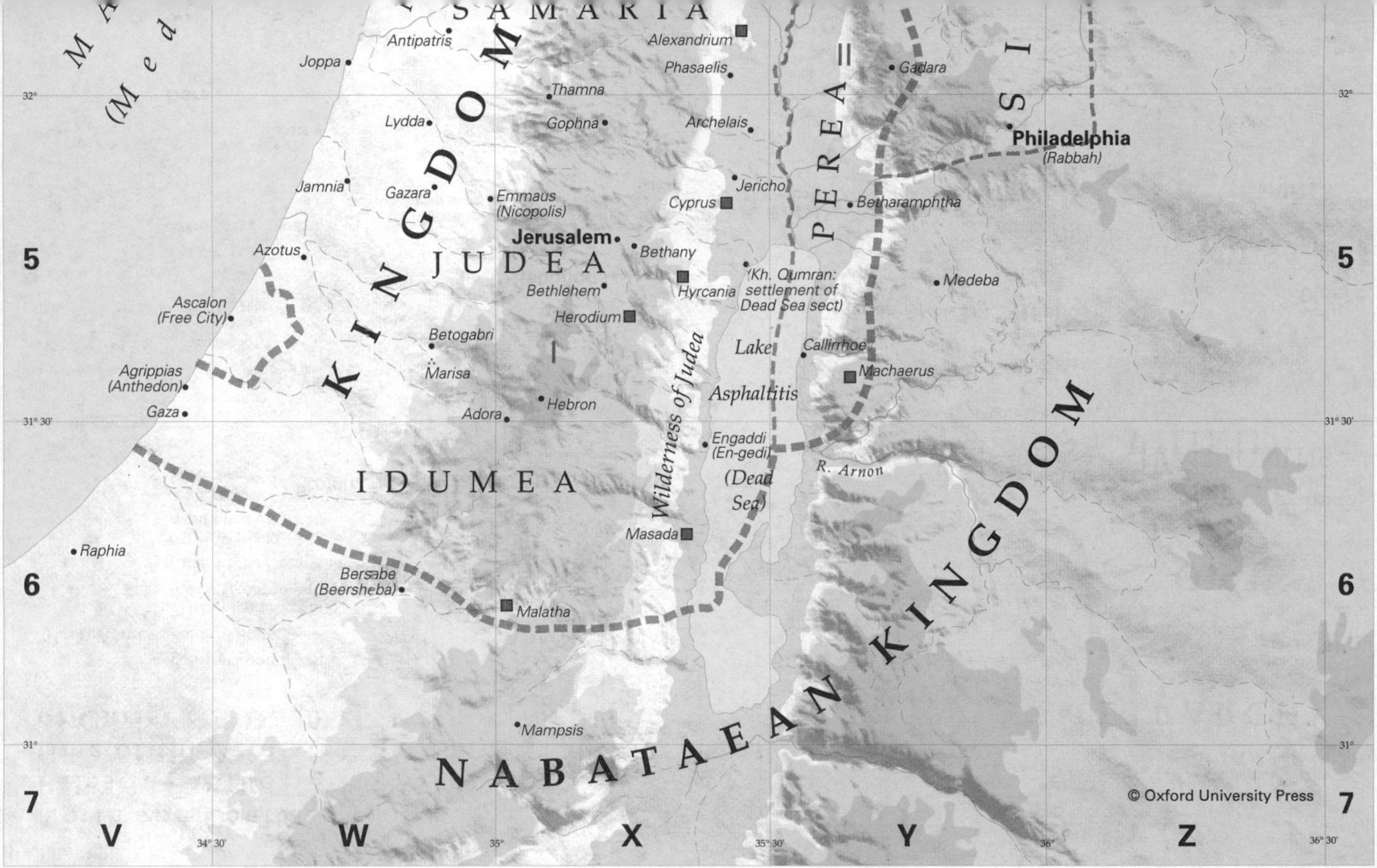


OUTER BORDER SHOWS 10 MILE SUBDIVISIONS

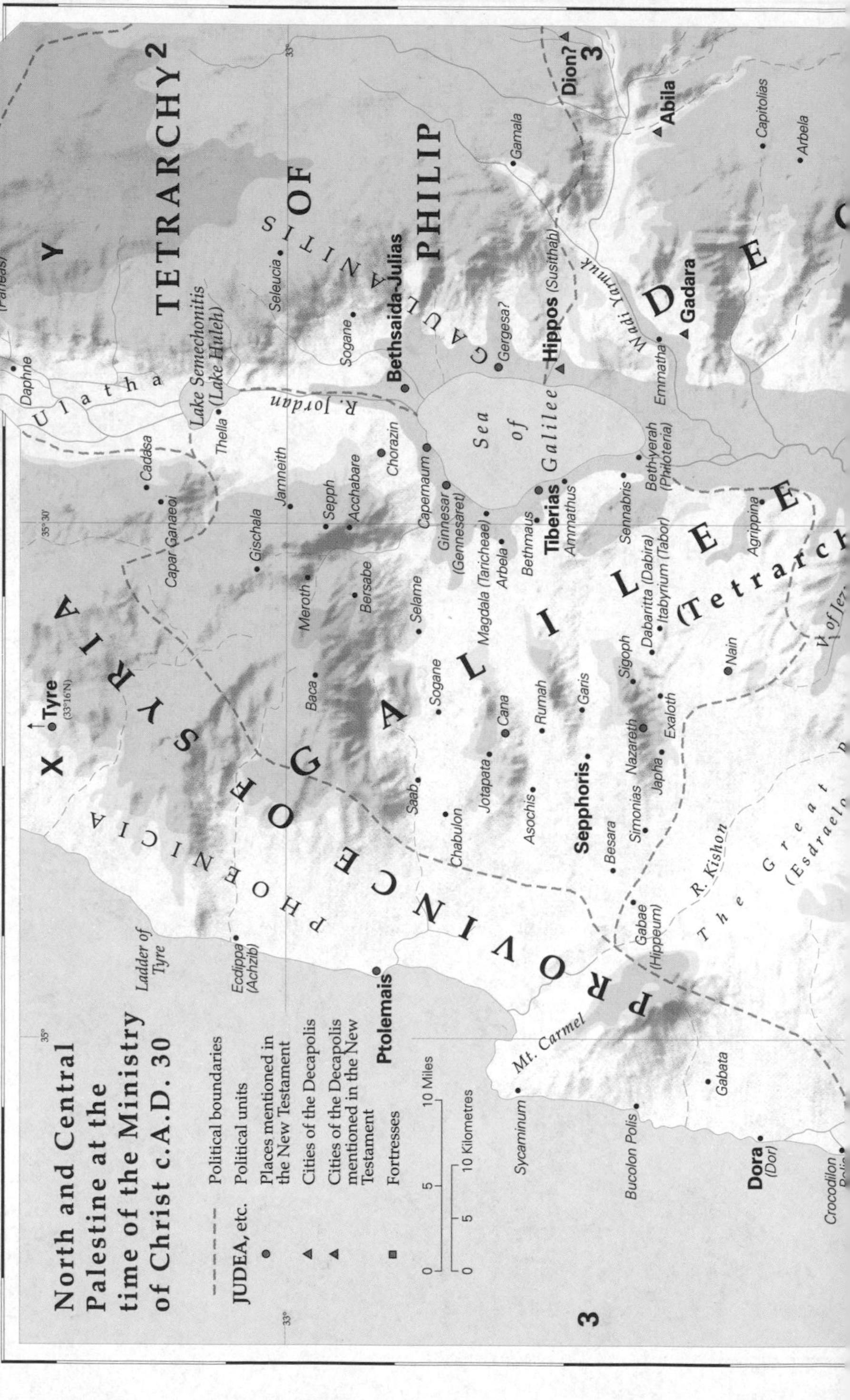
North and Central Palestine at the time of the Ministry of Christ c.A.D. 30
Political boundaries
JUDEA, etc. Political units
Places mentioned in the New Testament
Cities of the Decapolis
Cities of the Decapolis mentioned in the New Testament
Fortresses
0 5 10 Miles
0 5 10 Kilometres
TETRARCHY OF PHILIP
PROVINCE OF SYRIA
GALILEE (Tetrarch
DE
PHOENICIA
GAULANITIS
Ulatha
Caesarea Philippi (Paneas)
Daphne
Lake Semechonitis (Lake Huleh)
Thella
Cadasa
Capar Ganaeoi
Gischala
Jamneith
Sepph
Acchabare
Chorazin
Capernaum
Ginnesar (Gennesaret)
Magdala (Taricheae)
Arbela
Bethmaus
Tiberias
Ammathus
Sennabris
Beth-yerah (Philoteria)
Agrippina
Dabaritta (Dabira)
Itabyrium (Tabor)
Nain
Sigoph
Garis
Exaloth
Nazareth
Japha
Simonias
Sepphoris
Besara
Rumah
Asochis
Cana
Jotapata
Sogane
Chabulon
Saab
Baca
Meroth
Bersabe
Selame
Tyre (33°16'N)
Ladder of Tyre
Ecdippa (Achzib)
Ptolemais
Gabae (Hippeum)
R. Kishon
The Great (Esdraelo
Mt. Carmel
Gabata
Sycaminum
Bucolon Polis
Dora (Dor)
Crocodilon Polis
Seleucia
Sogane
Bethsaida-Julias
R. Jordan
Sea of Galilee
Gergesa?
Hippos (Susithah)
Gamala
Emmatha
Wadi Yarmuk
Gadara
Abila
Dion?
Capitolias
Arbela
35°
35°30'
33°
3

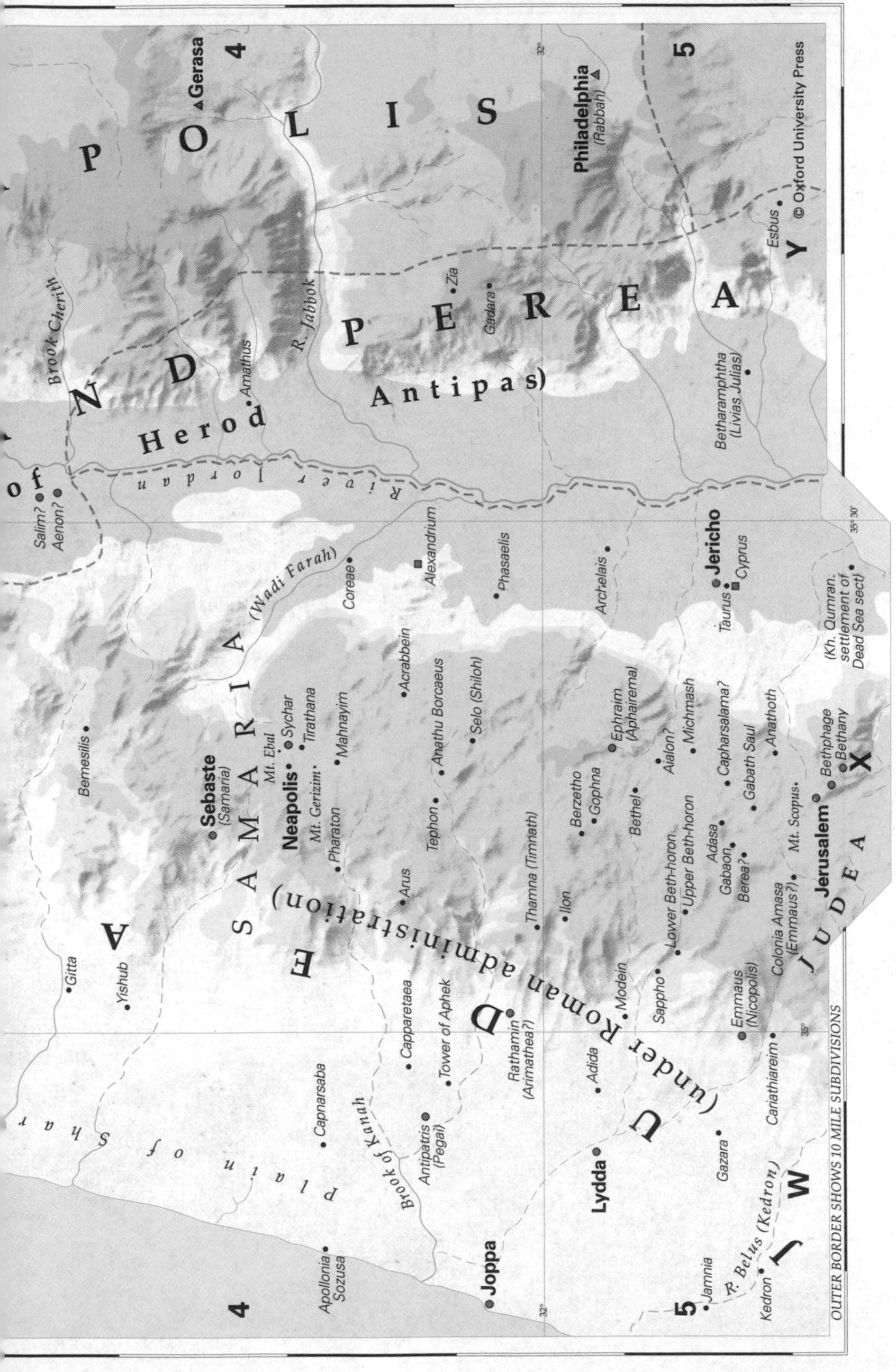


© Oxford University Press

# MAP 14

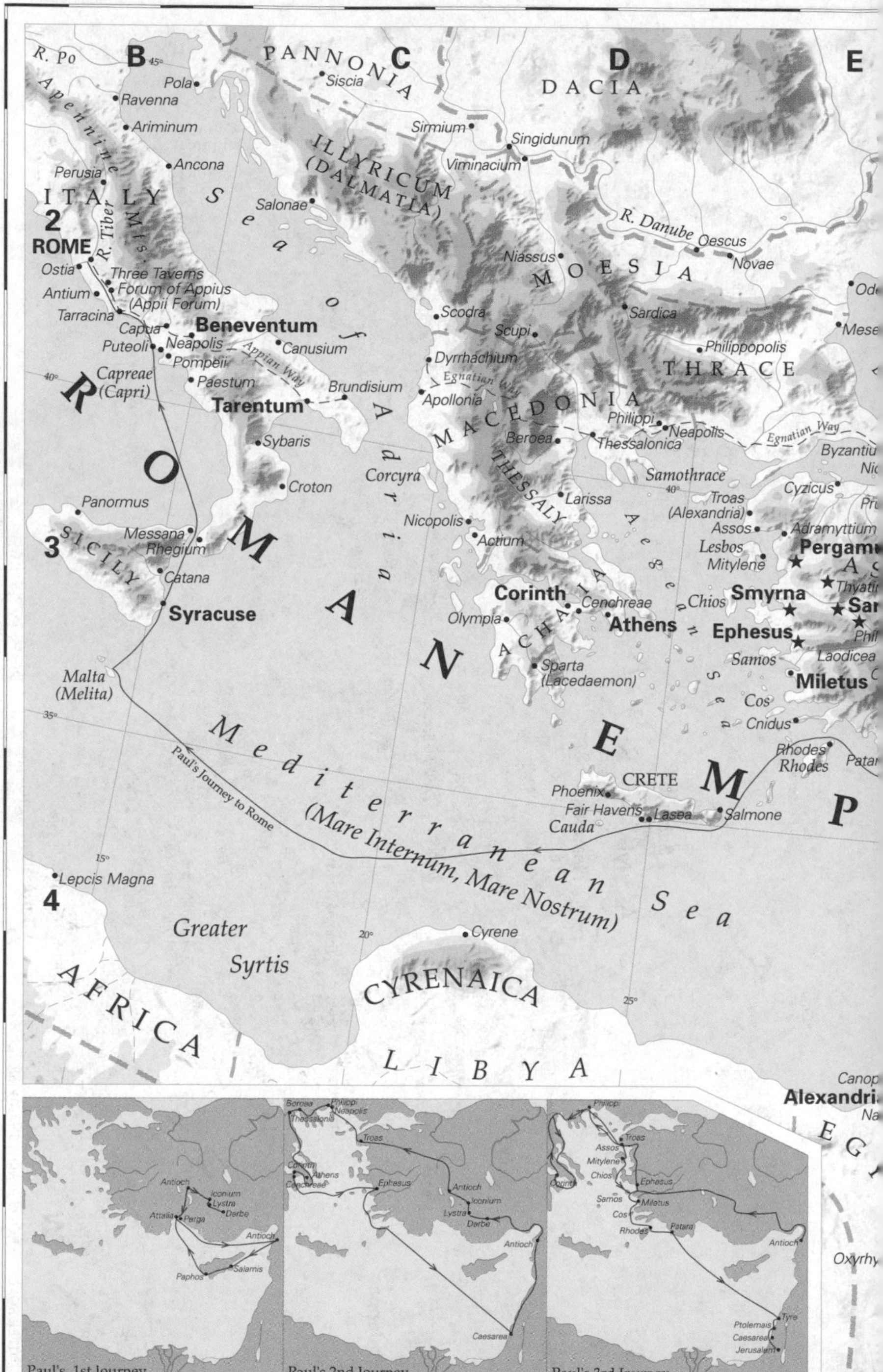
B
C
D
E
2
3
4
R. Po
PANNONIA
Siscia
DACIA
Pola
Ravenna
Ariminum
Apennine Mts.
Ancona
Perusia
ITALY
R. Tiber
ROME
Ostia
Three Taverns
Forum of Appius
(Appii Forum)
Antium
Tarracina
Capua
Beneventum
Puteoli
Neapolis
Pompeii
Canusium
Appian Way
Capreae
(Capri)
Paestum
Brundisium
Tarentum
Sybaris
Croton
Panormus
SICILY
Messana
Rhegium
Catana
Syracuse
Malta
(Melita)
Sea of Adria
Sirmium
Singidunum
Viminacium
ILLYRICUM
(DALMATIA)
Salonae
R. Danube
Oescus
Novae
Niassus
MOESIA
Sardica
Scodra
Scupi
Philippopolis
THRACE
Dyrrhachium
Egnatian Way
Apollonia
MACEDONIA
Philippi
Neapolis
Beroea
Thessalonica
Byzantiu
Corcyra
Samothrace
Cyzicus
THESSALY
Larissa
Troas
(Alexandria)
Assos
Adramyttium
Nicopolis
Actium
Lesbos
Mitylene
Pergam
Aegean Sea
Corinth
Cenchreae
Chios
Smyrna
Thyati
Sar
Olympia
Athens
Ephesus
Phil
ACHAIA
Samos
Laodicea
Sparta
(Lacedaemon)
Miletus
Cos
Cnidus
Rhodes
Rhodes
Patar
Ode
Mese
Nic
CRETE
Phoenix
Fair Havens
Lasea
Salmone
Cauda
ROMAN EMP
Paul's Journey to Rome
Mediterranean Sea
(Mare Internum, Mare Nostrum)
Lepcis Magna
Greater
Syrtis
Cyrene
CYRENAICA
AFRICA
LIBYA
Canop
Alexandri
Na
EG
Oxyrhy
15°
20°
25°
35°
40°
45°
Antioch
Iconium
Lystra
Derbe
Attalia
Perga
Antioch
Paphos
Salamis
Paul's 1st Journey
Beroea
Philippi
Neapolis
Thessalonica
Troas
Corinth
Athens
Cenchreae
Ephesus
Antioch
Iconium
Lystra
Derbe
Antioch
Caesarea
Paul's 2nd Journey
Philippi
Troas
Assos
Mitylene
Chios
Corinth
Ephesus
Samos
Miletus
Cos
Rhodes
Patara
Antioch
Tyre
Ptolemais
Caesarea
Jerusalem
Paul's 3rd Journey
OUTER BORDER

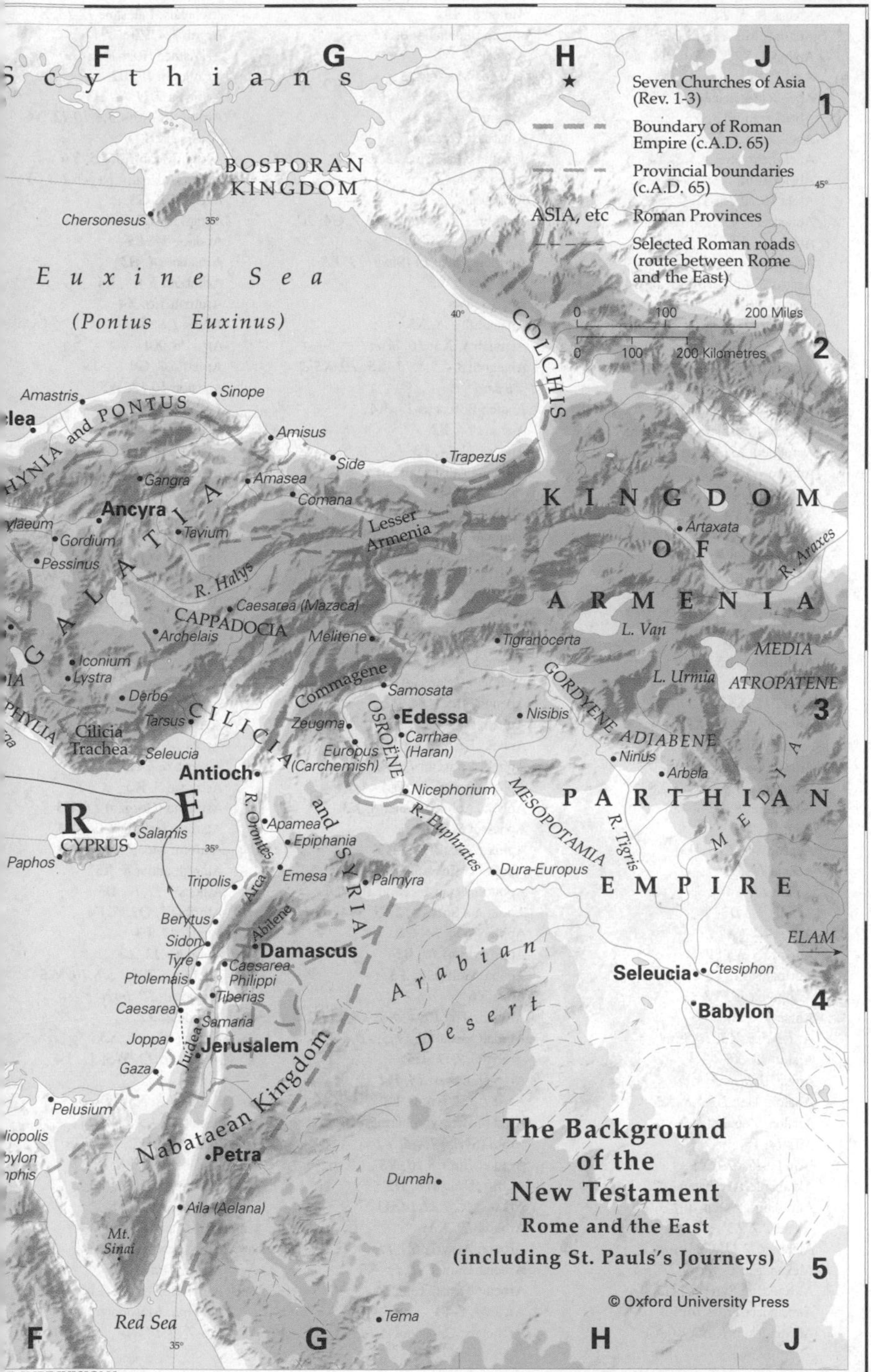
F
G
H
J
Scythians
Seven Churches of Asia (Rev. 1-3)
Boundary of Roman Empire (c.A.D. 65)
Provincial boundaries (c.A.D. 65)
ASIA, etc
Roman Provinces
Selected Roman roads (route between Rome and the East)
0
100
200 Miles
0
100
200 Kilometres
1
2
3
4
5
45°
35°
40°
BOSPORAN KINGDOM
Chersonesus
Euxine Sea
(Pontus Euxinus)
COLCHIS
Amastris
Sinope
BITHYNIA and PONTUS
Amisus
Side
Trapezus
Gangra
Amasea
Comana
Ancyra
Tavium
Gordium
Pessinus
GALATIA
Lesser Armenia
KINGDOM OF ARMENIA
Artaxata
R. Araxes
R. Halys
Caesarea (Mazaca)
CAPPADOCIA
Archelais
Melitene
Tigranocerta
L. Van
MEDIA ATROPATENE
L. Urmia
GORDYENE
ADIABENE
Iconium
Lystra
Derbe
Commagene
Samosata
Edessa
Nisibis
OSROËNE
Carrhae (Haran)
Zeugma
Europus (Carchemish)
Tarsus
CILICIA
Cilicia Trachea
Seleucia
Antioch
Ninus
Arbela
PARTHIAN EMPIRE
MEDIA
Nicephorium
MESOPOTAMIA
R. Tigris
R. Euphrates
R. Orontes
Apamea
Epiphania
SYRIA and
CYPRUS
Salamis
Paphos
Tripolis
Arca
Emesa
Palmyra
Dura-Europus
Berytus
Abilene
Sidon
Damascus
Tyre
Caesarea Philippi
Ptolemais
Tiberias
Caesarea
Samaria
Joppa
Judea
Jerusalem
Gaza
Arabian Desert
ELAM
Seleucia
Ctesiphon
Babylon
Pelusium
Nabataean Kingdom
Petra
Dumah
Aila (Aelana)
Mt. Sinai
Red Sea
Tema
The Background of the New Testament
Rome and the East (including St. Pauls's Journeys)
© Oxford University Press

# INDEX TO MAPS